Talent, Truth and Energy

75 Years of Service to Journalism

by
BERT N. BOSTROM

Professor of Journalism
Northern Arizona University

The Society of
Professional Journalists,
Sigma Delta Chi
Chicago, 1984

For the spouses of members of the national board of directors,
who, through the years, have been willing to sacrifice quality time with their husbands and wives that they might provide the Society with incalculable hours of continuing, dedicated service.

and for Pearl Luttrell,
whose friendly spirit and loyal devotion to the members and chapters of the Society while serving as a vital part of the headquarters staff for more than twenty-five years will always be remembered.

The Society of Professional Journalists
Sigma Delta Chi
75 Years of Service

TABLE OF CONTENTS

FOREWORD:

I didn't know much about Sigma Delta Chi when Bob Cooley, journalism chairman at Northern Arizona University, suggested in early 1968 that I join the Valley of the Sun professional chapter in Phoenix. I knew so little, in fact, that, while the initiation was impressive, I heard few of the words during the ceremony at Gene Pulliam's R & G Ranch, concerned that the ritual might end with a dunking in the nearby pool.

My true initiation to the Society came more than a year later when I heard national treasurer (and 1971-1972 national president) Guy Ryan, of San Diego, read the words from the ritual, "We welcome...association with those who seek modestly but with faith to perpetuate a profession...that lays its own claim to service on a vigilance that knows no midnight and a courage that knows no retreat..." I've been caught up in those phrases and in the work of the Society ever since.

Thus, it should be no surprise that, on May 31, 1980, while serving as vice president for campus chapter affairs, I asked the officers and Russ Hurst in Milwaukee about what I might do as a volunteer when I completed my term eighteen months later. Hurst, perhaps only to make conversation, suggested that the seventy-fifth anniversary of the Society was just four years away and it might be appropriate to have a book written concentrating on the most recent twenty-five years in the Society's history. Charles C. Clayton, of course, had written *Fifty Years for Freedom*, published in 1959 for the Society's fiftieth anniversary, documenting Sigma Delta Chi's early history. I almost came out of my chair with enthusiasm for the project. The seeds planted that day germinated and, I hope, have flowered in this volume. Shortly after I was granted a sabbatical leave to do the research for the book, the final plans for writing the official history of the Society from 1959 through 1984 were accepted by its board of directors.

After reading Clayton's book, I began my sabbatical semester spending two weeks of January 1982 at the Society's Chicago headquarters, working through drawers filled with long-untouched documents, correspondence, newsletters, reports, books of board minutes, convention transcripts, and photographs. Hurst and new executive officer Russ Tornabene directed me toward additional documents stored in other places at headquarters, and Pearl Luttrell, a staff member since 1959, provided a continual flow of information from her almost faultless memory. I returned to Flagstaff armed with two large boxes of reports, photocopied data and some original documents, a set of *The Quill* from 1932 to that time, and a travel budget that would allow me to visit each Society past president.

I was blessed in my endeavor with the fact that twenty-three of the Society's presidents beginning in 1959 were available for tape-recorded, on-site interviews. (Only V.M. (Red) Newton, president in 1959-1960, and Buren McCormack, president in 1961-1962, had died.) During the seven months of my leave, I visited with twelve of the twenty-three past presidents in their homes and offices, in hotels and in restaurants. After returning to my job as a professor of journalism at NAU in August 1982, I continued to travel for an additional year, using weekends and national convention week to interview ten more past presidents. I conducted the interview with the twenty-third past president – Robert M. White II – by telephone. My travel also included visits with Hurst, former *Quill* editor Charles Long and current editor Ron Dorfman, Society parliamentarian Charles Barnum, First Amendment counsel Bruce Sanford and 1978-1983 FOI chairman Bob Lewis, 1979-1984 finance chairman Howard Dubin, and headquarters staff members Tornabene, Luttrell and Roger Boye. All told, the live interviews included thirty-three persons in eighteen cities from New York City to Vista, California, and from Portland, Oregon, to Little Rock, Arkansas. Eleven interviews were conducted in Chicago.

In addition to the taped telephone interview with White, I recorded telephone interviews with fourteen past and present Society officials – including 1960-1962 executive officer Warren K. Agee. Agee also sent a detailed letter, describing his years in office, along with an extensive set of his records. Voluminous files of materials came, at my request, from Casey Bukro and David Offer on ethics, Ken Reiley and George Wolpert on the admission of women, and Lewis and Clark Mollenhoff on freedom of information. The extensive list of tape recordings, publications and other resources found in the bibliography have been placed in the archives at national headquarters and are available to those who wish to hear or view them. I believe the records gathered therein represent the most nearly complete set of data on the Society's history ever compiled.

Beyond the archival material used for this book, I should mention the scores of telephone calls to chapter presidents, committee chairs, headquarters personnel, regional directors and national officers through which information was checked and re-checked and additional facts to fill small holes were gathered. If I have had one regret in collecting the material for the book, it is that I was not able to interview every regional director who had served since 1960, more of the professional chapter presidents, and more campus chapter presidents and advisers. Their input would have added greatly to the total picture presented, but time and resources did not permit.

The writing of the manuscript began during Labor Day weekend, 1982, and continued, as time permitted within my teaching schedule, through May 1983. Working full-time at the video display terminal during the summer and part-time during the early months of fall, I completed all of the book, except for the chapter on the campus and professional chapters, by October 1983. I spent the months through February 1984 writing the final chapter, editing, and updating the manuscript.

A word about the inclusion or exclusion of content and its arrangement is in order. A history of this type can be nothing more or less than the perspective of the author and those with whom he talks or corresponds regarding events that occurred during the partial lifespan of the organization. There will be those who will be pleased that certain events have been given the attention due them in this volume. Others will be disappointed that certain events were subordinated unduly, overlooked, or omitted. Obviously, not everything could be included. While I have been an active participant in much of the recent history, I have tried to act as a reporter, presenting an account of what has happened and, as much as possible, removing myself from making judgments. I hope I have been successful in that effort. I extend apologies to any member whom I may have inadvertently overlooked.

I am responsible, however, for setting the pattern of arrangement for the book. You will find Units I and III presented in chronological order, where such an arrangement is necessary to demonstrate continuity. Unit I deals with the early history and the period of transition from professional fraternity to professional society. Unit III deals with the Society as it entered the decade of the 1980's. The greater portion of the book – Unit II, dealing with the landmarks of Hurst's nineteen years as executive officer – has been arranged topically. In this way, the reader who wishes to follow the Society's development in working toward freedom of information; the growth of the Sigma Delta Chi Foundation; the frustrations of bringing about the admission of women, a code of ethics, and a change in the name of the Society, may do so without having to read through a series of chapters to find out what happened in a given year. The internal organization of each chapter in Unit II, however, has been treated chronologically. The final unit of the book – presenting the history of *The Quill*, the record of accomplishments of campus and professional chapters, and notes on some special persons in the Society's recent past – has been organized by subject matter as well. I hope the reader will find the arrangement useful and readable. I am especially pleased with the Appendix in the book, in which some information, never before gathered together, may be found.

My friend, Howard Graves, said once, "The Society of Professional Journalists, Sigma Delta Chi, is a microcosm of journalism in America." He was speaking of the goals and aspirations, the strides forward and the setbacks, the great days and those filled with frustrations, the chapters and the national leadership of this far-flung organization. I believe the reader will find that Graves was right on target.

ACKNOWLEDGEMENTS

Robert M. White II, Society president in 1966-1967, during one of our conversations, mentioned the oft-quoted verity, "Success has many fathers, but failure is an orphan." He was referring to his belief that every SPJ,SDX president, past or present, simply was part of a succession of leadership responsible for the Society's major accomplishments though they may have culminated in that person's year as president. The same may be said of any success this book may have as a chronicle of the Society's most recent twenty-five years. Although I have been involved directly in researching, writing and editing this volume, it has been the direct and indirect contributions of dozens of persons that led to its ultimate completion.

I am especially grateful to the members of my family for their acceptance that this project was of such personal importance and for their sacrifices in giving up husband and father on many occasions when research trips or writing intervals prevented me from being with them.

The project could never have been undertaken without the cooperation of Northern Arizona University president Eugene M. Hughes, vice president Joseph Cox, dean Charles Aurand and department chair Ray Newton. who joined in granting me the sabbatical leave essential for the completion of the major portion of the research. I am indebted to my department colleagues – Stan Bogue, Larry Bohlender, Jim Files, Dal Herring, Manny Romero, Martin Sommerness and George Taylor –

who accepted extra responsibilities during and following my leave and who provided continuing encouragement throughout the project, and to student, Karla Kipp, who helped with corrections.

Within the Society, I wish to express my appreciation to national officers Jean Otto, Howard Graves, Charles Novitz, Steve Dornfeld, Phil Record and Frank Sutherland and to other members of the board of directors for giving me the opportunity to research and write the book. Without their financial support as a board and their personal interest during the two-and-one-half years on the project, little could have been accomplished.

Executive officer Russell Tornabene not only has provided valuable information through the years but has been a constant source of advice and inspiration, for which I owe him a great deal. I am especially grateful for his help in facilitating the lease on the video display terminal on which this book was composed. I am indebted to Howard Dubin for arranging the printing and binding and to Virginia Holcomb for her work as Society coordinator at headquarters during the final rush to complete the project. In addition, I am grateful to the other members of headquarters staff – Roger Boye, Ron Dorfman, Jerry Eastman, Toni Henle, Deborah Ivan, Karen Kruty, Pearl Luttrell, Lois Martin, Grace Roberts, Mark Rosner, Mike Tarpey and Lois Usheroff – each of whom assisted with a myriad of detail work and who, despite busy schedules, made the research for this book a personal priority.

The twenty-four past presidents and the two dozen others – past committee chairs, *Quill* editors, regional directors and participants in special Society activities – whom I interviewed made my research a joy. Each gave freely of valuable time in personal research, providing information and documentation. Several served as gracious hosts during my visits with them. Their names are mentioned frequently in this book.

Two of these persons – former executive officers Warren K. Agee and Russell E. Hurst – deserve special note. Both men were meticulous in preparing voluminous and detailed information from memory and by making many of their extensive records available. In addition, Hurst wrote the introduction, lending his prestige in the Society and the journalism community to the book. Agee offered his skill and time in taking on the immense task of reading proof and assisting with the editing of the completed manuscript.

I am grateful to the Southern Illinois University Press in Carbondale, for granting permission to use material from *Fifty Years for Freedom*, by Charles Clayton, in the chapter, "The First Fifty Years Revisited;" and to Grid Publishing, Inc., Columbus, Ohio, for granting permission to use material from *Mass Media Law and Regulation*, Third Edition, by William E. Francois in the chapters on freedom of information.

Finally, I express sincere gratitude to William G. Hoyt, my friend, my primary editor and a distinguished author in his own right. It was he who turned a newspaper journalist and educator into an author through his patient counsel, continuing encouragement and genuine concern that the product be a worthy effort.

Bert N. Bostrom
Flagstaff, Arizona
February, 1984

iv

INTRODUCTION

By Russell E. Hurst
Society Executive Officer,
1962-1981

I won't attempt attribution. After all, I had heard the phrase more than once, and usually from a past national president. So who knows, it might have originated in the 'teens or 'twenties. But it speaks, as the saying goes, volumes:

"If there hadn't been a Sigma Delta Chi, someone would have had to invent it."

There are many good reasons for this, which in itself helps to explain the "why" of the organization's existence. It was not just a complusion to associate, for while that instinct runs deep in most people, it runs crash-bang into the average journalist's prideful obstinacy about joining *anything*. (In helping to organize new chapters I sometimes encountered an atmosphere approaching defiance, to which I learned to respond, "We're not here to push you or spoon-feed you. But we'll tell you what the Society is all about, and if you care about the things we stand for, we think you'll do it (organize) for yourselves." It usually worked.)

Among those many good reasons was, of course, simply a desire to talk shop in a little more formal way, to compare notes on how-we-covered-that-story, and to size up the competition from the "other" paper or the new broadcast station.

I think there was more than a touch of survival instinct in the mix, too. Journalists discover, usually sooner than later, that they are obliged to join forces against those who prefer to govern in secrecy. And there's nothing quite like the companionship of fellow professionals when you choose to march on city hall or the legislature. That's why freedom of information has always ranked number one in our members' perception of what is most important of all the Society's programs. Nor are we going to run out of cases or causes anytime soon, considering how deeply ingrained in human nature are the twin aphrodisiacs of personal greed and the lust for power.

And then there is the desire-need to be kept informed about your own business. The Society helps to fill that need in several ways, including a national magazine, *The Quill*; a variety of other publications from national headquarters, and, of course, the enormously valuable forums provided by chapter meetings, regional conferences, national conventions and specialized workshops. (But still paltry few opportunities for mid-career training, something the entire profession should get moving on.)

And of course awards programs that single out the best and hold it up for all to see and emulate; it's not only something to work toward, it's proof that you've arrived when your peers tell you so.

And the marking of historic sies in journalism – persons, organizations and places that have significance in the development of this craft that we love. Not a terribly splashy program, but oh how important that the Society is doing it.

And a good many more programs and activities, including the pleasure and ego-satisfaction of working with high school and college students and sensing their gratitude and excitement (and that first time you tried not to let slip that you were only three years out of school yourself).

Still, there were few tangible incentives to persuade a young reporter or student to part with precious dollars for the initiation fees: a *Quill* subscription and a membership certificate (that later may be framed) and a wallet card certifying a *professional* membership.

Belonging. Certifiable belonging. Being a professional among professionals. Sharing and reaffirming the idealism of the Society's founders as expressd in the initiation ceremony:

"Selfishness has no part in our ambitions. We strive first to bring to journalism a definition of service worthy of a great and honorable profession, and to translate that definition into fact by devoting his best to his daily work. Great truths are always simple, and the truth we cherish is so simple it needs no exposition. It is your individual responsibility to your profession.

"We welcome your association," the ceremony continues, "with those who seek to perpetuate a profession based on freedom to learn and report the facts; that believes in public enlightenment as the forerunner of justice; that is as jealous of the right to utter unpopular opinions as the privilege to agree with the majority; that regards itself as the interpreter of today's events and the mirror of tomorrow's expectations; that ascribes motives only when motives go to the heart of the issue; and, finally, that lays its own claim to service on a vigilance that knows no midnight and a courage that knows no retreat."

More than 100,000 new members have heard those words over seven and a half decades. Before 1970, most were initiated in a candlelight ceremony, with black-robed chapter members solemnly explaining each element of the Greek-letter symbolism (Sigma, talent; Delta, energy; Chi, truth). I think it is not an overwhelming loss that the old, lengthy ceremony has been abandoned by most chapters in favor of a shorter, modern version. Still, I think that it is a loss, especially to those who heard it or took part in it when it was done with quiet dignity and conviction.

Much else gave way that will not be missed, including overly formal enrollment procedures, student oaths to forsake all else for news-editorial journalism, and ostentatious clusters of silk lapel ribbons to denote honored members at conventions.

The constant is the spirit of professionalism. And, yes, there are a good many of us who believe journalism deserves to be ranked as a profession; also that objectivity is a goal much worth pursuing, and that there is most certainly a public right-to-know implicit in the democratic contract. (I personally reject the Tooth Faerie but enthusiastically embrace the possibility of the Great Pumpkin.)

★ ★ ★

How did those students get that piano from

*the lobby to the sixth floor of the Benjamin
Franklin Hotel during the 1975 national
convention in Philadelphia? Is it still there?*

★　★　★

The 1960's and 1970's saw record
growth in membership and chapters. The
Society matured and stabilized even while
undergoing deep-reaching changes that
included a complete overhaul of the by-laws,
admission of women members and a change
in the Society's name. At every step the
effort was put one brick solidly in place
before adding another. We operated with a
strict budget and still built financial reserves
that fortunately were in place when
inflationary crunches came. And we had
generous support from print and broadcast
organizations all over the nation for projects
that were not within our budgets.

The Society had always been thoroughly
professional in attitude and activities. Now
it cast off most of the final vestiges of
fraternity origins, including the "blood oath"
for students and closed-door initiations.
Membership procedures were streamlined,
simple-majority voting replaced stiffer
requirements, proportional voting was
established to reflect actual chapter size,
membership reinstatement was made easier
and cheaper, chapter assessments eliminated.

Activities grew at every level:
scholarships, gridiron shows, newsletters, a
new SDX Foundation with its own set of
programs, cooperation with journalism
schools, strengthened liaison with the legal
profession, dogged and successful efforts to
open public meetings and records, a new
code of ethics, expanded awards programs,
minority recruitment, fund-raising projects,
marking of historic sites, careers films and
literature, job-finding aids, seminars on
specialized reporting, joint activities with
other journalism organizations.

★　★　★

Much of Bert Bostrom's skillful compilation
in the pages that follow constitutes a success
story. Most histories of this kind do indeed
catalogue the triumphs and ignore the losing
days, which most of us have put out of our
minds anyway.

For the record, though, it should be

noted – maybe even emphasized as an object
lesson – that we experienced frustrations and
disappointments on a fairly regular basis.
And we accomplished great and good works
for the profession *despite* the built-in
limitations of being a *voluntary*
"organization" of rather loosely knit chapters
made up largely of non-joining, independent,
skeptical, overworked and underpaid
journalists who obviously met so many
deadlines in their workadaylives that one
more, from SPJ,SDX, simply was not to be
recognized. There *might* have been a year
when one-fourth of the required chapter
reports arrived by deadline. From painful
experience, we learned at headquarters to
build in ten-day or twenty-day cushions on
reports, the number increasing as more
board members, committee chairmen and
chapters discovered that extensions were easy
to come by. A stubborn or overly busy few
simply brought their reports to meetings or
spoke from notes that doubtless had been
compiled en route at 30,000 feet. No one
seemed to mind as long as the information
was on the table when it was time to vote.
Journalists are generally quick studies, and
they are trained to sift facts quickly. And I
always had the feeling that our national
boards and conventions arrived at sound
conclusions, even though burdened by the
democratic processes and occasionally
appearing hell-bent on repeating mistakes of
four years ago and having the same good
intentions in the process.

★　★　★

*From the viewpoint of some "outsiders" we
dealt with, we were a strange breed. The
hotel's convention coordinator, for example.
I mean there we were three weeks away from
a meeting planned for 1,100 people and only
200 registered in advance??! All those rooms
committed, waiters to be hired, food to be
ordered. "Are you sure they even know
about the meeting?" I was asked more than
once.*

*"They'll be there," I soothed over the
long-distance phone. "And please don't
forget the Bloody Marys and screwdrivers
for the breakfast meeting of past presidents."*

*"Hello? Hello? Did you say at
breakfast?!*

★　★　★

But back to the successes for a moment, because those are always more pleasant to deal with and our memories seem to accomodate them more easily. I was asked many times – and especially by officers of other organizations – what accounted for the truly outstanding years, of which there were a good many among the past 25 years.

The answer in several words is: hard work, balance and total effort. The hard work had to come from just about everyone from the national president down to the chapter member charged with turning off the lights. And the "work" part meant creative leadership as much as determination to see the job through.

Balance in this case quite literally meant something for everyone, without patronizing in the slightest. (One lesson learned early in organizational work is that you cannot please everyone all the time so don't expect to.) Still, man does not live by FOI alone. We had to keep in mind constantly that our members ranged from student to publisher, from copy reader to television anchor. In *Quill* articles and convention programming alike you had to hope to satisfy the varied needs and interests of our members.

And total effort meant that every wheel was turning: committees were charging along with interesting assignments; regional directors were out there traveling and meeting with local news executives and college presidents as well as their chapters; *The Quill* was brimming with timely, meaty articles and well-written to boot; members were attending meetings, writing letters AND paying dues; communication lines were wide open and humming; chapters were initiating larger groups of new members and doing it more than once a year.

And it was all happening without a lot of rah-rah and hype. Just minimal direction, really, because that's about all we could afford. It was happening because a lot of people *believed* that being a professional meant making contributions of time and effort to your professional society and, furthermore, whaddyaknow! you really do get out of something what you're willing to put into it.

Did anyone ever get a photo of famed Washington correspondent Merriman Smith sitting on the floor half the night rapping with students at a regional conference?

★　★　★

The Society has benefited greatly from uniformly strong – even brilliant – committee work. People in organization work know that much of the substance comes out of committees (despite all the bad jokes), and also that it's hard to get people to volunteer for the grind-it-out jobs and often you have to have a chairman willing to pick up pieces and put them together or the whole effort collapses. We have been singularly fortunate to turn up, year after year, people of exceptional dedication, intellect and energy to serve committee roles. There ought to be a special Hall of Fame for them somewhere, as well as for campus chapter advisers, professional chapter secretaries and the general chairmen of national conventions and Distinguished Service Awards ceremonies.

★　★　★

A special word about those SDX Distinguished Service Awards, which I had the privilege of administering for nineteen years. I got to know a lot about contests, and though I could easily be charged with bias, there is no question in my mind that the SDX Awards are the highest honors of the profession. Judgment is by peers, the judging is final and the results cannot be second-guessed or influenced by professional politics. (Oh, yes, newcomers, journalism too has its allegiances of personal friendship, geography, common business interests, etc.) In more than fifty years, we have never had a breath of scandal in the entire selection process – which by the way became something of a logistical nightmare as the entry total approached 1,500 and we had to use as many as eighteen or twenty judging panels in as many different cities.

Winners frequently told us that, in addition to the honor, they felt they had "really been presented" in a format that began with day-long "how-I-did-it" sessions and concluded with banquet formal wear, a multi-media show featuring the winners and an escorted walk under spotlights to center stage. They also had to be impressed by their audiences of keenly interested students and professionals who listened with rapt attention and asked awfully good questions. The DSA programs were, in fact, rated by many of our members as equal or superior in content to national conventions. And it was a stroke of genius on someone's part about 1960 to take the DSA show on the road, putting it in a different city every year after a long run in Chicago. That added luster to the Awards and the Society.

Perhaps in part because of the great prestige of the SDX Awards, the Society's other awards have come to signify the finest work, the highest achievement in all of journalism. Great care has always been taken in setting the criteria for the awards, and great care in selecting judges. With those ingredients in place, most contests need only a modest amount of review from time to time, simply to assure that advancing technology, for example, hasn't made an instruction obsolete.

Not incidentally, it has always bothered me that we (everyone, it seems) pay such niggardly attention to second- and third-place winners (losers?). "FIRST PLACE!" always gets the standing ovation while the seconds and thirds are slouching back into their seats, tripping on mike wires and bumping into chairs in silence. Veteran judges will attest, however, that selection of a winner among five or six finalists from among a hundred entries often comes down to almost a coin flip; there are only subtle shadings of difference in quality. Well, the winner is still the winner and take nothing away from that. But I've always found myself wishing for greater recognition for all those truly outstanding finalists each year.

★   ★   ★

SPJ,SDX has always had a public posture, evident in its convention resolutions, board statements and freedom-of-information actions. Little known are the behind-the-scenes roles of many officers and members who have been invited to mediate disputes between press and bar, students and administrators, members and their

employers, and in other cases where the expertise of a respected journalist was needed. You won't find that record in this volume – but it's worth noting that the Society's prestige has brought this kind of recognition.

Not much survives seventy-five years. Not very many growing things, darned few things that have moving parts. And relatively few companies and organizations. That SPJ,SDX has, with only a few whiffs of oxygen along the way, is a credit not only to strong principles and resolute leaders but also to a simple organizational structure. A majority of the Society's members belong to chapters. The chapters, professional and campus, send delegates to an annual national convention where their votes constitute the ultimate authority on everything the Society does. That leaves a substantial number of members, perhaps 40 percent, without direct voting representation since they don't belong to chapters. But delegates are reminded of this, urged to remember they are representing the interests of *all* members, and seem always to take the stricture seriously. The parochial or narrow-interest resolution was a rarity.

The Society's twelve regions elect their own directors to the national Board, and each region holds a spring conference. It's a small-scale convention but has no legislative powers. The twelve regional directors, four students elected by districts and six national officers elected by convention delegates make up the national board of directors, which governs in between conventions. Over the decades, as you will see in the text that follows, composition and character have changed. But while boards have differed on how to accomplish organizational objectives, they have a remarkable and most praiseworthy consistency in the pursuit of professional goals.

The chapter is the heart of the Society. This is where individual members find outlets for professional expression and opportunities for service. It is the one point in the whole structure of SPJ,SDX where professionals and students are meeting regularly to exchange ideas, review practices, sound alarms and join in a wide range of projects that affirm their commitment to the highest standards of the profession. You will find a separate chapter in this book on the role of the chapters – but it would take volumes simply to record their contributions to the development of the Society and the profession as a whole.

★ ★ ★

The same can be said of *The Quill*. The magazine has been of enormous value to the Society and the profession for more than seventy years. It has been the recorder of events, ideas, trends and practices. It has pictured journalism in all its stages of growth and all its moods. The magazine's articles and letters have reflected the greatness of the American press and scorned its failings. Perhaps no other publication in journalism has had a greater influence on generations of students and teachers, reporters and editors. Influence is difficult to measure and the claim may seem extravagant, but you should have listened with the editors and me over twenty years to the spoken praise, and read with us the flow of letters that affirmed *The Quill*'s ability to educate, inform and inspire.

If those aren't reasons enough to give the magazine highest priority among all the Society's activities, we now come to the overwhelmingly compelling reasons: the magazine is the *only* regular source of information about the Society for its members. And it is the only regular tangible evidence to many members that they hold an SPJ,SDX membership (remember the thousands of at-large members who have no chapter affiliation and thus no other ongoing contact other than *The Quill*).

Curiously, there is fresh debate with almost each new cycle of magazine staffs and boards of directors concerning the magazine's role. "House organ" for the Society? "Independent voice" of American journalism? Positive salesman of better journalism? Cerebral and critical? Practical and useful? (Brief pause while choices are made.) My answer is, *all* of the above, and probably more, given the resources, of course. Given the character of the magazine's audience – sharpshooters all! – there is no way that excesses would go

unnoticed and uncorrected.

★ ★ ★

A good many people are named in this book. They all deserve a place in the record. But as I read the galleys, I was struck by the fact that dozens – hundreds – of names are missing. Names of persons who really have earned special mention for service beyond the ordinary.

I know many of them well, have a brief acquaintance with many more, have only seen the names of others. They know who they are, but wouldn't expect any special attention. I want to take this opportunity to thank all of them for serving on committees, for keeping chapter books straight, for advising student chapters, for handling registration at regional conventions, for licking stamps, for sending reports to *The Quill* and our national newsletters, for hauling visitors to and from airports, for seeking out new members and spending time with them, for hauling supplies around in the trunks of their cars, for judging entries in this contest and that, for contributing to the SDX Foundation and the Legal Defense Fund, for volunteering to do all kinds of really cruddy jobs that had to be done. For being there. For being professional about it all.

★ ★ ★

Idealism has been the common thread, unifying spirit and moving force. An intellectual commitment to truth and fairness. Strange, one might think, for a profession of skeptics to be so sentimentally bound to "talent, energy and truth." Not at all; the skepticism is turned in directions other than the journalist's own creed.

We are a Society born of idealism, and can be quite glad of it; we will continue to grow professionally as long as we remember our origins. It's a faith that can be professed and expressed; or, for the shy, one that can be acknowledged quietly...a gut feeling...a silent imperative.

Wheaton, Ill.
February 1984

SDX: Its Birth & Transition

This history of The Society of Professional Journalists, Sigma Delta Chi – although its objective is to trace the growth and development of the Society from 1959-1984 – must, of necessity, begin at the beginning in 1909. One cannot assume that the reader has been privileged to read one or all of the three published histories delineating the incidents of the early years which set the philosophy and goals of Sigma Delta Chi. Nor can one assume that the reader will have knowledge of events near the end of Sigma Delta Chi's first fifty years which so manifestly impacted the organization as it approached its second half century.

To assure that the reader will have a perspective in which to place the history of the most recent twenty-five years, Unit I focuses on a brief look at five developmental periods, some extended, some of only a year or two in duration. They cover the birth and establishment of Sigma Delta Chi as a national honorary and later a professional fraternity (1909-1959); a closer look at the years of trauma and frustrations when its leadership perceived a "death trend " for the fraternity (1957-1959);" the efforts which led to its total reorganization as a professional journalistic society (1960); the transitional year which gave Sigma Delta Chi new life and vitality (1961); and the prologue (1962) to the decades of its greatest growth and achievement.

In taking this quick look back at the first fifty years, it, of course, would be impossible to chronicle all of the events, as significant as they may have been; to list all of the personalities and elected officers; or to identify each chapter as it became a part of the organization. For those interested in such detail, the author commends the aforementioned three histories: *The History of Sigma Delta Chi*, by Mitchell V. Charnley, published as a special issue of *The Quill* in 1926; *The Sigma Delta Chi Story*, by William M. Glenn, published in 1949; and *Fifty Years For Freedom*, by Charles C. Clayton, published in conjunction with the fraternity's fiftieth anniversary convention in 1959. Rather, the central point of this review will be to inventory those events, concentrating on the first five to seven years, which mark the beginning of developments and traditions affecting the Society today.

1

CHAPTER 1

The First Fifty Years Revisited

DePauw University was not unique among college campuses in the early 1900's. Founded by the Methodist Church in 1837 as Asbury College, a private, liberal arts college, it was a small school with 700 students in the quiet community of Greencastle, Indiana, some forty miles west of Indianapolis. It had the usual complement of academic programs for the day and a social atmosphere based in several active fraternities and sororities. By January 1909, the campus newspaper, in only its first year as a daily publication, was looked upon dubiously by influential faculty and the student body and "had failed to attain any great eminence or respectability," according to Charnley.

DePauw University *Daily* editor-in-chief LeRoy H. Millikan had been thinking for several months that, while other groups of undergraduates, drawn together by a mutual expectancy of professional life in the same field, had bound themselves by fraternal ties, yet in journalism, fraternalism had been completely neglected. "Why not organize a journalism fraternity?" he asked his friends L. Aldis Hutchens and Ralph C. Mann. With some skepticism, the two accepted the idea after a few days and the three young journalists approached their student colleagues on the *Daily*. The group, including Marion H. Hedges, Gilbert C. Clippinger, Eugene C. Pulliam, Charles A. Fisher and Paul M. and Foster Riddick, agreed to join in founding a journalistic fraternity. Toward the end of March, Edward H. Lockwood, William M. Glenn and Laurence H. Sloan were invited to join the fledgling organization. Mann, however, soon found himself forced to leave college and Foster Riddick indicated his interest in journalism did not extend beyond the college newspaper, leaving those ten young men to become the founders of Sigma Delta Chi.

It is interesting to note that, fifty-four years later, another DePauw student, John M. (Jock) Taylor, was recognized officially as a founder of the fraternity by the Sigma Delta Chi board of directors, meeting in Norfolk, Virginia. Before Taylor could be honored as the eleventh founder, it was determined with the help of the three remaining founders living in 1963 –

East College at DePauw University, Greencastle, Indiana, where LeRoy H. Millikan met with his friends in the offices of the University *Daily* and planned the formation of an honorary journalistic fraternity that would become Sigma Delta Chi.

Pulliam, Glenn and Riddick – that while Taylor had, indeed, been on the campus at the time of early discussions about the formulation of a journalistic fraternity, he had dropped out of school in January 1909 and did not participate in the final stages of the founding. Taylor did return to school the following year, however, and while the records were lost and his enrollment in Sigma Delta Chi was delayed twenty-one years until 1931, Glenn established that Taylor joined his brothers as a member of the first group to be initiated into Sigma Delta Chi, May 2, 1910.

As the seed of the organization germinated by early April, several principles and prerequisites for membership of the yet unnamed fraternity had developed. Charnley records that, "They longed dimly for 'better journalism,' both amateur and professional; they talked of a truthful, honorable press, one not dominated by commercialism; and they believed that by

planting journalistic ideals in student newspapermen, they would make great strides toward their goal. It was decided that only upperclassmen who had done notably good work in journalism, and who expected to make journalism their life's work, should be elected to the proposed organization. Thus, from the start, the professional ideal which caused so much trouble later was an integral part of the organization's plan. It was also decided that the fraternity should be honorary, not social, in nature, although it was taken for granted that it would follow with fidelity the conventional Greek-letter fraternity design." Founder Eugene Pulliam said later, "We didn't know what we were creating. We only knew what we believed."

The generally accepted birth date for the fraternity is April 17, 1909 – the day the organization gained a name, Sigma Delta Chi. The founders met in a classroom on the top floor of West College. Millikan and Pulliam had been assigned the task of selecting a Greek-letter name. "We studied *Baird's Fraternity Manual* [the publication which officially recognized such organizations] much more diligently than any college textbook on our shelves," Millikan said later. "We became desperate. We were flunking in Greek. And then the gods came to our rescue. Gene and I were secretly wearing pledge pins – known as 'Sigma Deltas' – of Kappa Kappa Gamma sorority. [The two men were said to have been serious about two girls in the sorority.] We said, 'Say, how would it sound to add Chi and make it Sigma Delta Chi?' There you are, Sigma Delta Chi. The fraternity was named." In an aura of secrecy, Pulliam suggested the name, and, after some argument, it was adopted because it was euphonious and because it was thought to be different from other Greek-letter combinations. They did not know that previously there had been a society by this name at Yale. Millikan's proposal for "colors" to represent the fraternity – black (for printer's ink) and white (for paper) – were adopted at the same meeting.

In his book, Glenn told a somewhat different story than did Charnley and Clayton on the first discussions about a

3

Al Bates (left), Sigma Delta Chi executive secretary from 1929-1934 and chairman of the headquarters committee for the fraternity from 1942-1946 when there was no full-time administrative officer, pictured with Bernard (Barney) Kilgore, president of *The Wall Street Journal*, and Henry Rieger, Region 11 director, at the 1965 national convention in Los Angeles where Kilgore was the keynote speaker and Rieger was convention chairman.

fraternity, how the name and colors were selected and who among the recognized founders were involved in those decisions. Chapters two through five of his book credit Glenn and Sloan with much of the early work. Dates and places, however, are consistent in each author's report.

The secrecy which surrounded these early meetings ended May 6 when the ten founders, in single file and with solemn faces, paraded in to morning chapel late enough to be observed by everyone, sat in the front row and announced the formation of Sigma Delta Chi. Pulliam had been assigned to write the story which appeared in the *Daily*:

The curiosity of the college world was aroused this morning by the appearance of ten men wearing black and white colors. The enquiries of the students as to the purpose of the organization, if such it might be, met with no response from these men, but

on being interviewed by a reporter for the *Daily* they finally gave up their secret, or at least part of it.

The announcement that a new Greek letter interfraternity, known as Sigma Delta Chi, has existed at DePauw for many months will come as a surprise to everybody but the members themselves, who have quietly worked out their ritual, insignia, ceremonies and constitution before letting the existence of the fraternity become known. They have held their meetings in various places, sometimes under very peculiar and interesting circumstances, in order to preserve secrecy.

Sigma Delta Chi has appropriated to itself an entirely new field, that of journalism. Observing the success of the fraternity idea in other professional fields, such as law and medicine, it occurred to these ten men, or eleven, as their number originally was, that the idea was also practicable in the field of journalistic endeavor. It is their intention to include among its members only those men who expressly intend to engage in either newspaper or other literary work as a life's profession. Membership will hereafter be granted only to upperclassmen who have proved their sincerity and ability by consistent effort in college publications. Thus, the fraternity will, in time, acquire an honorary character, which will operate as an incentive in the development of literary talent. Nor will its influence be limited to the college world alone. The fraternity expects to establish chapters in other colleges and universities in which daily newspapers are now published. In the course of years, it is hoped that the roll of alumni will contain the names of many prominent journalists and authors. By binding such men together in the true fraternity spirit and inspiring them with common ideals, a larger spirit of idealism will be injected into the press of this country. It will be seen from this also that the organization is not intended to displace or conflict with the existing press clubs. The two fields are rather adjoining than overlapping.

The charter members of the Alpha chapter are representatives of the best that is in DePauw. They are men of ideals, aims and ability. Their activities have not been confined to one line of college interest. All of them, however, have had experience in journalistic or literary work outside of college.

The details were hardly in such apple-pie order as the *Daily's* story indicated. The general principles were quite clear, but the ritual, insignia, ceremony and constitution had been worked out only in a very tentative sense. Before the end of the term, a motto, "Talent, Energy, Truth," had been selected and fitted to the name. Sloan is reported to have said, "Now, what we have to do is to go through the dictionaries and find out what 'Sigma' means, what 'Delta' means and what 'Chi' means, and see if we cannot get an analogy between the three Greek letters and the exalted profession of journalism." It

Eugene C. Pulliam (left), one of the ten founders of Sigma Delta Chi in 1909, received the Wells Memorial Key from Theodore F. Koop at special ceremonies in 1969. The Wells Key, named in honor of Chester Wells, who died while serving as fraternity president in 1913, is the highest honor the Society can bestow on one of its members.

was three years later, in 1912 at the first national convention, that the significance of the Greek letters was announced. Sigma represented the Greek 'sophia,' and was translated as talent or genius; Delta meant 'dynamis' or energy; and Chi stood for 'chaios' or truth.

As the fall semester got under way, the enthusiasm for the fraternity slowed almost to a stop. Millikan, Hutchens and Lockwood were graduated and Pulliam left college to enter active journalism. Internal bickering pervaded the Alpha chapter throughout the second year of its existence and had it not been for the hoped for, but not anticipated, quick interest from two other universities in forming chapters of Sigma Delta Chi, the organization might have died out. Just before Christmas 1909, word came first from Lee A White and others at the University of Michigan as well as from a group of men at the University of Kansas, stating that they had heard of the organization of the fraternity and were interested in joining as chapters. Members of the Alpha chapter wrote the men from Kansas:

We are a young organization, hardly past the formative stage, but with high ideals and with a possible future. If you wish to join us in the plan to extend the fraternity through the larger colleges of America; if you wish to share with us the burdens of early failures and the exhilaration of later success; if you like our idea, and wish to come in this thing and help make it go – then you are more than welcome.

The Beta chapter of Sigma Delta Chi was chartered February 22, 1910, at Lawrence, Kansas, closely followed on March 18 by the Gamma chapter at the University of Michigan at Ann Arbor. Alpha chapter had had glory thrust upon it. The two new chapters, coming on their own initiative, joined the movement in what had to have been the most fortunate event in the fraternity's early history. The word spread rapidly. By year's end, the Writers' Club at the University of Denver was chartered as the fourth chapter. And early the next year, two more – the University of Washington and the University of Virginia – were on the rolls of the now "national" organization. Purdue, the first chapter to be installed in person by Alpha chapter members (the first five had been accomplished by mail) and Ohio State joined the growing list of chapters by June, 1911, followed within the next year by Wisconsin, Iowa and Illinois, bringing the number of chapters in mid-1912 to eleven.

It was in 1912, as well, that the first effort at a publication began. The Alpha chapter, acting as a clearinghouse, invited other chapters to send in a monthly letter, with sufficient copies so that all the chapters' letters could be mailed the first of each month to every chapter. The plan failed eventually; but it was here, just the same, that *The Quill* had its beginnings. Early records do not reveal why the name for the magazine was chosen or who selected it.

With chapters from coast to coast, thoughts turned to holding a first national convention and the development of a centralized authority to administer the affairs of Sigma Delta Chi. Sloan issued a formal call for such a meeting January 20, 1912, proposing Greencastle as the site and presenting an agenda. He asked that each chapter come with plans for a fraternity publication, a new system of fraternity

government, a definite expansion policy and ritual changes and contitutional amendments. Financial arrangments for the travel, including pooling and the equal sharing of railroad expenses, along with the central location of the Alpha chapter at DePauw, assured the selection of Greencastle as the host city. Chapters responded at once and promised not only to send delegates, but to try to persuade alumni members to attend. All but two of the chapters – Washington and Virginia – were represented by delegates when the first national convention of Sigma Delta Chi was called to order April 26, 1912.

The work done toward the building of a significant organization in three business sessions over two days was monumental. Laurence Sloan, the guiding spirit in the founding three years earlier and the member of Sigma Delta Chi whose efforts had brought the fraternity nationwide attention, was elected by acclamation as the first national president. The remainder of the first slate of national officers included George K. Thompson, Iowa, as vice president; Roger F. Steffan, Ohio State, secretary; Robert C. Lowry, Purdue, treasurer; Lee A White, an alumnus of the Michigan chapter, historian; W. Pyke Johnson, Denver, alumni member of the executive council; and George Marsh, Kansas, undergraduate member of the council. White urged that the word "professional" be substituted for "honorary" in the constitution so as to establish definitely the status of the fraternity. Although this suggestion was left to the constitution committee to study, it marked the beginning of a long effort by White to make such a change – a change in 1916 that Charnley said "strengthened the fraternity in purpose 100 percent." The constitution committee was also instructed to make the constitution non-secret and to decide on the status of a man once a member of Sigma Delta Chi who later should give up journalism. Walter K. Towers, Michigan's official delegate, made a strong attempt to admit advertising men to the fraternity, championing them as journalists in the Sigma Delta Chi sense. The effort failed.

The matter of *The Quill* was a priority

item for the fraternity's leadership. It was decided to issue the magazine as a continuing fraternity publication six times a year. A limit of $20 was placed on the cost of each edition and each member was assessed $1 per year as a subscription rate. Frank Pennell of Michigan was named its first regular editor. Consideration of the constitution and revisions of the ritual dominated much of the convention's time. Wanting to avoid offending members of the Alpha chapter, to whom the ritual's every line had sentimental virtue, the delegates worked carefully to eliminate its flowery nature, and succeeded. More importantly, the revised ritual – still secret until that time – was put on paper. The ritual included a brief oath of allegiance for new pledges, an oath of office, directions for memorial services in case of death of chapter members and a ceremonial for initiation. In addition, the convention set a $25 initiation fee for new chapters and $4 national dues for each member, and assessed each chapter $20 for fare and Pullman expense of convention delegates. A numbering system for pins (and ultimately for membership cards) was adopted with the number one to be assigned to the new national president, down through the officers, then through the chapters in order of their founding and after this through new members in order of their registration. The convention also approved a charter for a twelfth chapter – the University of Pennsylvania. It was reported that votes on several issues were shouted from passenger cars as the train pulled out of the station after midnight April 27, thus ending the convention.

During the following year, little attention was given to chapter achievement, methods of advancing journalism or anything but the mechanics of growth and organization. Sloan, Lowry and Steffan were caught up in further expansion of the fraternity and concentrated on lining up additional colleges and universities for potential chapters. Missouri, Texas, Oregon and Oklahoma chapter petitions were approved but two others, those of Kansas State Agricultural College and Columbia, were blackballed – a procedure allowed by the convention. The officers were concerned

as well about *The Quill*. Pennell failed to get a single issue of the new magazine put together on schedule, complaining that he found it impossible to get responses from many of the chapters; others had written so vaguely and ineffectually that there was no news in what they said. Vol. I, No. 1, dated December, 1912, was finally completed and mailed to each chapter in February 1913. It was a modest magazine of twenty pages in a six-by-nine-inch format and included four pages of editorials; one devoted to a letter of greeting from the fraternity's first honorary president, Governor Chase S. Osborn of Michigan, who was elected during the convention, and fifteen pages of chapter letters. The cover was on glazed paper and bore, in addition to its name and the name of the fraternity, a large reproduction of the badge. While Pennell managed to publish two additional issues before the 1913 convention, complaints by the officers abounded and the editorial offices were moved to Denver University with Pyke Johnson as editor. Johnson's ambitions for the magazine were less than successful as well and the next issue did not appear until 1914, although it contained pictures of the officers, several articles on journalism and some chapter news.

The second convention opened May 2, 1913, in Madison, Wisconsin, with twelve of the sixteen chapters represented by delegates. Given the realities of the financial condition of the fraternity (it had only $105 in the treasury) and the problems in news gathering, the delegates voted to publish *The Quill* only three times a year, but added a $10 assessment per chapter to finance the magazine. As it turned out, the chapters were negligent in paying that assessment, contributing to Johnson's frustrations in producing the magazine on a regular basis. The issue of membership surfaced again, this time dealing with the interpretation of journalism as including both the business and editorial side of newspaper, magazine and publicity work. The convention recommended a strict interpretation of the constitution's language that kept the organization purely in the news field. It also reduced the national membership dues to $3 and made a three-fourths vote of chapters sufficient to grant a charter. In addition, it empowered the executive council to grant a charter to Kansas State Agricultural College when that school was deemed to have made its journalism program permanent. In what turned out to be a most important step, the delegates approved a recommendation seeking endorsement of Sigma Delta Chi by the Association of College Journalism Professors, an organization which later developed into the present Association for Education in Journalism and Mass Communication. That endorsement came during the following year and, because it meant that at least one faculty member in a school would be morally obligated to take an interest in Sigma Delta Chi, it had the effect of establishing the system of advisers to the undergraduate chapters.

Chester A. Wells of the Wisconsin chapter was elected national president without opposition. The future looked bright, for a new spirit of professionalism and activity for the fraternity was evidenced in Wells' vigorous and enthusiastic leadership in the next two months. Following his graduation in June, however, Wells contracted a throat infection, was hospitalized in Madison for what was thought to be a minor operation, suffered a severe hemorrhage, and died September 1 at the age of twenty-six. The Wisconsin chapter, that fall, proposed that a Wells Memorial be established in his memory and that a key be given each year to the retiring president of the fraternity. The proposal received prompt and enthusiastic approval. Sloan, president of the fraternity for 1912-1913, is officially recognized as the first recipient of the Wells Memorial Key, but by the time of the next convention, a separate key was awarded to past presidents and the Wells Key was awarded, as it is now, to a member for outstanding service, regardless of whether the person holds or has held offices in the Society. Fraternity historian Lee White was the first to receive the Wells Memorial Key under its new designation in May, 1914.

The roll of chapters was altered in the months before the 1914 convention opened May 1 at Ann Arbor, Michigan, with Pennsylvania and Virginia giving up their charters and the addition of Indiana University, Nebraska and Iowa State. Roger F. Steffan, the driving force in the formation of the Ohio State chapter and the fraternity's first national secretary, was elected president. The up-and-down fortunes of *The Quill* took an important, but in reality a short-lived step forward, at the third convention when delegates approved a plan to charge a $5 initiation fee for new members with $3 to go into a permanent *Quill* fund. The plan entitled each member to a five-year subscription to the magazine with the subscription price thereafter to be $2 for three years. Johnson, despite his problems with the magazine during the previous year, was re-elected editor and dates for publication were set for October, January, April and late May. Finances plagued *The Quill* and the fraternity. The national organization was in debt by as much as $380 within a year and Steffan cancelled plans for a 1915 convention. Much of the debt was attributed to *The Quill*, which had spent $700 against $400 received for the magazine from dues. Johnson, who told Steffan, "No *Quill* until the past dues bills are paid," resigned and fraternity vice president Carl Getz, a journalism professor at the University of Montana, was named editor. Getz, however, found the same problems and after publishing five issues, turned the editorial reins over to White, then on the faculty of the University of Washington. With the help of a gift from former Governor (and national honorary president) Chase S. Osborn and the payment of a special assessment by chapters, all debts were paid and White published a cut-back issue of the magazine in April, 1916.

To further complicate the fraternity's dilemmas, Steffan, re-elected president on a referendum vote, had attempted to resign that presidency in November 1915, because of the pressures of a new job. When no one was willing to step in and assume the post, he worked as he could to prepare for the May 4-6, 1916, convention in Columbia, Missouri, although he did not attend that meeting. Only two national officers were present at the seventh anniversary convention, but twenty-two of the twenty-five chapters were represented. In their most important decision, the delegates voted to strike the word "honorary" from the name of the organization, a necessary prerequisite to the strict emphasis on professionalism they sought. Robert C. Lowry, for four years treasurer of the fraternity when "there was nothing to treasure," was elected national president. He remained in that office for three years, a time which saw World War I disrupt the efforts of local chapters and the national organization as well. No national conventions were held in 1917 or 1918. Felix M. Church, re-elected secretary at the Columbia convention, noted, however, that the fraternity was now organized on a more or less permanent basis, no vital changes in existing conditions or rules needed to be made and a convention really served the purpose of a school of instruction to delegates.

The disruption of the war had a devastating affect on the organization. Notwithstanding, 1917 was what Charnley called "the best year yet" from an internal, organizational standpoint. The severe deficits in the treasury were only a memory and White published *The Quill* on a regular basis. The magazine took on new importance in the next two years for it was the primary link between the national fraternity and the members who did not enter the military. It was estimated that when the United States entered the war, about 50 percent of the 1,250 regularly enrolled members had entered the service or some civilian counterpart, including about 95 percent of the 300 undergraduate members, leaving too few men in most of the twenty-eight chapters for regular meetings. All of the national officers were in the military. When Church resigned his secretary's post in favor of Robert E. White, a Detroit newspaperman, he wrote, "Just now our program is stationary....But finances are splendid, and the national treasury and *The Quill* are in the most comfortable position they've had in five years."

It was December 5, 1919, when Sigma Delta Chi convened its next national convention in Champaign, Illinois. Accomplishments at the two-day meeting measured up to the promise officers had seen in the fraternity's condition. Thirty-two chapters were on the rolls. Delegates ordered a special committee to "reduce to a code of ethics as many as possible of those high motives and lofty principles which actuate leading journalists in the practice of their profession," and directed that the code serve as a fraternity standard after its approval by chapters. Constitutional changes included an increase in the size of the executive council to nine men – four officers and five councilors}to be chosen from different sections of the country so that all chapters might have official advice near them. Church was elected president with Ward Neff, vice president of the *Corn Belt Dailies*, Chicago, first vice president; Cargill Sproul, associate editor of *Business*, Detroit, second vice president; and Norman Radder, assistant professor of journalism, University of Minnesota, treasurer. The new councilors included Harry Crain, *Capital City Journal*, Salem, Oregon; T. Hawley Tapping, Peoria, Illinois; Lyman Thompson, Chicago; Frank B. Thayer, Washington State College; and Glendon Allvine, *New York Tribune*. Lee A White, then at the Detroit *News*, was persuaded to remain as editor, he reported *The Quill* was in excellent condition with a circulation of 1,950 and a balance on hand of $825, something unheard of in its history.

TOWARD PROFESSIONALISM

White was to achieve his greatest victory, however, November 18-20, 1920, in Norman, Oklahoma, where delegates from thirty-one chapters (including five alumni chapters, Chicago, Seattle, Milwaukee, Detroit and Des Moines) gathered for the eleventh anniversary convention. Six years before, he had recommended that the secrecy provisions be struck from the fraternity's constitution only to be defeated overwhelmingly. Just the year before, the vote had been 27-2 to keep the secrecy provisions. But, slowly, he had been able to convince a few, most of them alumni, of the difficulty of convincing an experienced newspaperman that a secret grip and whispered Greek words were anything but "kid stuff," and the lack of need for such esoterica. Forced into a decision on the matter by a parliamentary maneuver, the chapters voted 17-14 against secrecy and, as the minutes of that meeting state, "This virtually abolishes secrecy in the Sigma Delta Chi fraternity." White's record of accomplishment in his battles for professionalism and openness as the hallmarks of the organization; his rescuing of *The Quill* five years earlier, bringing it to financial and editorial stability; and his devotion to the fraternity during the war years made it natural for the convention to elect him as its new national president. He was then not only the fraternity's outstanding figure but also the man to whom it was most indebted. Upon assuming the presidency, White convinced the convention to select professor Frank Martin of Missouri as the new editor of *The Quill*.

Because of the logistics of moving *The Quill* operation from Detroit to Columbia, Missouri, before the January 1921 issue, White edited that issue and included a "Hail and Farewell" editorial which, while not popular at the time even with Martin, set the tone for future editorial direction of the magazine. The function of *The Quill* was not to catalog at length the personal accomplishments of the fraternity, but to present "the foundation principles of the profession, and the ethical concepts which should guide the practitioner...things all too frequently not adequately handled even in schools of journalism; not to devote unnecessary space to news of undergraduate chapter trivialities, but rather to cater to a far larger class, the alumni; to become a magazine of real worth as far as its limited means and widely separated publication dates would permit." Martin, with the help of the Missouri chapter, brought out issues in April and October featuring new typography, many short articles and chapter news written as news stories and placed wherever makeup demanded. Approval at the 1921 convention in Ames, Iowa, of expansion of *The Quill* to eight issues a year demonstrated the improved financial condition of the fraternity but failed to consider the problems inherent in producing the magazine that often with volunteer editors and staff. It was no surprise, then, that Martin was able again to publish only four issues in the following year.

Delegates from the thirty-eight chapters were ready to re-elect White to the presidency, but he flatly refused, telling the convention it needed to stick with the well-established policy of selecting a new man each year to head the fraternity. He was, however, rewarded with the Wells Memorial Key. Kenneth C. Hogate, Detroit correspondent for *The Wall Street Journal*, was named president (Hogate was president of that newspaper at the time of his death in 1954 and his early involvement tying Sigma Delta Chi with *The Wall Street Journal* would pay off handsomely for the fraternity in the '50's and early '60's). He was followed in office by Ward A. Neff, elected in 1922 in Manhattan, Kansas. That convention saw another new national office created, that of alumni secretary, filled by Donald H. Clark of Des Moines, to fill the need of encouraging and developing alumni chapters. Clark's and Neff's work increased the number of such chapters to ten, with Minneapolis, Oklahoma City, Washington, Pittsburgh and St. Louis added. In addition, the groundwork for alumni chapters in New York, Philadelphia, Indianapolis, Toledo, Cleveland, Denver, San Francisco and Portland, Oregon, was done.

During Neff's year, a contest was established recognizing "the college paper reporter who performed the most notable piece of reportorial work." Known as the Iowa State Award, for it had been developed by that undergraduate chapter, and offering a gold watch as the prize, it was the forerunner of future competiton for collegiate journalists sponsored by the fraternity. In addition, a concerted two-year project to revise the ritual was undertaken and completed by White and Cyril Arthur Player, an Oxford University graduate initiated by the University of Washington chapter and in 1922 a distinguished reporter for the Detroit *News*. The rewritten version, approved by the Minneapolis convention in 1923, eliminated the flowery and stilted language in the initiation ceremony.

No doubt, Neff's greatest contribution came in the form of his proposal to set up a *Quill* endowment plan, the purpose of which was create and build a fund which should, in time, furnish enough revenue to support *The Quill*, pay an editor and prepare the way to giving Sigma Delta Chi "the best journalist's magazine in the world." At that time, *The Quill* was receiving $6 from the initiation fee of each new member, was published six times a year, and had total revenues of about $2,000, including $75 from advertising, while costs of producing the magazine amounted to more than $3,000. After hours of discussion at the November 20, 1923, meeting, the convention, by a vote of 34-9, created the *Quill* Endowment Fund by turning over $2,000 from the general fund. It also established a new initiation fee of $25 over strong objections of some members who said such a high fee would keep many eligible men from pledging the fraternity, with $15 to go to the Fund, $5 toward operating *The Quill*, and $5 to national headquarters. The Fund was set to become a reality and take effect in the fall of 1924. Meanwhile, the editorship of *The Quill* had passed from Martin to Chester W. Cleveland of Chicago.

Parenthetically, opposition to the Fund surfaced in each of the next few years but because it had become a part of the constitution, each attempt to get the required two-thirds vote of the chapters to change or abolish it failed. The constitution provided that the principal amount could never be used for operating the magazine. Only net income from the investments could go for that purpose. Clayton reported that the Fund grew quickly, reaching $11,108 by 1925 and $25,000 by 1927. Two years later, when earnings were first used to support *The Quill*, the Fund had reached $51,000. During the depression, economic conditions forced a change in the endowment plan. Initiation fees for undergraduates were dropped to $19, Clayton said, with $14 going to headquarters. Since 1937, the fund has been increased primarily by interest earned, but the principal amount still reached $100,000 in the late 1950's and was reported at $237,000 in the 1982 financial statement of the Society.

During the presidential terms of T. Hawley Tapping (1923-1924) and George F. Pierrot (1924-1925) prospects for new financial stability for *The Quill* led to demands for a better magazine. The

publication board recognized that need and felt it was time for a change in editors. When that problem was not solved by the 1924 convention in Bloomington, Indiana, an advertisement in the December issue of *The Quill* announced the search for a new editor. Mark L. Haas, a staff member of *The American Boy* in Detroit, was hired but he resigned in September 1926. The October issue that year was another milestone in the history of the magazine. It was the largest issue up to that time} 70 pages – devoted entirely to Charnley's *History of Sigma Delta Chi*. It also marked the beginning of a thirty-five-year association with Ovid Bell Press in Fulton, Missouri, which printed the issue.

The fraternity's first convention in the West, at Boulder, Colorado, in 1925, was significant only in that it selected Donald H. Clark as its president. Recognizing that the growth of the fraternity had reached the point that routine business was placing an undue burden on the national secretary, Clark began the drive to establish a national headquarters and employ a full-time man to administer Sigma Delta Chi. Delegates to the 1926 convention in Madison, Wisconsin, did not act on the proposal, but did settle, for a while, the question of a code of ethics, adopting the Canons of Journalism of the American Society of Newspaper Editors as the fraternity's standards. Clark, then chairman of the executive council, and his successor as president, professor Roy L. French of the University of North Dakota, doubled their effort for a headquarters. They proposed office space in Chicago at 836 Exchange Avenue in the building in the Chicago Stockyards occupied by the *Daily Drovers Journal*. The space would be provided at no cost by past president Ward Neff, whose offices were also in the building. Approval of the establishment of the new headquarters was one of the actions at the 1927 convention in Lawrence, Kansas, and the offices were opened in January 1928. New national president James A Stuart, managing editor of the Indianapolis *Star*, conducted a search for the office administrator. The council selected George Courcier, giving him the title of permanent assistant secretary of the fraternity and responsibilities for handling much of the detail work formerly entrusted to the national secretary. Courcier resigned the post in June 1929 and was replaced for five months by Theodore A. Berchtold. Robert B. Tarr of the Pontiac, Michigan *Press*, elected president by delegates to the uneventful national convention in 1928 at Northwestern University, and other members of the council were faced with the task of finding someone to succeed Berchtold. They selected Albert W. Bates, with Swift & Company in Los Angeles at the time. Bates was on board in Chicago a scant month before the 1929 convention in Columbia, Missouri. Beginning his tenure in association with new national president Edwin V. O'Neel, of the Indianapolis *Times*, Bates' provided vigorous leadership, allowing the fraternity to operate efficiently despite the beginning of The Great Depression.

Clayton said of Bates, "For the next five years, he was to prove an enthusiastic and diligent worker for Sigma Delta Chi. He inherited a complicated job, for shortly before he took over the post, the stock market bubble had burst, and the nation was headed for the worst depression in its history. Twice the fraternity was to honor him with the Wells Memorial Key: in 1938 and in 1945. His interest in the fraternity never lagged. Probably no one has served on as many committees or has done as much for the fraternity over so long a period."

One of Bates' first assignments was with *The Quill*, for which he was named business manager along with his other duties. When Haas resigned as editor in September 1926, a series of interim editors, including Pierrot and professor Lawrence Murphy of the University of Illinois, held the magazine together. Franklin M. Reck, accepted the editorship in 1928 and named Martin A. Klaver as managing editor; the two served until the fall of 1930. It was Klaver who, in association with Bates, changed *The Quill* to a monthly publication in January, 1930. For the past several years, it had appeared every other month. The issue also marked the first use of more than one color in the magazine. Soon after the 1930 convention in Columbus, Ohio, with Reck as president, Ralph L. Peters, a rewrite man for the Detroit *News*,

took over as editor. He was to remain as editor for nearly fourteen years, longer than anyone in the history of the organization.

The early years of the depression hampered the fraternity's operations to some extent, but did not diminish the enthusiasm of the officers or members. Approximately 200 members showed up for the 1931 convention in Minneapolis. In an historic move, delegates approved a proposal for honoring distinguished service to journalism. The plan called for six individuals selected each year for scholarly achievement to be awarded special gold keys. In June, 1932, the executive council named the winners of the competition. While no more gold keys were issued for the next six years, the present Distinguished Service Awards, formally established in 1939, are dated from that event. By 1932, however, the economic distress which nearly brought the nation to its knees had the same effect on Sigma Delta Chi. New president Charles E. Snyder, editor of the Chicago *Daily Drovers Journal*, found himself unable to reverse the financial straits in which the undergraduate chapters and national headquarters found themselves. He attempted to resign, feeling he was to blame for the situation, but the resignation was refused by the council. Snyder knew that attendance at the convention scheduled for Iowa State would draw only a handful of delegates and cancelled the meetings. In the absence of a convention, the officers remained for another year.

Financial problems of the chapters and the national organization dominated the 1933 convention at Northwestern University in Evanston, Illinois, at which Walter R. Humphrey editor of the Temple, Texas *Telegram*, became president. For the previous seven years, the initiation fee had been $25. But now, the students howled for relief from such a large payment upon joining the fraternity. It was noted that *The Quill* fund had now reached $75,000 and that, for four years, *The Quill* had been receiving operating revenues from accrued interest. Meanwhile, the $5 which went to headquarters wasn't enough, given the drop in the number of new members. The solution was unique and immediately effective. Initiation fees for student members were dropped to $19, ending the undergraduate clamor, and the division of the $19 was made to provide $14 to headquarters and $5 for *The Quill*, quickly restoring the national operating treasury to reasonable health. The only loser was the *Quill* Endowment Fund, which, as has been stated, grew on its own anyway.

TRAGEDY AND CELEBRATION

The fraternity's silver anniversary year – 1934 – was one of tragedy and celebration. The tragedy was a fire which burned national headquarters; the celebration, the twenty-fifth anniversary convention of Sigma Delta Chi. However, in April, before either of those events, Bates surprised the officers and members resigning as executive secretary. Bates told Humphrey he had accepted a position in Chicago with Swift & Company. The president and other members of council once again set about finding a replacement. The choice fell upon James C. Kiper, assistant to the dean of men at Indiana University.

Kiper reported for work on Friday, May 18, and one day later, the roof literally fell in on the fraternity. Bates recorded the events of that day in the next *Quill*:

Kiper and I had put in a sweltering day going over office routine, records, programs and other details. We left the office at 4 pm, roasting in a temperature of ninety-one degrees, and headed for a drugstore to get a cool drink. About 4:15 there was a rush of fire engines into the yards. It looked like a real thriller so we went into the yards to the Livestock Exchange Building and climbed nine flights to the roof to get a good view.

The flames gave off such a blistering heat that we could scarcely stand to look over the edge of the roof, even though we were nine stories up and nearly a block north. The fire had made a good start in the south pens, all of wood, and with a strong west wind behind [was] sweeping eastward toward the railroad tracks which separate the corral area from the cluster of buildings at or near the main entrance at the corner of Exchange and Halsted.

Before either Kiper or I could realize it, the flames had swept clear to the tracks and were eating their way northward toward Exchange Avenue. By the time we could dash to the ground floor and out onto Exchange Avenue they were lashing out into the street. Jim was strange to the yards, so he just hung on close behind, and we dashed. Fire engines were thundering down the street, through black smoke so dense it was impossible to see more than two or three feet ahead. We ran to the center of the street, held our breath, and ran as we never had before. Not tiny sparks but great burning chips of wood were falling everywhere. We managed to avoid them all and got through to the *Drovers Journal* Building. We were badly worried by then, but we still couldn't believe that the *Drovers Journal* Building would be taken.

Jim and I went to the second floor for the small fire extinguisher in the Sigma Delta Chi offices. I climbed out onto the roof of the *Drovers Journal* annex. I put out a few flaming embers. The flames were coming across the elevated railroad line bridge creeping toward our office windows about three feet from the bridge so I climbed up onto the elevated bridge and tried to stop the flames there. I must have made a ridiculous sight. It was plain that all hope was gone. So I climbed back into the building and Jim and I went to work on Sigma Delta Chi records. We managed to get the master enrollment card file and two stencil reels with *Quill* subscription addresses onto the *Drovers Journal* truck before it pulled away.

Then Kiper and I had to fall back to the vault, which was supposed to be fireproof. We rushed card files, scholarship award files, the petty cash box, the chapter enrollment records, three typewriters, a few drawers of odds and ends, the big permanent enrollment book, a *Quill* file, and a few other items into the vault. By then, the flames were all around the building. The front windows had caved in and the fire was shooting toward the back of the building. At the back of the building, the fire was licking at headquarters' window sills from the elevated railroad. Jim and I grabbed the cash book and the big alumni dues register and ran for the east door on the ground floor. Jim had to climb out a window. We ran like scared rabbits through streams of water, through a burning garage and across Halsted to my old flivver, which luckily I had parked just outside on Root Street. We got the record books into it, got it started, [Bates said in another article the car seemed to have the same get-the-hell-out-of-there attitude as they had, for it started on the first turn] and drove to a safe distance. The fire started at about 4:10 and the *Drovers Journal* Building was entirely gone by 5:30. I couldn't bear to go home without knowing the worst.

It was 11:30 before the flames had died down enough on Exchange Avenue for me to get over to the *Drovers Journal* Building. The sight was so terrible to behold that it ceased to be terrible, just as the excitement of it all had been so terrific that it ceased to be exciting. Nothing but a pile of bricks remained intact except a single concrete column. Up where the second floor had been was our steel vault, resting in that column of concrete. An air hole above the vault door was pouring out smoke, although the rest had died down.

Not until five days later was it possible to burn the vault door open with a torch. What remained of the once useful and effective records of national headquarters was a sickening sight, but a cause for jubilation at that. We had expected a total loss, but luckily not quite everything had burned. That water had reached the west end of the interior in time to leave partly decipherable many old vouchers, record books, *Quills*, and an extremely valuable Personnel Bureau [employment service] card file. Everything was at least partially burned, and only ashes remained of the bulk of the vault's contents, but the few items salvaged will save literally years of hard work for future officers.

Clayton's history reports that minutes of national conventions, files of *The Quill* and supplies of all kinds had gone up in smoke. All of the office equipment was destroyed as well as printed supplies accumulated over a period of years. The Chicago offices of *Editor & Publisher* were put at the disposal of the fraternity as a temporary headquarters until space could be obtained in "a dusty, wooden stall in a corner of the gutted Live Stock National Bank. Within six months, the masthead of *The Quill* carried the old address, 836 Exchange Avenue, for national headquarters. No sooner had the wire services reported the fire than members in all parts of the country began sending in offers of assistance. An alumni organization of directors and district chairmen started rebuilding the membership list.

The Quill did not miss an issue. The June issue, although delayed because all the mailing envelopes had been destroyed and new ones had to be printed, carried an editorial which said in part:

Something has been built up during those twenty-five years that flames could not destroy nor water weaken; that invisible and intangible something that has knit together a strongly unified organization that has attained an important place in the journalistic affairs of the nation. The program will go on; that is the tradition of the press. We feel that from the ashes will arise a stronger, more vital and alert, a more outspoken and united organization that has been tried by fire and found to be of enduring stuff.

President Walter Humphrey added his encouraging and optimistic view in the same issue of *The Quill.*

Although burned out of house and home, Sigma Delta Chi is going full speed ahead. It will take more than a fire to put a permanent crimp in the vigorous program of the fraternity, more than the loss of all records to erase the inspiration and impetus of twenty-five years of building. During the past few years, Sigma Delta Chi has been gaining in prestige, in influence and the esteem of not only its own membership but of the entire newspaper craft. This fire comes at a time when the fraternity's strength is at its peak. The rebound, therefore, should come with an unmistakable surge to answer the challenge of the emergency.

Nine of the ten founders of Sigma Delta Chi were living when president Humphrey, Kiper and other members of the executive council put the tragedy of the fire behind them and started planning for the silver anniversary convention scheduled for October 19, 1934, at DePauw University. Only Clippinger had died, in 1931. Forty-two undergraduate, seventeen alumni chapters and nearly 8,000 members were affiliated with the fraternity. *The Quill* published its silver anniversary edition with a white and silver cover in October featuring articles relating to the development of Sigma Delta Chi, journalism as a profession and education for journalists.

When the convention opened, every chapter except South Carolina was represented as were four of the founders – Millikan, Sloan, Pulliam and Riddick. In addition, six past presidents and alumni from across the country attended. John E. Stempel, copy editor for the New York *Sun* and later chairman of the department of journalism at Indiana University, was elected president.

Steady progress marked the years from 1935 through 1941. Without question, one of the most important events during that period occurred in 1936 when the Dallas convention approved a move for headquarters from the stockyards to the Pure Oil Building, just north of the "Loop" at 35 East Wacker Drive in downtown Chicago. Rent was to be $60 per month. It would be an address familiar to members for forty-three years. A house ad at the bottom of page twenty in the December *Quill* announced, "We Moved to 35 E. Wacker Drive December 19, 1936." Several moves were made in the years following, but, until 1981, always within that thirty-plus-story building near the Chicago River.

The 1937 convention changed what had been alumni chapters to "professional chapters" and designated the so-called

"active chapters" as "undergraduate chapters." In yet another event which has impacted the organization since its inception, Ralph Peters, who in 1937-1938 doubled as *Quill* editor and president of the fraternity, suggested in the final report of his term that Sigma Delta Chi inaugurate a comprehensive program of Distinguished Service Awards to replace the ignored gold keys. After a year of study, delegates to the 1939 convention in Palo Alto, California, adopted the plan, which called for awards in general reporting, editorial writing, foreign correspondence, Washington correspondence and radio news writing. The winners were to receive a medal and an engraved citation. They were to be selected by a carefully picked group of judges, representing all fields of journalistic endeavor and all parts of the country. In addition, a set of awards was established at the college level honoring the best collegiate newspaper and the best collegiate photographer, along with a citation for excellence in journalism for one man in each graduating class of every college or university with a chapter of Sigma Delta Chi. The first set of awards for work done in 1939 were presented at the 1940 convention in Des Moines, Iowa.

At the Des Moines meeting, SDX president Irving Dilliard told the executive council at its preconvention meeting that he had a plan to mark historic sites in journalism which would be an excellent annual observance to call attention to National Newspaper Week. The project was approved and a committee was appointed to study financing and possible sites for a first marking. The committee made its recommendation to the 1941 convention in New Orleans, suggesting that the first site be in Bennington, Vermont, where had stood the press of Anthony Haswell, editor of the *Vermont Gazette*. The site, approved by the delegates, was selected because of Haswell's courage in challenging the Alien and Sedition Acts passed in 1798 under the administration of John Adams, and on August 16, 1942, the marker was unveiled.

Other significant innovations made during those pre-war years were changes in the constitution which established a vice president for alumni activities – an officer who would succeed to the presidency – in 1935 (Frank McDonough, associate editor of *Better Homes and Gardens* was selected); a vice president for expansion the following year (Mitchell Charnley of the University of Minnesota was elected); and vice president for undergraduate chapter affairs in 1938 (Willard R. Smith, Wisconsin manager for the United Press, was named). National presidents for those years were: Carl P. Miller, Pacific Coast edition, *The Wall Street Journal*, Los Angeles (1935-1936); Tully Nettleton, Chicago, editorial writer, *The Christian Science Monitor* (1936-1937); Peters, rotogravure editor, the Detroit *News* (1937-1938); George A. Brandenburg, Chicago editor, *Editor & Publisher* (1938-1939); Elmo Scott Watson, editor, *Publishers' Auxiliary*, Chicago (1939-1940); and Irving Dilliard, editorial writer, the St. Louis *Post Dispatch* (1940-1941). Convention sites included Champaign-Urbana, Illinois (1935); Dallas (1936); Topeka, Kansas (1937); Madison, Wisconsin (1938); Palo Alto, California (1939); Des Moines (1940); and New Orleans (1941).

THE WAR YEARS

The Japanese attack on Pearl Harbor followed the New Orleans convention by less than a month and the pressures of wartime activities had a profound effect on Sigma Delta Chi both at the local chapter and headquarters levels. Many members of undergraduate chapters enlisted in the armed forces and others were drafted. It soon became evident that most undergraduate chapters would either have to suspend activities for the duration or function on a limited scale. Professional chapters found waning interest of their members in meetings and projects. Newly elected national president Palmer Hoyt, publisher of the Portland *Oregonian*, canceled plans for a 1942 convention early in that year and then was faced with the resignation of James Kiper as executive secretary. The council decided not to replace him for the duration of the war. The council itself, with members occupied with their own affairs, decided to cease meeting. Former executive secretary Bates, still working in Chicago, agreed to chair a special headquarters committee and

joined past president George Brandenburg and Carl Kesler, state editor of the Chicago *Daily News*, in administering the few national activities which remained. Mrs. Helen K. Pilcher was left in charge of the office to manage routine operations. The fraternity was all but shut down. Because no convention met, Hoyt served as president for two years until going to Washington as domestic director of the Office of War Information in July, 1943. The council elected Willard R. Smith, associate editor of the Madison, Wisconsin *State Journal* to succeed him. The near-dormant condition of Sigma Delta Chi continued through late 1945. No national conventions were scheduled in 1943, 1944 or 1945.

Even *The Quill* was affected. During the first eighteen months of the war, *The Quill* was able to continue its regular monthly schedule, but with the July 1943 issue, it was decided to publish only six times a year until the return of peace. Editor Ralph Peters explained in the July-August issue that the picture was bleak. Under wartime conditions income from the endowment fund dwindled and initiations dropped to almost nothing. As to an alternate source of income, he wrote, "One of the sources from which it is hoped to obtain additional revenue is from advertising. Now let us be frank about advertising. *The Quill* is not begging; it wants no gift advertising; no 'blackjack' advertising; no handouts. Its influence in policy and in its editorial columns, needless to say, are not for sale." Color was dropped and the size of the magazine was cut back to sixteen pages. It was, however, just about the only continuing contact between the national operation and individual members in those four years. A year later, Peters underwent an emergency operation for appendicitis and died August 30, 1944. One of the weaknesses of *The Quill* at that time was the fact that there was no provision for an assistant who could take over in an emergency. National president Willard Smith edited the September-October issue, Bates agreed to put out the November-December issue and Kesler edited the next two. In July 1945, Kesler was formally named editor. Clayton, who later would become *Quill* editor himself, said, "Under Kesler's direction, *The Quill* not only would retain its high professional stature but would become an even more powerful voice in journalism." Early in Kesler's editorship, advertising began to pick up and the July-August 1946 issue was one of the most successful in attracting advertising to that date.

Smith, like Hoyt, served two years as president and was followed by Barry Farris, editor-in-chief of International News Service in New York, for the 1945-1946 term of office. It was during presidency that the council became active again and decided to hold a national convention in 1946. With the help of Bates, Brandenburg and the Headline Club of Chicago, plans were laid for a convention November 21-23 in Chicago. The council's next task was to select a new executive secretary, a post vacant since 1942 when Kiper resigned. In November 1945, a job description for the new position was published:

> We are now ready to employ a full-time executive secretary who will also direct the Personnel Bureau and publish *The Quill*. We need a man who has journalistic talent and also a flair for business and promotion. He should be able to manage an office and its personnel; sell advertising; work well with editors in the placement of members in editorial jobs. He should understand or be able quickly to grasp the needs of editors in all fields from publications to radio and publicity. He should have a good personality, be able to make friends easily, address audiences with poise and persuasion, and have enough instinct for organization to see that the detailed records are efficiently kept at national headquarters. Above all he must believe wholeheartedly in the aims and purposes and in the practical worth of Sigma Delta Chi.

The choice fell upon Victor E. Bluedorn, a returning veteran who had graduated from Iowa State University and had been publisher and editor of the *Scott County Tribune* in Walcott, Iowa, before the war. Bluedorn was twenty-nine when he assumed the office in April 1946. He set out to rebuild the undergraduate and professional chapters – a task necessary to effect any revitalization of the national organization. By the Chicago convention, he had helped to reactivate five undergraduate chapters and one professional chapter and had petitions for a new undergraduate charter from Oklahoma A & M and four professional chapters from Miami, Florida; Fort Worth, Texas; and Brookings, South Dakota, ready for convention action.

One hundred and fifty delegates and friends registered for the Chicago convention and elected George W. Healy, Jr., managing editor of the New Orleans *Times-Picayune*, as president for 1946-1947. In an important decision, the convention took steps to reinstitute *The Quill* on its regular monthly schedule under Kesler's editorship beginning with January 1947. The magazine, however, was still having financial problems and continued to be limited in its number of pages. Press freedom had been an important element in Sigma Delta Chi's purpose since its founding in 1909, but the 1946 convention, in a way, formalized the commitment, naming a committee on freedom of the press headed by Kent Cooper, general manager of The Associated Press. Accepting the challenge given it, the new ad hoc committee, made up of six of the nation's leading journalists, went to work. Its primary focus was on a bill pending in Congress which would authorize the setting up of an official global information service.

Issuing a statement on its own volition in May 1947, opposing the provision in the bill to establish a government news service, the committee set off a furor within the fraternity. Delegates to the 1947 convention in Washington, DC, were highly critical of the committee's autonomous action and passed a resolution stipulating that all committee reports bearing on public policy be first submitted to the executive council before being released to the public. The importance of free press issues, however, was too much to ignore.

SOME IMPORTANT CHANGES

John M. McClelland, Jr., editor of the Longview, Washington *Daily News*, had been named by Healy as chairman of a structure committee to study changes needed to provide the framework for growth and prestige. His committee recommended the establishment of three new permanent committees, among them an advancement of freedom of information committee. After adoption of the report, incoming president Luther Huston, manager of the Washington, DC bureau of *The New York Times*, named Clayton, an editorial writer for The St. Louis *Globe-Democrat*, to head the committee. A second committee, recommended by McClelland's report, was to study press ethics and Huston named McClelland to head that committee. Both groups made their initial reports to the convention the following year in Milwaukee.

The structure committee also proposed seventeen amendments to the constitution and by-laws. While some of the amendments were rejected, some of the others that were passed dealt with efforts to encourage the development of professional chapters. The committee's report said that, in Sigma Delta Chi's first thirty-eight years, sixty-two undergradute chapter charters had been granted while fewer than fifty were active. Of those amendments adopted, three are especially significnt. A program of naming three "Fellows" of Sigma Delta Chi each year was established. The amendment provided that a fellows committee composed of three immediate past presidents be established to screen candidates and make recommendations annually to the convention. The program, with very few modifications, is still carried on today. A second amendment changed the title of the executive secretary to executive director (it was changed to the present title, executive officer, in 1960) and spelled out the duties of the office for the first time. The third amendment provided for the creation of a business manager for *The Quill* and the appointment of associate editors.

By the time of the 1948 convention in Milwaukee, membership had reached a reported 16,247, there were forty-nine undergraduate and thirty-six professional chapters and *Quill* circulation had reached an all-time high, surpassing 8,000. A record 242 delegates heard McClelland report the ethics committee recommendation that the fraternity work toward the drafting of an ethical code. There had been no effort in this direction since the 1926 convention voted to use the Canons of Ethics of the American Society of Newspaper Editors. Clayton was named by 1948-1949 president Neal Van Sooy to chair the press ethics committee which was assigned the task of working on a code. It was an effort which, over the next twenty-five years, would cause more than a few vigorous floor fights at conventions beginning with the 1949 neeting in Dallas. The committee's report there proposed a code to be enforced by an impartial board of review authorized to cite flagrant violations and invoke the power of public opinion. It spelled out the obligations of accuracy, fairness, decency, and community leadership. The convention voted to defer action and refer the problem to yet another ethics committee and, again, Clayton was named chairman by new president (and *Quill* editor) Carl R. Kesler.

The first convention held in the Southeast, in 1950, convened November 8 at the plush Sans Souci Hotel in Miami Beach, Florida. While the convention had its serious discussions, the hotel's private beach and a wide variety of other entertainment took its toll. Clayton's book records that because of the pressure of other business, the expected debate on press ethics did not materialize. In fact, so much entertainment had been provided that the convention ran behind schedule. Unfortunately, the confusion brought on a heart attack for Kesler, who was trying to expedite business on that Saturday afternoon. McClelland took over the chair, later presided over the annual banquet, and was elected president to succeed Kesler, who later recovered.

Freedom of information, the lingering problem of developing an ethics code, and membership qualifications dominated discussions in the fifties. V.M. (Red) Newton, managing editor of the Tampa *Tribune*, took over as chairman of the national advancement of freedom of information committee, a post he would hold for more than ten years. The fiery and outspoken Newton time and again took on the highest offices and elected officials in the nation, including the President. His reports and accomplishments made spectacular reading in *The Quill* and lively discussions at the conventions. The beginning of another long freedom of information battle – to negate the effects of Canon 35 of the American Bar Association prohibiting courtroom photography – took place in 1954 with a convention resolution condemning the ABA position. Decisions not to decide on the ethics code dotted convention business sessions in those years. The need for enforcement and the extent to which a code would enforce journalistic responsibility were elements which split committees and convention sessions year after year. The question of "freebies" surfaced at the 1956 convention in Louisville, Kentucky, when the committee's report recommended that all newspapers tighten their standards of ethical operation by issuing instructions to their staffs to prohibit the acceptance of gifts. That report was accepted, but development of a full code was, again, left to another year. Payment of national dues was made compulsory for membership in 1954 at Columbus, Ohio. By 1957, the convention was told that while 16,000 members were paid up and active, a total of 9,253 had been dropped from the rolls. At that time, more than 27,000 members had been initiated, 1,976 had died and twenty-one had been expelled. Although it had little impact on the membership, an important step in protecting the leadership of the national organization was adopted by the 1957 convention in Houston and effected by the executive council the following March: Sigma Delta Chi became incorporated under the laws of Illinois March 10, 1958.

Presidents of the fraternity in the fifties included Charles Clayton (1951-1952); Lee Hills, executive editor, Detroit *Free Press*, (1952-1953); Robert U. Brown, president and editor, *Editor & Publisher*, New York (1953-1954); Alden C. Waite, president, Southern California Associated Newspapers, Glendale, California (1954-1955); Mason Rossiter Smith, editor and publisher, *Tribune Press*, Gouverneur, New York (1955-1956); Sol Taishoff, editor and publisher, *Broadcasting – Telecasting* magazine, Washington, DC (1956-1957);

Robert J. Cavagnaro, general executive, The Associated Press, San Francisco (1957-1958); and James A. Byron, news director, WBAP AM-TV, Fort Worth, Texas (1958-1959). Taishoff was the first man with broadcast connections to become president of the fraternity and Byron the first broadcaster to reach that office. Conventions were held in Detroit (1951), Denver (1952), St. Louis (1953), Columbus, Ohio (1954), Chicago (1955), Louisville, Kentucky (1956), Houston (1957) and San Diego (1958).

By the mid-fifties, the officers were looking toward the golden anniversary convention scheduled for Indianapolis November 11-14, 1959. Clayton, who took over as editor of *The Quill* upon Kesler's death in 1956, was named chairman of the fiftieth anniversary committee. Elaborate plans for the celebration included a trip to Sigma Delta Chi's birthplace at DePauw University. Eugene S. Pulliam, managing editor of the Indianapolis *News* and son of founder Eugene C. Pulliam, was named general chairman for the convention.

Clayton did what many observers called an impossible job by producing the 132-page golden anniversary edition of *The Quill* and, when he couldn't find anyone else to do it, writing a 244-page history of Sigma Delta Chi, *Fifty Years for Freedom*, published April 17, 1959.

Given the buildup in *The Quill* and the attitude of the membership that everything connected with the fraternity was rosy, anticipation of the best-convention-ever caused Sigma Delta Chi officers to project the highest attendance in history. Few, if any, of the 600 delegates to the gala convention were aware the fraternity's leadership had become convinced Sigma Delta Chi was in a severe state of deterioration, nearing organizational insolvency. The paradox was indeed striking. In the midst of celebrating fifty years of apparent triumphs, the fraternity's executive council was wrestling with strategies to stave off what appeared to be a "death trend" for Sigma Delta Chi. But even those eleven men on the council could not envision the metamorphosis Sigma Delta Chi would encounter in the first twelve months of its second half century.

CHAPTER 2

Toward a Professional Society

The genesis of the introspection which led the executive council of Sigma Delta Chi to determine that the fraternity in 1959 was in feeble condition at best came in the two or three years just prior to the fiftieth anniversary convention in Indianapolis. It might have been the financial condition of the fraternity, the failure of members to pay national dues or need for the revitalization of failing chapters, but it was the knotty problem of membership eligibility and the controversy which surrounded it in 1957 and 1958 which pried off the lid and intiated the fraternity's self evaluation.

National president Sol Taishoff, editor and publisher of *Broadcasting* and *Telecasting* magazines, had made up his mind it was time to face squarely the problem of the membership status of public relations men in the fraternity. When the council had convened for its mid-year meeting, April 12, 1957, at the Sheraton Hotel in Chicago, the public relations issue was first on the agenda. Taishoff's agenda asked, "Are public relations practitioners journalists as defined in the fraternity by-laws and eligible to be initiated as members? What should be the rights of public relations men who are presently members in good standing?" Councilor Robert M. White II, editor of the Mexico, Missouri *Ledger*, remembers, "It was a case of deciding whether or not Sigma Delta Chi was going to be a 'newsman's' organization rather than a 'media' organization."

The council's action was decisive in favor of a purist position. On a motion by councilor V.M. (Red) Newton, Jr., managing editor of the Tampa *Tribune*, and seconded by Taishoff, the policy on professional membership was amended to read, "Advertising, publicity and public relations men are not considered as being within the professional field of journalism and are specifically excluded in the fraternity's definition of journalism." Previously, only the field of advertising had been excluded by name. Membership eligibility for public relations men had been a continuing problem since the phrase "dissemination of public information, excepting..." was added to the policy in 1937. Former executive director Al Bates

The 1958-1959 SDX officers were instrumental in rebuilding Sigma Delta Chi from a professional journalism fraternity on a "death trend" to a vital journalistic society. Five of the six served as national presidents. They are Robert J. Cavagnaro, president in 1957-1958; Buren McCormack, president in 1961-1962; James A. Byron, president in 1958-1959; Robert Root, vice president for undergraduate chapter affairs in 1958-1959; E.W. (Ted) Scripps II, president in 1960-1961; and Robert M. White II, president in 1966-1967.

said at that time, "This doesn't mean that all press agents or public relations people are eligible." The policy was in limbo and almost unmanageable until 1952. The executive council that year, made eligibility dependent upon the preparation and dissemination of information in the "public interest" as opposed to that in the "private interest." The 1952 version provided that those public relations practitioners who are writers for civic organizations, social agencies, benevolent or philanthropic foundations, educational institutions or departments of government except military and those who have "an acceptable background of experience in news work for newspapers, magazines or in broadcasting" were working in the public interest and could be looked on with favor for membership. The 1957 executive council action moved to make these persons ineligible for membership as well as those working for the "private

interest." Not only did the policy change deny new membership to public relations men, it cast members who were then actively engaged in public relations practice in the role of "associate" members without voting and office-holding rights.

Minutes of that April 12 meeting made the motivation clear: "There was a general feeling that public relations had grown into such an enormous industry, the original character of Sigma Delta Chi as a journalistic fraternity was being threatened." Robert Cavagnaro, general executive of The Associated Press in San Francisco and vice president in charge of professional affairs, notified chapter presidents of the action by letter and through an article in the June 1957 *Quill*. Records of immediate reactions by chapters and public relations members are skimpy, but by the November convention in Houston, the battle lines had been drawn.

White recalls that he and Edward

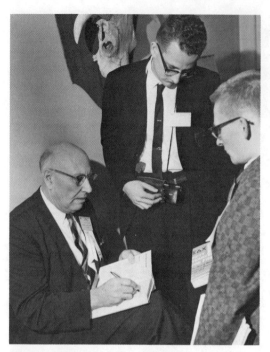

Charles C. Clayton (left), author of the fraternity's golden anniversary history, *Fifty Years for Freedom*, autographs a copy of his book for delegates at the 1959 national convention in Indianapolis. Clayton was Sigma Delta Chi president in 1951-1952 and was editor of *The Quill* from 1956-1961.

Lindsay, editor of the Lindsay-Schaub newspapers in Decatur, Illinois, and the fraternity's vice president in charge of undergraduate chapter affairs, had decided to give up their seats on the executive council. However, upon arriving in Houston, "we learned the public relations people, many of whom were close friends, were going to kick us off the board because of the PR issue. We both decided to fight and worked like hell to get re-elected to the board." The effort to replace the council which had adopted the new policy could have had far-reaching effects had it succeeded. All council members were elected to one-year terms and stood for election at each national convention. Thus, with a concerted effort, the entire council could have been unseated. The attempt at Houston failed and rotating terms of three years for council members were instituted with the reorganization of Sigma Delta Chi in 1960. Resolutions sent to national headquarters or brought to the convention floor predicted ominous results if the council's decision were allowed to stand. The Buckeye (Akron, Ohio) professional chapter stated, "...to destroy the relationship that exists among newspaper people, radio and television newsmen and public relations men ultimately would destroy the fraternity in the Akron area and perhaps elsewhere." Calling the disqualification of present public relations members unfair, unwise and unjust, the Tri-State (Pittsburgh) chapter resolution charged that the action "...could do great harm to the fraternity."

White had been designated by president Taishoff as parliamentarian for the convention and when the president asked White to rule on whether a motion by a delegate (who was also a public relations practitioner) was in order, White properly ruled it out of order. The delegate stood and shouted, "You're completely ignorant and incapable of making a ruling!" White very calmly responded, "If you'll forgive my ignorance, I'll forgive your rudeness." It was in this tone that the lengthy and emotional debate took place, but, when all had been heard, the delegates decided to postpone action until the 1958 convention in San Diego and called on incoming national president Cavagnaro to appoint a special committee to prepare a report on "membership eligibility provisions of the constitution as they relate to the future character of the fraternity." Cavagnaro selected longtime Sigma Delta Chi friend Bernard Kilgore, president of *The Wall Street Journal*, to chair the committee. Kilgore had his select panel at work on the project December 16 in Chicago. For six months, the committee reviewed options and expressions from the membership and by late June 1958, had its report ready.

The Kilgore Report, as it became known, was printed in the August 1958 *Quill* and called for two basic changes. First, the elimination of the "associate" member category, with all post-college members in good standing to be referred to as professional members. This meant that members involved in public relations would regain full-privilege status. Second, the report called for the deletion of the 1937

Bernard (Barney) Kilgore (center), president of *The Wall Street Journal*, and a key figure in the 1960 reorganization of Sigma Delta Chi, is pictured with 1964-1965 Society president Ralph Sewell (left) and 1966-1967 president Robert M. White II. Kilgore, national treasurer in the mid-1950's, and for whom the Kilgore Freedom of Information Internships are named, arranged for McKinsey and Co. to prepare the study which led to the reorganization.

phrase, "preparation or dissemination of public information," from the definition of journalism in the fraternity by-laws. Thereby, the Kilgore Report would rule out initiation of public relations men in the future.

The September issue of the magazine carried a full-page ad, paid for by the Texas Association of Sigma Delta Chi, a loosely-knit group of five professional and seven undergraduate chapters in Texas with a record of activism in freedom of information and other journalistic issues. The ad, which flatly rejected the Kilgore proposals and called for delegates to defeat the Kilgore Report in San Diego, argued that, "Many a newspaper editor across the nation will say some public relations men perform definitely journalistic functions. Any journalism professor aware of the facts in today's method of gathering and disseminating news will agree." It declared that the Texas Association of Sigma Delta Chi and its

affiliated chapters believe that the public relations men who fit that category "should be considered eligible for active and professional membership in Sigma Delta Chi." The ad concluded, "Causing the fraternity to retract within the narrow membership area is not the way to keep Sigma Delta Chi vigorously 'professional' and 'journalistic' if the fraternity is to remain true to its historic ideals and keep faith with its founders."

A storm of letters and counter ads reached *The Quill* offices quickly and no fewer than nine full pages of letters and ads were published in the October and November issues. Past national president Walter R. Humphrey (1933-1934), editor of the Fort Worth *Press*, took the Texas Association to task both for representing all Texas chapters and for opposing the Kilgore Report. Humphrey said, "The [Texas] state association has not discussed the Kilgore Report or voted on it, although its directors,

23

Buren McCormack (left), Society president in 1961-1962, presents a special certificate of appreciation to Dr. Warren K. Agee upon the completion of Agee's tenure as executive officer. Agee became executive officer in November 1960 and resigned to accept an administrative post at Texas Christian University in July 1962.

I understand, approved using the ad. None of the college chapters had even met between the time the Kilgore Report was published and the time of this ad in September's *Quill.* The ad may represent the position of Texas Sigma Delta Chi's; I don't know. But it does not represent action by chapters nor does it represent state convention action on the Kilgore Report because the convention has not met." Humphrey, a member of the Kilgore committee and chairman of the membership eligibility committee which reported in Houston, said further, "We of Mr. Kilgore's committee believe its proposals are the best possible for the future strength of the fraternity."

The October issue also included a full-page ad from a group of public relations consultants and executives endorsing the Kilgore Report. Headlined, "We Thank You for Restoring Us to Full Membership," the ad, signed by Bates, then a public relations consultant in New York, and among others, public relations executives

from General Motors, Sears Roebuck, U.S. Steel and NBC, said, "We accept your tighter definition of journalism. Although we prepare and disseminate news stories, we admit we do so, at least in part, in the interest of our clients and employers. Newsmen, on the other hand, generally work without obligation to any special interest. Both activities may well be in the public interest but there is a fundamental difference which is important to Sigma Delta Chi." The three columns of type concluded, "The Kilgore Report suggests a solution to a problem that has been tearing Sigma Delta Chi apart....We agree with its findings and recommendations and...hope that both college and professional chapters will approve the report and instruct their delegates to vote for it at the convention."

Walter Burroughs, publisher of the Costa Mesa, California *Globe Herald and Pilot* and a victim of executive council action depriving him of full membership rights many years earlier when he had spent time as an advertising and public relations executive, wrote, "Journalism and public relations are mutually exclusive....Opening the door to domination of Sigma Delta Chi by unthinking or non-professional public relations men, however well intentioned, is the beginning of a death trend [for the fraternity]." Lindsay wrote, "Sigma Delta Chi will decide at the San Diego convention whether it will be a fraternity of newsmen or public relations men. It can't be both." And White, in a short letter, added, "I favor the adoption of the Kilgore Report. It will keep news the basis of Sigma Delta Chi. Not advertising. Not public relations. Not social science or home economics or engineering. But news....Without the support, the recognition, and the respect of news mediums and newsmen, Sigma Delta Chi is thirty." Even the immediate past president of the Public Relations Society of America, Dan J. Forrestal, wrote that he "endorsed this [Kilgore] report heartily." With his committee the clear symbol of controversy, Kilgore remarked in his own dry way one night during the convention in San Diego, "I'd just as soon be famous for some other reason than the Kilgore Report." But after two hours of debate and discussion at the November 22 business session, the delegates endorsed the report, 70-24, ending the two-year debate but leaving the question of its effect on membership in doubt.

THE WHITE REPORT

Elation on having the public relations issue resolved had not subsided before a new and more potentially-damaging problem faced the executive council. Meeting after the San Diego convention, the council heard retiring fraternity treasurer Buren McCormack and executive director Victor E. Bluedorn report that the fraternity had lost $27,000 in general operating funds in the fiscal year ending July 31, 1958, and an additional $8,300 in the first three months of fiscal 1959. The gravity of the financial report is best explained by the fact that the $27,000 deficit was greater than the total monies collected from members' dues in fiscal 1958 and just over 25 percent of the fraternity's gross annual income, $107,500,

Victor E. Bluedorn (right), executive director for the fraternity from 1946-1960, presented a special certificate in 1959 to Kenneth Whiting, the 30,000th member to join Sigma Delta Chi since its founding in 1909. Bluedorn's fourteen years was the longest tenure of any person who served as the top administrative officer for SDX until Russell E. Hurst's nineteen years from 1962-1981.

for that year. At the direction of the council, new national president James A. Byron, executive news director of WBAP AM-TV, Fort Worth, Texas, and the first broadcaster to become national president, appointed a special committee to study the operations of the fraternity, to determine whether or not all expenditures were necessary or justified for carrying out its mission, and to recommend means of balancing income and outgo. Further, Byron instructed the committee to study and evaluate the effectiveness of headquarters operations and recommend corrective measures. White was named to chair the committee and was joined by McCormack, vice president and editorial director of *The Wall Street Journal*, Burroughs and Lindsay. The committee convened in mid-February 1959 with members spending several days at national headquarters in Chicago studying records, procedures and correspondence and analyzing financial statements. Formal work began with a meeting February 18 which lasted all day and well into the night, with and without Bluedorn present.

From those deliberations, the committee developed the outline of the White Report, although White credits Burroughs, as committee secretary, with formulating the language and preparing the report for the council. White edited the final document. Burroughs had begun his work even before the February meetings. "After talking to student members and professional members, I had determined that, by this time, the members were not getting (a) any help in activities or (b) any inspiration. I started asking why it was that the student and professional members were feeling low in their minds and had no particicular pride in the fraternity." When the White Report was presented April 14, 1959. at the council's meeting at *The Wall Street Journal* offices in Washington, DC, its revelations – more far-reaching than had been anticipated – were startling and struck directly at the fraternity's nerve center.

With considerable regret, the committee reports to the executive council that in this, the fraternity's fiftieth year, the fraternity appears to be on a death trend which will require some positive and courageous action on the part of the council to reverse and change back to a growth trend. The committee finds that there is a continuing weakening of the base of the fraternity – the enthusiasm, understanding and performance of the undergraduate chapters. This weakness is now being extended to the professional chapters. Principal responsibility for this deteriorating situation must be charged to inadequacy of the national headquarters operation.

The conclusions in the thirteen-page report, it stated, were based upon observations of the committee members and information secured at headquarters as well as data received from chapters and members. However, it continued, "...analytical examination of audited statements confirms the sickness of the fraternity." The $27,000 general operations deficit for fiscal 1958, "...while serious in itself, is symptomatic of

a more serious malady so far as the general health of the fraternity is concerned." Pointing to the fact that while initiation income between 1955 and 1958 demonstrated apparent growth in membership, concomitant increases in dues from members stayed approximately the same from year to year. Income from dues in 1956 amounted to $25,337. In the same year, money from initiations reached $21,205. The committee expected a substantial increase in membership dues income the following year, but found an increase of only $170 to $25,507. A similar pattern was evident in 1958 with an increase of only $363 to $25,870 in membership dues while the 1957 initiation fees totaled $18,452. "The inevitable conclusion is that there is constantly diminishing interest in the fraternity and in its objectives" because while new members are being initiated, continuing members are not renewing memberships by paying dues. The report continued:

When it is considered that the reported general operating loss has increased from $293 in 1953 to $27,000 in 1958, it becomes apparent that if the present trend is allowed to continue, it is a matter only of a few years until the fraternity will become insolvent.

In the opinion of the committee, this danger of financial insolvency is a lesser danger than the general loss of vigor of the fraternity.

If the recent trend on membership continues, the fraternity will become insolvent so far as purpose and achievement are concerned – as well as financially insolvent.

White and some of the other members, looking for obvious ways to cut expenses, identified the executive director's salary of $11,500, his *Quill* advertising commissions of $5,117, Christmas "bonus" of $221, stipend for editing the SDX News section of *Quill* of $600 and retirement expenses of $2,623 – a total income package of $20,000 plus. "In comparison with the total income of managers of effective trade associations...it is rather more than such a position normally pays." But savings in various areas – including the salary and benefits of the executive director – was not the answer. The report said:

> The fraternity is in the position of any organization which is failing in its purpose. To succeed, it must make membership in the fraternity so desirable that members will desire to continue as members and pay dues. Instead of attempting to balance the budget, we should take a positive step which will ultimately increase income.

The report recommended that dues income be increased through retention of current members and increasing the number of initiates – particularly professionals. In addition, it recommended that a strong effort be made to reverse the "death trend" of undergraduate chapters by concentrating on efforts to build appreciation for the fraternity and, thus, activity and effectiveness, along with building the number of graduate members. To accomplish this, the committee recommended the establishment of a "sales department" at national headquarters headed by a field secretary "…whose primary assignment would be to visit both undergraduate and professional chapters systematically; to carry to them the message of the fraternity; to inspire them to carry on the work which each chapter of the fraternity should assume." It is ironic that the council, having taken a purist attitude about membership, found itself in need of a good public relations man. The field secretary called for would be paid from funds generated from as many as 100 continuing members who would pay $100 as a "contributing membership" or, if necessary, from the fraternity's reserves. Interestingly, the committee recommended against a general increase in dues. "An increase might price membership out of the market to an extent that there would be so little increase in total income, the problem would remain unsolved."

Minutes of the April 14, 1959, meeting in Washington, DC state only that the White Report was approved and would be followed up by a committee headed by president Byron, with Cavagnaro, Burroughs, McCormack and Newton as members. White did not continue on the committee because of his pending appointment in

August 1959 as president and editor of the New York *Herald Tribune*.

But within the council, the tenure of executive director Bluedorn was under fire. Minutes of an April 20, 1960, council meeting state that Bluedorn "had been warned one year earlier" about his performance and the inadequacy of the national headquarters operation. Burroughs recalls a conversation with Bluedorn. "I talked to him and told him he was slipping."

While the specifics of the field secretary recommendations of the White Report were not implemented by the council in 1959, a modified version would be included in reports of subsequent committees and adopted by the council and convention. However, the identification of problems in the report began a process which would carry the fraternity toward total reorganization and bring about the end of Bluedorn's fourteen-year association with Sigma Delta Chi.

REORGANIZATION AND THE McKINSEY REPORT

The festive aura in which Sigma Delta Chi launched its second half century in Indianapolis, November 11-14, 1959, masked the real problems which had surfaced during the preceding year. But that was understandable. The more than 600 delegates to the golden anniversary convention and the executive council were caught up in the excitement of the moment and had reason to celebrate.

Sheer growth in number of members since Sigma Delta Chi's founding in 1909, with the 30,000th member having been initated in August 1959 seemed reason enough. The Alpha chapter at DePauw University had spawned seventy undergraduate and fifty-three professional chapters in nearly every state. A sentimental, thirty-five-mile bus trip by delegates to the DePauw campus in Greencastle, Indiana served to emphasize the fraternity's apparent prosperous evolvement from humble beginnings. Vice President Richard Nixon and NBC-News Washington commentator David Brinkley, along with Sigma Delta Chi founders Eugene C. Pulliam, William M. Glenn and Paul M.

27

Riddick, were among the speakers and guests. Even national president Byron, in what had to be the great irony of the convention, joined in the celebration. Although Byron had knowledge of the ominous projections in the White Report, a continuous decline in paid memberships, past and looming fiscal deficits and questionable leadership from the fraternity's executive director, Byron, apparently receiving his information from Bluedorn, believed he was providing an accurate, though optimistic report when he said in his president's report:

Financially, your fraternity is sounder than ever, as the treasurer's report will show you. Income exceeded expenses by more than $14,000. Gross receipts of nearly $140,000 were the highest for any year in history. As to membership, we enrolled 1,147 men last year.

The financial statement for the fiscal year ending July 31, 1959, which was given to delegates verified Byron's comments. However, no data on how the fraternity allegedly had recovered from an $8,000 deficit for the first three months of the fiscal year or had increased its income from $107,500 to $140,000 in a single year can be found in minutes or financial documents for that year, and, according to Burroughs, the information probably was provided by Bluedorn.

The largest single issue of *The Quill* in the organization's history to date – 132 pages – carried stories of the fraternity's triumphs in freedom of information, ethics and the maturation of Sigma Delta Chi to a place of national prestige. In that November 1959 issue, editor Clayton said:

If there is one development of the last half century which can be said to exemplify the period, I think it is the development of the concept of journalism as a profession, worthy of a place in society with medicine, law and the ministry. Such a concept implies a history of service, a prescribed code of ethics and an established system of professional training. Sigma Delta Chi was among the first to place emphasis on this concept and has worked

constantly through the years to strengthen it. Sigma Delta Chi has kept pace with the changes of the years and contributed leadership to them through its research program, its insistence on journalism as a profession, its militant fight for freedom of information, and its awards program. It is unique among organizations in its field in that it is the only one which includes in its membership all phases of the profession, from the student still with stars in his eyes to the men who write and edit today's news.

Clayton's book on the history of the fraternity, *Fifty Years For Freedom*, published by Southern Illinois University Press April 17, 1959, provided yet another source of pride for members. "I tried many times to persuade someone to write the history because of my teaching schedule in the Department of Journalism at Southern Illinois University at Carbondale and my work as editor of *The Quill*. Finally, when time began to run out, I did it myself and completed it in less than three months," Clayton said. A former reporter, city editor, editorial writer, and assistant to the publisher of the St. Louis *Globe Democrat*, Clayton had served Sigma Delta Chi in nearly every important role in the 1940's and 1950's, including a year as national president in 1951-1952. He had been a member of the executive council, was a winner of the Wells Memorial Key, highest honor the fraternity can bestow on a member, was first national chairman of both the freedom of information and press ethics committees in 1948 and 1949, and was chairman of the fiftieth anniversary committee in 1959. Although no records provide accurate figures, the best estimate is that between 4,500 and 5,000 copies of the book found their way into public and private libraries.

The salute to Sigma Delta Chi's history from all directions and the air of certainty which pervaded the Indianapolis convention left the delegates and the national membership at large with little inclination to look behind the scenes. E.W. (Ted) Scripps II, national vice president for professional chapter affairs and vice president of Scripps-Howard newspapers in Washington, DC in

1959, remembers the delegates had no knowledge of the White Report or any of its conclusions. "So much of the strength of the membership and so many of the delegates at the convention in Indianapolis were undergraduates. They were not really interested, at that time in their lives, in the long-range future of the fraternity." A member of the executive council since 1955 and its youngest member at age thirty, Scripps added, "Only the top echelon and some of the professional members were in a position to see what the fraternity could contribute to American journalism. The problems didn't filter down to the general membership." Ralph Sewell, assistant managing editor of *The Daily Oklahoman* and *Times*, Oklahoma City, and newly-elected executive councilor, reinforced how few in the membership knew of those problems. "I was state chairman for Oklahoma in 1959 and had no idea of what shape the fraternity was in when I went on the council." Sewell, who was not in Indianapolis and was notified by telephone of his election, recalls, "The battle was internal to the council. Those of us out in the hinterlands were involved with our local concerns and, for the most part, were in the dark about such things as the White Report."

With the conclusion of the celebration and convention program, incoming national president V.M. (Red) Newton, Jr. wasted little time in bringing that battle back to the forefront. Although the minutes of the November 14, 1959 meeting do not carry mention of it, the naming of a special committee on organization and administration with Burroughs as chairman at Indianapolis is confirmed in the minutes of both the April 20, 1960, and August 6, 1960, meetings of the executive council. Along with Burroughs, the committee members were Kilgore, Taishoff, Floyd Arpan, professor of journalism at Northwestern University; William Kostka, public relations counselor of Denver, Colorado; and Don Carter, executive director of The Newspaper Fund of *The Wall Street Journal*. The special committee apparently was considered a committee of the council and was not listed in the March

1960 *Quill* as one of the standing national committees appointed by Newton. The net result was that its work remained internal and the general membership still did not know of any of the fraternity's problems.

Before leaving Indianapolis, the council also took another step in easing Bluedorn out of office. As was the custom, the council set the executive director's salary each November, but in this case, meeting in executive session, it kept Bluedorn in his job only on a month-to-month basis. The exact language of the resolution, moved by Lindsay, seconded by Scripps and adopted unanimously, stated:

> That Victor Bluedorn be continued in his present employment at the rate of $11,500 per year plus retirement benefits and also plus 15 percent of the net income from advertising sales from *The Quill*, pending action on the 1960 report of the special committee charged with drawing up a proposal for reorganizing the administration of the fraternity and of the 1960 report of the advisory committee to the publication board of *The Quill*."

That advisory council to the publication board was charged to look at the fiscal administration of the magazine and the relationship of the executive director to *The Quill*. The council also unanimously adopted a further resolution, moved by Burroughs and seconded by Scripps, restating a past policy keeping the executive director in a position subordinate to the national president, thus giving Bluedorn close supervision until the committee reports were in. Upon Bluedorn's return to the meeting at the end of the executive session, Newton explained the two resolutions and the reasons for making the executive director's continued tenure dependent upon the reports of the committees. Bluedorn acknowledged the explanation and thanked the council.

To begin its work, the committee on organization and administration met in Chicago on several occasions at no expense to the fraternity. Burroughs suggested they return to the grass roots for information. directing that a survey be taken of all professional and campus chapters. With that project under way, the committee turned to another source for help. Burroughs recalls, "We decided to consult the guy who had played the major role in solving the public relations problem two years earlier – Barney Kilgore." Kilgore, who had considerable experience studying the problems of business corporations, trade associations and newspapers, suggested the fraternity should call on the best management consultants available to get the viewpoints of outside experts who would not become involved with emotional, fraternal or personal feelings. He approached his friend Marvin Bower, managing director of McKinsey and Company, Incorporated, a prominent national management consulting firm. There was no way the fraternity could afford its services, but in a bold move, Kilgore asked Bower to have his company, as a public service, make a study of the organization and administration of Sigma Delta Chi and to recommend the organization and methods whereby the objectives of the fraternity more nearly could be achieved. Bower accepted the challenge. and the firm, which had offices in five American cities including Chicago, agreed to take on the project at no charge to Sigma Delta Chi. Burroughs issued the formal invitation to McKinsey and Company on April 8, 1960.

Meanwhile, the executive committee of the council, which included only the five officers, received the report of the advisory council to the publications board, chaired by Marvin Shutt. Although copies of that report do not exist in Sigma Delta Chi headquarters, the fraternity's officers said the Shutt committee report "appeared to be excellent" in its recommendations on the future of *The Quill*. However, because McKinsey and Company was asked to do a complete study on the fraternity, including *The Quill*, the officers convinced the executive council at its April 19, 1960, meeting in *The Wall Street Journal* offices in Washington, DC that no action be taken on the report until the McKinsey Report was received.

Reporting to the council the next day on the work of the committee on organization and administration, Burroughs outlined the

details of the McKinsey study then in progress. He also shared the results of the questionnaires, which indicated that the undergraduate chapters appeared to be weaker than in 1959 and still to be weakening at a rate faster than that of the professional chapters. Proposals by professor Arpan for a crash program to revitalize the undergraduate chapters were received enthusiastically but then set aside, again, to give McKinsey and Company a clear shot at approaching its study of the fraternity as a whole.

With the reports of the two committees appointed in Indianapolis accepted, though in both cases only as interim reports, the matter of the tenure of Bluedorn took center stage. Minutes of that critical executive session on April 20, 1960, read:

Certain political activities of the executive director, apparently aimed at holding on to his present method of operating, at his present total rate of compensation, rather than to put into effect improvements in operating methods were discussed. The secretary reported the recommendation of the special committee on organization and administration: That it appeared inevitable that the present executive director must be replaced, notice to be given him at this time that the final report of the committee based on the McKinsey and Company study might recommend termination of his employment.

After long discussion, the consensus of opinion of the meeting was, clearly, that the recommendation of the special committee did not go far enough; that, instead, an immediate change should be made so that there would be no obstacles in the way of following the recommendations of McKinsey and Company when received. It was moved by Sewell, seconded by Hicks, that the executive committee be directed to take steps immediately to terminate the employment of Victor E. Bluedorn as executive director and to devise means of filling the gap created hereby until the report of McKinsey and Company could be received along with a job description for a chief administrative employee of the fraternity.

The employment of a replacement should be deferred until receipt of the McKinsey and Company report; and that the executive committee be authorized to keep Bluedorn on the payroll for six months at his basic salary [$956 per month].

Sewell remembers his motion well and recalls, "Vice president for undergraduate chapter affairs Maynard Hicks, executive councilor Frank Angelo and I were freshmen on the Council....We were skeptical but the conversation around the room went on for about an hour in that executive session. In the end, we were convinced this was the right thing to do." Others who were present at the meeting agree. Hicks said, "Sewell and I knew from our own experiences and from many conversations with other SDXers that Vic Bluedorn was no leader in crisis. He had personal problems and carried them into business hours. The SDX office was inadequately run, slow to respond, and undependable. So Hicks and Sewell teamed." Carter said there were no surprises in the motion. "The tone of the reports which had been submitted and the gloomy predictions about the future of Sigma Delta Chi unless changes were made left no doubt in my mind as to what should be done." Arpan remembers Bluedorn was not devoting all of his time to Sigma Delta Chi just before he was terminated. "He had his fingers in a couple of financial arrangements out in Wheaton, Illinois, which took a lot of his time and the council felt he wasn't devoting 100 percent of his attention to the fraternity."

Attending his first council meeting, having been elected in absentia in Indianapolis, Angelo knew immediately where the problems were. "It was obvious that 90 percent of the problems in the fraternity had to do with the relationship of Bluedorn and the fraternity." Bluedorn's apparent personal attitude and his relationship with the council were identified by Warren K. Agee. He remembers that when he moved into Bluedorn's office upon becoming executive officer, a framed organization chart on the wall showed

"Executive Director" at the top and "Board of Directors" beneath. Interestingly, Angelo recalls, "While the old-timers on the council had come to the conclusion that something had to be done, it was the three rookies, Sewell, Hicks and Angelo, who provided the final impetus to get the job of terminating Bluedorn done."

The roll call vote was unanimous in favor of the Sewell motion. President Newton, who was not at the meeting because of illness, was called and voted "aye." White, also absent from that meeting, subsequently requested the secretary to record his concurrence with the motion. Acting for the officers, Burroughs and Carter went to Chicago headquarters the following Monday, April 25, to notify Bluedorn he had been terminated by the executive council and to set the wheels in motion for the headquarters staff to keep the office operating until an interim executive director could be selected. Bluedorn was at home that morning, having cut his hand severely during the weekend. Burroughs called him from the headquarters and related the decision of the council. Accepting the option to resign rather than be fired, Bluedorn announced his decision officially, May 6, 1960. It was not until the June 1960 *Quill* was circulated that Bluedorn's resignation was known to the general membership. In his letter to president Newton, Bluedorn explained that his decision was prompted by his "obligation to his family and his plans for the future." He continued, "Each of us must occasionally re-examine his position. I have thought about this for a long time, particularly recently. Now I feel it would be a propitious time for me to make a change that will provide more adequately for my family and perhaps return to active journalism." *The Quill* article also announced that president Newton had named professor Arpan as acting administrator of the fraternity.

Arpan, who had decided to take a teaching position at Indiana University, accepted the job "because I believed in Sigma Delta Chi and somebody had to do it. I was the only member of Burroughs' committee from the Chicago area and he asked me to do it. It was going to be a short term, as far as I was concerned, because I had already resigned my faculty commitment to the Medill School of Journalism at Northwestern. I said, 'OK, I'll do it for part of the time but give me an opportunity to find somebody else to serve temporarily until we can get a permanent executive officer.' " Arpan began his work almost immediately after Bluedorn's resignation and was completely in charge of fiscal and program responsibilities in his tenure as acting administrator. Even though he had completed his teaching responsibilities at Northwestern, driving in from Evanston and spending about half of each day in Chicago represented a substantial sacrifice. Arpan had major responsibilities as director of the United States Information Agency's Multi-National Foreign Journalists Project, which brought journalists from seventy-eight nationss to study methods and operations of the press in America. He also had connections with the summer National Institute for High School Journalists at Medill, a program he had founded and directed for twenty-five years. For previous years of service to the fraternity, during which he had been vice president for undergraduate affairs and associate editor of *The Quill*, Arpan was awarded the Wells Memorial Key in 1958. He would be honored again by the organization, in 1979, with the Distinguished Teaching in Journalism Award. Arpan turned to Charles E. Barnum, also a journalism professor at Northwestern, to assist with the foreign journalists project and, in July, to be his replacement as acting administrator.

"Arpan maneuvered the thing so that the committee appointed me to this responsibility," Barnum said. "I had to make the same trips to Chicago almost on a daily basis. I had received permission from my dean to take time away from classes, especially in the fall, to take care of the day-to-day duties of the administrator in the office." Barnum, who had been active in Sigma Delta Chi for eight years, credits members of the headquarters staff, especially Pearl Luttrell, for keeping the operation going effectively. "Pearl absolutely was indispensable. She occupied a relatively minor position there, but she was a major

force in getting that thing together." Arpan agreed. "Pearl was a real jewel. I think she was one of the saviors of Sigma Delta Chi in those days. She was very non-political and provided information when we needed to keep things going without getting involved in the problems of the office. I relied on her a great deal in those days." Barnum stayed on the job through the meetings of the executive council on the McKinsey Report in July and August and directed many of the preparations for the national convention in New York the following November. Both Arpan and Barnum received plaudits from the council for administering the fraternity's affairs from May through November. "It was very difficult for anyone to be running the fraternity," Scripps recalls. "Both men filled in very loyally and were most deserving the the the praise that came." Perhaps Hicks summed up the feelings of those on the Council about the interim administrators. "Those two men did more part time than should have been expected. Their service is one among the golden chapters in Sigma Delta Chi history. What could have been a total transitional mess that might have sunk the organization was handled brilliantly by Arpan and Barnum. And, in November, they dropped out of the interim authority with graciousness and modesty and aid for the incoming Warren Agee."

With all of the problems, the fraternity operated smoothly in the summer of 1960, perhaps because all involved knew the McKinsey Report had the potential of offering Sigma Delta Chi a vigorous and productive future. McKinsey and Company and its executive in charge of the study, Walter J. Talley, Jr., had no preconceived notions about Sigma Delta Chi. None of its executives were members of the fraternity. They were given free access to the records and to a study of the staff and operations of the headquarters office. They studied the history, constitution and by-laws of the fraternity, interviewed thirty leaders of Sigma Delta Chi in various parts of the country and arrived at tentative conclusions as to the objectives of the organization and the programs needed to achieve them. Talley, who had left McKinsey and become an executive with the Union Oil Company of

California by the early 1980's, remembers, "During and after our interviews, it was obvious to us that Sigma Delta Chi was at a critical point in its growth. Most of our findings represented a distillation of thoughts developed from those interviews." On July 8, McKinsey and Company representatives met with the committee on organization and administration in Chicago to discuss the results of the study. Based on those discussions, the McKinsey staff refined the proposals and presented the finished document to Burroughs July 15, only fourteen weeks after receiving the invitation to do the study.

Talley presented the twenty-four-page report to the council August 6, 1960, at the McKinsey offices in Chicago. It made eight suggestions for major changes:

1. Reorganization of national headquarters under an executive officer who would be more responsive to the leadership of the president and board of directors.

[The new title, executive officer, to be applied to what had been called the executive director, came at the insistance of Burroughs who, drawing from his military experience, thought, "The job was to be executive officer to the president, not to be the commander himself."]

2. Reorganization of the executive council to a board of directors to include eleven regional directors, plus officers, with directors to be elected for three-year terms.

3. Elimination of vice presidents for expansion and professional chapters in favor of a first vice president who would be president-elect.

4. Curtailment of responsibility of the vice president for undergraduate affairs.

5. Abolishment of the board of publications and transfer of its duties to the board of directors.

6. Hiring of a fulltime executive editor for *The Quill* to make it a more professional publication.

7. Changing the name of the fraternity to Sigma Delta Chi, The Society of Journalists.

8. Increasing the dues from $5 to possibly $10 a year.

Additionally, the plan would eliminate the state chairmanship system in effect, replacing it with the eleven regional directors; provide financial assistance to undergraduate chapters, establish new goals; and set up regional conferences in addition to the national convention. The report contained a table of organization for the proposed Society's administration and a map showing how the nation would be divided into the eleven regions – a plan which, with a few small changes and the addition of a twelfth region thirteen years later, stood at the organization's seventy-fifth anniversary.

A twist of fate may have allowed the fired Victor Bluedorn to influence the McKinsey consultants and ultimately their recommendations. An unsigned, forty-seven-page document titled, "A Plan of Action for Sigma Delta Chi," possibly prepared by Bluedorn, but clearly written in mid-1959 by someone with significant knowledge of the fraternity and its problems, was circulated to council members just before the Indianapolis convention. None of the past presidents or others involved during this time period and interviewed for this book was able to identify the author of "A Plan of Action...." However, first-person references to administrative actions within the fraternity taken or requested by the writer appear on several pages of the document, lending credence to the premise that Bluedorn was its author. One of those references asks for "immediate blanket approval of this report so I can proceed to develop specific and detailed plans in collaboration with the national president." Burroughs refused to give Bluedorn credit for originating the ideas, although he admitted the beleagured executive director may have written the document. "I am quite certain he took the ideas from someone else, perhaps McCormack, who, I remember pointing out that what Sigma Delta Chi needed were groups of officials all over the country to see that more professional chapters were established and that the undergraduate chapters were kept properly active."

McKinsey's Walter Talley recalls that he and his staff definitely used the document and that it had an impact on their findings. "While I don't recall who had written it, the plan represented a part of the input and supported our own thinking on the importance of eleven regional directors making up the larger part of the new board of directors." As it turned out, at least five of suggestions in the "Plan of Action" found their way into the McKinsey Report.

Among a myriad of other things, the "Plan of Action..." called for (1) twelve regional directors to be elected for three-year terms; (2) the board to include the national president, vice president, secretary and treasurer; (3) the elimination of the offices of the three vice presidents; (4) changing the organization's name to Sigma Delta Chi, the American Society of Journalists; and (5) raising the dues. The only points included in the McKinsey Report not touched on in "A Plan of Action..." were those referring to the executive director, the elimination of the publications board and the hiring of a full-time editor for *The Quill*. Barnum, who remembers the report, but couldn't verify the author, said, "I wouldn't minimize the effect of the document on the McKinsey Report." The irony concerning Bluedorn, who was terminated in part because the executive council believed he would be a hindrance to any attempt to reorganize the fraternity, especially that of McKinsey and Company, having played a significant role in that reorganization makes the assumption of his authorship of "A Plan of Action..." even more interesting.

There is no doubt that the executive council was impressed with Talley's presentation and the report as a whole. Although he had been on the council for less than a year, Sewell remembers that the McKinsey proposals concerning the name and emphasis of Sigma Delta Chi were recommendations whose time had come. "It was a kind of natural transition which, in fact, had already begun. We were just recognizing that it was happening with the growth of the professional chapters and the prepondrence of membership among the professionals. The council members felt the concept of the fraternity was a thing of the past, tied only to the campus chapters, and those members represented only about 10

percent of the total membership." Scripps concurred. "I realized the word 'fraternity' could be a turnoff for the professional side of the organization. I was trying to get the emphasis on the word 'professional.' The word 'fraternity' had the connotation of an honorary society, which we didn't want. It wasn't an honorary; it was a society of professional journalists."

The concept of moving the new Society closer to the members with the introduction of eleven regional directors was important to Burroughs. The selection of executive councilors under the pre-McKinsey system gave some consideration to geographical regions of the country, "but, for the most part," he said, "the men selected were tapped by other members of the council because they were good men. Basically, I was so strong for the eleven regional directors because by having members located across the country, the new board would be able to get good intelligence about the Society in each area of the nation. We couldn't have one man inspiring everybody every place. The idea was that we should get good regional men who were good journalists in the first place. Men who could take the time to go visit the chapters and talk to the members – primarily the undergraduates. But it would also be a needed help in serving the professional chapters, especially those which had members living in wide geographical areas." Angelo's concerns about the development of professional chapters were answered in the McKinsey Report. "While I wasn't opposed to the work the fraternity had done with the collegiate chapters, I had the feeling that the fraternity was so hung up on wanting to help kids it had almost turned the organization over to them. The reorganization plan recognized the needs of the students but also turned more toward the needs of the professionals." Hicks recalls, "It was probably Burroughs, speaking late in the discussions and as the leader for change, who summarized for those with any lingering doubts: 'These changes have to be swallowed if we are going to survive.' Someone else from his side of the table added almost as an amen, 'It's either that or down the drain, and, by God, I won't let this organization go down the drain.' "

When the council returned from a lunch break at 1:30 pm that August 6, Scripps moved that the council commend McKinsey and Company and the committee on organization and administration for their able work and that the plan be adopted as best suited to the future growth, development and continued strength of Sigma Delta Chi. Newton seconded the motion. During the discussion, Burroughs raised the point that to adopt the plan in its entirety would be to endorse McKinsey and Company's financial recommendations – including a $20,000 salary for the new executive officer. Burroughs asked Scripps to rephrase his motion to "adopt the plan in principle but without accepting its financial recommendations." Scripps and Newton agreed and the motion was carried unanimously.

HIRING A NEW EXECUTIVE OFFICER

With the McKinsey Report adopted, the council turned to another pressing matter – selecting a new executive officer. Feelers had been set out among those close to the national reorganization effort for nominations. Barnum recalls, "I don't know how much response we received in total, but several nominations came in for each of two men – William R. Shover, assistant director of public relations for the Indianapolis newspapers, owned by Sigma Delta Chi founder Eugene C. Pulliam, and professor of journalism Alvin Austin of the University of North Dakota." Burroughs' committee had invited both men to Chicago for the August 6 meeting and the council interviewed each.

Austin, in fact, had offered himself for the position in a letter to Kilgore, Newton and Burroughs on July 30. He wrote, "I have given a great deal of thought to this position since the vacancy arose last spring and I have come to the conclusion that it offers a challenge in which I definitely would be interested." Citing his work as vice president in charge of undergraduate affairs from 1952 through 1955, Austin indicated that his experience in working on the council and having received the Wells Memorial Key in 1955 demonstrated his dedication to the fraternity. Although only one week went by between the time he sent his letter of interest and the interviews in Chicago, Austin said he had second thoughts. "I can recall that I went to the interview with a great deal of uncertainty in my mind. I had offered myself to do this job for Sigma Delta Chi, but I really didn't want to give up my position as professor of journalism and chairman of the department at North Dakota." Shover, who had been co-chairman of the 1959 Indianapolis convention celebrating the fraternity's fiftieth birthday and more recently Director of Corporate and Community Relations for *The Arizona Republic and Phoenix Gazette*, recalls his involvement. "Either Burroughs or Lindsay called me and explained why they needed me. I wasn't sure at all that I wanted to leave Indianapolis because Mr. Pulliam had said he had plans for me with his newspapers. I couldn't talk to him because he was out of the country, but decided I'd go to Chicago with the intent of accepting the position, if selected, only on an interim basis for a year or so at the most and to try to get a leave of absence from the papers. When they asked me what I'd have to have in salary, I told them $18,000, which didn't seem to set very well. I didn't know they had just set aside McKinsey's recommendation for a $20,000 figure as too high."

At the conclusion of the interviews, considerable discussion arose concerning the qualifications of the interviewees and their responses to questions concerning the McKinsey Report. Lindsay pointed out that the wording in the report clearly favored consideration of someone well acquainted with journalism education, as emphasis was heavy on the undergraduate chapter program. After a long discussion, the council decided not to decide and notified each of the candidates that the council had postponed action on hiring an executive officer. The council told Shover and Austin that steps would be taken to interview other candidates although both should consider themselves active candidates until further notification.

The council, however, knew it had to move quickly to find a new executive officer.

Scripps remembers that in addition to finding someone who would meet the needs of Sigma Delta Chi at the undergraduate level, "We were looking for a young person who had the vitality and enthusiasm to do the job we wanted done and someone who had a good presence among the professionals – someone who was respected by the journalism industry." Chairman of the board and past president James A. Byron thought he had just the man – a man with whom he had worked at the Fort Worth *Star-Telegram* (before he became news director at WBAP), whom he had seen initiated to the Fort Worth professional chapter in 1947 and who had been chairman of the department of journalism at Texas Christian University from 1950-1958. He was Dr. Warren K. Agee, dean of the school of journalism at West Virginia University.

Byron didn't waste any time contacting his former colleague. "Jimmy telephoned me in Morgantown, West Virginia, at the conclusion of the August 6 meeting in Chicago," Agee said. "I also got calls from Charlie Barnum and Don Carter. They said Sigma Delta Chi needed a man with strong professional and academic credentials to lead in the revival of the fraternity. They said I was the exact person neded for the job." In addition to his academic background, Agee had spent eleven years as a staff member of the *Star-Telegram*, and had a broad knowledge of journalism education through the Association for Education in Journalism, a respected organization he had served as president in 1958. "Jim said I was needed to begin my duties by the time of the national convention that November. He said he realized that this was short notice, but that he and others would tell West Virginia University president Elvis Stahr, Jr., of the fraternity's urgent need. I responded that I had just built a new home on a hill overlooking the city and with a fine view of the mountains; that my daughter Kim was in junior high school and would have an adjustment problem in moving to Chicago (my younger daughter Robyn was only two years old); that I had grown to love West Virginians; and that I still had important things to do as dean of the school of journalism. I promised that I would do

some serious thinking about the offer with my wife Edda.

"Soon after the telephone call from Chicago, Don Carter visited Edda and me in our home in Morgantown. He explained the McKinsey recommendations, said the fraternity badly needed strong leadership at this crucial period and added: 'Warren, we need you. If you are a praying man, you will get down on your knees and pray about this – and accept!' He said the new society not only needed to regain the support of professionals – those whose interest had lagged – but also was in poor shape on a number of campuses; some journalism deans and directors, he reported, were threatening to close down their Sigma Delta Chi chapters."

Carter remembers "working" on Agee. "I had known Warren Agee from my work with The Newspaper Fund and thought he was the man for the job. I stressed with him the platform that this position with Sigma Delta Chi would afford him broader service in the field of journalism and how much we needed someone of his professionalism and interests to accept the job." Barnum, too, said he "worked hard to convince Agee to accept the job." He added, "Warren was a close, personal friend and I felt he was the man for the job. I don't know how many times I called him trying to get him to accept, but it was quite a few times."

Agee recalls he made his decision "after much agonizing, one night about ten o'clock at the Association for Education in Journalism convention at Pennsylvania State University after Carter and others had talked again with me there. I accepted the position because I was persuaded that I was greatly needed and because I caught a vision of what a strengthened Sigma Delta Chi could mean to the journalism world and American society." His wife, Edda, was an important sounding board in the decision-making process. Although both of them were somewhat apprehensive about the Chicago winters and the potential health-related aspects therein, she remembers her husband saying, "I can't let Sigma Delta Chi die....I just can't. I've got to go to Chicago and do what I can." Writing to his colleagues at West Virginia University upon his resignation there, Agee said:

> We in education, as well as persons
> in other walks of life, live in terms of
> the future: dreaming, and working,
> toward a society of better institutions –
> yes, better communications media.
> There are many avenues toward the
> realization of those dreams. Without
> intending to dramatize my move, let me
> ask your indulgence, and cooperation,
> while I dream – and work – to learn if
> all is gossamer or if we can actually
> move even one small step toward a
> stronger, better press and broadcast
> media and, consequently, a better
> world. With your help, I am convinced
> that we can.

The executive council unanimously
selected Agee for the post only three weeks
after adopting the McKinsey Report. His
appointment was announced in the October
1960 *Quill*. Shover recalls that when he
heard the council had passed him by in favor
of Agee, he was not disappointed. "I hadn't
thought much about the council putting us
off. And Mr. Pulliam, upon his return from
overseas, told me he didn't want me to go to
Chicago. When I told him, 'But that's your
organization. Perhaps I can go and help
them out for a while.' he replied, 'They can
get somebody else.' As it turned out, he did
have plans for me in 1962 when I made the
move to Phoenix." For Austin, his personal
conflict of wanting to retain his posts at the
University of North Dakota and his desire to
serve Sigma Delta Chi was resolved for him.
"My doubts probably showed up in the
interview," he said.

On the hiring of Agee, president Newton
told the membership, "We are delighted to
secure a man of such broad experience in the
field of professional journalism as well as a
recognized authority in academic circles. We
now feel certain that Sigma Delta Chi will
forge ahead with its plans for reorganization
to a new position of strength in American
journalism."

Agee moved his family to Wilmette,
Illinois – a northern suburb of Chicago –
and began his duties November 1. In one of
his first priorities on the job, he met with
representatives of McKinsey and Company
and was delighted to learn that the
consultants had corroborated that he "was
the man for the job."

THE 1960 NEW YORK CONVENTION

With the new executive officer hired,
president Newton and other members of the
council faced the challenge of convincing the
chapters to adopt the McKinsey Report at
the New York convention. Under Newton's
direction, a twenty-page paper was prepared
and sent to all campus and professional
chapter presidents and secretaries. The
document contained a letter from Newton
outlining the history of the reorganization
process, statistics on comparative dues
structures with other professional and trade
organizations, a letter from the committee on
organization and administration, a summary
of the McKinsey Report's recommendations,
and the language changes proposed for the
Sigma Delta Chi by-laws. The package was
mailed in late October leaving little time
before the November 30 opening of the
convention for a real campaign to "sell" the
proposal. Hicks, as vice president in charge
of undergraduate affairs, got out "restrained
memos to advisers...urging for change and
building confidence in the reports of the
committees and the council." Changing to
the name "society" was not too easy to sell,
he said, "because 'society' was considered
feminine and received laughter and scorn in
many places, most especially in the branch
of the organization for which I had
responsibility." Barnum remembers the
mood of the council members just before
New York. "When we went to the
convention, we were uncertain as to the fate
of the report. We weren't certain the desire
was there among the membership and
delegates to accomplish the goals we had set
forth. It was touch and go." Talley agrees
the feeling of uncertainty was apparent. "It
was for this reason that I was asked by the
executive council to make the New York
presentation – a factual boil-down of the
actual report."

Burroughs opened the Thursday,
December 1, business session's discussion of
the McKinsey Report with a history of the
events leading to the proposals to be
considered by the delegates. He introduced
Talley, who presented the report and its

recommendations formally. With the document before the delegates, chairman of the committee on by-laws Cavagnaro followed with his committee's recommendation for adoption, whereupon president Newton announced that the vote on the recommendations changes in the by-laws would take place the following morning.

Calling not only for the adoption of the changes proposed by the committee on organization and administration and McKinsey and Company but for a "series of dynamic programs as the integral part" of the reorganization plan, Arpan led off the Friday, December 2, session. In what may have surprised the council, Elmo Ellis, delegate from the Atlanta professional chapter, moved adoption of the report in total. The motion was seconded by Herb A. Probasco, delegate from the University of Nebraska. Before any discussion from the floor could take place, Barnum, acting as parliamentarian, advised president Newton that the vote on the changes would have to be taken one at a time rather than as a group. Barnum, still uncertain at that time as to what the delegates would do on the vote, recalls, "It was the impression of the leadership that the delegates didn't know the in's and out's of the reorganization plan as well as they should. Action was coming too fast. I didn't want to allow even the appearance of ramming the report down the delegates' throats. That could have had disastrous results down the road even if it had passed." President Newton thanked Ellis for his motion and declared that the convention would proceed to consideration of the various proposals.

Guy Ryan, delegate from the San Diego professional chapter, moved that the delegates take up proposal 10 – dealing with the new structure of the board of directors and calling for eleven regions, each with a regional director to be elected to a three-year term – as its first consideration. Ryan said that unless proposal 10 was passed, the remaining proposals would be without meaning. The motion was seconded by Richard Hildwein, delegate from the Central Illinois professional chapter, and was carried without dissent. Cavagnaro, representing the San Francisco professional chapter,

moved adoption of proposal 10 with Joseph Quinn, delegate from the Los Angeles professional chapter, seconding. Attempts to change the number of regions from eleven to ten – with region nine being eliminated – were defeated overwhelmingly on a show of hands and the convention approved the regional concept as presented, 77-16, thirteen votes more than the two-thirds majority needed to amend the by-laws.

As adopted, Region One included the Northeastern states, New Jersey, most of New York and Eastern and Central Pennsylvania; Region Two encompassed Maryland, Delaware, the District of Columbia, Virginia, North Carolina and the eastern tip of West Virginia; Region Three included Tennessee and the five southeastern states; and Region Four included Michigan, Ohio, Western Pennsylvania, the western tip of New York and most of West Virginia. The original Region Five included Wisconsin, Illinois, Indiana and Kentucky, with Region Six made up of Minnesota, North Dakota and South Dakota. Region Seven encompassed Iowa, Missouri, Nebraska and Kansas with Region Eight including Oklahoma, Texas, Arkansas and Louisiana. The mountain states of Wyoming, Utah, Colorado and New Mexico comprised Region Nine, with Region Ten including the northwestern states of Alaska, Washington, Oregon, Idaho and Montana. Region Eleven was made up of Arizona, California, Nevada and Hawaii.

Returning to the top of the list of McKinsey proposals, Newton called for motions regarding proposal 1 – changing the name of the executive director to executive officer – and proposal 2 – which changed the name of the executive council to the board of directors. Both proposals were adopted by wide margins. Proposal 3 dealt with the change in the name of the organization. Hildwein moved adoption of the name proposed by the Burroughs committee – Sigma Delta Chi, The Society of Journalists, a Professional Fraternity – and received a second from Ellis. During the discussion, Kenneth Eskey, delegate from the Pittsburgh professional chapter, offered a substitute motion to change the proposal and, thus, the name to Sigma Delta Chi, Professional

Journalistic Society and that the word "society," be substituted in every section thereafter in which the word "fraternity" occurred. The substitute motion was seconded by Ed O. Meyer, delegate from the Richmond professional chapter. The vote was 79 ayes and 12 noes. The fraternity designation was out and Sigma Delta Chi had become a professional *society*.

C. Forrest Brokaw, delegate from the Eastern Oklahoma professional chapter, pointed out to the convention that all of the remaining proposals, except proposal 13 – dealing with an increase in dues – were for the purpose of making the by-laws implement the plan and that no objection to them had been expressed in earlier discussions on Thursday. He therefore moved that proposals 4,5,6,7,8,9,11,12 and 14 be adopted as a unit. Following a second by Richard Fitzpatrick, (no affiliation listed in the minutes), the vote for adoption was 87-1. Taking up proposal 13, Cavagnaro moved adoption and Quinn seconded. It was evident that the delegates had, indeed, come to New York with the intention of adopting the entire package in principle. Two attempts to amend the motion to lower dues for certain classifications of members were defeated, 64-24 and 71-22. A further attempt to submit the dues proposal to the membership at large by referendum also was defeated, 88-7. President Newton then called for a vote on the Cavagnaro motion, which carried, 83-18.

Adoption of the McKinsey Report left only the business of filling the elective offices called for in the document. E.W. (Ted) Scripps II was elected national president and chairman of the board of directors, Buren McCormack was named first vice president, Walter Burroughs was elected secretary and Theodore F. Koop, director of Washington news and public affairs for CBS, was named treasurer. Arpan, now a retired professor at Indiana University, was elected vice president for undergraduate affairs. Outgoing national president Newton kept a seat on the new board of directors as an ex-officio member.

Under the reorganization plan, the newly-elected regional directors were added to the board. Those first regional directors were: Region One, H. Eugene Goodwin, director of the school of journalism at Pennsylvania State; Region Two, R.K.T. Larson, associate editor for public service for the Norfolk-Portsmouth, Virginia, newspapers; Region Three, Edward G. Thomas, public information manager for the Southern Bell Telephone and Telegraph Co., Atlanta; Region Four, Frank Angelo, managing editor of the Detroit *Free Press*; Region Five, Edward Lindsay, editor of the Lindsay-Schaub newspapers, Decatur, Illinois; Region Six, James Borman, news director of WCCO Radio, Minneapolis; and Region Seven, Robert M. White II, co-editor and co-publisher of the Mexico, Missouri *Ledger* and president and editor of the New York *Herald Tribune*. Elected for Region Eight was Ralph Sewell, assistant managing editor of *The Daily Oklahoman*, Oklahoma City; Region Nine, William Kostka, president of William Kostka and Associates and publisher of the *Colorado Transcript*, Golden, Colorado; Region Ten, J. Ernest Knight, editor of the Tacoma, Washington *News-Tribune*; and Region Eleven, Raymond L. Spangler, publisher and columnist of the Redwood City, California *Tribune*.

In his presidential report to the convention, Newton sounded an optimistic note, telling the delegates that the new Society had a record number of dues-paying members, 16,304, and that the number of professional and campus chapters had reached fifty-eight and seventy-five respectively. But he pointed to continuing problems of rebuilding interest among the undergraduate chapters and removing *The Quill* from its status as a "step-child of Sigma Delta Chi." Reminding the delegates that the McKinsey recommendations called for strengthening campus chapters, he said, "The undergraduate program is the base not only of Sigma Delta Chi but of all journalism and perhaps the very base of free American government. If we in journalism today do not expend of our time, energy and talents in the development and promotion of journalism among our young people, who then is to fight for freedom tomorrow?" *The Quill*, he said, faced "a crossroads of destiny," and he hoped that the magazine "would not continue to meander down the haphazard road of a house organ." Newton added, "We need a publication which has constant impact, not only on national journalism but on the nation."

As what was, perhaps, the most important national convention from a business standpoint in twenty-five years adjourned in New York City, December 3, 1960, three years of work and turmoil ended on a triumphal note. The McKinsey recommendations were in place with only a change in the name as proposed failing to survive. The new board of directors was sworn in at the close of the Saturday morning business session. A new executive officer, Warren K. Agee, was on the job. Sigma Delta Chi had turned an important corner.

Among the men who gathered for a past presidents' and Wells Key breakfast at the 1966 Pittsburgh convention were many who led Sigma Delta Chi through its traumas of the late 1950's and through the reorganization of the early 1960's. (Seated from left) Walter Humphrey, Buren McCormack, Floyd Arpan, George Wolpert, Alvin Austin, Barney Kilgore, and Ralph Sewell. (Standing from left) Ted Scripps, Ted Koop, Donald Clark, Walter Burroughs, Charles Clayton, William Kostka, Bob Cavagnaro, James Byron and Sol Taishoff.

CHAPTER 3

███████████████

An Agenda for a New Direction

Agee had made his first address as executive officer to his colleagues in Sigma Delta Chi at the New York convention opening with a story:

> In all of his six years, the little boy had not spoken a word. His parents were frantic; they feared he was subnormal.
>
> Then one morning at breakfast he said in loud, clear tones: "Mom, this toast is burned."
>
> His mother shrieked with joy and clasped him in her arms. "Son! Son!" she exclaimed. "Why haven't you spoken to us before?"
>
> "Well," the boy replied, "up to now everything's been okay."

When the delegates to that convention recognized the "burned toast" condition of Sigma Delta Chi and adopted the leadership's recommendation to restructure Sigma Delta Chi following the McKinsey plan, Agee was delighted. He had told the convention his goals for the organization. "I believe it is possible to develop a spirit of professionalism among our present and future newsmen that will cure many of journalism's ills. I see in Sigma Delta Chi a tremendous reservoir of strength for the upbuilding of journalism and journalism education in this country." By utilizing this reservoir, he said, "we can obtain this commitment to the ideals of journalism, to the goals of high ethical standards and to top-notch performance."

As Agee set out in his first months on the job to re-establish Sigma Delta Chi as a growing and respected force in American journalism and to move the Society toward building a stronger, better press, Scripps recalls the executive officer did it "with enthusiasm and a lot of grace and dignity, which wasn't easy." Scripps noted that the administrative detail at national headquarters to implement the McKinsey Report was a massive task in and of itself and working with the Chicago staff, where some loyalites to Bluedorn still existed, made it all the more difficult. "He did an amazing job under the circumstances." Agee's agenda might have been beyond the reach of many, but, as his wife, Edda, noted later, "Warren worked his heart out for

Walter Burroughs, Sigma Delta Chi president in 1962-1963, was considered by his colleagues to have been the driving force behind the move to bring the fraternity from its "death bed" condition in 1959 to its status as a newly-energized professional society in 1960.

professional journalism like a race horse. But that work was also his hobby." In an address to the Detroit professional chapter shortly after the New York convention, he told his audience his first assignment had been to charter the new chapter at Las Vegas, Nevada. Drawing on the analogy that Las Vegas was a city famous for its gambling industry, Agee said:

I am going out to do some gambling. I am gambling my time, all my years of academic and practical experience, my so-called middle years. I am placing all my chips on one big gamble, one big bet. I am betting that Sigma Delta Chi, now in its fifty-second year, and now reorganized to come to grips with the real problems of American newsmen, will be forged into a truly professional society of journalists, with all that the meaning of the words imply. After all, you are

gambling your time and your efforts the same as I. I think we have drawn a winning hand. Let's play it to the hilt and see what happens.

Scripps saw his job as national president as one of "implementing the McKinsey plan without disrupting the old hands who weren't sure that change was the right way to go. When you come in as president of an organization that, just before you take over, has rolled over a few times, you've got to spend that year cementing things back together in a new shape without upsetting too many apple carts doing it or at least making people think you aren't upsetting apple carts." While Scripps traveled the country visiting scores of chapters and reapplying the glue as needed, he emphasized that the strength of the national organization truly was in the viability of the local chapters. "That was what the reorganization was all about – to build on the fact that Sigma Delta Chi was the only journalistic organization with a powerful voice for professionalism and freedom of information at the local level as well as at the national level. If the local chapters were strong, the national organization was going to be strong without hardly lifting a finger."

Agee was on the road as well, acquainting members with the goals of the "new" Sigma Delta Chi and inspiring them to emphasize professionalism as against the former predominantly social and honorary emphasis of most chapters. His travels that first year carried him some 25,000 miles visiting thirty-six professional chapters and thirty-three undergraduate chapters in thirty states from Florida to Washington and from California to Massachusetts. Building membership and establishing new chapters were high on Agee's list of priorities in 1961. The increase in national dues from $5 to $10 didn't slow the executive officer in his pursuit of members. In his first months in office, Agee obtained the services of Lester Davis, *The Wall Street Journal*'s circulation specialist, and revised the content and scheduling of the dues renewal notices and invited inactive members to rejoin the organization. The campaign's success was noteworthy, for chapters, with Agee's help, enrolled 1,258 new members – 549

Phil Dessauer (left), chairman of the national convention in Tulsa, Oklahoma, in 1962, meets with Society executive officer Russell E. Hurst and *Quill* executive editor Clarence O. Schlaver. The 1962 convention was the first for Hurst as executive officer. Dessauer later became Region Eight director and was elected the Society's national president in 1978.

professionals and 709 students – a gain of more than 200 over the preceding year. In addition, nearly 300 inactive members returned to full, active membership, paying a $5 reinstatement fee and the 1961 dues. Six new professional chapters – Las Vegas, Mid-Carolinas, Florida East Coast, Southeast Louisiana, Orange Coast and Nashville – along with four new campus chapters – Arizona State, Wyoming, East Texas State and Columbia – were chartered, bringing the total to 143.

But Agee and Scripps knew the base for continuing future growth of the Society – the undergraduate chapter – was still a weak link. Agee's theme in speeches across the nation was one of building the prestige of Sigma Delta Chi with young journalists. "We have fallen short on the university campuses where the future newsmen of our nation are being educated. We have lacked a continuing series of dynamic programs designed to hold the interest of our undergraduate members and their instructors. On some campuses we are regarded as strictly an honorary organization and journalism majors join simply because they feel it is an honor." He told the Detroit professional chapter, "We hope to encourage more joint meetings of undergraduate and professional chapters. President-elect Buren McCormack of *The Wall Street Journal* is now trying to formulate a design for a national series of programs that will bring our student members and our professional members into frequent contact. By so doing we hope to raise the prestige of the news profession, both within and without. We hope by so doing to interest many more young people in journalism as a career and to hold and nurture their interest through their years of education and well into their first journalism jobs. We can solve our national shortage of able, trained talent if we operate as a professional society; young people will, in effect, be banging at our doors. And newsmen, who are trained as professionals and who think as professionals, should be able to command an ever-increasing share of the income of our respective media – salaries should go higher, thus helping to solve another of our recruiting problems."

Scripps, who was probably Sigma Delta Chi's youngest national president at thirty-one since professional members began to assume national offices, had a close affinity with the campus scene. His journalism professor at the University of Nevada at Reno, Al Higginbotham, had been a moving force to get Scripps elected to the national executive council in 1955, just three years after he had completed his education there. Believing that the drive to re-interest members who had deserted local professional chapters and drives to interest potential new members could be tied to rebuilding undergraduate chapters, he said, "Professional chapters should give all the assistance possible to the undergraduate chapters in their area, not only to strengthen the chapters, but also as an inspiration to their membership. It has long been my contention that the undergraduate program that serves the undergraduate members and chapter best is one that is closely integrated with the local professional chapter. Whenever possible, undergraduates should be invited to join professional chapter programs and to join in discussions dealing with professional affairs. In this way, the undergraduate feels he is a closer part of the national organization and, perhaps more important, it will stimulate his interest in journalism."

A new alliance between Sigma Delta Chi and other journalistic organizations was yet another priority on Agee's agenda. He had told the 1960 convention, "Not only do we desire to strengthen our own organization as much as possible, but there is much to be achieved through closer cooperation with other groups such as the American Society of Newspaper Editors, the American Newspaper Publishers Association, the Radio Television News Directors Association, the Association for Education in Journalism, Theta Sigma Phi, and magazine groups. All of them have committees or programs concerned with ethical standards, with finding and nourishing talent, with raising the effectiveness and the status of their own operations in the public eye. Sigma Delta Chi holds a unique position among all of these groups; our membership cuts across almost all of them. We should be able to serve as a catalytic agent to stimulate the efforts of all these organizations to solve common problems." Through personal contacts, Agee was able to set up breakfast meetings for Sigma Delta Chi members during conventions of the other organizations and was able to build knowledge of and interest in the Society with state press associations. In so doing, Agee said, "I hoped to raise the status of Sigma Delta Chi in the thinking of practicing newspeople. Responding to a McKinsey and Company inquiry as to what he thought about Sigma Delta Chi, Turner Catledge, then managing editor of *The New York Times*, is reported to have replied, 'They're a jolly good bunch of fellows.' "

REGIONAL CONFERENCES

Work to give Sigma Delta Chi greater visibility at the local and regional levels as well as bringing the national organization closer to individual members – 9,000 of whom were not affiliated with chapters – took the form of the establishment of regional conferences. The McKinsey Report had called for "sponsoring joint regional meetings and seminars of nearby college and professional chapters to discuss professional subjects of mutual interest," and newly-elected regional directors were charged with the task of establishing such conferences. The first regional conference was held in Region Eleven on the campus of California Polytechnic State University (then a state college) in San Luis Obispo, October 21-22, 1961, with the department of journalism as host. Although a campus chapter was not chartered there until 1965, the site was selected by Regional Director Ray Spangler and the sponsoring Los Angeles and Northern California (San Francisco) professional chapters because it provided an attractive place near the ocean, midway between the two cities. Agee arranged for the Chicago headquarters to blanket the four-state area with a direct-mail invitation to chapter and at-large members – something that would continue for each regional conference in the future – and 165 delegates registered for the two-day conference, chaired by Robert W. Goodell, editor of the San Luis Obispo *Telegram-Tribune*. In his letter inviting chapters and at-large members, Spangler wrote, "I urge all members to attend in order that they might learn about the progress of the 'new' Sigma Delta Chi and by their participation in this regional meeting strengthen its structure and add to its stature." Almost all the nine professional and eight undergraduate chapters in the region – including the two from Arizona universities, along with chapters from Hawaii and Nevada – were represented. Most of the delegates, however, were from the Los Angeles and San Francisco areas. The conferees paid a $6 registration fee covering the meetings and two meals and $5 single room rates (or $3.50 double occupancy with connecting bath) at the Motel Inn, across the street from the campus. Students from the Los Angeles and San Francisco-area campus chapters were granted $10 each by the Los Angeles and Northern California professional chapters to help defray their travel expenses.

Henry Rieger, of the Los Angeles professional chapter, arranged for a panel, "A Model Student-Professional Chapter Relationship," setting the tone for the conference. Originally, two other panels on "The Press Conference: News Source or Space Thief?" for professionals and "Job Opportunities for the Undergraduate" for students were set to run concurrently. Students and practitioners alike, however, agreed that such segregation no longer represented the new, strong professional emphasis in Sigma Delta Chi, so all delegates heard both panels. Luncheon speaker Paul Veblen, executive editor of the nearby Santa Barbara *News-Press*, attacked tactics employed by members of the John Birch Society in fostering its views. Afternoon speaker William N. Cothran, news director of WRON-TV, San Francisco, criticized the failure of radio and television newscasters to check out stories before broadcasting them in the name of instant coverage, while Michael O'Connor of the San Diego *Union*, discussed news service responsibilities in covering Latin-American affairs. Demonstrating the breadth of participation in the conference, panelists also included Dr. Walter Wilcox, chairman of the graduate journalism department at the University of California at Los Angeles; R.T. Kingman, public relations coordinator for General Motors Corporation; Dr. Charles M. Hulten, chairman of the journalism department at the University of California, Berkeley; Tom Cameron, Los Angeles *Times*; Leif Erickson, Associated Press, San Francisco; William Flynn, *Newsweek*, San Francisco; Jere Witter, KPIX, San Francisco; Clif Dektar, American Broadcasting Company, Los Angeles; John Moon, managing editor of the *South Bay Daily Breeze*; Charles Katzman, Santa Monica *Daily Outlook*; Jack Starr, UCLA journalism student; and Ken Inouye, president of the Sigma Delta Chi chapter at the University of Southern California.

Agee represented the national officers and board at the conference and, in his dinner address, called for more professionalism in journalism and an expansion of such programs as the Society's freedom of information campaigns, which had sparked laws in most states guaranteeing free access to public records. Agee complimented Spangler, Goodell and the host chapters, commenting that the conference "was an unqualified success and would serve as a model for conferences in other regions during the next year." Spangler remembers the conference was "an excellent meeting with an outstanding program. It was short and quick and kept the people interested. In keeping with the origins of Sigma Delta Chi on a college campus, he said, "The initial organization of the conference was based primarily on an association with the collegiate atmosphere and we had decided it should be sponsored by a college. We had great food. The college was very generous with us. They grew their own beef there and we had a tremendous steak dinner Saturday night."

A FULL-TIME EDITOR
FOR *THE QUILL*

The building of Sigma Delta Chi through membership recruitment, regional conferences, affiliation with other national journalistic organizations and, of course, the general acceptance by the continuing membership of 16,000 of the annual dues increase from $5 to $10 led to almost immediate financial improvement for the Society. By November 1961, Agee was able to report to the members that, "We closed our books for the fiscal year with a total net gain of $23,000 after all bills were paid. The figure compares with a total net increase of $7,617 for the previous year. As a result, we were able to employ our first full-time editor of *The Quill* and provide the necessary quarters and clerical assistance in our Chicago offices; to pay the minimum travel expenses of our regional directors; and to budget a sum toward assisting weak student chapters during the coming year."

Scripps noted that one of the image problems Sigma Delta Chi had was with *The Quill*, which at that time had a circulation of 17,000. "It needed more attention that it had been getting or than any one man who was doubling as executive director could give it regardless of his abilities In the long run, one of the best decisions we made was to establish a full-time editor and have him on the staff in Chicago." That pressing problem regarding *The Quill* had been a priority set by the McKinsey Report. It stated, "Developing the magazine into a really inspiring professional journal requires hiring a full-time executive editor who should have some qualifiying experience, be an outstanding young man, and report to and work closely with the executive officer. The executive editor's duties will include having complete charge of the publication of *The Quill*, preparing and issuing informational releases regarding the activities of the Society under the direction of the executive officer." In addition it called for "an imaginative advertising solicitation program with the practice of paying commissions on

advertising to headquarters staff to be eliminated." The elimination of the publications board also was recommended. Clayton had been editing the magazine as a volunteer, part-time effort from his offices in St. Louis and later at Southern Illinois University in Carbondale. Former executive director Bluedorn had been serving as business and advertising manager, collecting the advertising commissions in addition to his salary. Clayton was disappointed in the McKinsey Report suggestions and later recalled: "I thought it [the hiring of an executive editor] would expand the headquarters' staff too much, wouldn't achieve anything any different, and was a waste of money. It could have been continued as it was without any problems whatsoever." Clayton said he had had no input to the McKinsey task force relating to a job description, the editorial function or the changes in the business side. "When the time came to implement the changes McKinsey recommended, I already had been awarded a Fulbright grant for study in Formosa and entertained no thoughts of applying for the full-time job. I had too many other irons in the fire."

As the search for a new editor-business manager began, Agee said, "We worried about the possible conflict of interest in this dual job, but we knew that the Society could not then afford two people for these functions. I don't know how the actual job description evolved, but we wanted the ablest man possible who could wear both hats." Advertisements were run in *The Quill* and elsewhere seeking to fill the position. President Scripps had named a selection committee made up of Sydney R. Bernstein, then editorial director of *Advertising Age* magazine; David Botter, a professor of magazine journalism at the Medill School of Journalism at Northwestern University; George Brandenburg, long-time Chicago representative of *Editor & Publisher*; and the executive officer. Agee recalls, "The number of applicants suffered because of necessary budget restraints. The McKinsey Report had recommended a salary of only $8,000. We received a half-dozen applications including one from Clarence O. Schlaver. C.O. had been managing editor of *Office*

Appliances, one of the nation's largest trade journals in Chicago and a former newspaper reporter and editor with the Kewanee, Illinois *Star-Courier* and the Chicago *Daily News*. We concluded that Schlaver could handle the job competently because he had been a member of Sigma Delta Chi for many years and was familiar with professional issues. In addition, he was experienced in drawing layouts and general magazine editing and in obtaining advertisements." Schlaver's appointment as executive editor of *The Quill* was effective July 1, 1961, with his first issue as editor to be in September.

After Schlaver's appointment was announced in the July issue of *The Quill*, president Scripps opened the September issue with a full-page letter to members outlining the goals for a new age in the magazine:

> This issue marks the beginning of another chapter in the history of Sigma Delta Chi, for this issue introduces what we hope will come to be a revitalized and inspiring magazine for our Society. It would be impossible, and probably a mistake, to try to make over this magazine completely in one issue, but we are confident it marks the beginning of a new era for *The Quill*. It is hoped that *The Quill* will become a truly important and successful magazine in the field of journalism, a magazine which surveys and interprets today's journalism while stimulating its readers to collective and individual action for the good of our profession.

He called on the membership to help, "first and most fundamentally with articles which inform, interpret, or predict within the journalism scene, and in so doing perhaps stir worthwhile controversy; photographs which are candidates for 'Photo of the Month'; and cartoons which arm the typewriter with a hammer and those which supply succinct humor. And last, but certainly not least, we need your objective criticism, both pro and con, for after all this magazine belongs to Sigma Delta Chi and all its members. To succeed, it must be what you want it to be and the best way for the new executive editor to know what that is, is for you to write and tell him."

Rather than using space in the magazine

for his own views on what the new *Quill* should be and do, Schlaver wrote to each of the chapter presidents October 9, 1961. "One of the primary suggestions in the McKinsey Report," he said, "related to a tie-in between the national office and *The Quill* for better chapter programs. In the October issue of the magazine and the November issue, now being prepared, I believe there is material which can be the topic or at least a stimulant for fall and winter programs." Pointing to Ira Lurvey's guest editorial, "Too Much of Too Little, Too Fast, and Too Loud" in the October issue, Schlaver suggested a topic for lively debate at a local chapter meeting. "Is news choking itself by too much speed? Should newspapers be concerned with interpretation rather than 'hot off the press' news or fragmentary information, which, forsooth, is often erroneous as Lurvey suggests? Should emphasis be placed on headlines, rather than accuracy and interpretative analysis on radio and television?" He called attention to an article, "Color Makes Cold Type Hot," suggesting a meeting focusing on suburban newspapers, on which offset printing was taking hold, with editors talking about their problems, trends in publishing, perhaps their defense or chest-beating as opposed to the metropolitan press. Yet another article, "The Public Relations Man as City Editors See Him," offered chapters the opportunity to array PR practitioners against city editors in a lively, no-holds-barred discussion regarding the place of the PR person in the journalism sun. In the upcoming issues, he said, members would find articles on "The Electronic News: How Free?" and the report of the Society's freedom of information committee. "There's a wealth of material for a big night by the local Sigma Delta Chi chapter – ideas for getting local media and government figures to sound off." He concluded his letter, "What I am trying to say is that *The Quill* can suggest programs. Here at national headquarters, Warren Agee and I stand ready to help when you call on us. Personally, as the new editor, I want to make *The Quill* a vital force in discussion of our profession. If your magazine, and it really is that, doesn't hit the mark, let me know. And if it does, I would like to hear from you too." By the end of the year, the letters were coming in from across the nation with compliments on the "new look." One brief letter stated, "The change is certainly in keeping with the Society's forging ahead into a second half century of service to journalism."

A SUBSIDY FOR STUDENTS

The Society's growing financial stability, which allowed for the hiring of a full-time editor of *The Quill*, brought about a further service to undergraduate chapters by the end of the reorganizational year. Meeting during the fifty-second anniversary convention at the Hotel Fontainebleau in Miami Beach, October 25-28, 1961, the board of directors voted to appropriate $10,000 for transportation of student delegates to the 1962 convention in Tulsa, Oklahoma. Moved by Spangler and seconded by Arpan, the resolution changed the system for assisting student delegates to attend national conventions started at the Society's first convention at DePauw University in April 1912. Student chapters had paid pro-rata travel expenses from a required assessment on professional chapters through the 1961 convention. That assessment for the sixty-six professional chapters was abolished in separate action at the Miami Beach meeting. It was pointed out that assistance to the student chapters was one of the principal objectives in the McKinsey reorganization report and that the new travel subsidy would set this particular objective in motion. "Underwriting this expense will help solve a major problem confronting most of our student chapters," incoming national president Buren McCormack said. "It will enable them to concentrate on professional programs rather than money-making activities that often have scant relation to their news work and journalism studies." While the board didn't know, in 1961, whether $10,000 would cover the full cost of transporting delegates to the Tulsa meeting, it is interesting to note that, by 1963, the concern of the board turned to what to do with the surplus in travel funds for students not needed to pay those travel expenses. At the May 10-11, 1963, meeting in Dallas, the board agreed to use money left over from the

travel funds for Tulsa and add enough additional to pay one-half of the campus chapter advisers' travel expenses to the 1963 convention.

FOI IN THE SPOTLIGHT

Sigma Delta Chi's continuing emphasis on freedom of information did not suffer in 1961 while efforts to institute organizational changes took the spotlight. V.M. (Red) Newton stepped out of the presidency following the New York convention and back into his role as chairman of the FOI committee with the same zeal he had maintained in his previous eight years as chairman. Concentrating on the cloak of bureaucratic secrecy which enveloped America's foreign aid program, Newton's committee report stated, "Secrecy regarding foreign aid should end not only to give the American people their rightful knowledge of the expenditure of their tax funds but also, and equally important, to give world opinion a true picture of American efforts to improve the lot of distressed peoples." The report stated further that the only glimmer of light which reached the American people on the expenditure of its foreign aid funds had come from congressional investigations and from such books as *The Ugly American* and *A Nation of Sheep*. Addressing the record of President John F. Kennedy in the first months of his administration, Newton said, "As far as Sigma Delta Chi and other news groups are concerned, the record indicates that continued watchfulness is needed. The statements of principle by President Kennedy are not enough and only an informed and persistent criticism of unjustified secrecy will bring about changes. The full test for the Kennedy administration will come as problems arise that might bring some embarrassment. Careful review of how President Kennedy and his cabinet members handle these situations will give us a full view of what freedom of information means under pressure." Scripps also took on the President. In a speech before the Milwaukee professional chapter in May, Scripps referred to a suggestion by Kennedy that the press adopt self-censorship of news affecting the national security. "I would venture to say that through the years and especially in recent months the press of the United States has shown itself to be more responsible regarding release of information injurious to national security than this or past administrations. I think that any voluntary censorship plan would tend to become permanent and could become non-voluntary."

Sigma Delta Chi, during the reorganizational year, made an equally giant stride with another institution – the Internal Revenue Service. Although Sigma Delta Chi had dropped the word "honorary" to become a stated professional organization in 1916, it had been classified by the IRS as a "social group." Agee approached the agency with a request for reclassification based on the actions taken at the New York convention changing the organization from a fraternity to a professional society. On May 10, 1961, the Internal Revenue Service recognized Sigma Delta Chi as a society of full professional stature and declared that its 137 chapters and 16,000 members were entitled to exemption to federal income tax under section 501(c)(6) of the 1954 code, putting the Society in the same tax category as the American Bar Association and the American Medical Association. Agee said, "The new ruling was based on the Society's activities in helping to foster the education of future newsmen for all media, professional seminars and other programs, publishing *The Quill*, conducting a vigorous freedom of information campaign on state and national levels, presenting awards for distinguished service in journalism, marking historic sites in journalism, and generally uplifting the ethical conduct and professional standards of newsmen and news media throughout the United States."

For the individual members, the ruling meant that annual dues, both national and local as well as other necessary expenses incurred by members in promoting Sigma Delta Chi activities, henceforth were deductible for income tax purposes. Necessary expenses entailed by members in attending conventions and other meetings that advance the Society's numerous causes also were identified as deductible, Agee said.

Speaking for the Society, Scripps said, "Sigma Delta Chi is pleased to have this further public recognition of its role as the professional society of journalists. We are promoting a rapidly developing program on seventy-six college campuses, in sixty-one professional chapters and in newsrooms throughout the nation designed to increase the effectiveness and prestige of journalists, the individual news media and the profession itself. The IRS ruling will help us accomplish these aims."

Of the items on Agee's agenda in 1961-1962 which did not deal with reorganization under the McKinsey plan, many were crowned with success, while only one was a frustrating failure. On the plus side, Agee recalls, "In order to increase the advantages of membership, the headquarters office wrote to forty-five American and foreign press clubs asking them if they would admit visiting Sigma Delta Chi's as guests upon presentation of their membership cards. I received favorable replies from clubs in Milwaukee, Minneapolis, Cleveland, Indianapolis, Houston, Galveston, Las Vegas, Los Angeles, San Fransisco, Palm Springs, and Columbus, Ohio in the United States and from Vancouver, Montreal, and Toronto, Canada, as well as Rome, Italy." Satisfying as well were Agee's successful efforts to get the national convention to charter special chapters in London and Korea to begin the internationalizing of Sigma Delta Chi, and the beginning of the opening of chapter meetings and initiations to the public. On the latter, Agee remembers attending a meeting of the Central Ohio professional chapter in Columbus where the first television coverage of a Sigma Delta Chi initiation took place. He also served as "guide" for the Colorado professional chapter in early 1962, when 180 delegates to a Colorado Press Association convention witnessed the initiation of twenty-three newsmen to Sigma Delta Chi, marking the first such initiation opened to the public. This 'first' was at the instigation of former national president Palmer Hoyt, editor of the Denver *Post*."

One of the biggest jobs, Agee said, was planning for the national convention in Miami Beach, "a mammoth undertaking for a neophyte." The convention attracted New York Governor Nelson Rockefeller;

McGeorge Bundy, special assistant to President Kennedy on national security; and space expert Robert R. Gilruth as speakers. Headquarters operations and staffing also received Agee's attention. "I was able to increase the staff in the national office by 40 percent and establish a retirement plan to help protect the financial security of headquarters personnel. In addition, the staff and I revised all of the headquarters manuals, booklets and letters."

The major disappointment in Agee's first twelve months on the job came when he endeavored, unsuccessfully, to move the national office to a less expensive location in a city other than Chicago. "I was told before arrival that I could work toward this end. I found that almost all items of continuing expense – salaries, office rental, services and commuting – were higher in Chicago than in other cities in which I had lived. Since few members ever visited headquarters personally and ours was mostly a mail and telephone operation, I felt that almost any other location with reasonable access to an airport would be preferable. Members of the Chicago Headline Club, however, strongly objected to this proposal and worked against it. I learned too that Pearl Luttrell, who had become an extremely valuable employee with considerable Sigma Delta Chi experience, could not move to another city. I scouted for less expensive quarters in or near the Loop, but nothing better was found."

Despite the few disappointments which came with the job, by the time the national convention met in Miami Beach, October 25, 1961, Agee counted the year a real success. He heard president Scripps tell the delegates, "A renewed interest in Sigma Delta Chi is evident in all our fifty states. I believe that our Society for the first time in its recent history has now the opportunity to become the professional journalistic society." When Agee addressed the convention, he said, "Eleven months ago your national officers and directors and I, as your new executive officer, accepted the mandate of the fifty-first anniversary convention of Sigma Delta Chi to carry out the reorganization and reinvigoration of our Society in terms of the philosophy and the actual recommendations of the McKinsey plan. This we have attempted to do, and I am happy to report that major strides have been made." Outlining the progress made in 1961, Agee said, "My hat, were I wearing one today, would be off in salute to the men of Sigma Delta Chi, to the giant strength and the equally giant potential of our Society in meeting both the problems of journalism and the problems of our democracy." He concluded his remarks, "It's been a great year for Sigma Delta Chi, a year of both experimentation and progress, but the best is yet ahead. With your continuing devotion to our ideals and objectives, Sigma Delta Chi will move steadily forward toward the realization of our mutual hopes and dreams."

FROM AGEE TO HURST

The successes which marked the year of change from professional fraternity to professional society were gratifying for national president Buren McCormack and first vice president Walter Burroughs as they assumed the top two elective offices in Sigma Delta Chi following the Miami Beach convention in 1961. They had been in positions of leadership in the organization from the days of the Kilgore Report on eligibility of public relations practitioners for membership through the White and McKinsey Reports and, in 1962, provided the continuity on the new board of directors. They had seen a major portion of their dreams for Sigma Delta Chi manifested, especially as the board assumed much more active control of all operations of the Society. Scripps acknowledged that, while he was in the spotlight as president in 1961, McCormack and Burroughs continued to be driving forces behind the scenes as the reorganization plan was effected. Referring specifically to Burrough's support during his presidency, Scripps said, "He did all the dirty work and I got all the glory." McCormack and Burroughs presented contrasting styles of leadership over the years, yet worked together as a dynamic and efficient team. McCormack, according to his colleagues, was a quiet, strong influence on the society and kept a level head in helping to direct the changes as they took place, but had no desire for personal aggrandizement. As Sigma Delta Chi president, he was graceful but determined, employing the style he had used as he moved through the executive ranks with *The Wall Street Journal* to become vice president and editorial director. Conversely, Burroughs, outspoken, energetic and forceful, was ready and willing to be on the battle lines. When the unpleasant side of things came along, which was bound to be in any reorganization of that type, he often took what was, at the time, the unpopular position. The respect in which he was held by his fellow council and board members, however, just as often won him the day despite his rough-and-tumble nature.

Thus it was with two venerable and dedicated stalwarts of the Society at the helm that Sigma Delta Chi literally took to the road in 1962 continuing the revitalization process. Burroughs traveled to Moscow, Idaho, to install the Palouse Empire professional chapter January 13 while McCormack and Agee were on their way to Norfolk, Virginia, to charter the Tidewater professional chapter January 14. Six weeks later, March 10, McCormack flew to London to charter the first international chapter of the Society. Agee and Burroughs joined forces in Kansas City, speaking at the first Region Seven conference March 10.

The establishment of the full complement of regional conferences, following up on the first such conference in Region Eleven in October, 1961, was effected early in the year. Region Six held its first conference February 17-18 in Minneapolis. April conferences included Region Three in Atlanta and Region Five in Chicago both on the 13th and 14th, with Region Eight meeting in Lubbock and Region Ten in Seattle, April 28-29. Region Two convened in Williamsburg, Virginia, May 4-6 with Region Nine meeting in Grand Junction, Colorado, and Region Eleven in San Jose, California, May 5. Region One scheduled its conference May 11-12 in New York City. The thirtieth annual Awards for Distinguished Service in Journalism program was held in conjunction with the Region Four conference in Detroit, May 12.

At headquarters, Agee opened the tenth annual drive for open records and open meetings laws in states where they did not exist. Writing to more than 2,000 members in eleven states, Agee pointed out that the legislatures in Missouri and Nebraska, without a dissenting vote, had adopted Sigma Delta Chi-sponsored open records laws. The Society had targeted Arizona, Georgia, Kansas, Michigan and Mississippi for the open meetings law drive and Colorado, New York, Rhode Island, South Carolina, Virginia and West Virginia for legislation in both the open meetings and open records areas.

But while the Society continued to move forward and much activity was apparent at the national, regional and local levels in the first three months of 1962, Agee was going through what he called "a period of severe mental anguish." In a letter to president McCormack, April 8, Agee revealed his dilemma:

A deanship provides an opportunity for service, together with remuneration and prestige, second only to the presidency or the chancellorship on a university campus. Such an opening occurs only once in every ten years or so at Texas Christian University [where he had received his bachelor's degree and where he had been a faculty member and later chairman of the Department of Journalism for ten years] in my home community of Fort Worth. Two months ago, Dean Cortell K. Holsapple died, and I have been importuned to return to accept the position of Professor of Journalism and Dean of the Fort Worth College of the university. For personal and family reasons, as well as those of a professional and academic nature, I feel compelled to accept this offer and, most reluctantly, to relinquish my position as Executive Officer of Sigma Delta Chi.

He asked to have his resignation effective June 30 so that he could assume his new duties July 1 to prepare for the fall semester. His letter continued:

The personal reasons scarcely require recounting: the wear and tear of frequent travel and the abnormal family life that is its natural accompaniment, the poor Chicago weather and the hardships of its cruel winters, Mrs. Agee's severe sinus infections, the daily commuting involving almost two and one half hours, the extremely high cost of living on Chicago's North Shore which substantially negates a most generous salary, and other factors, most of them related to the difficulties of northern metropolitan living.

Nineteen years later in a personal letter to the author of this book, Agee remembered the decision-making process which led to his resignation and said that, in addition to the deanship of the Fort Worth College (Evening Division of Texas Christian University), he had been offered what he thought was a wonderful and unique opportunity to help establish a School of Communication at TCU, something which ultimately failed to materialize. But he added, "I had lived in Fort Worth for forty-one years and my children were born there. Although I was offered a salary $5,000 less than I was making with Sigma Delta Chi, I knew that the living costs were much lower than on the North Shore of the Chicago metropolitan area and, as it turned out, I felt no decrease in salary and was able to build a new residence without difficulty." On the professional level, Agee remembers, "I knew that I could not long remain out of the academic stream if I wanted to make academic journalism my career henceforth." In his letter to McCormack, he said:

I am resigning only with the knowledge that, during the past seventeen months, Sigma Delta Chi has been led through its period of crisis and is well on the high road of renewed acceptance and accomplishment. The pattern of the reorganization program has been tested, at least in part, and found to be sound. We have accomplished, through the diligence of many persons, during this period of less than two years what some of our leaders had anticipated would take at least three or four. Accordingly, I consider that the mission which I undertook when I left West Virginia University has been subtantially performed although my period of service has been curtailed through circumstance.

Agee told this author that any doubts about leaving the post without having accomplished what the board had hired him to do were relieved upon talking to the man who had recommended him for the position of executive officer – his friend, former colleague and past Society president James A. Byron. "When I talked with Jim at that time, he said, 'Warren, we only wanted you to remain long enough to help establish new directions for the Society.' " He concluded his April 8 letter of resignation:

I am prepared to work closely with whoever succeeds me, both immediately and in the months and years ahead. I shall seek to follow through this year in every way possible to assure that the transition is orderly and that the plans for the national convention continue without interruption. Clarence Schlaver is available, of course, to lend extra assistance during this period and our office staff can carry on many of our functions with little guidance. Needless to say, I shall continue my strong support of, and assistance to, Sigma Delta Chi throughout the years ahead.

I am deeply grateful for the wholehearted support that you and other members of the board, as well as our past presidents and numerous key members of our Society throughout the country, have given to me. One could not hope for finer and more understanding employers and associates than all of these men have been.

In the announcement of Agee's resignation carried in the May *Quill*, McCormack praised the executive officer. "He has made a very fine contribution to the growth and development of the Society. He has given freely of his talent, time and energy to move Sigma Delta Chi ahead." The president noted that the names of many people were under consideration as a successor to Agee and that the board of directors hoped to have a new executive officer selected at the regular spring board meeting in Detroit, May 11. With that date only little more than a month after Agee's April 8 letter, the process of selecting a replacement moved quickly.

Agee had told McCormack that Dean

Burton W. Marvin of the William Allen White School of Journalism at the University of Kansas had expressed interest in the job but no mention of contact or interviews with Marvin appears in any official records. Rather, the search, which attracted two dozen candidates, focused on two men, Henry Rieger of Los Angeles and Russell E. Hurst of Minneapolis.

Burroughs, with the help and encouragement of Spangler, approached Rieger, his long-time friend and United Press International bureau chief in Los Angeles, to consider applying for the post. Rieger had a strong record of service to Sigma Delta Chi at the local and regional levels, having been a key member of the committee which planned the first regional conference in October 1961. "At the time, it sounded like it was something I wanted to do," Rieger said. "I accepted the opportunity to go to Detroit to meet with the board of directors with full intention of accepting the job should it be offered to me. In fact, I had extensive conversations with members of the board the day before the board decision and, although I was not confident I would receive the nod, I was excited about the possibility."

Hurst was an editorial writer for the Minneapolis *Tribune* in early 1962 when he was approached about the job. "I believe it was Paul Swensson, who was Executive Director of The Newspaper Fund for Dow Jones, [the parent company of *The Wall Street Journal*] who called me at home on behalf of Buren McCormack and proposed that I consider this opportunity to take over as Executive Officer of Sigma Delta Chi." Swensson had known Hurst since 1953 when Hurst went to work for the *Tribune* and Swensson was managing editor of the newspaper. "I later learned that my name had come up from at least three different sources – from Swensson, from Warren Agee and from Dr. Ed Emery, Sigma Delta Chi campus chapter adviser in the school of journalism and mass communication at the University of Minnesota. My immediate reaction was 'no!' for I was enjoying tremendously what I was doing in Minneapolis. By coincidence, I had been invited to speak in Colorado Springs at the Broadmoor Hotel at the Council on Religion in International Affairs. McCormack, learning that I was going to be there – and it turned out that he and his wife and daughter were going to be there on vacation that weekend – invited me to have breakfast with him. I had thought about the job for a few weeks but really had no thoughts of moving. Following that Colorado Springs meeting, I was invited to make a full submission of my biography and so on, and meet with the board of directors in Detroit May 11.

Agee's connection with Hurst stemmed from days at Texas Christian University when Hurst, returning from Air Force duty, enrolled as an undergraduate journalism student while Agee was chairman of the department. "As a student of mine at TCU, Russ was editor of *The Skiff*, the campus newspaper, and was a key person in holding the department together during my year's absence completing my Ph.D. residency at the University of Minnesota. He had gained both newspaper and radio experience in Fort Worth and then went on to Minnesota where he earned the master's degree. The Minneapolis *Tribune* hired him originally to cover the oil exploration and the legislatures in North and South Dakota." It was he, Agee said, who, after talking with Hurst on the telephone about the job and finding some interest expressed, contacted McCormack and helped arrange the Colorado Springs meeting. Agee talked with McCormack after the Colorado Springs meeting and learned that the two had hit it off well. "I was confident, even before Detroit, that McCormack would recommend Hurst to the Board and that he would accept the position. Knowing that, in Hurst, the Society would have a successor who could carry on the work in a highly efficient manner, my decision to step down was made much more confortable," Agee said.

Hurst had joined Sigma Delta Chi as a graduate student at the University of Minnesota February 20, 1953, and was a charter member of the reorganized Minnesota professional chapter in 1956. At the time of his nomination for executive officer, most of his activities had been only in campus chapter and professional chapter programs. "I had met some of the national people coming through while I was on the ladder for the professional chapter – treasurer at the time – but I didn't know a whole lot about the national level of operations of the Society. I had only about the same awareness as any other member about the reorganization of the Society, reading about it in *The Quill* and hearing about it from delegates returning from the national convention."

The prestige of the people who had contacted him and with whom he had met and talked "was a pretty powerful influence," Hurst said, in helping him decide to become a full-fledged candidate for the job. "What really persuaded me, however, was an opportunity to work with THE national journalism society [Hurst's emphasis] and to have a role in doing the things that Sigma Delta Chi was involved in on a national basis – the publication of a magazine, the opportunity to work with professionals all over the country. I was strongly persuaded from the start that the things the Society stood for were the things I believed in and the things I wanted to do. I felt very humble about even being considered for this job – scared too." When Hurst arrived in Detroit May 10 for the final interviews, he was not at all confident he would get the job. "Hank and I had dinner together at the Statler Hilton Hotel the night before the board meeting, both of us saying, 'I know you're going to do a good job, Hank,' 'I know you're going to do a good job, Russ.' I didn't know until later that Rieger was seriously considering withdrawing as a candidate."

Rieger confirmed the dinner meeting conversation with Hurst and recalled the sleepless night which followed. "I went up to my room and sat down thinking, 'Is this something I really want to do?' I started doing the old-fashioned 'plus and minus' list. To this day I really don't know what caused me to make the decision, but, at six o'clock in the morning, I came to the conclusion that I really wanted to continue to be a newsman – a career I had spent much of my life developing. I woke up Walter [Burroughs] at that hour and told him, 'I'm sorry, but I've determined in all fairness to Sigma Delta Chi and myself, I've

determined that being executive officer is not what I want to do. I'm sorry we've carried this thing this far, but I'm going to withdraw as a candidate.' Walter was upset and asked me to reconsider but, when I said I was firm, he accepted my decision."

When the board of directors convened at nine o'clock, in the first item of business Rieger appeared before the board to withdraw his name from consideration as executive officer. Of the board's subsequent interview with Hurst, the minutes state only that "Russell Hurst spoke and was questioned about his candidacy for executive officer." The board then went into executive session and Region Eight Director Ralph Sewell moved, with Region Five Director Dennis Orphan seconding, that the president try to hire Hurst as executive officer at a salary of from $14,000 to $15,000 per year. (Schlaver's salary was set at $13,000 with the remainder of the staff salaries to be left to the discretion of the new executive officer.) The motion carried unanimously. Angelo recalls, "Hurst wasn't well known while Rieger had an active record in serving Sigma Delta Chi in the West at least." He admitted he had come to the meeting favoring the hiring of Rieger but was so favorably impressed with Hurst's remarks during the interview that he changed his mind and was happy with the selection of the man from Minneapolis. McCormack, apparently, was able to negotiate immediately with Hurst. The minutes of the same meeting record Hurst's expression of appreciation and delight along with that of his wife at having been selected for the position. The board, on Burroughs' motion with many seconds, expressed its appreciation to Agee for his many contributions during his twenty months of service. Agee responded with thanks, saying it had been a gratifying experience and that working conditions had been ideal.

HURST BEGINS HIS WORK

Hurst arrived in Chicago May 30, 1962, and was on the job the next morning. Working for the next few weeks with Agee in briefing sessions, he learned the job quickly. A number of the board members later reflected on their surprise and pleasure with the manner in which Hurst grasped his new responsibilities and was in command of his job almost immediately. Perhaps the most demanding of the group, Burroughs, said, "He studied hard in learning his new trade. He talked to many members of the board and, right from the start, he was excellent – well, I wouldn't say excellent, but he was very good. Much of the credit for continuing the progress has to go to Hurst, along with McCormack." Sewell, who had just been elected treasurer in Miami Beach, added, "I'm sure Russ's family saw little of him in that first year for he was on the road almost immediately. He made a terrific early record traveling and getting acquainted." Region Eleven Director Spangler agreed. "Hurst took over remarkably well. There was some shock in the organization at Agèe's departure, but Russ took over quietly and competently." As fine a job as Agee had done, Angelo remembers Hurst came in at a very tough time. "There were still a lot of cross currents going on and he handled them very well. When you look at the job he did in the light of the times – the still limited finances and and the hard, hard work of keeping some of the chapters alive, he made a wonderful start." The retiring Agee's confidence in Hurst's ability was reflected in his farewell statement to the membership in the July, 1962 *Quill*. In part, it said, "Our advances are evidence of the loyalty and the teamwork of thousands of members who have made our Society great. Please permit me to thank you personally and to commend to you our new executive officer, Russell E. Hurst, who, with your continued support, will give Sigma Delta Chi outstanding service during the years ahead."

If the board members and Agee were surprised that Hurst was immediately effective so far as his day-to-day duties were concerned when he arrived in Chicago, they had to have been astonished that this man, with little inside knowledge of the reorganizational goals and objectives of the Society at the national level, was so in tune philosophically with them. That philosophy was expressed in his opening statement to the membership in the July 1962 *Quill*. He said:

One of the first things every newsman learns (painfully sometimes) is that it's dangerous to make an assumption about anything. I feel there is little chance of my going astray, however, in assuming that my principal goals as executive officer are also yours as a member:

To aid Sigma Delta Chi toward increased stature and membership.

To encourage journalistic professionalism of the highest level attainable.

To seek to influence increasing numbers of talented young people to enter journalism; to hold them in journalism once they become professionals.

There are many facets to each of these goals, of course; the Society's freedom of information and awards programs, *The Quill*, marking of historic sites, professional and undergraduate programs and relations, regional activities, workshops, seminars and so on. And there are other facets still awaiting our discovery and development. The only risk I foresee is in the assumption that Sigma Delta Chi will advance by its own momentum. It won't. The Society's growth in recent years has been the result of dedicated effort by individual members and officers. Our future growth will likewise be in direct proportion to the amount of talent and energy each member devotes to the Society's programs and activities.

I am confident of the future. I pledge an efficient headquarters operation. And I look forward to meeting you and cooperating with you in the continuing development of Sigma Delta Chi as a vital force in American journalism.

From the outset, Hurst had an awareness of the importance of the Society's local chapters and individual members to its goals and objectives. "That was the key to the future of the Society," Hurst said. "It was and is a voluntary organization and as long as the individual members were motivated and the chapters continued in what I felt was the most important role structurally within the whole of the Society, then the Society would continue to grow."

Taking his commitment and motivational effort on the road, Hurst visited sixteen chapters in his first four months in office. The "outstanding examples of professional programming" he saw first hand made him set as his first goal the development of chapter programs which, in turn, he said, would give them added strength, the ability to bring in new members and help to build the Society as a whole. He encouraged regional directors to become more directly involved through regular visits to campus and professional chapters. The result, he reported at the national convention in Tulsa, was the enrollment of almost 1,500 new members in fiscal 1961-1962, during Agee's tenure, an increase of about 200 more than the previous year.

Direct visitation was only part of Hurst's plans for communication with local chapters. Within those first months, he laid plans for publication of *Replate*, an occasional summary of chapter programming ideas and fund-raising projects along with reports to chapter officers of important decisions and plans of the national officers and board of directors. He recruited professor William Baxter of Howard College, Birmingham, Alabama, to compile news from chapter newsletters along with information from the national office. While there had been some success in earlier efforts at an officers' newsletter – *Trading Post* from 1954 through 1960, edited by headquarter's personnel, and *Here's How* from March 1958 through September 1959 edited by Robert A. Lerner of the University of Missouri. *Replate*, from its first issue in March 1963, became a permanent informational tool used by chapters and has been continued under several names, most recently *News and Views*, a monthly publication. Headquarters' files indicate *Replate* was taken over as a national office function with the June 1964 issue as have all newsletters since.

Hurst continued Agee's connection with allied organizations, traveling to national meetings of the American Society of Newspaper Editors, Associated Press Managing Editors Association, Radio Television News Directors Association, Association for Education in Journalism and Theta Sigma Phi, the women's journalistic organization.

At the same time, work at national headquarters was at a fever pitch with efforts related to producing the fiftieth aniversary issue of *The Quill* for November 1962. Hurst became fully immersed with Schlaver and others in the Chicago offices in compiling and editing the 108-page special issue devoted to "American Journalism: Past, Present and Future." From that experience, he not only gained a greater respect for the magazine but developed a real love affair with *The Quill*, something which would last through his nineteen years as the Society's top administrator. He told the board, "I have been working as closely with Schlaver as my other duties permit, scouting for manuscripts, consulting on various stages of editing, proofreading and writing book reviews."

Those first months brought about the beginning of an effort to fulfill another of Hurst's early goals – to work actively to recruit young persons to journalism. Following through on a suggestion by Richard Hixon, president of the New Jersey professional chapter, Hurst met with directors of the Boy Scouts Exploring Service to discuss possibilities of Sigma Delta Chi cooperation in sponsoring Explorer posts in journalism. He made arrangements for a booth at the 1963 national convention of the American Personnel and Guidance Association, where he noted there would be "an excellent opportunity for us to reach some 5,000 to 6,000 high school and college counselors with career information on journalism. Many of them are totally unaware of the opportunities in our field," he said. He asked president-elect Burroughs to appoint a committee to review available career literature and suggested that "such a committee consider the possibility of developing a distinctive SDX careers brochure. Headquarters receives regular requests for such materials and rather than passively waiting for such requests, I think we should be putting career materials out aggressively in fulfillment of our goal of attracting young people to journalism." His report to the Tulsa convention further suggested the organization of speakers bureaus, workshops and other programs for the enrichment of the profession, for the inspiration and recruitment of high school and college students, and for the advancement of public information about journalism and journalists.

While much, if not most of the credit probably must go to the departed Agee and the national officers, it is significant to note that first indications that the Society's long-standing financial problems apparently had been solved came in a Hurst suggestion to the board in Tulsa. The new executive officer reported that about $40,000 in the Society's checking account could be transferred to a savings account. While expenses had increased partially because the Society had underwritten travel expenses to Tulsa for campus chapter delegates and advisers and headquarters had moved to larger facilities still on the eighth floor of 35 East Wacker Drive, income for the 1961-1962 fiscal year was up by $30,000. Hurst remembers that in addition to substantial savings in the *Quill* Endowment Fund, there were small amounts of money in several separate accounts scattered around the Chicago area. A combination of reasons, no doubt, accounted for the surplus,

he said. The probability remains, however, that the board action in Tulsa to set up a savings program for the Society in general was probably the beginning of the Sigma Delta Chi invested reserves, an account which had grown to more than $200,000 when Hurst resigned as executive officer in 1981.

The Tulsa convention, November 14-17 at the Mayo Hotel, attracted nearly 550 delegates. Burroughs, who had been at the forefront of the reorganizational drive some five years earlier, became national president. Announcing his election, *The Quill* editor commented, "All through the years, Burroughs has been called in by the heads of business organizations in all parts of the country to help them solve knotty problems. On this account he could also be called 'Doctor' Burroughs, for he has been and still is in demand as a business physician and surgeon." Certainly he had worked his surgical magic on Sigma Delta Chi for as he assumed the Society's top elective office, the transformation of a weak and, perhaps, dying journalistic fraternity to a growing and vibrant professional society of journalists had been completed. Hurst was firmly in control of the day-to-day operation of the Society and a bright and promising future lay ahead for Sigma Delta Chi.

UNIT II

███████████████

The Hurst Era:
A Legacy
of Landmarks

The rebuilding of the Society and its resultant impact on the future of the organization during the years dominated by Burroughs, Kilgore, McCormack, White and Agee, as revolutionary and successful as they proved to be, was to serve as only the foundation for a Sigma Delta Chi whose years from 1962-1984 would be the most progressive in its history.

It is far more than simple coincidence that for nineteen of those years Hurst was the Society's executive officer. Under his leadership and that of the officers and boards of directors working with him, Sigma Delta Chi matured and expanded in every facet of its operation from record growth in number of members and chapters to a broad extension of traditional programs and the development of significant new projects. The landmark decisions of delegates at forthcoming conventions as well as of the officers and boards were to be as momentus as those of the founders in 1909. Indeed, some of the changes to come would be more revolutionary – especially to long time members – than the reorganization in the late 1950's and early 1960's.

Among the events during the Hurst years which would bring Sigma Delta Chi to a new level of prominence in American journalism, we shall now examine the movements and struggles which brought about the admission of women to the Society; the change of the name of the organization; the writing of a strong, new code of ethics for journalists; the evolution of vigorous and effective freedom of information and First Amendment programs at the national and local levels; the development of the Sigma Delta Chi Foundation; the building of additional prestigious awards programs; and the beginning of efforts to recruit, train and establish a place for minority journalists in the profession. Some of these milestones positively affected the growth in number of members and chapters – a milestone in itself – while others were effected because of that growth.

Hurst took little personal credit for those substantive and positive changes, suggesting that many persons were involved in planting the seeds, nurturing their growth and bringing them to maturity. The fact remains, however, that all of those programs and others were begun, extended, facilitated or completed during the tenure of Russell Hurst as executive officer.

58

CHAPTER 4

■■■■■■■

The Modern-Day "Mr. SDX"

LeRoy H. Millikan, Eugene C. Pulliam, Paul Riddick and the other founders of Sigma Delta Chi probably would have joined Hurst's contemporaries in calling him "Mr. SDX." No other member of the fraternity or, later, the society spent as many years in full-time service to the organization as Hurst and few, if any, were as actively involved in the operation of Sigma Delta Chi for so long a period even as volunteers.

Sigma Delta Chi was in its eighteenth year as a fraternity of journalists when Hurst was born in 1927 and was approaching its golden anniversary when he became a member as a graduate student at the University of Minnesota in 1953. By the time Hurst had spent four months on the job as executive officer in October, 1962, more than 35,000 men had joined SDX since 1909 and the Society had 79 campus and 69 professional chapters with 13,200 members "in good standing" on the active roles. Every national officer who served during his years as executive officer credits Hurst, in great part, with providing the impetus and inspiration leading to that growth, which made the Society the largest journalism organization in the world.

Upon presentation of the Wells Memorial Key to Hurst on his retirement, April 25, 1981 in Cincinnati, one speaker said, "If you seek his legacy, look about you." He was speaking of the student and professional members present as representative of 28,000 Society members recognized at that time to whom Hurst had dedicated his talents and energies. The individual member and chapter were always Hurst's first priority. He believed they were not only the life blood of the Society, but the very reason the Society existed. The efforts he made in working with the elected officers and boards in developing the Society's multitude of programs were devoted to serving that individual member, whether reporter, editor, broadcaster, photographer, or media executive.

Even before he had his feet firmly on the ground in all of his varied administrative roles, Hurst seemed to be everywhere – at national conventions of the Society and other journalism groups, SDX regional conferences and local chapter meetings, and with groups

Russell E. Hurst, an editorial writer for the Minneapolis *Tribune*, was hired May 11, 1962, as Society executive officer and served in that post for nineteen years - longer than any other person.

of journalists hoping to charter a chapter – preaching the gospel of Sigma Delta Chi. For most of his tenure, he was not just at the center, he *was* the center of Sigma Delta Chi, the person to whom everyone looked and about whom they thought at the mention of the Society's name. While an expansion of the Society's efforts in joining with other journalistic organizations in broader ventures in the late 1970's brought others to the national limelight, Hurst retained his status as a one of the few prominent leaders in American journalism.

If Hurst had a professional love within the context of his job for anything other than the members of the Society, it was *The Quill*. He believed the magazine was the single most important activity of the Society. "It provides the information link to all of our members, serves as a forum for discussion of controversial ideas in the field and keeps the membership up-to-date on everything that is happening in the field," he

said. "Many of our members are not affiliated with any campus or professional chapters and *The Quill* is their only link with the national organization. Freedom of information and ethics would rank high in importance as programs in the Society, but *The Quill* has always been first." He took great pride in the magazine. Recognizing that other journalism publications serving different purposes had done commendable work, he believed that *The Quill* had uniquely filled its role since 1912 as "the outstanding publication in journalism over that period of time."

Hurst, along with executive editor C.O. Schlaver and later with editors Charles Long and Naomi Donson, set the philosophy of the magazine as not only to be a journal to serve the interests of the profession, describing trends and practices in the field, but to make the magazine useful to members, students and teachers as an instructional tool. In addition, he saw the

60

role of *The Quill* as a stimulus to growth of the Society, reporting on activities of the organization to the membership.

Believing that *The Quill* operation should be a team effort, Hurst spent long hours on the magazine, often taking that work home with him. "It was almost impossible to put out a monthly magazine for what is the most critical audience in the world, an audience of journalists, singlehanded. I frequently found myself reading articles, reading proofs, and discussing story ideas with the editors. As I traveled, as the editor traveled, and later the assistants, we always traveled with, among other objectives, a principal objective of seeing if we could develop future article ideas and identify authors. If we ran into a prospective advertiser, we would encourage that advertiser to consider *The Quill* as a vehicle."

Given his belief in the importance of the magazine to the Society and its members, Hurst agonized over the fact that inflationary factors and periods of recession often necessitated a cut in number of pages in issues of *The Quill*. One fiscal decision was even more distressing. "Somewhat to my surprise, the board decided to cut back the number of issues from twelve to eleven in 1975. I had hoped that that would not happen, frankly." It was news of chapter activities and announcements of actions of the board and the officers which suffered in reducing the size of the magazine and the number of issues. But Hurst turned to *Replate* and its successor, *NEWSletter*, in an attempt to keep chapters apprised through their officers of activities and policy changes in the Society.

THE HURST STYLE

Before examining the Hurst years in detail as they relate to landmark events in Sigma Delta Chi history, it is important to understand the Hurst style as identified by the national presidents with whom he worked and by Hurst himself. William Small, a former president of CBS and NBC News and more recently president of United Press International, who was the Society's president in 1974-75, observed Hurst from the perspective of a local chapter member, national committee member, regional director and national officer. "Hurst made a greater contribution to the Society than anyone else in the twenty years since reorganization," he said. "Of course, that was natural because he was the on-going glue that held us together. He was efficient, self-effacive, and had good ideas. Every president I knew found Hurst the most valuable asset during the year of his presidency."

Working with the Society's all-volunteer board of directors in which new members replaced others each year was no easy task for the executive officer. Change in styles and strength of leadership, differences in personalities, and shifts in priorities for programs and policies surfaced every year, sometimes dramatically, with the election of the new national president. Some presidents and executive committees assumed office with a "take-charge" style, while, quite naturally, others adopted a more passive role in leading the Society. As the administrative leader charged with providing continuity from year to year, Hurst regularly found himself in a period of readjustment. "I got to know these people as they came on the board and worked up the ladder toward the presidency, so in some respects, I could anticipate the kind of year it would be. I had to prepare myself for a period of adjustment and usually it developed rather quickly," Hurst recalls. Bob Chandler, editor of the Bend, Oregon *Bulletin* and national president in 1970-1971, said, "Hurst had the rare ability to keep a constant course for an organization where each new president felt he should change the direction of the Society to fit his own style." In that atmosphere, Hurst believed his role was "to keep the gears moving and assure that continuing programs which might not have the priority originally established by a previous administration were not ignored." As boards evolved, Hurst tried to absorb all of their ideas and provide a sense of perspective on how goals might be reached or problems solved. It was all in the timing, however.

Many of the past presidents with whom he worked characterized Hurst as a listener and facilitator. He would sit silently through long discussions by the board members, taking note of all that was said, raising questions only in his own mind. William B. Arthur, 1968-1969 national president, recalls, "Hurst believed that a board was a board and that the executive officer should not inject himself into the decision-making process. It was the board's place to discuss and make policy." To pop in early in discussions with serious questions about how a new program might be financed or to relate that a similar program had been tried ten years earlier and failed for lack of resources, Hurst said, "would have the effect of killing the free flow of ideas, the momentum of a new inspiration." The Hurst style was to wait until all the elected representatives had had their say. "But when I sensed there was a developing consensus among the members, I posed some hard questions about cost factors and other possible problems," Hurst said. At many board meetings, he frequently played the role of devil's advocate. Hurst recalls that when the board would reach a certain point of discussion nearing a decision on an important matter, it became common for all the members to turn and look at him asking, "OK, what's wrong with it?" Alf Goodykoontz, president in 1977-1978, noted that that was an important moment each time. "Russ was superb in his attention to detail. Lots of us who were president were good at suggesting ways to do things, but weren't so cognizant of ways to pay for them," 1978-1979 president Phil Dessauer added. "He was the cool and restraining voice in board meetings. He would generally put his finger on what the problems were and he was usually right." At times, the board would move in directions with which Hurst did not agree. But, Chandler remembers, "He was the best soldier in the world. Whatever the deal was, he went out and put 100 percent into it to make it work."

While he asked the probing questions which needed to be put to a board excited about the prospect of a new program or direction, to get all of the necessary information on the table, Hurst's role was more positive than negative. As he gained experience over the years, he was able to provide information about how a project might be facilitated, assuring the board that it was on the right track. "Sometimes I had to curb my own excitement about an idea that was taking form," Hurst recalls. On numerous occasions, he would identify people, organizations and other resources around the country which would be valuable in helping to move what was only an idea through developmental stages to manifestation. Thus, calling on Hurst's knowledge and considerable skills for facilitation, it was nearly as common for the officers or board to turn to the executive officer asking not "What's wrong?" but "How can we do this?"

Hurst was especially effective during the period of change in the late 1960's and early 1970's, according to Ralph Otwell, a regional director and national officer during that time. "Those were years of ferment in the Society, what with the battles on and off the board surrounding the admission of women, the name change, adoption of the new code of ethics and major changes in the system of voting at national convention," said Otwell, who became national president in 1973-1974. " Without the strong administrative head of Russ Hurst to calm all the anxieties by board members and others and to keep everything on track, God only knows what might have happened," Another who joined the board as a regional director during those years. becoming president in 1975-1976, Robert McCord, agreed. "Hurst was the very model for performance by an executive officer of a national organization. He was the best organizer and the best worker with whom I've ever had the pleasure to serve."

Hurst's mind was always active in attempting to build policy and programs that would enhance the Society or American journalism. A conversation at dinner or correspondence with a colleague might provide the germination for an idea. But he was never concerned about who received credit – inside or outside SPJ,SDX – for the genesis of that idea. "My concern was always with the principle, the objective, and having it implemented and done well," he said. "It never bothered me that the Society itself did not get credit for a specific activity it initiated at the national level if some other group picked it up and ran with it." In all fairness, however, it must be said that Hurst, as well as the SPJ,SDX board of directors, took great pride in national leadership roles in such projects as developing model "sunshine" and shield laws, a strong new code of ethics for journalists, the First Amendment Congress, and the Freedom of Information Service Center.

While there was not always agreement between the board and Hurst during his tenure, only on rare occasions was there more than understandable disappointment or concern about a decision made or a policy adopted. As the relative styles of leadership – active to passive – among the elected officers changed from year to year, Hurst on occasion had to take a more directive role with the board, raising some eyebrows among more zealous members. When there were problems, it can be said that those same variant styles often played as great a role, if not a greater role, than the issues at hand. Such was the case in the most significant disagreement between Hurst and the Society's officers. As Hurst's tenure as executive officer neared the end of a second decade, he had established administrative procedures for day-to-day operation of the Society with which he was comfortable and in which he had confidence. There being no apparent need to change them, those procedures had gone virtually unchallenged and, for all intents and purposes, were supported by past officers and boards. During study of the need for an extensive fiscal reorganization of the Society in 1980, brought on by inflationary pressures and a decline in the Society's rate of growth, a clash of perceptions surfaced on the role of the executive officer vis-a-vis the officers and board. The resulting conflict of styles among strong-minded leaders, along with some apparent breakdown in interpersonal communication techniques, not unusual for any group of human beings trying to work in concert, let alone for journalists, overshadowed the reorganizational objectives being pursued. While Hurst maintains that those differences did not cause him to resign in January 1981, they were precursors to that action.

For the greater part of his nineteen years as executive officer, however, a spirit of cooperation coupled with lively debate dominated board and executive committee meetings. William C. Payette, president in 1972-1973, said Hurst's effectiveness in the long term was primarily because of the respect the officers and board members had for his knowledge and experience. That admiration and respect were perhaps best exemplified by 1964-1965 president Ralph Sewell. "We would pray upon taking office that Russ Hurst would not quit as executive officer before our year as president had been completed." Arthur, who was editor of *Look* magazine in his year as president, said Hurst understood the roles of the busy media executives who became president. "Many of us on the ladder lived in mortal fear of becoming president without Russ Hurst on the job – that before we took over the gavel, Hurst would be tempted to return to writing."

In the last year of his work, when discordance emerged regarding the role of the executive officer, Hurst's loyalty and dedication to the Society and the profession towered above operational disagreements with the officers. Jean Otto, editor of the Op-Ed Page of *The Milwaukee Journal*, and president in his last full year as executive officer, said, "He presented a sense of class to the rest of the journalistic world and to the public. He had a sense of personal honor and an honorableness about the profession and he stood very tall in this respect. He held the Society together when not very many people – the volunteers on the board and out in the chapters – could give it the kind of time that was needed."

In sum, Hurst's acknowledged abilities in administering a growing and often unwieldy organiation of journalists from 1962 to mid-1981, probably stemmed from his unswerving dedication to the profession at large. At the Distinguished Service Awards banquet in Omaha in 1971, Burroughs presented Hurst with a wrist watch from the past presidents of the Society. The engraved message on the back of the watch stated, "Past Presidents' Award to Russell E. Hurst in gratitude for a decade of outstanding service to the Society." Angelo characterized Hurst as "...a newspaper guy trying to put together an organization rather than an organization man who happened to have been a newspaperman." In any case, Hurst earned the reputation as "Mr. SDX" and wore it with great dignity.

CHAPTER 5

FOI:
A Process
of Learning

On one occasion, an aspiring young lawyer addressed Sir William Blackstone in these words:

"Upon what fundamental ground, Sir William, and for what public purpose, does freedom of the press occupy a preferred position in the law of England?"

Blackstone replied:

"Young man, the press must be free to protect the ends of an ordered society; to sustain and support its basis institutions; and to defend the freedoms which constitute the most glorious aspect of our national heritage."

Kent Cooper, general manager of The Associated Press, had been an advocate of free access to the news for many years when his book, *Barriers Down*, published in 1942, brought attention to the need for the press in America to begin a vigorous fight for the people's right to know. His battles had centered primarily on free access to information in foreign capitals where his correspondents had been experiencing great difficulty. In this context, 1946-1947 Sigma Delta Chi President George W. Healy, Jr., appointed Cooper, the fraternity's national honorary president in 1926, to head a new national committee on freedom of the press, marking the first time the organization had made any effort in this direction.

Sigma Delta Chi, from its earliest days, had had concern for the Constitutional guarantees of a free press in the United States. The fact is, however, that other, mostly internal, conflicts dominated the fraternity in its period of growth and development and no efforts toward effecting any change in freedom of information matters are recorded through its first thirty-six years. Even the "Purposes" for establishing the fraternity, listed by the founders, emphasized only good fellowship among journalists, acquiring the noblest principles of journalism and fostering a higher ethical code. The "Purposes," extended in 1960 to include attracting talented young people to the journalistic field and raising the prestige of the journalist in the community, failed to identify freedom of information as an objective. It wasn't until 1978 that the Society's annual *Directory*

Raymond L. Spangler (far right), who as Society president in 1965-1966 helped to convince Congress to adopt the federal Freedom of Information Act, charters the California Central Coast professional chapter in 1967. Attending the chartering of The chapter, which later became the Los Padres professional chapter, are Haig Keropian, president of the Los Angeles professional chapter; Maj. Richard Hill, Vandenberg Air Force Base; John Rose, former California SDX chairman; Guy Ryan, Region Eleven director; Gene Lee, chapter vice president; Robert Lauffer, treasurer; and Paul Veblen, president.

included among those purposes "To work to safeguard the flow of information from all sources to the public so that it has access to the truths required to make democracy function and to protect our freedoms."

Cooper and the group of distinguished journalists of the time, including Hugh Baillie, president of United Press; Seymour Berkson, general manager of International News Service; Robert U. Brown, editor of *Editor & Publisher*; Richard Fitzpatrick, member of the Washington, DC professional chapter; John S. Knight, head of Knight Newspapers and national honorary president; and Donald D. Hoover, president of Bozell and Jacobs, Inc., called themselves the committee on world press freedom. Concentrating its efforts on the concerns of the wire services about access to news overseas, the committee occupied itself with a bill pending in Congress authorizing an

official global information service and setting up a government news service. That Cooper's committee took its apparent mandate seriously was made manifest May 14, 1947, when it released its own statement opposing the bill because it would have legitimatized government-operated "news services" abroad. The committee, however, as previously noted, did not clear the statement with the fraternity's executive council. Delegates to the national convention in Washington, DC, November 12, 1947, took exception to the committee's assumed autonomy in releasing the report. Healy defended the committee's action, pointing out that it had been ordered to "take an active and aggressive lead," but the convention adopted a resolution stipulating that all committee reports bearing on public policy first be submitted to the executive council. With that convention, the

Virgil M. (Red) Newton (right), the fraternity's president in 1959-1960, was honored in 1963 for his twelve years of leadership as chairman of the Society's freedom of information committee. With him is Society executive officer Russell E. Hurst.

committee on world press freedom, for all intents and purposes, was dead. Writing in the November 1959 *Quill*, James S. Pope, executive editor of the Louisville *Courier* and *Times*, said the committee "...was fine in concept, but was still-born." He noted it had become apparent that American journalists could not liberate much information overseas "until we had mastered the art at home."

Incoming president Luther A. Huston, manager of the Washington, DC bureau of *The New York Times*, wasted little time, however, in keeping the movement alive in the fraternity. Early in 1948, he appointed Charles Clayton as chairman of an advancement of freedom of information committee with instructions to report to the 1948 convention in Milwaukee. Brown, the only holdover from the Cooper committee,

was joined by Lee Hills, managing editor of the Miami *Herald*; Mason Rossiter Smith, publisher of the Gouverneur, New York *Tribune-Press*; and J. Russell Wiggins, managing editor of *The Washington Post*.

Clayton's new committee set the tone for all future freedom of information efforts for Sigma Delta Chi. Its report said:

We believe that this basic right – the right to know – includes freedom to speak freely upon all matters without fear, freedom to gather and disseminate information and opinion without censorship or suppression, and freedom of choice of sources of information without dictation, either by government or by private monopoly. We believe that a free press and a free radio can serve a free people only if all mediums of communication are economically independent and are unfettered by restrictions controlling newsprint, manpower, or sources of information. We believe that freedom of information, which is not hampered by nationalistic interests or regulations, nor restricted by discriminatory toll rates, nor muzzled by censorship, represents the best assurance of international understanding and world peace. We believe that it is the obligation of this fraternity to help preserve true freedom of information in the United States and to safeguard this basic liberty from encroachment, either by government or by selfish private interests.

Taking its cue from the need to put the freedom of information house in order in the United States, the committee called on the convention to condemn actions by courts and state legislatures in Rhode Island, Maryland and Illinois to impose gag orders on the press. With the convention's adoption of the report, the first substantial effort by Sigma Delta Chi in its history to effect change in freedom of information cases was a matter of record, and a permanent committee on freedom of information was established.

Fitzpatrick; Lyle Wilson, United Press bureau chief in Washington, DC; and Norman Isaacs, managing editor of the Louisville *Times*, followed as chairmen of the committee for the next three years. The

Meeting with members of the Milwaukee professional chapter during his term as national president in 1968 was Staley McBrayer (far right). McBrayer countered the American Bar Association's Reardon Report by forming Sigma Delta Chi-sponsored media committees in every state in 1968 to oppose the ABA's action. Pictured with McBrayer are Milwaukee-area journalists Frank Lodge, James Huston, Mel Kishner and John Engelbert.

195l convention delegates in Detroit heard Isaacs' committee report blast the fears of the military and "civilians in authority" that "the public may come to know too much." The report criticized the attempts at censorship and insisted that "the American public can be trusted to think straight when it gets the facts." The report so influenced the delegates that, for the first time, they adopted a national theme for the year: "Eliminate Press Barriers and Make the People Conscious of Their Right to Know."

THE "RED" NEWTON YEARS

Past president Palmer Hoyt, editor and publisher of the Denver *Post*, took over the chair of the committee for 1952. On his committee was V.M. (Red) Newton, Jr., managing editor of the Tampa *Tribune*, who would follow Hoyt and remain as chairman from late 1952 through 1963 even during his year as president in 1959-1960.

Newton was not only the most flamboyant freedom of information chairman in Sigma Delta Chi history, he was the spearhead for national FOI efforts for all of

journalism for twelve years. Pope, in his *Quill* article, said, "This man has a built-in blaze of fury for the concealers of public information. When his flame-thrower is unleashed, he doesn't give a hoot in hell whether the target is a Florida sheriff or a United States senator or even the White House." Calling Newton's freedom of information committee reports "gold mines of new data and inspiration," Pope said in 1959, "Newton's spirit, his astounding vitality in battle, his omniscience about everything going on in every state have been vital factors in all that has been accomplished. His 1957 report was the most comprehensive single document I have ever seen on news suppression at every level and depth. Some of our colleagues think Newton hits too hard now and then, antagonizing some of our potential friends. His net value probably makes such risks negligible. And his speeches and letters have made FOI a living reality to many public officials who otherwise would never have heard of it."

Those who served with Newton on the committees joined Pope's appraisal. Al

Austin, professor of journalism at the University of North Dakota, called him "bombastic," and said, "No case was too big or too small for him to tackle. He went at all of them with a relish." Clark Mollenhoff, who would become national FOI chairman in 1966, recalls, "His letters were filled with fiery rhetoric that displayed his passionate and intense desire to run over everything and everyone who stood in the way of a free press." Newton broke up the committee's work into sections, assigning parts to various members. Austin wrote the Latin American section of the annual report, while Mollenhoff concentrated on the federal government. "Occasionally, Newton would rewrite some section of my Washington report to jazz it up a little. But, in time, he mellowed and accepted the fact that I would try to be as tough as would be warranted."

Many of Newton's annual reports were filled with letters to state bar associations as well as government officials, from the President of the United States to the Defense Department, two of his favorite targets. His language was uncompromising. Battling the New York State Bar Association over a canon which restricted the free flow of information on court cases, Newton wrote in 1957, "I feel that a self-centered and self-controlled class of lawyers, divorced from the public by its own codes, regulations and technicalities, smacks too much of the old French nobility of the long robe. In this country, a farmer's son could learn law by the fireside and become President." When, in two 1959 news conferences, President Dwight Eisenhower refused to answer questions by Mollenhoff on secrecy in government agencies but said, "There has been no administration in my memory which has gone to such lengths to make information available so long as the national security and national interest of this country [are] not involved," Newton fired off a letter to the President. Newton cited cases in which just the opposite was true, stating, "It would take a super-Houdini to navigate the mushrooming maze of the federal bureaucracy which places a restraining finger upon every phase of living of every American citizen." A letter in 1962 to Arthur Sylvester reminded the assistant secretary of defense

that "Sigma Delta Chi is keeping a permanent record of these abridgments of our free government so that our grandchildren, yours and mine, may know for sure the identities of those responsible and the exact incidents leading to the elimination of freedom from the American way of life."

Some in the Society were concerned that Newton's style was becoming counter-productive. Others, including William Small, believed that while Newton's rhetoric may not have done much good in specific cases, he was part of the all-important, on-going educational campaign that made government officials aware that the press was there. Small, who was then news director at WHAS-TV in Louisville and who had been brought on the FOI committee in 1960 to cover the emerging free-press problems of radio and television, said, "I am fully convinced that if the Society had not been involved in terms of free press issues, we would be far more compromised today than anyone believes."

STATE OPEN MEETINGS AND OPEN RECORDS LAWS

If the effectiveness of early freedom of information efforts by the Newton committees at the national level was not entirely clear, quite the opposite was true as they related to state issues. Pope wrote, "Sigma Delta Chi's main achievement, of course, has been in stimulating state laws for open meetings and open records." While committees headed by Clayton, Fitzpatrick, Wilson and Isaacs focused attention on FOI problems in various states, it was Newton's committee that did the basic research, setting the stage for successes to follow. Reports of the early 1950's provided chapters and members with information on which states had such laws and reprinted the language of the stronger laws for use by journalists hoping to get legislation passed in their states. A 1953 study of state open records laws by the committee revealed that only twenty-eight of the states had laws giving the public the right to inspect their governmental records. The report stated, however, that nearly all of those "rights" could be turned on or off at the whim of state officials. A

President of the United States Gerald R. Ford scheduled a nationally-televised news conference before the 1974 national convention in Phoenix, It was the only time in the Society's first seventy-five years that a US President had addressed an SPJ,SDX convention. Freedom of information was on the delegates' minds for Ford's first official act as president related to the press had been to veto a bill broadening access to federal documents under the 1966 FOI Act.

similar study in 1955 on open meetings laws provided the news that only nine states had anti-secrecy laws of one kind or another. It reported, however, that the number of states with open records laws had decreased to twenty-two. While all journalistic organizations of the day were concerned about the lack of needed legislation in a majority of the states, it was Sigma Delta Chi which took the lead to remedy the situation.

In a bold move in 1956, the FOI committee launched a major national campaign for open record and open meetings laws in those states not having such statutes. The center of the campaign was the publication and distribution of model laws in both categories. Drawing on the strong points in laws already in force or those prepared for introduction, the language in the model statutes was strong and absolute. The open meetings statute was written using the language of a proposed law introduced in Florida three years earlier. A copy of the

model law is included in the Appendix of this book.

Publication of the model laws was only the first step. The committee also helped to organize campaigns in 1956 to enact the proposed statutes in more than twenty states and reported the progress of the drive on a regular basis. The results were to be significant. Reporting to delegates at the 1957 national convention in Houston, Newton wrote, "The Sigma Delta Chi model laws for open government records and open government meetings were introduced in the legislatures in fifteen states, and this promptly precipitated a running fight from coast to coast in which the politicians' plaintive, unctious and sanctimonious squawks bounced against the blue. But when the last political bleat had whistled across the Mississippi, the legislatures of eight states had adopted the law guaranteeing open government records, bringing to twenty-nine the number of states having such legal safeguards. And the legislatures of six states had adopted the law stipulating open government meetings, bringing to seventeen the number of states having such statutes."

Inspired by the work of advancement for freedom of information committee and by successes in other states, more Sigma Delta Chi chapters took the lead with their state legislatures. In 1959, the number of states with open meetings laws had reached twenty-three and those with public records statutes had reached thirty-two. Pope, whose own FOI efforts were centered in the work of the American Society of Newspaper Editors, called the Sigma Delta Chi campaign, "...a miraculous piece of effectiveness in this new field in so short a time."

While other national organizations, state press associations and individual media worked to get laws passed either by themselves or in joint effort with an SDX chapter, Hurst said "A great deal of the credit for the adoption of those laws must go to Sigma Delta Chi and the efforts of professional chapters and, in many cases, campus chapters. Educational campaigns in some states took three or four years. In other states, a dramatic, concerted effort by chapters in a given year achieved the goal quickly." He added that many of the accomplishments, some by individual members, went unreported. After giving a series of speeches to chapters in Ohio about the need for a public access law and finding little enthusiasm for the task, Hurst said that, upon returning to Chicago, he received a telephone call from an SDX member, Murray Seeger, whose broadcast station had been shut down by a labor dispute. "He asked for all the information we could send him about the needed legislation, saying, 'I've got about ten days. I'd like to go down to the legislature and be a one-man lobbying effort before the lawmakers.' We sent him the materials, he did his lobbying and the bill was passed. There are scores of examples such as that where individuals and chapters worked successfully for FOI laws."

National Sigma Delta Chi headquarters supplied the ammunition and the committee, with several years of experience in hand, provided the chapters with step-by-step, how-to-do-it information based on knowledge gleaned from both successes and failures in various state campaigns. The Nevada SDX chapters helped to push that state's first open meetings law through the legislature early in 1960. That same year, the University of Nebraska campus chapter partially funded a study which demonstrated the need for legislation for public access to records in that state. The study led to the Nebraska legislature's adoption of an open records bill by a vote of 43-0 in 1961. Sigma Delta Chi chapters in Missouri worked successfully to have the Society's model open meetings law passed in 1961 as well. By the end of that year, the national FOI committee reported that many states had adopted the SDX model laws. "Over all, the national freedom of information picture has improved...particularly in the thirty-five states which have adopted open records laws and the twenty-six states which have open meetings laws on the books," the report stated. The parade of SDX members testifying before legislatures and building support for open government continued at a slower, but no less vigorous pace in the next ten years. Progress made by 1971, as reported by national FOI chairman Richard Kleeman, was substantial, with the right-to-know scoreboard showing forty-one states with open records laws and thirty-eight with open meetings laws.

A victory celebration might have been in order in 1983 when, with Mississippi's adoption of an open records law, all fifty states had an open records law and some type of open meetings law, according to Tonda Rush of The Reporters Committee for Freedom of the Press. Instead, chapters had already become occupied with working to seek stronger administration of and the strengthening of existing laws, to close loopholes, and to prevent repeal of certain provisions on the books by resurgent government and business interests. As one observer said in 1984, "We've won a great many battles for openness at the state and local level, but the war is far from over."

THE JOINT MEDIA COMMITTEE

While those battles were common in the states from 1953 through 1983, a parallel series of freedom of information conflicts on the national scene began in the 1960's. Theodore F. Koop, vice president of the CBS Washington, DC operation, was elected president of the Society in 1963. Newton's fiery disposition was still apparent, but Koop believed that Newton's style had outlived its usefulness. "He had become a one-man show," Koop said. He recalls that, upon knowing he would be elected president, he began looking for a way to ease Newton out of his twelve-year tenure as chairman of the advancement of freedom of information committee. He took the direct approach naming Julius Frandsen as committee chair for 1964. Frandsen, bureau chief for United Press International in Washington, was a stark contrast to Newton in style and approach. Clark Mollenhoff, in 1983, a journalism professor at Washington and Lee University, who worked for both men on the committee, remembers, "Dealing with Frandsen was entirely different from dealing with Red Newton. Frandsen was experienced in dealing with the Washington scene and did not shoot from the hip under any circumstances. He had a caution that came from being in a supervisory capacity in a Washington wire service operation. Just as dedicated to the principles of a free press, he also understood that there were occasionally situations involving newsmen who could not be defended or where the defense had to be circumscribed carefully. Frandsen, as contrasted to Newton, would occasionally suggest some wording change that would tone down or qualify a report. Usually those changes improved the report and made the SDX position more tenable in a period when many press officers in government were looking for something to criticize in the reports."

Meanwhile Koop was busy moving in another direction with press coverage problems. Following the assassination of President John F. Kennedy in November 1963, the Warren Commission and others criticized the press for parts of its coverage of the events in Dallas and the investigations which followed. During a conversation with Alfred Friendly, managing editor of *The Washington Post*, the two men found a mutual interest in trying to solve the problems inherent in press coverage of a

news event of such magnitude, thereby attempting to prevent situations which would place the news media in a bad light. Koop and Friendly, who was also chairman of the freedom of information committee of the American Society of Newspaper Editors, decided it was important that others be involved. Following a meeting of the Sigma Delta Chi board, which approved the idea, Koop announced in a news release dated May 8, 1964, "Sigma Delta Chi will seek to initiate joint discussions with other media organizations on freedom of information problems." In addition to SDX and ASNE, those invited included representatives from the Associated Press Managing Editors, the American Newspaper Publishers Association, the National Association of Broadcasters, the National Press Photographers Association, the National Editorial Association, the Radio Television News Directors Association and the American Newspaper Guild. Participation by those from ANPA, the NAB, the editorial writers and the Guild was limited and short-lived. The others, however, sat down together to hammer out solutions to the problems facing the news media and formed what was called The Joint Media Committee on News Coverage Problems. It was the beginning of significant joint efforts among those variant and self-oriented organizations which would impact all matters of freedom of information and First Amendment conflicts from that time forward.

The Joint Media Committee, while perhaps intending to tackle an agenda including the Warren Commission Report, press-bar relations and associated problems, concentrated on the single item which caused Friendly and Koop to initiate the plan. Koop remembers, "It wasn't so much a freedom of information committee then. We were concerned about how do you cover a big story that falls into your lap?" The result was a first draft of a document titled, "Orderly Procedures for Mass Coverage of News Events." As one of his final agenda items as SDX president, Koop took the draft to the Sigma Delta Chi board meeting in December 1964 in Kansas City. The board was impressed with the document and incoming President Ralph Sewell asked

Koop to remain as the SDX representative on the Joint Media Committee as it continued its work. The final draft was submitted by the Joint Media Committee to the various sponsoring groups, receiving approval from the SDX board in Philadelphia, May 7, 1965. "CBS paid for having 50,000 copies of 'Orderly Procedures...' printed and they were mailed to every imaginable government official – governors, county commissioners, mayors, sheriffs – anyone who might have to deal with a major news event," Koop said. In part, the brief manual urged government officials to plan ahead. "We urge those responsible for events that are bound to attract wide news coverage to make advance preparations that common sense dictates for orderly newsgathering....Even in unexpected happenings – crises, accidents, police actions and the like – there are almost always opportunities for the governmental, civic, police or other authorities in charge to arrange measures by which the media can do their job in an orderly fashion and with a minimum of confusion,"

The document on orderly newsgathering brought about some positive results if only in drawing attention to the subject. Of greater import in the long run, however, was the establishment of the Joint Media Committee which drafted it. Koop and Friendly were convinced the group could effect a wide range of cooperative efforts utilizing the talent and resources of SDX, APME, RTNDA, ASNE and NPPA, and would lend greater clout to a particular issue than any organization might be able to muster on its own. Others on the committee, however, found themselves more interested with internal concerns and the Joint Media Committee was dormant for several years. "They all came back, however," Koop recalls, "when the American Bar Association brought forward its Reardon Report on fair trial and free press in 1967."

THE FEDERAL FOI ACT

Sewell reappointed Frandsen as national FOI chairman and with both Koop and Frandsen in Washington, DC, the Society turned its attention toward passage of a federal freedom of information act, an effort

which had been going on for nearly ten years but without much enthusiasm. Only a handful of reporters and editors in Washington, DC were interested in the enactment of any federal open records laws. Mollenhoff, Washington correspondent for the Des Moines *Register* at that time, said, "Most of the editors in the capital believed that working to benefit other reporters' ability to gather information would only serve to negate the advantage their top reporters had through their own contacts. More editors from news media in the country at large were interested in such a project, but perhaps only Wiggins, executive editor of *The Washington Post*, and I took an active interest in Washington, DC" When Attorney General William P. Rodgers made an issue of the doctrine of executive privilege in the Eisenhower administration in 1958, Mollenhoff, Wiggins and Harold Cross, counsel for the American Society of Newspaper Editors, and a few others joined with a congressman from California, John E. Moss, chairman of the House Foreign Operations and Government Information Subcommittee of the Committee on Government Operations, in the drive for a federal freedom of information act.

During Newton's term as Society president in 1960, Sigma Delta Chi assisted Moss in drafting language for a bill, but Congress turned a deaf ear. Attempts from 1961 through 1965 failed as well, but each SDX president, along with Newton and Frandsen, stayed with Moss and Senator Edward V. Long of Missouri in efforts to get the legislation off the ground where it would be visible to the news media and the public. President Lyndon Johnson opposed the bills from 1964 through 1966 and, according to Mollenhoff, threatened to make Moss *persona non grata* politically. "Fortunately, Moss was the kind of stand-up guy who stood on principle and fought the battle through to the end," he said.

Mollenhoff became chairman of the freedom of information committee appointed by 1965-1966 president Ray Spangler. His work for nine years on the committee and his residence in Washington, DC gave him the insight which helped to direct the Society's efforts in the final push for passage of the

Freedom of Information Act in 1966. Both houses of Congress passed the bill unanimously and President Johnson signed the bill July 4 of that year. "The flourish with which Johnson conducted the signing ceremonies made some persons believe Johnson had been in support of the bill all along," Mollenhoff said. "But just the opposite was true." Mollenhoff's 1966 FOI report stated, "In general, the new statute follows the recommendations of Sigma Delta Chi for this kind of legislation....The measure provides that any person shall have access to the records of all executive branch agencies. There are nine categories of records that are exempted from coverage including items involving national defense and foreign policy." Moss, in a June 28, 1966, letter to Spangler, wrote, "I shall always be grateful to Sigma Delta Chi for the guidance and assistance in setting the stage for the legislation and in helping to get it through."

Mollenhoff wrote Spangler July 10, "If we had nothing but the federal information law this year it would be enough....For me, it is a great relief to get the bill through Congress and signed. I've been working on it for twelve years and I had wondered if it would ever be passed. Now we will have to see that it is administered properly." The FOI report, published in November, warned "The full impact of this legislation will not be realized until after July 4, 1967 – the date it becomes operative. Even this gain must be viewed as only a potential bright spot until the press has had time to examine how it is administered by the Johnson Administration. An atmosphere of censorship and secrecy has characterized the Administration's policies, particularly at the White House and the Pentagon. The activities and attitudes expressed by high officials of the Johnson Administration on information policies should serve as a warning that there could be efforts to twist the open records law into a closed records law....Two different bureaucrats can use the same law in different ways. And the same bureaucrat can use the same law differently on different days of the week, depending on the issues involved. There will still be plenty of room left for the use of that all-too-rare

journalistic talent – enterprise." Despite those warnings in 1966, Mollenhoff reflected sixteen years later that, "Passage of the Freedom of Information Act was a high point for FOI efforts in the 1960's because it was so necessary as a tool to open the door for gains we have made in the years since." In his letter to Spangler, Mollenhoff said that he hoped newsmen would use the law, "when they have good cases in jurisdictions where the attitude of the courts is inclined toward an open government view." The comment was a paradox of sorts in that, in the same letter, he referred to two other free press issues involving the courts which caused great concern in the Society in 1966 – the Annette Buchanan case in Oregon and the Sheppard decision by the United States Supreme Court – both of which would lead to long-term battles involving Sigma Delta Chi.

STATE SHIELD LAWS

Buchanan, a 20-year-old managing editor of the University of Oregon's *Daily Emerald*, was found guilty of contempt of court and fined $300 by Circuit Judge Edward Leavy for refusing to testify as to the identity of her sources for a story on the use of marijuana on the campus. There was no state law in Oregon to grant the reporter a right to protect sources and Buchanan declined on the grounds that she was bound by journalism tradition to protect her sources. The Sigma Delta Chi Board voted one of its largest legal defense grants to date, $1,500, for her appeal and issued a statement commending her for her stand. "Her actions have been in the best tradition of the press in protecting sources regardless of whether the law in the jusisdiction carries protection for the journalist. She deserves the support of Sigma Delta Chi and every other journalistic organization for standing firm....The conviction of Miss Buchanan should be appealed. The prosecutor should be the subject of the sharpest condemnation if he persists in further efforts to make her talk prior to the time she has exhausted her appeals. Public opinion is on the side of Miss Buchanan. This alone should be enough to frighten ambitious prosecutors from pursuing this course in the future. In that respect, the Buchanan case has been most helpful.''

While the Buchanan case probably pushed journalists in some states to adopt shield laws allowing reporters to protect sources of information, there was sharp division in and out of the Society on the matter. A dozen states already had such laws, but some journalists believed that even absolute shield laws could be repealed or weakened and that the First Amendment, along with journalistic tradition, was the best long-term protection for the news reporter. Nevertheless, there was interest in getting shield laws adopted. As with the open meetings and open records laws, many of the successes went unreported. Steve Dornfeld, who would become president of the Minnesota professional chapter, a regional director and president of the Society, recalls that in the late 1960's, while he was a member of the University of Minnesota campus chapter, a friend had been cited for contempt for refusing to reveal a source. ''I was a little disappointed that the Minnesota professional chapter wasn't doing anything about it, so I wrote to Hurst at national headquarters and got a copy of a model shield law, took it over to the legislature and wandered the halls of the capitol. I found some sponsors and got the bill introduced. It took us three tries, but we got our shield law passed.''

Delegates to the 1971 national convention in Washington, DC approved a Sigma Delta Chi model shield law and distributed it to chapters, encouraging them to seek passage of such legislation where it was not then on the books. The model law, which appears in the Appendix of this volume, was limited rather than absolute, but the board in adopting the enacting resolution and the convention delegates who ratified it were convinced that it would be improbable that an absolute law would be acceptable to state legislatures. Copies of the model law were mailed to presidents, secretaries and advisers of all professional and campus chapters in states where no such law was on the books. Only nineteen states had shield laws in 1971, according to FOI chairman Kleeman's report to that convention. It is interesting to note that,

once again, Sigma Delta Chi was out front among national journalism organizations in efforts to get legislation passed attempting to assure that the free flow of information would not be inhibited. It is also important to understand that the move came six months before the Supreme Court would rule such legislation appropriate in its next important press case.

That case, involving Earl Caldwell in California, Paul Branzburg in Kentucky and Paul Pappas in Massachusetts, brought the question of First Amendment protection to even greater prominence. Caldwell, a Black *New York Times* reporter in San Francisco, had refused to enter a federal grand jury room, contending that his very presence before the secret grand jury hearing would irreparably damage his confidential relationship with his news sources in a militant Black community. Caldwell was cited for contempt by a federal district judge, but, the ruling was overturned by the Ninth United States Circuit Court of Appeals. Sigma Delta Chi joined with the American Society of Newspaper Editors in filing a friend-of-the-court brief supporting Caldwell before the United State Supreme Court. Branzburg was an investigative reporter for the Louisville *Courier-Journal*, who, Kentucky courts claimed, was not covered by that state's shield law because he wrote accounts showing he had witnessed a crime – the manufacture and sale of illicit drugs. Pappas, a New Bedford, Massachusetts, television newsman, spent a night at Black Panther headquarters to report on an expected police raid. When the raid failed to occur and Pappas therefore reported nothing, he refused to answer the questions of a grand jury investigating racial unrest. Massachusetts did not have a shield law and state courts held that the First Amendment did not protect him from the duty of giving such testimony.

The Supreme Court agreed to join all three cases. In its *Branzburg v. Hayes* decision of June 29, 1972, the Court in a 5-4 ruling written by Justice Byron White, said, ''The issue in these cases is whether requiring newsmen to appear and testify before state or federal grand juries abridges the freedom of speech and press guaranteed by the First Amendment. We hold that it does not. The First Amendment does not relieve a newspaper reporter of the obligation that all citizens have to respond to a grand jury subpoena and answer questions relevant to a criminal investigation, and therefore the Amendment does not afford him a constitutional testimonial privilege for an agreement he makes to conceal facts relevant to a grand jury's investigation of a crime or to conceal the criminal conduct of his source or evidence thereof."

In one of two dissenting opinions, Justice Potter Stewart wrote, "The Court's crabbed view of the First Amendment reflects a disturbing insensitivity to the critical role of an independent press in our society....The Court thus invites state and federal authorities to undermine the historic independence of the press by attempting to annex the journalistic profession as an investigative arm of government. Not only will this decision impair the performance of the press' constitutionally protected functions, but it will, I am convinced, in the long run, harm rather than help the administration of justice." Justice William O. Douglas, in a separate dissenting opinion, was more concerned about how the ruling would hinder the effectiveness of the press in serving the people's right to know. "Today's decision will impede the wide-open and robust dissemination of ideas and counterthought which a free press both fosters and protects and which is essential to the success of intelligent self-government," he wrote. "I see no way of making mandatory the disclosure of a reporter's confidential source of the information on which he bases his news story....The function of the press is to explore and to investigate events, inform the people what is going on, and to expose the harmful as well as the good influences at work. There is no higher function performed under our constitutional regime....A reporter is no better than his source of information. Unless he has a privilege to withhold the identity of his source, he will be the victim of governmental intrigue or aggression. If he can be summoned to testify in secret before a grand jury, his sources will dry up and the attempted exposure, the effort to enlighten

the public will be ended....When we deny newsmen that protection, we deprive the people of the information needed to run the affairs of the nation in an intelligent way....Now that the fences of the law and the tradition that has protected the press are broken down, the people are the victims. The First Amendment, as I read it, was designed precisely to prevent that tragedy."

The Court's majority took the narrow view in the Caldwell, Branzburg and Pappas cases, but did leave open the possibility of federal and state legislative relief. "...Congress has freedom of determine whether a statutory newsman's privilege is necessary and desirable....There is also merit in leaving state legislatures free, within First Amendment limits, to fashion their own standards in light of the conditions and problems with respect to the relations between law enforcement officials and press in their own areas," Justice White wrote. In Sigma Delta Chi's response to the decision, national FOI chairman Richard Fogel, assistant managing editor of the Oakland, Caliornia *Tribune*, wrote, "Sigma Delta Chi is disappointed at the tenor of the majority opinion and apprehensive as to its possible effects."

Even before the Court's decision was handed down, attention had focused as well on the case of William T. Farr, a former Los Angeles *Herald-Examiner* reporter, convicted on more than a dozen counts of contempt for refusing to reveal the names of attorneys who supplied him information, in violation of Judge Charles Older's gag order, for a story he wrote during the Los Angeles trial of the Charles Manson "family." While Farr believed he was protected by the California shield law as a newsman, the California State Court of Appeals held that the shield law had to give way to the right of a judge to control his own court. The California Supreme Court refused to hear the case. By the time it reached the United States Supreme Court, *Branzburg v. Hayes* was in place and the high Court refused to review Farr's appeal. The case drew national attention when on November 16, 1972, Judge Older sentenced Farr to an indeterminate term on the civil contempt convictions, meaning Farr faced the possibility of serving a life sentence if he did not reveal his sources. Farr was released temporarily three and one half hours after he entered the county jail. He was flown by Sigma Delta Chi to Dallas, Texas, where he and Peter Bridge, a reporter for the Newark, New Jersey *Evening News*, jailed for twenty days for not revealing sources for a story, addressed the national convention of the Society. November 21, Farr was ordered back to jail where he spent forty-six days until he was ordered released by United States Supreme Court Justice Douglas pending appeals. *The Quill* reported in February 1963 that Farr's time in jail was the longest by any newsman in United States history for defying the courts. Farr continued to pursue the appeals processes. In a June 20, 1974, hearing in which a number of prominent American journalists testified on Farr's behalf, Los Angeles Superior Court Judge William H. Leavit ruled that the news profession had established a moral principle to protect its sources. Since Farr could be expected to live up to that principle, the indeterminate sentence would serve no further purpose. Shortly thereafter, Judge Older resentenced Farr to the maximum penalty for one count of civil contempt – five days in jail and a $500 fine. Farr appealed again but lost in the the United States Court of Appeals in 1976. Again, the Supreme Court refused to review the case.

The Los Angeles professional chapter of Sigma Delta Chi provided impetus in raising money for Farr's appeal process and focusing national attention on the case. That drive brought about a national fund-raising effort for Farr and several other reporters, including Bridge, Joe Weiler, a reporter for the Memphis, Tennessee *Commercial-Appeal*, and Harry Thornton of WDEF-TV in Chattanooga, Tennessee. The fund, supported by SDX chapters across the country, had reached more than $4,000 by the time Farr was released.

As previously noted, the Society had already been moving toward having state shield laws passed where necessary to protect confidential sources, and by late 1973 eight more states had adopted such laws, several of them using the SDX model bill. But

responding to the Supreme Court's apparent willingness to respect federal shield legislation, Sigma Delta Chi's officers, especially Small, national secretary and chairman of the Joint Media Committee in 1973, were actively involved in seeking the right formula for a federal statute acceptable to journalists and to the Congress. More than fifty bills had been introduced in the House and Senate since the *Branzburg v. Hayes* decision, some of them absolute in nature and many with strings attached. Small and his Joint Media Committee members met repeatedly with members of the House Judiciary Committee members, supplementing their discussions with written exchanges. They settled on supporting a bill sponsored by Rep. William S. Cohen of Maine if it were amended in several ways. The original Cohen bill provided absolute privilege in all state and federal proceedings short of the trial level, including grand juries, and qualified privilege in civil and criminal court actions. The amendments agreed upon included broadening the definition of "newsman" to include news media executives and corporate entities to prevent grand juries from bypassing the reporter and going to his superiors or the company for the material he gathered, deleting language which would permit a reporter's source to waive privilege, and revising a section that orginally would have waived these protections in a libel case if the defendant based his defense on the reporter's information.

The bill's title was changed from the "Newsman's Privilege Act of 1973" to the 'Constitutional News Source Protection Act of 1973" to make clear reporters were seeking only their First Amendment rights and not some special privilege. Small called the result "an extremely strong bill and, realistically, as far as we can expect the House of Representatives to go." He saw no chance of an absolute bill and took issue with those who said that, failing an absolute bill, journalists in general and Sigma Delta Chi specifically should fall back on the First Amendment. "I think those who make this claim are only kidding themselves," he said. "The Supreme Court in the Caldwell-Pappas-Branzburg decision stated flatly that this was not so and invited legislation to clarify the situation. As for the argument that inviting Congress to prepare a qualified bill is inviting a subsequent Congress to pass harmful legislation, it should be noted that nothing exists to prevent Congress at any time from passing mischievous legislation."

While neither the Cohen bill nor any other proposed federal shield legislation became law by the mid-1980's, the history of Sigma Delta Chi's work in this area would be incomplete without detailing efforts made to effect reasonable federal solutions to the problems of keeping sources confidential. This is true especially in the light of, among others, the Fresno Four case in 1975-1976, the Myron Farber case in 1978, the Paul Corsetti case from 1979 to 1982, and court decisions in civil cases involving Jay Shelledy in 1977 and Bill Gagnon in 1981, which might very well have been moot had Congress seen fit to pass the Cohen bill.

A Fresno, California, city councilman was indicted in November 1974 by a Fresno County grand jury for allegedly accepting a $4,000 bribe. Superior Court Judge Denver Peckinpah issued a gag order restraining anyone involved in the case from talking about the case in public and sealed the grand jury transcripts. Joe Rosato and William Patterson, reporters for the Fresno, California *Bee*, published a story January 12, 1975, which was said to include some of the secret grand jury findings. Judge Peckinpah called the two reporters and the newspaper's managing editor, George Gruner, before him and ordered them to reveal the source of their information. When the two reporters and Gruner refused to reveal the source on the grounds that they were protected by the California shield law and that they had not received the information from any person covered by the judge's gag order, Judge Peckinpah held them in contempt of court. Peckinpah also questioned another reporter, Jim Bort, who upon refusing to disclose how the newspaper had obtained the grand jury report, was held in contempt as well. The "Fresno Four," as they became known, were found guilty of contempt a total of seventy-three times. The California Court of Appeals overturned eighteen of the convictions on the grounds of

limited protection under the state's shield law, but upheld the remaining fifty-five, ruling, as in the Farr case, that when the shield law conflicts with the power of the court and may interfere with a fair trial, the shield law must give way. California's Supreme Court and the United States Supreme Court declined to review the case. While the case was on appeal, Judge Peckinpah retired from the bench and, in 1976, following the Court's refusal to review, the case went to Judge Hollis Best, who imposed an indeterminate sentence on the four newsmen, sending them to jail September 3, 1976. The judge agreed that the sentence was coercive and that Patterson, Rosato, Gruner and Bort could be freed as soon as they complied with the court's original order to reveal the source. After serving fifteen days in jail, the newsmen were granted a hearing in which journalists, including the Fresno Four, testified to the long-standing journalistic ethic which prevents reporters from revealing sources. Judge Best accepted the fact that the four were unlikely to reveal the source because of that commitment, determined that the indeterminate sentence would be punitive, and sentenced each to five days in jail, the maximum sentence allowable in the case. Since each had already served fifteen days, they were released from custody following Best's decision.

Myron Farber, a *New York Times* reporter, investigated the deaths of three hospital patients who died from overdoses of the drug curare in New Jersey. The series of articles led to the indictment of Dr. Mario Jascalevich. Farber repeatedly refused to hand over his notes to the court and was jailed for a total of thirty-nine days. The case was markedly different from the Farr case in two ways. First, while the courts at least considered the California shield law as it related to Judge Older's demands on Farr, Farber and *The Times* were never granted a hearing either by the New Jersey courts or by the United States Supreme Court to determine if the reporter's notes were protected by the New Jersey shield law. This, despite the fact that the Supreme Court, in *Branzburg v. Hayes*, had invited state legislation in matters of the confidentiality of reporter's sources. Second, Farr was asked to identify the name of a specific attorney who passed information to him. In the Farber case, he and *The New York Times* were issued subpoenas for "all notes, all records, all memoranda, all correspondence and all recordings of all interviews with all witnesses for the prosecution and all witnesses for the defense." In the Farr case and in those of Branzburg, Caldwell and Pappas, there was reason to believe that they had specific information which probably was not available from any other source. In Farber, the justification for requesting what amounted to 5,000 documents, virtually the entire *New York Times* file in this case gathered over four months of investigation, was a single affidavit by the defense counsel that, based on "his information and belief," something in those files, he wasn't sure what, would be helpful for the defense. There was no showing that any of the information was critical. There was no showing that the information could not have been obtained from other sources. Farber had said that if it could be shown that any specific document was highly critical, he might have been willing to talk. Farber and *The Times* paid a total of $286,000 in fines. The New Jersey case had a happier ending than most in that the state law was revamped by the legislature in 1980, giving absolute privilege to reporters and editors not to turn over their notes or disclose sources even if they are sued for libel. The New Jersey Supreme Court upheld the new law in a landmark May 1982 decision. Former New Jersey Governor Brendan T. Byrne, hours before he left office in January 1982, formally ended the Farber case by pardoning Farber and *The New York Times* for the 1978 contempt conviction and ordering the return of the fines against them.

Corsetti, a reporter for the Boston *Herald American*, obtained a telephone interview in 1979 with a prison inmate and published a story which said the inmate had implicated himself in a murder case. Corsetti named the inmate in his story and, when he was brought to trial, Corsetti refused to testify as to the content of the interview because, he said, at least two police officers had the same information. Since Massachussetts legislators had refused to pass a shield law, Corsetti was cited for criminal contempt and sentenced to ninety days in jail. Two-and-one-half years of appeals ended when the state Supreme Judicial Court ruled in 1982 that, "The public has a right to every man's evidence," and Corsetti was ordered jailed. After spending eight days in jail, Corsetti's sentence was commuted by Massachussetts Governor Edward J. King and the state's Executive Council. King, who failed to pardon Corsetti and, thereby, clear his record, said he believed Corsetti was guilty of contempt but had suffered enough.

In one of the civil cases, Lewiston, Idaho *Tribune* newsman Jay Shelledy, was convicted of contempt and sentenced to thirty days in jail in 1977 for refusing to reveal his source for a story which resulted in a libel suit against his newspaper. Shelledy quoted an unidentified police officer as saying that a former Idaho narcotics agent acted hastily in shooting a youth he was arresting. The Idaho Supreme Court, in a 3-2 decision in 1978, upheld the sentence, saying there was no statutory newsman's privilege in Idaho and that public policy required all competent adults to testify in legal actions unless specifically exempted by statute. It rejected Shelledy's argument that the action violated the First Amendment. The United States Supreme Court refused to review the case. The judge made a second major decision in the case, withdrawing his jailing order after advising the plaintiff he would strike the defense of the newspaper in return for not jailing Shelledy.

In Pueblo, Colorado, Gagnon, a statehouse reporter for the *Chieftain and Star Journal*, was ordered jailed in 1981 after refusing to disclose the identity of a confidential source and produce documents provided by the source during a $1.5 million civil lawsuit filed against the publishers of the two Pueblo dailies. He maintained that having to reveal the information was a violation of his First Amendment rights – Colorado did not have a shield law – and that the court had other sources available with the same information. The Colorado Supreme Court upheld the Freemont County district judge, saying that he had not abused his power, and ordered Gagnon to reveal the information or go to jail. On November 24, 1981, the district judge dismissed the case against the Pueblo newspapers and made moot the contempt conviction against Gagnon.

Scores of similar cases in which newsmen were jailed for failing to reveal sources were reported in the years following *Branzburg v. Hayes.* The total number of such cases is incalculable because of the number which were publicized only in their local areas. From 1972 to 1984, only seven additional states passed shield laws, bringing the number to twenty-six in 1983 with only twelve of those states having laws which provided absolute protection. In an additional ten states without shield laws, the courts recognized some form of qualified privilege for reporters, leaving fourteen which had either rejected such legislation or had not had any cases dealing with the issue. At this writing, the Society of Professional Journalists, Sigma Delta Chi, was leading an effort to build a new model shield law and work toward getting that legislation passed in the twenty-four states which had no such laws on the books. But while this battle with the courts was in progress, another conflict dealing with the press-bar relations was boiling furiously.

FREE PRESS AND FAIR TRIAL

In the same year that the Buchanan case lit a fire under the protection of confidential sources issue, 1966, the United States Supreme Court announced its decision in the *Sheppard v. Maxwell* case, sparking a new First Amendment/Sixth Amendment controversy which would still be in evidence nearly twenty years later. Samuel H. Sheppard was convicted in a highly-publicized 1954 murder case in Cleveland, Ohio. In overturning the conviction, the Court did not blame the press, but stated that Sheppard was deprived of a fair trial "because of the trial judge's failure to protect Sheppard sufficiently from the massive, pervasive and prejudicial publicity that attended his prosecution....The court's fundamental error is compounded by the holding that it lacked power to control the publicity about the trial. From the very inception of the proceedings, the judge announced that neither he nor anyone else could restrict prejudicial news accounts....and he reiterated this view on numerous occasions....The carnival atmosphere at trial could easily have been avoided since the courtroom and the courthouse premises are subject to the control of the court." In its conclusion, the Supreme Court said, "The courts must take such steps by rule and regulation that will protect their processes from outside interference. Neither prosecutors, counsel for defense, the accused, witnesses, court staff nor enforcement officers coming under the jurisdiction of the court should be permitted to frustrate its functions."

The Court noted, however, that there was a need for public scrutiny of the judicial process. Quoting from a 1948 decision, the Court's opinion stated, "The principle that justice cannot survive behind walls of silence has long been reflected in the Anglo-American distrust for secret trials....A responsible press has always been regarded as the handmaiden of effective judicial administration, especially in the criminal field. Its function in this regard is documented by an impressive record of service over several centuries....The Press does not simply publish information about trials but guards against the miscarriage of justice by subjecting the police, prosecutors, and judicial processes to extensive public scrutiny and criticism....And where there was no threat or menace to the integrity of the trial, we have consistently required that the press have a free hand, even though we sometimes deplored its sensationalism." The previous quotes notwithstanding, in offering judges and attorneys in criminal cases a series of possible solutions to the problems of pretrial and trial publicity including changing the venue, delaying the trial, and extending the jury-selection process, the Court also listed the right of a judge to shut off the flow of most information about a crime by ordering officers of the court not to discuss with or provide data to the press.

From the time the Court agreed to review *Sheppard v. Maxwell,* Sigma Delta Chi president Spangler warned of possible peril for the press. In a December 1, 1965, speech to the Northern California professional chapter in San Francisco, he said, "Of all recent developments in free press, fair trial controversy, the most serious is the Supreme Court's decision to review the *Sheppard* case." And in a speech at Stanford University February 14, 1966, Spangler said, "The United States is moving toward British-style control of the press in which the law is almost entirely judge-made and judge-controlled because of the Court's involvement in the Sheppard case." Describing the average citizen's concept of free press and fair trial, he said, "When a crime is committed by someone else, he wants to know all about it; that's free press. But if the crime involves him, he wants it kept out of the paper; that's fair trial." But even Spangler admits he did not foresee all of the ramifications of the June 6, 1966 Supreme Court decision.

In October of that year, an American Bar Association study group, headed by Justice Paul C. Reardon of the Supreme Judicial Court of Massachussetts, recommended that in pending criminal cases police, prosecutors and defense attorneys be restricted from making public "potentially prejudicial information" in order to protect juries from having too much knowledge of a case before hearing the testimony in the courtroom. Obviously picking up on the Supreme Court's *Sheppard* decision and needing no higher authority to effect such rules for its members than its own House of Delegates, it appeared that what had taken place earlier that year in Arizona in the Charles Schmid murder case and in the Richard Speck murder case in Illinois, where "gag orders" had been issued by judges, would become the general rule rather than the exception. Mollenhoff, in the 1966 FOI report, called the Reardon committee report "a most disturbing development in the area of press and bar relations. While it may be well intentioned, the Reardon Report carries with it the potential for unduly curbing newspapers and even destroying the watchdog role of the press in the criminal law enforcement field."

But even while the American Bar Association was beginning to seek input from those institutions which might be affected by the Reardon Report, judges and police officials were already establishing new rules concerning what crime information the press would be allowed to have and what procedures had to be followed in reporting arrests and trials. The American Newspaper Publishers Association, which had been conducting its own two-year study on "the people's right to know," including an examination of the proposed Reardon Report, came out strongly in January 1967 against its adoption by the ABA. "The people's right to a free press, which inherently embodies the right of the people to know, is one of our most fundamental rights, and neither the press nor the bar has the right to sit down and bargain it away," the ANPA study said. "Indeed, there can be no fair trial without a free press, and without fair trial, no freedom can exist. There is no real conflict between the First Amendment, guaranteeing a free press, and the Sixth Amendment, which guarantees a speedy and public trial by an impartial jury. The presumption of some members of the bar that pretrial news is intrinsically prejudicial is based on conjecture and not on fact....There are grave inherent dangers to the public in the restriction or censorship at the source of news, among them secret arrests and ultimately secret trial. Rules of the court and other orders which restrict the release of information by law enforcement officers are an unwarranted judicial invasion of the executive branch of government. There can be no codes or covenants which compromise the principles of the Constitution."

Mollenhoff and Robert M. White II, who became Sigma Delta Chi president following Spangler, in a joint statement, commended as "fully documented and persuasive" the ANPA report and said, "It is totally in accord with the Sigma Delta Chi conviction that there must be a free press with the right to cover and criticize all law enforcement and judicial matters....Any bar association policies or actions that tend to curb free press reports and commentary would also tend to encourage secrecy and the intolerable abuses that are inevitable in a star chamber proceeding." White asked

Koop, already involved through a revitalized Joint Media Committee effort to get the Reardon Report modified, to be Sigma Delta Chi's representative at an ABA hearing in Honolulu in the summer of 1967. "I thought it was necessary to have a broadcaster there to emphasize the dimension of the potential effect of the Reardon proposal," White said. For a day and a half, representatives of the news media sought to convince Justice Reardon and his colleagues that modification was warranted. Koop recalls that the die was already cast by the bar association members by the time most of the hearings were held. Even as the newsmen debated with Reardon and his committee, elsewhere at the ABA's Honclulu meeting a panel of trial judges endorsed the Reardon recommendations "without reservation."

Delegates to the SDX convention in Minneapolis were told late in 1967 that the Reardon committee wanted to forbid lawyers from releasing information relating to pending criminal cases, including prior criminal records, existence of a confession and identity of witnesses, and would have the courts adopt the ABA canon as their own rule. Further, law enforcement agencies would also be gagged and limited to minimal information such as the fact of arrest, name and age. In addition, the Reardon Report recommended contempt power against lawyers, police or reporters who wilfully disseminate "extra-judicial" statements designed to affect the outcome of trials. The delegates adopted a resolution urging the American Bar Association to use the "utmost caution and deepest reflection upon the proposed adoption of binding rules of conduct which would effectively abridge the constitutional guarantee by extra-legal process and effect by rule of the Association what is specifically denied under the law to the Congress of the United States."

When the ABA House of Delegates met in Chicago, February 19, 1968, Koop, representing the Joint Media Committee, SDX and RTNDA; Michael J. Ogden of Providence, Rhode Island, representing the American Society of Newspaper Editors; and D. Tennant Bryan, newspaper publisher from Richmond, Virginia, representing the American Newspaper Publishers Association, testified before the group of attorneys. Koop said, "I suggest we should be talking about releasing a maximum rather than a minimum of information. The public needs more, rather than fewer, facts if it is to evaluate realistically the current crime wave....Public confidence in effective law enforcement can stem only from knowledge, never from secrecy." Koop picked up some support from a number of the delegates, primarily from Western states where the bar and press had voluntarily worked out guidelines for pre-trial publicity and reporting on actual proceedings. "We pledge continued and accelerated efforts to bring about voluntary compacts between the bar and press in every state. We plead with you to join us in this endeavor," he said. The press hoped it had a trump card in bringing the offer of a $150,000 study, to be done by the ANPA, which would survey 3,000 trial judges to determine whether in their opinion pre-trial publicity has influenced juries.

The results of the voting in which the 289 members of the House of Delegates shouted down (later confirmed by a 176-68 head count) any attempt at delay, and thus accepted the Reardon Report, was described best by C.O. Schlaver in his March 1968 column in *The Quill*. "Davids of the press, using principles for slingshots, fought valiantly against the Goliaths of the American Bar Association....It seemed almost predestined that the Davids would fall against the odds that were almost insurmountable. It was not likely that the ABA hierarchy was about to dump a Reardon Report study costing an estimated $250,000 in money and almost three years in time to prepare. Yet this observer was proud of the sharp lances thrown deftly and courteously against their legal adversaries by Ted Koop, Mike Ogden and Tennant Bryan....Defenders of the freedom of the press, besieged for statements following the House of Delegates vote, hadn't lost their composure as they were questioned about 'What now?' They had expected to lose but the strain was displayed in their faces, disappointment nurtured by their devotion to the cause of a press unhampered in its duty to report and to interpret."

White was furious. Upon adoption of the Reardon Report, the now past president of the Society said in a speech that it was perhaps time for Congress to investigate the ABA. "Through its rules and regulations, it exerts vast powers in every state in the land; in every city in the land; in every village in the land; yes, even in the federal courts. No private organization should have such power." J. Edward Murray, managing editor of the Phoenix, Arizona *Republic*, who had traveled thousands of miles and used his voice and typewriter for three years in a losing cause, said, "In criminal cases of high interest and serious concern to the public, the press will have no recourse except to fight back." And fight back it did with newly elected SDX president Staley McBrayer and the Society's chapters and members leading the way.

McBrayer, publisher of two daily and four weekly newspapers in the Houston, Texas, area, immediately announced plans to form news media committees in each state to oppose state and local adoption of the American Bar Association recommendations. Noting that adoption of the Reardon Report did not automatically put its provisions into effect because state bar associations, the state courts or the state legislatures would have to approve such major changes, McBrayer said, "We invite all other media organizations to join us, and also all concerned lawyers and judges. We commend those members of the bar who have already expressed concern about the hazards to fair trial inherent in the ABA's proposals. The nation's press fully shares the bar's concern over protecting the right to a fair trial. We invite lawyers and judges to share our concern that the public be kept fully informed on the administration of criminal justice." Working with Mollenhoff and the national FOI committee, within weeks McBrayer had named coordinators in all fifty states assigned (1) to convene as soon as possible a committee of news media representatives and interested members of the bar to lay plans for a coordinated effort to oppose the Reardon Report; (2) to report to SDX headquarters on the situation in that state; and (3) to keep SDX headquarters advised regularly on all press-bar developments in the state. Before those committees could become fully organized, local chapters were put to the test quickly in two cases of national prominence: the assassination of Martin Luther King in Memphis, Tennessee, in April and the assassination of Robert F. Kennedy in Los Angeles in June. Judge W. Preston Battle in Memphis issued a ten-point order which included a prohibition for any person connected in any way with the case "to take part in interviews for publicity and from making extra-judicial statements about this case from this date until such time as a verdict is returned in this case in open court." Immediately upon its issuance, John Means, president of the Mid-South professional chapter of Sigma Delta Chi, protested the order, calling it "the most amazing legal order since the Alien and Sedition Act." In California, Superior Court Judge Arthur L. Alarcon issued similar highly-restrictive orders to protect the rights of accused Kennedy assassin Sirhan B. Sirhan.

The first protest came from Larry Sisk, California state coordinator for opposing the Reardon Report and chairman of the California freedom of information committee, set up as a state committee by past president Spangler and approved by the SDX board in 1966. "By invoking some of the recommendations of the American Bar Association's Reardon Report, Judge Alarcon's order makes the recommendations effective even before their final adoption by the association and before the Reardon recommendations are considered by the State Bar of California," Sisk said. In California and other states, however, the drive to oppose adoption of the Reardon Report at the local level was fully under way. Hurst called the efforts, "One of the best demonstrations of the ability of SDX marshaling its forces in a time of crisis through a coordinated national campaign and finding dedicated members to volunteer in all of the states and go to work on this problem." The temporary failure suffered in adoption of the Reardon Report by the ABA House of Delegates served an interesting purpose, he said. " We had been comfortable in many press-bar relations for a number of years. But out of that experience and with the establishment of the state committees, press and ABA members met, often using SDX chapter meetings as a forum, and found out we had more in common than in differences, that we were reasonable people, and that there were avenues available to develop cooperative approaches. There is no doubt in my mind that Sigma Delta Chi's efforts softened the blow of the defeat in Chicago."

Sisk's committee offered a typical example of the approach – notifying the State Bar of California of its desire to begin discussions on the issue. Out of that opening dialogue, John H. Finger, president of the State Bar, issued a statement which said it welcomed such discussions and was in no way bound to any action or recommendation of the ABA "nor should it be assumed that the State Bar Board of Governors will agree with either the approach to the problem or the substance of the rules recommended in the Reardon Report." In Wisconsin, Richard Leonard, editor of *The Milwaukee Journal* and SDX coordinator, called a meeting in May which saw the beginning of a permanent Wisconsin freedom of information committee that took as its first task to oppose implementation of the Reardon Report in that state. Within a year a set of voluntary press-bar guidelines was in place in Wisconsin.

But California and Wisconsin were only the beginning. By late 1969, Sigma Delta Chi headquarters had been notified by coordinators that in nineteen states press-bar voluntary guidelines were in place and in another seventeen states such guidelines were under discussion. As was true with the problems in instituting state shield laws, some Society officials, including White, favored staying with First Amendment rights as the source for press-bar relations instead of instituting voluntary guidelines. "The courts ultimately are in charge and can twist such guidelines any way they wish any time they wish," White said. Perhaps, in the long run, White may have been right, for in 1982 the Supreme Court of the State of Washington, a state which was a pioneer in voluntary guidelines, made those guidelines mandatory and required that reporters

assigned to cover criminal trials agree to abide by those rules. Shortly thereafter, a number of state press associations disassociated themselves from voluntary press-bar guidelines. But, in 1969, the trend was definitely toward voluntary agreements among the news media, bar associations and judges. So much so that even United States District Judge Edward J. Devitt of St. Paul, Minnesota, chairman of the ABA Legal Advisory Committee on Fair Trial and Free Press, which succeeded the Reardon committee, supported the concept of voluntary guidelines as one, though not the only, acceptable system. And new ABA president Bernard G. Siegel of Philadelphia backed up his announced intention to work for greater press-bar cooperation by naming Richard M. Schmidt of Washington, DC, general counsel of the American Society of Newspaper Editors, as chairman of the ABA standing committee on public relations.

While Sigma Delta Chi remained at the forefront of the battle, lest one believe that the effects of the Reardon Report were made ineffective across the nation, in hundreds of courtrooms judges were implementing gag orders, almost manifesting the caption on a 1968 Stayskal editorial cartoon appearing in the Chicago *American*. The cartoon showed the press in the witness chair, and a judge, attorneys and even jury members wearing ABA buttons with one attorney jumping up and down shouting, "We don't care if there is no evidence that you newsmen threaten fair trials...You're guilty! guilty! guilty!" The Society's 1972 FOI chairman, Richard Fogel, of the Oakland, California *Tribune*, in a study of the press-courts situation for his convention report, noted that on August 11, 1972, Los Angeles Superior Court Judge Julius A. Leetham went the full route, ignoring the California voluntary guidelines and issuing an order against all media, prohibiting them from publishing or broadcasting anything about a case he was handling except that which transpired in court. Sigma Delta Chi issued a strong protest and joined other organizations supporting a legal challenge instituted by the Los Angeles *Times*.

By the early 1970's, news organizations and Sigma Delta Chi chapters were commonly appealing judges' gag orders and, in some cases, violating the orders as tests of those orders. Jack C. Landau, director of the Reporters Committee for Freedom of the Press, noted that, in every case since *Sheppard* which was fully litigated and involved a constitutional challenge to a judge's gag order, the press had been upheld. While they pointed to the potential of a new trend, those court victories were of little help to the press in covering criminal cases, for before the judge's order was ruled unconstitutional by a higher court, the pretrial and trial proceedings had been completed, in effect, allowing the judge to have his way during those critical time periods and, in many cases making the issue moot. Meanwhile, those reporters who risked contempt convictions for violating a gag order found no comfort in the final decision in a 1975 Louisiana case. When two New Orleans reporters violated a gag order, they were found in contempt. A circuit court of appeals found the lower court's gag order invalid, illegal and void, but held that it had to be obeyed until overturned. The United States Supreme Court refused to review the case. Gilbert M. Savery of the Lincoln, Nebraska *Journal*, writing in the 1975 FOI Report, said, "Encouraged by the high court's inaction in this matter, judges in lower courts around the country were applying gag orders with greater frequency." Savery, of course, didn't know it at the time he wrote his 1975 roundup on free press-fair trial, but, within a few weeks, he would find the most famous gag-order case of the decade in his own backyard.

On Sunday, October 19, 1975, Charles Erwin Simants was apprehended in Sutherland, Nebraska, and charged with six counts of first-degree murder for the slaying of a family the night before. Savery's synopsis of the events of the next eight months was carried in the 1976 FOI Report. Lincoln County Judge Ronald Ruff, in an open-court session October 21 to hear motions on ordering restrictions on press coverage and closing the preliminary hearing to the public and press, agreed to a prosecution motion, joined by the defense, to restrict coverge because of publicity, and a

gag order was effected. It marked the first time in Nebraska, which had had voluntary press-bar guidelines since the early 1970's, that a gag order had been issued. Seeking to resolve the situation through the appellate process rather than violating the order, the Nebraska media carried their appeal to Judge Hugh Stuart's Lincoln County District Court. Stuart narrowed Judge Ruff's order but retained the gag and made the voluntary bar-press guidelines a formal order of his court. When the Nebraska Supreme Court failed to act, the media went to United States Supreme Court Justice Harry A. Blackmun, asking for a stay. In two separate opinions, on November 13 and November 20, Blackmun left the matter to the Nebraska Supreme Court and prodded the court to act. The Nebraska Supreme Court, in its decision, allowed most of Judge Stuart's gag order to stand. The United States Supreme Court eventually agreed to hear the case, but denied the motion of the the Nebraska Press Association and other plaintiffs in the case to expedite review or stay the gag order pending Simants' trial. Meanwhile Simants had been convicted of murder and sentenced to death.

The Nebraska newsmen fighting the gag order were not alone. Hurst and 1975-76 Society President Robert McCord had a major part in calling a meeting of various news organizations in Reston, Virginia, to plan a joint effort in the case. The result of that meeting was a friend-of-the-court brief joined by The Society of Professional Journalists, Sigma Delta Chi, and sixteen other news organizations to be presented before the United States Supreme Court. While the brief, in itself, provided the Court with strong support for the Nebraska Press Association, *et al*, and undoubtedly impressed the Court with this unanimity of position by the national media, it also marked one of the first times the press found itself of one voice on a major issue and prompted similar future efforts. McCord, executive editor of the Little Rock, Arkansas *Democrat*, not only called for action on the part of newsmen to fight the growing gag order trends in general, but arranged for a national drive among Society chapters to assist the Nebraska Press Association in paying its more than $100,000 in costs for the case. Speaking at the University of Kansas, McCord said that all possible avenues of protest, including violation of gag orders, should be taken to stem the tide of gag orders engulfing the nation. "Every time a judge issues a gag order, other judges read about it and follow suit," he said. He noted that, despite the New Orleans ruling, violation of gag orders in cases "where that seems to be the most appropriate method – and that has to be done on a case-by-case basis – will let the judges know they have serious opposition and that the press is not simply lying down and accepting these unconstitutional orders." On the financial side, McCord asked his board of directors to lead the way. Meeting in Rochester, New York, the board responded by bringing its total contribution from the Legal Defense Fund to $2,000, and asked chapters and individual members to make contributions. Within a month of the board's action, chapters from Virginia to Seattle and from North Dakota to Oklahoma were sending contributions. In addition to $1,200 raised by the Nebraska chapter, $500 came from Fort Worth's professional chapter; $250 from the Western Washington chapter; and $100 each from Buffalo, St. Louis, Dallas, Brookings, South Dakota, and Warrensburg, Missouri. The Phoenix newspapers made a $1,000 contribution through the Valley of the Sun chapter and the New Orleans *Times Picayune* sent another $1,000 through that city's professional chapter. Records from the Nebraska Press Association archives reveal that a total of $6,862 was contributed by Sigma Delta Chi campus and professional chapters by August 30, 1976.

The United States Supreme Court heard oral arguments on the case April 19, 1976. Media reports on those hearings, based primarily on questions put to attorneys representing the Nebraska courts, seemed to point to a favorable decision by the Supreme Court. On June 30, the Court held unanimously for the Nebraska Press Association. One of the key portions of the Court's decision declared that, "The case is not moot simply because the order has expired, since the controversy between the parties is capable of repetition, yet evading

review." In the main, the Court said, "While the guarantees of freedom of expression are not an absolute prohibition under all circumstances, the barriers to prior restraint remain high and the presumption against its use continues intact. Although it is unnecessary to establish a priority between First Amendment and Sixth Amendment rights to a fair trial under all circumstances, as the authors of the Bill of Rights themselves declined to do, the protection against prior restraint should have particular force as applied to reporting of criminal proceedings. The heavy burden imposed as a condition to securing a prior restraint was not met in this case." The Court's decision, however, fell short of making all gag orders unconstitutional, much to the distress of the press. In effect, the Court said that trial courts could issue gag orders although their validity would be difficult to sustain.

The Nebraska Press Association's partial victory did have the effect of slowing the rate at which gag orders were issued. Five weeks after the June 30 decision, the American Bar Association's House of Delegates, while refusing to recommend elimination of judicial restraints on publishing information in the public domain, did agree to procedures suggested by Landau by which a judge should hold a public hearing and set forth facts and reasons to explain the necessity for proposed restrictive orders. The statement of the ABA's Legal Advisory Committee on Fair Trial and Free Press, which drafted the guidelines, said: "The media and persons other than the parties have a sufficient interest in the alternative measures for protecting a trial against the influence of prejudicial publicity, including the closing of the courtroom, that they should be given the opportunity to assert free press and speech and public trial considerations into the court's deliberations." The press, understandably, was not satisfied with that course of action and took further steps to get the Reardon Report modified.

Scott Aiken, the Society's FOI chairman in 1977 and 1978, among other actions, testified for the Society before the ABA's Task Force on Fair Trial and Free Press, chaired by Judge Alfred T. Goodwin of the United States Court of Appeals for the Ninth

Circuit. "The judge and his committee desire to expand the press' ability to report on the legal system's operation," Aiken said in his 1977 report, but he warned, "The ABA delegates at large, however, are probably less than enthusiastic about revising the fair trial, free press standards...." Judge Goodwin's ABA committee, however, did recommend to the House of Delegates in 1978 a new standard for the section on the conduct of judicial proceedings in criminal cases. Stating that it was being made "...in response to the Supreme Court's decision in *Nebraska Press Association v. Stuart*," Standard 8-3.1 – Prohibition of direct restraints on media – stated: "No rule of court or judicial order shall be promulgated that prohibits representatives of the news media from broadcasting or publishing any information in their possession relating to a criminal case." In the commentary accompanying the new standard, the committee said, "While the mode of the Court's reasoning in *Nebraska Press Association* does not foreclose the possibility that prior restraints on the press can be imposed under extreme circumstances, the benefits of a *per se* rule against such a measure are overriding." The House of Delegates approved the change in standards at its August 1978 meeting.

Any relief which might have come as a result of the ABA's modification in the Reardon rules on publication of available information had little chance to occur because of yet another case already decided in the New York Court of Appeals and headed for the United States Supreme Court.

Paradoxically, in the same year – 1976 – that the Society's board was meeting in Rochester, New York, to marshal forces to raise money and support in the Nebraska Press Association case, about 100 miles away Seneca County Judge Daniel A. DePasquale had closed to the public and press a pre-trial hearing on admission of evidence in a murder case. The Gannett Company, owner of two newspapers and a television station in Rochester, appealed the decision and won its case in the Appellate Division of the New York Supreme Court. The New York Court of Appeals, however, reversed the appellate division decision upholding Judge

DePasquale, stating that while criminal trials could be presumed to be open, a judge had the discretion to seal a pre-trial proceeding. In its 4-2 decision, the court laid down a general rule for New York. "At the point where press commentary on those hearings would threaten the impaneling of a constitutionally impartial jury, pre-trial evidentiary hearings in this state are presumptively to be closed to the public." The decision led to closure of pre-trial proceedings throughout the state almost immediately. The United States Supreme Court agreed to review *Gannett v. DePasquale* and held hearings in November 1977. Its July 2, 1979, decision upholding the New York Court of Appeals and Judge DePasquale was met with disbelief in many quarters given the general tenor of the *Nebraska* decision. Upon reflection, however, it was clear the Supreme Court had acted on Chief Justice Warren Burger's suggestion in *Nebraska* that pre-trial hearings might be closed.

The 5-4 decision carried with it a major change in interpretation of the Sixth Amendment's guarantee of a "public trial." Justice Potter Stewart, in one of three concurring opinions, wrote, "The Constitution nowhere mentions any right of access to a criminal trial on the part of the public; its guarantee, like the others enumerated, is personal to the accused." Justice William Rehnquist carried it a step further. "...[S]ince the Court holds that the public does not have any Sixth Amendment right of access to such proceedings, it necessarily follows that if the parties agree on a closed proceeding, the trial court is not required by the Sixth Amendment to advance any reason whatsoever for declining to open a pretrial hearing or trial to the public." Justice Harry A. Blackmun, dissenting, said, "Publicity is essential to the preservation of public confidence in the rule of law and in the operation of courts. Only in rare circumstances does this principle clash with the rights of the criminal defendant to a fair trial so as to justify exclusion. The Sixth and Fourteenth Amendments require that the states take care to determine that those circumstances exist before excluding the public from a hearing....Those circumstances do not exist in this case." Within a day of the *Gannett v. DePasquale* decision, defense attorneys across the country were requesting and getting closed pre-trial hearings. Even more ominous, judges were granting motions closing the trials themselves, based on the language in Stewart's and Rehnquist's opinions. Thus, while the press, following the *Nebraska* case, could publish information already in hand or in the public domain, the courts, in turn, effectively had blocked the availability of information at its source in the *Gannett* decision.

The Society, using its network of campus and professional chapters and its state FOI coordinators, joined with the Reporters Committee for Freedom of the Press in monitoring the nationwide effects of the *Gannett* case with chapter members and others, calling in reports on court closures in their areas. The results at the end of August showed that ten trials had been closed and pre-trial proceedings had been closed to public and press at the rate of one per day. By early October, seventy-five closures had been noted. The monitoring during the fall and winter months demonstrated closures still averaging one per day. During the fall, in public speeches made by the various justices, the confusion was even more evident. Chief Justice Burger said in Flagstaff, Arizona that the decision applied only to pre-trial hearings, while Justice John Paul Stevens, speaking in Tucson, Arizona, said the Constitution does not bar the closing of trials if the defense and prosecution agree to it. Even Justice Blackmun, who called the ruling "an outrageous decision, totally in error," said, "...[I]f the defense, the prosecution and the judge agree to close the trial itself, the courtroom shall be closed."

Following up on the data collected, the Society joined the Reporters Committee and six other news organizations in an amicus brief in another case, *Richmond Newspapers v. Virginia*, on appeal to the Supreme Court, hoping to clear up problems left by *Gannett*. Virginia's Supreme Court had upheld the trial judge's decision to close the trial. The amicus brief said, "This Court's ruling in *Gannett* has caused such widespread confusion in the legal community that it must be rectified before our traditional system of open criminal proceedings is entirely transformed into a chain of secret hearings...." Noting the ambiguity in the language of the *Gannett* opinions, the brief asked the Court to reexamine its reasoning in *Gannett*, even in terms of excluding the public from pre-trial hearings. If the decision were to stand, the brief asked that the Court make it clear that the ruling applied only to pre-trial hearings. Many in the legal and journalistic communities saw the Court's acceptance of the *Richmond* case as a convenient vehicle to settle the issues left by *Gannett*, but believed the decision in *Richmond* might be another close ruling.

Meanwhile individual states were addressing the matter of closed pre-trial and trial proceedings. Legislatures and state supreme courts in Arkansas, Pennsylvania, Maine and Connecticut made it more difficult to effect closure. Even the New York Court of Appeals, which had upheld DePasquale, altered its position in another case filed by The Gannett Company in 1979, reversing a lower court's pre-trial closure laying out specific guidelines that would have to be followed if the public and press were to be excluded from such hearings and stating, "We did not mean to suggest that closure would be necessary or even appropriate in all pre-trial proceedings."

One year to the day following its *Gannett* decision, the United States Supreme Court handed down its ruling in *Richmond Newspapers v. Virginia*. Seven of the nine justices agreed – with Rehnquist dissenting and Justice Lewis Powell not participating – that trials must be open, but leaving the Gannett decision on pre-trial closures intact. After reviewing historical developments in criminal trials, Chief Justice Burger concluded, "From this unbroken, uncontradicted history, supported by reasons as valid today as in centuries past, we are bound to conclude that a presumption of openness inheres in the very nature of a criminal trial under our system of justice." And answering the State of Virginia's contention that the Constitution nowhere states that trials must be open to the public, Burger pointed out that although not all specific rights – including the right to privacy, the right to travel and the right to be presumed innocent – were not expressly guaranteed in the Constitution, the Court recognized that they were as indispensable as those explicitly defined. The decision for openness in criminal trials was not absolute, however. While Burger said that in *Richmond*, the Court for the first time was asked to decide whether a criminal trial may be closed to the public without any demonstration that closure is required to protect the defendant's right to a fair trial, "or that some overriding consideration requires closure," and while he noted that the Court had answered, "No," the very language implied that even trials might be closed under extraordinary circumstances. The Justice Department, in early fall 1980, issued guidelines to United States government attorneys regarding judicial closures, which, while they required demonstration of a "substantial likelihood" that a person's right to a fair trial would be denied or that ongoing investigations would be seriously jeopardized, they left the door open for Burger's "overriding considerations."

Writing in *The Quill* in September 1980, Lyle Denniston, Supreme Court reporter for the Washington *Star*, suggested that the *Richmond* decision was "filled with promise, but not with assurance. It remains to be tested further. The legal rules that govern newsgathering will be the central preoccupation of the Court as it works its way through a still-growing docket of press cases." Denniston's analysis seemed to verify the Reporters Committee update of August 15, 1980, which reported that, since the *Gannett* decision, there had been 272 motions to keep the press out of courtrooms, including the granting of thirty-three of forty-seven requests to bar the press from trials. While the *Richmond* decision, reinforced by the Court's 6-3 *Globe Newspaper Co. v. Superior Court* decision in 1982, was hailed by Society leaders as a landmark in seeking openness in criminal trials, individual judges' and attorneys' attempts at closure of both trials and pre-trial hearings continued to spark the Society and other press organizations to appeal for relief. The Society's First Amendment

counsel in 1982, Bruce Sanford, said, "Access will be the major area of First Amendment legal developments for the remainder of the twentieth century." Those so-called voluntary guidelines for press-bar relations turned sour in 1982, when Judge Byron Swedberg, of a Superior Court in the State of Washington, demanded that the news media would have to agree in writing to abide by the state's voluntary guidelines before they would be admitted into court. While every newspaper in the state as well as radio and television stations complained that Judge Swedberg was making the guidelines mandatory and that reporters were being subjected to prior restraint and would face contempt of court charges if a judge felt they had violated any signed agreement, an appeal to the Washington Supreme Court resulted in Judge Swedberg's ruling being upheld.

To counteract such problems, and led in many cases by Society members and chapters, First Amendment coalitions were developing in more and more states in the early 1980's to keep lawyers and judges better informed, as well as to aid newspapers and broadcasters in fighting closure orders. Further, chapters were publishing and distributing handbooks for reporters and editors on what to do in cases in which they were denied access to public meetings, records or the courts. Taking its cue and title from the Pennsylvania First Amendment Coalition, the Grand Canyon professional chapter in Flagstaff, Arizona, produced a "Media Survival Kit." It included step-by-step advice prepared by attorneys from the Brown and Bain law firm in Phoenix on what to do if excluded from access to such meetings or hearings. That extensive document, covering state and federal law, became the "Arizona Reporters' Handbook on Media Law," published jointly in 1981 by the Grand Canyon chapter, Brown and Bain and the Arizona Newspapers Association. That project served as a springboard for the beginning of the Arizona First Amendment Coalition, sponsored and funded by the Society's six professional and campus chapters in Arizona, Arizona Newspapers Association and Arizona Broadcasters Association. From its beginning, it has been directed by Bernie Wynn, a member of the Valley of the Sun professional chapter in Phoenix and political writer for *The Arizona Republic*.

Exemplary of continuing efforts to close avenues to reporters was an attempt made early in 1981 by members of the American Bar Association to institute new, restrictive rules on dissemination of information relating to arrests and pre-trial hearings through a document called The Uniform Information Practices Code. First Amendment counsel Bruce Sanford's leading role for the Society in challenging that effort is detailed later in this book.

CHAPTER 6

FOI: The Battle Continues

Thus far, we have traced the Society's successes and setbacks with federal and state court systems and the American Bar Association in keeping sources confidential and gaining access to criminal proceedings. But the Society was active in yet another conflict with the ABA and the courts – the use of cameras and tape-recording devices in courtrooms. A brief history of the canons of the bar association and decisions by the federal courts on the subject will place the controversy in perspective with the Society's other freedom of information and access battles.

CAMERAS IN THE COURTROOM

The ABA preceded the federal government in establishing rules related to cameras in courtrooms. Following Bruno Hauptmann's execution – he had been convicted in 1935 in the kidnap-murder of Charles Lindbergh's son – the ABA established a special committee on cooperation between press, radio and bar. That committee's report termed the Hauptmann trial, "...the most spectacular and depressing example of improper publicity and professional misconduct ever presented to the people of the United States in a criminal trial." From that report, the bar association, in 1937, adopted Canon 35 of its Canons of Professional Ethics, calling for a ban on photographing and broadcasting courtroom proceedings. While the canon did not have the force of law, state bar associations and judicial councils adopted the rule, and the prohibition against cameras and microphones was effected. The canon, as amended in 1952 and 1963, expanded the ban to include television. Even after years of debate and lobbying by various press groups. which argued that the state of the art in each field was such that it need not interrupt the decorum of the court, Canon 35 was superseded by Canon 3A(7) in 1972 in a new Code of Judicial Conduct. It said, "A judge should prohibit broadcasting, televising, recordings, or the taking of photographs in the courtroom and areas immediately adjacent thereto during sessions of the court or recesses between sessions." The new canon did allow some exceptions to prohibiting cameras in the courtroom. They

A youthful William Small, while working at WLS Radio in Chicago and WHAS in Louisville, became involved in the battle for cameras and recording devices in American courtrooms from the late 1950's through the 1970's. Small, who was vice chairman of the FOI committee for several years, became Region Two director from 1969-1971, and was national president in 1974-1975.

included providing for presentation of evidence or perpetuation of a record, for ceremonial purposes, or for recording or reproducing court proceedings only for instructional purposes in educational institutions. The latter exception could be done only if the means of recording did not distract from or impair the dignity of the proceedings, all parties and witnesses gave consent, and the reproduction would not be

shown until the proceeding had been concluded and eleven direct appeals had been exhausted.

The ban on photography and broadcasting of federal criminal proceedings came in 1946 with the adoption of Rule 53 of the Federal Rules of Criminal Procedure. An amendment in 1962 extended the ban beyond the courtroom itself to the "environs" of the court – a term often left open to interpretation by the individual court – and to "all judicial proceedings" rather than solely to criminal cases.

State bar association procedures and the federal courts came together in 1965 in the case of Billy Sol Estes, who was convicted in a trial on a state charge of selling farmers non-existent fertilizer, tanks and equipment. The trial was televised because of Estes' flamboyant personality and his connections with the White House and covered by at least twelve photographers using motion picture and still cameras. Estes appealed on the grounds that he was denied Fourteenth Amendment rights to due process because of the televising and broadcasting of the trial. The United States Supreme Court in *Estes v. Texas* in 1965 reversed the conviction in a 5-4 decision, with Justice Tom Clark basing his argument on the psychological effect of judge, jurors, defendant and witnesses being "on television" rather than on the possible tendency of television to disrupt order in the courtroom. In his opinion, he wrote that the possible effects "are real enough to have convinced the Judicial Conference of the United States, this Court and the Congress that television should be barred in federal trials...." In addition, he wrote, "...[T]hey have persuaded all but two of our states to prohibit television in the courtroom." One of those two remaining states revised its court rules to prohibit broadcasting and photography following the *Estes* decision.

The National Press Photographers Association led early fights to eliminate or modify the federal and state rules. Sigma Delta Chi members may well have battled the rules as well, but the national organization and its committee for advancement of freedom of information did not take a formal stand until 1952, four years after that committee was formed. In its section on television and the news, the committee's report stated, "Denial of the right of television (and of radio) to employ the tools of their trade – the microphone and the camera – to disseminate information is censorship." But the committee apparently was concerned only with the broadcast media's rights to cover city council, legislative and other administrative meetings or hearings and did not challenge the court

bans directly. The report continued, "Sigma Delta Chi certainly is on record that it is sympathetic with the contention that television should enjoy the same rights as all other elements of the press. But it also is reasonable to note and remind television that, all through these vigilant years of campaigning – a ceaseless battle for freedom of and access to information – the press has made exceptions. That is part of press responsibility, and must be part of television's responsibility."

Two years later, the committee's report addressed the matter of the courts' prohibition of news cameras in courtrooms. "Your committee is convinced that a reasonable solution could be worked out wherein news pictures could be obtained in the courtroom without abridgment of decorum and dignity, but that this will be reached only if all newspapers, radio and television get together so that public opinion is brought into the matter." In response, the delegates to the 1954 convention adopted a resolution urging the fraternity to confer with officers of the American Bar Association regarding Canon 35. NPPA members, with the permission of the ABA, covered an association conference in Lincoln, Nebraska, and presented evidence at the ABA's national meeting in August 1955, of having completed the task without disturbing the Lincoln conference. The bar association took no formal action and commentaries of members, particularly judges, showed little disposition to relax the barriers. Newton's committee, now with broadcaster Ted Koop of CBS News in Washington as a member, continued to hammer away at what it called "The Right To See," informing judges and attorneys of scientific advances in camera technology and cataloging 132 successful attempts to use cameras in courtrooms from 1955 through 1958. Calling attention to the Colorado Supreme Court's lifting of that state's ban on photographing courtroom trials, the committee's report called the February 26, 1956, decision, "...[T]he first time in U.S. journalism that a court of such stature – or any court – had found that visual media does not detract from the dignity and decorum necessary to the conduct of courtroom proceedings...." What appeared to be a breakthrough in 1958 – the House of Delegates agreed to hear arguments from press groups including Sigma Delta Chi on modifications to Canon 35 – resulted in two votes to defer action and plans to establish a new committee to study evidence on the effect of photographs and broadcasts on witnesses, juries and defendants.

By the end of the 1950's, the outlook for anything but the mildest kind of liberalization in Canon 35 by the ABA was doubtful. The new committee, after meeting with representatives of eight press organizations, favored no changes in the rules. Individual judges, however, still seemed willing to consider entry of cameras into courtrooms, the most prominent being Chief Judge Charles S. Desmond of the New York State Court of Appeals. In March 1960, Judge Desmond said, "I would not resist an experiment designed to show whether trials can be televised without bringing visible equipment into the courtroom." Bill Small of CBS News, Washington, replaced Koop on the Society's FOI committee in 1960 when Koop became a national officer. Small testified for Sigma Delta Chi before the ABA's special committee in Chicago, February 18, 1962, and, in a stinging speech, said, "Suspicious as Canon 35 is of my profession, it seems to me that it is even less trustful of the judges who preside in American courts. The very instances of departure from Canon 35 which have worked so well are evidence of the judge's power over his own court (and, we would contend, his wisdom in its conduct). We contend that Canon 35 in its paranoid fear of modern journalistic technology, discredits the judge as well as the journalist in its fear of the conduct of both. I know of no responsible jurist who would willingly permit anything to impair a trial but, equally, I know of no responsible journalist who would want to impair justice. Further, should judge or journalist disturb proper due process, our law in every state permits appeal on the grounds of mistrial. Our judicial checks and balances are the best protection, not antiquated Canons....I suggest to you that practice has shown that the tools of journalism can serve justice in quiet dignity which will broaden public

understanding of our courts. As these practices become commonplace the various arguments, real and imagined, against their use will evaporate."

The day following Small's testimony, a continuing conflict within the press on First Amendment rights of the print media vis-a-vis radio and television's coverage of trials surfaced. The Chicago *Tribune* editorialized, "Contrary to what seems to be the majority opinion among editors, we think Canon 35 is all right. We believe its provisions are sensible, that they meet a real need, and that if they are altered materially, the courts and the processes of justice will be degraded." Two months later, Robert P. Early, managing editor of the Indianapolis *Star*, wrote in the ASNE *Bulletin*, "Besides ignorance displayed by the spokesmen for the press, television and radio groups regarding constitutional rights of a defendant, they tried to tie in the television and radio industry as a part of the free press. The television and radio industry operates through government license. Purpose of that industry is to sell merchandise over the people's airwaves using as a device to trap viewers and listeners – entertainment, sports, educational and so-called news and public service programs." Even Barney Kilgore, already a folk-hero among Society members for his work in the reorganization, did not see the need for protecting the rights of radio and television newsmen. In a 1962 article for *The Quill*, Kilgore wrote, "I would like to suggest that we are going to get the issue of freedom of the press obscured dangerously if we try to stretch it to fit the radio and television industries that operate and apparently must operate for some time in the future under government licenses....The argument that freedom of the press protects a licensed medium from the authority of the government that issues the license is doubletalk." Small would have no part of that. His rebuttal in the following issue of *The Quill* stated, "If we are going to follow Kilgore's shunning of broadcasting's First Amendment rights to its conclusion, we are to assume that it would permit or even encourage government to control, to censor, to suppress broadcasting freedom of expression....To write off First Amendment freedoms in broadcasting is to stifle the one broad avenue presently available for competition of voices in the marketplace of ideas. The opposite side of press freedom's coin is freedom from the press...."

Small and his broadcast colleagues in and out of the Society were faced not only with dissension from among the printed press, but with the new federal revisions, regarding its Rule 53 to include television and extending coverage to the environs of the court. In March 1962, the Judicial Conference of the United States, made up of the eleven Federal Court of Appeals Chief Judges and a district judge elected from each of the eleven circuits, unanimously stated, "The Judicial Conference...condemns the taking of photographs in the courtroom or its environs in connection with any judicial proceeding, and the broadcasting of judicial proceedings by radio, television or other means, and considers such practices to be inconsistent with fair judicial procedure and they ought not to be permitted in any federal court."

The ABA's special committee took note of both the lack of agreement within the press and the Judicial Council's action in reporting to the full body in August. Although what it called its "interim report" was, in the main, negative toward any revisions to Canon 35, it delayed any final recommendations until February 1963. Meeting in New Orleans, the House of Delegates sounded the death knell to hopes of any change in the Canon when, in a virtually unanimous vote, the 250 delegates approved the special committee's request to retain all substantive portions of Canon 35. The action was another setback, but not nearly so disastrous to attempts to modify the ABA's rules as the Supreme Court's *Estes v. Texas* decision in 1965. While Canon 35 did not carry the weight of law, the Supreme Court's ruling did, and the issue, at least at the national level, was placed in a deep freeze which would not show any signs of thaw when the ABA adopted its 1972 Code of Judicial Conduct replacing the infamous Canon 35 with Canon 3A(7), or for years thereafter.

Placing its emphasis on what might be accomplished at the state and local levels and on those successes in which individual judges had allowed television and still cameras in their courts, the Society kept the issue alive through convention resolutions and the work of the national FOI committee and headquarters staff with chapters and individual members. Although it would take ten years, slowly and sporadically some results began to show. By 1977, cameras were allowed in courtrooms in Alabama, Colorado, Georgia and Washington but only with the consent of both parties in a proceeding. California had had an experiment with cameras in courtrooms and Texas had permitted cameras in appellate courts only. Florida's Supreme Court, on an experimental basis, opened all courtrooms to television and still cameras in 1977, while in Wisconsin the Supreme Court authorized a short-term experiment for television stations in Milwaukee Municipal Court. In addition, Montana and Minnesota judges agreed to form commissions to study opening the courts to cameras. Shortly thereafter, experimental approval turned to permanent approval in state after state, while Supreme Courts and legislatures in additional states cleared the way for even more experimental efforts.

Other than the 1956 rulings in Colorado, it is to Florida, where courts were opened fully to cameras permanently and on a regular basis by its Supreme Court May 1, 1979, that the news media point to their greatest success. No major problems were encountered in Florida by judges, prosecutors or the press in the two-year experiment, including the sensational, televised trials of Ronnie Zamora and Theodore Bundy. Interestingly, it was another case which began during the two-year experiment in Florida which brought the issue of cameras in state courtrooms to the United States Supreme Court for the first time since *Estes*. The Court, in 1980, agreed to hear *Chandler v. Florida*, a case in which two former Miami Beach policemen were convicted of a 1977 burglary in a televised trial and were sentenced to seven years in prison. A Florida appellate court upheld the conviction and the state's Supreme Court refused to review the case based on its 1979 decision admitting cameras on a permanent basis. On January 26, 1981, the United States Supreme Court ruled unanimously that the Constitution does not prohibit a state from experimenting with electronic and photographic coverage of the courtroom. In his opinion, Chief Justice Burger did not overrule the *Estes* decision of 1965, but because there was no evidence of prejudice of constitutional dimensions, he said, "...[T]here is no reason for this Court either to endorse or to invalidate Florida's experiment." The decision in *Chandler v. Florida* can be read as a narrow ruling and may have invited similar cases in which the defendant's rights might be damanged by photographic coverage. But its effects gave the go-ahead to any state wishing to move ahead with such coverage of courtrooms.

The final barriers were down; Canon 35 and its successor, Canon 3A(7), had been circumvented; and the drive was on to open courts to cameras and recording devices in states without such provisions. Bill Small's suggestion to the ABA's special committee of almost exactly nineteen years earlier that, as cameras in the courtroom became commonplace, "the various arguments, real and imagined, against their use will evaporate." had come true. Only the long-standing Rule 53 of the Federal Rules was left unshaken and it remains intact today. Many of the states without rules admitting cameras were quick to join those which did. By 1981, thirty-four states had permanent or experimental rules in place and that number grew to thirty-nine one year later. Specifically, in 1982, twenty-two states had adopted permanent rules for coverage in either courts of original jurisdiction or appellate courts and, in half of those, no consent was needed from anyone other than the judge in criminal trials. In the seventeen states with experiments, only six required consent from other than the judge in criminal cases. The eleven states without any rules admitting cameras to courts were Illinois, Indiana, Michigan, Mississippi, Missouri, Nebraska, Oregon, South Carolina, South Dakota, Vermont and Virginia, but even in five of those states, new rules were being considered.

Meanwhile, the American Bar Association, finding itself outflanked and passed by in more than three-quarters of the states in the controversy, bent severely but didn't break entirely. Meeting in August 1982, the ABA's House of Delegates voted, 162-112, to modify substantially its opposition to cameras in the courtroom for the first time since 1937. One must read beyond the first few lines of Canon 3A(7) to locate the change, for its opening language remains, "A judge should prohibit broadcasting, televising, recording or photographing in courtrooms...." The modification came after the prohibition stating, "...[E]xcept that under rules prescribed by a supervising appellate court or other appropriate authority, a judge may authorize broadcasting, televising, recording or photographing of judicial proceedings in courtrooms...consistent with the rights of parties to a fair trial subject to express conditions, which allow such coverage in a manner that will be unobtrusive, will not distract trial participants, and will not interfere with the administration of justice." Commenting on the need for the new language, one ABA spokesman said, "It looked like we were still in the Dark Ages, with most of the states having made changes contrary to the Canon." William O. Seymour, FOI chairman for the National Press Photographers Association, which had battled the ABA barriers from their beginning and who, along with NPPA's Joe Costa, had made the final pitch for the news media, preferred to credit all of the national press and broadcasting organizations including The Society of Professional Journalists, Sigma Delta Chi, for standing firm in the forty-five years it took to get the ABA to change its position.

Just how many Society chapters and members had input into effecting the tremendous changes in the 1970's and early 1980's cannot be determined. It is important to note, however, that national convention delegates kept the issue alive, adopting resolutions in 1972 and in every year since 1975 urging the courts to facilitate photographic and recorded coverage and urging chapters to work toward that goal. And, as Hurst pointed out, the number of chapters and individual members who worked toward various freedom of information objectives, including cameras in the courtroom, without seeking recognition, remains significant.

THE EQUAL-TIME CLAUSE AND FAIRNESS DOCTRINE

Broadcast news media have been a vocal opponent of these two regulations as discriminatory against radio and television since each was conceived. The same division among the print and broadcast areas of the press evident in the Canon 35 conflict kept the Society relatively impotent for many years, but, by the mid-1960's, Sigma Delta Chi began to take a stand in support of radio and television. Because of the federal rules involved, the efforts were limited to national lobbying for change.

The Equal-Time Clause, also known as the equal opportunities requirement, or Section 315, requires that if time is given or sold by a broadcast station to a candidate for political office, equal time on the air must be given or sold to all other legally-qualified candidates for that office. It stemmed from the Radio Act of 1927, was transferred intact to the Communications Act of 1934, and was amended in 1959 to exclude, with some exceptions, bonafide newscasts, news interviews, news documentaries and on-the-spot coverage of news events during an election campaign. The regulation's provisions were temporarily suspended through congressional adoption of Senate Joint Resolution 207 in 1960 for the presidential race to permit broadcasting of the Nixon-Kennedy debates. The Federal Communications Commission, in a 5-2 vote, modified the rule once more in 1975, holding that live broadcasting of presidential candidates' entire news or press conferences, and under certain circumstances, candidates' debates, would be exempt from equal-time requirements because they were bonafide news events.

The Fairness Doctrine was developed in 1949 out of an FCC decision reversing an eight-year prohibition against editorializing on the air by broadcast stations, and it became a part of Section 315 in 1959. Dealing with a broad spectrum of issues rather than election campaigns, the

regulation stated: "[W]hen a broadcast station presents one side of a controversial issue of public importance reasonable opportunity must be afforded the presentation of contrasting views." The constitutionality of the doctrine was upheld in 1969 when the United States Supreme Court ruled, 8-0, in the *Red Lion Broadcasting Co., Inc. v. FCC* and the *U.S. vs. Radio Television News Directors Association* cases that it is the right of the viewers and listeners, not the broadcaster, which is paramount. The decision stated that nothing in the First Amendment prevented the government "from requiring a licensee to share his frequency with others and conduct himself as a proxy or fiduciary with obligations to present those views and voices which are representative of his community."

Early Sigma Delta Chi efforts regarding the rights of radio and television to have equal status with their print counterparts concentrated on gaining access by broadcasters to meetings and sessions of governmental agencies, much of that tied to the use of cameras and microphones in legislative hearings *et al*. As late as 1959, the annual FOI report simply noted, in its lead article in the "news camera" section, the changes approved by Congress in the equal-time rules. Reporting what "they"–the broadcasters and specifically RTNDA–were trying to accomplish in effecting changes in the Equal-Time Clause and the Fairness Doctrine seemed to be the extent to which the Society's FOI committee gave attention to the problems throughout the 1960's. *The Quill* gave the two issues broader coverage during that time, providing space for prominent radio and television journalists, including Small, to spell out the inequities between print and broadcast journalism and the need for change. Speakers and panelists at national conventions, as well, focused on the problems. But only in 1965 is there documentation of official action by the Society in the form of a convention resolution which endorsed proposed legislation in Congress for absolute repeal of the equal time provision, calling it, "unnecessary, archaic and in direct derogation of the First Amendment to the Constitution." Individual Sigma Delta Chi members were speaking out in opposition to specific applications of the FCC rules and testifying before committees seeking repeal of both regulations, but, generally, they were identified with their broadcast organizations rather than the Society.

Sigma Delta Chi began a more direct role in 1971 when Small, then vice chairman of the FOI committee, lent the Society's name and influence to an alleged Fairness Doctrine problem revolving around the CBS documentary, "The Selling of the Pentagon." The United States House of Representatives Commerce Committee, chaired by Rep. Harley O. Staggers, hoping to demonstrate that the documentary violated Fairness Doctrine standards, issued a subpoena to CBS News president Frank Stanton asking to examine outtakes from interviews used in the production of the broadcast. Stanton refused to produce any of the unused material, stating, "We will take every step necessary and open to us to resist this unwarranted action of a congressional committee and to keep broadcast journalism free of government surveillance. Too much is at stake for us to do less." Staggers countered, saying that broadcasting was different from newspapers and Congress had a right to investigate its unused material. Stanton's continued refusal to answer the subpoena for materials brought a committee vote seeking House approval of a citation for contempt of Congress against the CBS News president.

Sigma Delta Chi issued a statement July 8, 1971, in the form of an open letter to the members of the House of Representatives. Urging the representatives to kill the contempt citation, the letter stated, "Approval of this citation would be a severe blow to our cherished, constitutionally guaranteed freedom of the press, of which broadcast journalism is an integral part. Such action, endorsing efforts of governmental agencies to snoop into non-broadcast material, would serve to intimidate and harass all newsmen in the future....Sigma Delta Chi takes this occasion to reaffirm its stand against any interference with the crucial role of the news media in freely presenting information to the American people....Fishing expeditions such as the one undertaken by the Commerce Committee must be stopped if constitutional liberties are to be preserved." In an unusual move, the members of the House refused to support Staggers and his committee majority.

Using a parliamentary manuever, the House returned the matter to the Commerce Committee, effectively killing the contempt citation against Stanton. Later, the FCC, following its own investigation, ruled that "The Selling of the Pentagon" had met all requirements of the Fairness Doctrine and, of greater import, that matters of editorial judgment belonged with the journalist rather than with any government body.

While some print journalists continued to challenge the right of broadcasters to equal treatment under the First Amendment, the Society made its position clear in 1975. In a strongly-worded statement reaffirming its opposition to the Fairness Doctrine and the Equal-Time Clause, the board of directors noted, "The First Amendment states that Congress 'shall make no law abridging freedom of the press.' Yet every time the FCC raises questions about the free exercise of journalistic judgment, it does so in violation of the First Amendment. There must be no distinction made between the rights of broadcast and print journalists under the First Amendment."

The Federal Communications Commission, in a 5-2 vote, September 25, 1975, made it possible to broadcast debates between presidential candidates of the two major parties, exempting the debates from the Equal-Time Clause for the first time since Senate Joint Resolution 207 temporarily suspended the Clause so that the Kennedy-Nixon Debates could be aired in 1960. Called the Aspen Institute rule because the rules were worked out at a meeting in Aspen, Colorado, the 1975 ruling said broadcasters were free to carry debates without subjecting themselves to equal time demands from all other candidates as long as a third party – which turned out to be the League of Women Voters – sponsored the debates, and the debates were aired live or within twenty-four hours of their taping.

While the Commission's decision was

considered, by many, as a considerable breakthrough in the Equal-Time Clause battle, delegates to the 1975 convention in Philadelphia adopted resolutions calling for the FCC to repeal its Fairness Doctrine and Congress to repeal the Equal-Time Clause provisions of Section 315 of the Communications Act of 1934. Little more than a year later, Society president Richard Leonard urged all chapters and members to join the Society's national campaign to extend all First Amendment rights to broadcasters by urging their congressmen to support passage of the First Amendment Clarification Act of 1977. Robert Lewis, vice chairman of the FOI committee, and Val Hymes, Region Two director, testified before the Senate Communications Subcommittee in favor of Senate Bill 22, which would have repealed the Fairness Doctrine and Equal-Time provisions as well as allow cameras in the House and Senate sessions. The measure died an early death in the 1977 session.

For the next five years, the national committee continued to monitor what it called abuses of FCC powers but saw no possibility of modification, let alone repeal, in Congress until Mark Fowler became FCC chairman in April 1981. In a near about-face on September 17, the Commission recommended that Congress repeal Section 315, including both onerous provisions. But Fowler's proposal met with negative reaction on Capitol Hill, especially from Rep. John Dingell, chairman of the House Commerce Committee, and Rep. Tim Wirth, chairman of the Telecommunications Subcommittee. By late 1983, although support in Congress for Fowler's position was growing, consideration of any changes in Section 315 remained bogged down in congressional committees. Although a 1983 proposal by Senator Robert Packwood of Oregon to institute a Constitutional amendment deregulating the broadcast media and effectively eliminating Section 315's Fairness Doctrine and Equal-Time Clause was set aside, the FCC made its own modification concerning equal time and the presidential debates.

On November 8, the Commission announced that it was broadening the Aspen Institute rule allowing broadcasters to sponsor debates among political candidates without triggering equal time requests from candidates not included in the debates. It also lifted the requirement that debates be aired live or within twenty-four hours. The National Association of Broadcasters and Radio Television News Directors Association, which brought the petition for the change to the FCC, were elated. Spokespersons for the two organizations said the new rules would permit viable candidates on the national, state and local levels opportunity to present their credentials and positions to their communities.

While some of the burden had been lifted, the onus of the remainder of the Fairness Doctrine and Equal-Time Clause regulations remained in tact in early 1984.

ZURCHER v. STANFORD DAILY

On April 12, 1971, the *Stanford Daily*, the campus newspaper at Stanford University, published a special edition including photographs of a disturbance on campus two days earlier in which nine policemen were injured. On the day of publication, Palo Alto, California, police arrived unannounced at the newspaper's offices armed with a search warrant and, for about forty-five minutes, searched filing cabinets, desks and photographic laboratories, read reporters' notes and other matters, looking for any information and photographs that might help them identify those who had assaulted the officers. They found nothing that assisted them in their investigation.

Richard Fogel, an at-large member of Sigma Delta Chi's Freedom of Information Committee, met with the Society's board of directors May 8 in Las Vegas, Nevada, to request support for a pending federal law suit to be brought by the *Stanford Daily*. Even before legal counsel had been obtained to determine if the newspaper had a case, as alleged, under the First, Fourth and Fourteenth Amendments, the board adopted a motion expressing outrage at the use of a search warrant to gain indiscriminate information from the newspaper and set aside funds from the legal defense fund to be provided when needed by the campus newspaper. Following up on the board's action, the FOI committee issued a statement: "This search of a newspaper office, thought to be unprecedented in the annals of American journalism, is clearly a violation of propriety and privacy – and not one bit less loathsome for having been perpetrated against a campus newspaper rather than an established, independent publication. Nor do circumstances preceding and surrounding the search by Palo Alto police and Santa Clara County district attorney's representatives justify this use of the search warrant to invade a free and independent newspaper and snoop into confidential material gathered by its reporters and photographers. We join President Richard Lyman of Stanford University in condemning this disgusting raid as 'deplorable and threatening the full freedom of the press,' and we subscribe also to Attorney Anthony Amsterdam's declaration that *The New York Times* might just as well move its files out on 42nd Street and let the police department use them for branch research if this sort of thing is to be allowed." Sigma Delta Chi's contribution to the *Stanford Daily's* defense fund was set at $500.

The newspaper's suit, filed under the U.S. Civil Rights Act in federal district court against Palo Alto police chief James Zurcher and several others, sought an injunction against any further searches and a declaration that the one that had led to the action violated the First, Fourth and Fourteenth Amendments. The district court in 1972 held for the *Stanford Daily*, stating that the Fourth Amendment prevented the use of a search warrant against any person not suspected of a crime unless there was a showing that a subpoena, if served, might result in destruction or removal of the sought-after material. The court further ruled that the First Amendment would apply when the innocent third party was a newspaper. The United States Court of Appeals affirmed the opinion of the district court judge, but, on May 31, 1978, the United States Supreme Court reversed the decision of the lower courts in a 5-3 decision, declaring that a newspaper's offices – or any innocent third party's premises – may be

searched when there are reasonable grounds to believe that criminal evidence may be on the premises. As it did in the *Branzburg v. Hayes* decision, the Court invited legislative action against possible abuses of its decision. Between 1971 and the time the Court ruled, at least fourteen other search warrants for criminal evidence had been issued on the news media, according to reports in *The Quill*.

The Society of Professional Journalists, Sigma Delta Chi, was among the first to respond. Small, Lewis, and Grant Dillman, Washington manager for United Press International and 1977 national FOI chairman, testified June 22 before a Senate judiciary committee considering some of twelve bills introduced in Congress since the decision. Lewis said, "Material coming into newsrooms on a confidential basis is likely to contain raw information – some true and some not – that is in the process of being checked for verity. And there most certainly could be confidential personnel reports and private business records. The idea of turning police loose to prowl through the files is an unthinkable violation of freedom of the press, and stirs thoughts of a police state." The Society did not wait for the Congress to act, however, and, urged by president Alf Goodykoontz and FOI chairman Scott Aiken, it organized a drive encouraging chapters to work for state laws regulating third-party searches. Working in cooperation with the Reporters Committee for Freedom of the Press, the campaign was off the ground quickly. California became the first state to pass legislation prohibiting suprise police searches of newsrooms, its law taking effect January 1, 1979. Connecticut, Illinois, Nebraska, Oregon, Texas and Washington followed with similar legislation requiring that a subpoena be issued for materials wanted and allowing for a challenge to such a subpoena. No challenge was possible when a search warrant was issued. The Texas bill went a step further, allowing for protection for all citizens against searches, not just for the press, a position the Society had taken in working toward passage of a federal statute. It was that very issue – whether all citizens or just the press should be protected – which almost killed the bill in

Congress. President Carter's Administration wanted to apply a subpoena-first rule only to the media. A compromise was reached primarily covering news personnel and the Privacy Protection Act of 1980 was passed by Congress, taking effect January 1, 1981. The law required law enforcement officers at all levels of government to use subpoenas rather than search warrants to obtain a journalist's work product such as notes and article drafts. It provided less protection against a search for written and printed matter, audio and video tapes, photographs and film and negatives. Newsroom searches were permitted if the journalists were criminal suspects, if the materials sought were the fruits of a crime, if it were necessary to prevent death or injury or the destruction of evidence, or if a subpoena had failed to produce the materials.

THE PENTAGON PAPERS

The New York Times on June 13, 1971, printed a summary of a top-secret 7,000-page government document, "The History of U.S. Decision-Making Process on Viet Nam Policy," identified in short as "The Pentagon Papers." Almost immediately, the Nixon Administration threatened court action to halt publication if The Times did not comply voluntarily and claimed that publication of the classified document violated provisions of the Espionage Act. The Times refused to comply. Two days later, the government was able to convince a federal district court judge to issue a temporary injunction against further publication of the document. The Times complied with the judge's order and ceased publication of "The Pentagon Papers" on June 16, marking the first time since 1800 in United States history that prior restraint had been invoked successfully against the press. Sigma Delta Chi issued a statement June 17 which suggested, "....[O]n the basis of what has been published thus far, the apparent collision of the constitutional rights of a free press with the requirements of national security have been greatly overstated....Careful distinction must be drawn between damage to national security and endangering American lives on the one hand, and possible embarrassment to

governments, or to individuals now or formerly holding positions in government on the other. An overriding concern, we believe, is the right of American citizens to be fully informed about the decisions of their government – and about the processses leading up to those decisions....We are confident that, upon careful weighing of the issued involved, the ultimate decision of the courts will hold that First Amendment rights of a free press are paramount in this case and will permit The Times to continue publication of its articles." Before the issue would be settled for the moment by the United States Supreme Court, three other newspapers – The Washington Post, the St. Louis Post Dispatch and the Boston Globe – were restrained from publishing information from "The Pentagon Papers." In a 6-3 decision June 30, 1971, that left a great many doubts in the minds of the press about what might happen in a similar future case, the Court said that the government in this case had not met the heavy burden of showing justification for prior restraint, and publication resumed.

THE OFFICIAL SECRETS ACT: AMERICAN STYLE

In response to a pressing need for overhaul of the Federal Criminal Code, the Nixon Administration prepared a voluminous document which was introduced in Congress in early 1973 as Senate Bill 1400. Buried deep within the bill's 680 pages was a provision which carried dire implications for the press. Known as the Official Secrets Act, the proposed legislation made it a felony punishable by from three to seven years in jail and fines of from $25,000 to $50,000 for government officials to disclose almost any kind of defense and foreign policy information, whether or not its disclosure would endanger the national security. Further, it would similarly punish reporters who received the information and all responsible officials of their publication or broadcasting companies unless they promptly reported the disclosure and returned the material to a government official. The law would also provide the same penalties for government officials who knew about an unauthorized disclosure and failed to report their coworker's action. Part of the law made a crime of any unauthorized disclosure of what was determined as classified information. Finally, the act expressly prevented officials who disclosed such information from defending their action by proving that the information was improperly classified. The law in force at the time covering national security leaks required the government to prove the information in question affected national security and that the defendant meant to harm the country by releasing the information to an enemy. Those who ascribed motives to the Nixon Administration's purposes in proposing the changes drew direct lines between the leak of "The Pentagon Papers," allegedly by Daniel Ellsberg, to *The New York Times* and other newspapers and the language in S.1400.

The Society's board at its spring meeting in Omaha May 5 called on Congress to reject the proposals. One month later, Grant Dillman, Sigma Delta Chi's representative on the Joint Media Committee, testified before the Senate Judiciary Committee, stating that, "We are not talking about classified or national defense information. We are talking about information that is not supposed to be made public only because some government agency, for whatever reasons, has not authorized its release." Dillman also questioned whether Washington *Post* reporters Carl Bernstein and Robert Woodward would have been able to break the Watergate story if such a law had been on the books. "I think not," he said. "The threat of jail would have had a chilling effect on their sources, particularly if word had been passed that national security was involved. Watergate is only the most dramatic example of the hobbles legislation of this kind would put on enterprise reporting. Or even day-to-day reporting. There is a very real danger that it would reduce Washington correspondents to 'handout reporters' in the worst sense of the term." Partly because of the impact of testimony by press organizations and because the bill was opposed by Sen. Sam Irvin, chairman of the Judiciary Committee, it died, only to be replaced by the Ford

Administration's version, introduced as Senate Bill 1 in 1975.

Containing many of the provisions incorporated in S.1400 but removing the exclusion of proof of misclassification as a defense, S.1 was expected to pass Congress in some form but died in committee in 1976. Before its demise, efforts were under way to effect a compromise. Sen. Edward Kennedy, the main architect of the compromise, insisted the bill have a new number – it became S.1437 – but it was still referred to as "Son of S.1." Many of the provisions that could have extended espionage laws to the press were removed and much of the press attention and outrage abated. An interesting aside on the bill was that, as amended, it would have allowed reporters to ignore a gag order and immediately publish or broadcast the information in question without filing an appeal to challenge the order's validity. If the judge attempted to impose criminal contempt penalties against the reporter, the reporter could appeal, claiming that the gag order constituted a prior restraint and, if successful, would be free of any contempt penalties. The bill passed the Senate, 72-15, in 1978 but was still pending under various other number designations in the House Judiciary Committee in mid-1983. Bob Lewis, chairman of the SPJ,SDX freedom of information committee from 1978 through 1983, said, "When the provisions which would have hamstrung the press were eliminated and, for all intents and purposes we had won our battle there, we turned our interests to more urgent problems." The ten-year effort by Congress to revise the Federal Criminal Code continued as of this writing but was stymied by other than press issues.

IN SUM: 1946-1978

Given the list of major and minor victories in the freedom of information "war" for the first thirty-two years Sigma Delta Chi was an active combatant, it would be easy to ignore the losses and declare a distinct advantage for the Society and the press in general. A more realistic assessment, however, might be to say that journalists were bucking a continuing hurricane-force wind generated by the executive, judicial and legislative branches of government at all levels and coming from different directions at different times for those three decades. For every step the press moved straight ahead toward its First Amendment goals on one front, it was blown back a step or more on another or was knocked to the side and forced to retrench and get back on track. Many contend, that despite the defeats, journalists had gained substantial ground, pointing to advances in open meetings, open records and shield laws in the states, along with successes in stopping efforts by government to build new roadblocks. Others direct attention to pre-trial closures, refusal by the appellate courts to review violation of shield laws and the continued harrassment and jailing of reporters, suggesting a probable loss of ground or a stalemate at best. Both sides agree that the press was better armed to do battle in the late 1970's than it was in 1946.

There is general agreement among past presidents and FOI chairmen of the Society that Sigma Delta Chi was an effective force in those years and total agreement that it was more effective on the local and state level than with the federal government. All agree, as well, that it was a slow process, one of learning what to do and how to do it during the 1950's and into the 1960's. That was true of all of the press organizations. But when the early lessons were learned through experience, and the freedom of information drive was on in earnest, it was the unique organizational structure of Sigma Delta Chi which cast it in a leadership role among press groups. Almost all the press associations had knowledgeable and dedicated national boards of directors and many had full-time professional staffs ready to work. But only Sigma Delta Chi, with its scores of professional and campus chapters and thousands of individual member journalists, had substantial troops in the field to pursue the objectives and effect the strategies set by national leaders.

The Society's objectives were simple: everytime the press was confronted by government attempts at any level to inhibit the free flow of information or there were signs a confrontation was imminent, chapters and members were alerted to resist and or take the offensive. The involvement in numbers by chapters and individual members in those years, while recorded in part in *The Quill*, *Replate*, *NEWSletter* and the annual FOI reports, can never be fully established. As Hurst noted, "There were so many cases, largely unreported by chapters and individual members, where the Society provided the ammunition from the national level and the local members did the work and had a significant impact in effecting change or successfully fighting off challenges to a free press."

The strategies in the First Amendment and freedom of information struggles were more subtle. Knowing that government closure of access to news could be made quickly with the passage of a law or through a court decision and that it might take years to effect changes, the Society adopted the position that a patient, yet determined, approach would pay off best. At the national level, the FOI committee and the Society's officers pounded away year after year to help to bring about passage of the federal Freedom of Information Act, modification of the American Bar Association's Reardon Report, and equal First Amendment treatment for broadcast news media, and to meet the challenges brought with nearly every administration to keep the public and the press from knowing what it was doing. In the states and local communities, chapters and individual members had to work for two, three or even more years to realize success in passage of open meeting, open records and shield legislation or ordinances. Challenges to court orders, in which chapters and the national Society assisted with appeals, took years in many cases. Often the battle was won, but even when it was lost, there was no lack of desire or commitment to seek another case or cause and continue the fight. Bob Chandler, Society president in 1970-1971, perhaps summarized both Sigma Delta Chi strategy and effectiveness when he said, "It matters not if we are unable to win a complete battle over any FOI problem in a given year. We must continue to guard and protect the right of the American people to know what their governments do for, and to them."

CHAPTER 7

▆▆▆▆▆▆▆▆▆▆▆▆▆▆▆

FOI:
A New
Commitment

The Birmingham, Alabama, convention in November 1978 was a landmark insofar as freedom of information efforts by The Society of Professional Journalists, Sigma Delta Chi, were concerned. President Alf Goodykoontz and his successor, Phil Dessauer, managing editor of the Tulsa, Oklahoma *World*, didn't set out to alter dramatically the Society's priorities or plan of attack in FOI. As with many turning points in the Society's history, it was a matter of the preparatory work done by past leadership, the coincidental coming together of events and people at a certain time and place, and to Goodykoontz and Dessauer's great credit, the seizing of the moment.

President Goodykoontz had set "Future Directions for the Media" as the theme for the convention and he brought an impressive array of speakers and panelists to Birmingham, many of whom would play some part in the Society's about-to-be-expanded FOI endeavors. Among the guests were Allen Neuharth, president of The Gannett Company and president of the American Newspaper Publishers Association; William Hornby, vice president of the American Society of Newspaper Editors; Joseph Shoquist, president, Associated Press Managing Editors Association; Paul M. Davis, president, Radio Television News Directors Association; Ann Daly Tretter, president, Women in Communications, Inc.; and Mary A. Gardner, president, Association for Education in Journalism. On the FOI front, Goodykoontz scheduled Myron Farber, *The New York Times* reporter who had been jailed for refusing to disclose his sources of information when ordered to do so by a New Jersey judge; Jack Landau, executive director of the Reporters Committee for Freedom of the Press; and Scott Aiken, SPJ,SDX freedom of information chairman.

The future directions of the media theme turned out to be future directions in freedom of information. Neuharth said the press was under attack, noting, "The courts have really leveled their guns, and have scored a few direct hits, but the walls are still standing." He maintained that since times have changed, so must the weapons of the press. "The time has come to get the

Bruce W. Sanford, Rep. Jim Wright of Texas, and 1983-1984 Society president Phil Record on the steps of the US Capitol in Washington, DC. Beginning in the early 1980's, Society officers made contacting key congressional leaders an important and continuing part of SPJ,SDX freedom of information activities.

public on our side – to have the public know the true meaning of freedom of the press." Farber reviewed his case for the delegates and said, "The press must do a better job in explaining to the public that reporters are not seeking a special privilege for themselves...but are merely trying to inform the people." And Landau issued a call to arms in the FOI battles. "The courts have sent our reporters to jail, held our editors in contempt and fined our publishers....We

have no choice...but to fight back....Perhaps we should start thinking more about fighting on our own turf of public opinion." Aiken added, "We can't stand on simple arguments any more. We have to thrash this thing out....We have to be willing to lobby, to spend our money and energy....We should not be intimidated."

Dessauer, the incoming SPJ,SDX national president, hoped the session with the leaders of the other major, national

104

Robert Lewis served as chairman of the national freedom of information committee from 1978 through 1983 - the years when the Society made FOI its highest program priority and increased its dollar support for FOI from $1,000 to more than $70,000 per year.

journalism organizations would lead to closer ties, especially in the freedom of information area. He saw the possibilities of expanding on the accomplishments of such ventures as the Joint Media Committee and the seventeen-organization effort in the *Stuart v. Nebraska* amicus brief. He told his colleagues that a weakness of individual organizations is that they "react to a problem, not prevent it. We should not merely respond to crises." Hornby called for a task force approach. "A coalition works best if it's addressed to a specific project....We have to be sure we do have a unified voice." From a philosophical standpoint, Gardner and Tretter noted that their organizations had adopted free press resolutions which were the same as those backed by SPJ,SDX and other organizations. And looking at the potential for cooperation, Davis and Shoquist agreed that given economic considerations, a broadly-based organization would be appropriate in addressing common FOI problems. While the speeches and panels

were spread over two days of the convention, the ideas came together to spark a resurgence of the drive to build the Legal Defense Fund and to provide the beginning for four significant new projects: a cooperative effort with the Reporters Committee, which had established the FOI Service Center; a drive toward hiring a First Amendment counsel for the Society; the establishment of The First Amendment Congresses; and the establishment of Freedom of Information Day. What happened in November 1978 was not to disparage the giant strides made in FOI through three decades of dedicated work by SPJ,SDX and other groups. Without that history, no further advancement would have been possible. But taken together, the four projects conceived, if not born, in Birmingham marked the commencement of an even more vital era in, and greater priority for, freedom of information within the Society.

THE LEGAL DEFENSE FUND

Money to finance what its leaders and members hoped to accomplish in fighting for First Amendment rights had always been the Society's major stumbling block. The problem in the early days had been overcome to some extent by capitalizing on the massive reserve of volunteers within the organization and non-members who were proselytized by SPJ,SDX officers and professional staff. Hurst remembers that while no formal legal defense fund existed when he took office in 1962, there were funds earmarked in the Society's operating budget for assisting member and non-member journalists, campus and professional chapters and the commercial and student news media in freedom of information litigation. The amounts were small – $100 to $300 in most cases. With the exception of the years when contributions to such cases as those involving Annette Buchanan, the Nebraska Press Association and the *Stanford Daily*, total allocations for a year rarely exceeded $1,000. "One must remember," Hurst said, "$250 bought a lot of services especially in the light of additional contributed services. If you got to a problem in time and resolved it before it became a full-blown legal case, as we often

First Amendment counsel Bruce W. Sanford joined the Society's freedom of information team February 1, 1981.

did, a small amount of money plus the available expertise was enough. It is easy to overlook the fact that those contributed services by members and others over the years probably amounted to millions of dollars." By the early 1970's, the board noted the significance of the work being done by the Reporters Committee for Freedom of the Press and made annual contributions to its work. The board also made special grants from its operating funds for freedom of information research and cataloging of cases, its most prominent contribution being an annual allocation to the Freedom of Information Center at the University of Missouri.

When the cases of William Farr and Peter Bridge gained national attention in 1972 and chapters, along with individual members, began making contributions to be used in those and other cases, the Society's board of directors, meeting in Dallas November 15, formally established the "Sigma Delta Chi Legal Fund," later to be referred to as the Legal Defense Fund. On a motion by national secretary Ralph Otwell

and seconded by Region Seven director Bill Kong, the board opened the fund with the $1,600 on hand and issued an invitation to chapters and members to add to it. By April 1973, the fund had reached $6,000, much of that coming on the basis of the Farr and Bridge publicity. With dollars on hand and coming in for the Legal Defense Fund, the board was able, for a while, to increase the number of grants, although the amounts remained small. As an example, responding to calls for help on legal cases, in May 1975 the board allocated $732 to participate with RTNDA in an appeal of the NBC "pensions case"; gave $200 to aid the *Northern Star*, a student newspaper at Northern Illinois University, in its effort to obtain compliance by university officials with the state open meetings law; provided $200 to the Greater Miami professional chapter, which was supporting a *Washington Post-Newsweek* petition to change Florida's rules to permit television and still cameras and sound recording devices in courtrooms; voted $200 to aid a Maui, Hawaii, editor in a case involving alleged supression of his publication by local government officials; and gave $200 to the *Texas Observer*, an independent bi-weekly newspaper fighting a $5 million libel action. In November of that year, the board voted grants of $200 each from the Legal Defense Fund to aid the Nebraska, Des Moines and Mid-Carolinas chapters in freedom of information cases and another $200 to assist Dan Hicks, Jr., crusading editor of the *Monroe County Observer*, Madisonville, Tennessee, in his effort to survive attempts to force him out of business. While it was clearly the publicity surrounding the major national FOI cases that caused chapters and members to make contributions, the majority of dollars moving out of the Legal Defense Fund went to assist with relatively obscure cases. Further, while those prominent cases happened irregularly, those small, but important local cases kept coming week after week. The grant of $500 to help in the *Stanford Daily* case in April 1978, brought the Legal Defense Fund down to $600.

It was with this news that the officers went to Birmingham in November hoping to raise some interest among the delegates to

Jack C. Landau (right), who, as director of the Reporters Committee for Freedom of the Press, cooperated with the Society in establishing the FOI Service Center in 1979, received an SDX Distinguished Service Award for Washington correspondence in 1967 from Society president Staley McBrayer and executive officer Russell Hurst. He was named an SDX Fellow in 1978.

the national convention in replenishing the fund. What happened there couldn't have been predicted even by the most optimistic officers. The Thursday, November 16, luncheon featured Farber as the major speaker and the announcement of the outstanding campus and professional chapters for the year. When Ohio University was named the top campus chapter for 1978, its president, Alan Alder, rushed to the podium to receive a certificate and a check for $100. Perhaps inspired by Farber's speech or simply by the established need, Alder returned the $100 – something his or any campus chapter could have used for local activities – saying that it should go to the Legal Defense Fund. Before the thunderous applause from a standing

audience had subsided, Region Six deputy director and Milwaukee *Journal* reporter David Offer saw an opportunity and sent a note to the podium asking that all professional and campus chapters from Wisconsin meet briefly after the luncheon. In that meeting, Offer suggested that those chapters and the individual members follow up on Ohio University's contribution to the Fund and make their own donations. By late afternoon, Offer had a number of checks and some cash in hand and asked for permission to make the Wisconsin presentation during the evening banquet. During the afternoon, Landau and Aiken, along with Akron, Ohio, attorney David Lieberth, sounded the FOI alarm in their panel and the several hundred delegates who

Bruce W. Sanford and Society president-elect Steven R. Dornfeld listen to testimony by Salt Lake City newsman Ted Capener on the federal Freedom of Information Act before a congressional committee, July 15, 1981. Sanford regularly assisted Society officers and FOI committee members prepare statements on key First Amendment issues and often testified before Senate and House committees for the Society.

attended walked away disturbed, if not distressed, at the outlook for freedom of information. That evening, Neuharth's biting address brought the message home again. When it was time for Offer to go to the podium, he put the money in a breadbasket from one of the banquet tables and took the Wisconsin contribution to the microphone. Mentioning the Ohio University contribution and what the Wisconsin delegates had done, he encouraged other chapters and individuals to make their own donations to help build the Legal Defense Fund. "Operation Breadbasket" was under way. Within minutes, table after table sent a representative to the podium each carrying a breadbasket filled with checks and cash contributions of from one to twenty dollars. Offer, along with other persons on the stage and in the crowd, became "cheerleaders" in a pep-rally atmosphere and excitement filled the room as the dollars mounted. By the

time the dinner meeting ended, delegates and their chapters had poured more than $2,000 into the Legal Defense Fund, a figure which would climb to $2,600 by the convention's final session. It was the single largest boost given the fund since it had been established six years earlier.

The enthusiasm for building the fund spilled out of Birmingham, carried by delegates to their home chapters, and thousands of more dollars flowed to the Society's Chicago headquarters. Nearly every regional conference in early 1979 repeated the "Operation Breadbasket" effort. While only between 100 and 200 delegates attended any given regional conference, the dollar amounts grew and grew, each conference challenged by the preceding regional meeting. Region Two raised $339; Region Six, $700. Region Eight director Phil Record, joined by national secretary Howard Graves, preached "commitment and sacrifice" for the Legal Defense Fund at the

Region Eight conference like an evangelist preparing a crowd at a revival to do battle with the Devil, the delegates in Huntsville, Texas, contributed more than $900. Record and Graves took their "preachin' and shoutin' for FOI" to Region Nine in Denver, Colorado, and the result was a $1,300 boost for the fund. By the time the last regional conference was history, "Operation Breadbasket" had raised an additional sum of $4,000.

Back home in the local chapter meetings, the drive had almost as much enthusiasm. Two chapters sold "Warren Burgers." The San Francisco State University campus chapter "barbecued" Supreme Court Chief Justice Warren Burger at a student activities fair and raised $50 selling hamburgers and burn ointment urging students to, "Buy a Warren Burger – Help put the bite back in the First Amendment." Professional chapters turned over profits from newsmaker luncheons and gridiron shows to the fund. The June *Quill* reported that twenty-nine campus chapters and twenty-six professional chapters had made contributions, which, along with a $5,000 donation from Harte-Hanks Newspapers, brought the total to more than $29,000. What had been a $600 Legal Defense Fund balance a year earlier had swelled to more than $30,000 by mid-summer 1979. While the magic of the excitement emanating from the Birmingham convention waned somewhat and "Operation Breadbasket" with it, drives for the Legal Defense Fund continued into the 1980's. Hundreds of individual members contributed each year and chapters made support of the fund an annual project. Special events were scheduled at national conventions nearly every year. A celebrity memorabilia auction at the 1981 convention in Washington, DC raised $4,115 and "The First Amendment Follies," produced at the 1982 Milwaukee convention by Joann Noto, Central Michigan University; Jim Corbett, University of South Carolina; Sharon Applebaum, University of Kansas; and John Allison, California State University at Long Beach, campus representatives on the national board, raised nearly $4,000 for the Legal Defense Fund.

Again, in 1983, chapters and individual members answered the call for the Legal Defense Fund. In three cities – Chicago, Kansas City and Los Angeles – special benefit pre-release showings of the major motion picture, *Under Fire*, netted more than $5,500 for the Legal Defense Fund. Fund chairman Mike Hammer noted in his report to the board in November 1983, that more than $20,000 had been raised since the previous convention, not including a special series of fund raisers at the San Francisco convention which brought in another $2,000 plus.

The sometime "Sigma Delta Chi Legal Fund" of 1972, dependent for its limited resources on occasional small contributions, had become an established and viable part of the Society's freedom of information campaign. While the money kept coming in through the early 1980's, the dollars were, just as quickly, being directed not only toward individual cases as in the past, but into such projects as the FOI Service Center and funding for the Society's First Amendment counsel.

THE FOI SERVICE CENTER

President Goodykoontz had two things on his mind in setting up the Birmingham convention program. One was the deepening concern about freedom of information problems and the lack of resources to fight those battles. The other was the potential connection of national journalism organizations. When Goodykoontz asked Landau, executive director of the Reporters Committee for Freedom of the Press, to participate in the FOI panel, the two concerns seemed to merge. Landau, an attorney and Supreme Court reporter for Newhouse Newspapers, had helped to found the Reporters Committee in 1970 and had struggled for eight years to keep its head above water financially while trying to establish it as a viable force in federal freedom of information matters. He had brought together a prestigious group of reporters determined to fill what they perceived as a major gap in the collection of primary research data on First Amendment issues that could provide the basis for litigation as needed. Generally, the

Reporters Committee was among the first, if not the first, to respond when public and press rights to information were jeopardized anywhere in the nation. Using the legal and journalistic expertise within its board of directors and others associated with the movement, the Committee prepared amicus briefs, filed suits and provided counsel for reporters and editors. The Society's effective role in state and local FOI matters and in some national cases was well-established, but Goodykoontz recognized Landau's committee as "the leader among journalism groups in the 1970's on the national scene, especially in federal cases." He knew, as well, that if any one person had his finger on the pulse of the freedom of information situation at large, it was Landau. Several times during 1978, Region Seven director Ron Willnow suggested to Goodykoontz that the Society be in touch with Landau. Goodykoontz approached Landau about the possibility of a joint Society and Reporters Committee freedom of information projects.

The convention's busy schedule did not allow for the meeting during the day. The only time Goodykoontz could find was 10 pm Friday night following the awards banquet. He invited Landau, Hurst, members of the board of directors and a few national FOI committee members to his suite in the Hyatt Hotel at that hour. More than twenty persons attended, including all of the Society's officers and a majority of the board. Upon his arrival in Birmingham, Landau did not know that he had been nominated or would be elected as a Fellow of Sigma Delta Chi at that convention. The three Fellows of the Society are elected each year by convention delegates to recognize outstanding editorial performance or contributions to the elevation of journalism as a profession. The honor bestowed on him and the Reporters Committee and the enthusiasm generated among the delegates by his FOI panel speech certainly set a positive tone going into that exploratory meeting. The mood in the room was electric. This writer had just been elected to the board of directors and shared the excitement of some present about what might develop when two powerful groups joined forces. Negative electricity was present as

well, as there were others of the Society who believed Landau and the Reporters Committee tended to try to capture the spotlight in any of its joint ventures. They doubted that any measure of cooperation could be effected between the two proud organizations. Landau, alone in representing the Reporters Committee, had some concerns about having his organization subordinated by SPJ,SDX as well.

Goodykoontz asked Dessauer, who would be president the following day, to share in leading the discussions. The questions and answers among the participants centered on what kind of cooperative effort would be possible. Two specific suggestions came out of the meeting. One dealt with the possibility of "sharing" a full-time lawyer who would operate out of the Committee's Washington, DC office, but who would work for SPJ,SDX, giving the Society access to the Committee's extensive files and expertise. The second was a note by Landau that the area of state open records and open meetings laws would be an area in which both organizations could work together and benefit each other. It was well after midnight when Dessauer said he sensed a definite interest among the board members present to pursue the discussion further and in detail, leading toward joining forces in some meaningful way. Landau said he was personally intrigued with the idea but wanted to consult with his executive committee. He agreed, however, to keep in touch with Dessauer and Hurst on a possible connection.

To some extent, Dessauer shared the apprehensions of board members who doubted the two groups could come together. "We didn't want to be swallowed up by the Reporters Committee and, I'm sure, the Reporters Committee didn't want to be swallowed up by us," he said. "But we were frustrated by the turn of events of the time in FOI matters. When our own professional standing and the core of our ideas were being attacked, we felt we really ought to go the extra step to try to do something. We wanted to hire our own attorney, but knew we couldn't afford to do that. A connection between the Society and the Reporters Committee seemed to be a logical alternative and I think most of us left the meeting with a positive feeling."

At the Saturday board meeting following the Birmingham convention, the matter was discussed again with enthusiasm. Region Four director David Lieberth noted that Landau's feeling for the connection apparently had grown since the night before and that he had mentioned the possibility of a seat on the Reporters Committee board for an SPJ,SDX member. Region Six director Steven Dornfeld moved that the board authorize the national officers at their January meeting to hire a full- or part-time lawyer or law or journalism student to do legal research on FOI matters. The officers would be empowered to exercise their judgment on all details after reviewing results of fund-raising efforts and considering future FOI needs. "There may not have been any reference to Landau's organization in the motion," Dornfeld recalls, "but clearly the intent of the motion was to explore some kind of connection with the Reporters' Committee." Region Twelve director Frank Sutherland seconded the motion and it passed unanimously. Sutherland, one of the "young Turks" on the board, remembers asking himself, "What are we here for if not for FOI? I believed The Reporters' Committee would never have had to been formed if SPJ,SDX and other journalistic organizations had met their obligations to freedom of information. Our decision to become involved in 1978, for me, was one developed out of some guilt and I was happy to see this new beginning."

With a mandate from the board in hand, Hurst and Dessauer conducted an exchange of conversations and correspondence with Landau during December, and definite progress was made. The annual January officers' meeting of the Society was scheduled for Washington, DC for the express purpose of meeting with Landau at his offices in the capital city. With his primary work focusing on federal issues, laws and court decisions, Landau and his board hoped the joint effort with the Society of Professional Journalists might help close a major gap which existed in freedom of information research being done by his office – that of cataloging statutes and case

law relating to state open meetings and open records. Although calls came to his staff of attorneys asking for information and advice on the subject, the Reporters Committee either had to spend much time digging up the data needed or had to refer the caller to another agency. So far as he knew, such a library on state FOI problems did not exist anywhere in the country. Communication among the three men centered on general areas of agreement based on the preliminary discussions in Birmingham about a shared attorney-researcher.

Dessauer; Hurst; past president Goodykoontz; president-elect Jean Otto, editor of the Op Ed Page for *The Milwaukee Journal*; secretary Howard Graves, Chief of Bureau for The Associated Press in Portland, Oregon; treasurer Charles Novitz, manager, News Syndication, ABC News, New York; and vice president for campus chapter affairs Bert Bostrom, professor of journalism at Northern Arizona University in Flagstaff, Arizona, gathered in Washington January 20, 1979, meeting first at the Capitol Hilton Hotel with Washington-area FOI committee members to discuss the proposed connection with the Reporters Committee and a financial commitment of $3,000 per year to help the SPJ,SDX FOI committee with its work in secretarial, telephone and mailing costs. Moving to the Reporters Committee offices, the officers discussed a specific proposal from Landau. It concerned adding a research attorney to Landau's staff to begin the project of collecting all state open meetings and public records statutes along with related case law. The attorney would be housed in the Reporters Committee offices and, through a telephone "hot line" there, would serve SPJ,SDX chapters and members, along with national officers and headquarters staff, answering legal queries. The attorney would also spend time providing information and advice to non-Society callers regarding his research and on general FOI problems which found their way to the Reporters Committee. Landau said his best estimate was that the cost for the attorney would be about $25,000 per year for salary and secretarial help, and he asked the Society officers to assume two-thirds of that cost, or about $17,000 per year. In return, Landau proposed, the attorney would spend two-thirds of his time on projects determined by the Society and its committee and one-third of his time on projects for the Reporters Committee. While he was eager to get more than a one-year financial commitment from SPJ,SDX, his own excitement about adding this important phase to his organization's work caused him to agree to take even a one-year plan to his board. "The discussions left all of the officers with a good feeling about the possible connection," Dessauer recalls.

When the Society officers reconvened their meetings at the hotel, there was consensus on moving ahead as quickly as possible. They had been impressed by what they saw as Landau's commitment to accuracy through primary research, what Dessauer called "a first-class way of doing the job." Although Hurst was behind the idea fully, he reported that the Society was already in the throes of probable serious financial problems largely because of a decline in the growth rate of new members and a continuing substantial inflation rate. "If you go ahead with the project, where do you propose to get the money?" he asked. "You've just agreed to allocate $3,000 to our FOI committee and, with the $17,000 for our share of the research attorney, you're talking about $20,000 for this year and perhaps for years to come. May I remind you that the Legal Defense Fund has a total of fewer than $4,000 and there are no provisions in this year's budget for such a program?" The influx of contributions to the Legal Defense Fund following the Birmingham convention had not yet started, nor was there any real indication at that time that it would happen. Bostrom remembers a short, but deafening silence. "But almost immediately there was a sense of confidence among the officers that this project could be pulled off. We couldn't say how, but we knew it could be done." Dessauer put the feeling into words. "Don't worry, Russ," he said. "We'll get the money." If worse came to worse, Dessauer recalls, "I was ready to go to the Society's reserve fund to get the thing started." Otto said she was ready to take on the project on faith. "My feeling was that this was what we ought to be doing," she

said. "If we were going to have an impact on FOI, we couldn't go about it by just waving a flag – we had to have a concrete project and go ahead and do it." She added that the costs of fighting major legal battles after the fact could be much greater and, "We could avoid those big problems if we had proper legal information going in." All of the officers believed the new project would be well received by the membership, which ultimately would have to pay the bills. Graves said, "It would mean the Society is interested in the individual reporter rather than just in the big national issues. Providing journalists with a qualified attorney hired by the Society to whom they could take their questions and problems on either state or federal First Amendment law would be a tremendous step forward." Newly-elected treasurer Novitz said he had no doubt that the project was worth doing and "we would find a way to make it happen." With that, the officers voted unanimously to support a one-year agreement with the Reporters Committee, in which SPJ,SDX would pay two-thirds of the cost, up to $17,000, of hiring an attorney-researcher.

In a February 7, 1979, letter to the national board apprising it of the officers' action, Dessauer reported that he had received a letter from Landau stating that his executive committee was "very excited about the project" and had approved it. Dessauer told the members through the March *Quill* that they would have an attorney who would be available to advise them on FOI problems. "We regard this as a major and vital step in strengthening our resources in this period of heavy litigation for the press. The services such a lawyer can provide our membership and chapters on a daily basis will be of inestimable value." Meanwhile, Landau was busy searching for an attorney to fill the position. He recommended Peter C. Lovenheim, 26, a Cornell Law School graduate who had received his undergraduate degree, summa cum laude, in journalism and political science at Boston University and had been a reporter for The Associated Press in that city. When the board met in Denver April 27 to consider the hiring of Lovenheim, the Legal Defense

Fund's account had zoomed past the $20,000 mark, assuring that money was available for a one-year program. FOI vice chairman Lewis reported that he had interviewed Lovenheim for the Society and recommended his employment. Sutherland and Region Eight director Phil Record were worried about the financing. "We were putting a lot of faith in the membership that they would come through with dollars in support of this effort," Record recalls. "They had demonstrated they were worthy of that faith by their actions in Birmingham and thereafter in contributing to the Legal Defense Fund and it was worth the risk involved." Following a discussion of concern over the need to enumerate the specifics of the attorney's duties and the desire of some board members to be assured that the Society would not be pouring dollars into the Reporters Committee coffers without proper credit to the Society, a motion to effect the agreement by hiring Lovenheim, effective May 1, 1979, was adopted with one abstention.

Lovenheim spent more than half of his time in the first six months on the job collecting copies of state and federal freedom of information acts and related data needed to establish the center as a viable resource. Landau provided the help of law students working at the Reporters Committee offices for four months to help gather the materials and when he reported to the board in November 1979 at the New York City convention, he wrote, "In our state files, we have complete texts of all forty-nine state open records acts, open meetings acts and many privacy statutes. These are supplemented by summaries, indices, or actual copies of state attorney general opinions and court decisions interpreting these laws. All of this material is catalogued in a master file-book indicating what material is on hand from each state. The file-book is updated as soon as new documents are received. As a result, the FOI project now has as complete a library of state freedom of information materials as any public interest group doing work in this field." In addition, Lovenheim and the Reporters Committee law students began to write complete analyses of open record laws

in several states – a project which, it was discovered took much more time than anticipated after several were completed, and was given a low priority in future years – and gathered primary documents on the federal Freedom of Information Act and related case law. Even while Lovenheim and the law students were gathering information, the telephone calls and letters had begun to come in. More than one hundred calls and letters were received from thirty states, the District of Columbia and the Virgin Islands during the first six months of the experiment. But by November 1979, the FOI Service Center was a operative project. Announcements listing the services available and the telephone number to call were on their way to SPJ,SDX chapters and to newsrooms across the nation. The board's pleasure with the work completed was expressed in its unanimous consent to continue to fund the joint project at Landau's request through December 1980.

Lovenheim extended the original services of the FOI Service Center in the next year, writing a special booklet, "How to Use the Federal FOI Act." The Center published 10,000 copies of the booklet, making it available at no cost to SPJ,SDX convention delegates and giving it wide distribution across the nation. He also published a federal legislative FOI update in May and November 1980, including a summary of bills enacted or pending before the House and Senate; made public appearances before SPJ,SDX chapters and civic organizations; testified before congressional committees against proposed modifications in federal freedom of information laws; and worked with the Society's FOI chairman, Bob Lewis in helping to prepare further testimony, letters to Congressmen and other government officials, and media alerts on urgent problems to be sent to chapters and news organizations expressing the need to become involved in lobbying efforts. When Landau and Lovenheim reported to the SPJ,SDX board in November 1980 in Columbus, Ohio, they said the number of calls and letters from journalists had grown to more than 700 for the year – with half of them reportedly coming from SPJ,SDX members – assuring the board that the "hot line" was being used regularly. Their report stated, "...[T]he first eighteen months' operation of this project has more than justified the prediction of the need for an FOI Service Center. We have found over and over again that reporters don't even know how to read their own state acts, much less how to use them; that all too often they are intimidated by government officials who clearly are withholding information; that government had devised a whole series of techniques – including delays and high research and reproduction fees – to discourage the press from using the acts; and that the reporters tend to feel helpless and hopeless when faced with these problems...[T]he frequent use of this Service Center already should justify the continuation of this project on a long-term basis as envisioned originally when it was established as a joint venture. It is clearly a successful effort so far to put some life into the state FOI acts and to provide meaningful and prompt research to journalists who wish to use the state and federal acts." Landau announced at the meeting that Lovenheim had decided to leave the Center to pursue his career further in communications law and that Ms. Tonda Rush, an attorney who had worked at the Reporters Committee for about a year, was being recommended to replace Lovenheim. Rush, 29, who had journalism and law degrees from the University of Kansas and had been a reporter for the Lawrence, Kansas *Journal-World* for five years, was confirmed unanimously by the board.

In the next three years, Rush continued the work Lovenheim had begun, but with the wide publicity the Center was receiving in print and by word of mouth, the work load centered primarily on answering "hot line" calls and letters requesting information and advice. By mid-1983, calls and letters were coming in at the rate of one hundred per month and increasing, Rush said. The state FOI files were being updated regularly and "The Library," as Rush called it, "is, without doubt, the most complete, current source of information on laws, changes in laws, attorney general and court decisions on those statutes." The Lovenheim booklet on using the federal FOI Act turned out to be

one of the most popular and widely distributed publications of the FOI Center and was updated by Rush in 1983. "We thought the 10,000 copies would last a long time, but since 1980, we've sent out more than 30,000 booklets, making it the most successful single venture the Center has tried and contributing to its total success," she said. Rush's title at the Center was changed formally from research attorney to director of the Center in November 1982. She resigned in October 1983 to become a legislative aide with the American Newspaper Publishers Association.

Landau's hope for an extended commitment from the Society for FOI Service Center funding did not receive SPJ,SDX board approval. Instead, the board, still influenced by nagging conflicts with Landau over the question of for whom the director was working and to whom the FOI Service Center "belonged," voted annually for one-year extensions through December 1983. With other freedom of information projects well underway – including the hiring of its own First Amendment Counsel – the board of directors, in November 1983, voted to accept Landau's suggestion for a three-year phase-out of the Society's direct participation in funding the Service Center. The board agreed to provide $10,000 toward the Center's operation through June 1984, and to provide $5,000 for each of the next two years – 1985 and 1986.

HIRING BRUCE SANFORD

"The coincidence of the Landau connection and our FOI chairman, Bob Lewis, appointed by Dessauer, in Washington, DC made us a lot more knowledgeable about where the problems were and where we could have an impact," Otto said. "Out of that, it was almost natural to take the extra step of getting our own attorney." But retaining legal counsel specifically for the Society was not a new idea. Other journalism organizations had brought First Amendment attorneys within their staff organizations many years earlier and SPJ,SDX had entertained the idea since the 1950's, only to be hamstrung by limited budgets.

Hurst recalls, "I felt the need for many years of having an able, experienced FOI counsel immediately accessible anytime. Headquarters regularly received calls from members asking to help extinguish legal brush fires." Although the luxury of having an attorney on board was not possible then, he said, "We were fortunate to have had the contributed services of newspaper, broadcast and press association attorneys all over the country who stepped in when we were in a tough spot and provided legal advice, prepared briefs and assisted chapters, individual members and the national organization in resolving FOI problems – services which amounted to hundreds of thousands of dollars over the years in the cause of press freedom." Society presidents Koop, Spangler, White and McBrayer, whose terms coincided with most of the battles with the American Bar Association in the 1960's, knew that legal counsel would have been of tremendous help. White said, "We were journalists talking to lawyers and judges and while we did the best we could, as it turned out what we needed was a lawyer to be able to communicate effectively with those lawyers." Presidents Ralph Otwell and Bob Chandler were strong supporters for the idea in the early 1970's. The subject was discussed and dropped for fiscal reasons year after year until Otwell, as national president, tried to make it high priority in 1974, and Goodykoontz brought the matter to the board's attention again a year later at its Philadelphia meeting. He suggested that a study of the Society's resources needed to be made, perhaps toward the hiring of an attorney to deal with FOI problems. President Small said a good general counsel could be very expensive, but that perhaps an attorney with interest in the First Amendment would agree to work for the Society if SPJ,SDX covered out-of-pocket expenses. Hurst and president-elect Richard Leonard went to Washington in 1976 to discuss with Landau the possibilities of hiring legal counsel, but, again, according to Leonard, "Finances were the big stumbling block." Given impetus from regional directors Willnow and Dornfeld, Goodykoontz, upon becoming national president in 1977-1978, reinstituted the call

for retaining legal counsel, making it an agenda item to be discussed in Birmingham. That meeting, of course, led directly to the Reporters Committee connection the following year, the success of which provided further impetus for such a project.

When Jean Otto became president in 1979, she reappointed Lewis chairman of the Society's FOI committee. Lewis, Washington correspondent for Newhouse Newspapers, had been the Society's FOI vice chairman in the capital for four years, testifying before congressional committees and frustrated by times having to represent SPJ,SDX without the aid of legal counsel. On March 16, 1980, in Williamsburg, Virginia, he and Dornfeld, a former FOI committee member and now national treasurer, discussed the need for a Society attorney and the fact that perhaps this was the time to go back to the board with the idea, especially since the Legal Defense Fund seemed to be healthy. Dornfeld urged Lewis to prepare a memo for board consideration. The result was a 300-word letter to president Otto which spelled out the needs as he saw them. He wrote:

A recent experience illustrates the handicap the freedom of information committee operates under because we don't have our own lawyer.

After testifying before the Senate Intelligence Committee on the Central Intelligence Agency charter, I received a call from Rep. Les Aspin's aide on the House Intelligence Committee. He had read about SPJ's concerns with the [U.S. Supreme Court's] *Snepp* decision [upholding pre-publication clearance contracts for CIA employees] and wanted to discuss the possible remedies we had mentioned....This was a chance for SPJ,SDX to get some input in the legislative process. To do so, however, we needed a lawyer. I ended up calling Dick Schmidt, general counsel of ASNE, and Dick Kleeman of the Association of American Publishers, and eventually a meeting was set up with Aspin's people. That, in turn, led to another hearing confined to the Snepp situation.

In my opinion, it is unfortunate

that an organization with our resources and reputation must ask other groups for free legal assistance. We probably are in a position to attract the best media lawyer available. We should be providing others, including our chapters and members, with legal aid, not vice versa.

In his letter, Lewis outlined possible responsibilities for a general counsel including: to initiate legislation, prepare amicus briefs, monitor and analyze federal legislation, develop SPJ,SDX positions on legislation, help prepare testimony on such legislation, represent the Society on the Joint Media Committee and be available to answer questions of officers, chapters and members on legal questions. In a separate note to Dornfeld, Lewis mentioned Schmidt as a possibility, saying he "would be great but I have questions about how he would wear two hats, SPJ and ASNE." He added, "Schmidt says he has talked to the ASNE people and they would be agreeable if he worked something out with SPJ." Dornfeld and Lewis went to the Region Two conference that spring and obtained adoption of a resolution to the national board urging the hiring of a general counsel.

Upon receiving the documents from Lewis and the Region Two delegates, the board, meeting in Seattle May 9, 1980, instructed the Society's officers to explore how it could finance a full-time attorney and to move ahead if possible. President Otto called together the officers, including Dessauer, Graves, Novitz, Dornfeld and Bostrom along with executive officer Hurst, in Milwaukee, Wisconsin, May 30 through June 2 to review the budget for fiscal 1981 and see if dollars for an attorney could be found within the operations budget rather than looking to the Legal Defense Fund. The budget appeared to be tight at best and the officers were determined that the Society would not operate in the red the next year. But rather than dumping the idea of hiring legal counsel, the officers reset a great many Society budget priorities and cut what they believed were unnecessary or less-important items in the budget for fiscal 1980-1981. In so doing, the officers allocated $7,500 for February through July 1981 to pay a basic

fee for a legal counsel. Within a month, Otto named a search committee made up of Lewis, Goodykoontz, Novitz and Region One director James Plante to talk to attorneys in Washington, DC, where the board believed the legal counsel should be located. The search committee was limited, however, to offering a $15,000 annual retainer. While one candidate for the job noted that $15,000 was what a law firm might collect for filing a routine annual report with the FCC, Lewis said, "We had some signs that law firms would consider SPJ a good client and be interested in taking us on on a part *pro bono publico* basis." The position was advertised by word of mouth in the Washington legal community and six candidates were interviewed by Lewis, Goodykoontz and Novitz September 19, 1980. The committee's unanimous recommendation was Bruce W. Sanford, a former *Wall Street Journal* reporter who had represented United Press International and Scripps Howard Broadcasting in First Amendment cases during his eleven years of experience with free press issues. Novitz was impressed with Sanford because of his media work and because he was aware of the Society and its goals. "But also because the nature of the clients at Baker and Hostetler meant that he would be 'our' legal counsel. They did not represent another journalism organization," he said. The committee wrote, "He demonstrated a good grasp of SPJ,SDX's needs and a willingness to give more time to the Society than the retainer, on its face, justifies." Sanford, 35, a member of the legal firm of Baker and Hostetler and who had just moved from that company's Cleveland office to its offices in Washington, DC, was a *cum laude* graduate of Hamilton College with a Juris Doctor degree from New York University's School of Law. He was the author of a best-selling handbook, *Synopsis of the Law of Libel and Right of Privacy*, written in non-legalese and used in newsrooms across the country; a frequent contributor to *The Columbia Journalism Review*; and an instructor at the American Press Institute. Sanford had been active in working with the ASNE and ANPA freedom of information committees, but had not been involved with any SPJ,SDX First

Amendment cases. He had taken part in the First Amendment Congresses in 1980 and was impressed with the Society's leadership in getting that organization off the ground. "I had the distinct impression that something new was going on in the Society of Professional Journalists," he said. He recalled that he thought his inexperience in legislative matters was a plus for him. "I think that some people believed that my lack of a track record on Capitol Hill was a virtue in that I was not identified there as representing the bottle-cap industry or the trucking or oil industries."

Lewis took his committee's recommendation to the board November 19, 1980, in Columbus, Ohio. where Sanford made an informal presentation of how he viewed the best possible role for a First Amendment counsel to the Society. He divided the total role into three subcategories: general representation, legislative affairs and judicial affairs. Under general representation, he suggested the counsel could advise the board and freedom of information committee, as requested, on First Amendment and other matters; assist in developing and promoting its own distinct voice in First Amendment matters; enhance public recognition of the aims and achievements of the Society in First Amendment matters and counsel local chapters, as needed, on First Amendment and other legal matters including referrals to competent local counsel. In the legislative area, he suggested counsel could develop and communicate distinct Society positons on proposed legislation, prepare and deliver testimony before Congress, work with congressional staff and representatives of other press groups to influence certain legislation, mobilize a government relations "strike force" to organize the mechanics for influential members to write letters and telephone congressmen at crucial stages in the legislative process, and develop meetings between SPJ,SDX members and key Congressional leaders. On the judicial front, he said counsel could report to the membership on the practical effects for working journalists of court decisions, work with local chapters on "test case" litigation, and prepare *amicus curiae* briefs in cases of

particular significance to the Society. Sanford told the board it would be a privilege for him to work for the Society and accept the challenges which would lie before him as its First Amendment counsel. He said he understood the financial limitations of the Society and found the amount authorized as a retainer acceptable.

Following brief discussion on the search committee's finding, Region Five director Casey Bukro moved that the board accept the committee's recommendation and retain Sanford, effective February 1, 1981, when the first $7,500 payment would become available. Willnow seconded and the motion was passed with one dissenting vote and one abstention. Dornfeld especially was pleased. "Thinking back on my six years on the board as a regional director and as an advocate for freedom of information programs in the Society, I was happy. This had to be one of the few major actions by the board on FOI matters during that time," he said. "In modern times, Bob Lewis deserves a great deal of the credit for his work in retaining legal counsel and giving the Society more visibility on freedom of information issues." After thirty-four years of active participation in the freedom of information arena, the Society of Professional Journalists, Sigma Delta Chi. had its own First Amendment counsel.

SANFORD'S FAST START

While his contract did not take effect for more than two months, Sanford was on the job immediately. He recalls, "The world didn't stop until February 1. One of the things that happened in December and January was the Uniform Information Practices Code, which reared its ugly head in a very menacing way, and none of the professional press organizations were doing very much about it." The American Bar Association was about to give its seal of approval to the code, which came down heavily on the side of privacy regarding the release of information which would otherwise be available to the public and press. If the ABA House of Delegates were to approve the code at its winter meeting in February 1981 in Houston, Sanford said, "It would go shooting out as a model code to state legislatures, where with ABA approval uniform codes tend to go gliding through." Sanford decided that although there was little time to work on building a case, efforts to move the code forward had to be stopped. Along with others from his law firm and with Lewis's help, Sanford organized a drive among national press organizations to try to convince the ABA to delay adoption or reject the code completely. Research was done and Sanford prepared a hard-hitting letter to be signed by representatives of as many press associations as possible and sent to the president and board of governors of the American Bar Association.

"I'm still proud of that letter," Sanford said. "It didn't pull any punches. In fact it was so strong that a couple of press organizations didn't want to sign it. They wanted to send their own one-paragraph letter in which they would say, "We agree with everything they say, basically...,' but they didn't want their names on the letter itself because we were being so vehement at certain points." The letter, dated February 4, 1981, and signed by Sanford for the Society and by Erwin G. Krasnow, general counsel for the National Association of Broadcasters, and Arthur B. Sackler, general counsel for the National Newspaper Association, stated the case clearly:

A description of the Code's general deficiencies...should elucidate our conviction that the Code in its present form is nothing less than a badly conceived, blunt instrument for state and local governments to use in obstructing several decades of progress toward insuring that citizens receive the information to which they are entitled. Unlike the Federal Freedom of Information Act...and many derivative statutes passed by at least twenty-five states, the Code elevates vague notions of individual privacy above the public's interest in unfettered access to information kept at taxpayers' expense. Indeed, the Code's section on and exemption for privacy places the burden of proof on those, including the press, who seek access to government documents. Thus, the Code flatly reverses the presumption, contained in

the federal statute and the majority of state laws, that government cannot withhold information absent explicit statutory authorization....In other ways, the Code provides government officials with enlarged opportunities to conceal embarrassing information from the public view....[I]t authorizes the decision for secrecy to be made by a potentially self-interested bureaucracy rather than by the legislative branch after public debate on explicit and narrow exemptions....[I]t elevates the government bureaucrat to the position of censor, providing him with the means to prevent the public from scrutinizing his performance and that of his agency.

Sanford had to leave for China just before the ABA meeting, but before he left he arranged for the mechanics of supplying copies of the joint letter to the press representatives covering a briefing in Houston on the position of the signatories and to get copies to the members of the ABA board of governors before its general session. He and his colleagues also arranged for four respected ABA "insiders" to speak to the issue on the floor of the meeting if needed. In a personal note to Lewis upon completing the job, Sanford wrote, "All this has consumed an incredible amount of our time, but we hope that the effort will be successful at stopping the Uniform Code in its tracks." It was. The House of Delegates pigeonholed the Code and it did not surface again. Sanford believes there were two major factors which made the ABA withhold approval. "First and foremost was the strength of our argument that the Code was ill-conceived and needed further study and was very, very controversial. But nobody had said that to them. Nobody had said this is an awful, awful Code, it is badly structured. You don't create this kind of hybrid where you take two bodies of constitutional law and try to balance and push them together. You just don't do that." Secondly, he said, "I made a great many phone calls to a lot of people in the ABA prior to that meeting and asked them to speak to board of governors members." Lewis agreed on both counts. "Dick Schmidt had been keeping us aware of this potential problem with the Code but I was pretty much leaving it in his hands. The next thing I know, here it is about to be adopted by the ABA. SPJ wouldn't or couldn't have done anything about it on its own. It's a perfect example of why we needed a First Amendment counsel."

It is worth noting here the stark contrast between the valiant but fruitless efforts of Koop and his colleagues before that same body in 1967 and 1968 when the Reardon Report was adopted and the words of Society president Bob White, "...[W]hat we needed was a lawyer talking to those lawyers..." Graves, who had become president in Columbus, agreed with Lewis. "If we hadn't had a First Amendment attorney, we never would have become involved in that issue. Even if we had, we would not have been as effective. Sanford couldn't have done it alone either in all likelihood. It was a cooperative effort, an effective combination. He provided the legal expertise and we provided the name of the organization and the numbers of members nationwide. It was a good marriage." Sanford knew what to do and how to do it. "I just instinctively know how and what I can say to judges and other lawyers that will not tune me out, so they won't start talking emotionally or irrationally about the irresponsible press," he said. His action turned back a tide, sweeping toward an almost sure major setback for the public and press, with two months of demanding and precise work and a couple of carefully-worded letters. And all of this before he received a dime from his new client. The Society of Professional Journalists was out front again on the national FOI scene.

Upon beginning his formal arrangement with SPJ, Sanford believed that the Society had the best idea of what it wanted and what the level of activity was going to be. "It became apparent very quickly, however, that the level of activity was much higher than anyone had originally anticipated and it wasn't going to slow down," he said. As the tri-partite FOI effort in cooperation with Sanford began, Sanford's effectiveness was immediately apparent. On the legislative scene, "Bruce greatly strengthened our ability to analyze and draft statements to deliver to Congressional committee hearings," Lewis said. "For those of us who are accredited to cover those hearings, we cannot lobby, and Bruce was able take on that duty and organize others around the nation to call congressmen at certain critical points, give SPJ's position and and ask for their support." In just one year, Sanford was able to capitalize on the existing SPJ freedom of information network and establish an increasingly elaborate and effective grassroots lobbying organization. "There are some incredibly effective persuaders, such as Howard Graves, in the Society," Sanford said. "With their personal connections with various members on The Hill, we could get things done." Graves made three trips to Washington in early 1981 and credited Sanford with setting up meetings with important people in the Congress and backgrounding him on the issues to make him, as president of the Society, an effective spokesman. Using what Graves called Sanford's "diplomatic and tactful manner," the new general counsel was able as well to provide advice on what bills were worth fighting for or against and what tactics would work with members of Congress. "Sanford was aggressive, alert, and saw areas in which we could work," Graves said. Of equal import, "He complemented the work of the FOI committee and, likewise, Lewis was very supportive of Sanford."

The very fact that Sanford and Lewis gave a new level of importance to individual Society members, as a network of monitors on state and federal FOI problems, made that network even stronger. When issues developed that would have national significance, local members were kept informed through a monthly FOI column in *The Quill*, special mailings and alerts; through a monthly bulletin called *The Washington Report*; and through an expanded national FOI report. With a major financial assist from The Gannett Company, the FOI committee's report took on a new look in 1981, with illustrations and individual stories on almost each federal and state issue written by members of the network. Further, copies of the eighty-two-page 1982 report and the fifty-two-page 1983 report were mailed to all professional members of the Society and widely distributed in Washington, DC and in state capitals across the nation. In addition to Gannett's financial contribution toward publication of the reports, Gannett News Service personnel in Washington actually wrote many of the stories and did the layout for the tabloid newspaper. Kilgore FOI intern Sharon Appelbaum assisted with that task as well in 1983.

Sanford made the first of a series of major addresses before large groups of civic leaders, as well as separate talks with local press groups in San Diego, California, and Portland, Oregon, within months of the beginning of his work for the Society. "You have to go to work and get something accomplished and then you have to tell people what you have done," Sanford said.

Early in 1981, at Lewis's suggestion, the FOI committee broadened its scope into international affairs. Liz Schevtchuk, of the National Catholic News Service in Washington, DC, and one of four deputy committee chairs, drafted letters to the governments of South Africa, Haiti, Korea and the Peoples Republic of China along with nations in Central and South America, protesting sanctions against reporters. Working with Dr. Barbara Wolter Hartung, assistant professor of journalism at San Diego State University, Schevtchuk contacted the U.S. State Department, and chairs of Senate and House committees regarding matters involving foreign journalists. In addition, Schevtchuk, prepared the Society's position paper in response to the United Nation's UNESCO-sponsored "New World Information Order." The proposals included in the study of the "New World Information Order" included plans to license journalists; to tie officially press freedom and rights of journalists to so-called "responsibilities" in reporting; to establish special training for journalists which the Society said, could be subverted by some repressive regimes into indoctrination or detention of journalists; and to redress "current imbalances and inequities" through the NWIO instead of through news organizations and governments of UNESCO. Presented at a special

conference in Taillores, France, in May 1981, the SPJ,SDX paper cautioned: "It is essential that all proposals, no matter how well-intentioned, be carefully scrutinized for opportunities for abuse by those who place less value on a free press. The focus of the proposals must move away from regulation and toward freedom and independence for journalists and media organizations."

In the judicial arena, Sanford believed it was important to take positions that would be appealing and persuasive with the judge in a particular case or the judiciary in general. "What we wanted to do was to be a forceful and effective voice, but thoughtful, modulated – but not necessarily moderate – and measured in our approach to preparing amicus briefs." SPJ,SDX had, for many years, joined others signing their briefs, what Lewis called "taking from the plate of the other organizations," partially because of financial considerations. Sanford said, however, "If you are going to be taken seriously, you've got to be part of the leadership," meaning that the Society had to be willing to pay for such briefs rather than allowing others to pay and simply signing on. In the only two FOI cases in the Supreme Court in 1982, *The Washington Post v. The Department of State* and *FBI v. Abramson*, Sanford wrote the *amicus* briefs on behalf of the Society of Professional Journalists, Sigma Delta Chi, which was joined by other press organizations, reversing the former practice.

By early 1983, the Society had had an important impact in a number of FOI and press freedom cases during Sanford's two-year tenure and because of his work with the officers, Lewis and the FOI Committee. On the Agents Identity Bill, pushed by the Central Intelligence Agency, which made it a crime to publish the names of CIA agents even of those agents' names appeared in the public record, the Society played a part in getting the bill modified to the point where "it doesn't have as great a threat to press coverage as it would have in its original form," Lewis said. Dornfeld added, "For some reason, other press groups had chosen not to deal with that bill. We were literally alone. Some of them had economic baggage to carry and have concerns other than freedom of information. Our only interest has been in FOI. We haven't had to worry about cable television, about postal rates and the like. We have concentrated on First Amendment issues and we're unique in that respect."

Sanford and Lewis organized a major campaign to modify the bill, including an attempt to change the language requiring the government to prove that reporters had a "specific intent" to do damage by printing the name of a CIA agent instead of the "reason to believe" language in the CIA-sponsored bill. The 1981 national SPJ convention was in Washington when the bill was before a Senate committee and Sanford mobilized delegates to talk to key senators, attempting to convince them of the the need for the Society's proposed language. "We almost won that one in the Senate," Sanford said. "It was very, very close. The CIA had to send its former director and then the Vice President of the United States, George Bush, to lobby and twist some arms. No one can compete with that kind of clout on a bill like that." he said. Although the Agents Identity Bill passed the Congress with the "reason to believe" language, and the defeat was an agonizing one for Sanford, he said, "We certainly did snatch out of the jaws of that defeat a victory in the form of the House Committee Report which stated the bill did not apply to working journalists." Of equal import, he said, was "the effort itself of getting Society members involved in direct action with members of Congress. It galvanized the Society's lobbying effort and served as a prelude to our fight over the Federal Freedom of Information Act, which, in many ways was even more important."

The Reagan Administration had been trying for some time to modify substantially and to weaken the FOI Act. It had attempted to exclude the CIA, the FBI and parts of the business community from provisions in the act. "We managed in 1982, with other press groups, to stop it when the Reagan Administration had more support in Congress than it did after the 1982 elections," Lewis said. Sanford, who had arranged for SPJ officers to testify on the Act, said in 1983, "It was significant that we beat the business community in

1982, that we beat the FBI and that the CIA was sufficiently impressed with our show of force over the Agents Identity Bill that they did not push the national security exemption and in 1983, watered down what they asked for in S.1324." Lewis added, "I think we're in a much better shape in Congress on the FOI Act than we were in 1982 having picked up allies in both the House and the Senate." In his report to the 1983 convention in San Francisco, Sanford called the weakened version, "little more than a bill to alleviate the unique and especially cumbersome administrative burden of FOIA compliance at the CIA." He and 1984 Society FOI chairman Tony Mauro, however, indicated they would still oppose certain sections of the bill. In addition, the committee, in conjunction with several other journalism organizations, organized a 1983 nation-wide petition drive seeking grass-roots' support for the defeat of attempts to weaken FOIA.

Lewis testified April 21, 1983, before a Senate Judiciary subcommittee chaired by Sen. Orrin G. Hatch, the author of one of two sets of amendments before Congress that session. Lewis urged Congress to fine-tune the Act to make it more effective in providing the American people with information about its government and asked that expanded exemptions be made only with "broad evidence of overwhelming persuasiveness – not with statistical nonsense, myth-making or hyperbole." Sanford, meanwhile, did a complete analysis for the SPJ officers and board on the Hatch amendments (S.774) and an alternative bill (S.1034), sponsored by Sen. Patrick J. Leahy, outlining the Society's position. A vote on the Hatch amendments was stalled late in 1983 with the help of key senators. The Society's representatives were scheduled to testify further against the bill in the spring of 1984.

Sanford and Lewis took steps as well in 1983 and 1984 to try to shortstop an attempt by the Reagan administration to control the flow of sensitive information – the President's National Security Directive. Sanford told the San Francisco convention, "The directive requires all government officials who have access to special intelligence information – about 120,000

persons – to submit to the government for pre-publication review, anything they write or want to say about their experience with government. The directive would prohibit, obviously, high officials of one administration from criticizing the foreign policies of a succeeding administration without first submitting their criticisms to their successors for clearance. This absurd situation would deny the public from the views of former officials and the lessons of their experience in government."
Representing the Society, Sanford and CBS News journalist Bob Schieffer testified in late October before a House committee noting the grave consequences – including Sen. Charles Mathias' warning that the directive would impose a "virtual vow of silence" for life on government employees – if it were allowed to become effective. SPJ,SDX continued to work against the directive during early 1984 and, on February 15, won what 1982-1983 president Steve Dornfeld called "a significant victory," when the Reagan administration announced it was withdrawing the two most objectional parts of the directive – requiring government employees to seek prior approval for publication or speeches regarding their government service and the provision requiring lie detector tests to check for sources of leaks of classified government information.

Dornfeld had attacked another of President Reagan's administrative orders on October 25, 1983 – refusal to allow full press coverage of the United State's invasion of Grenada, a small island in the South Caribbean allegedly being made a client-state for Cuba and the Soviet Union. For three days following the invasion, the United States government imposed a complete news blackout, denying Americans first-hand reporting from Grenada and forcing them to rely on government handouts and Radio Havana for news. Not until the sixth day, was the press allowed to cover Grenada in any way resembling coverage of past American warfare. In a letter to the President, Dornfeld wrote, "Both the unprecedented news blackout of an announced military action and the subsequent orchestration of limited press coverage of the invasion deprive the American people of much-needed information about crucial steps taken by their government. While we realize there may be a need for restrictions on press access in times of combat, the blackout instituted by your administration is an unneeded overreaction that runs counter to our American traditions of an informed citizenry." Calling for a adoption of a resolution by delegates to the 1983 convention condemning the news blackout – it passed unanimously – Sanford said, "What you must realize is that the censorship during the episode in Grenada is not an isolated event. To the contrary, it is part of a pattern of activities that have given the Reagan administration, after three years in office, easily the worst record of any modern presidency on the issue of openness in government. The Reagan presidency is an administration hell-bent on secrecy." Sanford said that at the urging of the Society and other press organizations, Congress was likely to listen to press concerns in the future. "But," Sanford added, "the threats to open government will not evaporate, not so long as the White House treats information as poison."

In addition to providing the legal expertise on specific cases as they evolved, Sanford helped the Society to develop what was, perhaps, a new philosophy regarding involvement in freedom of information cases. Discussing what some called the "erosion of press rights in the 1970's and 1980's, Sanford said, "Only the alarmists and the knee-jerk hysterics talk about erosion of press rights. It's a very slippery and non-meaningful phrase." While saying that libel law is no longer as favorable to the news media as it was in the late 1960's, nonetheless he pointed to advances in the area of access. "Press rights are expanding in what some judges would call an alarming rate. Look at the *Richmond Newspapers* decision. Where was that First Amendment right before the Court's ruling existed? Look at what Justice Stevens calls, '...the First Amendment right of access to important information about government.' That gives you a constitutional right to police blotter information if you carry it all the way down. I think you have to analyze each area and say here's a threat to First Amendment freedoms and here's an area where the courts and legislatures are showing a great sensitivity toward adapting First Amendment freedoms to twentieth century phenomena." He warned that for the Society or any press group to assume a posture over application of First Amendment freedoms to the emerging forms of technology and the new forms of electronic media would be dangerous. "If we posture in that area, the public is going to tune us out – the public including the courts and congressmen. They are just going to think, 'Oh, those guys, they want all they can get their hands on all the time. They want it whether it's the name of a rape victim or anything else. They just want to know everything and they're not going to get it.' It is not a time to posture, it is a time to be thoughtful. That firm conviction on my part is what forms the backdrop for a lot of my advice to the Society."

Sanford's reflective approach and continuing, aggressive work on libel cases, federal legislation and problems with the judiciary, and his publication of "position papers" for SPJ,SDX, impressed the Society's leaders with each succeeding month from February 1981. It was obvious soon thereafter, however, to Lewis and the officers that the $15,000 retainer was far too little to cover the growing volume of work Sanford was doing. In preparing the 1981-1982 Society budget, the officers recommended to the board that the retainer for Sanford be increased to $30,000 per year, with an additional $5,000 to be set aside for expenses in preparing briefs and other costs. When the board approved the higher amount, it was noted that in just three years the Society had made a significant, almost unbelievable new financial commitment to freedom of information. Figures from 1978 showed SPJ,SDX had budgeted a total of less than $1,000, including Legal Defense Fund contributions, for freedom of information. In 1981-1982, with a $19,000 agreement for the FOI Service Center, the $35,000 amount designated for First Amendment counsel, $3,000 for the freedom of information committee, and other contributions, the total commitment from the budget and the Legal Defense Fund, had surpassed $60,000.

The dollars allocated for Sanford's services were considered to be well spent by the Society's leadership. "For the first time," Dornfeld said, "we have been able to produce really polished, well-researched testimony to present before congressional committees and forcefully speak out on issues rather than limping along behind another press group echoing what they've had to say." Otto added, "Sanford's value can not be overestimated. Because he has kept officers and board members informed of what legislation is coming up and has helped us to understand the issues, it has been possible for board members to talk to chapters with a clear concept of what has been going on in Congress, the courts and the regulatory agencies." The image of The Society of Professional Journalists, Sigma Delta Chi, had improved as well, both with other press organizations and with the public. While Sanford had a great deal to do with that, another area which helped as well was the organization of The First Amendment Congresses, a project in which Otto had a leading role.

THE FIRST AMENDMENT CONGRESS

Six months before the Birmingham convention in 1978, Goodykoontz had suggested to *Quill* editor Charles Long that it might be a valuable project for the magazine to investigate the number and type of journalism organizations in the country. Intrigued by the idea, Long asked Warren K. Agee, at the University of Georgia, to work on the endeavor, and the result was a special issue of *The Quill* in November 1978 on "The Journalism Organization." Agee's research turned up 119 organizations which wholly or in part involved news-editorial journalism and covered thirteen pages in the magazine.

Goodykoontz followed with his panel on "Future Directions for Professional Journalism Orgnizations" in Birmingham, to which he attracted the leadership of the most well-known and respected national journalism groups. Dessauer represented the Society on the panel, which drew only a very small assembly of delegates. Dessauer was discouraged by the turnout but fascinated by the discussion and determined to follow up in some way during his administration. "It occurred to me that what we had seen there in the representation of these organizations on the panel was only a slight touch of what the potential was and that there was no real coordination among the groups. I was also conscious of the problem of trying to achieve coordination against the suspicion of some group trying to take over or build an empire or do something that some other organization would resent." Realizing that SPJ,SDX was in a singularly unique position to take the lead in such a project because the Society was an umbrella organization of all news media and none of the others was, Dessauer asked president-elect Otto at the January officers' meeting in Washington to chair a special projects committee of the Society to address two issues. First, to see what could be done in bringing these diverse news organizations together to discuss what they might do in concert on First Amendment issues and, second, to work toward establishing a vehicle to arouse public awareness on First Amendment issues and to begin a dialogue with the public on those issues. "My long-range goal was to establish the role of SPJ,SDX as the coordinating organization whenever problems might arise in journalism – something we had the machinery to do – to bring in other groups toward solving those problems."

Otto, whom Goodykoontz had asked to moderate the panel of organiztion leaders, had corresponded with the panelists and set the direction for discussion among those leaders and, thus, was informed about what had happened in Birmingham. But as for being asked to lead a followup project, she said, "It was sprung on me in Washington and, while it was terribly exciting, it was all very nebulous – just a 'see what you can do' assignment." Otto had been interested in building public confidence in the press for several years. As the newly elected treasurer of the Society in 1977, she delivered a speech at the Region Two conference in Richmond, Virginia, where she said, "The greatest danger to press freedom would be to have the general public believe that freedom was designed to insulate reporters from being accountable." Later, she would say, "The more I read and the more I studied, the

more I became convinced that the problem lay both within and without journalism – with the reaction of the public to what a lot of journalists had become." Returning to her home in Milwaukee, she turned to Agee's articles on "The Journalism Organization" in the November *Quill* to find out just what organizations might be appropriate for such a venture. In early February 1979, Otto wrote letters to respected national organizations which spoke for a large number of people and particular segments of the media. They included the American Newspaper Publishers Association, American Society of Newspaper Editors, National Association of Broadcasters, National Newspaper Association, Radio Television News Directors Association, National Broadcast Editorial Association, National Conference of Editorial Writers, Associated Press Managing Editors Association, Reporters Committee for Freedom of the Press, United Press International and The Associated Press. In her letter, she noted the public reaction to the press and the way it performs and asked if those organizations were sufficiently interested in looking into these problems to join others in joint discussions. "Almost all of them responded with let's do something or let's talk about it," she said. In one of the letters, Herbert Hobler, First Amendment chairman for the NAB, wrote that he had already designed such a proposal. "He said he wanted to have a large "congress" to get together and just talk. It didn't have a sense of direction and it wasn't exactly the same as what developed, but I suggested he bring his ideas to any first meeting." Nine of the organizations, along with SPJ, sent representatives to a meeting March 3l, 1979, at the O'Hare Hilton in Chicago. They were Hobler; Shoquist, *The Milwaukee Journal*, representing APME; Jim Donahue of ANPA; Paul Davis, WCIA-TV, Champaign, Illinois, representing RTNDA; Robert Kieckhefer of UPI in Chicago; Bill Boykin of the Inland Daily Press Association, representing NNA; Robert T. Barnard, Louisville *Courier-Journal*, NCEW; Joy Koletsky of the Reporters Committee; Ed Hinshaw, WTMJ, Milwaukee of NBEA; and John Curley, Gannett Washington

Bureau, representing SPJ,SDX along with Hurst and Otto. A representative of ASNE was not present although that organization had indicated an interest in participating. A clear indication of the lack of any previous, genuine coordination was the fact that few of the participants knew each other. "Many were total strangers. They got together in that room and had to introduce themselves, explain what their organizations were and what they were doing. In personal relationships, we started from scratch." Otto went in with a plan, however. Using Hobler's preliminary idea, she presented possible projects and even dates, having found that Benjamin Franklin's birthday was January 17 and James Madison's birthday was March 16. "The chemistry was right and a spirit was born in that meeting," she said. The spirit turned into almost immediate action. Otto's report on the meeting said:

The group reached early agreement that it was interested in proceeding with a conference....on the public perception of freedom of the press and educating the public to the fact that any encroachment on a free press dilutes the public's right to know....on educating the public to what it has lost and stands to lose by apathy and antipathy toward its First Amendment rights.

It was agreed that a first conference would be a one-day meeting designed to capture public attention. A second and longer seminar, with fewer participants, would follow within months. This would take the form of workshops in which journalists and other selected persons would explore various problems in depth and, after meeting in small sessions, bring proposals to the entire group for action.

It was suggested and agreed that these two meetings would be called First Amendment Congresses.

Otto credits Hobler with coming up with the name for the First Amendment Congresses. The remainder of the specific plan, she said, was a joint effort in the spirit envisioned when she wrote the letters. The group decided to have its first Congress on Franklin's birthday, January 17, 1980, in Philadelphia's Independence Hall; to invite nationally prominent speakers including, they hoped, Supreme Court Justice Potter Stewart or William Brennan; and to ask national pollster, George Gallup, Jr., to conduct a survey of public attitudes toward the press the results of which would be announced at the Congress. Hobler arranged for that survey at no cost by telephoning Gallup, his neighbor at home, before the meeting ended. They determined that the audience for the Congress would be "...members of the public – people who have constituencies to whom they can take the ideas generated at the meeting," including, as possible examples, the League of Women Voters, the PTA, the American Bar Association, labor unions, platform committees of the political parties, the National Education Association, the ACLU, and the US Chamber of Commerce. Dissemination of the information to the public at large was of major concern and the group decided to ask the Public Broadcasting Service to televise the entire proceeding and come up with a one or two-hour program to be televised nationally and that the networks be asked to give the Congress broad coverage. With the first program plan outlined as well as they could, the group set the second First Amendment Congress for Williamsburg, Virginia, eight weeks later on March 16, Madison's birthday. The group explored speaker possibilities and came up with a list of more than thirty, most of whom were nonjournalists. The planners believed members of the public should do the talking, with the journalists doing the listening.

Turning to financing the ventures, they decided to ask each co-sponsoring organization to contribute from $500 to $1,000, depending upon the resources of each, to establish a working fund. In addition, they considered possible foundations which might be tapped to assist with the project. Finally, the group established working committees for program, arrangements, invitations, publicity, film and transcript, and finance. The steering committee would be chaired by SPJ,SDX's Otto and would be made up of the persons attending that Chicago meeting plus a representative of ASNE.

All of this was simply a plan of the representatives of the ten organizations thus far involved but it did not carry the official blessing of any individual group, including the Society. To facilitate the plan, the group set an April 30 deadline for all organizations to make firm commitments of co-sponsorship and planned its next meeting for June 28 in Washington, DC to take the next steps. All the press organization boards approved the concept and pledged financing as requested. ASNE did join the group, represented by William Burleigh of the Cincinnati *Post*, as did The Associated Press, represented by Lou Boccardi of its New York offices. It was the foundations to whom Otto turned first for financial assistance, however, and they responded handsomely after the Congress steering committee was able to get itself tax-exempt by joining with an existing foundation. "I think the beginnings were successful, at least in part, because the other groups perceived that SPJ,SDX had no particular ax to grind in calling the group together," Otto said. "They didn't feel threatened by the Society Other organizations could have accomplished the same thing, but it would have been more difficult."

Dessauer said the logic of the project and the need were so plain that he wasn't surprised that the organizations came together so quickly. "Disunity had been so evident in holding back progress in other freedom of information work that it was obvious that it was time for a unified voice with the public and to let it know what the concerns of the press are all about," he said. As far as the speed by which it was accomplished was concerned, Otto said, "I had a sense of urgency about the project even in writing the orignal letters. When the group came together in Chicago, the members shared that urgency. About halfway through those discussions, Kieckhefer leaned back in his chair and said quietly, but emphatically, 'Let's do it!' "

By fall, the basis of the program was established, following the guidelines set in Chicago, and on November 2, 1979, letters went out to about 300 representatives of the public and press inviting them to

Philadelphia January 16-17, 1980. The letter, signed by Otto, said:

The goal of this meeting is to begin a dialogue between the public and both print and broadcast journalists. We look for direct and frank conversation between those whose responsibility it is to deliver information and opinion and those who need facts and points of view to make the sound decisions required of democratic government....Sponsors of the Congress believe that you can make a crucial difference in the public's perception of what a free press means, why it is essential to democratic government, and why it is the right of every American. We urge you to attend and to speak your views frankly, to share the concerns of other articulate and thoughtful people, and to join the effort to enlist the public in protecting its stake in the First Amendment.

Keynoter at the Congress was John Henry Faulk of Madisonville, Texas, who, as a CBS radio personality in the early 1950's, had been a victim of the Aware, Inc. and House UnAmerican Activities Committee purges. "The genius of our Constitution, the genius of the First Amendment, is that it protects those ideas and those opinions that we loathe and despise with the same force that it protects those that we cherish and live by," he said. Other speakers included Gallup; Millicent Fenwick, US congresswoman from New Jersey; Ernest Morial, mayor of New Orleans; Jerome Barron, dean of the George Washington University School of Law; Oregon state representative Ted Bugas; Judee and Michael Burgoon, researchers from Michigan State University; Sidney L. Berger, an attorney from Evansville, Indiana; Thomas J. Donahue of the US Chamber of Commerce; Gary Bryner, administrative assistant to the president of the United Auto Workers; A.H. Raskin, associate director of the National News Council; and Dr. Norman Graebner, professor of American history at the University of Virginia. Journalists on the program included Dan Rather, CBS News; Robert Toth, Los Angeles *Times*; Eugene Patterson, St. Petersburg, Florida *Times*;

and Anthony Lewis, *The New York Times*.

Gallup's poll on public attitudes about the press was revealing. He found a majority of the persons polled did not know what the First Amendment said, nor understand what it meant, and that about a third of the public believed that curbs on the press were not strict enough – painting a clear picture of the problems facing the press. Calling for public education in her remarks, Otto said:

> Many of us in journalism have become convinced that the greatest danger to a free press is not Supreme Court rulings that close courtroom doors, not courts that send reporters to jail for not revealing the source of their confidential information, not legislatures that pass overly broad privacy laws, and not administrative agencies that close their records. Rather, we believe it is the lack of public concern about such rulings and laws that presents the greatest danger to the free flow of information and ideas upon which a free society depends. We hope you will help people understand that the First Amendment right of a free press belongs to all of us.

The representation of speakers and delegates who attended the sessions in The First Bank of the United States Auditorium was in almost direct line with the plans laid ten months before in the first planning session. Likewise, the second Congress in Williamsburg March 16-18, followed the original plan to the letter. The impact of the Philadelphia Congress and an address in Williamsburg by columnist James J. Kilpatrick sparked the 150 delegates, in a full day of twelve workshops, to come up with ideas and projects by which the words from the Philadelphia Congress might be made manifest. They brought recommendations to a full session during which twelve resolutions and about 250 projects for action were adopted. Closing the second Congress, Otto told the delegates she hoped they would make known to the public, legislators, lawyers and journalists the types of resolutions passed and "help implement what you have decided to be done. It is going to take time. We can't

change the face of the country, or public opinion, with a single meeting."

In her report to the Society's board May 9 in Seattle, she wrote, "The contribution by SPJ,SDX of $1,000 seems to have been a sound investment, one that paid off not only in added prestige for the Society but a genuine contribution to an improved climate for journalism throughout the country." She mentioned that, without the help of Fred Beringer and the Philadelphia professional chapter of SPJ,SDX for the first Congress and Goodykoontz and Norman Beatty and others from the Richmond professional chapter at Williamsburg, the entire project would not have been possible. She said later, "One does not just descend on a city and have a First Amendment Congress. It took logistics and, once again, the Society's broad and wide spread organization helped to assure the successes we had." Her report to the board continued:

> If the Congress is able to follow through on the recommendations, we can look for a wide and intensive effort at educating various groups about the relevance of a free press in American life. Efforts are to be directed at the general public, at the media, at the legal profession, at legislators, in journalism and law schools, in high school and grade schools, in organizations and elsewhere. Such a project clearly will be years in being accomplished and will call for perseverance on the part of all sponsoring organizations. It will also call for assistance, where possible, from cooperating organizations, some of which bring special skills to the task....The conclusion now appears to be a long way off and it seems appropriate to assume that this project will never be ended.

She told the board that she had been able to raise $140,000 for the project, mostly from grants from journalism foundations and that about $60,000 remained to carry out the mandates of the delegates. Although PBS did not televise either of the Congresses nationally, one grant from Johnson and Johnson made possible the filming of the Congresses, and videotapes made from that film, were circulated to chapters and civic groups around the nation. Otto concluded her report with a note that, "An additional benefit has been seen in several local First Amendment Congresses around the country. I would like to see these encouraged, as they reach a level that could not be touched by the limited number of people at the national Congresses." To support that hope, she prepared "Guidelines for a First Amendment Congress", which were distributed through the Society, and among others, to groups planning such events.

Otto was elected to remain as chairman of the steering committee for the First Amendment Congress. After helping to organize it on a more permanent basis as a project of the Sigma Delta Chi Foundation, she wrote a set of bylaws which led to its incorporation as a separate foundation within a year of the Williamsburg meeting. Otto, who became editor of the editorial page of the *Rocky Mountain Daily News* in Denver, Colorado, in 1983, was elected the first chairperson of the Congress and was re-elected annually through 1984. "If you would have told me that that meeting with Phil Dessauer to 'see what you can do' would have led to the formation of a new organization that would be nationally known in three years, I would have said 'You're crazy. There's no way in the world it could happen. Who needs another organization?'" she said. "And the enthusiasm is still there in all of the organizations. We're just beginning to grow up in how we can work together. Our main emphasis now is in educating the public and educating the press to issues relating to the First Amendment." Although the Congress did not start the annual national Freedom of Information Day celebration, that activity is one of the primary educational projects in which it participates each year.

A NATIONAL DAY FOR FOI

Jim Bohannon, a newsman for WRC Radio in Washington, DC, was doing some feature work for the station in 1979 when he became fascinated with number of special "days," "weeks," or "months" celebrating what he called "artificial, contrived things specifically designed to promote something which otherwise would be unpromotable –

such as national hot dog month." A member of the Society's national freedom of information committee, Bohannon had an idea while attending the national convention in New York City in November of that year. He told chairman Lewis and the committee members, "If we can promote that kind of thing, then surely something as eminently worthwhile as freedom of information deserves its own day." Lewis encouraged Bohannon to take his idea to the SPJ,SDX board at its meeting following the convention. The board liked the idea and, upon a motion by Region Two director Val Hymes, voted unanimously to establish a Freedom of Information Day and publicize it nationally.

Otto, who had just become national president, worked with Lewis, Bohannon and Hurst in setting Madison's birthday, March 16, as an annual day of recognition of the importance of freedom of information. Hurst and the national headquarters staff notified the Society's chapters, publicized the event through *The Quill* and sent news releases to media around the country announcing March 16, 1980, as the first national Freedom of Information Day. Hurst's staff suggested that chapters prepare public service announcements for broadcast on local stations and editorials for publication in newspapers and on the air and provided samples of materials which could be used. Bohannon obtained proclamations from city officials in the Washington, DC area and the technique was duplicated in cities and states from coast to coast by SPJ,SDX chapters. The new unofficial "day" was promoted, as well as the First Amendment Congress in Philadelphia. With only two months to promote it, the first celebration was only a limited success outside of the two Congresses, but the seed had been planted and had already started to grow. Otto had asked several members of Congress to co-sponsor the needed bills to declare March 16 as Freedom of Information Day. Sen. William Proxmire of Wisconsin introduced Senate Joint Resolution 196 to establish the day officially and was joined by Rep. Henry Reuss with a similar resolution in the House of Representatives. Proxmire's resolution passed in the Senate but Reuss was unable to obtain the necessary number of co-sponsors to effect passage in the House in 1980. A similar effort in 1981 failed for the same reason, and the idea of establishing congressional approval for the day was dropped for the time being. Otto reported late in 1983 that new interest had developed on Capitol Hill and another drive would be made to seek congressional support for the day in 1984.

Tack Nail, executive editor of *Television Digest* and a long-time member of the freedom of information committee, also helped to bring national attention to FOI Day. In March 1981, he helped arrange for Graves and Lewis to appear on the Mutual Broadcasting System's "The Larry King Show," a midnight to 6 am radio talk show with a listening audience of more than six million through 250 stations. Graves, who had participated in a First Amendment Congress in Fairbanks, Alaska, Saturday, March 14, arranged to fly all night arriving in Washington, DC late Sunday to participate on the Monday night, March 16 broadcast. During the three-hour appearance, Graves and Lewis answered questions on free press and First Amendment issues from callers nationwide, giving Freedom of Information Day a new dimension.

Along with SPJ chapters and the co-sponsoring organizations of The First Amendment Congress, other national organizations picked up on the FOI Day idea, securing proclamations from governors, mayors and other government officials in 1981, building the program substantially.

Following a third year of growth of the project, president Dornfeld named Bohannon chairman of the 1983 Freedom of Information Day effort. Bohannon prepared a "do-it-yourself kit" for local chapters on events which could be a part of FOI Day, including working with local radio stations on, to be a part of, talk shows and expanding the program of news releases, public service announcements and editorials for publication in newspapers and on radio and television stations. Having returned to Washington to join the Mutual network staff, he arranged for Dornfeld to appear on "The Larry King Show" March 16, 1983, an appearance he said is likely to be an annual Freedom of Information Day event in each future year. The Society's *News and Views* newsletter carried stories of chapter activities throughout the nation during the spring of 1983, demonstrating that Bohannon's seed of an idea in 1979 not only had germinated and grown, but had reached full flower.

A FINAL WORD ON FOI

Freedom of information has not been the province of the Society alone since its efforts in the field began in 1946. Sigma Delta Chi was among the first of the national journalistic organizations to become involved and was an effective force throughout those early years. Its impact, recorded herein, speaks for itself. It is obvious, however, that other national and state journalism associations, the news media and individual journalists have played equally-important roles in the fight for the free flow of information, carrying the battle to the courts, legislative bodies at the national, state and local levels and executive administrations. But it is just as obvious that The Society of Professional Journalists, Sigma Delta Chi, has been in the forefront of almost every national and local battle for nearly forty years. By 1978, the Society's claim to leadership in FOI was clearly established. Since its Birmingham convention, the Society has made quantum leaps both in programs and in leadership. Novitz credited the hiring of Sanford as legal counsel as the major step in assuming that leadership. "He proved to be everything the search committee hoped he would be – bright, energetic, a great champion for us, a fine politician, a great organizer and a man who understands the possibilities and could tell us what should be done and what can be done."

Dornfeld noted that with the Society's willingness to take a leadership role in FOI has come the desire by newspapers and other media to seek out SPJ,SDX as *the* organization to turn to for help in state and national cases. "I think that speaks well for the progress we've made," Dornfeld said. About that same progress, Lewis said in 1983, "Even with our strong record in FOI, especially in the states, from the 1950's through the 1970's, we still grew in stature from a pigmy to a giant on the national level in the last five years." The depth of the long-term commitment to freedom of information and the importance of keeping an attorney/lobbyist as an integral part of that program was, perhaps, best exemplified by Frank Sutherland, who would be president of the Society as it began its fourth quarter century. Sutherland said dollars for First Amendment counsel and FOI activities "would be the last money I'd cut out of our budget." Graves' assessment of the 1978-1983 development supports that theory.

"The Society's presence and visibility improved strikingly in those years, given the accomplishments with the FOI Service Center, the First Amendment Congresses, Freedom of Information Day and the work of our own legal counsel. Other organizations, our own members, journalists in general and the public know that SPJ,SDX is not just a fraternal or social group, but that it has purpose, and it is made up of activists in the vital freedom of information fight."

CHAPTER 8

The SDX Foundation

Sigma Delta Chi was in the throes of turmoil in April 1960. Executive director Victor Bluedorn was about to be fired by the executive council and McKinsey and Company had been invited to formulate a reorganizational plan to revitalize the fraternity. Yet Burroughs, McCormack and Newton demonstrated their confidence in the organization's future by recommending establishment of a fund to provide dollars for special projects at the national level. Newton appointed Floyd Arpan to head a committee "to investigate the feasibility and appropriate methods for Sigma Delta Chi to establish an educational fund."

Because the reorganizational effort dominated the board and headquarters staff's time in the following eighteen months, little was done about the proposed fund until Apran reported his scholarship committee's findings at the October 26, 1961, board meeting in Miami Beach. He suggested the establishment of a "Sigma Delta Chi Foundation to promote educational and charitable activities [to be] conducted by Sigma Delta Chi." He pointed out that if such steps were taken, it would be important to consult tax attorneys and to incorporate such a foundation as a separate, but integrated, part of the Society. The board found the idea acceptable and McCormack asked Arpan to continue his study. With more details in hand, Arpan returned to the board May 11, 1962, in Detroit and received permission "to complete the study and file incorporation papers as [the committee] sees fit." The completed document and articles of incorporation were presented November 14, 1962, at the national convention in Tulsa and approved, formally establishing the SDX Foundation. The Foundation's charter read: "To aid, encourage and promote education for the field of journalism; to aid, encourage and promote the education and training of those persons who intend to enter journalism or those persons already in journalism; and to take all lawful steps in furtherance of the foregoing purposes...."
Money to support the Foundation's work was to come from contributions from anyone interested, and McCormack told the convention that, "Many such persons have contributed and others have expressed the

National secretary Frank Sutherland, 1983-1984 president Phil Record, and 1982-1983 president Steven R. Dornfeld with Sen. Patrick Leahy of Vermont on the occasion of the awarding of the Society's First Amendment Award to Leahy in 1982. The award program, which had honored nearly twenty-five persons and organizations by 1984 for exemplary work on First Amendment issues, was initiated in 1975.

desire to do so." Hurst had seen the need to attract talent to journalism from his first days as executive officer. In one of his early speeches on his personal philosophy concerning goals and objectives of the Society, Hurst had said that Sigma Delta Chi needed to "keep open our manpower lifelines by encouraging young men and women to enter journalism." He saw the Foundation's potential in this area as substantial to meet what he called "a critical need" throughout the 1960's.

If dollars arrived at national headquarters for the Sigma Delta Chi Foundation in the first six months of 1963, they were few in number. President Burroughs attempted to get the Foundation on track financially, appointing a ways and means committee made up of five prominent newspaper publishers to study and design a plan for the Foundation. Few, if any,

suggestions came from the committee by the time the board met in Norfolk, Virginia, in November of that year. It would be for Ted Koop, the incoming 1963-1964 national president, whose interests as an executive councilor were evident in first discussions in 1960, to make the Sigma Delta Chi Foundation a viable force in the Society, though it would take him nearly three years to do so. The Norfolk convention delegates elected the first formal Foundation board, naming Koop; first vice president and president-elect Sewell; Carter, then managing editor of *The National Observer*; Robert W. Chandler, Region Ten director and editor of the Bend, Oregon *Bulletin*; and James S. Copley, chairman of The Copley Press, Inc., to that board. No board officers were elected at that time.

Koop, who became the Foundation's first president in late 1964, recalls, "We had

Sol Taishoff (left), Sigma Delta Chi president in 1956-1957, was named a Fellow of the Society in 1963. Making the award is Theodore F. Koop, 1963-1964 national president, and the "father" and first president of the Sigma Delta Chi Foundation. Under Koop's leadership, the Foundation sponsored lectures by SDX Fellows on college campuses beginning in 1965.

no money whatsoever," and the Foundation did little to carry out its mandate through 1964 and early 1965 except for a $100 grant to the University of Missouri Freedom of Information Center. Spangler said there was controversy about what the Foundation should be in its formative stages. "Some members of the board felt the Foundation should in no way become an activist group. It should raise money, invest it and use it for beneficial purposes." The grant for freedom of information purposes seemed to fuel that controversy. Its first recorded project was concurrent with its first substantial dollar contribution. Koop said the Foundation board had let the officers and national board know that a financial commitment would be necessary if anything of significance was to be done. "We didn't ask for funding," Koop said, "We demanded it."

DOLLARS FOR THE FOUNDATION

National treasurer Staley McBrayer

took the lead at the national board's May 7, 1965, meeting in Philadelphia, recommending that the Society take $25,000 from its cash reserves to provide funds for the development of an active educational program by the Foundation. The board approved McBrayer's motion. In separate actions, the board increased Foundation board membership to seven and recommended that 1965-1966 national president Spangler, past-president Sewell and regional directors Kleeman and Angelo represent the national board, with Koop, Carter and former executive officer Agee as at-large members. Koop responded to the financial gift with a proposal that the Foundation sponsor a writing awards contest to recognize "outstanding, original manuscripts on journalistic problems, practices, standards, instruction and research." Providing $500 in cash prizes, including a $250 first award, the contest was approved, to be judged on the basis of

William C. Payette, Society president in 1972-1973, and Richard Leonard, president in 1976-1977, presided at ceremonies marking an historic site in Baraboo, Wisconsin, honoring Ansel N. Kellogg and the first newspaper syndicate.

"contributions to a fuller understanding by journalists and/or the public of the role and responsibilities of journalists as practitioners and journalism as a profession." First winner of the writing award, announced at the June 1966 Distinguished Service Awards meeting in Des Moines, Iowa, was professor Verne E. Edwards, Jr., chairman of the journalism department at Ohio Wesleyan University, for an article, "Let's Revive Newspaper Editorials." The contest apparently had only a two-year run and, interestingly, the second winner was Robert S. McCord, editor and publisher of the Little Rock, Arkansas *Times*, who would become the Society's president in 1975-1976. His article, "Don't Leave Out The Fun," also concentrated on the need for and excitement of editorial writing.

Koop had only just begun to get the Foundation off the ground with the writing awards. He knew that if Sigma Delta Chi was to become known on college campuses as a truly professional organization, the national body had to take further action. In attacking this problem, he developed a plan which would mark the Foundation's first major program. He noted that, since 1948, Sigma Delta Chi had honored outstanding professional performance by journalists in its "Fellows" awards, but made little use of honoring those journalists beyond recognizing them at annual conventions. With money in the Foundation account for the first time, he convinced its board to sponsor the Sigma Delta Chi Foundation Lectures, announcing his idea to the membership September 1, 1965. Under Foundation auspices, three lectures – to be given by the most recently elected SDX Fellows if possible – would be presented each year at universities and colleges with campus chapters of the Society. The series would be designed, "To promote the highest standards of journalism through searching, candid examination of professional problems." All expenses would be borne by the Foundation, including those of the lecturers and the host chapters. Lecture sites would be selected from applications by campus chapters wishing to act as hosts. To facilitate the beginning of the lecture series, the Foundation postponed its basic rules for one year and selected the first three Sigma Delta Chi chapters established – DePauw, the University of Kansas and the University of Michigan – as host chapters. Paul Miller, a 1963 Fellow and president of Gannett Newspapers and The Associated Press, delivered the first lecture December 1, 1965, at Michigan. Turner Catledge, executive editor of *The New York Times* and a 1964 Fellow of the Society, spoke at Kansas December 2 and Robert U. Brown, also a 1964 Fellow and president of *Editor & Publisher* magazine, presented the third lecture at DePauw, December 10. The first competition for chapters to be host to the 1966 Foundation Lectures by Fellows elected in 1965 attracted more than a dozen applications. The University of Southern California was selected as the site for the presentation by David Dietz, a science writer from the Cleveland, Ohio *Press*, Ohio University was host to Wes Gallagher, general manager of The Associated Press; and the Columbia University Graduate School of Journalism was selected to be host to Mark Foster Ethridge, long associated with the Louisville *Courier-Journal* and a lecturer at the University of North Carolina at Chapel Hill. "None of the lecturers was paid an honorarium," Koop said. "We simply paid their expenses and most of them were delighted to deliver a lecture on a college campus." For the students who attended those lectures, Koop said, "We got all kinds of fan mail from the chapters. I don't think they were ever so pleased with a program sponsored by the Society and they were able to get so much from these speakers." While not all Fellows elected since that time have delivered lectures on college campuses, the Sigma Delta Chi Foundation's series of three lectures each year continued through the mid-1980's, with other outstanding journalists selected by the Foundation board acting as substitutes for Fellows as needed. Koop himself was a Foundation lecturer October 3, 1972, when he addressed students and professionals at

Gregory Waskul (left), a journalism student at California State University at Northridge, received the 1975 Barney Kilgore Memorial Award and a check for $2,500 from 1975-1975 Society president Robert McCord.

Northeastern University in Boston. "I've never been so well received in my life. I spent an entire day with the students, not just for the evening dinner speech. I can tell you from my experience that having Foundation lecturers on campus means more to the students than you can possibly imagine."

Because the board believed its role should be only in providing funding and advice rather than operating another permanent enterprise, the Foundation turned down a 1965 invitation by Willard Kiplinger, publisher of *The Kilplinger Letter*, to join him in establishing a Washington Journalism Center for the study of journalism. That center, with which Koop later worked independently of Sigma Delta Chi, provided national internships and seminars on current issues in the press for many years. But Koop, Sewell, Spangler and others were about to launch yet another major project which would keep the Foundation's board active.

AL BALK'S CAREER FILM

Koop, re-elected president of the

Charles Barnum (center), long-time Society parliamentarian, interim executive officer in 1960 and vice president for campus chapter affairs from 1964-1966, received the Wells Key from 1970-1971 national president Robert W. Chandler as 1971-1972 president Guy Ryan listened.

Foundation, notified the Society's board in Los Angeles in November 1965, that the Internal Revenue Service had granted the SDX Foundation tax-exempt status, thereby encouraging its board to seek contributions from the business community – the Society's Code of Ethics prohibiting acceptance of gifts from non-journalism organizations was not adopted until 1973 – as well as from Society members and chapters. With the potential of more dollars for the Foundation, its board voted to underwrite a film on journalism recruitment, a project discussed for two years by the Sigma Delta Chi journalism careers committee but set aside for lack of resources. Several films had been available on freedom of the press, the mechanics of publishing and broadcasting, and careers in one or more journalism specialties, but none dealt with the general subject of career opportunities in various branches of the booming field of journalism and mass communication.

While the Foundation provided the dollars, Koop said it was Al Balk, a free-lance writer and later a feature editor for *Saturday Review*, who was the driving force

behind the film project. "It was very gratifying, a relief and somewhat exciting when we received word of the go-ahead on the film," Balk recalls. "Nothing had been done like it and some of us believed very strongly in it. There was a shortage of journalists at the time and we wanted to do something about that situation."

Koop arranged a meeting with Robert C. Doyle, one of the nation's most respected television and documentary film producers. He had been director/producer of coverage of national political conventions and other major events for NBC-TV and later director of television for the National Geographic Society. for which his specials for CBS-TV had won numerous prizes. Balk, who served as executive producer; Doyle; and Koop met several times in evolving the general structure of the film. A major breakthrough took place when *World Book Encyclopedia*, a division of Field Enterprises Educational Corporation in Chicago, offered the services of the firm's movie producer, Telecine Film Studios, Inc., and paid all expenses connected with a producer's travel to all field filming. With Doyle having to withdraw

136

from the project because of commitments at
National Geographic, final details of the
film's story line were shaped by Balk,
Telecine president Byron L. Friend and
Robert H. Dressler, director of audio-visual
services for *World Book*. Woven throughout
the film, in fast-moving semi-documentary
style, were sharply-edited film clips of major
news events, scenes of newspersons at work
and the comments of six successful young
journalists about their careers. Balk
approached Walter Cronkite of CBS-TV to
narrate the movie to give the film prestige.
Cronkite agreed to do the narration at no
charge. "Walter did not need any special
stroking or front-office encouragement to do
the job," Balk said. "He was for it from the
start. He was always gracious about doing
things for and about journalism. In fact,
while we were setting up to film his segment,
we needed to move a desk to a better
position and proceeded to do it. The union
film crew said they could not photograph the
bit unless the proper union man moved the
furniture. We were dismayed because there
was no such union man present and we were
on a limited time schedule. Cronkite played
peacemaker, discussing the situation quietly
with the camera crew, got the matter settled
without problem and we proceeded to shoot
the narration." The six featured journalists,
all of whom contributed their services, were
Tom Wicker, Washington bureau chief of
The New York Times; William Normyle,
space technology editor of *Aviation Week
and Space Technology*; Eddie Barker,
director of news and special events for
station KRLD-TV, Dallas; Karl Fleming,
Los Angeles bureau chief for *Newsweek*;
Garrett Ray, editor and publisher of the
suburban Littleton, Colorado *Independent*
and Arapahoe *Herald*; and Lois Wille,
Pulitzer prize-winning social problems
reporter for the Chicago *Daily News*.
Officials of local television stations in cities
across the country donated the services of
television crews to film and interview the
journalists at work. All three major
networks – CBS, ABC and NBC –
contributed newsfilm footage or money to
help underwrite the movie's distribution.
Balk, who edited *Columbia Journalism
Review* from 1969 through 1973 and went to

Accepting the Barney Kilgore Memorial Award in
1978 from Phil Dessauer, national president in
1978-1979, was Linda Mari Tiara, a journalism
student from the University of Hawaii. From 1969
through 1982, the Kilgore Award was a $2,500 cash
prize, sponsored by the Sigma Delta Chi
Foundation. The Kilgore awards were changed to
become $4,000 freedom of information internships
in 1983.

World Press Review as editor in that year,
said the contributed services by Telecine and
the television stations in various cities "made
all the difference in getting the film done.
We didn't have any real money to do the
motion picture and without the help of all of
those who participated, there wouldn't have
been a film."

Titled, *That the People Shall Know –
The Challenge of Journalism*, the twenty-one
minute, l6mm, black-and-white, sound film
premiered at the November 1966 national
convention in Pittsburgh. Delegates were
told that the film was available for free
showings through Modern Talking Picture
Service in New York City and that prints
could be purchased for $50 through national
heaquarters. Within four weeks of the
convention, more than 100 requests for the
film were received, including bookings by
eighty high schools in states from New York
to California and from Alaska to Mississippi.

Fifty prints were purchased immediately by
the Knight Foundation, Inc., for distribution
to high schools and audio-visual centers
through SDX chapters in Knight Newspaper

cities. In addition, six Society chapters purchased prints for use with career-day audiences in their cities. In a further move to enlarge the potential audience, Hurst obtained clearance for use of the film in unsponsored showings on both commercial and educational television.

The audiences swelled with each passing month and Hurst told the board a year later in Minneapolis that the film had had 3,000 showings, including more than 2,000 in high schools, and that it had been viewed by more than 200,000 persons. Sewell, who called the making of the film, "the most important and gratifying project of my term on the board and with the Foundation," told the board the Foundation had paid out only $8,700, some of that from special cash contributions, for making the film, purchasing prints and supporting the free-loan distribution to schools. "I don't believe much of that money was used for the production of the film," Balk said. Hurst agreed. "Balk did a superb job of working on the film and, at several times, had to do the project with practically no money compared to what it cost to make a film in those days. Another film that we knew of and of about the same length, done about the same time, cost more than $75,000," Hurst said.

Balk received the Wells Memorial Key at the 1967 Minneapolis convention for his work with the journalism careers committee and on the motion picture. Described by Burroughs as "the man who made things move and got things done," Balk said, "I was one of the younger persons who had received the Wells Key and it was a surprise and a high moment for me. I had really thought of the careers committee work as an assignment that needed to be done but didn't expect it would lead to such an award." Balk, in turn, presented the Wells Key to Koop in Atlanta in 1968 for his long record of service to the Society as national president, as founder of the Joint Media Committee and for what Spangler called "giving life to the Sigma Delta Chi Foundation," before leaving its board in 1967. Balk remembers that event as another high moment for him. "I had always thought highly of Ted. He was a great

credit and help to the Society. Just to be standing on the same stage with him was a real honor," Balk said.

KILGORE IS HONORED

The day before the opening of the 1967 convention, Barney Kilgore died in Princeton, New Jersey, at the age of fifty-nine. Kilgore, whose quiet, behind-the-scenes but pervasive role in Sigma Delta Chi through the late l950's and early l960's leading to the rebuilding of the organization has been documented in this book, was eulogized at the convention and in the December 1967 *Quill*. His close associate at *The Wall Street Journal* and colleague in Sigma Delta Chi, Buren McCormack, wrote, "It was typical of Barney Kilgore that he never sought any acknowledgement or credit for what were major contributions to our Society. But the officers and directors of the Society knew full well how much he had done. It was no surprise to them, then, that Barney Kilgore was awarded the Wells Memorial Key in 1959, was chosen a Fellow of Sigma Delta Chi in 1960 and was elected national honorary president in 1965. [Kilgore, who was initiated as a member April 27, 1927, at DePauw University, had also been a member of the executive council and served as national treasurer in the mid-1950's but would never accept nomination for the Society's presidency.] Sigma Delta Chi had rewarded Barney Kilgore in every way it could for a lifetime of devotion to an organization that he loved and toward which he devoted his great talent and energy."

A special committee composed of past presidents Cavagnaro, Byron and Burroughs and Region Three director Ed Thomas proposed to the closing session of the Minneapolis convention that a memorial to Kilgore "be perpetuated by an annual award in his name. As the delegates stood in tribute to Kilgore, Cavagnaro read a memorial tribute. "Barney Kilgore was not just a Sigma Delta Chi, he was the epitome of it. Barney Kilgore did not write the ritual of Sigma Delta Chi, he lived it. The symbolism of Sigma Delta Chi is *talent, energy and truth*. In Barney Kilgore this was not mere symbolism. He exemplified talent and energy and he lived truth. The name of Barney Kilgore will be well known to members of Sigma Delta Chi as yet unborn for, while he was not Sigma Delta Chi, Sigma Delta Chi in its truest sense could be Barney Kilgore. Sigma Delta Chi today, the modern Sigma Delta Chi, is greatly the work of Barney Kilgore. After half a century of existence, there were needed changes, and the name of Barney Kilgore is stamped indelibly upon most of the significant ones which were made...."

In conjunction with Sigma Delta Chi Foundation president Bob White and its board, the special committee, with the blessing of the convention and the national Society board, set about to plan an appropriate continuing program to honor Kilgore. When Cavagnaro, Burroughs and Thomas reported in Atlanta in November 1968, the Kilgore Memorial Award, a $2,500 cash prize funded by the Foundation was established to be awarded to an outstanding college journalism student and member of the Society. Nominations were to be submitted by professors or journalism school or department administrators based on the student's news work during his or her college career and had to be accompanied by a supporting letter from the president of the nominee's college or university. A screening committee would narrow the field to five finalists, who would be required to write a thesis on some phase of journalism. A select committee of top journalists would then determine the winner, who would be brought to the 1969 convention in San Diego, expenses paid, to receive the first $2,500 Kilgore prize. The Society's officers recommended that an additional $15,000 be provided by the Society for the Foundation to assist with the Kilgore award and the continuing film program. While Society funds were contributed to the Foundation on a regular basis for many years, becoming its primary source of revenue, president Angelo appealed to chapters to send funds for the SDX Foundation projects. Although there is no record of the amount generated from the appeal, many campus and professional chapters did respond with contributions of from $100 to $500.

The first competition attracted twenty-five nominees, with Douglas A. Stone, a senior in journalism at the University of Minnesota, named as winner of the 1969 Barney Kilgore Award. The other four finalists included Michael V. Adams, Texas Christian University; Roger C. Boye, University of Nebraska, who in 1971, joined the Society's headquarters staff in Chicago as news editor of *The Quill* and in 1983 was general manager of the magazine and the Society's first director of development; Albert Carl Stepp, Jr., University of South Carolina; and Lawrence L. Thomas, San Diego State College. Stone had worked as a reporter for the Minneapolis *Tribune*, was a reporter intern for the St. Paul *Dispatch*, was managing editor of his campus newspaper, *The Minnesota Daily*, and was president of the University of Minnesota campus chapter of SDX. In the "statement of journalistic philosophy" accompanying his entry, Stone had stressed the importance of honesty, understanding, thoroughness, responsibility and leadership. The complex issues of modern society require greater press efforts than before to provide coverage in depth so that public understanding may be increased, he wrote.

For the next thirteen years, the Foundation awarded the cash prize to other outstanding college journalists, adding additional cash awards of $200 for the four runners-up beginning in 1979. A list of the winners appears in the Appendix of this book. With the Society's priorities turning toward freedom of information issues in the early 1980's, the SDX Foundation ended its $3,300 cash award program in 1982, changing the Kilgore Memorial Award to the Kilgore Freedom of Information Internships. The new competitive program offered two college students the opportunity to spend a ten-week summer, fall or spring term in Washington, DC working on research and writing projects with the national freedom of information committee, the FOI Service Center and the Society's First Amendment counsel. The internships, scheduled to be a permanent program of the Foundation, were open to journalism seniors, graduate students and law students with journalism backgrounds. Work space and academic supervision was provided by the journalism faculty at George Washington University, assisting recipients who desired academic credit for their work. Student winners received $2,000 stipends for the internships, thus increasing the total Foundation commitment in dollars for the Kilgore program to $4,000. Sharon Appelbaum, a senior at the University of Kansas, and David Freedman, a 1981 Northwestern University journalism graduate and a law student at Columbia University, were named the first winners of the internship competition in 1983.

A NEW CAREER FILM

As the Kilgore Award program was being started in 1968, the Foundation's board and its president, Frank Angelo, were making plans to produce a new careers recruiting film to replace the "aging" *That the People Shall Know*. In his appeal for funds for the Foundation, Angelo noted that more than 600,000 students had seen the film by early 1969. Prints of the film were wearing out, issues discussed by the film's cast of characters were out of date and styles were changing, he said. Rather than make new copies, the Foundation board decided to move ahead with a new film. Hurst approached ABC News producer Charles Novitz, long active as a Society member since his initiation at the University of Illinois in 1950's, a past president of the New York Deadline Club and deputy director of Region One, asking him to take on the role as executive producer. About accepting the job, Novitz wrote, "Of healthy ego, of extraordinary confidence, at the right price (necessary expenses), and with time and interest because of a network job that demanded too little, about one-eighth of a nano-second elapsed before 'yes' was out of my mouth and I was embarked on a two-year expedition." Novitz called the success of the earlier film, which ultimately had an audience of well over one million viewers, "a remarkable product for its time," and recalls that its success was a spur rather than intimidating. "I screened the first film over and over until I'd nearly memorized the lines and also sought out similar films such as the one done by the Radio Television News Directors Association." Almost immediately,

he determined that he wanted a simple, straight-forward, "real people" approach which would capitalize on the idioms of the day, those which would appeal to a youthful audience. "We wanted to encourage young people to pursue education, and ultimately careers, in news. Secondly, we wanted to give the audience an idea of what journalists are like, what it is they do, and *why* they do their jobs, beyond making a living." As the concept for the film developed, Novitz approached Hollywood producers for permission to use sequences from the feature films *The Graduate* and *Zabriskie Point* and was able, after months of correspondence, to obtain clips from each which ultimately led off his film. He also negotiated for use of a film short, *Kinestasis 60*, produced by Charles Braverman, a fast-cut montage reviewing the top news events and personalities of the just-past 1960's. Presenting ABC News colleague Harry Reasoner with the possibility of narrating the new film, Novitz found him ready and willing. "One of the things that has delighted me about the Society is that many newsmen, having knowledge of the work by Sigma Delta Chi, were willing as fellow professionals to participate in what they felt was an important project." The stars of the film again included Walter Cronkite but concentrated, as had the previous film, on outstanding journalists who may not have been well known or were not as easily recognized at the time. The film included segments featuring Seymour Hersh, the Pulitzer Prize-winning free-lance writer; Liz Trotta of NBC News; Jim Hoge, editor of the Chicago *Sun-Times*; Hal Bruno, of *Newsweek*; Phil Record, of the Fort Worth *Star-Telegram*; and Mike Hill, a Black reporter for the Washington *Post*. Novitz followed the same process as Balk in obtaining contributed services from television news directors and station managers across the nation to film the sequences and interview the reporters and editors in action. "We got turn downs from nobody. We told them 'here's somebody we'd like [to have interviewed], here's some questions we want them to answer, here's how long we want it to be, here's the kind of film stock we want it shot on,' and it came back in about a

140

week exactly to specifications.''

While the normal cost for producing a film in that period was a minimum of $1,000 per minute, the twenty-six-minute, color, 16mm, sound film was put together for less than $5,000. "Much of that cost was for the one paid employee, a film editor who worked for me at ABC on the daily syndicated news service," Novitz said. Novitz produced the story board, wrote the narration and coordinated the effort, which culminated in a pre-screening of the film given the title, *The Journalists*, at the 1971 national convention in Washington, DC. He continued to work on final editing and production of the film through the winter and spring of 1972 and the motion picture was ready for distribution in October 1972. Once again, Modern Talking Picture Service, Inc., circulated the film on a free-loan basis, while it was available for purchase at $80 per print. And, as with the first film, audience counts mounted quickly with more than 2,000 showings for 100,000 high school students by February 1973. Novitz said he recalled figures provided by Modern Talking Picture Service showing that more than three million persons saw the film in its ten-year life span. And when *The Journalists* was withdrawn from wide circulation in the early 1980's, it was as much because of the poor condition of the remaining prints as it was that the film was becoming outdated.

THE FOUNDATION TODAY

With several programs established and operating, the Foundation's directors in the mid-1970's settled into managing those programs – the Foundation lectures by SDX Fellows, the Kilgore Awards program and circulation of the careers film – rather than looking to major new projects which might make excessive demands on its growing, but still limited, resources. In the next few years, opportunities arose which allowed the Foundation to "sponsor" additional programs. One such was the $5,000 Eugene C. Pulliam Fellowship for Editorial Writers, approved by the Society's directors and the Foundation as a continuing program in November 1977. With the program funded by an annual grant by Mrs. Nina Pulliam to honor her husband, the fellowship's cash

prize was to go to an outstanding editorial writer on a daily newspaper in the United States or its territories. Applicants had to have had a minimum of five years' full-time editorial writing and be under age forty. Purpose of the grant was to encourage young editorial writers to renew their personal resources and develop new or specialized interests through travel, study or a combination of both. First winner of the prize, awarded in 1978, was Ross MacKenzie, editor of the editorial page of the Richmond, Virginia *News Leader*. Beginning in 1980, Mrs. Pulliam increased the amount of the single prize to $10,000 each year. The name was later changed to the Eugene C. Pulliam Award, with no age limit nor minimum length of service as an editorial writer included in the qualifying requirements.

A second major award program – The Frank W. Corrigan Internship – was begun through the SDX Foundation in 1983 by Mrs. Mae Doris Corrigan to memorialize her husband. Corrigan, who died in 1982, was an editorial writer and senior business editor at *Newsday*, a daily newspaper on Long Island, New York, and the winner of the Society's 1973 Distinguished Service Award for an editorial predicting the Arab oil embargo and coming energy crisis. The ten-week internship, scheduled to begin in the summer of 1984, was to enable a journalism graduate to write and edit business stories on *Newsday* under the direction of that newspaper's staff. Each annual winner would receive $325 per week for the ten weeks plus transportation to and from New York.

Another addition to Foundation-sponsored activities was the Taishoff Memorial Fund, established in 1983 with a $25,000 bequest from the *Broadcasting*/Taishoff Foundation. The grant was given in memory of Sol J. Taishoff, SDX president in 1956-1957, and the first journalist from the broadcasting industry to become president of the Society. Taishoff was a founder of *Broadcasting* magazine in 1931, and, more recently, editor of the publication until his death in 1982. He was one of the Society's most ardent advocates for free-press rights for broadcasters and was active with SPJ,SDX throughout his life. Criteria for awarding the first Taishoff fellowship were developed in 1983 to provide funds for one-day seminars for professional broadcast newspersons to be conducted by Society chapters with the assistance of commercial and public broadcast stations. The seminars would feature top on-air, production and management personnel discussing themes and topics of concern for broadcast newspersons.

The Foundation's help with the First Amendment Congress has been discussed earlier, but the Foundation continued to support the Congress, now incorporated on its own, with annual financial contributions.

To include only the widely-publicized and more dramatic projects sponsored by the Sigma Delta Chi Foundation would probably leave the reader with the sense that it has created a legacy of worthwhile activities through the years. But that would ignore the more functional, yet generally unknown, endeavors without which the total program of the Society could not have been accomplished. Though limited by its charter and tax-exempt status concerning what projects it may fund, the Foundation has been the heart of many of the educational programs, such as those dealing with careers in journalism.

In the early 1960's, before he took on the role of producer of the first careers film, Balk wrote a pamphlet called, "The Big Story – Ten Questions and Answers About the Booming Career Field of Journalism and Communications." Originally compiled as a service of the Headline Club of Chicago, "The Big Story" was the centerpiece of careers materials produced by Sigma Delta Chi. Balk's writing, and cartoons by P.J. Hoff, a weatherman for WBBM Television in Chicago, who used his cartooning ability as part of his daily weather show, made the pamphlet readable and attractive. Hurst recalls, "Nearly every day at headquarters the mail or telephone calls would bring requests from junior high school and high school students for information on vocational opportunities in the media. We treated those requests with a high priority because we knew that the Society's interest and help

over the years turned many a bright student toward journalism and, after all, that was one of our purposes as an organization." Tens of thousands, perhaps several hundred thousands of "The Big Story" booklet were sent out before it was withdrawn in 1981 as an active project. The booklet was kept up to date by headquarters staff and was totally revised by staffer Halina Czerniejewski in the mid-1960's. The Society also gathered other journalism careers materials from various sources, putting together a package to provide greater help to those making requests. Often, it was Foundation money which provided for printing and mailing those materials.

For many years, the annual Freedom of Information Report was circulated only on a limited basis. The Foundation officers in the early 1980's determined that the report was a vital tool in educating members and the public at large on First Amendment issues and funded the mailing of the FOI Report on a broad scale. In the same freedom of information area, the Foundation made regular grants to the FOI Center at the University of Missouri, the Washington Journalism Center and the Reporters Committee for Freedom of the Press for research and study of important issues.

Aware that University travel budgets in the early 1980's were woefully insufficient at best, the Foundation established a grant of $1,000 to be awarded a journalism professor or instructor to attend one of four 1981 conferences at the Washington Journalism Center. The program continued at least through 1984. The Foundation also administers The Julian Fund, a growing endowment provided by past vice president for campus affairs, James Julian, a retired San Diego State journalism professor. Guidelines for use of dollars from that fund were being developed in 1983, aimed at supporting projects and travel by SPJ,SDX campus chapter advisers.

While continuing education and professional development have been important concerns of the Society for several decades, recent concentration on developing in-service training for journalists gave the Foundation yet another project to support. Under the direction of Dr. Ralph Izard of

Ohio University and Lillian Lodge Kopenhaver of Florida International University, the professional development committee began work in 1982 on preliminary plans for a nation wide program of educational programs which, it was hoped, would be sponsored and funded by the Foundation. In 1983, the Foundation provided grants totaling $5,000 to various SPJ,SDX chapters to conduct professional development seminars. A long-term goal and priority set by the Society board and the Foundation trustees has been to raise enough money for the Foundation to support a full-time director of continuing education as a part of the headquarters operation in Chicago.

Despite its already extensive program of activities developed since 1962, the Sigma Delta Chi Foundation with its liquid and non-liquid assets valued at $354,900 in August 1983, continued to expand its projects, primarily in the field of professional development.

THE SOCIETY HONORS
THE BEST IN JOURNALISM

Recognizing those journalists who set standards of excellence in singular accomplishments or through years of service to the profession has been an important part of the Society's agenda since its first national convention in 1912. In the seven decades that followed, a dozen major awards programs have been established by Sigma Delta Chi to spotlight achievements in journalism or service to the organization. Ranging from the Wells Memorial Key, which honors those who have served the Society in exemplary fashion; to the Distinguished Service Award, which annually recognizes journalistic performance in sixteen categories; to the First Amendment Awards, a tribute to individuals or organizations that have worked to strengthen freedom of the press, the citations for excellence have become special manifestation of the purposes for which Sigma Delta Chi was founded. Several of these awards programs have been detailed earlier in this chapter because of their connection with the Sigma Delta Chi Foundation. The significance of those and

the other honors for journalists established by the Society – recognized by members and non-members alike as some of the most prestigious in the nation – have earned them a distinctive place in its history.

NATIONAL HONORARY PRESIDENTS

The eighteen college students who were delegates and alternates to the first Sigma Delta Chi national convention at DePauw University in 1912 chose to honor a professional newsman to whom they might look for inspiration in their idealistic pursuits. Because the fraternity's leadership would, of course, be college men, they settled on the title "National Honorary President" for their honoree – Chase S. Osborn, editor and publisher of the Saginaw, Michigan *Courier-Herald*; governor of the State of Michigan at the time; and the father of one of the fraternity's members at the University of Michigan. Osborn, in many ways, became a patron for Sigma Delta Chi during its formative years, contributing money to help keep the fraternity and its magazine *The Quill* afloat and participating in conventions as a speaker and panelist. For eight years, convention delegates chose Osborn as their national honorary president until, in 1919, they selected H. F. Harrington, dean of the Medill School of Journalism at Northwestern University, to succeed him. The list of the forty-six men elected to that honorary office through the years amounts to a "Who's Who" in American journalism. They included William Allen White, publisher of the Emporia, Kansas *Gazette*; Kent Cooper, executive director of The Associated Press; Hugh Baillie, president of United Press; John S. Knight, president of Knight Newspapers; Arthur Hays Sulzberger, publisher of *The New York Times*; Roy W. Howard, chairman of the executive committee of Scripps-Howard Newspapers; James S. Copley, chairman of Copley Press, Inc.; Paul Miller, president of Gannett Newspapers; Dr. Frank Stanton, president of CBS; Kilgore; and Pulliam.

Apparently believing that the practice of electing a national honorary president had become passe' by the late 1960's, the board recommended that the office be abolished and delegates to the 1969 convention approved the suggestion without debate. The last journalist to be honored by the Society in that capacity was the late Nelson Poynter, president of the St. Petersburg, Florida *Times and Independent*, who completed his year as national honorary president in November 1970.

THE WELLS MEMORIAL KEY

Chester A. Wells, president of the University of Wisconsin chapter in 1913, was one of the fraternity's most vigorous and enthusiastic members. Wells' journalistic talents had earned him the editorship of the university's literary magazine and the post of managing editor on the student newspaper. Upon graduation in June, he was scheduled to begin teaching journalism classes at the University of Oklahoma. Hoping to capitalize on his positive spirit about the future of Sigma Delta Chi, delegates to the May 3, 1913, convention in Madison elected him national president. In August, he contracted a throat infection and was hospitalized for what was expected to be minor surgery, but during the operation he suffered a severe hemorrhage. He died September 1, 1913, at the age of twenty-six.

The Wisconsin chapter that fall proposed that a Wells Memorial be established to honor him and that a key be presented each year to the retiring national president of the fraternity. The suggestion met with swift and enthusiastic approval and Laurence H. Sloan, who had been the fraternity's first national president, received the first Wells Memorial Key when he finished his two-term assignment. The following year, delegates decided to change the award and present it to a member to recognize outstanding service to the fraternity, whether he had held office or not. From that time on, the Wells Memorial Key has been the highest honor the organization can bestow on a member. Lee A White, an alumni member from the University of Michigan, who had helped to organize the first national convention in Madison, was presented the Wells Key in 1914. White was named recipient of the Key again in 1921 after his year as president. He and Albert W. Bates, who served as full-time executive

director of fraternity from 1929-1934 and was chairman of the headquarters committee from 1942-1946, were the only members to be awarded the Key on two occasions.

Until 1972, it was not unusual for the Wells Key to be presented to a man who had served as president at some point in his career. In fact, the majority of winners had been past national presidents. Further, since the fiftieth anniversary year, only four non-presidents – Kilgore in 1959, Wolpert in 1962, Balk in 1967 and Pulliam in 1969 – had been awarded the Wells Key until 1972, when Chandler proposed that just the opposite be done in the future. "Being elected president of Sigma Delta Chi is the greatest honor any person can enjoy in this Society. Therefore, no president or past president should receive the Wells Memorial Key – the greatest honor the Society can bestow on a member. That honor should be reserved to those who work for the Society in extraordinary ways but never make the ladder or become national president," he told his colleagues on the board. It was agreed that he was right and those who served as chair of the awards committee accepted the idea with the provision that, in certain cases, it might be appropriate that a past president receive the award for service performed since his presidency. For the next twelve years, the Wells Key, presented as the highlight of the national convention's Friday night banquet, was awarded only twice to persons who had served as president of the Society – Small in 1979 and Goodykoontz in 1982. The ten non-presidents who received the award were Barnum in 1972, Copley in 1973, Kong in 1974, Julian in 1975, Rieger in 1976, Davis in 1977, Agee in 1978, Lewis in 1980, Howard S. Dubin in 1981 and Bukro in 1983.

A second Wells Key was presented in 1981 at the Distinguished Service Awards regional conference in Cincinnati, marking only the second time in the Society's seventy-two year history that two keys were awarded in one year. Both Carl Getz, for his work on *The Quill*, and Roger Steffan, president of the fraternity from 1914-1916, won the Wells Key in 1915. The special 1981 key went to the recently resigned Hurst in recognition of his nineteen years of service as the Society's executive officer. Hurst's reaction on receiving the Wells Memorial Key was typical of the emotions of many recent recipients. In an April 28, 1981, letter, he wrote, "That moment in Cincinnati was one I will always cherish. You know, I really was trying to make some appropriate thank-you remarks, but nineteen years worth of splendid memories were flooding my mind – memories of dedicated people and working together, accomplishments and striving, always striving, for the best we could bring to the Society and the profession. So about all I could muster up at that moment was 'thanks.' If my heart hadn't been in my throat, I would have added that the key with my name on it is truly shared with you and every member I've had the privilege to be associated with over the years. That's the way I'll always think of it."

THE SIGMA DELTA CHI DISTINGUISHED SERVICE AWARDS

The Society of Professional Journalists, Sigma Delta Chi, in 1982, celebrated the fiftieth anniversary of its program recognizing excellence in reporting, editorial writing, photography, research in journalism and public service. In an elaborate ceremony in Williamsburg, Virginia, the Society honored journalists' performance in sixteen categories: general reporting; television, radio and magazine reporting; Washington and foreign correspondence; editorial writing; editorializing on television and on radio; editorial cartooning; news photography; public service in journalism by a newspaper, a magazine, a television station, and a radio station; and research about journalism.

The special 1982 awards program, edited by Charles and Kathy Fair of Virginia Commonwealth University, traced the history of the Sigma Delta Chi Distinguished Service Awards and noted contemporary trends in awards for achievement in journalism. The competition was not always as broad nor as prestigious nationally as it has become in later years, but its humble beginnings in 1932 were intended to reward journalistic excellence. Charles Fair's comprehensive research and writing on what have become known as "The DSA's"

provide the best synopsis of the development of the awards. He wrote:

The SDX national awards program was first proposed in 1928 by John Dreiske, president of the Northwestern University chapter, but the SDX executive council took no action on the matter until the 1931 convention voted to present special gold keys to six men each year for their contributions to "the dignity and responsibility to the profession of journalism."

Those first recipients were Paul Scott Mowrer, European bureau chief for the Chicago *Daily News*; Philip Hale, music and drama critic for the Boston *Herald*; Franklin P. Adams, columnist for the New York *Herald Tribune*; Alexander Dana Noyes, financial editor for *The New York Times*; Jay N. (Ding) Darling, syndicated editorial cartoonist for the Des Moines *Register* and *Tribune*; and Casper S. Yost, editor of the editorial page of the St. Louis *Globe Democrat*.

The awards were presented in the spring of 1932, and with the Great Depression into its depths, the attention of journalists, as well as that of SDX, turned from contests to survival. In the next six years, the only awards were $50 grants for journalism research, which went to four journalism professors, including Alfred McClung Lee, who had chaired the committee that established the research awards competition in 1934.

It was in 1939, at the urging of *Quill* editor and past president Ralph Peters, that the national convention established the present Distinguished Service Awards competition. The gold keys of 1931 were replaced, however, by bronze medallions, and the first of these were presented for work completed in 1939. The competition included entries in general reporting, editorial writing, foreign correspondence, Washington correspondence, radio news writing and courage in journalism.

Since the awards program was begun in 1931, more than 700 men and women and their news organizations have received these coveted awards. And the DSA has become one of the most respected honors bestowed in journalism.

In an interesting bit of research, Fair also traced the subject matter which has been the focus of winning entries, revealed that two amateur photographers had beaten out professional news cameramen for awards in that category and listed those who had had the greatest success in winning the major prize. He found that two general topics – civil rights and international crises – have dominated the awards through the years, and that J. Parke Randall, an architect who was also an amateur photographer, won the DSA in photography in 1960 for a series of pictures of the collapse of a grandstand at the Indianapolis 500 race, while John P. Filo, a student at Kent State University, was awarded a DSA in 1970 for his photographs of the day National Guardsmen fired on student protesters on his campus. Among news organizations, the Associated Press had won twenty DSA's through 1983 and the Los Angeles *Times* and CBS had been awarded eighteen each. Paul Conrad, an editorial cartoonist for the Los Angeles *Times*, earned five DSA's through 1983 – more than any other individual journalist.

Judging panels for the Distinguished Service Awards are selected from among Society members and non-members across the nation, each of whom has established a reputation for journalistic excellence in his own right. While the list of judges often is published, the identity of judges for a specific category, whose decision is final, is never revealed. It is easy to start an argument among journalists about whether the DSA's have achieved a level of prestige above or equal to the Pulitzer Prizes, organized twenty-two years earlier than the Sigma Delta Chi awards. While the matter may be simply academic, it is worth noting that Clayton's history of the fraternity quoted an early DSA winner as saying, "I rank this above the Pulitzer because it is truly the judgment of my peers," and that this author had heard recent winners comment seriously in the same manner.

From the early 1940's until 1962, the awards were presented at a special spring banquet held alternately in Chicago and New York City. The DSA's ceremony was made a part of the Region Four conference in Detroit in 1962 and has been a part of regional conference programs in the spring of each year since that time. All of the winners since 1939 are listed in the Appendix of this book.

A CONTEST FOR STUDENTS

Competition for collegiate journalists had a much earlier start than the DSA's with an undergraduate chapter providing the impetus. The Iowa State Prize, established in 1923 to stimulate undergraduate reportorial work, was open to all college journalists regardless of membership in the fraternity and had as its prize a gold watch. No records could be found regarding how long the contest was in effect, but when Sigma Delta Chi established the DSA's in 1939, it also provided a permanent competition for student journalists in its Student Press Contest. The convention established "a national contest to determine the best selection of editorials, feature stories, sports stories and straight news stories published in a college or university newspaper each school year. The winner in each division will be awarded a medal." The convention also approved a photo contest for undergraduate members only, with first, second and third prizes to be made for "spot news pictures, feature pictures and sports pictures." The *Michigan Daily* won three of the four writing awards with Temple University's *News* capturing the feature-writing competition when the prizes were given for the first time in 1940. In photography, South Dakota State students won first prizes for sports and feature pictures, with a Northwestern University student taking first in the spot news category. Through the years, the Student Press Contest expanded to thirteen categories including divisions for magazines, radio and television. It was strictly a national competition until 1970, with entries being sent to national headquarters and a committee of professional journalists selected to judge the contest.

In April 1970, Bostrom, an assistant professor of journalism at Northern Arizona University, and Dr. Joseph Milner, professor of journalism at Arizona State University, were returning from a meeting of Rocky Mountain-area college journalism students in Sun Valley, Idaho. Neither had been very much pleased with the meeting and decided they would begin taking their students only to the Sigma Delta Chi regional conferences in the future. But since not many students had expressed interest in attending past SDX regionals, the two educators discussed just what it was that had attracted students to the conference they had just left. They settled on the fact that the awarding of prizes to winners of a series of contests in various newspaper and magazine categories was the major drawing card. "Why can't we get SDX to have a regional competition in those same categories?" Milner asked. He contacted Region Eleven director Henry Rieger, who expressed an interest, said he would take up with the board the idea of expanding the Student Press Contest to a preliminary judging at the regional level with regional winners sent to national for the final competition. The board, seeing the possibility of increased interest in regional conferences, adopted the idea quickly and the Mark of Excellence Contest was born.

The Quill announced the new program in January 1971 reporting that the Mark of Excellence Contest "would honor outstanding individual writers, newscasters, magazine editors and photographers at colleges and universities which have SDX campus chapters. There are no fees required and the contest will feature open competition, not restricted to SDX members and not restricted to publications on campus." Entries published or broadcast from February 1 of one year to February 1 of the following year would be eligible to receive appropriate awards at the regional conferences each spring in a semi final competition, with the regional winners considered for national prizes. A special plaque is presented annually to the national winners. The number of entries in 1971 was disappointing, but, by the following year, 1,940 entries were received in the regional contests, an record for the Society's student press contests.

Throughout the 1970's, a not-so-favorite pastime of the national board was to consider the expansion of, and changes in

the Mark of Excellence competition. Suggestions on new categories, the need for deletion of others and changes in the rules came from students, campus chapters and the campus chapter activities committee. And on each occasion the board considered altering the competition, the debate became long and heated at times. At its April 1980 meeting in Seattle, the board took a long look at the competition, which by then was attracting 3,000 entries or more, determined to set its parameters and rules for the next five years. Only minor changes have been effected since that time.

The 1982-1983 Mark of Excellence Contest offered students the opportunity to compete in sixteen categories in four divisions. In the newspaper division, awards were presented for editorial writing, editorial cartooning, spot news story, depth reporting, feature article and best all-round student newspaper. Magazine students could compete for awards for the best all-around student magazine and the best nonfiction article. The six broadcasting categories included radio and television spot news on deadline, news with no deadline and documentary. Photography awards were presented for best news photo and best feature photo. A complete list of winners is found in the Appendix.

OUTSTANDING GRADUATE AWARDS

At the same 1939 national convention in which the Student Press Contest and DSA's were established, the board decided to honor "one man in each journalism graduating class of every college and university represented by a campus chapter of SDX." The award would be based on "character, scholarship and the competence to perform journalistic tasks." Selection of the winner of the citation for excellence in journalism would be made by a special committee, formed annually, to be made up of "the president of the Sigma Delta Chi chapter, the chapter's faculty adviser and a professional member of the fraternity who is a graduate of the college or university."

That program continued through the mid-1980s with only minor modifications – substituting "an officer" of the chapter for "president," and, of course, allowing women graduates to be considered equally with men. Special certificates were prepared for presentation to winners in local ceremonies, with the list of all of the outstanding graduates published in *The Quill*.

THE HISTORIC SITES

The Des Moines convention in 1940 provided the beginning of one more landmark program for the fraternity – the selecting of an historic site connected with the history of American journalism. The idea came from 1940-1941 Sigma Delta Chi president Irving Dilliard, who told the executive council at its preconvention meeting that such a plan would be an excellent annual observance to mark National Newspaper Week. Receiving the approval of the council, the proposal was submitted to the convention, which voted to establish the program but failed to provide funds for it. However, it did authorize Dilliard to appoint a committee to initiate the project. Dilliard named Floyd Shoemaker, secretary of the State Historical Society of Missouri, as the first chairman.

Shoemaker's committee made its recommendation to the 1941 convention in New Orleans, suggesting that the first site be in Bennington, Vermont, where the press of Anthony Haswell, editor of the *Vermont Gazette* had stood. The site, approved by the delegates, was selected because of Haswell's courage in challenging the Alien and Sedition Acts, passed in 1798 under the administration of John Adams. Haswell, a country editor, had been fined and imprisoned for his outspoken protests against the drastic restrictions of the press. A $500 donation from an anonymous member solved the problem of financing the marking, and arrangements were begun to plan an elaborate ceremony for the unveiling of the first historic site marker. However, the United States had entered World War II, speakers were unable to accept engagements, gasoline and tire rationing was in effect and travel was difficult. Finally, on August 16, 1942, the marker was unveiled, but unfortunately without the elaborate ceremony that had been planned.

A second historic site was not dedicated until 1946. It honored James King, founder, editor and publisher of the

San Francisco *Daily Evening Bulletin*, who was assassinated by a politician after fighting corruption in municipal government. Since then, the Society has marked at least one historic site each year and in a number of years as many as three, honoring the men and women who played important roles in American journalistic history. Among the journalists honored with bronze markers at the sites where they worked were Elijah Parish Lovejoy, editor of the Alton, Illinois *Observer*, and a militant abolitionist who was also assassinated for his beliefs; William Allen White, publisher of the Emporia, Kansas *Gazette*; Ernie Pyle, World War II correspondent; H.L. Mencken, author and newspaperman; Benjamin Franklin; James Gordon Bennett; Horace Greeley; William Randolph Hearst; Joseph Pulitzer; Lincoln Steffens; Supreme Court Justice Hugo Black and pioneer radio news analyst H.V. Kaltenborn. Individual places marked because of their historic significance included The Associated Press offices in Washington and New York City; the Chillicothe, Ohio *Gazette*, oldest newspaper in continuous publication west of the Allegheny Mountains; the Augusta, Georgia *Chronicle*, oldest newspaper in the South publishing; the Chicago *Tribune*; the Chicago *Defender*, a pioneer in the publication of Black newspapers; *The Wall Street Journal*; the *Christian Science Monitor*; *Freedom's Journal*, the first Black newspaper published in the United States; and DePauw University, where Sigma Delta Chi was founded. All told, seventy-two sites were marked as national historic landmarks by the Society through 1983. Each was selected from among a series of annual nominations by a national committee which checked thoroughly on the credentials of the place or person considered for the honor. Another thirty-seven sites with local or regional significance to journalism have been marked by chapters of the Society since that alternate program began in 1950. A complete list of the markings appears in the Appendix of his history.

DISTINGUISHED TEACHING IN JOURNALISM AWARD

Although Sigma Delta Chi's roots were nurtured, in part, by journalism educators, the Society waited until 1966 to honor professors each year for their teaching ability, contributions to journalism education and contributions toward maintaining the highest standards of the profession. First among his national colleagues to receive the Distinguished Teaching in Journalism Award was professor A.L. Higginbotham, of the University of Nevada at Reno. Higginbotham had been vice president for campus chapter affairs for two terms and, in his forty-three years of teaching had become one of the nation's most respected and admired educators. He had been president of the American Society of Journalism School Administrators; president of Kappa Tau Alpha, journalism's scholastic honorary; editor of *The Journalism Educator*; and a member of the American Council on Education for Journalism. Higginbotham was recognized at the 1966 national convention in Pittsburgh, although he was on a foreign tour and could not be present.

Four professors from the University of Minnesota – Mitchell V. Charnley in 1968, J. Edward Gerald in 1975, Edwin Emery in 1980 and George S. Hage in 1983 – were honored with the award. Through 1983, Minnesota remained the only university to have more than one winner.

THE FIRST AMENDMENT AWARD

Bill Small spent much of his professional life working for freedom of information from his early days at WLS Radio in Chicago, through his involvement with RTNDA , as senior vice president of CBS News, and as president of both NBC News and United Press International. For the Society, he was a fourteen-year member of the freedom of information committee before becoming Region Two director. It was no wonder, then, that as Society president in 1975, he initiated the idea for the new SPJ,SDX First Amendment Awards.

"We had the Wells Key, honoring contributions to a Society member, and the DSA's, recognizing journalistic excellence in a given year. We had a need to recognize people who had made serious and ongoing contributions to the free press," Small remembers. He presented the idea to the

board at the spring conference in El Paso, Texas, May 2, 1975, suggesting that it not be a competitive program, but open to all who qualify in the eyes of the national board. "The board accepted my idea with real enthusiasm," Small said, "and immediately selected the Reporters Committee for Freedom of the Press as the first recipient." Small presented the citation to the Reporters Committee in ceremonics on Independence Mall at the convention in Philadelphia the following November. During the ceremony, he announced the second award would be made to retiring Supreme Court Justice William O. Douglas.

As guidelines for the award were developed, the board determined that there would be no limit in the number of awards to be presented in any one year. Should there be six worthy nominees, as there were in 1976, six First Amendment Awards would be presented. Further, achievements at the national and local levels would be treated equally because the contributions of those nominees who never attracted national attention in FOI battles were as significant in every respect as of those whom the spotlight had singled out. The 1976 winners included Bill Farr, the Fresno Four, former CBS News correspondent Daniel Schorr and past Society president Ray Spangler. But they also included the Medford, Oregon *Mail Tribune*, for its successful fight leading to the repeal of a state law which had limited access to criminal information and the Media of Nebraska Committee, for its work in the *Stuart v. Nebraska* case.

The other individuals and organizations presented the First Amendment Award through 1983 represented a broad spectrum of American life and included editors and publishers of several small newspapers, major media or their executives, the organizer of The First Amendment Congresses, attorneys and members of Congress. Not only has the First Amendment Award "served its purpose well in its first decade," as Small said, but it has become a prestigious addition to the Society's program of freedom of information activities.

DISTINGUISHED ADVISER AWARD

From Sigma Delta Chi's earliest days,

the level of activity and the contributions of its campus chapters have risen and fallen in roller-coaster fashion. It was not unusual for an inactive chapter to rise from its ashes and reach great heights for five-to-ten years in membership, programming and service to the Society and the profession, only to slip back again for several "down" years. Hurst and Pearl Luttrell at the national headquarters, the latter of whom observed the phenomenon for twenty years, were able to document that, in their peak years, campus chapters were blessed with outstanding advisers. "The connection was clear cut," said Hurst. "Many of these dedicated educators gave literally hundreds of hours each year working with student officers and members, inspiring them to accomplish great things." From her knowledge of working with the advisers, Luttrell knew which chapters would be active, vigorous and growing parts of the Society. "There were a great many wonderful advisers through the years, but a few stood out for the services they performed over a long period of time," she recalled.

The minutes of a few board meetings during the 1960's and 1970's carry mention of the need to do something to recognize the work of advisers, but nothing was done. During his term, vice president for campus chapter affairs Ralph Izard of Ohio University and his campus chapter activities committee believed it was time to honor the best among the advisers. He took his idea to the board April 28, 1978, and received unanimous support for the establishment of an award for a Distinguished Campus Adviser. The question of how to single out one national winner each year when there

were so many qualified candidates was settled by a determination to honor four advisers – one in each campus district – each year, with presentations to be made at each winner's home regional conference. Guidelines set up between April and November called for a nominee to have been an adviser for at least three years; made significant contributions to local chapter leadership; demonstrated support for the profession, the Society and individual student members; and participated in activities of the national organization. It was determined that only those currently active as advisers would be considered.

The first four designated as Distinguished Campus Advisers were Paul Atkins, West Virginia University; James Highland, Western Kentucky University; Merrill Bankester, Memphis State University; and Robert Warner, University of Wyoming. Each received a plaque and standing ovations at the spring 1979 regional conferences. To no one's surprise, each winner's chapter had won or would win awards as the outstanding national or regional chapter in judging separate from the Distinguished Campus Adviser balloting.

During the next four years, sixteen more advisers were selected, representing eleven of the Society's twelve regions – demonstrating that the reservoir of outstanding advisers was, indeed, deep. They are named in the Appendix. With what were the obvious choices of those with long records of service honored in the first five years of the competition, the board voted in 1983 to give the award greater future prestige by selecting only one winner each year beginning in 1984.

CHAPTER 9

███████████████

Admission of Women to the Society

The claim of The Society of Professional Journalists, Sigma Delta Chi, to be "the largest, oldest and most representative organization serving the field of journalism" will start an argument with women initiated to the honorary for women in journalism, Theta Sigma Phi (now Women in Communications, Inc.) at least insofar as the word "oldest" is concerned. Both organizations were founded in 1909. Theta Sigma Phi, however, claims April 9 as its founding date at the University of Washington while the generally-accepted date for the formal beginnings of SDX is April 17, eight days later. The proximity of time in the founding of the two groups does serve to underscore the beginning of more than sixty years of the separation of membership for men and women in the two most prestigious, grass-roots journalism organizations in the nation. There was no argument about separate organizations for men and women in the early years. A fraternity was a fraternity and an honorary for women was only for women. That was understood and accepted. When Sigma Delta Chi changed its status from an honorary fraternity to a professional fraternity in 1916, both organizations required a commitment to a career in journalism as a prerequisite to membership and the two groups participated with each other in convention programs as early as 1921. There were times, no doubt, when individual members and even boards of directors questioned themselves about the necessity for two separate bodies serving basically the same function, but if there were any formal efforts initiated to join SDX and Theta Sigma Phi, they were dropped quickly.

Within Sigma Delta Chi, concerns about membership eligibility centered on admitting public relations and advertising practitioners in addition to newsmen. Even in the massive reorganizational effort in 1959 and 1960 there is no recorded discussion of attempting to include women as members to help build the membership nor do McKinsey Report discussions allude to that possibility. The philosophy of the founders that Sigma Delta Chi was an organization of men bound together "in a true fraternity spirit"

William B. Arthur, Society president in 1968-1969, was surrounded by newswomen from the Buffalo and Niagara Falls, New York, area who picketed his appearance before the Greater Buffalo International chapter during 1969. The women were protesting the Society's failure to admit women to membership. Arthur promised to make membership for women a priority during his administration and presided during the November 1969 convention business session in San Diego where the by-laws were changed admitting women for the first time in the Society's sixty-year history.

dominated the thinking of their thousands of "heirs" for more than fifty years. Hurst, who admits that the subject probably had been discussed informally many times over the years and that many individual officers or board members might have legitimate claim to making an early attempt to facilitate admission of women to Sigma Delta Chi, recalls telling the Society's officers not long after he had been named executive officer, "It is inconceivable to me that the Society could develop along the lines it wanted to take as *the* professional society of journalists and, at the same time, eliminate from eligibility for membership what is about one third of the population of newsrooms of the country." Hurst had been executive officer for only six months when a brief letter from

Theodore Berland, a free-lance writer and member of the Chicago Headline Club, appeared in the November 1962 *Quill*. While he was probably not the first to write an appeal for admission of women, his letter no doubt spoke for all who had or would join the battle. He wrote:

Now that SDX is a professional society, and has thrown off the medieval shackles of a fraternity, how about going all the way and including women in the membership? This may seem radical to oldtimers but this is an era of integration and the presence of women in other professional societies is quite normal and non-disrupting.

The letter from Berland, who in 1983 was chairman of the journalism department at Columbia College in Chicago and, interestingly, was among the first men to join Women in Communications, Inc., when it accepted males, may have raised some interest as well as some eyebrows, but didn't attract a published rebuttal.

It was another two years before the issue surfaced again and then only in the internal workings of the Society's membership committee, chaired by Dessauer, associate editor of the Tulsa *World* In an August 23, 1964, letter addressed to the "Gentlemen of the SDX Membership Committee," Dessauer asked for their help with suggestions to solve or alleviate the problems of weak professional chapters and journalism schools with too few undergraduates to form a chapter. Saying that, "Membership is the key to a bigger and better SDX," he encouraged inclusion of "other ideas, information or suggestions you believe should come to the attention of the membership committee." What he received in return from Kenneth C. Reiley, chapter secretary of the San Diego professional chapter and an associate editorial consultant for Copley Newspapers, would sound the opening "charge!" for a five-year battle royal. Reiley's long letter, dated August 27, labored through a series of pros and cons on suggested remedies until the bottom of page three, where he wrote:

I would like to make this suggestion, and I'll probably be ridden out of town on a rail for it. I'd like to see professional newswomen admitted to membership....I can't see why a career woman, as perhaps an assistant women's editor, can't be a member when the women's page makeup man is....I don't see why we can't initiate a woman who meets the qualifications of the men -- two years experience and actively engaged in gathering, editing, disseminating or directing the editorial policy of a news medium.

This may be too far afield, but I am dead serious about allowing women into SDX. If necessary, do not initiate them into undergraduate chapters, where the opposition to such a move seems to be settled. If the girls show they are going to be career newspeople

Robert W. Chandler, national president in 1970-1971, applauded a speech by Daniel Schorr of CBS News during the San Diego convention in 1969. While Region Ten director, Chandler was one of the first members of the board of directors to support actively the admission of women to the Society.

by getting jobs and staying with them for two years, allow the professional chapters to initiate them at their discretion. We invite the Southern branch of the California Press Women to attend our meetings and they turn out in force. They are honorable, ethical and dedicated journalists and they should not be discriminated against just because they wear short pants.

Reiley's letter did not provoke any favorable committee or board of directors action by November, but it may well have caused him to be named vice chairman of the membership committee for 1965. He remembers he had begun work as early as 1958 toward clearing the way for admission of women. "My sympathies toward women stemmed from the twenty-one years I spent as a reporter/editor before joining SDX [in 1957]. The women in the newsrooms did the same work, but got less pay, fewer chances to advance and just got kicked around. It wasn't fair. It was a disgrace to the profession. I can't recall anyone on the

The Society's 1968-1969 board of directors which endorsed the by-laws change to admit women to Sigma Delta Chi included: (clockwise from left) William C. Payette, William T. Kong, Robert McCord, Wallace Allen, Frank Wetzel, Zeke Scher, Fred Barger, Staley McBrayer, William Day, Ralph Otwell, Henry Rieger, Larry Thomas, Wayne Markham and Clarence O. Schlaver. (Standing from left) Robert W. Chandler, Frank Angelo, William B. Arthur, Charles Long, Dr. Warren K. Agee, and Eugene Methvin. Not pictured was Guy Ryan.

committee being adamantly in favor of admitting women but me." Dessauer, who continued as committee chair in 1965, agrees. "The committee never did take any formal action in recommending or not recommending Reiley's position to the board, " he said.

Reiley's determination to carry his idea to the board caused him to write Hurst asking for a place on the agenda at the May 7, 1965, board meeting in Philadelphia. "If Sigma Delta Chi is to retain its identity as the true professional journalistic society, it cannot rightfully ban these professional journalists because of their sex," he wrote. "The national membership committee is pledged to increase the rolls of Sigma Delta Chi. If the number of men in journalism continues to decline while the number of women increases, you can see that we have a fairly hopeless task ahead of us." Reiley

received his hearing and scored a small victory when the board instructed president Sewell to refer the matter to the full membership committee, asking that a report be returned for presentation to the board at its November 10 meeting in Los Angeles. Dessauer's committee again could not reach any decision. In its report Dessauer wrote: "The results of our voting – and sampling of chapter opinion – is so mixed that I cannot report a recommendation from the committee. In all fairness, I believe this issue will have to be laid before the membership in order to get a true reflection of the over-all sentiment." The board "received" the report without action.

Reiley anticipated the board's response and, working with UCLA campus chapter president Don Harrison, he arranged to take the fight to the convention floor. Reiley prepared a resolution demanding a vote on the matter and Harrison addressed the delegates, saying:

> In the last two days of convention, I have been able to meet many delegates and I have heard many reasons why women shouldn't be admitted to Sigma Delta Chi. Did you know that women are incapable of reaching a rational decision and that they come to grips with issues not on the basis of fact but on the basis of emotion? Did you know that women would inhibit our convention sessions? And that we wouldn't be allowed to exercise our full vocabularies during the meetings if women were admitted?....I, for one, could never take the position that women are any less able than men, or that their contributions to Sigma Delta Chi would be any less impressive than those of our male members....If we defeat the proposal to admit women to Sigma Delta Chi, we ought to be honest and change our name to Sigma Delta Chi, men's journalism honorary.

While they could not muster enough support to change the by-laws and force a vote on the issue in Los Angeles, they were successful in getting enough delegate support for a modified resolution to instruct the board to prepare a by-laws proposal in time for the 1966 national convention in Pittsburgh which would allow for admission of women to Sigma Delta Chi. Dessauer remembers, "It was Reiley's persistent effort to make it an issue and, perhaps, because its time had come, that brought the debate to the convention floor." Incoming president Spangler appointed Reiley as the 1965-1966 membership committee chairman, but, fearing that there would not be enough time at the Pittsburgh convention to debate the issue fully, he asked Reiley to begin a year-long dialogue with members on the subject. As quickly as the notice of the convention's action was published in *The Quill*, opposition began to form.

THE GREAT DEBATES

To facilitate discussion, Reiley asked George Wolpert, a member of the Milwaukee professional chapter board and a staunch opponent to admitting women, to

Jean Otto became the first woman to serve as a national officer of the Society in 1976 when she was elected national treasurer in Los Angeles. Elected national president in 1979 in New York City, she was the only woman to hold that post in the Society's first seventy-five years. In 1979 and 1980, Otto was the spearhead of the drive to establish the First Amendment Congress and served as chairman of the Congress after its incorporation.

prepare a statement giving his reasons. In a March 31, 1966, letter sent to all professional and campus chapters and to the national president of Theta Sigma Phi, Wolpert wrote:

> [We are] asked why we oppose membership for women. We think that the shoe is on the other foot. Those who favor the idea should present valid reasons for their stand. They must come clean, stating where the idea originated, with what individual or group, and tell why. We know that it did not originate with Theta Sigma Phi, nor from any one individual newswoman. The ranks of Theta Sigma Phi would be decimated if Sigma Delta Chi raided the organization of its members. We would be guilty of

George Wolpert received a kiss on each cheek
April 21, 1970 from Ruth Wilson (left) and Laurie
Van dyke, among the first women members
admitted to the Society's Milwaukee professional
chapter. Looking on was 1969-1970 Society
president Frank Angelo. Wolpert, who led a
vigorous campaign against the admission of
women from 1975 through 1969, was awarded the
Wells Memorial Key in 1962 for years of dedicated
service to the national society.

meetings with wives. Sigma Delta Chi
insists upon being known as a
professional society of journalists, and as
such, it is comparable to those
professional organizations serving
medicine and law.

We respect the right of women to
enter the profession of journalism, and
we acknowledge that there is talent and
brilliance among them, but if we are to
survive as a fraternity of journalists, if
we are to grow and command the
respect of the profession, then we must
continue to be what we were born to be
– a fraternity of journalists in the literal
sense of the word. The alternative
means sacrificing all distinctions,
altering our objectives and by-laws,
foregoing our unique position, diluting
our strength and ending up just another
society of journalists for the sake of a
wild idea!

Seventeen years later in a March 5,
1983, letter to this author, Wolpert recalled,
"When Ken Reiley began his campaign in
the open, in 1966, to raise the barrier and
admit women; when national officers began
looking the other way following a stand
against women, it was time to fight....It is
paradoxical that any member who took an
oath to live up to the ideals of Sigma Delta
Chi would initiate a movement to admit
women when no woman journalist had ever
raised her voice in protest against exclusion.
That, no doubt, was because Reiley was
inducted as a professional without
background of the college orientation which
emphasized the traditions of SDX."
Referring to the potential destruction of
Theta Sigma Phi, he wrote, "I wanted no
part of that genocide."

The publicity about Reiley's campaign
and partial success in Los Angeles, coupled
with Wolpert's strong letter to chapters
precipitated discussion in many of the
Society's regional conferences during the
spring of 1966. In one of those conferences,
the Region Five meeting in Gilbertsville,
Kentucky, April 23, the major focus of the
program centered on the pros and cons of
admitting women to the Society. That
meeting brought Reiley face-to-face with
Theta Sigma Phi national president Marjorie
Paxon.

causing the deterioration and demise of
a fine sister organization.

Why, after fifty-seven years of
steady growth into a world-wide
membership of men engaged in every
field of journalism, should Sigma Delta
Chi, now the largest and most select
organization serving journalism,
suddenly lose its virility? If the
founders of Sigma Delta Chi, who
showed foresight in setting standards for
the fraternity that would encourage its
growth, had a moment's thought that
eventually membership should be
extended to women, there would have
been some suggestion of this in their
intent.

The danger of becoming social is
imminent if we admit women, especially
in campus chapters. There is even
evidence of such a trend now among
professional chapters which have

Only men were among the new members being initiated to the Society by president William B. Arthur at the 1969 San Diego convention; however, one day after this photo was taken, Arthur presided over the business session during which delegates overwhelmingly voted to change the by-laws to admit women to Sigma Delta Chi.

In her debate with Reiley, Paxon said her entire board opposed admission of women to Sigma Delta Chi.

I must confess, fellows, that I have never felt I was culturally deprived, or disadvantaged or rejected by my peers because I couldn't join SDX. Now, SDX is getting ready to vote on admitting women to membership. Why? Has all the talk about equal rights suddenly made you think you are somehow being unequal to women? If that's the case forget it. There's a wide difference between equal opportunity on the job and equal opportunity of membership. If this is the argument, then we in Theta Sig had better start worrying about whether we are discriminating against men....But this certainly isn't the answer....Theta Sig and SDX have many of the same aims and purposes. We have been good friends and have worked together in many cities. We would like to keep it that way. We would much rather cooperate than compete. And make no mistake, if SDX admits women, we will be forced to compete with you for membership....It's being said that if SDX admits women, Theta Sig will be killed. No, we won't be killed. We're tougher than that. But no Theta Sig that I've talked with doubts that we will be hurt, particularly at the student level.

She posed several pointed questions, asking if Sigma Delta Chi would be as concerned as Theta Sigma Phi in cases of discrimination against women in and out of newsrooms. She asked what chances women would have to hold office, other than the traditional post of secretary, in chapters or at the national level and whether the Society would give attention and space to specialized articles of interest to women in *The Quill*, areas in which Theta Sigma Phi offered both opportunities and outlets.

Kenneth C. Reiley, a member of the San Diego professional chapter in 1962, started a personal seven-year campaign to allow the admission of women into the Society. Reiley, who became national membership chairman in 1966, spoke at meetings across the nation, wrote letters and magazine articles, and lobbied at national conventions from 1965 through 1969 before seeing his efforts bear fruit at the 1969 national convention. Reiley later served as Region Eleven director from 1976-1979.

In short, what will you offer to women members besides the chances to pay dues? The answer, it seems to us on the Theta Sig board, lies not in admitting women to SDX, thereby weakening our organization and drastically changing the character of yours, as it surely will. Rather, the answer lies in devoting more time to finding ways of working together on such projects as interesting young people in careers in journalism, job placement, and joint events with top speakers. Our board will be happy to meet with your board or to send representatives to a meeting to consider cooperative ventures. Such a move would combine our strengths on projects of mutual concern and at the same time give each organization the opportunity to concentrate on its specialized viewpoints

and the specialized needs of our members....As women, we know there will always remain one basic difference – yes, and other differences too between the sexes. Would you really want it any other way?

Reiley responded just as firmly before the Region Five delegates. Answering Wolpert's question about who originated the idea, Reiley said, "I cannot tell a lie. I did it, with my little hatchet, Mother Washington. I did it because approximately twenty-five percent of the working journalists are women. I did it because Sigma Delta Chi does not tell the truth when it calls itself *'the* professional journalistic society' when it does not represent, nor admit, twenty-five percent of the journalists." He continued, "The 1966 *Directory* of Sigma Delta Chi, in defining the Society, says, 'It is the only professional organization that embraces all kinds of journalism as well as all ranks of journalists,' It does not embrace women, but that's not a bad idea. It defines journalism as 'the direction of the editorial policy of, the editing of, the preparation of news and editorial content of newspapers, magazines, press or syndicate services, professional or business publications, radio and television; and the teaching of journalism so defined.' Women, then, are journalists and should be embraced."

Commenting on the possible demise of Theta Sigma Phi, he said, "In my state, California, there are three Theta Sig [professional] chapters, at San Diego, Los Angeles and San Francisco. Yet there are hundreds of newspapers, radio and television stations scattered throughout the state – all with women working for them. There are only two student chapters in the state – at Stanford and Southern California. On the other hand, there are nine campus chapters of Sigma Delta Chi." On eight of those campuses, he said, all of the women who are journalism majors cannot join a campus chapter of any professional group – Theta Sigma Phi or Sigma Delta Chi. "It simply is not fair to ban ninety percent of the female journalism majors just because Theta Sig has two campus chapters in a state of eighteen million persons. And it is an insult to Theta Sig to suggest that they will be

Val Hymes, a Washington, DC, television correspondent and Distinguished Service Award winner in radio news, was the first woman elected as a regional director. She served as Region Two director from 1974 through 1980.

'wrecked' if college women are admitted to Sigma Delta Chi."

On May 6, 1966, in Des Moines, Iowa, it was time for the Sigma Delta Chi board to face the issue squarely. While board members did not have any choice about preparing the mandated by-laws change for the Pittsburgh convention, they voted, 9-2, against adoption of the very by-law they wrote admitting women to the Society. The minutes did not carry the names of those who were opposed to membership for women, but it was clear they were influenced by several factors. White remembers, "There was a keen recognition of the importance of some of the chapters – including the Milwaukee professional chapter – which were violently opposed to the issue. We were still building from a very weak base and, needing the support of all of our chapters, we didn't want to alienate them." Angelo, who opposed the by-laws change strongly, said his basic concern was for

Theta Sigma Phi. "The women had a viable group in Theta Sig and I thought that rather than having SDX admit women, we ought to consider merging the two groups." William B. Arthur, then managing editor of *Look* magazine and the newly-elected national treasurer, agreed with Angelo and worried about the possible effect on Theta Sigma Phi. Arthur had led a short-lived campaign on the board in Dallas, May 10, 1963, to have a committee appointed to study the possible integration of the Society with Theta Sigma Phi, but his motion failed. Chandler, on the other hand, said he supported Reiley's movement from the beginning and cast one of the two minority votes. Spangler recalls, "I favored admission, but made a definite attempt to stay out of the conflict in my role as president of the Society." No doubt, pressure was exerted on the board by long-time members of Sigma Delta Chi, including past presidents. In a July 13, 1966, letter to Wolpert, Robert U. Brown, president in 1953-1954, said he hoped the integration movement could be stopped quickly. "I believe that if we do not, it will eventually kill Sigma Delta Chi." Arthur recalls that the influence of the "fraternity-types" was the primary factor on the board for the negative vote.

Reiley and Wolpert presented final pre-convention arguments in the October *Quill*, with Reiley stating that SDX "is the only professional society of any stature which so discriminates [against women]....Sigma Delta Chi does not have the right to set up double standards of eligibility, bypassing the 'talent, truth and energy' of one of three professionals it pretends to represent." Wolpert called attention to the fact that Theta Sigma Phi delegates, meeting in convention in August, had voted unanimously against SDX membership for women, and concentrated on the possible destruction of Theta Sigma Phi. "Let's be sensible in Pittsburgh," he admonished.

REJECTION IN PITTSBURGH

President Spangler scheduled extra time for the floor debate in Pittsburgh, November 12. Reiley knew many delegates had come instructed to vote against admission of women and that the major opposition probably would come from the campus chapters. In his remarks, he said, "It is up to you to decide whether your chapter members would vote the way you have been instructed if they had heard the arguments presented here. If you think they would have voted differently from the way you have been instructed, then it is your obligation to be honest with them and with yourself and vote the way you think is right." But when the vote came on the change in by-laws admitting women at both the campus and professional levels, the delegates soundly defeated it, 96-47. Reiley then turned to his counter proposal that women be admitted only through professional chapters after they had worked as newspersons for two years. A motion to order the national board to prepare a by-laws change which would effect that "foot in the door" change was defeated, but only by two votes, 49-47. "The same forty-seven delegates supporting the original change voted for the second motion, but forty-seven other delegates abstained," Reiley recalled. Most of them didn't want to vote, he said, because they had come instructed only on the first issue. Spangler said that, after the close second vote, "I knew the matter wouldn't go away."

The election of at least two of the new regional directors who joined the board in Pittsburgh – Ralph Otwell, assistant to the editor of the Chicago *Sun-Times* and Region Five director; and Zeke Scher, of the Denver *Post* – assured that Spangler would be right. Both joined Chandler and Spangler in trying to convince others on the board that, despite the defeat in Pittsburgh, the time had come for positive action on membership for women. Otwell said, "I was very outspoken [following Pittsburgh] to the point where I'm sure I alienated some of my older friends in the Society." But one of those he helped to convince was McBrayer, a member since 1949, who recalls, "Some of us who enjoyed the fraternity status for all those years simply found the idea hard to accept, but we began to come around." The board took no action during 1967, but president White knew that while the issue was not on the agenda for the national convention November 15-18 in Minneapolis, it would surface again.

In the pre-convention board meeting,

Scher attempted to prevent a new floor fight by introducing a motion for a by-laws change admitting professional women to be considered the following year in Atlanta. His motion was defeated and, sure enough, the matter was brought before the delegates, again, by the UCLA campus chapter. UCLA chapter president Robert L. Suffel presented a petition calling for a referendum on the question. Members of the by-laws committee advised that the proposed language contained certain deficiencies and urged that the matter be delayed until the 1968 convention in Atlanta. Following debate, the UCLA delegate announced that his chapter members still intended to pursue the referendum early in 1968 despite a vote by the delegates urging them to reconsider. Scher was successful at the board meeting following the Minneapolis convention in getting the board to agree to draft a by-laws change admitting professional women only and in having it as part of the convention business in Atlanta, thus assuring that if UCLA did not press for a referendum, the matter would still be considered in 1968.

But UCLA did persist and, upon obtaining support from the necessary number of chapters, submitted a referendum to be voted on by mail ballot. The referendum stated:

> To amend all applicable sections of Parts I and II of the By-Laws pertaining to professional members, Fellows of Sigma Delta Chi, officers, trustees and the executive officer; to delete the words "he," "him," "his," "himself," "man," and "men," and to substitute the words "her or she," "him or her," "himself or herself," "man or woman," and "men or women"

respectively.

Ballots were mailed to campus and professional chapters February 1, 1968, with an April 5 deadline for return. Suffel and Wolpert provided articles for the February *Quill* restating positions of each side. Suffel relied on information provided by Reiley, while Wolpert continued his familiar theme, adding only, "While you are being implored to vote for women, ask youself if you want a woman president one day?" Only 102 of the 179 eligible chapters returned ballots, but, by a 67-35 vote, the move to admit women was defeated soundly again. A few of the national board members had been unhappy at the UCLA chapter's bold maneuver and, when the referendum was defeated, they proposed at the board's May 3 meeting in Cape Canaveral, Florida, that the issue be dropped from the business to be considered in Atlanta. "By a narrow vote," the minutes of that meeting report, the board rescinded its Minneapolis vote to seek a convention vote at the November 1968 meeting, and no by-law change was offered in Atlanta, eliminating the possibility of settling the issue there. All that could be done in Atlanta was to have the delegates order that the issue be brought up again in 1969 in San Diego, which is exactly what happened.

Round five of the battle royal began with letters to the editor of *The Quill* and discussions at regional conferences. Reiley and Wolpert were still in the forefront of the conflict, planning strategy, writing letters and preparing articles for publiction. Reiley scored his most important victory May 9, in Rochester, New York, when in a near-complete turnaround, the national board voted unanimously to support a by-laws change admitting women as members. The language in the motion, proposed by Chandler and seconded by treasurer Guy Ryan of San Diego along with Region Eleven director Hank Rieger, did not directly state that women should be admitted, but removed any reference to sex in the by-laws, effectively dropping all barriers to the admission of women. Chandler suggested further that a letter be sent to all chapters informing them of the board's action and requesting that chapters send delegates uninstructed on the issue to the national convention in San Diego. Agee, then vice president for campus chapter affairs, added that a poll of campus advisers showed that more than three-fourths of the advisers and two-thirds of the chapter presidents believed admission of women would increase the effectiveness of their chapters.

THE TIDE CHANGES

Arthur, president in 1968-1969, had been satisfied for some time that irreparable damage to Theta Sigma Phi was not likely to happen and that merger with the women's group was not a possibility. He turned his efforts toward effecting adoption of the change by the convention. Reflecting on the change in attitude by the board, Arthur attributed part of it to the makeup of the board and some to an acceptance that the time for admitting women had come and was now all but fact. "We were somewhat concerned as well that the threat by the UCLA administration in late 1968 to return that school's campus chapter charter if women were not allowed as members would spread to other campuses." he said. "My feelings were very strong, simply on the basis that women had earned a place in the Society." When Arthur went to Buffalo, New York, to address the Greater Buffalo International chapter in June, he was greeted outside the meeting hall by a group of women picketers demanding admission of women to Sigma Delta Chi. In his speech at the chapter's annual Ladies' Night dinner, he told the members and picketers, "My single platform for this year is to see that women are admitted to SDX. I suggest to you that this goal will become reality before the year is out."

Wolpert and Reiley continued their debates prior to the convention outside *The Quill* in *Seminar* magazine, a quarterly review for newspaper people published by Copley Newspapers. Reiley had copies of the magazine sent to each chapter and placed additional copies in the hands of the delegates after they arrived in San Diego. In that September 1969 issue of *Seminar*, Reiley attempted to shoot down each of Wolpert's earlier arguments. A supremely confident Wolpert wrote in rebuttal, "Twice [before] Ken and I have debated this issue. Twice Ken has lost. But he's not a quitter and neither am I. Even overwhelming and repeated defeat does not deter Ken from his insatiable desire to take women into Sigma Delta Chi....There are many outstanding, talented women journalists but with few exceptions they are sojourners on the way to matrimony, motherhood and matriarchy....If Ken and his minority group merely seek a diversion to enliven a convention, the time and effort can be directed to more fruitful issues. If they continue to force the will of the overwhelming majority to abdicate, the 1969 convention should make it clear that the issue is settled permanently." Just a few weeks later, the issue would be settled "permanently," but not in the way Wolpert had anticipated.

Some board members believed that one of the founders, Eugene C. Pulliam, would become involved in the controversy, perhaps in San Diego. Region Eight director Bob McCord, influenced in great part by Chandler's stand on the issue, joined the advocates for admission of women late, but in an active way. In what he called "an uncharacteristic move on my part," McCord wrote Pulliam asking him not to use his tremendous prestige to influence delegates to vote against the issue. Whether or not the letter had any effect, Pulliam did not become directly involved on the question of admission of women.

VICTORY IN SAN DIEGO

The debate on November 15, 1969, at the El Cortez Hotel lasted more than two hours. The long-standing arguments were presented one more time, but just minutes before a vote was to be taken, a surprised convention heard Larry Cohens, president of the Bradley University campus chapter, say, "Our chapter has a girl vice president. She's a girl, but nevertheless she is my vice president and she will remain vice president of our chapter no matter how the vote goes." Applause shook the room. Steve Hiney, delegate from Oklahoma State University and a member of the credentials committee, challenged Bradley's voting rights under the circumstances. President Arthur responded, "It is highly irregular to have a woman as vice president of a chapter. Perhaps we can take care of that in a moment." But Wolpert, who by coincidence was chairman of the credentials committee, countered, "The credentials committee had no knowledge that the vice president of that university chapter was a woman. Obviously, the reports were falsified....I think we should reconsider...to deny them voting privileges in fairness to the other campuses that have complied with all the rules." Arthur and his parliamentarian decided to move ahead with the vote rather than discuss removing

Bradley University's voting rights and, upon hearing a motion and second to close debate, called for that vote. Turning to the main issue on admission of women, Arthur called for a show of hands in favor of the by-laws change. As the delegates in favor raised their hands and it was apparent they would carry the day, thunderous applause and cheers filled the room. On the call for "all opposed," only about one quarter of the delegates raised their hands. President Arthur paused, then said:

> Ladies and gentlemen, Sigma Delta Chi will now admit women into the Professional Journalistic Society.

Instantly, Charles McFadden, a delegate from the Minnesota professional chapter, was at the microphone. "At this moment in history, we would like to make the first nomination of women....The chapter passed on these women and we have duly examined their qualifications...I would like at this historic moment, if I am not out of order, to nominate several women for membership." President Arthur told him the proposal was out of order and the Minnesota chapter's attempt to be first in initiating women failed.

None of the officers or board members was surprised with the adoption of the by-laws change, but nearly all were amazed at the overwhelming favorable vote. Reiley's never-quit attitude had paid off. "Of course I was overjoyed," he recalls. "I had taken a lot of beatings for about ten years, but I felt I was right and I still feel that way."

Wolpert was stunned and disappointed. When he returned home, he sent a buxom, Barbi-type doll, dressed, in a low-cut outfit to Arthur. Attached was a note which read, "To: Bill Arthur: The man who became confused in a parliamentary procedure and allowed a weak resolution to become a constitutional amendment and tear to shambles a great he-man Society in allowing women to become members of SDX." In his March 5, 1983, letter to this author, he wrote, "At no time did I feel I was fighting a losing battle. Right up to the final count I felt we had a chance to win and I know there are others to this day who wish we had." It should be noted here that five days after Wolpert mailed that letter along with the rest of his extensive file on his losing battle, he died at the age of 79 of a heart attack in Milwaukee. George Wolpert hadn't changed his mind nor his attitude on the issue nearly twenty years after the battle had begun. A short note executive officer Russell Tornabene sent to members of the board announcing Wolpert's death said, "Five-five, spunky, dapper, energetic George Wolpert was initiated as an undergraduate at Marquette in 1926. He began a love affair with SDX then which continued until his death March 10. George was campus reporter for *The Milwaukee Journal* while at Marquette, became a full-time reporter upon graduation in 1929 and remained so until he became a public relations consultant in 1931. He was president, in 1950, of the Milwaukee chapter and served three terms. He served on the national board several years. George Wolpert was a fixture at the national conventions, serving as chairman of the credentials committee at many of them. He won the Wells Memorial Key in 1962 and he cherished that honor. His final convention was in Milwaukee in 1982." Despite his feelings on the admission of women, Wolpert's love affair with SDX did last, for, in his will, he left substantial cash gifts to the Milwaukee professional chapter and the Society's Legal Defense Fund.

In St. Bonaventure, New York, an elaborate plan to be the first chapter in the nation to initiate women to the Society had been under way for more than a month. Anticipating the action in San Diego, but noting that the by-laws required membership applications to be submitted thirty days in advance of an initiation, the St. Bonaventure campus chapter had sent enrollment forms October 15 to Chicago, where Pearl Luttrell had placed them in a special file. "We knew dozens of other chapters would think of initiating the first women, but our hope lay in being foresighted enough to get our applications in on time to assure the legality of the effort," said Russell Jandoli, chairman of the department of journalism at the school. The initiation was set for Monday evening, November 17, precisely at 6 o'clock. Chapter adviser Harry Kennedy called at 4:32 pm Eastern time November 15, reporting the by-laws change had passed

"without a hitch," and the plans were made final. Upon his return to New York early Monday morning, Kennedy checked with the Society's Chicago headquarters only to find that Trinity College of Hartford, Connecticut, had also scheduled a Monday evening initiation. As it turned out the University of Georgia and Baylor University had made the same plans. The St. Bonaventure chapter chose the formal initiation ceremony because of the solenmity of the occasion in the Terrace Room of the Castle Restaurant across the street from the campus. A sleet and rain storm delayed the arrival of some of the initiates, causing the chapter's officers great concern. "What if Trinity had met all the requirements and had started at 6 o'clock?" asked Greg Mitchell, chapter president. By 6:25, all participants were present and the ceremony began. All went as planned until John Coleman, editor of *The Suburban Press*, Orchard Park, New York, and chief initiating officer of the Greater Buffalo International Chapter, began to read the pledge, asking the ten initiates, including seven women, to repeat the phrases after him. "I... do hereby promise...on the honor I bear myself as a gentleman..." Coleman realized that wouldn't work and quickly edited the printed words after only a second adding "...or a lady..." Jandoli reported the oath ended at 6:27, and by 6:35 the ceremony was complete. The women students initiated included Janet Bodnar, Homestead, Pennsylvania; Nancy Hultquist, Warren, Pennsylvania; Charlotte Kuzmich, Waterbury, Connecticut; Linda Mitchell and Patricia Stepien, both of Niagara Falls, New York; Peg Stomierowski, Orlean, New York; and Sister Dianne Salt, SMIC, Allegany, New York. The three men initiated that evening included one student, Kevin Donovan, Rochester, New York, and two professionals, Ken Wielosynski, editor and publisher of the Franklinville, New York *NewsTime*; and Frank A. Ragulsky, instructor in journalism at St. Bonaventure. The celebration which followed the historic moment was dampened only by the thought of waiting for official word from Chicago that St. Bonaventure had indeed been first to initiate women to Sigma Delta Chi. "Our sense of history never seemed so keen," Jandoli remembers. "We expected that we would have the first married woman [Linda Mitchell was married to the chapter president] and the first religious woman [Sister Dianne] and even the first woman from New York, Pennsylvania and even Connecticut. But it was the main distinction we were after and for which we had planned and worked so hard." The January 1970 *Quill* carried both story and photograph on the St. Bonaventure initiation, reporting that those initiates "were the first [women] to be officially enrolled at headquarters as SDX members." Hurst, who had missed the San Diego convention – the only one he did not attend in his nineteen years as executive officer – because back problems had caused him to be hospitalized, recalls, "We checked the first enrollments very carefully and were fully satisfied St. Bonaventure was first to initiate women."

The race to be *the* first was over but that didn't deter other chapters from trying to be *a* first or gather some other distinctive recognition relating to bringing women into the Society. With 207 professional and campus chapters scattered over the nation, many of which did not notify headquarters of their "accomplishments," *The Quill* has had to be the source of documentation for the other "firsts." The Minnesota professional chapter claimed to be the first to nominate women for a professional chapter, while Chicago's Headline Club asserted it was the first professional chapter to initiate women, with ten women joining at its December 4, 1969, meeting. Reiley's San Diego professional chapter, of course, was also among the first to admit women. The University of Tennessee staked claim to the largest early class of women initiates, bringing seventeen into its chapter December 7, but was surpassed quickly by the University of Nebraska, which initiated forty-three coeds. The Alpha chapter of Sigma Delta Chi at DePauw University, though not the first to add women to its membership, did enroll an important woman January 30, 1970, when it initiated Nina Pulliam, wife of SDX founder Eugene C. Pulliam, to membership. Pulliam had not opposed the admission of women in any

formal way at the San Diego convention.

Using the phrase "may be the first" or alluding to firsts with a question mark in future stories on initiation of women, *The Quill* reported Barbara Gardner of the University of Nevada as the first woman to be elected president of a chapter, February 17, 1970, at Reno. Election of the first woman president of a professional chapter did not occur for more than two years, a significant fact in and of itself, when Carmela Martin of the Roseville *Press Tribune* took over the reins of the Central California professional chapter. Kathy Snyder of the Des Moines *Register* and her father, Joe Snyder, editor and publisher of the Gallatin, Missouri *Democrat*, were said to be the first father-daughter team in the Society, and Jil Won of Seoul, Korea, initiated by the Washington State University chapter, the first international coed to join a campus chapter.

The rush to bring women into Sigma Delta Chi brought an immediate surge in the membership roles, with 119 women enrolled and applications for membership from another 148 by mid-January 1970. Even those chapters which had opposed the change in membership eligibility joined the parade. Early in the year, the Milwaukee professional chapter, with Wolpert looking on, initiated twenty-four women, and by April 15 the number of women who had become members reached 479. At the end of the Society's fiscal year, July 31, more than 1,100 women had joined SDX, helping to set a record, 2,890 new members in one year. Changes of other types were inevitable as well. Hurst announced in September 1970 that in addition to the traditional membership pins and keys, special key pendants and emblem charms were available from headquarters. More than 100 women were among the 900 persons who attended the Society's national convention in Chicago in November 1970.

The membership roles soared in the early 1970's. Professional chapters alone, which had initiated 600 men in 1968-1969, reported 838 new members in the first year after women were admitted, 942 in 1970-1971 and 1,306 in 1971-1972. On the campus scene, women's colleges were now eligible to have Sigma Delta Chi chapters. In 1971, Good Counsel College – now Pace University – in White Plains, New York, was the first girls' school to receive an SDX charter. Membership growth was even more dramatic in the campus chapters. Members initiated as college students numbered only 1,272 in 1969. One year later, with women joining the campus chapters, 2,284 students were enrolled. The number increased to 2,588 in 1971 and reached 3,127 in 1972. As might be expected, the enrollment surge leveled off in the mid-1970's, with new campus chapter members totaling 2,879 by 1975.

A WOMAN ON THE BOARD

With women as members of Sigma Delta Chi helping rather than hindering the progress of its chapters, there remained to be settled only Marjorie Paxson's concerns of how women would be treated at the national level and the future of Theta Sigma Phi.

It had taken two years for a women to be elected president of a professional chapter, and there was a similar time gap as well in the election of the first woman to the national board of directors. Appropriately, it was a student, Caroline Ross Pokrzywinski of Iowa State University, who had that honor, taking her seat on the board as a campus representative in November 1971. Students had served on the board as selected, non-voting members for many years until 1970, when four campus chapter members were elected for one-year terms representing specific geographic districts and given voting rights. Mrs. Pokrzywinski, initiated at Iowa State in 1970 and among the second group elected to the board, represented Regions Five, Six and Seven. The following November, Natalea Brown, Oklahoma State University, won a seat as a Campus Board Representative and in 1973 three women, Marti Weirich, Northern Arizona University; Jane Winebrenner, University of Illinois; and Leslie Ciarula, University of Bridgeport, were elected to the board.

Winning a seat as a regional director took longer – until 1974 – while electing a woman to the "ladder" as national treasurer, where she could ascend to the Society's presidency, wouldn't come until 1976. When Goodykoontz was elected Society treasurer at the Phoenix convention, he vacated his Region Two directorship and Val Hymes, the first woman inducted into the Maryland professional chapter and a special correspondent for Group W Television in Washington, DC, ran unopposed to complete Goodykoontz's term. Hymes had entered the national spotlight in 1973, winning the Society's Distinguished Service Award in Radio Reporting for her WTOP-Radio coverage of the May 15, 1972, attempted assassination of Alabama Governor George Wallace. An outspoken member of the board in her first year, Hymes was nominated from the floor to run for national treasurer at the 1975 convention in Philadelphia against Region Eight director Dessauer and Region Ten director Frank Wetzel, chief of bureau for The Associated Press in Seattle. When the votes were counted, Hymes had 179, Dessauer, 136 and Wetzel, 47. There are as many stories as there were persons involved in the campaign about who twisted whose arms, what alliances were formed and what else may have happened after that first vote and before the necessary run-off between Hymes and Dessauer. But the result of the second balloting showed Dessauer elected with 213 votes to Hymes' 124. At the same 1975 convention, the delegates amended sexist language out of the by-laws, eliminating the masculine pronouns.

JEAN OTTO ELECTED TREASURER

Despite Hymes' defeat in Philadelphia, a surge of support to elect a woman as treasurer developed – enough so that the 1976 nominating committee almost assured it would happen, presenting only two women as candidates for the post. Jean Otto, an editorial writer for *The Milwaukee Journal*, and Nancy Graham Baltad, a staff writer for the Los Angeles *Times*, were the committee's nominees and, once again, Hymes was nominated from the floor. Otto had been twice president – 1974-1976 – of the Milwaukee professional chapter, which was named the Society's outstanding chapter of 150 members or more for each of her two terms. Baltad was the 1973-1974 president of the Los Angeles professional chapter.

"Bill Small called and asked me if I would run," Otto said. "I was flattered, of course, but I really gave away my options on making the decision personally when I went to my editors and the publisher at the *Journal* asking, 'Am I going to have the time and will you support me financially in this five-year commitment?' Dick Leonard, the *Journal's* editor, [who, by coincidence, was the Society's president-elect at that time] played no role that I know of in my nomination, but encouraged me to accept it. I talked with my husband [Lee Baker, a public relations consultant in Milwaukee] and received the same encouragement." Once she gave Small a positive answer, Otto said, "I hadn't set my heart on winning but I was determined to give it my best shot." Delegates to the Los Angeles convention reported it was Otto's speech to the delegates which brought her victory on the first ballot. Otto concentrated on the state of the Society and issues relating to the need for a free press, telling the delegates just what she believed the Society of Professional Journalists, Sigma Delta Chi should be doing. "Somebody told me later, 'You had a lot of nerve giving that kind of speech to the convention,' but what else should I have talked about?" she recalls. The vote was 188 for Otto, 119 for Hymes and 42 for Baltad. Hymes continued on the board as Region Two director, a post she held through 1980, and worked as a vice chairman of the freedom of information committee for several years thereafter. Coming onto the board as an officer without the advantage of having been a regional director did not deter Otto from learning the ropes quickly. While she had to familiarize herself with all the issues confronting the board and, more importantly, get to know the other officers and directors, she was an immediate advocate for more active participation in freedom of information battles. She moved through the offices for three years, ascending to the presidency in New York, November 17, 1979.

Perhaps it was because Society members believed that now that women had reached the board level and one had become national president, they thought "now, we've got that behind us." Perhaps it was for a myriad of reasons, but nonetheless, in elections between 1976 and 1983, only two women were nominated for a regional directorship, one in Region Two and one in Region Ten, both of whom were defeated, and none sought the treasurer's position. Only through election of women students as campus board representatives in those years was there further inclusion of women on the board until November 1983.

When Dornfeld became Society president in 1982, he had the opportunity to do something about the lack of representation of women on the board, a concern he had shared with others since his election as a regional director in 1973. Convinced that there were qualified, interested women among the membership who simply needed a gentle push toward seeking election, he named a 1983 task force on women, chaired by Linda Kramer, assignment editor for KOIN-TV in Portland, Oregon. In his letter to Kramer, he said, "It is embarrassing and unacceptable that the eighteen professional members on the board do not include a single woman." He said what had been called the "old boys' network" which may have kept women from running for office in the past was long since gone and that something else may be wrong. Kramer, twice president of the Willamette Valley professional chapter, agreed to take on the job with the help of national secretary Sutherland. After notices in *The Quill* and *News and Views* suggesting that women who might be interested in seeking office or working on the task force contact her attracted only a few responses, Kramer wrote to Otto. "I asked if she would write a letter which I could disseminate as widely as possible to women who had held chapter office or a national committee post to encourage them to consider running for the board." Otto responded promptly. In her open letter to women members of the Society, Otto said the dim prospects for women moving into national office and assuming leadership was "...unfair, not merely to the one-third [of the membership who are women], but to all of those journalists who have a right to look across the board for leaders in this organization....Having served as president, I can tell you that the experience is not only challenging and demanding but intensely rewarding at a personal level. There probably is no way that a woman in journalism can get acquainted with so many different people in so many parts of the country. No way in which she can call upon her own inherent talents and interests to further the cause of journalism and the First Amendment. Granted, it takes enormous commitment. One cannot always do this kind of job well while pursuing a very demanding journalistic job, but it is worth asking employers whether or not they would support us in these activities and then making the personal commitment to go out and do what needs to be done."

Kramer accompanied Otto's letter with one of her own. She also wrote all regional directors asking them to scout for possible women candidates and to appoint women as deputy directors whenever possible. While the responses from the regional directors seemed to be positive in nature, some of the early letters from the women seemed to point to the problems with their employers, getting support from employers, and the like. "None of them answered saying, 'Here I am, ready to go!,' and it didn't look promising." But the interest Kramer's task force generated on its own or the spur it offered to women who had been interested in the past to become candidates in 1983 proved to be significant. By June 1983, three women had declared as candidates for the Region Two directorship, and two had declared intent to run in Region Three. At the San Francisco convention in November, Rosanne Brooks of Fairchild Publications in Washington, DC, was elected Region Two director and Georgiana Fry Vines, assistant metro editor of the Knoxville, Tennessee *News-Sentinel*, was elected Region Three director. Kramer said, "We were hoping to be able to find a woman as a candidate for treasurer to join the ladder toward becoming president," but that effort was in vain, at least for 1983.

THETA SIGMA PHI CHANGES

But what of the dire predictions that Theta Sigma Phi would be doomed if Sigma Delta Chi elected women to membership in 1969? Whatever happened to Theta Sig?

That organization's national magazine, *The Matrix*, carried the names of sixty-five campus and forty-five professional chapters accredited by that organization in its August 1966 issue. The best estimates available show a paid membership of about 4,500 in the late 1960's. Three years after Sigma Delta Chi admitted women to its membership, Theta Sigma Phi, meeting in Houston, Texas, in August 1972, made two major changes in its by-laws, admitting men to membership and changing its name to Women in Communications, Inc., the name by which it is known today. Kay Lockridge, elected to serve as the organizations' president for 1984-1985, said, "I think the move by SDX to invite women to membership may have been the impetus for Theta Sigma Phi to expand beyond its traditional role as an honorary for women in journalism and to reach out to men and women in the broad field of communications – public relations, advertising and the like – as well as editorial journalism." No matter what caused the organization to widen its eligibility guidelines, apparently it was the right move, for its membership in 1983, according to WICI headquarters in Austin, Texas, was more than 12,000 with about 150 chapters. While Women in Communications does not identify its members as male or female in its membership files, a spokesperson in Austin said the men who are members are primarily advisers to campus chapters. Lockridge estimated that probably no more than 5 percent of the members are men.

Thus, the promise of the destruction of Theta Sigma Phi upon admission of women to SDX did not happen. Not only did each organization prosper, though in slightly different ways, they resumed their long-standing cooperative and friendly relations. In fact, it is not uncommon for members of one organization to belong to the other. Initiated to Theta Sigma Phi in 1962 as a graduate student at Syracuse University in the days when that organization was primarily an honorary, Lockridge joined Sigma Delta Chi just months after the 1969 SDX convention in San Diego. A past president of the Society's Deadline Club in New York City, where she worked as a free-lance writer in the early 1980's, and active on a number of national committees for the Society of Professional Journalists, Sigma Delta Chi, Lockridge said, "The national presidents of Women in Communications, at least from 1980 through 1983, held dual memberships."

MINORITY RECRUITMENT AND PLACEMENT

Anyone who took a look at the people attending a national convention of the Society of Professional Journalists, Sigma Delta Chi, during the early 1980's saw the same thing as was found at that time in most of America's newsrooms – predominantly white faces. Unfortunately, the picture had not changed much in the fifteen years the Society had placed an emphasis on recruiting Blacks, Mexican Americans, Orientals and Native Americans for jobs in journalism. That is not to say the Society or any other national journalism organization accomplished nothing, but it does indicate successes were limited. The vast majority of SPJ,SDX members, then and now, have not been in jobs where they made hiring decisions, had a direct impact on employment practices, or established priorities for journalism schools. More than anything else, the Society was able to throw a bright light on the problem nationally, focus attention on what needed to be done and what could be done, and concentrate on specific projects which would have impact primarily at the local level.

Recruitment and placement of minority journalists had had no priority with Sigma Delta Chi from its beginning through the mid-1960's. The Society's leadership admitted later that it simply didn't give any attention to what was a developing problem until the release of the report of the National Advisory Commission on Civil Disorders, which sought to discover the causes of the summer riots of 1967 in Los Angeles, New York City, Newark, New Jersey and Detroit. The Commission's report stated, "[Our] concern with the news media is not in riot reporting as such, but in the failure to report adequately on race relations and ghetto problems and to bring Negroes into journalism....The journalism profession has been shockingly backward in seeking out,

hiring, training and promoting Negros. Fewer than 5 percent of the people employed by the news business in editorial jobs in the United States today are Negroes. Fewer than one percent of editors and supervisors are Negroes, and most of them work for Negro-owned organizations....News organizations must employ enough Negroes in positions of significant responsibility to establish an effective link to Negro actions and ideas and to meet legitimate employment expectations. Tokenism is no longer enough. Negro reporters are essential, but so are Negro editors, writers and commentators....We urge the news media to do everything possible to train and promote their Negro reporters to positions where those who are qualified can contribute to and have an effect on policy decisions."

There is no question that persons in minority ethnic communities were concerned about the lack of numbers of minority journalists in the news media long before it became evident to the broad spectrum of media organizations and news executives. But referring to the late 1960's, when active recruitment of minorities began, Hurst said, "I don't think Sigma Delta Chi entered the scene late. We were involved in an active kind of role as early as the problem had been identified," The first record of offical action taken by the Society is dated May 3, 1968, when the board pledged financial support to a scholarship program for American Negroes sponsored by the American Newspaper Publishers Association. That program was effected in the fall of 1968 when ANPA's Foundation announced grants totaling $14,000 for twenty-six Black journalism students attending eighteen universities. The board also instructed the journalism careers committee to develop specific recommendations for action on minority recruitment. Its chairman, Paul Swensson, a professor of journalism at Temple University, moved quickly to get the Society involved in the general effort to seek out and encourage minority youths to enter journalism. As the former executive director of The Newspaper Fund, a careers-oriented arm of Dow Jones and Company, publisher of *The Wall Street Journal*, Swensson had been in the forefront of the earliest movements of that kind. Speaking for

Sigma Delta Chi at the August 27, 1968, convention of the Association for Education in Journalism, Swensson challenged the journalism educators and Society members to broaden their search for talented young Blacks and other minority group members and prepare them for news careers. He said a recent survey revealed that only ninety-nine non-Caucasian students were enrolled in 110 departments of journalism. Michigan State University's campus chapter was one of the first SDX chapters to become involved when it joined in funding two $4,000, four-year scholarships for Black journalism students.

THE ATLANTA RESOLUTION

Swensson addressed the board at its national convention in Atlanta, November 20, suggesting that Sigma Delta Chi needed to become more deeply involved. He urged the board to increase its distribution of career literature and the recruiting film, perhaps create a new film "incorporating the Negro message," and encourage chapters to provide scholarship aid for minority students. Chandler asked that the matter be sent to the resolutions committee in time for possible action at that convention. When Swensson had presented his report to the convention and the resolutions committee brought its resolution to the floor, Jesse B. Brown, a Black student at the University of Houston, addressed the delegates. DeWayne Johnson, a journalism professor at San Fernando Valley State College in Northridge, California, remembers, "Brown's stirring speech – it did start the adrenalin flowing – resulted in adoption of the resolution which presented a possible solution to 'the communications vacuum that presently exists between the majority white population and the minority group members' toward careers in journalism and their employment." The resolution stated, "This convention does instruct the national president to establish a permanent committee on the national level to implement the recommendations of the journalism careers committee, and to administer a Sigma Delta Chi program to encourage and recruit minority group journalists, said committee to be established by December 31, 1968."

Incoming president Arthur appointed Ernest Dunbar, a senior editor for *Look* magazine, as the new committee's first chairman. Dunbar, a Black newsman with more than sixteen years experience, believed the Society had not taken the action with the vigor which was called for to that time, but he agreed to take on the assignment.

Working with Jesse Brown, by then a reporter for the NBC television outlet in Houston, Dunbar drafted a resolution for the 1969 convention in San Diego. The resolution called for six action programs, several of which had been suggested in Atlanta, to be undertaken by the Society. Among the new projects proposed was one which asked that Sigma Delta Chi join with the Association for Education in Journalism to create a journalism council that would work full-time on the problem of minority recruitment. Two joint sections requested the establishment of "regional, intensive journalism institutes specifically designed to prepare minority group persons to enter journalism." The first requested a national register of "qualified newsmen with teaching skills who are willing to serve – at full pay – on the staff of the institutes." The second called for obtaining "commitments from the publishing and broadcasting industry of a $1 million fund to pay for room and board, stipend and instructors' salaries for these institutes." Yet another program suggested in the resolution would have had the Society set up a series of regional conferences, in conjunction with local newspaper, magazine, radio and television personnel, for guidance counselors from high schools and colleges with predominantly nonwhite populations to train them in recruiting minority students for journalism careers.

The language of the report printed in *The Quill* about resolutions adopted in San Diego leaves little doubt that the delegates passed over Dunbar's resolution for another, more broadly-worded statement of purpose. *The Quill* reported in December 1969, that the convention "encouraged the American Newspaper Publishers Association and newspapers to continue their minority recruitment [and] financial assistance programs and to include Mexican-Americans, Asian-Americans, American

Indians, and other minority groups, as well as Blacks and Puerto Ricans."

Dunbar said later, "I was disappointed in the outcome and felt that people in the journalism community who were in a position to make a meaningful difference were not ready to take on the kind of action that the committee and I suggested." Now chief of publications and editor of *The Lamp* for Exxon Corporation in New York City, Dunbar has not been active within the Society in minority recruitment programs since that time. But he said in 1983, "I find I can be most effective now in talking to individuals who are looking for job opportunities or seeking guidance and, on the other hand, I talk to people in the business whom I know and try to steer people in that direction."

Edward J. Trayes, professor of journalism at Temple, provided a revealing look at the state of Black enrollment in eighty-three journalism schools and Black newsmen on thirty-two newspapers in sixteen of the nation's largest cities in an article in the April 1969 *Quill*. He found that only 128 of the 6,418 journalism majors at those schools were Black and that only 108 of 4,095 working reporters, desk men, photographers or news executives were Black. Among the 532 executives, only one was Black. In a follow-up article in the September *Quill*, Melvin Mencher, an associate professor of journalism in the graduate school of journalism at Columbia University, challenged newspapers and broadcast media to do more than mouth platitudes and become active in recruiting minorities for news jobs. "There is a deep reservoir of talent available in every community. It is as close as the nearby post office. It exists in government offices and public schools...the places members of minority groups have looked to for employment while business has kept its doors closed to them....Broadcasting stations and newspapers can find able men and women anxious to make mid-career changes from jobs in which they are underutilized or for which they are overqualified....Individual stations and newspapers can train these mature recruits on their own; they can pool their resources for industry-sponsored

training programs; or they can participate in one of the foundation-sponsored programs for schooling these potential employees."

President Angelo asked Johnson at the San Diego convention to become chairman of the careers committee. Johnson, who had prepared a minority recruitment brochure, "There is a future for you in journalism," distributed through national SDX headquarters to high schools and colleges across the nation, was ready to continue his work. On January 8 and 9, 1970, he met in New York City with Angelo, Hurst and a few others to discuss a new plan of attack on minority recruitment. Johnson had prepared a specific action program which included five goals: "(1) To make minority youth feel they were wanted and needed in journalism and to point out to them how to achieve such a goal; (2) to make publishers and editors aware of the need to hire minority youth and to point out where they may be found; (3) to organize Sigma Delta Chi chapters on Negro college campuses and to make minority youth and professionals aware of opportunities in Sigma Delta Chi membership; (4) to make every Sigma Delta Chi member and all chapters aware of the opportunity for service to this large segment of young people and to get them involved; and (5) to call attention to the Urban Coalition's Skills Bank, to scholarship possibilities, and to other avenues of opportunity open to minority youth in journalism."

Johnson recalls, "Angelo and Hurst responded enthusiastically to my suggestions. I returned to California and used the spotlight of the Region Eleven conference in Monterey, April 18, 1970, to call attention to the need to develop our program." In his speech to the conference, Johnson told Society members that while giant strides had been made in the 1960's in human relations and social justice, "We cannot allow ourselves to believe that we have done anything more than make a start." As an additional incentive, he prepared an extensive list of what individual members and chapters could do about recruitment of minority youths into journalism. He took his program to the national spotlight through an article in the July 1970 *Quill* in which he

170

spelled out the details outlined in New York and Monterey. Emphasizing the frustration of establishing meaningful goals only to find hopes unfulfilled when it is time for a committee chairman to write an annual report, Johnson called on individual members to become involved rather than assume that "all of us" will get the job done.

Johnson's enthusiasm for this and other projects in the Society over the years usually made things happen. But in working toward building minority jobs, he was told he had to "be patient," something he found difficult to do. Unable to make the kinds of strides for which he had hoped, in his report to the 1970 convention in Chicago Johnson said, "Headway is much too slow in the recruitment of minority group newsmen. The psyche of those recruited is too often abused by others of the minority group who sneeringly resort to the convenient 'Uncle Tom' epithet. The psyche is often sinfully abused by non-minority fellow workers in the profession." President Angelo told the board in Chicago that the Philadelphia professional chapter had contributed $1,000 to be used to help in minority recruitment and, at Angelo's suggestion, $500 of that money was made available to the Association for Education in Journalism for its minority internship program. In addition, the Chicago convention delegates adopted a resolution urging again the creation of a minority recruitment film. Novitz's work on the second careers film, *The Journalists*, treated the subject, but as had been the practice, the motion picture dealt with a general approach, encouraging youths of all races to consider journalism as a career.

TRAYES BECOMES MINORITIES CHAIR

Trayes updated his 1968 survey on Blacks enrolled in journalism schools and employment of Blacks by newspapers in the September 1970 *Quill*, finding that more journalism graduates were available but newsroom ratios remained small. He was named chairman of the minority recruitment committee by Chandler early in 1971. Chandler had committed himself to working toward establishing SDX chapters at predominantly Black schools. With the help of Trayes and vice president for campus

chapter affairs H.G. (Buddy) Davis of the University of Florida, two such schools – Texas Southern University in Houston and Lincoln University in Jefferson City, Missouri – were granted charters at the 1971 national convention in Washington, D.C. Trayes set his sights on another major project during 1972 – an attempt to set up a nationwide effort to provide opportunity for local contact between minority students considering journalism careers and experienced journalism professors. His minority recruitment committee set up a network of advisers at fifty-two colleges and universities in thirty-one states to meet with minority youths, primarily of high school age, on journalism careers and to help match up potential media employers and those minority journalism graduates seeking full-time professional employment.

During the twelve years Trayes was chairman of his committee – he held the position through 1982 – the Society made regular financial contributions to the Association for Education in Journalism Minority Summer Internship program and its Job and Scholarship Referral Service. The committee introduced or inspired resolutions at nearly every national convention on topical issues relating to discrimination in hiring, advancement or educational opportunities for minorities. Continuous attention to problems for ethnic minorities led to establishment of task forces and adoption of resolutions on equal treatment for other minority journalists, including women, and the handicapped. In addition three more Black schools – Florida A & M University; Clark College in Atlanta, Georgia; and Howard University in Washington, D.C. – received charters for SPJ,SDX campus chapters. Trayes' 1978 report to the convention in Birmingham summarized the substantial progress made in the ten years since the Society had become active in minority recruitment. The report stated that more Blacks were working on major metropolitan newspapers than in 1968 but the proportion of Blacks in newsrooms was still well below the Black population in those cities. Specifically, Trayes reported, of the 3,619 full-time news executive, desk, reporting and photographer positions listed by the twenty-five daily newspapers participating in the new survey, 206 were held by Blacks, almost double the number reported ten years earlier. Eighteen Blacks held executive positions on newspapers, compared to one in 1968.

THE MILWAUKEE EXPERIMENT

President Graves added a new dimension to the Society's programs on minorities in 1981 when he appointed a special task force on minority journalists, with Walter Morrison, an editorial writer for *The Milwaukee Journal*, as its chair. Following up on an idea by past president Jean Otto, Morrison's task force helped to organize a workshop for minority students at his newspaper and *The Milwaukee Sentinel*. "The workshop was premised on the sensible notion that, if minority students were to be attracted to careers in journalism, the approach should be made during the high school years." Established as a pilot program for other chapters and media to emulate, the seven-week workshop was planned and conducted by the Milwaukee professional chapter with coordination handled by Mary Ann Esquivel, Margaret Hoyos and Kevin Merida, all *Journal* reporters. Fifteen minority ninth grade to high school senior students from the Milwaukee area were invited to attend the weekly two-hour sessions, during which they heard presentations by local newspaper and television executives, editors and reporters. In addition, they were given information on planning college careers and financial aid opportunites from Dean James Scotton of Marquette University's School of Journalism. A final luncheon featured, as the speaker, Acel Moore, a Pulitzer Prize-winning reporter and columnist from the Philadelphia *Inquirer*. Evaluations on the workshop prepared by the three coordinators revealed enthusiasm for the project on the part of both the students and participating journalists. Guidelines for other chapters hoping to conduct such a workshop were made available through Society headquarters.

The problems of interesting minority students in choosing journalism as a career and seeking equal employment and promotion opportunites for minority journalists were not solved in the Society's – or the profession's – first sixteen years of work. All the work was just a beginning toward the long-range goals. But, as Johnson wrote in reviewing those years, "Something must have worked, judging by the complexion of the media in the early 1980's. The advice to 'be patient' had some validity."

CHAPTER 10

A New Name
A New Code

Delegates' voting patterns at national Society conventions have been as unpredictable as November weather patterns in the host cities. The vast majority of campus and professional chapter delegates is different from year to year because the leadership of those chapters changes each year. In addition, the grass-roots, widespread nature of the organization brings together in convention a diverse group of student and professional journalists, each with local, often special interests and concerns. A national issue which may have been the focus of floor fights for years may well be an entirely new question to most of the delegates at a given convention. Thus, the Society's officers and board members have learned to expect the unexpected and to accept surprise as commonplace. This was the setting as representatives of the 245 Sigma Delta Chi chapters gathered to consider four major propositions at the sixty-fourth anniversary convention in Buffalo, New York, November 14, 1973. Two of the issues – the name of the Society and a code of ethics – had been debated for decades. The other two – proportional voting and the geographical makeup of the regions – had been discussed for at least five years. The delegates in Buffalo, however, were about to face each issue squarely and change the organization as much as the admission of women four years earlier.

SDX BY ANY OTHER NAME...

The ten founders in 1909 had chosen the name – Sigma Delta Chi, honorary journalistic fraternity – with little apparent controversy. At the fledgling organization's first national convention in 1912, however, a conflict about the name surfaced, centering on the word "honorary," with those opposing the use of the word stating that it kept Sigma Delta Chi from recognition as a "professional" group. The name was changed in 1916 when seventeen delegates voted to drop the word "honorary" from the name. None of Sigma Delta Chi's early historians indicated exactly when the organization officially adopted the words, "professional journalistic fraternity," but references to the organization in the 1920's add the word "professional" and it may be

William C. Payette (left), president in 1972-1973, presided over the 1973 Buffalo convention at which both the name of the Society was changed and the Code of Ethics was adopted. He is pictured with executive officer Russell E. Hurst and Sigma Delta Chi co-founder Eugene C. Pulliam.

assumed that the new designation was effected, for all intents and purposes, in 1916.

The Greek letters themselves came under attack in 1922 when a committee of delegates to the Manhattan, Kansas, convention said it believed the name meant little to those outside of college circles. "Present policy of the fraternity must necessarily extend further into the actual field of journalism....In doing so, some provision for changing the name of the fraternity may become necessary outside of the undergraduate field." The report was accepted but pigeon-holed, and no further attempts to change the name were brought to the floor until the 1936 convention in Dallas. Delegates there made an attempt to draft a new constitution which would "transform the Sigma Delta Chi fraternity into a national organization of practicing journalists to be known as the American Institute of Journalists." The convention took no action on the proposal, killing the idea. Delegates faced the name issue once again in 1937 and voted down a motion to substitute the word

"society" for "fraternity," an effort which was defeated again in 1947.

When the long and painful period of introspection in the late 1950's culminated in the McKinsey and Company study on reorganization in 1960, the name of the fraternity was one of the key issues presented. The McKinsey Report stated, "If Sigma Delta Chi intends to gain further national recognition as a professional society of journalists, we recommend that the present designation be changed from Sigma Delta Chi – Professional Journalistic Fraternity to Sigma Delta Chi – The Society of Journalists." At the December 2, 1960, convention business session in New York, all of McKinsey and Company's recommendations were adopted except one – a change in the name of the organization. With a motion on the floor to adopt the suggested name, Kenneth Eskey, Pittsburgh professional chapter delegate, moved to make the name, "Sigma Delta Chi, Professional Journalistic Society," substituting the word "society" each time the word "fraternity" appeared in the

174

constitution and by-laws. Ed O. Meyer, delegate of the Richmond professional chapter, seconded, and after a show-of-hands vote, Newton announced the motion had been adopted, 79-12. The name had been changed for only the second time in the organization's fifty-one year history, but Sigma Delta Chi remained the primary designation.

Changing Sigma Delta Chi to a society spurred those who believed that as long as the Greek letters remained, the complete evolution of the organization to a professional orientation would be hindered. Delegates to the 1961, first-ever regional conference sponsored by Region Ten in San Luis Obispo, California adopted a resolution calling for a change in the Society's name to the Society of American Journalists, with undergraduate chapters to be known as Sigma Delta Chi, but the resolution fell on deaf ears. Bob White, as Region Seven director, was among the first on the new board of directors to broach the subject. He commented May 11, 1962, that members "have a difficult time explaining what Sigma Delta Chi means" and said he was not satisfied that it was the best name for the Society. In that November, national convention delegates in Tulsa rejected the idea overwhelmingly. An informal poll of the board at its Tulsa meeting showed "general opposition," but White suggested the matter "should be reviewed in the near future." White carried his quiet campaign on the board to Dallas, May 10, 1963, when he expressed the hope that the Society keep alive the possibility of changing the name. He offered an alternative, The American Society of Journalists, but had little, if any support. Walter Burroughs may have been listening, however, for in his presidential report to the 1963 convention in Norfolk, Virginia, Burroughs noted, "During the three years [since reorganization] many hundreds of news stories regarding Sigma Delta Chi have been published. Very seldom is Sigma Delta Chi referred to as 'Professional Journalistic Society.' About half the time we are still referred to as a 'fraternity.' I am not proposing any action at this time. I simply want to get it on the record that a correction is needed some

Charles Novitz, Region One director for a single year when the name of the Society was changed in 1973, did not favor the change. Nine years later, as the Society's president in 1981-1982, he opposed dropping the Greek letters, Sigma Delta Chi, from the end of the Society's name. The proposal to drop SDX from the name was defeated by a narrow margin at the 1982 Milwaukee convention.

day." Region Ten director Bob Chandler jumped at the opportunity. Chandler had earned the reputation among his colleagues on the board of taking the unpopular position when he believed something needed to be done. "I plead guilty to believing enough that the name had to be changed to have been an early advocate for such a move," he said. At Chandler's suggestion, vice president for campus chapter affairs Al Higginbotham moved that the board appoint a committee to make a concerted drive to change the name of the Society in accordance with the recommendations of president Burroughs. Chandler was named to chair the committee. Sigma Delta Chi co-founder Eugene C. Pulliam apparently had heard of Chandler's committee work for, in

Ralph Otwell, as treasurer of the Society in 1971, addressed the Washington, DC convention, telling the delegates they should support a change in the name of the Society. "The handwriting is on the wall, and it's not Greek," he said. The by-law change failed in Washington, but was adopted in Buffalo two years later.

1964 at a social gathering in conjunction with the Distinguished Service Awards ceremony in Phoenix, Pulliam approached Chandler. "Pulliam was very unhappy about any name change,"Chandler recalls. "As one of the founding members, the name Sigma Delta Chi was written in stone so far as he was concerned." Chandler remembers Pulliam saying, "You know we disagree strongly on something." Chandler said he replied, "That's right. The difference is, Gene, this time I'm right." Chandler may have been right, but the board refused to take any action toward a change in name until it was forced to do so. The 1964 convention in Kansas City also set aside an attempt to change the name to Sigma Delta Chi, The Society of Journalists.

Delegates to the 1965 national convention in Los Angeles must have been bound to upset some of the Society's most valued traditions. In addition to mandating that the board bring a by-laws change to the 1966 convention in Pittsburgh on admission of women to membership, they adopted a resolution calling on the board to prepare another change for Pittsburgh – this one to eliminate the Greek letters from the Society's name and to propose three possible new names for consideration by those delegates. Incoming president Ray Spangler, who had been handed the mandate for a name change, was deeply opposed to the idea. "I recognized two things," he said. "There was difficulty with the Greek letters in confusing the Society with a fraternity and an honors group with a professional group. But on the other hand, there was wide recognition of what Sigma Delta Chi was all about over the years and it had won wide acceptance and understanding. Out of respect for Gene [Pulliam] and out of my own inclination, I didn't want to see the name changed. But if it had to be changed, I wanted to see that those Greek letters survive as at least part of the name." Before the board met May 6-7, 1966, in Des Moines, an article, "To Alter? To Alter?" appeared in the April *Quill*. Written in seeming tongue-in-cheek style by DeWayne B. Johnson, the article was in response to a letter he had received soon after the November convention as campus chapter adviser at San Fernando Valley State College, Northridge, California (now California State University at Northridge) inviting him and other members of the Society to submit possible names to national headquarters. While the article addressed both the admission of women and name change issues, regarding the elimination of the Greek letters in the name, Johnson chided the board with questions it had to consider, including the differences between campus and professional chapters and the fact that the Society had international chapters. To conclude his article, Johnson listed thirty-five possible names including everything – in alphabetical order – from The American Academy of Journalists to The U.S. National Academy of Journalism and The World Congress of Journalists. Whether Johnson's list was included is not known, but the Des Moines board minutes report that "some fifty possibilities" were

THE SOCIETY OF PROFESSIONAL JOURNALISTS,
SIGMA DELTA CHI

Code of Ethics

THE SOCIETY of Professional Journalists, Sigma Delta Chi believes the duty of journalists is to serve the truth.

WE BELIEVE the agencies of mass communication are carriers of public discussion and information, acting on their Constitutional mandate and freedom to learn and report the facts.

WE BELIEVE in public enlightenment as the forerunner of justice, and in our Constitutional role to seek the truth as part of the public's right to know the truth.

WE BELIEVE those responsibilities carry obligations that require journalists to perform with intelligence, objectivity, accuracy and fairness.

To these ends, we declare acceptance of the standards of practice here set forth:

RESPONSIBILITY:
The public's right to know of events of public importance and interest is the overriding mission of the mass media. The purpose of distributing news and enlightened opinion is to serve the general welfare. Journalists who use their professional status as representatives of the public for selfish or other unworthy motives violate a high trust.

FREEDOM OF THE PRESS:
Freedom of the press is to be guarded as an inalienable right of people in a free society. It carries with it the freedom and the responsibility to discuss, question and challenge actions and utterances of our government and of our public and private institutions. Journalists uphold the right to speak unpopular opinions and the privilege to agree with the majority.

ETHICS:
Journalists must be free of obligation to any interest other than the public's right to know the truth.
1. Gifts, favors, free travel, special treatment or privileges can compromise the integrity of journalists and their employers. Nothing of value should be accepted.
2. Secondary employment, political involvement, holding public office and service in community organizations should be avoided if it compromises the integrity of journalists and their employers. Journalists and their employers should conduct their personal lives in a manner which protects them from conflict of interest, real or apparent. Their responsibilities to the public are paramount. That is the nature of their profession.

3. So-called news communications from private sources should not be published or broadcast without substantiation of their claims to news value.
4. Journalists will seek news that serves the public interest, despite the obstacles. They will make constant efforts to assure that the public's business is conducted in public and that public records are open to public inspection.
5. Journalists acknowledge the newsman's ethic of protecting confidential sources of information.

ACCURACY AND OBJECTIVITY:
Good faith with the public is the foundation of all worthy journalism.
1. Truth is our ultimate goal.
2. Objectivity in reporting the news is another goal, which serves as the mark of an experienced professional. It is a standard of performance toward which we strive. We honor those who achieve it.
3. There is no excuse for inaccuracies or lack of thoroughness.
4. Newspaper headlines should be fully warranted by the contents of the articles they accompany. Photographs and telecasts should give an accurate picture of an event and not highlight a minor incident out of context.
5. Sound practice makes clear distinction between news reports and expressions of opinion. News reports should be free of opinion or bias and represent all sides of an issue.
6. Partisanship in editorial comment which knowingly departs from the truth violates the spirit of American journalism.
7. Journalists recognize their responsibility for offering informed analysis, comment and editorial opinion on public events and issues. They accept the obligation to present such material by individuals whose competence, experience and judgment qualify them for it.
8. Special articles or presentations devoted to advocacy or the writer's own conclusions and interpretations should be labeled as such.

FAIR PLAY:
Journalists at all times will show respect for the dignity, privacy, rights and well-being of people encountered in the course of gathering and presenting the news.
1. The news media should not communicate unofficial charges affecting reputation or moral character without giving the accused a chance to reply.
2. The news media must guard against invading a person's right to privacy.
3. The media should not pander to morbid curiosity about details of vice and crime.
4. It is the duty of news media to make prompt and complete correction of their errors.
5. Journalists should be accountable to the public for their reports and the public should be encouraged to voice its grievances against the media. Open dialogue with our readers, viewers and listeners should be fostered.

PLEDGE:
Journalists should actively censure and try to prevent violations of these standards, and they should encourage their observance by all newspeople. Adherence to this code of ethics is intended to preserve the bond of mutual trust and respect between American journalists and the American people.

Adopted 1926, Revised 1973

received from more than two dozen chapters. Fulfilling its mandate, the board selected three names: Sigma Delta Chi, The Society of Journalists; American Society of Journalists (Founded as Sigma Delta Chi); and American Journalism Association.

Consensus of the board was that these three would give the convention a choice ranging from retention of Sigma Delta Chi as the first element of a new name to a clean break with Greek-letter identification. However, the board also approved a motion recommending to the convention that Sigma Delta Chi be retained as an element in any new name approved by the delegates. The convention did not have to consider an alternative name for, after debate, the delegates voted 125-19 against changing the name at all.

NEW SUPPORT ON THE BOARD

The debate returned to the board level for the next two years. With the addition of Region Five director Ralph Otwell to the board in 1966, Chandler and others had a new ally for changing the name. "I thought at that time that the total elimination of the Greek letters was unrealistic, but my goal from day one of my national involvement was to de-emphasize the Greek aspect in the name," he said. "I wanted to switch the emphasis based on work with students where I got the distinct impression that Sigma Delta Chi was a 'Stigma Delta Chi.' There was a strong aversion to anything that was Greek on many campuses, especially at the larger schools, and I believed that if we wanted to attract the kind of young journalist we would need in future years, we simply had to get rid of the onus of the fraternal or social organization." Otwell and Chandler were able to build enough support on the board by May 9, 1969, to have a by-laws proposal approved with only two dissenting votes to change the name to The Society of Journalists and to have it presented at the convention in San Diego in November. Preparing for that convention, Arthur knew that, once again, both the admission of women issue and the name change would cause major floor fights. "It seemed to me that we had a better chance on the question of membership for women than for changing the name of the Society in San Diego, so I decided to take up the name problem first. I had hoped that, if the name remained intact, one tradition would have been saved and that the other might sail through," Arthur said. As it turned out, he was right.

BUT A FOUNDER IS OPPOSED

The word was passed that Pulliam would be in San Diego to make a personal plea for votes against one or both of the issues. However, instead of opposing both by-laws changes, Pulliam chose not to enter the debate on the admission of women and concentrated on the name change. Illness prevented him from attending the meeting, but he sent a statement which was read to the delegates. He wrote:

For sixty years, the undergraduate members have gone out into the professional world to become real leaders in their chosen field. The undergraduate chapters – and this is the reason [I am writing] – are the fountainhead of this organization and its traditions. They have been developed in an atmosphere of enthusiasm and hope for a journalistic career while they were still students in college.

To change the name to the Society of Journalists would be to abandon the undergraduate chapters, because the undergraduate members are not journalists. They just hope to God that some day they will be....I believe that if you change its name, Sigma Delta Chi is not going to enjoy the position and the status it now has.

Just a word in closing. Many of you are members of Phi Beta Kappa. All of you know what Phi Beta Kappa is and what it symbolizes. Wouldn't you be shocked and surprised if you read in the morning papers that Phi Beta Kappa had changed its name to The Society of Intellectuals?

Many persons who attended the San Diego convention seem to remember Pulliam's comment on Phi Beta Kappa to have concluded, "...if you read in the morning papers that Phi Beta Kappa had changed its name to The Society of Brains," but the official transcript of the proceedings carries the language used above. Pulliam's personal request to save the name Sigma Delta Chi had a profound impact on the delegates, especially those from colleges at which the Greek letter name was not a problem, for they voted, 94-54, against a name change.

The vote was closer than it had been in Pittsburgh, but general consensus among the members was that, given the two-to-one vote, the issue was dead. But not to Otwell.

Casey Bukro (second from left) and Ralph Otwell (right) were two of the leaders in formulating the Society's new Code of Ethics and implementing it throughout the nation. Bukro, chairman of the professional development committee from 1972-1973 and later Region Five director, wrote much of the language adopted as the Code in 1973, and was one of its strongest advocates. Otwell, Society president in 1973-1974, spent much of his time that year traveling across the country explaining the Code and seeking its adoption by local chapters. With Bukro and Otwell were executive officer Russell E. Hurst (left) and Northwestern University journalism professor Dr. Curtis Mac Dougall, the 1967 Distinguished Teaching in Journalism Award winner.

Named chairman of a special by-laws committee following the 1970 convention in Chicago, he brought the matter to the board at its spring meeting in Las Vegas, Nevada, in May 1971. He told the board, "While recognizing the traditions of sixty-two years associated with Sigma Delta Chi, and the accomplishments of the organization which are identified with those three Greek letters, [the committee] voted to change the name to reflect more clearly the greatly broadened activities, the vastly expanded purposes and the immense changes in the communications industry that we serve." A new by-laws proposal would have the delegates to the Washington, DC, convention in 1971 select from among another set of three alternative

names: American Association of Journalists (Founded as Sigma Delta Chi); Society of American Journalists (Founded as Sigma Delta Chi); and Association of Professional Journalists (Founded as Sigma Delta Chi). The position of the board in favor of a name change clearly was apparent. Not only did it approve the proposed by-law, but a straw poll among the members showed a preference for The American Association of Journalists.

Otwell opened the debate in Washington with a strong statement on the need for a change in name. "The handwriting is on the wall, and it's not Greek," he said. More than twenty-five delegates spoke on the issue, including Ben Avery, delegate from the Valley of the Sun professional chapter in Phoenix, who read a letter from Pulliam asking the delegates to turn down a change of name. Once again, the delegates never got to selecting a new name. In the closest count in the six years the issue had reached the floor, they voted, 96-83, against changing the name in any way. But this time it was the professional chapters that gave the name Sigma Delta Chi support by the wider margin, 45-34. The campus chapter delegates' vote was only 51-49 against any change. The board accepted the decision with regret and, although Otwell and Chandler, among others, still believed firmly the name change had to come, it agreed to sit on the issue at least through the 1972 convention in Dallas. That did not stop some chapters from pursuing the matter and, working through the resolutions committee, they succeeded in bringing the matter to the floor in Dallas, requesting that a by-laws change be presented in 1973 at Buffalo. The delegates would have no part of it however. Upon hearing about the defeats in Pittsburgh, San Diego and Washington, they thought the matter should be set aside for at least another two years and voted 108-62 against the resolution. Meanwhile, believing something had to be done about its own "identity crisis" and acting on its own, the Minnesota professional chapter of Sigma Delta Chi had changed its name to the Minnesota Professional Journalism Society, a chapter of Sigma Delta Chi. The national board gave its blessing after the fact, May 5, 1972.

Shortly after the Dallas meeting, newly-elected treasurer McCord, acting as an individual member and not as an officer, began his own campaign. "Anybody who had represented the Society in testifying on such matters as freedom of information knew we had to have a change in the name," McCord recalled. "You would identify yourself as a member of Sigma Delta Chi only to have some committee member attempt to embarrass you by asking 'What's Sigma Delta Chi, a high school fraternity or a secret society?' Anybody who went through that just once, for God's sake, just had to be committed to getting the name changed." He wrote to 120 chapters asking

each to sign petitions to bring the name change question to Buffalo. His own preference for a name was The American Society of Journalists, Sigma Delta Chi. When the board convened its May 4, 1973, meeting in Omaha, Nebraska, McCord had received fewer than ten petitions along with several letters of complaint. "I was very much discouraged. I had written many of the chapters I had visited over the years and, as happens with groups like ours, the chapter presidents put the letter aside and never got around to answering," he said. Telling the board he had failed in his effort, he said he would write those chapters that had signed petitions, reporting the same results. Hurst noted, however, that if he received ten petitions, a by-laws proposal must be submitted to the convention. "I thought it took a lot more petitions than that to get the job accomplished, but when Hurst said we needed only two or three more to reach the goal, we had no trouble in getting them." When the final petition arrived, the number had reached twelve, enough to assure the matter would be on the agenda in Buffalo. Four campus chapters sent petitions, those at the University of Toledo, Columbia University, University of Colorado and University of Iowa. The eight professional chapters were St. Louis, Northeast Georgia, Tidewater Virginia, Northwest Ohio, Western Washington, Chicago Headline Club, Los Angeles, and Willamette Valley. The by-laws proposal as submitted to delegates in advance of the convention stated "...to amend the by-laws...the name of this organization shall be: The American Society of Journalists, Sigma Delta Chi." This time there would be no need for two separate votes – one on whether the name should be changed and one on what the name would be. There would be one vote on the name itself and that would be that.

A NEW NAME FOR THE SOCIETY

The by-laws committee, chaired by Charles Barnum, met before the business session in Buffalo to map strategy for the floor debate. Perhaps it was because the convention was being held near the Canadian border, but in committee discussions it became apparent that McCord's proposed name might present some problems, given that the Society was international in nature. With chapters in the United Kingdom and Korea, it was evident that the word "American" would not be appropriate after all. Wanting to avoid that kind of debate, the committee began discussing a possible last-minute amendment to its own by-laws proposal. After some time, Lew Cope, a science reporter for the Minneapolis *Tribune* and the president and delegate from the Minnesota Professional Journalism Society, began playing with the words in the name of his own chapter. Cope suggested the name, The Society of Professional Journalists, Sigma Delta Chi, as a possible solution to the dilemma. The committee adopted Cope's idea and decided that it would offer the amendment at the very opening of debate, trying to get that out of the way before the expected emotional discussion began.

Barnum presented the by-laws change in its original form on Saturday morning, November 17, 1973. President Bill Payette recognized Cope, who presented the planned amendment and the explanation for the committee. Bob Rawitch, delegate from the Los Angeles professional chapter, opened the debate, pointing out that one of the local newspapers had incorrectly identified Sigma Delta Chi in its story on the opening of the convention. "They called it a National Journalism Fraternity," he said. "So long as SDX is the front part of our name, we are going to be in the minds of many, many people, a fraternity, an honorary organization, instead of a professional society." Rawitch was the only delegate to speak before the amendment passed easily on a voice vote. Turning to the main issue, president Payette recognized Bill Close, delegate from the Valley of the Sun professional chapter, who said, "May I candidly point to next year and the fact that the convention will be held in Phoenix, Arizona, the home of one of the two living founders of SDX. Mr. Pulliam is unalterably opposed to the name change." Close asked permission to read part of a letter from Pulliam, which said: "Again, you are asked to approve a name change for

SDX. Consider...carefully what you lose if you accede to this urge for a new name....The history of similar organizations founded on college campuses and expanded to adult professional life shows that SDX alone survived....Please don't destroy the one unique organization which has given American journalism new life, new ideas and new inspirations year after year...on American colleges." Close added one final observation. "Somehow it seems to me just a little bit impertinent, a little bit impolite and in poor taste to change the name of this organization and then partake of the hospitality of Mr. Pulliam next year." McCord answered Close saying, "It seems to me that this proposed change has its ideal in that it maintains the old, but also interjects the new element into our title that does identify us. There is no suggestion by anyone that there be less emphasis on the front of the name than on the back of the name so, therefore, our jewelry, our stationery, our emblem, whatever part of the old we wish to retain for as long as we wish to retain it, will stay with us."

Cope returned to the floor to try to allay the fears of those who thought subordinating the name Sigma Delta Chi would be injurious. When the Minnesota chapter changed its name, he said, "I was a bit of the traditionalist and was worried about the loss of the name SDX, but it has worked out beautifully. It has helped us before the legislature. We no longer have a problem of 'What are you?' and I think it has helped in recruiting, particularly in getting many women who remembered it from the fraternity link. In short, a chapter change of name has helped Minnesota. While I was a traditionalist at first, I am a total convert and believe the national [organization] can benefit from a name change." According to the official transcript of the session, representatives from only two campus chapters – the University of California at Berkeley and Columbia University – joined the discussion and both of them supported the change. Others who spoke in opposition or offered alternatives included Region One director Charles Novitz, Twin Tiers professional chapter delegate Chet Horner and Nevada professional chapter delegate

Dick Frohnen. The full debate took only thirty minutes and although a voice vote seemed to indicate adoption of the name change, a formal count was taken. President Payette, in announcing the result said, "Welcome, professional journalists. Your vote is 113 yes, 77 no. I remind you that Sigma Delta Chi is still part of our name and tradition."

McCord said he didn't know of the change from the American Society of Journalists to the Society of Professional Journalists until the amendment was introduced on the floor. "I wasn't disturbed at all with the change at that moment. I was so interested in getting the name changed, I accepted it willingly. It wasn't long, however, before I began to think we hadn't done as well as we might have. The use of the words 'professional journalists' seemed redundant to me and I wish we had given it a little more thought." Writing in *The Quill*, Halina Czerniejewski noted, "There was little immediate fanfare, some shock," after the vote. And she asked, "After sixty-four years of SDX, how long would it take for SPJ to become a household term? But then, that was one of the arguments in favor of the change, wasn't it?"

STILL AN UNWIELDY NAME?

Between McCord's concern for redundancy and the time required in selling SPJ,SDX to the members and the media which would cover future Society events, the controversy continued even after Buffalo. Otwell traveled more than 45,000 miles visiting chapters as the Society's president in 1973-1974. "No one was really very happy with the new name," he said. "Those who had sought a name change were interested in something far more dramatic than The Society of Professional Journalists, comma, Sigma Delta Chi. And, of course, those who had opposed the change were unhappy about the whole thing. The risk during the entire year was to avoid becoming apologetic about it. The constant refrain was, 'If the Society doesn't like the new name, it can be changed again.' " Insofar as the use of the name by the media was concerned, the eight-word title proved to be too long for efficient use in print or on the air. The Greek letters, while at the end of the name and left there intentionally as a compromise with the traditionalists, continued to plague the Society's leadership in several ways. Few chapters referred to themselves as The Society of Professional Journalists or even SPJ, let alone SPJ,SDX in local communication with members or the media. They preferred to call themselves SDX. This was true especially with the campus chapters. Added to that was the fact that the Greek letters still provided many in the media with apparent reason to refer to the organization as a fraternity. The national officers had tried to resolve an identity crisis but in the years from 1973 through 1978 found themselves with a new name and the same old problem.

Near the end of Goodykoontz's term as president in 1978, he had had enough of those problems and set out to use what prestige he had as the Society's leader to effect a change. In his oral report to the Birmingham convention, he departed from his published report and told the delegates, "SPJ,SDX should change its name to The Society of Journalists. I will ask the national board to prepare a by-laws change in time for the 1979 convention in New York to try to accomplish that goal." Pointing to numerous instances of incorrect usage by chapters, committees and the media, including his own newspaper, he said the title is "still confusing the public and ourselves. Of course, we are proud of our Sigma Delta Chi heritage and would want to retain the name in such activities as the Distinguished Service Awards and the fine programs of the Sigma Delta Chi Foundation." Goodykoontz carried his concern to the board's April 27, 1979, meeting in Denver and formally moved that such a by-laws change be prepared. Sutherland seconded. Region Eight director Phil Record said that because everyone seemed to be having difficulty getting the name correct, he felt such a change should be a priority, but Region Five director Casey Bukro asked, "If we already have an identity crisis, what will another change do to us?" Vice president for campus chapter affairs Bert Bostrom noted that the New

York convention would be asked to approve a dues increase for professional members and that two controversial issues might be too much to ask at one time. "The dues increase should have the higher priority this year," he said. Goodykoontz's motion was adopted, 11-9, but. a few weeks later, Goodykoontz decided perhaps that the name change proposal would be inappropriate in 1979 after all and he asked Hurst to poll the board by mail. The action to take that by-laws change to New York was reversed, 18-3. From that moment, however, it was not a question of whether such a change would be brought up again, but when?

All the Society officers except one, Novitz, during the early 1980's believed as did Goodykoontz, but they weren't convinced The Society of Journalists was the right name to offer convention delegates. In 1981, president Howard Graves determined that the time was right to approach the membership once again. In his president's column titled, "Beach This Whale," in the November *Quill*, he wrote, "Ladies and gentlemen of The Society of Professional Journalists, Sigma Delta Chi, it is time to find us a new name. We are not a fraternity. We are a profession. That cluttered, unwieldy, unclear name, as one former national president wrote me, is a redundancy....The cover of the September issue of *The Quill* identified this organization as 'The Journalism Society of the '80's.' If we are to be that, let's beach this whale. Let us eradicate the fraternal connotation....Our seventy-fifth anniversary will be celebrated in 1984. Perhaps we can present ourselves a gift on that occasion with a new name. I hope so." Because the November 1981 issue of *The Quill* was circulated about the time delegates to that year's national convention were gathering in Washington, DC, one can not be certain that Graves' column influenced delegates to action there. But a possible new solution to what the board and many members perceived as a problem with the eight-year-old name was presented in the form of a resolution at that convention. The resolution pointed out all of the problems aired earlier and, while it stated that the name Sigma Delta Chi would be preserved as part of the name of the Distinguished

Service Awards and the Sigma Delta Chi Foundation, it concluded, "Be it resolved that this organization begin the process that will change its name to the Society of Professional Journalists and that this convention approve a by-laws revision to be presented to the 1982 convention for consideration." In what appeared to be an indication that the time for another name change was at hand, the delegates in Washington approved the resolution to be sent to Milwaukee the following November.

THE DELEGATES KEEP SIGMA DELTA CHI

Clearly the name change issue was the primary topic of conversation when the delegates assembled for the business session November 13. After reading the proposed amendment, president Novitz, who had spoken in opposition to the original name change in 1973, added, "As I have made abudantly clear, with all due respect for the continuing friendship [with my fellow officers], your president is one of those who opposes this change." Past-president Graves followed with the presentation for the name change, telling the delegates that in his travels for the Society to more than fifty cities in 1971, on many occasions he had to stop and explain to those in the media and to others just what Sigma Delta Chi was. Graves also read from a number of letters and news stories published during the past several months in which the name had been misused or the organization had been referred to as a fraternity. The delegate from the University of Wisconsin at Eau Claire, who did not identify herself, responded asking Graves, "Is it the Society's fault that other people can not get our name right?" She pointed out that much of the material distributed at the convention and the Society letterhead referred only to the Society of Professional Journalists and did not include the words Sigma Delta Chi. "We have not changed our name as yet. How can others be expected to get our name right when our own leadership can't get our name right?" Past president Otto, speaking for the name change, said, "I think it is essential that when we do the things that the

Society is moving into doing, that we have an identity which clearly marks what we are. When we go on Capitol Hill and before other groups, they see the three Greek letters, which are a proud and honored part of our tradition, and the immediate image is, this is a Greek, honorary group of some kind, and they ask, 'What kind of group is this? What kind of impact does it have across the broad spectrum of American society?' When you read The Society of Professional Journalists, however, immediately you get a different impression. Images and salesmanship are overdone in our society. Nonetheless, we live in this society and we are subject to the same kind of impressions that everyone else is. I suggest that we maintain our Greek letters on our awards and for the Foundation, but I'd like to make [our name] simple for all those people out there who don't know what we are. That's what this name change is all about." The delegate from the Greater Buffalo International professional chapter took the traditionalist point of view suggesting, "We have had the name Sigma Delta Chi since our founding in 1909. It's a cumbersome title now, I agree. But I am willing to tolerate that inconvenience rather than seeing Sigma Delta Chi deleted from our title." John Feeley, Colorado professional chapter added, "When someone spells my name wrong or gets the name of my newspaper wrong, I try to maintain a controlled level of rage. I do not change my name; I do not change the name of my newspaper. I try to educate the [offender] and write back, saying, 'You are an idiot' or something to that effect. We should [as an organization] maintain a controlled level of rage when someone misidentifies us and try to correct it." The questions of recruiting members on college campuses and maintaining a chapter on certain campuses with and/or without the Greek letter identification received attention in delegate speeches, but since chapters on both sides of the issue were able to document that either name would cause problems, the arguments seemed to have little effect on other delegates who, for the most part, had come with minds made up. Maynard Hicks, a professor of journalism at California State

University at Northridge and a member of the organization since 1927, chose to defend the name change proposal despite the fact that his roots went back to fraternity days. "I praise your interest and consideration that you change and simplify the name in the interest of economy of space [in newspapers and magazines] and in the interest of ending this yearly madness," he said. The debate lasted approximately thirty-five minutes. When president Novitz announced the result of the voting, the proposal to delete Sigma Delta Chi from the name was defeated, 151-142.

It is important to note here that, since 1973, voting at national conventions had been on a proportional system giving chapters with greater membership from two to as many as ten votes, while chapters with fewer than fifty members having only one vote. In the case of the nine-vote margin, a change of position by only one or two chapters voting against the name change would have changed the decision, making it even closer than the vote count itself indicated. It is also interesting and probably significant that ninety-three chapters were absent or denied voting rights on the name-change question in Milwaukee. Eighty-six professional chapters were present for the vote, with fifty-six chapters absent. On the campus chapter side, 139 chapters were present and voted, with thirty-six chapters absent and one chapter present but with no voting rights. It had become common for chapters to fail to send delegates to national conventions because of financial problems at the local level for several years, but the absence rate at the Milwaukee was among the highest, if not the highest, in recent history. Within minutes of the decision on the name change, Resolution Five, placing a five-year moritorium on future convention votes on any change in the Society's name, was adopted, 135-134. The national officers and parliamentarian reported, however, that one convention may not bind another's action and, given the nine-vote margin on the name change, it was obvious the issue would be back at future conventions as The Society of Professional Journalists, Sigma Delta Chi, moved toward its fourth quarter century.

SOMETHING OF VALUE:
A CODE OF ETHICS

"To advance the standards of the press by fostering a higher ethical code, thus increasing its value to the profession," the founders had written as one of their purposes in 1909. There was, of course, no formal code of ethics either within the fraternity's constitution or anywhere in the profession at that time. Attempts to draft such a code were not begun until 1919 when delegates to that convention appointed a special committee charged "to reduce to a code of ethics as many as possible of those high motives and lofty principles which actuate leading journalists in the practice of their profession." But future conventions could not agree on the language or extent of any code until 1926, three years after the American Society of Newspaper Editors' Canons of Journalism had been published. Resolving their inability to come together on a Sigma Delta Chi code of their own, delegates in 1926 simply adopted the ASNE Canons as the standards by which SDX members would "practice their profession."

Ethics continued to be a topic of concern at national conventions through the 1940's, but, for the most part, officers and members concentrated on specific incidents in which actions of journalists were questioned. When Neal Van Sooy, editor and publisher of the Santa Paula, California *Chronicle*, became Sigma Delta Chi president in 1948, one of his first official acts was to name a press ethics committee, with Charles Clayton as chairman. That committee's report to the 1949 convention in Dallas caused a furor and provided headlines in news trade journals the following week. The committee's report presented the first tangible code of ethics drawn by the fraternity in its history, but proposed that it be enforced by an impartial board of review authorized to cite flagrant violations and invoke the power of public opinion. It spelled out the obligations of accuracy, fairness, decency and community leadership. It was too much for the delegates to accept and they called for more study by Clayton's committee. In 1951, the ethics committee provided delegates the choice of two codes,

one prepared by a majority of the committee and the other a minority report. After a long debate, the delegates voted to table the committee's report.

Norman Isaacs, managing editor of the Louisville *Times*, became chairman of a new committee on ethics and news objectivity in the mid-1950's and its 1956 report caused another stir, but little apparent policy change. One aspect of the report, which recommended that all newspapers tighten their standards of ethical operation by issuing instructions to their staffs to prohibit acceptance of gifts, caused the greatest debate. Clayton's history of Sigma Delta Chi states, "Despite some of the comments from the floor, the report was accepted." Accepted, perhaps, but there is no available record which indicates that the "no gifts" guideline was added as an appendage to the ASNE Canons, making it "official." The study of a possible Sigma Delta Chi code of ethics continued when president James A. Byron appointed Bill Small, then news director of WHAS Television in Louisville, as chairman of the ethics committee in 1958. "We didn't get very far on a code," Small said. "What the committee did try to do was to collect a series of articles on ethics which, in effect, would be position papers on ethics. The articles appeared on occasion in *The Quill*. One hope, which was never fulfilled, was that they would be published as a single volume which would be useful in a course in journalism."

It would be unfair to say that in the early 1960's the Society practiced "situational ethics" – deciding upon the ethical thing to do and what might be politically astute given the circumstances of a particular situation. But failure through the years to come to grips with what ought to be in a Sigma Delta Chi code did force the board to look at each problem or potential problem on an individual basis. The Ford Motor Company's College Editors' Conference and Mustang Test-Drive Program in the spring of 1964 did get the board's attention. Ford's conference with forty-four college editors was scheduled "to discuss and exchange views on the automobile business and the growing youth market for automobiles." Following the conference, the company provided each editor with a new demonstration car to drive back his campus and to use at no cost for the remaining weeks of the spring term. "We hoped to give the editors a chance to make an exhaustive and personal evaluation of this new product. We hoped that the presence of the Mustangs on the campuses would attract the attention of other students to our new car – a car which we believe has a special appeal to young people," a Ford spokesman said. The Sigma Delta Chi board responded by adopting a resolution at its May 2, 1964, meeting criticizing Ford Motor Company for providing the editors with new cars. "It is the unanimous decision of the directors that such a promotion violates the professional journalistic ethics upheld by Sigma Delta Chi. The practice of accepting gifts or favors from politicians, public relations men and advertisers long has been deplored by responsible journalists. We see no difference between offering automobiles to college editors and the free-loading favors sometimes offered to professional newsmen. Promotions of this nature appear to legitimatize corporate favors among the press, especially inexperienced journalists. We strongly urge that Ford abandon any such favors in the future." Ford's vice president for public relations answered, "In sponsoring the program, we were neither offering favors nor suggesting that participation in the program involved a *quid pro quo* in the form of special publicity treatment."

The incident with Ford focused attention on questionable activities by corporate entities relating directly to Sigma Delta Chi, especially helping with financial contributions to sponsor official events and special programs at the annual conventions. President Koop had addressed the subject in a memo to board members in July 1964. But the Tidewater professional chapter attacked the potential ethical problem directly. It sent a resolution to the board in time for its meeting at the November convention in Kansas City, Missouri, calling for "prohibition of financial support from profit-making organizations outside the journalism profession for official convention functions." Aware of financial considerations, specifically those in local chapters serving as hosts for a convention, the board recognized the problem, but couldn't bring itself to cut all of the ties with corporate America. In a policy statement on convention hospitality adopted in Kansas City, the board said, "Newspapers, broadcasting stations and other news organizations desiring to sponsor a meal, reception, or otherwise contribute financially to the success of a convention, are cordially invited to do so. The board is concerned about accepting contributions from non-industry organizations. It does not wish to prohibit them but requests that organizations invited to contribute are carefully screened, that no pressure is used, and that no public credit is given. As for non-industry sponsorship of women's activities, the host chapter is asked to consult the national president about individual events. Organizations sometimes desire to provide their own hospitality outside the official convention program, such as offering breakfast daily or maintaining open house in a hotel suite. The board does not encourage such activities, but since they are unofficial it cannot formally regulate them."

At the same convention, the professional development committee, chaired by Don Carter of *The National Observer*, outlined its goals for the Society, some of which addressed questions of ethics. As its first long-range objective, the committee said it wanted "to examine the pressures on the news reporters and editors – particularly the gift, junket and related job problems. What constitutes a conflict of interest for a journalist? What side jobs related to journalistic duties should be rejected to insure high professional standards?" Listed separately, but a part of the problem which needed attention, was the exploration of "the utilization of a newsman as chairman of the publicity committee for civic drives, charities and other interests." Further, the report stated, the committee needed "to study and propose codes of ethics to govern the professional actions of members of the various media in their dealings with each other." Incoming president Sewell listed "upgrading professional performance during a technological revolution" as one of his goals for 1965, but he did not favor any all-consuming code of ethics which spelled out everything that might put a newsperson in a compromising position. Sewell believed the Society needed to continue to monitor ethics for journalists but, he said, " We all knew what we should and should not do, what would and would not compromise us. I think we followed this thing [ethics] out the window. As far as being compromised by the International Telephone and Telegraph breakfasts, which served a purpose for the undergraduates, or by Bill Burk's Santa Fe suite, it didn't happen." Looking at the period of the mid-1960's and the type of reporting that was going on, Bob White, president in 1966-1967, recalls, "Without any question, ethics were of tremendous importance. But I don't think any of us thought our ethics were being questioned. We were not caught up at that time in investigative reporting."

None of the presidents of White's time were concerned about establishing the long-sought code of ethics, but each had his own ethical issue which he sought to enhance. White's concern was for advancing the standards of performance in journalism through concentration on accuracy. "Accuracy is our only reason for existence. If we don't have accuracy we don't have anything," he said. In his speech in April 1967 at DePauw University dedicating a Sigma Delta Chi marker there, he said, "Each new generation of newsmen must do still better, must make and take constantly improving tools and with them hew still finer the accuracy needed to serve better the minds of men."

For Staley McBrayer, president in 1967-1968, it was objectivity. In his annual report to the convention in Atlanta, he wrote, "SDX points the way to fairness – reporting both sides – objectivity for the professional reporter – evven as difficult as it may be at time. It would seem the essence of professionalism for a reporter who feels he cannot be objective to a point of professionalism to level with his editor and ask to be relieved of his assignment." McBrayer remembered "advocacy journalism" was coming into vogue during

his administration, and journalists, especially young journalists, were telling him "You can't be objective today. You've got to tell your side." Visiting the college campuses, McBrayer said he told the youthful reporters, "[Some of] you call yourselves Christians. Well, that means Christ-like. Yet you wouldn't dare say that you are Christ-like. But it's your belief and the standard you'd like to move toward. That's the same dedication you must make to objectivity. You have always to be trying to be objective. You may not ever reach it but it's a hell of a lot better to be trying than to say there's no use." McBrayer believed Sigma Delta Chi's successes in raising journalistic standards would raise public confidence in the press. "The public must be made aware that there is a professional communication organization to which they can look with confidence," he said.

Vice President of the United States Spiro Agnew attacked the credibility and ethics of the press in November 1969 when he said the press operated from a "privileged sanctuary" and "it is not fair and relevant to question its concentration [of power] in the hands of a tiny and closed fraternity of privileged men, elected by no one, and enjoying a monopoly sanctioned...by government." He added, "As with other American institutions, perhaps it is time that the networks were made more responsible to the people they serve." Reaction from the press was quick and severe, bringing the added charge by many inside and outside the media that the press was thin-skinned and could hand out criticism but couldn't take it. SDX President Frank Angelo, took the view that the press should be looking at itself with greater candor. Addressing the East Tennessee professional chapter at its installation ceremony July 24, 1970, he listed three major concerns of the public concerning the news media: lack of precision in presentation of the news by not being accurate in fact or perspective, feeling that the media were involved in overkill in news coverage, and believing there was a lack of balance in news coverage. "The primary problem is that most people want the press to tell it like it is – from their point of view. We do distort the view unless we

187

print a balanced version. Truth is hard to come by and we must start [in our search for truth] by being more demanding of ourselves." Angelo was not an advocate for a code of ethics, but his drive for self-examination by the press probably renewed the effort at writing such a code.

Chandler supported Angelo's response to Agnew. Addressing the Region Two conference in 1971, he said, "In our hearts, we know our critics are right. And it hurts. We must recognize the validity of some of their suggestions. We have some blemishes and, if we're honest, we'll admit it. Today's critics have lumped [good media and bad media] together. Our job is to tell it like it is....If there are any flaws, it is our duty to correct them." Chandler also favored and was willing to take a more direct approach toward a code. "The ASNE Canons, which we had adopted, had been written long before and our ideas of ethics and what was ethical behavior had changed in the meantime." he remembers. "The original guidelines were so broad as to not really give much guidance to anybody. It would have been just as well to have written one which said, 'I agree to abide by the Golden Rule and the Ten Commandments.' I thought it was time to update those guidelines." Chandler has been credited by his contemporaries on the board with providing the first, strong push from the national level toward developing specific new standards for journalists. In his 1971 speech to the Washington, DC convention, he said, "I think our organization is going to have to take stronger steps in the future to help correct the shortcomings of our business....It is up to us not only to rise to the defense of those [in the press] who are attacked, but to point out to our own people the error of their way when they have in fact erred. We pride ourselves in exposing evil in government or the professions. We should pride ourselves in putting our own conduct under the light of publicity." Chandler's Bend, Oregon *Bulletin* was one of the four newspapers involved in early press council experiments and he was a member of the Twentieth Century Fund study committee which recommended the founding of the National News Council. "Those experiences had

caused me to do more reading and pay more attention to the ethical problems of journalism than I would have otherwise."

BUKRO'S COMMITTEE TAKES THE LEAD

Guy Ryan, who followed Chandler as president, also believed the Society could best answer critics of the press by using its prestige to demonstrate that journalists were concerned about their performance standards. Upon taking office, he told the Nevada professional chapter, "Some of our people have forgotten that we work for the public." Honest journalism, performed with the highest integrity, is the job of journalists in the 1970's, he said. Ryan named Casey Bukro, a reporter for the Chicago *Tribune*, as chairman of the professional development committee, a move that would lead directly to the formulation and adoption of the code Ryan saw as necessary. On that committee, he placed Dornfeld; Offer; and Haig Keropian, of the Van Nuys, California *News*, each of whom would play leading roles in developing the code. Later in Oshkosh, Wisconsin, Ryan told students at the University of Wisconsin at Oshkosh, "Our integrity is being impugned, our motives are being questioned, our performance is being criticized and our beliefs are being challenged. I don't have to remind you that the very concept of a free press is on trial. And the jury is not very friendly."

When the national board gathered in Milwaukee May 5, 1972, it wrestled with the need for a "purity code" to be applied further than just to non-media support at national conventions. Region Three director Rhea Eskew, reporting for a study committee on sponsorship of chapter activities, recommended that local chapters be urged not to permit participation by non-media organizations. Discussions of working toward drawing up a broadly-based purity code were resolved when the board adopted a motion calling on chapters only to follow a policy similar to those moderate guidelines already established for chapters that are hosts for a national convention. The debate within the board, however, was an indication that its members were becoming aware that something such as a more rigorous code was necessary in the immediate future to replace or at least modify and update the ASNE Canons. In his speech that August to the Association for Education in Journalism, Ryan continued his responsibility theme, calling those who practiced advocacy journalism "journalistic Judases." He told the journalism educators, "They are selling us down the river, playing into the hands of our detractors, widening the credibility gap."

Bukro decided, independently, that the professional development committee should do something about the matter of ethics. In a September 7, 1972, letter to his committee members, Bukro wrote, "Professional development is a logical outgrowth of professional concern and involvement in activities designed to enhance professional performance....I am proposing that our committee enter a new phase in which the emphasis will be on concrete proposals to this end....Ethics has a high priority these days among newsmen and news readers. Some people believe there should be a regular program on ethics at each chapter. Since the meaning of objectivity in news reporting seems to be in question more than ever these days, ethics is an urgent and meaningful topic for all chapters." Offer, a reporter for the Milwaukee *Journal*, responded, "Your comments on the importance of ethics are totally valid and for several years I have wondered what SDX could or should do. While I am not certain that the idea you mention [chapter programs] is the answer, I am delighted and impressed that thinking is moving toward the problem of journalistic ethics."

Ryan traveled as much or more as Society president in 1972 than had any of his contemporaries, thanks in great part to the support of his employer, James S. Copley, publisher of the San Diego newspapers and chairman of Copley Newspapers, Inc. Apparently Ryan got his message across in speaking to chapters across the country and through reports of those speeches in *The Quill*. By the time of the 1972 convention in Dallas, there was an awareness of the problems of ethics confronting journalism and a growing desire, if not demand that the Society play an increasing role in setting higher standards. In his presidential report to the Dallas convention, Ryan, although not mentioning the need for a code by name, said, "We've got to prove to readers of our newspapers, listeners to our radio newscasts and viewers of our television news that the media are, indeed, honest, reliable and responsible. And that's going to take a little more dedication by practitioners to the principles of Sigma Delta Chi." As further evidence of that developing interest, several chapters and individual members submitted resolutions dealing with ethics for consideration by the Dallas convention. Goodykoontz, chairman of the 1972 resolutions committee, remembers, "Those resolutions dealt with specific instances where journalists had been challenged for apparent unethical behavior and were directed at getting the Society to take a strong stand on journalistic ethics. Offer, who was on my committee, did a good job of bringing those variant resolutions into one acceptable and useful document." Offer recalls, "The finished resolution was an amalgam of three or four individual resolutions which were too narrow in scope to be offered to the convention and which didn't present a national picture we could ask the delegates to address. We were able to put together a strong statement, however, and the delegates responded by adopting it intact." The resolution stated, "The credibility of the working journalist is the key to successful, responsible and professional journalism...and must be jealously guarded by all members of Sigma Delta Chi." The resolution called on members "...to be aware of the dangers of losing public confidence....The credibility of the news media may be endangered when practicing journalists become personally involved in political campaigns, when they accept part-time employment – paid or unpaid – as agents of candidates or parties, when organizations of journalists engage in political endorsements, or when journalists accept gifts from news sources....Sigma Delta Chi states its firm belief that ethical journalists at all levels should refrain from any of these activities which may discredit journalism as a profession and bring the integrity of individual [news media] into question."

While the resolution didn't specifically codify the elements brought forward, it did accomplish three things. First, it served as an indicator that those delegates were as eager, if not more eager, than the board in raising the ethical standards for journalists; second, it spelled out those concerns which had received only casual attention to date; and third, it provided the impetus to the professional development committee to move ahead with a formal approach toward codification. Offer had seen to it that Bukro's professional development committee would be involved in carrying out the mandate of the resolution. "I wrote the final paragraph, [That this resolution be referred to the national professional development committee for study and program proposals] with the specific intent that there be a call for action and to give Casey [Bukro] the support of the convention to do what he clearly had in mind."

William Payette, president of United Features Syndicate in New York, who became president in Dallas, reappointed Bukro as chairman of the committee. But, because the convention had called for program proposals rather than for a new code, Bukro began to cast about for an appropriate direction in which to carry out his mission. "It was Hurst who steered me toward focusing on a new code of ethics," Bukro said. "He had observed what was happening on the board and in the Society and believed the old ASNE canons were outdated, too general in nature and needed to be replaced with a modern code." Armed with the dual impetus of the resolution and Hurst's suggestion, Bukro went to his committee with a June 4, 1973, letter suggesting that the 1926 code made no provision for electronic media and posing these questions. "Should we update it and make it known to the public that the press is guided by a code of ethics? What should we say about moonlighting, second jobs, reporters being involved in politics, free trips, gifts, and community affairs? What about editors and publishers who participate in fund-raising drives or serve on boards of community organizations? Does objectivity suffer when reporters and editors help shape

community decisions by serving in civic posts? What about press credentials and privileges. Do we lose or gain if we set ourselves aside as a privileged group? Do we need press cards or should we prescribe conditions for their use? Should they be used for free parking? Can we strengthen the role of journalists by emphasizing the rights of private citizens, since journalists represent the public?"

When Bukro returned from a Chicago *Tribune* assignment in Alaska in August, he was fired up about the task of writing a code of ethics. "I was inspired by my trip and somehow wanted the code to have the feeling of grandeur and majesty I had felt in Alaska." Nine enthusiastic responses from the committee had arrived – from Offer, Keropian, Wendell Phillippi, Noel Wilson, Bob Liming, Cliff Rowe, Sherman London, Sidney Elsner and Dorman Cordell – on Bukro's return to Chicago. Later, Bukro would receive responses from committee members Todd Hunt and Paul Hood. There were the expected conflicts within the committee on accepting gifts, service in civic organizations or political involvement, and the problems with holding a second job. "I had to get busy with my homework because the time had come to put feelings into words on paper and, as committee chairman, that job fell to me. I started doing research on ethics, looking at other codes and studying the state of journalism and some of the history of SDX." As he began to develop the language for a draft of the code, Bukro remembered one of his journalism professors at Northwestern University, Jacob Scher, and "his ringing lectures about the rights and responsibilities of journalists – one balancing the other. When I sat down to write the code in mid-August 1973, I asked myself, 'How would Jake do this?' Some of his declarations came back to me and I wrote them in. 'Our constitutional role is to seek the truth as part of the public's right to know the truth,' and 'Media should not pander to morbid curiosity about details of vice and crime.' Scher was inspiring and that's what I wanted the code to be. He gave me a sense of idealism about journalism, and I tried to convey that idealism in the code." Bukro's sense of the history of the Society played an important role as well. "I wanted to make the code our own, reflecting the Society's own ideas," he remembers. "So I went to our initiation ceremony for some of our own ideals such as 'with faith to perpetuate a profession based on freedom to learn and publish the facts...that is as jealous of the right to utter unpopular opinions as of the privilege to agree with the majority.' And, of course, the ideas of members of the committee added their own flavor. With all this whizzing around in my head, the writing seemed to flow."

Bukro sent his first draft of a new code of ethics to the committee and to Hurst August 22. He wrote the members, "After several readings of the answers you sent...it is clear that those suggesting strong measures outnumber the moderates. The sentiment seems to be the issues we are dealing with...call for strong measures, even unorthodox measures. A dominant theme, not only in the answers you gave but in much of the current literature on a free press, is that press integrity is not only a question of what we know to be true of our behavior. It also involves what the public believes to be true, whether that impression is true or false....The draft of the proposed revised code takes a strong stand. Feel free to change it. But let me caution you on a major point. The code of ethics must reflect what we stand for. It must be some sort of positive statement. The more modifiers, exceptions and qualifications we throw in, the fuzzier it will be."

The exchange of correspondence with committee members continued through October and differences among them on specific language began to resolve themselves. Because committees charged with tackling similar tasks of writing codes in the 1950's and 1960's had foundered on minority disagreements, Bukro stressed the need to go along with "the mainstream of thought on the committee," or a majority rules concept. "It was democratic and it kept us from getting bogged down. When it wasn't absolutely clear, I exercised my authority as chairman to make a call, based on the fact that the chairman is expected to have the clearest sense of a committee's

mission and a sense of the attitudes of the committee." Throughout the process of writing second and third revisions, about 80 percent of the code stood as it was written in Bukro's first draft, evidence that giving Bukro credit as the code's author is, indeed, appropriate.

Only the matter of how to deal with the questions of gifts to journalists remained as a major point of contention. As item one under "Ethics," Bukro had written, "Gifts to journalists or their employers should be condemned. Free travel and other privileges that might be offered to journalists should be discouraged, since they set journalists apart from the public they serve." Wilson had offered the language, "Gifts to journalists or their employers, although acceptable when clearly in the interest of a free flow of accurate information, should be quickly rejected when there is the slightest evidence that they may be calculated to distort the observation or interpretation of events." Offer disagreed with Wilson and wrote, "I feel that newsmen must not only remain unobligated to outsiders but they must maintain the appearance of independence." Bukro, who said, "My feeling was that Wilson's version left a great deal open to individual interpretation," wanted the democratic process to apply. But he also wanted all minority views to be examined fully before a final decision was made on the language to be presented. The committee changed the wording on the gifts section, taking the strongest stand possible. As item one under "Ethics," the committee wrote, "Gifts, favors, free travel, special treatment or privileges can compromise the integrity of journalists and their employers. Nothing of value should be accepted."

THE BATTLE THAT NEVER OCCURRED

Hurst and Payette recall the revolutionary nature of some language in the proposed code – especially regarding acceptance of gifts, called "freebies" by everyone involved – was expected to cause vigorous debate on Saturday, November 17, 1973. Hurst said, "There was considerable anticipation that there would be a long discussion. Committee members and board members were prepared to discuss and defend the idea of having this revised code." Payette recalls that Bukro and Hurst had warned him "there was going to be one hell of a floor fight on the code." Payette wanted to keep the entire voting procedure "as simple as possible." Since the delegates had had opportunity to read and study the new code, Bukro's presentation as committee chairman lasted only about two minutes. "I didn't think there was any need to do much more than to get the debate started and let her rip," Bukro remembers. He moved adoption of the code and stepped back as Payette took the microphone, asking for a second, which came immediately. Payette paused, expecting the beginning of debate only to find no one seeking recognition. After a few seconds it became obvious there was no discussion forthcoming and Payette said, "The adoption of [this report] has been moved and seconded. All in favor?" He was greeted with a chorus of "Ayes." "Opposed?" he asked. The delegates were silent. "It really caught me by surprise that there had been no call from the floor for discussion before the vote was taken," Hurst said. "My immediate thought was, 'Did the delegates fully comprehend what they had just approved unanimously?' I grabbed Bukro by the arm as he was leaving the podium and asked him, 'Do you think they really understand what adopting this code really means to them and to the Society?' When he said he didn't know, I suggested that perhaps the question should be put to the delegates again, just to be certain they understood what they had approved." Bukro returned to the podium and interrupted Payette, who was about to move to the next order of business. Payette moved aside and Bukro, once again, but in more detail, told the delegates the ramifications of the new code and that in adopting the code they were not only lending the prestige of the Society to the strongest new code of ethics for journalists in the nation, but were urging all members of the Society to abide by its tenets – a set of tenets that "had teeth." Payette said, "All right. I think we have already accepted it. If you would like to vote on it again, fine. All in favor, please say aye." The delegates shouted "Aye." Payette said, "Opposed?" Once again, there

was no response. "It is adopted," Payette said. No doubt, that occasion marked the first and perhaps the only time in the Society's history to date that delegates had approved a far-reaching policy statement twice and done so unanimously each time. A copy of the SPJ,SDX Code of Ethics can be found in the Appendix to this book.

It must be noted here that a reading of the transcript of that November 17, 1963, session, while it indicates that, indeed, two votes were taken and each was unanimous, it gives a slightly different version of who brought the issue to the floor a second time. Bukro brought the version presented herein to this author's attention and, after checking it with Hurst and Payette, the author was convinced the transcript is in error.

SPJ,SDX was not the only journalism organization to have worked toward higher professional standards in the early 1970's – the Associated Press Managing Editors and other groups were evaluating their codes and canons – but, the Society's new Code of Ethics was in place in November 1973.

IMPLEMENTING THE CODE

The delegates in Buffalo apparently were convinced that the new SPJ,SDX Code of Ethics was needed and that its strict language was appropriate, but, as new president Ralph Otwell began to visit chapters in the next few weeks, it became equally apparent that perhaps another set of Society members, had they been delegates in Buffalo, might not have voted in the same manner. "There was a lot of hostility among many members. Unfortunately, the focus was on the 'freebies' which seemed to upset more people than all the rest of the code put together." Otwell said if there was one weakness in the code, it was in the section which stated journalists should accept nothing of value without defining what it was which had value. "We got into a lot of meaningless discussions about, 'Well, can you accept a free meal, can you accept a book or a calendar at Christmastime?' The question was 'of what value' and 'how much value' and the code didn't answer that question." But where there was conflict about the strong provisions of the code in some circles, there were others who not only accepted its provisions but also set about to establish means of enforcing it. The code, after all, ended with a pledge which said, "Journalists should actively censure and try to prevent violations of these standards." Otwell noted, "The whole thing was getting off on the wrong track. We had word that some chapters were holding 'star chamber' proceedings concerning members who were violating one part of the code or another with the aim of throwing them out of the chapter. It was a totally undemocratic process without due process or, sometimes, not even giving those accused the chance to answer the charges. The code, insofar as those chapters were concerned, was in serious risk of becoming an embarrassment to the Society." Otwell was faced with having to meet both problems headon.

At the Region Ten Conference in Spokane, Washington, April 19, 1974, Otwell said, "You've got to remember that the new SDX Code was not engraved on stone tablets and handed down by Moses as he descended from Mt. Sinai. It is simply a code handed down by a committee in Buffalo. Some chapters have organized ethics committees to run unethical journalists out of town on a rail. Any journalist ought to be given a chance to reply. Before charges are made and reputations are damaged, you've got to be sure you are on safe ground. There are real problems with any code and the real problem to this one is how to implement it. Ours is not a licensed profession and it is protected by the First Amendment. Any reckless implementation would be dangerous." Pointing to parts of the code he thought were more important, Otwell added, "Real attention should be directed toward conflict of interest – reporters who moonlight in public relations and take leaves of absence to work on assignments that can be influenced by their regular news jobs."

Bukro was on the road during 1974 as well talking to chapters and at regional conferences about the development of the code and why it was written. He called the code "our declaration of independence – independence from the old hangups which plagued journalism," and urged self-restraint from inside the profession, not outside.

While Otwell concentrated on the need to be aware of conflicts of interest and to correct them, Bukro was concerned about those "freebies." He said the public did not have confidence in politicians on the take and they didn't have confidence in media on the take. Addressing the common practices of accepting free tickets to events for reporters and going on junkets paid for by businesses and associations, he said, "Paying our own way is part of the costs of doing business." In answer to those in audiences who said free tickets and other gifts amounted only to "peanuts," Bukro said he usually pointed out that Paul Poorman of the Detroit News had tallied up the value of all gifts and freebies to that paper, which amounted to $76,000 in one year.

The furor which seemed to be developing across the nation prompted Otwell early in 1974 to ask president-elect Bill Small to develop guidelines for implementation of the Code of Ethics which, it was hoped, when sent to chapters, would defuse the situation. Small's document, adopted by the board in May 1974, stressed that the code was voluntary in nature and that an educational campaign would be necessary to effect its provisions. "A chapter of the Society of Professional Journalists, Sigma Delta Chi, should understand that the emphasis is the positive one of encouraging observance of the Code of Ethics," it stated. "Chapters should take an affirmative role in seeing that others in and out of journalism, those who do not belong to this Society, are informed about the Code....Because the Code is new, adherence will come only after the profession and the public are educated. Its intent is to discourage many existing practices, some of them entrenched by years of observation....In time, hopefully, it will be accepted by all as the normal way for journalists to conduct themselves."

While there was controversy, it should not be assumed the Code of Ethics was unpopular and unused. As with most revolutionary ideas when put into action, the loudest, most often-heard comments came from the vocal few who objected to individual parts of the code. Hurst knew not only of the complaints and problems but also of the hundreds, if not thousands, of members who believed the statement of ethical standards was the most relevant and important addition to the Society's arsenal in the fight for credibility and who made it a personal as well as professional philosophy. As an example, Hurst said, "Within the first year, more than twenty major newspapers, along with many radio and television stations and press associations, adopted the SPJ,SDX Code as their own. In addition to that, the Society could take credit for having assumed another important leadership role at the national level. Within a couple of years, other national organizations had revised their codes or written new codes based in part on the statement of principles adopted by SPJ in Buffalo. We really don't know how many news organizations simply used our code as their own because many of those adoptions were unreported, but it was a significant number – far more than we might have anticipated."

Meanwhile, Offer, who had urged continued study and development of programs on ethics through some type of committee, was named chairman of the professional development committee. Bukro had been elected Region Five director in Buffalo and was busy in that role as well as with his travels discussing the code. During the year, Offer's committee recommended that to make the code as effective as possible as quickly as possible, it should be given far wider dissemination that it had received. Both local chapters and national officers were encouraged to pursue endorsements of the Code of Ethics by news organizations and associations and that those endorsements, when made, be widely publicized. In addition, the committee recommended that the Society work with other journalistic organizations, encouraging them to set the highest possible standards. Asked by Otwell to come up with suggestions on how to handle grants to the Society from foundations, including those affiliated with non-media organizations, the committee proposed that the leadership "be alert to the peril of ethical blindness that could lead us to assume cynically the worst about all who wanted to help us advance our goals."

One of the first newspapers to adopt the code was *The Milwaukee Journal*. Its

editor, Richard Leonard, had been elected national treasurer of the Society in Buffalo, but he had been an advocate of a stronger ethics code for some time. Leonard said, "This Code is a worthy statement of principles for our staff and for journalists everywhere." He had the Code printed and posted in the newsroom. "We ran the code in full as a quarter page in the paper to let our readers know we believed in its principles. What was most pleasing to me was the support we got from the staff, especially the younger reporters. They rallied around it; they thought this was great." Leonard not only publicized the Code, he instituted all of its provisions. Tickets to athletic events, concerts and the like, which had been provided free to the newspaper were paid for by the newspaper. Christmas gifts coming to the newspaper and its staff members just a month after the convention were returned to senders. "We were also concerned about conflict of interest and we tried to set the example of cleaning house and enforcing the Code here on the *Journal*. The use of the Code was important to the public as well. After we printed the code, our readers, on occasion, would write and let us know if they felt we had violated our own Code of Ethics. Sometimes they were right and sometimes they were wrong, but they were aware of these new standards and they had something with which to measure our performance." Leonard spoke as often as he could on the need for making the Code an important part of the journalist's professional life. In one speech, he said, "To those who are overestimating the importance of ethics, I say the future of the free press may very well depend on how ethical journalists can be. A hostile public will not support the concept of a free press. A free, responsible press – yes. A free, irresponsible press – no."

Leonard had a good fix on the national impact of the Code in its first several years of implementation. In his work with the Associated Press Managing Editors Association, he had sent out questionnaires to managing editors before and after the Buffalo convention concerning the use of codes or the principles included therein. He found that while 70 percent permitted reporters to accept free trips in 1972, only 40 percent permitted such trips after the SPJ,SDX Code was in place in 1974. He asked, "Do you have a stated policy on outside work, conflict of interest and free gifts?" Fewer than 2 percent said they had such a policy in 1972, while 35 percent reported a policy had been adopted in 1974. "There's no doubt we were making considerable progress. The news media were not using only the SPJ Code, but our Code made media executives aware of the importance of putting some kind of code into effect," Leonard said.

When McCord became president in November 1975, he set as one of his primary goals the hanging of a copy of the SPJ,SDX Code of Ethics on the wall of every newsroom and journalism school in the country. Knowing that handing out a simple piece of paper wouldn't get the job done, to set the example, wherever he traveled or spoke, he presented a framed copy of the Code to editors, reporters and chapter members so that it could be hung on a wall immediately and he encouraged others to use the same technique. By the end of 1976, McCord had placed more than forty Codes across the nation and had talked personally with the heads of five large newspaper groups about the code. His attitude toward the Code was exemplified in a speech to the Kansas State campus chapter shortly after he became president. "Of all the things we've done in the past few years, drafting the Code is at the top of the list in importance."

Some members of the national board, including Bukro, wanted stronger enforcement of the Code as it became more widely known. McCord, in a letter to Offer, asking him to stay on as chairman of the professional development committee, said, "I honestly believe we are a year or two away from the type of enforcement that I think most of us would like to see. There is great ignorance out there about the Code. It would be unfair to turn chapters into star chambers, enforcing rules that many of the journalists in their area had no hand in making and did not even know existed." Offer told Bukro early in 1976, "Each time we, through our chapters or as a national organization, refer to the Code of Ethics in specific matters of journalistic practice, we accelerate the process of making adherence to the Code a matter of routine and that, after all, is what you and I want the most....[Enforcement] has been the focus of my attention for the last two years. I both wanted to avoid misuse of any censorship power and to establish some system for making enforcement practical. I submitted such a system to the board and, as you well know, it was rejected. I was, obviously, disappointed in that decision. However I was impressed with some of the arguments of those who voted against my proposal. I told Bob [McCord] that his decision to emphasize wide distribution of the Code provided greater direction and emphasis on the Code than any past president of the Society had ever given."

A different type of problem than anyone had anticipated with the Code came to light January 26, 1976, when the Valley of the Sun professional chapter in Phoenix voted to replace the SPJ,SDX national Code with its own version. Ginger Hutton, president of the Valley of the Sun chapter, said, "We wanted a local code that would upgrade ethics but would also be more practical and easily adhered to within the managerial and economic framework of the local media. We believed that, because of its strictness, the national Code was being pretty much ignored." Don Bolles – the same *Arizona Republic* reporter who died almost five months later, June 13, the victim of the blast of a bomb placed under his car June 2 – served as chairman of that chapter's ethics committee and wrote a good portion of the revised version. He said, "What is considered acceptable practice among ethical newsmen violates the national Code," and noted that provisions that "nothing of value should be accepted" was too strict. The Valley of the Sun Code stated, instead, "Each member of the Valley of the Sun chapter must decide for himself when he believes that any gift or consideration is intended to compromise his or her integrity." The Code modified nearly every section of the national document to avoid a code which Bolles said was "so strict that it simply is being ignored."

McCord wrote Hutton May 3, 1976,

stating, "I wish to express my concern and disappointment at the attempt of the Valley of the Sun chapter to rewrite and weaken our Code of Ethics of the Society. I believe that your action is a step backwards in our national effort to upgrade ethical standards in our profession....Perhaps there would be more merit to your revisions if your claim that the Code was being ignored was accurate. I can assure you that this is not so. The Code of Ethics is fast becoming the accepted standard of journalistic conduct." When the Valley of the Sun chapter reaffirmed its stance on using its own Code rather than the national version, McCord went to Phoenix to address the chapter September 15. "I come here not in the role of a headmaster to rail at you for rewriting the dictionary but as a colleague who wants to convince you of the need for a strict code of ethics and one that can be universally observed," he said there. "Rules of conduct shouldn't be discarded simply because they can't be put into effect immediately....There's the implication that Arizonans are, well, different. I don't accept that at all. You people are as ethical as any other journalists – certainly you try to be. We can't have different sets of standards....I think journalists need agreement on many things. Mind you, I am not saying that stations and papers should not be different, not retain their individual personalities and policies. I am talking about agreement on matters of public policy, such as fairness and...abridgement of freedom of the press....Guidelines are needed, and badly, not because we want to be loved, but because we want to be believed. And no one will believe anyone he does not respect." McCord wrote Offer the following day, "The trip to Phoenix was not as rough as I thought, and I think maybe I did a little good....I suggested that they take our Code and adopt their own implementation Code, and I think they may do that." He was right, for in October, with about thirty members present, the Valley of the Sun chapter voted to rescind its Code.

The SPJ Code of Ethics became more widely known, not only through dissemination of the document in newsrooms but, as Hurst recalls, "It was published in more than a dozen journalism textbooks [a number that had increased to more than twice that number by the mid-1980's], giving it added prestige and allowing it to reach an audience of students many of whom never joined the Society." The professional development committee continued its work toward further implementation of the Code in the late 1970's with Harry Fuller, an editorial writer for the Salt Lake City, Utah *Tribune*, and Margo Pope, an education writer for the Jacksonville, Florida *Times-Union*, as chairs. When Jean Otto became national president, she changed the name of the committee to the ethics committee and named Marvin Garrette, assistant managing editor of the Richmond, Virginia *Times-Disptach*, as its chair. During Garrette's year, Offer's continuing interest in the ethics area prompted him as Region Six director to center his 1980 regional conference at Green Bay, Wisconsin, on an ethics debate using the Socratic method. Beginning with a complex hypothetical case, a trial lawyer questioned leading reporters and editors extensively on ethical questions about pursuing a story. Garrette was a member of the panel questioned and, along with committee member Mike Hammer, a reporter for *The Daily Oklahoman*, took note on how the program was developed. The experimental project was videotaped with cassettes made available to chapters which wanted to duplicate the program. Garrette picked up on the project and his committee developed formal guidelines for chapters and organizations planning a program on ethics. The guidelines, written by Offer, Hammer and Garrette, were distributed widely as a program idea on ethics and included in the 1981 and 1982 ethics committee reports.

Garrette asked professor John DeMott of the Memphis State University department of journalism to take on a project for the committee. DeMott researched all of the available literature on ethics and produced *The Ethics of Professional Journalists: An Annotated Bibliography of Suggested Readings*, which was published for the Society in 1980 and circulated widely in the next several years to chapters, working reporters and editors and journalism educators.

A NEW, LARGER ETHICS REPORT

The annual report of the committee had been duplicated and included only as a part of the delegates' notebooks at national convention until Fred Behringer, vice president and executive editor of the Montgomery Publishing Company in Ft. Washington, Pennsylvania, took over as chairman on appointment by president Graves in 1981. Behringer believed the report needed wider distribution and should be more than just a synopsis of committee actions. He asked his committee members to gather and write articles on current topics dealing with journalistic ethics. Montgomery Publishing Company agreed to set the type and print the booklet at no cost to the Society. The 1981 ethics committee report was another step forward in the committee's attempt not only to focus attention on ethics, but to provide direction and a survey of current information of national significance. Several thousand of the twenty-four-page booklets were distributed at and following the 1981 Washington, DC convention and served to inspire the committee and the national leadership to do even more. Behringer's 1982 ethics committee report, again set and printed by his company, was a tabloid-size, thirty-two-page newspaper filled not only with topical information but with opinion and speeches on ethics by noted journalists, including Isaacs; Kurt Luedtke, author of the screenplay for the film, *Absence of Malice*; John R. Finnegan, executive editor of the St. Paul, Minnesota *Dispatch – Pioneer Press*; Robert W. Greene, assistant managing editor of *Newsday*; and Tom Johnson, publisher and chief executive officer of the Los Angeles *Times*. Behringer reported that more than 8,000 copies of the report were mailed by the Society to members and other organizations during the year. During the summer of 1983, the Society received a $7,000 grant each year in 1983 and 1984 by Capital Cities Communications to fund the mass printing and mailing of the ethics report.

President Dornfeld, who, along with Offer and Bukro, knew that enforcement of the SPJ,SDX Code of Ethics remained the biggest problem in making the code effective, took a new course toward establishing a method for enforcement in 1983. Dornfeld appointed a special subcommittee to the ethics committee, chaired by Bukro, to study and prepare guidelines for chapters to use when called on to investigate a violation of the Code. As this book went to press, that committee had not completed its work.

TOWARD GREATER DEMOCRACY

In its first convention in 1912, Sigma Delta Chi's voting procedures were predicated on the delegate from each chapter having one vote on matters of constitution, policy, budget and the like. As fraternity alumni began to form their own chapters and even when, in 1937, the collegiate chapters were designated as undergraduate chapters and alumni chapters became professional chapters, there was no reason to alter those procedures. Quite naturally, because they were the long-established body of the organization, undergraduate chapters, later to be called campus chapters, always have outnumbered professional chapters and, thereby, have had controlling strength at national conventions.

By the time of the 1960 reorganization, the number of campus chapters had reached sixty-six while professional chapters numbered fifty. Yet, among the 12,000-plus members of the Society, a growing majority were professionals – alumni of campus chapters or, in many cases, initiated directly by a professional chapter. In addition, the central focus of the organization had turned from a campus fraternity to a professional orientation. It was no wonder then that a few of those professional members began to question the fact that the students had the majority of votes in the Society's supreme legislative body, the national convention. Some, no doubt, challenged the maturity of the students who had the power to direct this now national and prestigious organization. But most of those who questioned the system of voting were concerned that college students were quite naturally more interested in campus problems than in journalistic issues of national import. As the gap narrowed between the number of campus and professional chapters during the 1960's and as the gap widened in the number of members of professional members versus the number of student members, the issue of voting rights became more evident in direct proportion.

Another element fueled the fires of discontent beginning in 1961. At the national convention in Miami Beach, the national board voted to underwrite the travel expenses of official student delegates to the national convention in Tulsa the following year. Student delegates had been partially subsidized in their travel expenses since the 1912 convention, but this action, which would be carried out through the 1970's, assured that student delegates would attend the national conventions. Professional chapter delegates, on the other hand, had to raise travel funds through their local chapters or pay their own way. When, in 1969, the number of professional and campus chapters each reached 101 but the proportion of professional to student members had grown to 80-20, even the national board believed something had to be done to equate voting strength to membership strength.

Meeting in Rochester, New York, May 9, 1969, the board approved a motion by Chandler that would change the voting procedures if adopted as a by-laws change by the San Diego convention that November. Chandler's proposal was that each chapter have a minimum of one vote and an additional vote for each twenty-five members or portion thereof, based on the number of members of a chapter in good standing. The delegates in San Diego, perhaps overwhelmed by the more dramatic issues of the admission of women and a possible change in the name of the Society or perhaps because the student delegates outnumbered their professional counterparts, would have no part of weighted voting at future conventions. They tabled the issue but directed the national board to study the issue further and report at the 1970 convention in Chicago. Hurst noted the historic role of student members in Sigma Delta Chi as it applied to the controversy. "You must remember that student members had always been treated and still are treated as equal participants with professionals in legislative

and executive matters in convention. That tradition is as strong as the organization itself." And he reminded, "Even many professionals remember their campus ties and what the recruitment of members at the campus level has meant to the Society through the years. The campus chapters and student members have always been the backbone of Sigma Delta Chi."

The board tried the "one-man, one-vote" formula in its deliberations in Oklahoma City the following spring. Among two by-laws changes it proposed at that meeting, the weighted-voting measure provided that, for convention and referendum voting, each chapter be given a number of votes equal to the number of members in the chapter in good standing. Since there were far more members in professional chapters than in campus chapters, the professionals would have the majority of votes in convention despite the fact that student delegates might continue to outnumber them at conventions. Whether the second by-laws proposal was tied to the first as an incentive to students to support weighted voting is speculative, but the board also proposed that student members be elected to the national board with full voting rights. Before that time, students had served on the board as part of an appointed, non-voting student advisory committee. The Chicago convention delegates turned down weighted voting, but approved the annual election of four student members with voting rights to the national board.

The influx of women to membership immediately thereafter swelled the ranks of both campus and professional chapters, but in the next three years the number of new campus chapters chapters exceeded the number of new professional chapters by as many as twenty, giving the students a decided edge in voting strength once again. Thus, proportional representation in voting at conventions returned as an issue before the board. Small and Region Ten director Frank Wetzel led the 1973 drive to change the way in which voting was to be conducted. Both noted that, on the basis of fairness to the predominantly professional membership in the Society, a change was needed. Following a lengthy discussion

198

which also included consideration of giving members-at-large – those not affiliated with a chapter – voting rights at conventions, the board approved a by-laws proposal which would give chapters with fewer than fifty members one vote, with one vote being added for each additional fifty members or part thereof. No representation was to be provided for at-large members. There were continuing concerns that the measure would be defeated once again in Buffalo, but during the floor debate James Wigton, a student member of the national board from Ohio State University, told the delegates that the four campus board members were unanimous in favoring the by-laws change on proportional voting. He pointed out that, of the reported 26,800 members of the Society, 78 percent were professionals. Comparing the voting strength of the campus chapter delegates, representing only 22 percent of the membership, with the proposed weighted voting change, he said the new system would give the professionals a 60-40 ratio in number of votes, still a smaller ratio than the division of total membership. Allaying any fears that the few large professional chapters would then be in the dominant position, Wigton said that the voting strength of the eleven largest chapters combined would amount to only fifty-six of 367 total votes. Surprisingly, there were no negative comments from the floor and the measure was adopted unanimously by voice vote. At conventions following the Buffalo meeting, national headquarters staff calculated the number of members in good standing in each chapter and assigned the number of votes for each chapter on the basis of the formula adopted.

OFFICER NOMINATIONS CHANGED

In a somewhat related matter to the move to proportional voting, the delegates in Buffalo were the first to have a choice between two candidates for each national office. Since fraternity days, nomination of national officers was handled by a nominating committee which simply "tapped" one person to run for each office. Seldom, if ever, were there nominations from the floor; thus anyone selected to be nominated for treasurer would doubtless be

elected and move up the ladder, having a clear path to the presidency. The system had worked efficiently through the years, for a board member who had served as regional director and had as much as six years' experience in national affairs generally was selected as the candidate for treasurer. The incumbent treasurer would be nominated automatically for national secretary and so on through the ladder. The process of nominating a new regional director worked the same way. The national nominating committee would select a single nominee from a region and present him or her to the national convention, almost always without opposition.

The traditional method was upset at the 1972 national convention in Dallas. Graves in Region Nine and Novitz in Region One challenged the nominating committee's choices, were nominated from the floor for directors of their respective regions and each was elected. Their elections were an outgrowth of feelings by many that the standing method for nominations was a "closed system." A resolution presented at Dallas provided an alternative. It instructed the national nominating committee "to nominate more than one qualified, able candidate for top national offices." The resolution was adopted, 83-67, with the mandate to be carried out in time for the elections in Buffalo.

Otwell and McCord, among others, were adamantly opposed to the idea and each considered refusing nomination as one of two candidates for president and secretary, respectively, in Buffalo. Both were concerned that the new method of selecting the top national officers could result in the election of a person with no board experience and little understanding of contemporary issues facing the Society. "The ladder provided a way in which anyone moving into the presidency would have the necessary experience at the national level and the chance to hone his leadership skills," McCord said. A second factor causing them to oppose the nomination of two persons for each office was that the result would bring campaigning for office to the conventions. "I didn't want the elections to turn into popularity contests or to have the convention dominated, even in part, by the type of political campaigning with posters and buttons that had divided other national organizations," Otwell said. But the die had been cast and the will of the Dallas delegates was carried out in 1973. In the first-ever contested races designed to be that way in the Society's recent history, Otwell defeated Richard Fogel, assistant managing editor of the Oakland, California *Tribune*, 148-42; Small defeated John R. Finnegan, executive editor of the St. Paul, Minnesota *Dispatch – Pioneer Press*, 177-12; and Leonard moved up from Region Five director to national treasurer, defeating Bukro, 125-63. Bukro, who had had considerable exposure as the person who brought the ethics question to Buffalo but who had not served on the board, put on a colorful, but relatively quiet campaign for the treasurer's post. When he was defeated by Leonard, he sought the directorship of Region Five to replace Leonard there and was elected without opposition. McCord's race was much tighter, but he was elected national secretary, defeating M. Charles Reid, Jr., assistant metro editor for the Orlando, Florida *Sentinel Star*, 99-90. As it turned out, the incumbent officers were advanced and a board member became national treasurer to start his way up a less-sure ladder. Of the national officers, only James Julian of San Diego State University, the incumbent vice president for campus chapter affairs, did not have to face opposition. He did, however, have to run formally for a second term and was re-elected without a challenge from the floor. Until 1973, the vice president for campus chapter affairs had served one, two and three-year terms. The fact that Otwell, Small and McCord were elected, however, did not alter their opposition to the new system.

From 1960 through 1968, the person elected first vice president also had been designated as president-elect, lending strength to the ladder system. The 1969 San Diego convention, however, struck the title president-elect from the office in what was called "a more democratic" move. In an attempt "to restore continuity," at least in the case of the presidency, the board presented a by-laws change to the 1974

Phoenix convention, which it adopted, substituting the president-elect title for first vice president and meaning that the president-elect would become president without a further election. The requirement for a slate of two candidates for each of the other offices remained intact.

In the races for president, president-elect, vice president for campus chapter affairs and secretary in Phoenix, the incumbent board members were elected by even wider margins than in Buffalo, but this time the treasurer's race provided the excitement as two board members, Region Two director Goodykoontz and Region Ten director Cliff Rowe, were the nominees. Goodykoontz defeated Rowe, 171-159. When the incumbents won handily again the following year in Philadelphia with only the treasurer's race involving a close contest, delegates decided that candidates named to oppose incumbents potentially were serving only as straw men to fulfill the mandate of the 1972 resolution. They adopted a new resolution, 230-89, allowing the Society's nominating committee to nominate only one candidate for president-elect, vice president for campus chapter affairs and secretary. Two candidates, however, still would have to be named for the treasurer's post. Once elected treasurer, an officer reasonably could expect to move up the ladder toward the presidency. The final move by convention action regarding election of national officers came in Milwaukee in 1982, when the delegates returned the office of vice president for campus chapter affairs to a three-year term.

THE REGIONS ARE REALIGNED

The McKinsey Report in 1960 had proposed establishing regions of the country, each with its own director, to bring the Society closer to local chapters and individual members. With the adoption of the reorganization plan, the nation was divided into eleven regions with the breakdown based on the number of chapters and members in each designated area. The boundaries remained the same for twelve years until regional directors began to suggest the need for realignment. Some regions were too large, such as Region Eight, which had incorporated Texas, Oklahoma, Arkansas and Louisiana, and Region Three, which included Tennessee, Mississippi, Alabama, Georgia, South Carolina and Florida. Others which had too few chapters to be effective included Region Six, incorporating only Minnesota, North Dakota and South Dakota, and Region Nine, which included the sparsely populated states of Wyoming, Utah, Colorado and New Mexico. At its May 4, 1973, meeting in Omaha, the board proposed a by-laws change which would establish a new Region Twelve, which would take Mississippi and part of Tennessee from Region Three and take Arkansas and Louisiana from Region Eight. In addition, the board proposed moving Wisconsin from Region Five to Region Six, Arizona from Region Eleven to Region Nine, and South Dakota from Region Six to Region Seven. When the delegates considered the changes in Buffalo, they agreed to set up the new Region Twelve as proposed and to move Wisconsin to Region Six and South Dakota to Region Seven. However, all six Arizona chapters objected to being moved from Region Eleven and delegates amended the by-laws proposal to abide with their wishes. In the years from 1973 to 1984, all regional boundaries except those for Regions Six and Seven remained the same. South Dakota was returned to Region Six in 1978.

███████████████

New Goals for the 1980's

The Society's board of directors in 1973 was made up of five media executives, eight editors, three wire service chiefs of bureau, two university professors and four students. All but two of the thirteen professional newsmen on the board at that time had been tapped by the Society's leadership through the years to accept nomination as a regional director and/or a position on the ladder and none had faced competition in the elections. None of the past presidents of Sigma Delta Chi from 1960 through 1980 had made a conscious decision to "run" for the board before being asked to do so. It was the way the process of bringing new members to the board had been done for more than forty years and it had worked well. Executives and editors on the board had sought out their peers to join or replace them because they believed administrative experience and ability were needed to operate the Society effectively. Further, newspeople in the top echelon of their organizations would bring added prestige to Sigma Delta Chi.

The two 1973 board members who had sought seats on the board and come from outside the "system" were Charles Novitz, an editor in television news for ABC-TV in New York; and Howard Graves, chief of bureau for The Associated Press in Albuquerque, New Mexico. Both were former presidents of professional chapters and had been deputy regional directors – Novitz in Region One and Graves in Region Nine – and both had been bypassed by the nominating committee when their regional directorships came open in 1972. Support developed for each in his region and, upon arrival in Dallas for the 1972 convention, each had determined he would run from the floor, a rare, but acceptable practice, to oppose the candidate nominated for director in his region. The motivation in each case was a genuine interest in the Society and the fact each believed he had "something to offer at the regional and national levels." While both men fit the mold, bringing administrative experience and an appropriate title with them to the board, their elections, by comfortable margins, were an early signal that the "system" was about to be challenged by dedicated younger men and women who were at the reportorial level.

Casey Bukro's election in 1973 in Buffalo as Region Five director came after he was well known, at least at that convention, as the chairman of the professional development committee which presented the code of ethics there and as the unsuccessful candidate for national treasurer. Bukro, a past president of the Chicago Headline Club and an environment writer for the Chicago *Tribune*, called himself "a reporter-type" and became one of only a few reporters to join the board in a generation or more. Bukro was unopposed in being elected Region Five director because both he and Richard Leonard, the incumbent Region Five director, were the candidates for national treasurer and it was decided the loser would assume the regional position.

The other reporter elected unopposed to the board in Buffalo was Region Six director Steven R. Dornfeld, who covered the Minnesota statehouse for the Minneapolis *Tribune*. He had been an outspoken delegate on the name change and admission of women issues at previous conventions. At the 1971 convention in Washington, speaking for the name change, Dornfeld said he hoped the Society would become more representative of the membership and pointed out that the national board "seemed to consist entirely of aging, white, male editors and publishers," to which president Chandler responded, "How old do you think I am?"

Dornfeld remembers: "The national nominations committee really wanted to slate someone else, Lew Cope, for Region Six director. Cope, was also a reporter but a little older and less of a hell-raiser in my region. But Cope and my chapter along with others Region Six who wanted a stronger Sigma Delta Chi presence, more activity and to get regional conferences started again, decided I could handle the job and talked the committee into nominating me as its one candidate. We all had very strong feelings that we wanted to build the organization and we weren't happy with what had been happening as a result of the regional director that had been picked by national." Dornfeld said he may not have been nominated if Novitz's and Graves' attempts to run from the floor a year earlier

had not been successful. "Their election was a chastening experience for the Society leadership. If Novitz and Graves hadn't been elected, the national nominations committee might have been less interested in what we thought in the region." At the same Buffalo convention, another candidate who ran from the floor – Wallace B. Eberhard of the University of Georgia – was elected Region Three director.

The accepted mold for board membership had been cracked with the elections of Bukro, Dornfeld and Eberhard's and it was broken the following year in Phoenix when three more reporters won seats as regional directors. Val Hymes, special Washington. DC correspondent for Group W Television, was unopposed for Region Two director and became the first non-student woman on the board. Scott Aiken, foreign news analyst for the Cincinnati *Enquirer*, defeated two journalism educators, Ralph Izard of Ohio University and William Hall of Ohio State University, for the directorship of Region Four. And Frank Sutherland, an education reporter for the Nashville *Tennessean*, became the first director of the new Region Twelve, defeating Jim Bonney, general manager and editor of *Mississippi Today*, 7-6. With the Phoenix elections completed, the makeup of the board had switched dramatically. Eight of the fourteen professional newspersons had been elected either outside the "system" or as reporters and all of them were in the first year of what was likely to be a six-year tenure.

Goodykoontz, who was strong in his encouragement of the younger members to take an active role on the board and even seek national office, said, "I don't believe any of the continuing officers and board members saw the evolvement as confrontational, an 'us' and 'them' situation." Sutherland said the change in board membership was a reflection of what was happening in the Society. "After women came in in 1969, the whole nature of the Society turned a little younger. More young reporters were members than ever before."

The new majority did not assume control or attempt to effect major changes immediately. The Society's officers, after

203

all, had a powerful influence on policy and setting the agenda and each was a member of the establishment. Several of the new regional directors were in awe of, and all had great respect for, their older, executive-level colleagues on the board. All new directors understood there was much to learn and were dedicated to the best interests of the Society. They did, however, accept the role of "young Turks." Led by Dornfeld and Region Seven director Ron Willnow, a young city editor at the St. Louis *Post Dispatch*, and later by Sutherland, they raised questions and challenged the way things were done. Their interests, stemming from youthful, reportorial enterprise and idealism, were in stronger efforts in freedom of information, continuing reform in the election process, and advancement of women both in the newsroom and the Society. The advancement of the Society's goals and programs was not hindered by the young Turks. Rather, they helped to bring a healthy, fresh perspective to old issues, a development that was accepted fully by most of the officers. Then too, the board was not embroiled in the kinds of controversy which had enveloped it during the battles for admission of women, the name change, and weighted voting. It was, by comparison, a quiet period in the mid-1970's.

The coincidence of the election of the eight new board members within a three-year period, and the movement to require two nominees and a subsequent race for each regional directorship, made the youthful, reporter-types a fixture on the board for the next ten years. First, seven of the eight were re-elected without serious competition to second three-year terms. Second, had any publishers or editors wanted to gain a board seat, they would have had to submit to a contested election process, something for which they had already shown a distaste in the Society. The nominating committee, still dominated by the executive-level board members, decided in 1976 that only women would be nominated for the ladder. The election of Jean Otto, then an editorial writer for *The Milwaukee Journal*, as national treasurer in 1976 all but assured two things: that a woman and a member of the "new breed" would ascend to the presidency of the

Society. By November 1978, Novitz and Graves had been elected successively to the ladder as national treasurer and were succeeded as regional directors by James Plante, a writer for ABC News, New York, and Harry Fuller, an editorial writer for the Salt Lake City *Tribune*. Dornfeld, still a reporter as Washington, DC correspondent for Knight-Ridder Newspapers in 1984, and Sutherland, managing editor of the Hattiesburg, Mississippi *American* in 1984, were elected national treasurer in 1979 and 1981, respectively. Another reporter, Robert Lewis, Washington correspondent for the Newhouse Newspapers and the Society's freedom of information committee chair, became treasurer in 1982. Thus, among those who would be national president from 1979 through 1986, only Phil Dessauer, managing editor of the Tulsa *World*, president in 1978-1979, and Phil Record, associate executive editor of the Fort Worth *Star-Telegram* and Society president in 1983-1984, came to the board as an established editor or executive from the major news media.

In a short six years, the pendulum had swung from an executive-dominated board to a board made up of younger men and women, primarily reporters or editors who had reached management-level positions while on the board. Interestingly, as the young Turks assumed leadership as Society officers, they noted, with some distress, the lack of balance between the two spheres of influence on the board. "It was healthy to make the Society's leadership more representative of the membership, but I think it went too far," said Dornfeld in 1983. "We need a mix because the Society has benefited from some of those heavy-hitters from the executive ranks on the board and as officers." Dornfeld didn't regret the significant turn-around on the board, however. "Many of the high ranking journalists who were leaders of the Society before this whole changeover began were active participants in other journalistic organizations such as ASNE or ANPA. They couldn't devote as much time and energy to the Society as some of us who were reporters and lower-level editors have in the last six or seven years [prior to 1984]. The

Society has benefited from that as well. It has helped lead to what we've termed 'The New Activism' in the Society. But we've also paid a price for it – losing executives pretty much from the board and that's been unfortunate." The problem of bringing management-level journalists back to the board was compounded in that those on the national nominations committee in the early 1980's were not, themselves, executives and, therefore, not in a position to tap others in management to accept a position as a regional director or even start up the ladder as national treasurer. The new tradition which surely encouraged even more reporters to seek board seats and the election process in place in 1983 promised to extend further the imbalance on the board which had only one executive, eight editors, eight reporters or writers and one professor in addition to the four campus board representatives. Novitz, Dornfeld, Record and Sutherland made an attempt in 1983 to bring the pendulum closer to middle ground calling on past presidents still holding prestigious positions to assist in the search for news executives with a commitment to the Society to assume leadership roles. And the national and regional nominations committees were challenged to follow the same course to effect a better mix on the board. Their successes were yet to be determined when this volume went to press.

However, while they were still working their way toward leadership roles, the young Turks were encouraged with the progress they had made in a quiet way through the 1970's. They were justifiably proud of the new emphasis on freedom of information they had achieved in establishing the FOI Service Center and hiring legal counsel following the 1978 Birmingham convention. Their "New Activism" in FOI had led The Society of Professional Journalists, Sigma Delta Chi to new levels of prestige in the journalism community. And they were about to bring that same "New Activism" to bear on some organizational problems – a pattern of declining growth in membership, resultant general fiscal problems, and changes in priorities for the Society.

Before dealing with how the vigorous and determined new board dealt with those issues, it is important to recognize an additional fact – one which could not be identified until it was illuminated by the light of history. The six-year metamorphosis brought about a near total change in the perspectives from which the young Turks and their departed, executive-level counterparts viewed the Society's problems and possible solutions.

Chandler, Otwell, Small, McCord and Leonard in the early 1970's and their predecessors in the 1960's had operated from an "executive mentality." That is, their experience told them that to do something well, the deliberate approach was best in most cases. If you wanted to reach a goal, you took the time to set objectives and policies to effect their implementation, found a person in whom you have confidence, delegated as much authority as possible and turned that person loose, staying out of his way so he could do the job. That was the environment in which the officers since 1962 had worked with Hurst. Many of the arangements with Hurst were agreed to across the board table with little or nothing put in writing, except, of course the formal definition of the job of the executive officer. The working relationship between the board and Hurst was one of support, encouragement and confidence. When the board decided to change a policy, it simply communicated that change to Hurst through board deliberations and votes expecting him to effect the change. On some occasions, when Hurst sought direction or suggested the officers or board become more directly involved on a specific matter such as the development of a budget, they would offer some advice but deferred on a final decision to their executive officer. Some members of the board believed the officers and even the board itself, on those occasions, abdicated responsibility to Hurst. Perhaps so. But if they did, it must be said they firmly believed the details of the headquarters operation and much of the general work of the Society were Hurst's responsibilities. They had hired an executive officer to handle those duties so that they could deal with the larger picture during the limited time they, as volunteer leaders, had to spend on Society matters.

By contrast, the zeal of some of the new

leadership of the late 1970's, especially Dornfeld, Hymes, Sutherland and Bukro, came from a "reportorial mentality." Perhaps, this was a first opportunity to relieve frustrations of having seen problems and believing they knew how to solve them but not having the authority to effect resolution. Just as likely, the younger board members, as reporters, worked under tight, low budget situations and they saw some of the Society's operations as extravagant while certain projects they saw as important received little financial support. Graves and Novitz had had management experience but identified in many ways with the youthful element on the board. Thus, as control of the board converted to members of this total group, they brought with them an eagerness to take charge – a full-speed-ahead, do-it-now attitude. They were willing to give the time, were desirous of becoming involved and expected to have more input into the day-to-day operations of the Society.

It is important to note, however, that both the executives and the reporters on the board had one thing in common. Had it not been for the financial support of their respective newspapers, magazines, radio and television stations, networks and press associations, none might have participated for so many years or spent as many hours in volunteer service. The dollars provided them by their employers for travel, hotel bills, meals and the like amounted to a substantial sum. When added to the coverage of the board members' respective tasks at home

with other personnel while the board members attended meetings and conventions, it amounted to an almost incalculable fiscal contribution to the Society and the journalistic profession through several decades.

For all intents and purposes, the six-year changeover represented a 100 percent turn-around in the posture of the board on operating the Society, something that no one planned and that perhaps no one, including Hurst, saw coming. The paradox of it all was that the new officers apparently saw Hurst as the personification of the "old guard" just retired, while Hurst, in effect, had been the young Turk among a board of powerful and prestigious executives only a few years earlier. In addition, because the new leadership had not been a part of the long-standing, executive-style relationship between earlier officers and Hurst – viewing it only briefly and then from the periphery – they did not see what they were doing as changing the rules in the middle of the game. Hurst did, and said he regretted that previous executive committee and board members had not communicated with their eager successors how and why things had been done through the years.

Important and effective changes, leading toward a newly-energized Society would be made in the next two years. But those years would be marked by stress and, at times, mental anguish which, under the circumstances, seemed almost unavoidable.

CHAPTER 11

███████████

Challenges and New Priorities

The enrollment surge sparked by the admission of women had leveled off by 1973. Annual growth increments in the Society, at ten percent or greater for several years, slowed somewhat, almost imperceptibly, and Hurst kept the board informed about membership figures. He also noted that inflation had begun to deal a double blow to the Society in terms of increased costs of operation and falling revenues from members who ceased paying annual dues giving considerations at home higher priority than SPJ,SDX membership. *The Quill* was having to cut back in size because of inflationary pressures and a declining advertising revenue caused by the recession. The $15 annual dues for professional members had not been increased since 1968 and the one-time initiation fee of $17.50 for student members had not been increased since reorganization. Through the mid-1970's Hurst informed the board and membership of all of the signs pointing to fiscal problems. Bill Small, president in 1975-1976, said, "Hurst did a superb job of keeping us apprised of everything, not only of the moment but of the potential ones down the road." Small's report to the Philadelphia convention noted:"The Society enters 1976 healthy in many respects, but shaky in one – finances. On the brink of a deficit year last November, your officers voted not to increase dues." Instead, Small wrote to all the Society's life members who no longer paid annual dues asking them for a one-time contribution. "I was very pleased with the response from the life members, which helped in the short run. We got through 1975 with a small deficit, but we knew that over the long haul we had to do something about the dues structure," Small recalls. The board and convention delegates responded to the mini-crisis in 1976, hoping to stem the tide with a dues increase for professional members to $20 per year and a one-time fee of $22.50 for student members.

THE FISCAL CRUNCH ARRIVES

By mid-1979, however, inflation kept the pressure on the Society's finances despite recruiting campaigns, led by membership chairmen Goodykoontz and Graves, which had put initiation of new members back on a

It was a resolute Jean Otto who told the New York City convention delegates that if they would approve a major membership dues increase, as president in 1979-1980, she would direct the Society's officers and board of directors to examine the SPJ,SDX budget line-by-line, cutting out all unnecessary expenditures and establishing priorities for all of the Society's programs. The dues increase was adopted and Otto kept her promise.

growth pattern. Hurst informed the board that while the line had been held on expenses, income had fallen short of expected revenues by about ten percent and, to balance the books, the Society had had to dip into its reserves to make up a $54,500 deficit for fiscal 1978-1979. Inflation had soared to double-digit figures, surpassing twelve percent. The board knew it had to ask for another dues increase at the New York City convention. President Dessauer wrote to chapter officers and convention delegates explaining the situation. "The toughest job I have had since becoming president is to ask for a dues increase....In the last five years, our Society's expenses have risen forty-five percent while income has increased only thirty-five percent." Using Hurst's figures, Dessauer pointed to an increase of eighty-eight percent in postage, sixty-two percent for printing *The Quill*, another sixty-two percent for regional expenses, and fifty-two percent for general printing and supplies. Headquarters rent, including an increase in space approved in 1978, was up sixty percent while the five-year increase for staff salaries was forty-nine percent – much of that for two new staff positions since 1974. Dessauer asked for an increase from $20 to $30 for professional dues and an increase in the student initiation fee from $22.50 to $27.50. "Our other choice," he said, "is to cut back, trim activities and services to whatever level is necessary to operate in the black. If we do that, we will survive, but we'll be retrenching at the very time SPJ,SDX is needed more, not less." Novitz recalls, "The decision to seek a dues increase during a period of inflation reflected the ambition of that generation of officers to do more. There was a real commitment on the part of that board to use the assets of the society for purposes we judged as real and important."

At the board's meeting before the New York convention, Hurst warned, however, that with only a ten percent inflation factor and continuation of present levels of dues payments, the net gain from the proposed dues increase would be wiped out in fewer than two years. Sutherland, assigned to present the dues issue to the delegates November 17, 1979, asked incoming president Otto to be prepared to make a statement during the debate assuring the delegates that she and her board would be good stewards of the Society's finances. At the close of the seventy-five-minute debate, Otto said she sensed that "the convention was in no way prepared to vote a dues increase without some kind of responding action on our part." Addressing the delegates, she pledged, "The national officers will be concerned with every dollar of your money. We will be as cautious and frugal as we possibly can be." The convention approved all the dues increase proposals by large majorities, giving the Society what it needed but clearly expecting a close look at all future expenditures to avoid having to be faced with another increase in only a year of so. "Jean took her promise to the convention very seriously and I've always believed that was the turning point," Sutherland said.

During the Saturday post-convention

Society presidents during the mid-1970's made efforts to counter the growing impact of inflation on the Society's' operating budget. Pictured here are: (from left) Alf Goodykoontz (1977-1978); Robert McCord (1975-1976); William Small (1974-1975); James Julian, vice president for campus chapter affairs, (1972-1975); and Richard Leonard (1976-1977).

board meeting, Otto announced the formation of a finance committee to do an immediate study of the Society's fiscal policies and procedures. "In casting about for a chairman, I felt it was very important to find someone who knew how a business operated or ought to operate because most journalists don't have any experience with finance. I also wanted someone who was a good member and cared about the Society and who was in Chicago and had access to the headquarters office and staff," she remembered. Before she left New York City, she approached Howard Dubin, president of two book-publishing firms in Chicago, Manufacturers' News and University Book Publishers, Inc., and a past president of the Chicago Headline Club, asking him to take on the assignment. "I knew of his dedication to the Society and that, having run a business, he knew what figures meant on a bottom line and the components of how to get to that bottom

line. It was a fairly spontaneous response on my part to a real need and I believed he could do the job," she said.

Dubin accepted the position with the understanding Otto wanted a preliminary report of some kind at the officers' meeting in Philadelphia January 14, 1980. Others appointed to the committee were Bukro and past presidents Goodykoontz and Leonard. Dubin recalls, "We had to move quickly because it was already late November. Casey and I were in Chicago and decided to begin with an indepth interview with Hurst. I asked Jean [Otto] if she wanted Goodykoontz and Leonard to come to Chicago for the meeting with Hurst but she said that since our work was of a preliminary nature it wouldn't be necessary for the others to be there." Dubin and Bukro spent the greater part of a full day with Hurst asking how he and each of the others on the headquarters staff spend their time and on what tasks they were working. "We wanted

209

to find out just how the money allocated to headquarters was being spent and we asked tough questions," Dubin said. The two committee members determined they needed to talk to each of the key headquarters staff to obtain more information. "Hurst cooperated with us when we interviewed him but it was obvious he preferred we not interview the staff. But we thought it was important and went ahead," Dubin said. Reviewing his and Bukro's findings after the interviews, Dubin believed that some management techniques and personnel policies did not fall into line with what he perceived as common practice for organizations of that size. Both agreed that staff utilization needed improvement. "What was unfortunate," Dubin said, "was that because Hurst was personally responsible for the manner in which the office was run, anything we questioned seemed to reflect on him, which was in no way intended. We were there to help, not to hurt the operation." Bukro added, "We saw our mission as taking a fresh look at the headquarters operation in the context of present [1981] needs and priorities. The accent was on present needs, not the past." The final draft of Dubin and Bukro's preliminary report was not ready until a few days before the officers' meeting. Dubin carried the reports to Philadelphia, distributing them there.

THE PHILADELPHIA MEETING

The officers who gathered in Philadelphia included Otto, Graves, Novitz, Dornfeld, Dessauer and Bostrom, along with Hurst and finance committee members Dubin, Bukro and Goodykoontz. Otto suggested the officers meet without Hurst to discuss the report, but her colleagues insisted the executive officer be included. Because the report had been distributed after the officers and Hurst arrived in Philadelphia, only hours before the meeting, no one had had time to study the document in detail. Hurst challenged a number of Dubin and Bukro's assumptions and said parts of the report were inaccurate. Hurst said later that, while he had no objections to a review of headquarters operations, he was disappointed that the review was not made

by persons more experienced in administrative management. "I cooperated with Dubin and Bukro in every way I could," Hurst said, "including setting up the initial meeetings with other staff members. But I discovered at Philadelphia that we were 180 degrees apart on some things, including our perceptions of what the 'problems' were." Hurst recalled that he was dismayed that Goodykoontz and Leonard, the other two members of the finance committee and both past national presidents, had played no role in the preliminary study. "Here were two people with whom I had worked for years and who could have provided background and documentation on policy and operations that Dubin and Bukro said they wanted – yet, they were left out," he said. Goodykoontz recalls he was not happy with the manner in which the draft had been presented. "I made it clear that I was distressed at having had my name signed to that preliminary report when I had not had any part in its writing," he said.

In planning for the Philadelphia meeting, Hurst had prepared his own twenty-seven-page "Blue Book" filled with information aimed at assisting the board and finance committee "in assessing the Society's current programs and establishing future priorities." In his cover letter, Hurst wrote, "This report may provide a starting point for further studies, judgments and, ultimately, policy decisions by the Board and the national convention of delegates. I have included a list of some options for reducing expense, since the severe impact of inflation requires that the Society do some short-range and possibly long-range belt-tightening if income and expense cannot be kept in near balance. The options presented are only several of many that might be considered. And while each option has a positive value in the direction of economy, it simultaneously carries a negative value of reversing an action course previously determined to contribute in some way to the advancement of the Society. But the economic facts are harsh – and every organization and institution in the nation is having to face up to the harsh realities of inflation." Meanwhile, Dornfeld, as the newly elected

national treasurer, had made a trip to
Chicago to become oriented to his new post.
His discussions with Hurst and his
knowledge that the finance committee was
beginning to do research prompted him to
commence his own study of the Society's
fiscal condition. By the time of the
Philadelphia officers' meeting, he was
already involved.

The discussions in Philadelphia were
long and, at times, heated. Hurst said later
that he believed many of the concerns had
far more to do with form than with
substance. But out of the debate came a list
of more than a dozen cost-saving and fund-
raising measures drawn from Hurst's
suggestions, the finance committee report
and ideas from the officers. The largest
dollar-saving measure came with adoption of
a plan to cut travel subsidies for student
delegates to the national convention to one-
half of the cost of coach air fare and
elimination of the subsidy altogether for
chapter delegates whose schools were within
400 miles of a convention city. A full
subsidy had been provided all student
delegates since 1962, but rising air fares and
greater numbers of campus chapters caused
projections of costs rising to more than
$60,000 per year, far beyond the Society's
ability to pay. Among other cost-saving
measures approved were reducing travel
costs by officers and headquarters staff and
setting guidelines for travel to assure the
greatest benefit from dollars spent, selecting
and dedicating only one historic site per year
instead of the traditional three, studying the
possibility of a longer work-week for
headquarters staff and examining possible
savings in fringe benefits for staff, and
beginning the renegotiation of the
headquarters lease with the goal of reducing
costs and space either at the 35 East Wacker
Drive address or in other quarters. Hurst
said he was spending considerable time –
from as little as five percent to as much as
twenty percent of his time – on *The Quill*, an
amount the officers believed was excessive
given that the magazine had two full-time
editorial employees. After discussing the
possibilities of conducting formal time
studies to determine a breakout of time spent
by Hurst and his staff on various tasks, the

Jack Condon (left), chief financial officer of the
Fort Worth, Texas *Star-Telegram*, provided the
1980-1981 officers and board with what many
considered valuable assistance in the process of
evaluating the Society's fiscal priorities. He
received a plaque of appreciation from SPJ,SDX
president Howard Graves in 1981.

officers agreed that Hurst should monitor
that situation and review other belt-
tightening possibilities in Chicago. Graves
was satisfied that the finance committee's
examination of the headquarters' operation
had been healthy and useful. "Their frank
and open discussion of the operations at
headquarters and their list of
recommendations took a lot of courage.
They were hard-headed, but they were
practical," he said.

With the fervor of that portion of the
agenda behind them, the officers turned to
the issue of the magazine. *The Quill* had
become even more of a financial drain on the
Society than in the past because of increasing
costs and fewer advertising dollars.
Advertising sales efforts were limited to what
a part-time national advertising
representative could come up with and the
results had been less than gratifying. To

attempt to rectify that situation, the officers voted to hire a full-time internal advertising representative immediately on a six-to-nine-month experimental basis to determine if there was greater potential for attracting advertising to the magazine. Following the meeting, Hurst was able to obtain the services of Roger Boye for that task. Boye had worked as news editor of *The Quill* in the 1970's. The officers also voted in Philadelphia to approach the board at its May meeting in Seattle with a proposal to reduce the number of issues of the magazine from eleven to ten, effecting a saving of $9,000. In addition, they instructed Hurst regarding some changed procedures to be involved in publishing *The Quill*, with the goal of increasing efficiency and reducing costs.

Dornfeld was on a leave of absence from his newspaper to study at the University of Michigan for a year and had some time he could give to the whole matter of fiscal reform in the Society. He made a number of trips to Chicago following the Philadelphia meeting, continuing his own analysis parallel to that of the finance committee. "I had been on the national board for six years and had never gone through any kind of budget-making process," he said. "Two or three months into the fiscal year, the board would be presented with and be asked to approve a budget under which we had already been operating for some time and, at that, it seemed to be simply last year's spending pattern adjusted for inflation. I guess I always assumed the officers were doing more than we were doing, but I never paused and thought about it very much."

THE BOARD CONCURS

Informed by the officers of progress made on fiscal reform, the board made several important decisions upon convening in Seattle May 8. Dornfeld and Dubin revealed their studies had shown that costs to maintain student members after their first year of membership amounted to $6 per student per year in printing and mailing *The Quill* and general administrative expenses. Offer noted that the $6 would probably climb quickly given the pressures of inflation and that the board ought to be looking at

costs of at least $10 to maintain students as members. Some of the board thought asking students to "pay their own way" so far as membership was concerned would come too soon after the student initiation fee had been raised and travel subsidies had been cut. But the board voted to ask the November convention to approve an annual dues structure of $10 per year for student members to begin after those students presently enrolled had been graduated.

Boye's report indicated his brief time working full-time on advertising for *The Quill* seemed to be paying off, but that it might not be necessary for anyone to work full-time in the future. In the light of Boye's successes, Hurst recommended that the services of a part-time national advertising representative be discontinued and the board agreed. The officers' suggestion of reducing the number of issues of the magazine to effect cost savings was turned down.

Moving to the matters of internal operations at headquarters, the board chose not to deal with many of the issues Dubin's finance committee had raised, but Dubin had also presented a report on computerizing part of that operation. The board voted to take the first step toward automation by placing the Society's complete, active membership and *Quill* files into a data-processing format through an outside bureau. Novitz was pleased that while cutbacks were necessary and appropriate, the board had not stopped looking forward. He had approached the dues increase proposal in New York with a philosophy that expansion of the Society's programs was as important as budget control. Through all of the discussions in New York, Philadelphia and Seattle, Novitz said he was motivated by a statement by from Chicago architect Daniel Burnham: "Make no small plans. They lack the power to inspire men's souls."

Much of the discussion centered on the matter of the budget itself. Hurst and Dubin urged the board to set goals and priorities for each of the Society's activities and that the budget be drawn on the basis of those priorities. Dubin added that each program should be analyzed each year to determine if it should be continued or expanded or if it should be subordinated to new programs which may have been developed during the year. "I had been encouraging the officers and Hurst to accept the budget philosophy that if we had all this money and no existing programs, what programs would we invent?" Dubin said. Otto said if the Society were to move out of what she believed was an inefficient system, "We have to learn what a budget is, what it ought to do and how realistic it is. To do that, we must challenge every item in the budget. We have to challenge every income item and every expense to determine if our money is going for the right programs and causes." Dornfeld agreed recalling: "Every time we wanted to start a new program during my years as a regional director, there was never any money even though we were still in a growth period. Now we were in a financial crunch and we had to tie programs to dollars if we were going to assure the membership we were using their money effectively." Dubin's report had recommended direct participation by the officers and the board in the budget-making process.

Hurst told the board he would welcome renewed participation by the board on a level he had known in earlier years. Recent boards, he said, had delegated more and more responsibility to him in budget-making although he maintained there remained a continuing high level of consultation by mail and telephone and at board meetings where budgets were discussed and voted upon. This board, however, accepted the opportunity and authorized the officers to examine each line item of the 1980-1981 budget and make recommendations on setting dollar amounts based on program priorities. Among the income figures Graves believed had to be challenged were those figures tied to membership. "We didn't have anywhere near the number of 'active' members we were saying we had. Our letterhead carried the number 35,000 for our membership, but when you looked at the number of dues-paying members, it was fewer than 20,000," he said. Region One director Jim Plante noted that members probably assumed each of the 35,000 paid $30 per year to belong to the Society and that student members paid only a one-time

fee. Otto added, "Our members certainly had a skewed idea about what our annual income really was when they multiplied the dues amount by 35,000. We didn't have anywhere near the dues income our members thought we had." The board agreed in Seattle and although it didn't have an answer on what the publicized number should be, it indicated the matter should be examined carefully and an accurate number be used.

THE OFFICERS IN MILWAUKEE

Otto called a meeting of the officers for May 30 in Milwaukee to examine and recommend a budget for fiscal 1980-1981. She was joined by Graves, Novitz, Dornfeld, Bostrom, Dessauer and Hurst in a four-day marathon which proved to be a turning point in the Society's history.

Among the first things agreed upon in Milwaukee was that during the 1980-1981 fiscal year, the Society would operate in the black. There would be no drawing from the reserves to cover expenses. As Otto wrote in her summary of the meeting, "Any new programs or expenditures for the Society will have to be evaluated against available funds and will hinge on either having money available or discontinuing programs of lesser priority." Further, the officers decided that *Quill* expenditures would be limited to *Quill* income except for the $20,000 provided from Society funds for the magazine each year. Even that $20,000 was challenged and, as a part of the budget preparation, the officers voted to phase out the Society subsidy through the next three years.

Many cost-saving measures had already been approved, of course, but as the officers planned where the dollars should be spent for the next year, they eliminated some long-standing services, including the traditional membership certificates which hung on walls of members' offices across the nation. They cut back on contributions to other organizations, and adjusted priorities to fit available funds without killing any of the Society's major programs. Hurst's salary was frozen at its 1979-1980 level for at least one year. They recommended that when the current agreement with the Reporters Committee expired in December 1981, it not be refunded. Rather, the $17,000 contribution toward the research attorney's salary and expenses would be replaced by a $5,000 annual grant with the purpose of continuing to update the state FOI file and assure access by SPJ,SDX to those records.

As for new expenses, the officers had brought with them the mandate from the board to investigate the financial possibilities of hiring an attorney as First Amendment counsel. Dornfeld recalls: "When we carved out $7,500 for an attorney there in Milwaukee, it was the first time [since he had been on the board] we actually had set a priority and found the dollars in the budget itself for something which we had considered very important." FOI was clearly the priority item in the budget the officers prepared and was given more attention in actual dollars allocated in the budget than ever before. But in the way of new programs, the officers also gave first approval for a task force on what was called continuing education at that meeting and later took on the title of professional development. Otto asked Izard to chair the new task force and charged him to look into the possibility of Society-sponsored seminars, workshops and short courses designed to meet the needs of working reporters and editors.

For most of the officers who were not familiar with accounting practices or even reading a budget intelligently, the budget-making process was an awkward situation. Graves and Bostrom wanted more detailed information and explanation than was available on the surface. Graves not only wanted a balanced and forward-looking budget, he wanted one which the average working journalist could read and understand. "Only through persistence and determination were we able to get all of the information we needed to get a clear picture of our fiscal condition or to determine where we wanted to go and to be sure the membership would comprehend what we had done," he said. For Bostrom, it was his first experience in constructing a budget of that size – more than three quarters of a million dollars. "No question about it, we were very demanding of Hurst during those four days. Although he could not agree with every

decision we made – in fact he had serious doubts about some of them – he was gracious in accepting them and made every effort to cooperate with us," Bostrom said.

"Preparing the budget was not an easy thing to do," Otto remembers. "Anytime you challenge existing habits and procedures, someone is threatened whether they ought to be or not. It's the way life works. And to take control over something when you are learning in the process of doing causes a lot of emotional tension." Dornfeld recalls, "It was painful to take the budget and turn it inside out. It was painful too, I am sure, to the headquarters staff for they somehow thought that we were questioning their performance or their competence." Otto said she thought those officers were very sensitive to the fact that it was necessary to change the organization. "But there was a very real risk that we could destroy the cohesion and the loyalties of all of the past leaders. What we wanted to do was to bring the Society up to snuff without killing it. I think we did that in the process of self-examination," she said.

With the draft of the budget completed, the officers focused attention on three major items discussed briefly in Seattle, but set aside for further study – a possible move of the national headquarters to new facilities, job descriptions for all board members as well as the professional staff at headquarters, and the advertising sales position for *The Quill*.

Hurst had been notified by new owners of the building at 35 East Wacker Drive in Chicago that the rent for headquarters space would go from the 1980 annual rate of about $33,000 to as much as $60,000 per year over the course of the new five-year lease agreement offered the Society. In her report to the board, Otto said headquarters would have to be moved because of the rent formula that would become effective when the Society's lease expired at the end of December. "Alternatives are now under exploration including moving to other quarters in the Loop [the downtown section of Chicago], finding acceptable rental space in one of the suburbs, moving headquarters to the new center being built by the American Newspaper Publishers Association

214

in Reston, or buying a small office building in a Chicago suburb where other tenant(s) can help meet Society expenses on quarters. Hurst was authorized to contact a broker to do a more thorough search for a headquarters location in the Chicago area."

On the matter of job descriptions, the officers determined that, "We should consider not only what each of us does but what we believe we can and should be doing, in line, of course, with what is possible." Among the recommendations for job descriptions discussed in Milwaukee, the officers indicated their preference that Hurst spend no more than five percent of his time as executive officer on *The Quill*. Otto said later, "He clearly loved journalism and he enjoyed working on the magazine. It was his touch with journalism while he was administering the Society's affairs. But the officers and ultimately the board perceived that working on *The Quill* was not what they wanted the executive officer to devote his time to in the future. An editor of the magazine should be editing the magazine. When Hurst was working on the *The Quill*, he was not doing the kinds of creative, program-oriented, outreach projects that we believed were his responsibilities."

On the third item, the officers voted to offer Boye an opportunity to come on the headquarters staff in the fall as director of sales for *The Quill* and director of development for the Society. This was in line with Boye's suggestion in Seattle that a full-time advertising salesman might not be needed. As director of development, Boye would work on membership programs, help to supervise the transition to computerization and help develop fund-raising programs for the Society. Although the move would add a staff member at headquarters, the officers believed that increased revenues from advertising, the dollars saved on terminating the part-time professional advertising representative and an approved twenty percent increase in advertising rates for *The Quill* would cover almost all of the needed salary dollars. Boye began work in his new job in September 1980.

The report of the Milwaukee meeting and the budget draft were sent to all board members, who responded with only a few

suggestions and approval of the budget for the 1980-1981 fiscal year. While Hurst continually had provided board members with monthly budget reports comparing the current year to the previous year's figures and budget was a topic of discussion at every board meeting, the officers' total preparation of the 1980-1981 budget marked the first time in many years the board had looked at a completed budget before the beginning of the fiscal year for which it was to be in effect.

During the fall months, Hurst, Otto, Graves and Dubin investigated possible alternate sites for the national headquarters but they could not reach a consensus on any site at which they looked. The ANPA possibility in Reston, Virginia, began to dim when it was learned that the new Newspaper Center there would not be ready for occupancy for two years. During those same months, new *Quill* editor Naomi Donson began looking at alternatives to the arrangements in force for typesetting and printing the magazine and, along with Boye and Hurst, she believed it would be possible to effect some savings by moving to new companies for those services.

LOOKING TO OUTSIDE HELP

A few weeks before the 1980 convention in Columbus, Ohio, Otto and Graves, in concert with the other officers, decided to inivte both candidates for national treasurer to the officers' meeting the night before the national board meeting. The candidates, Record and Sutherland, were pleased to be invited, knowing that whoever was elected would be in tune with the continuing officers upon assuming office. A short while into the evening meeting, November 17, Record said that as a regional director he had always had trouble making sense out of the budget for the Society. "I prepared the $7 million editorial budget for the Fort Worth *Star-Telegram* and I understood that budget, but I couldn't understand the Society's budget of less than $1 million. I was especially concerned because I could find no way of monitoring the SPJ budget." he said. When he made the decision to run for national treasurer, he said, he took all the papers he had dealing with the Society budget to Jack

Condon, the new chief financial officer at the *Star-Telegram* and asked Condon if he could explain the figures therein. Condon had been with the accounting firm of Price-Waterhouse before joining the Fort Worth newspaper. "Condon took the figures home and studied them for several nights," Record said. "Then he called me and said, 'I can't understand the figures. I can't see how they arrived at these figures. There is no justification for the variances when one line item jumps dramatically from one year to the next,' " Condon had given Record a critique of the budget and, at the officers' request, Record reviewed Condon's recommendations. "I remember Jean Otto saying, 'This is what we have been looking for, this kind of critique from an outside source. He's asking the same kind of questions that I've been asking,'" One of the officers asked if Condon would perhaps be willing to come up here and spend a day looking at our office and our financial management procedures."

The following morning Record called *Star-Telegram* Executive Vice President and General Manager Phillip J. Meek and asked that if Condon were willing to do it, would Meek approve releasing his financial officer for one day to go to Chicago to take on the task the officers had discussed. Meek said that Condon was in the office at that moment and that Record could ask Condon of his interest. Condon said he would be willing to do the job and Meek not only approved the trip, but also offered to pay Condon's travel expenses. Upon learning of Condon's acceptance, Graves was delighted. "This was something that none of us had ever thought of. It was a tremendous opportunity," he recalls. "To me it was the epitome of what the Society was all about – that there were resources available if we would only tap them." All of the officers greeted enthusiastically the idea of having an independent, outside expert look at the Society's accounting practices and how its money was being managed. Sutherland may have identified the position of many of the regional directors when he remembered, "I was aware of what the officers had been doing in looking at the budget and the process of making the budget, but I didn't

realize until the moment Record and I met with the officers just how seriously they had taken the promise Jean [Otto] had made to the convention a year earlier." Regarding bringing in an outsider to take a hard look at the management techniques being used, Sutherland said, "It was obvious we didn't have the expertise. I wasn't particularly comfortable about bringing someone from outside the Society in, but I didn't see any other option and I said let's do it."

Hurst, one of the Society's strongest exponents for many years on using contributed services, had reservations. Record remembers Hurst's reaction. "This isn't a new idea." Hurst had said. "Upon taking office, many new treasurers have wanted to set up a bookkeeping system similar to those with which they were familiar." Hurst said his chief concern was that anyone studying the Society's budget and financial procedures should have a basic knowledge of the Society's purposes and activities, its financial history and operating guidelines as well as the limitations imposed by a small staff. "The headquarters had always operated with a small staff – our financial 'department' was one bookkeeper, period – and low budget," Hurst said. "I thought we performed minor miracles regularly in the volume of services we provided to our members and chapters, the board and the public. I was fairly well convinced that the management practices of a large corporation could not be laid down on us; there are just too few parallels between a large, metropolitan newspapers and a voluntary, not-for-profit national society of journalists. I was concerned, too, about the brevity of the proposed visit by Mr. Condon," Hurst added. "But I was just as interested as the officers in learning what he could do to assist the Society."

Incoming president Graves, sensing near consensus on bringing an outside expert in to look at the financial management of the Society, issued the formal invitation to Condon and dates were established with Hurst for Condon's visit. Several other continuing items of import to the impending changes in the Society were discussed at the board meeting before the convention. Hurst reported that final negotiations were under way for space at 203 North Wabash in Chicago for the national headquarters. Hurst said in his report, "If we are successful in completing the deal, we will have achieved quite an accomplishment in an extremely tight rental market." Dubin noted that computerization was under way and received approval of his suggestion that the project be continued using an out-of-office bureau for another six months before determining if computer terminals should be installed in the office. It should be noted here that in-office terminals were added in 1983.

Record was elected treasurer at the convention's business session. The proposed student dues structure was tabled by the delegates with orders to the board to provide more specific information and justification for the student dues throughout the spring of 1981 so that the issue could be discussed at regional conferences. The proposal for dues would then be brought to the 1981 convention in Washington for consideration. Bostrom remembered, "The debate on the dues showed a dominance of negative opinion and had it been voted on at the Columbus convention, it would have been defeated, I am sure. In postponing any action because they needed more data and in giving the board the opportunity to explain the need fully in 1981, they acted very responsibly. Given the circumstances, I couldn't have asked for more." Bostrom agreed to take on the responsibility of gathering the requested data and getting reports to chapters in early 1981.

At the board meeting at which he presided following the convention, Graves named Record to chair a planning committee. "We were playing our role as officers and a board from year to year and we weren't looking down the road to see where we were going or where we wanted to go," Graves said. He believed that it was necessary to tie the setting of goals and priorities for the Society for the next three to five years to the progress being made in the budgetary process. "I named Record as chair because he would be president of the Society in four years and would have the opportunity to effect ideas generated by the committee as he moved toward the

presidency," Graves said. Record immediately asked for input from all members of the board as well as his committee regarding their goals and priorities for the Society. Graves announced that the traditional January officers' meeting would be expanded to a full board meeting in Chicago to hear reports from Condon and the planning committee.

Graves was also determined to do more about the problem of the decline in numbers of new members being initiated by chapters. Graves named Bruce Itule of the Chicago *Tribune* as membership chairman for 1981. Itule said he believed the Society's future rested in recruiting professional members, not in increasing student members, and he addressed the possibility of an immediate direct-mail approach. He asked for an appropriation of $5,000 to be used by the membership committee to conduct a large-scale membership drive by direct mail. Region Four director Mike Kelly suggested a drive on a smaller scale as a test of effectiveness and moved an appropriation of $750 to conduct a direct-mail recruiting effort. David Offer urged that the test drive not be a token mailing, but that it be well thought-out, using lists of potential members and a well-designed invitation. Dubin, who had suggested the direct-mail approach in an earlier board meeting and offered to assist with the effort, agreed with Itule that with some help by Boye at headquarters, they could conduct such an effort with a small dollar amount, but wanted assurances that if the drive were successful, they might continue with the proposed larger project. The board gave its assurance and approved the test project with only a few dissenting votes. Within ten weeks, the committee's efforts were paying dividends. Although the committee had exceeded its budget by spending $1,012, the drive directly brought in $1,240 in new-member initiation fees, and more responses were coming in every day. Dubin had paid the extra $250 out of his own pocket to assure completion of the test mailing. At the January 1981 board meeting, Dubin was reimbursed and the board approved a Sutherland motion allowing up to $5,000 of any monies generated by a continuing membership drive through November 1981 to be made available to the membership committee for further mailings and drives.

A CHANGE OF ADDRESS FOR SPJ,SDX

Negotiations for moving headquarters were nearly complete by early December 1980. The nerve center of the Society of Professional Journalists, Sigma Delta Chi, had been in only two locations in fifty-three years. Ward Neff, a past SDX president and publisher of the *Corn Belt Farm Dailies* in Chicago, had hoped to consolidate the fraternity's activities by establishing a permanent headquarters in January 1928. He provided space at no cost to Sigma Delta Chi in the *Drovers' Journal* Building at 836 Exchange Avenue in the Stockyards of Chicago.

The move to the Pure Oil Building, at the familiar 35 East Wacker Drive address by the Chicago River and just blocks from the center of the downtown Loop, came in 1936. When Warren K. Agee became executive officer in 1960, headquarters occupied a few offices on the eighth floor. That space was cut back in an economy drive almost immediately, but, when *The Quill* was provided a full-time, on-site executive editor in 1961, office space was expanded to meet that need. Six years later, with Hurst as executive officer, the membership and activities of the Society growing rapidly, and Charles Long added to the staff as an administrative/editorial assistant, Hurst negotiated for larger quarters on the thirty-first floor. The Society's operation continued to grow and by the late 1970's, when Kathy Lieberman joined the staff as director of information, the headquarters was expanded again taking over all of that floor. According to Hurst, the Society leased space at 35 East Wacker Drive for longer than any other client in the building – forty-five years. But in 1980, with new building owners and the rent about to rise to the point where it would double in just five years, the officers and board had no choice but to find other quarters.

"We came within an inch of signing the lease for the Wabash Avenue site," Hurst said, "when a real-estate broker Dubin had alerted about the Society's lease problems

reported in December that the American Hospital Association was considering leasing office space to a not-for-profit organization in its building at 840 North Lake Shore Drive. The building, about six blocks north and three blocks east of The Loop in the Gold Coast section of Chicago's Near North Side, was at the corner of Pearson Street and North Lake Shore Drive, a stone's throw from Lake Michigan. Hurst, accompanied by Dubin and two realtors, examined the site and met with hospital association officials. "We found the eighth-floor office space very acceptable and the price much better than we were about to pay for space in a less-desirable building," Hurst said. "Over the next four to five weeks, we persuaded them we would be a good tenant for them and we were able to negotiate a lease."

Hurst told the board in January that instead of paying $60,000 per year in just five years (the 1980 rent was $33,177) to stay at 35 East Wacker Drive, or paying $36,000 for the Wabash Avenue site, "Total rent for the first year will be $27,020.84. The AHA building is modern and well maintained; the AHA officials have been most cooperative and supportive, even to the point of suggesting that we may be able to use some of their in-house services to save additional dollars. In short, it's a winner." Board members visited the site January 23, were impressed with the proposed facilities and a lease was signed with move-in set for January 31, 1981. The Society had a new address, 840 North Lake Shore Drive, Suite 801 West.

THE CHICAGO BOARD MEETING

Condon spent the three and one-half days of the week of January 5, 1981, in Chicago, meeting extensively with Hurst, looking over the headquarters operation but concentrating primarily on a review of internal accounting controls, budget compilation and preparation, and the conversion of membership and *Quill* mailing lists to computerization. He interviewed most of the office personnel and met with the Society's auditors and bankers. "I was most impressed with the staff's dedication and commitment to SDX," he wrote president Graves on January 15. Condon's report and its recommendations were sent to each board member, Hurst and Dubin, who had been reappointed finance committee chairman, a week before the scheduled board meeting.

Meanwhile, Record was organizing and preparing a report on Society priorities and goals for the next three-to-five years based on input from board members. "I had received perceptions on what we should be doing as a Society and where we should be going from most of the officers and regional directors by December 15 and distilled that information to five items which I took to the meeting in Chicago," Record said. When the board convened at the Schiller Park Holiday Inn near O'Hare Airport January 23, 1981, the first order of business was to consider those five items. Four of the goals were approved as written within the first half day of the three-day meeting. They included: (1) continued expansion of the Society's freedom of information and First Amendment efforts; (2) establishment of a national membership drive; (3) emphasis on continuing education programs and services, called professional development by the committee; and (4) initiation of a program to secure foundation grants and other income to assist development of both the professional development program and *The Quill*. The fifth goal, labeled as Priority One, was aimed at financial and administrative reorganization as outlined in Condon's report. Action on it was postponed until after the board had had opportunity to discuss that report. "All of the recommendations had come from board members and were simply compiled in a form they could consider, so approval was not unexpected. We did not assign numerical priorities to the goals. Each was given an equal priority," Record said.

The board, turning to the Condon's sixteen-page report, addressed its first point – suggestions for the administrative organization of the Society. It must be noted first that, while many on the board found the report a significant analysis and agreed with its recommendations, it represented only a different way of approaching the headquarters operation than Hurst had been using. Condon, who did not attend the session, wrote: "The basic organization of the Society, both from the admininstrative and internal control standpoint, is in need of a business manager function." He proposed six responsibilities for the business manager, none of which "currently is being fulfilled effectively." Condon suggested that a written procedural manual, containing all the financial and administrative controls by area, should be prepared including detailed job descriptions for the headquarters staff. He made recommendations on changing the system of handling cash receipts, billing, accounts payable and other bookkeeping procedures to what he considered a more efficient method. In addition, he challenged the preparation and reporting of the budget and called for the use a variance sheet which would explain the differences between the budget items for a coming year and the estimated or actual expenses for the current year. He indicated that formulating the budget on the basis of the prior year's costs plus an inflation factor and the formal board approval of the budget four months after it was in operation needed to be changed. Condon was especially critical of the Society's auditing firm. "The last management letter [recommending changes in fiscal procedures] received from the Society's independent accountants was in 1972. A written letter should be prepared each year and addressed to the board of directors and the finance committee," he wrote. "Whatever the reasons, it is inexcusable that SPJ has not received a management letter in eight years." Turning to the board's policies on investments, he wrote, "It is the practice of SPJ to utilize only one bank for its certificates of deposit. It may be worthwhile to shop around. Additionally, [the Society] should refrain from obtaining thirty-day or sixty-day notes. Ninety-day or longer have better rates."

Hurst said later, "Mr. Condon's remarks about investment policies illustrates how difficult it is for an outsider to understand our operations after a brief visit. The facts are that the largest part of our annual income, dues payments, arrived within a few months after the first billing. Funds not needed immediately were invested in both long-term and short-term notes. Maturity dates were matched to our needs for cash in the months ahead. And, yes, we bought thirty-day notes at the close end of the time scale, so that even the smallest amount of the money would draw interest. If we had tried to cash in a sixty-day or ninety-day note before it matured, we would not only have lost the interest, but also part of the principal in penalties. We monitored investments closely. I personally reviewed them each Monday. And we were certain our bank was competitive, which wasn't difficult, since Chicago banks and savings and loans advertised their rates."

Dornfeld, Otto and Dubin did not find Condon's findings or recommendations a surprise. "I didn't see the Condon Report as revolutionary," Dornfeld said. "To me, it was echoing, amplifying and enlarging upon things we had already begun to come to understand." Otto saw the report as affirmation of the finance committee's findings: "When the Condon Report, in essence, confirmed what our committee had found, that work achieved a lot of credibility that it might not have had otherwise." Dubin, whose finance committee had seen only very few of its suggestions implemented by that time, said he thought Condon's recommendations merely restated his committee's work. "Condon told me he agreed with many of our findings. However, some of his specific suggestions were impractical," Dubin said, "because here was a person coming out of a very large organization where they were able to do things that it would be impossible to do in a small-office situation."

Graves knew many of the board members had limited knowledge of the specifics discussed during the officers' deliberations which brought about the invitation to Condon to prepare the report. "I called an executive session on Saturday afternoon to explain the Condon Report and to have the board hear the officers' recommendation for a change in auditors," Graves recalled. "The board had to know what the officers had been doing. The Condon Report was something on which the board had to make a decision and it was not fully aware of all of the background on why the report was requested and why the officers were recommending a change in

auditors." Hurst and a representative of the Society's auditing firm, who was present to answer questions about its service to the Society, were excluded from the meeting, something Hurst did not understand or appreciate.

In nearly four hours of deliberation, the board accepted, in concept, much of the Condon Report, but took special interest in the matters of investment policies and a possible change in auditors. "Many of Condon's recommendations on internal procedures, especially in finance, were things our paid auditors should have been recommending for years and apparently hadn't been doing," Dornfeld said. "In my years on the board, I had never seen a management letter from the auditors. I don't think the auditors saw their role as working for the board but rather for the executive officer. They may well have been giving him valuable advice and counsel but they really weren't doing a service for the board. Whatever advice they were giving the executive officer, we weren't hearing about." Hurst said later that the auditors had provided advice through the years, and that he and past officers had implemented some of the suggestions and rejected others as impractical – much in the same manner as Dubin had dismissed some of Condon's recommendations. During the late 1970's, the auditors made few additional recommendations because, as they had examined the Society's business practices through the years, most of their suggestions for improvement were already in place or had been turned down as not appropriate for the SPJ,SDX operation, Hurst said. He added, "In recent years [prior to 1980-1981], I asked the auditors for advice mostly on technical matters – things such as how and where to set up a category of income or expense, or how to prepare some new government-type form. Things of that kind were of no great import to the board. As it was, I sometimes felt embarrassed by the length and detail of my reports to the board and wondered if anyone could possibly have the time to read them."

When the board returned to open session that evening, the board adopted a Dornfeld motion that the executive officer be directed to solicit proposals from several auditing firms including the one being used, specifying fees and services performed, including management letters to the board so that it might consider a possible change in auditors at its April meeting in Cincinnati.

HURST RESIGNS

Hurst was a very private man who took great pride in his work and in the accomplishments of the Society. He had been in the spotlight and had become known as "Mr. SDX," not because he had focused attention on himself, but because he had kept the Society out front in the journalistic community. While he believed he had done a good job, he preferred to let the evidence of his work speak for itself. His quiet, unassuming manner did not allow him to portray himself for an instant before the board or the membership as the reason the Society had progressed to its stature of leadership in journalism in 1981. He shared his innermost thoughts about his personal triumphs and disappointments as executive officer with very few of his associates. Working with scores of individuals on boards of directors and twenty national presidents had prepared him to deal with changes in styles and priorities through those nineteen years. But the past year had been difficult for Hurst, probably more difficult than most years. On January 18, 1981, one week before the board convened in Chicago, he decided to resign and submit his letter of resignation at the close of the board meeting.

The board had gone into executive session shortly after 9 pm to consider a number of line items in the budget. When it appeared that the last item had been covered, Hurst asked members of the board, "Are there any other questions at all on anything we've covered today?" When he was assured there were no more questions to be raised or agenda items to be covered, he said, "I have an annoucement to make." It was almost 10:30 pm, January 24, 1981, when Hurst reached for a sheaf of papers from his brief case and distributed his January 18-dated letter:

To the Board of Directors:

This is to notify you that I intend to resign as executive officer of the

Society effective June 1, 1981.

It has been a privilege and an honor to serve as executive officer these past nineteen years, but I feel that the time has come to pursue other career interests.

My deepest gratitude to you and your predecessors on the national board, and to all of the members of the Society who have worked so devotedly to advance the standards of our profession. I know that this spirit of dedication to professionalism is strong and bright throughout the Society, and that no worthy goal will be beyond our reach.

The June 1 date was chosen to permit an orderly transition. The board might wish to consider appointment of a search committee as soon as possible, allowing the committee three months in which to select a new executive officer. That would leave one month for us to work together at Headquarters so that my successor can become well-acquainted with the Society's structures and operations.

Meanwhile, of course, I will continue to commit my fullest energies to my duties and do everything possible to assure a smooth and effective transition.

Respectfully submitted,
Russell E. Hurst
Executive Officer

The author of this history was one of twenty-one persons who sat in stunned silence for a few seconds which seemed interminable until Hurst told the board he had been thinking about leaving the Society for some time and that that day's events had not prompted his decision to resign. Several board members asked almost at the same moment if there were any way Hurst would change his mind, but he said the decision was final. Graves adjourned the meeting but there were board members still sitting in quiet wonderment as much as thirty minutes later.

Record, in 1983, probably best summed up the feelings of the great majority of his colleagues on the board about Hurst's resignation. "It was my fervent hope that he would remain as executive officer and carry out the recommendations of the Condon Report and the planning committee," Record said. "Any weaknesses we may have perceived in the Society cannot all be attributed to Hurst....The boards had taken a 'Let Russ do it' attitude when Hurst was not an auditor, he was not a bookkeeper....We put a tremendous burden on Hurst when the boards had the fiduciary responsibility and I do not think the boards exercised that responsibility over a great many years. But Russ Hurst was 'Mr. SPJ,SDX.' His resignation was a thunderbolt. I loved and respected him. And I can say this. The Society would not be what it is today without having had Russ Hurst as executive officer."

Asked why she felt Hurst resigned, Otto said, "I'd like to take him at his word. I think, maybe, he didn't find the job a whole lot of fun any more. He saw the board veering off into other directions. The things he felt comfortable doing for a lot of years and really enjoyed, the board was challenging. He had been at the job for nineteen years and established a mentality toward the job. We all do that. We see a right way to do something and a wrong way to do something. When the board was demanding something different from him, he was no longer interested." Graves told the board the morning following Hurst's resignation, "I regret the loss of Mr. Hurst, but I believe the Society will be able to move forward and build upon the accomplishments achieved during Hurst's tenure."

The board members reconvened Sunday morning, January 25, to deal with the situation left them the night before. They released a statement written by regional directors Harry Fuller and Ron Lovell on Hurst's resignation:

For nineteen years as executive officer of the Society of Professional Journalists, Sigma Delta Chi, Russell Hurst has personified a conspicuous commitment to advancing the best in journalism. While executive officer, Mr. Hurst had devoted limitless energy and countless hours to helping make the Society a respected and effective spokesman for the highest principles of professional journalism.

On behalf of the membership, students and professionals, we express our deepest appreciation for his nearly two decades of exceptional counsel, leadership and inspiration.

The board of directors and national officers, SPJ,SDX, accept his resignation with profound regret. We respect his wishes in this regard and we have conveyed to him our sincere best wishes in attaining those personal goals he has decided to pursue full-time.

The words in the statement were in no way simply perfunctory. Those who had worked with him on the board through the years still hold him in the highest regard for his untold contributions to the Society and to American journalism. Other members of the Society, who knew him well along with those whose only contact had been at national meetings or in telephone conversations, have maintained great admiration for Russ Hurst. It was not unusual for those who were interviewed for this book to begin the conversation with, "How is Russ Hurst? What is he doing?," and, "Be sure to give him my sincere regards when you see him."

But, in January 1981, when the Society was to lose its executive officer in just five months, the first order of business for the board was to appoint a search committee to begin work screening possible candidates for the position. Graves named Otto to chair the committee and appointed past president Goodykoontz, Sutherland, and Dr. Perry Ashley, campus chapter adviser at the University of South Carolina, to serve with her.

The matter of the planning committee's remaining goal, that of implementing the financial and administrative recommendations of the Condon Report, was still to be decided. The board adopted the fifth goal with little discussion or debate, leaving no doubt that, despite Hurst's resignation, the board and officers were ready to complete the reorganization of the headquarters operation and the relationship of the officers and board to the executive officer. Graves, in fact, proposed that the Society hire a business manager as quickly as possible to learn the internal operations of the headquarters and help provide continuity after Hurst's departure. Any decision on that suggestion was postponed so that the board could consider all possible alternatives in line with the selection of a new executive officer.

Full implementation of the goals and priorities, of course, did not take place immediately. The priorities relating to freedom of information, fund-raising, the membership drive, and professional development programs and services were initiated in the main in budget hearings during the spring and summer of 1981 and all were instituted during the next two years. However, as Hurst and Dubin had anticipated, the specific recommendations on restructuring fiscal policies and controls and administrative functions listed in the Condon Report had to be studied further in line with what would fit within the limited financial means of the Society. "We agreed on the concepts in every case," Record said. "But we had to modify some specifics to make them appropriate to our operation. For instance, we did not hire a business manager. On further analysis, we gave our bookkeeper, Grace Roberts, some of those business-manager responsibilities. She carried out those duties well and has been a most effective professional staff member at headquarters."

Because of the traumatic events from December 1979 through November 1981, for Otto and Graves it was among the most difficult times in the Society's history to have been president. Otto knew her steadfast approach to the problems confronting the Society was not always popular with everyone. But she played her role in 1980 much as Walter Burroughs had played his in the late 1950's or Bob Chandler and Ralph Otwell had in the early 1970's. Each was willing to pay the price on a personal basis to put what each steadfastly believed was in the best, long-term interest of the Society.

In an article published in the September 1981 *Quill*, Record listed first among the ten events which he said had produced the positive, dramatic changes in the Society, "Jean Otto becomes national president in November 1979 in New York City. Many had talked about the need for change in the Society. Otto, realizing the trauma that lay ahead, decides to bite the bullet and show others how to do likewise." Two years later, Record said, "She had a strong, supportive board which pitched in behind her, but it was her leadership that got the job done."

Richard Leonard, Society president during 1976-1977 when signs of needed change began to appear, said, "[Difficult] things that we knew were coming, some of us decided not to face up to for one reason or another. You have a short term as president and, on some of the ongoing problems, you say, 'I'll leave that for the next guy.' Jean was able to do something that many of us had trouble doing – overriding personal relationships. I always felt so close to Russ Hurst, I don't think I could have taken the objective look she took at what needed to be done in terms of changing the Society."

Graves found his year as president equally difficult and believed the reforms initiated by Otto should be refined and given stability. Perhaps, more than any president before him, he traveled extensively visiting professional and campus chapters throughout the country to explain what was occurring within the Society and to dispel any grass-roots divisiveness. "There were many sleepless nights," Graves recalls, "because of the seemingly every-day turn of events at headquarters. I consulted with many of my board colleagues and local Society members during those tenuous times. Communication was imperative to be certain the Society membership, board and officers were not splintered. When I asked officers and regional directors for help, I received it willingly. Reason and calmness prevailed and I believe the result of the various reforms we set in place helped to bring about an invigorated and stronger organization."

CHAPTER 12

The Tornabene Years

The advertisement for applicants for the post of executive officer in the March 1981 *Quill* and in major newspapers across the country called for an "experienced journalist to direct activities and programs of the Society of Professional Journalists, Sigma Delta Chi" who would be asked to supervise and coordinate Chicago headquarters and 310 professional and campus chapters nationwide. It said the person chosen would be "expected to act as spokesman for the Society, to be knowledgeable about journalistic issues, to design and implement programs, and be able to speak and inspire support within and outside the Society." Although the deadline for applications was March 20, more than 120 persons responded to the ads. Search committee chair Jean Otto recalls: "Among the applicants we had some who were formerly extremely active in SPJ; some had never been members at all but who knew about the Society, some were management-types. As I reviewed all of the applications, it became apparent that we had strong managers with absolutely no understanding of what journalism or the Society were all about and that was very important to the committee. We also had loyal Society members without the kind of management experience we knew we had to have."

Shortly before the deadline, it appeared that the ideal candidate for the job was not among the 120 applications. Otto remembers receiving a brief, hand-written note from Sol Taishoff, president of the Society in 1956-1957 and founder, publisher and editor of *Broadcasting* magazine, which said, "Have you considered Russ Tornabene for executive officer? You couldn't do better." Tornabene had been director of public affairs for network news at NBC in New York City since 1975 and had been active in Society activities since he joined Sigma Delta Chi in the late 1940's. "I couldn't do much as chairman," Otto said, "for I had to believe that if he were interested he would have filed an application. The committee invited five candidates to be interviewed in Chicago on a Monday in early April, but Tornabene was not among them. "The Thursday or Friday before the interviews, on an impulse, I called

Russell C. Tornabene became the Society's eighth full-time executive officer June 1, 1981. A reporter and executive with NBC News for thirty years before assuming the SPJ,SDX administrative post, Tornabene was responsible for effecting plans for the major fund drive beginning in 1983 and for computerization of the headquarters operations.

Tornabene and asked him about his possible interest," Otto recalls. "He said he and his wife, Audrey, had discussed it but had not decided to take the step as yet." Otto told Tornabene the committee was meeting the following Monday and that if he were indeed interested, it would be best if he had an application in Chicago by Monday. "He told me that Bill Small, president of NBC News, was out of the country but would be back the next day and that he would have to talk to Small before making a formal application," Otto said. "I suggested that he go ahead and send in an application and then talk to Small. He could call me before the meeting to tell me if he were still interested and had the clearance to apply."

Tornabene had not entertained ideas of leaving NBC News. He had been with the network as a newsman and executive for thirty years. "It never occurred to me to

apply for the job of SPJ executive officer," Tornabene said. "When Jean called me, I almost scoffed at the idea. I was happy in my job, I was making good money, I had a daughter in high school in the New York City area, and I wasn't that young – fifty-seven at the time." Tornabene admitted, however, that Otto made him think about the position seriously. "She planted ideas with me and asked me what I was going to do in the next four or five years. That was as far as she could go, of course. For a couple of days, Audrey and I talked about the terrific dislocation for the family, the financial considerations and the new opportunity. After I talked with Bill Small, we decided to go ahead and I applied," he said.

The application was in Chicago on Monday morning and Tornabene called Otto to tell her to consider him a formal applicant. When the interviews were completed, the committee did not believe any of the candidates were right for the job, especially in the light of the new application from Tornabene. "Even without having interviewed Tornabene," Otto recalls, "we believed he was the only one who had management background, who had an understanding of journalism, who had been a long-standing, highly-dedicated member of the Society and knew what it was all about and what it ought to be doing. In short, he was the only one who had it all.

"Specifically, the committee was impressed with Tornabene's fiscal experience, something the Condon Report and finance committee had called for," she said. "We were pleased that he had been in broadcasting because that would say something about the Society's attitude toward broadcast journalism. He knew how to manage people, how to deal with an office staff, and he seemed to convey a presence of vigor and enthusiasm." Otto settled a few unresolved issues by telephone with Tornabene and the committee recommended him to the officers and board. A formal interview was set with the officers and board at its spring meeting April 22 in Cincinnati.

THE RIGHT MAN AT THE RIGHT TIME

Tornabene's background was

impressive. A 1949 graduate of Indiana University where he had been president of his campus Sigma Delta Chi chapter, Tornabene had served as a tank crewman in World War II and was recalled to active service in the Korean War where, in 1951, he was desk editor and chief correspondent for *Pacific Stars and Stripes*. A frequent contributor to *The Quill*, he joined WRC Radio in Washington, DC in 1951 as a news writer. He moved to NBC Network News in 1955 in Washington and was transferred to NBC News, New York in 1961 as manager of news operations. Seven years later he became general manager of the NBC Radio Network and in 1973 added the title of vice president for the NBC Radio Network. During his tenure as a newsman, he had coordinated coverage of trips to Europe, the Middle East and South America by Presidents Eisenhower, Kennedy and Nixon, was an editor or producer of news coverage at six of seven national political conventions since 1956, and covered space launches and manned space flights during the 1960's. He had served as an officer of Sigma Delta Chi chapters in Washington, DC and New York City, becoming president of the Deadline Club in 1975. His most recent Society activity had involved him in the 1979 New York City convention as editor and then publisher of the financially-successful *New York, New York* convention magazine.

The officers interviewed Tornabene for ninety minutes in Cincinnati and unanimously endorsed the search committee's action. Tornabene told the board in his final interview that he could be on the job to work with Hurst beginning about May 15 and could assume the position officially June 1. The board officially selected Tornabene as the Society's ninth full-time, paid executive officer on April 23, 1981. Tornabene accepted the position because, "It was an opportunity to do something worthwhile in the profession to which I owed a great deal. The opportunity was enormous, almost limitless."

As the board in Cincinnati considered effecting administrative and financial changes it had adopted in Chicago, members noted Tornabene's demonstrated strengths in several of those areas and, other than voting

Howard Graves, president of the Society in 1980-1981, probably traveled more during his five years as a national officer than any other person with a similar tenure. Believing that the campus and professional chapters benefitted from the presence of a national officer at their local meetings, Graves visited chapters in more than 150 cities in forty-seven states, extending into all twelve regions of the Society.

officially to change auditors, agreed to wait for their new executive officer to recommend and administer specific changes when he took over on June 1.

Hurst, of course, attended the Cincinnati meeting as executive officer. In his final report, he noted that membership numbers, revised to meet the requirement of the officers and board to include only active, paid members, had reached 28,355 (the number had been more than 35,000 before the officers and board, in 1980, decided to change the meaning of the word "active") and the number of campus and professional chapters had grown to 174 and 139, respectively, for a total of 313. His figures demonstrated a more than doubling of the active membership of 13,200 (had the 1980 definition of "active" been applied in 1962, that number would have been closer to 10,000 and active membership could have been said to have nearly tripled) and the 148 chapters when he became executive officer in

1962. Invited by the board to share his thoughts about the Society out of his nineteen years' experience, he closed out his official duties with these observations:

Don't mistake form for substance. Remember that headquarters exists to serve our members. Keep lines of authority and responsibility clear. Value the student members who are the lifeline of the Society and the profession. The money the Society spends on student members is an investment in the future.

The Quill is the Society's single most important product and must be of the highest possible quality even if it has to be subsidized. Computerization is an effective tool, but it should not be allowed to depersonalize the Society's relationship with members.

The Society is distinctive in its makeup as an organization of professionals; it is not to be compared with a trade association and its members should always be regarded as professional colleagues, not 'customers.' Not every activity has to be cost-justified. If a proposed program has merit and a potential for long-range dividends to the profession, find the money and the people to accomplish it.

Everyone in the Society must work conscientiously to realize our goals. Too much dependence must not be placed on any one person or committee. Service to SPJ,SDX is not for personal gain, but a 'stewardship,' an opportunity for service to the profession.

As has been noted earlier, president Graves presented Hurst the Wells Memorial Key for his service to the Society at the Saturday luncheon of the Distinguished Service Awards conference in Cincinnati.

While the talents and experience Tornabene brought to his new position when he arrived in Chicago in mid-May served him well on the job, he had much to learn about the myriad of details and programs around which the Society operated. He spent what he called "an extremely efficient two weeks" with Hurst working through mountains of files, becoming acquainted with the staff at headquarters and being briefed

Georgiana Vines, assistant metro editor, Knoxville, Tennessee *News-Sentinel* was named Region Three director in November 1983, becoming only one of four non-student women elected to the national board through 1984.

on continuing projects as well as the duties he would assume on June 1. "Just to learn what the landscape was, it was necessary to stay at headquarters, work long hours and ask direct questions in that very brief orientation," Tornabene said. "I will be forever in Russ Hurst's debt for the gracious and very efficient manner in which he organized all of his notes prior to my arrival in Chicago. Hurst devoted as much as nine hours each day to me, briefing me on what the organization was all about."

The new executive officer outlined his philosophy on the Society and its work in an article in the September 1981 *Quill*. "The Society must be vital if it is to meet its goals. Only through vigorous, orderly and organized effort will its program be accepted. And the Society must have a clear vision, one standing for the principles of professional journalism, one of commitment to a free and independent press, and one which serves members in a variety of cogent programs. For without a vision, we will plod."

Tornabene hit the ground running when he took the SPJ,SDX reins. Although he was fully aware of the apparent mood of the board to assume more control of the fiscal affairs of the Society and the resultant conflicts between the officers and Hurst, he did not tiptoe in, cautiously attempting to find his place in relationship with the twenty-two volunteers on the board who had hired him. He took immediate, bold steps to effect the reorganizational goals established six months earlier. "I saw the Condon Report and finance committee recommendations as a roadmap in alignment with what my experience had taught me." By mid-June, Tornabene had researched and participated in interviewing candidate-firms hoping to become the Society's new auditor and made the final selection. Armed with personal knowledge of investments and concerned with what the board had also perceived as less-than-acceptable return on the Society's investments, Tornabene set about to change the system of investing the reserves. "I realized quickly that we could earn a great deal more money from interest on our investments than the Society had been getting," he said. "It was more of a change in philosophy from depending entirely on a bank investment counselor to researching on our own and shopping for the best opportunities than in simply moving the funds." Within months, Tornabene had recommended and convinced the officers to move the funds temporarily to high-interest-bearing notes while research continued on the best placement of the Society's reserves. That move alone provided the Society with enough new income in twelve months to pay his first year's salary.

Morale among the professional and clerical staff at headquarters was, perhaps, at an all-time low. In fifteen months, they had experienced a change-over in executive officers, two changes in editors and several assistant editors of *The Quill* along with sundry changes in secondary staff positions. They were very conscious of the studies of

headquarters by the finance committee, Condon and the officers. Moreover, they were concerned, if not anxious, about how all of the reorganization would affect them.

Tornabene reorganized the office shortly after he arrived. But in doing so, he began a series of full-staff meetings each Monday morning. He kept all of the office personnel informed on possible changes in staff utilization as they were being considered and sought staff input on how best to effect those changes to keep the headquarters operation moving smoothly. Suddenly, professional staff, secretaries and clerks believed they were a viable part of a unit and morale soared from the depths to new heights. The office reorganization took the form of permitting every department head to be responsible for his or her department. "I really believe that if you are trying to do somebody else's job, you really aren't doing your own job. You are doing, not managing. There's an old 'saw' which goes, 'Organize, deputize, supervise and decide.' Ultimately I have had to decide, but as the system works, I really feel I am doing my job."

When the officers arrived for their second annual budget review June 26, Tornabene was firmly in command of his environment. There were still gaps in his historical perspective on certain programs and projects, but those were filled in as needed by the officers. "What really struck me about Russ Tornabene," Graves said, "was his positiveness and his 'let's try it' attitude. He was full of ideas and had a tremendous volume of enthusiasm. When we would run into a dilemma or hit a stumbling block of a fiscal or program nature, he found a way around it." Novitz was not surprised that his longtime New York colleague caught hold so quickly. "He was a fast-study, a good listener and solution-oriented," Novitz said. "His experience in management with NBC stood him in good stead, but it was the underpinnings of his Society experiences, having been involved in SPJ,SDX leadership at several levels, knowing the players, that made him 'Mr. Right' for the job."

Dornfeld remembers that Tornabene "brought a fresh perspective to the Society's

Rosanne Brooks, Fairchild Publications, Washington, DC, was elected to a three-year term as Region Two director in November 1983. She is pictured at a board luncheon with 1983-1984 campus board representative Gregory Gilligan, Ohio State University.

leadership. His expertise on management of the Society's money was a real contribution both in financial gain and in leadership. In addition, he was quite unflappable. There were so many possibilities for frustration and he handled them very well, especially with the board." The recently displayed aggressiveness to be involved more directly in manifestation of its policies on the part of the board was matched by aggressiveness on the part of Tornabene. While this might have instituted new conflicts, it did not. "The word 'control' was meaningless to me," Tornabene said. "At times, I took full control because I was given responsibility and authority to do a job. The board, from the beginning, said they wanted to know what I wanted to do and they would tell me if I could go ahead it with. It wasn't just a safety valve, it was getting the very best

from our resources. I felt very comfortable with the board from the very beginning. Communication was the key. I overcommunicate everything I do although sometimes I have been chided for deluging the board members with paper. But somewhere in their mail was every idea before it was implemented."

Tornabene's active participation in fiscal matters had much to do with successes in stretching *The Quill's* limited budget through internal manipulation. Editor Donson and general manager Boye had been able to effect considerable savings by negotiating new contracts for typesetting and printing. Tornabene examined the full implications in the production of the magazine. Because he had had experience in making money work for an organization, he noted that the $1,600 per month being spent for typesetting under the new contract was strictly an expenditure and he turned those dollars into the generation of new dollars in the form of useful and needed equipment. "Working in concert with the officers, I received approval from the board to terminate the typesetting contract and to purchase a typesetter/computer for *The Quill* at a cost of $1,600 per month for two years. At the end of that period of time, we owned the typesetter worth $25,000 and had cut our typesetting expenses from $1,600 to maintenance costs of $250 per month," he said. In addition, *The Quill* staff had greater control over typesetting and achieved later deadlines for the magazine's content. To better facilitate communication, after approval by the officers, he had a new, more efficient telephone system installed which helped to departmentalize the headquarters operation. He also had a telecopier installed allowing for speedy exchange of original documents which needed signatures or examination by the officers.

THE COMPUTER LENDS A HAND

Record books, file cabinets filled with cards and papers, and drawers of metal address plates sitting near an Addressograph machine – that's the way it was from the l950's through the 1970's at national headquarters. As happened with so many organizations during those two decades, there was never money in hand to move to a more modern system, especially a computerized one. But when a small office houses the records of 100,000 members along with the minutes and policies of scores of board and officers' meetings, important correspondence and the minutiae collected over fifty years, the records dominated the work space.

Relatively speaking, computerization came quickly, though thoughtfully, after it became a matter of serious discussion in 1980. Hurst administered the first efforts. A computer service bureau was retained to enter mailing lists for *The Quill* but little else, beginning in the summer of that year, replacing the Addressograph operation that had been used for more than twenty years. Dubin and Bukro, working together and separately, studied the opportunities for

efficiency further computerization would bring, along with its basic and programming costs. When Tornabene replaced Hurst, he began looking at the options of obtaining an in-house, stand-alone computer or continuing with the service bureau's computer but bringing terminals and a printer into the office so that operational control was in the hands of his staff. After thorough study, it was decided to go with the terminals and printer as an interim step. Long-range plans approved by the board in 1982 called for moving toward acquiring the Society's own computer when the board-appointed computer committee headed by Bukro believed the needs of the Society's headquarters had aligned themselves with what the more elaborate, but expensive, system can provide. In the meantime, new softwear was purchased to expand the capability of the terminals linked with the service bureau. By mid-1983, the system was installed and fully operational. Tornabene and the officers and board had effected savings enough between June 1981 and November 1982 to pay for the computer hardware and software without affecting continuing programs.

Addition of the computer terminals and printer along with the new softwear provided three major advantages almost immediately, Tornabene said. "First, it trained all of us on using the computer so that we can go from where we are to where we hope to go. Second, it made it possible to handle additions and changes in-house – we have literally thousands and thousands of those every year – and shortened the time for those record modifications from as long as from four days to three weeks down to one day. And third, that quick turn-around time on additions and changes made it possible for us to use the headquarters staff more effectively and efficiently." The computer has made it possible to offer additional services to the profession and to members as well. Looking toward the long-range effects of computerization, Tornabene said, "We will be able to do in-depth analysis on freedom of information to help us determine the position we want to take based on what has happened before and projections for the future. To do this, we will have to connect with large information banks but that will be within our capabilities." He said *The Quill* will not only benefit from the research capabilities of the computer but studies of the demographics of *The Quill's* audience may well help in attracting more advertising to the magazine. "The computer will be a tool that will allow us to do things that couldn't be done before in terms of staff and time in addition to doing things quickly."

As more information about the Society's members was added to the computer bank, faster and accurate services was available to members. No one was more aware of that advance than Pearl Luttrell, who, in her various jobs dealing with the membership and the Society at large, had been overwhelmed with hand work and short staff for twenty-five years. "We tried to get information members needed as quickly as possible but often it took several days to find the data, write a letter and get it mailed to them," she said in 1983. "Now we are limited only by the information we have – which in the main is a list of national and chapter officers – and the time-sharing problem of getting on the computer in supplying information while the member is on the phone. When we have our stand-alone computer in-house and there is no problem with time-sharing and we add more software and information about each member, we'll be able to give about any information a chapter member or officer needs and do it in a matter of minutes rather than days."

The computer was not the only piece of equipment added to headquarters which brought efficiency and more speed to office operations. Tornabene used dollars spent for outside services to purchase equipment for in-house use including a folder, collator, computerized postage meter and the Mergenthaler typesetter. On the postage meter alone, Tornabene said, "We saved hundreds of dollars a year having an exact amount of postage needed for the tens of thousands of pieces of mail we send out rather than using the spring-type meter which gave us an approximation." Again, members and chapters were the beneficiary not only in cost savings, but in producing needed materials quickly. "In ten minutes,

I printed out a list of the professional chapter presidents, made 100 copies and had them collated and folded ready to be placed in envelopes," Luttrell said. "We never could have done that before." An early project completed by the headquarters staff involved producing a directory for Region Ten of regional officers and campus and professional chapter officers including addresses and telephone numbers in five states. The computer supplied the information quickly, the type was set on the "Mergy," and after it was printed, it was collated and folded in office, Luttrell recalled.

The computer had been on-line for only a year by 1984, but already the effects had demonstrated that the Society was ready and able to handle the promise of the computer.

EFFECTING THE GOALS AND PRIORITIES

Tornabene found working with the changing volunteer leadership on the board less jarring than he had anticipated. "The officers who form the center of the Society's leadership have acted as a team," Tornabene said. "The current president might have a particular priority, but once that has been taken care of, he has gone back to the team concept." He perceived his role as executive officer as that of a coach working with that team. "The coach is on the bench, he isn't in the game. He has to call the plays and has to select the players, but he doesn't go on the field and play quarterback."

The finance committee and the Condon Report had recommended that job descriptions for the officers, executive officer and headquarters staff, along with fiscal and administrative policies and procedures, be put in writing and collected in a single volume. While some of that information existed, much of it was not in writing and that which was on paper was scattered among files and offices. Tornabene had taken on a similar project at NBC. Researching and collecting what had been achieved by Record's planning committee, including job descriptions approved by the board in Columbus and Cincinnati, Tornabene wrote and Record edited sections which needed to be added with the resultant publication of a forty-three page "Policies and Procedures" manual which could be read, used and modified as times dictated. "As the profession is dynamic, so must the Society be dynamic and dynamic means change." Tornabene said. "It means being sensitive to the need to constantly adjust those things which need modification and to be aware that we control change but none of its consequences. Using past experience, we need to understand how we can make our operations better, but we must be thoughtful in making change."

Otto proposed and hoped to establish a national member network program during 1981 in which professional chapters would appoint a local chapter member to assist new SPJ members moving to its city with information on housing, schools and other information needed to become settled. "Not only would SPJ members be helping other SPJ members," Otto said, "it would no doubt help in getting those new persons involved in the local chapter."

When the delegates gathered in Washington, DC for the November 1981 convention, Tornabene and the officers were able to report that the fiscal and administrative reorganization of the Society was all but completed and that the goals and priorities of the Society had been established and were being implemented. Long-term financial considerations were still a matter of concern, however. The delegates in Columbus a year earlier had required that before any dues structure for student members would be considered, full disclosure and justification of need for those dollars would be necessary. Vice president for campus chapter affairs Bostrom prepared and distributed a detailed analysis of the income from students and cost factors for maintaining student members during the spring of 1981. Discussions on the matter at regional conferences showed a clear division of opinion on the advisability of establishing dues for students and no one could predict how the vote would go in Washington. Bostrom presented the by-laws change to the delegates calling for approval of dues of $10 per year for student members beginning in January 1984. The two-year delay in implementing the dues program would allow

students who had joined the Society with the understanding they had to pay only the one-time $27.50 initiation fee to complete their student membership eligibility. Student delegates joined with professional delegates in approving the proposal as presented, 294-73. "Convention delegates, especially the students, have always responded in a positive way to the needs of the Society when they were provided with the full story," Bostrom said. "They gave us the opportunity in Columbus to justify that need; we did our job in supplying the information, so it was gratifying, but not really a surprise, when the 1981 convention approved the dues package for students." The membership services staff member at national headquarters, Jerry Eastman, sent a notice to all campus chapters in 1983 announcing procedures for administering the collection of dues the following January. On the basis of Eastman's explanation, Kathleen D. Griffin of the University of South Carolina sent in her 1984 dues payment of $10 to become the first student in the Society's history to pay annual national dues.

Novitz became the Society's national president in Washington and determined that the two previous years had provided so much focus on detail and self-examination that he said, "I thought 1982 was the time for the Society to recoup, consolidate and to move ahead." In his first president's column in The Quill, he announced his agenda, selecting two of the five goals and priorities established a year earlier – freedom of information, and professional development/continuing education. Further, he added improvement and development of The Quill as a new priority for the Society. It may have been that the goal for raising funds set in January 1981 included dollars for expanding the magazine, but Novitz gave fiscal stability and, thereby, enhancement of the editorial product its own identity as an important need to be addressed immediately.

Direction of The Quill had passed to the third editor in two years with Ron Dorfman's appointment in late 1981 to be discussed later and Novitz said, "My primary concern was to provide for Dorfman a nurturing environment to lay the groundwork not for a single, good issue, but for scores of good issues of the magazine. He needed to understand what the officers and board wanted in the magazine, that his autonomy was to be considerable, and that the magazine was his baby." Novitz continued the role of the publications committee chaired by Sutherland, believing it was an important element in the total picture to take undue pressures off Dorfman.

During Otto's term as president, Novitz had been involved in the decision to remove the *Quill's* subsidy from general Society funds and requiring the magazine to operate on its own and without deficit. "It occurred to me that in eliminating the so-called 'subsidy,' we were playing with numbers," he said. "Since the importance of the magazine was crucial to the Society, I didn't give a damn what we called the money. If *The Quill* needed the money, and if it were in my power, I was going to try to assure that the magazine had the financial potency to do the job we had said we wanted it to do." In setting the budget for fiscal 1982-1983, Novitz and Sutherland convinced a majority of the officers and board to reallocate income from membership dues and student initiation fees to provide a larger percentage for *The Quill*. Looking toward increasing the other major funding base for the magazine – The Quill Endowment Fund – the board, using the expertise of Tornabene and past presidents McCord and McBrayer, solidified an effort begun earlier to raise funds for that purpose.

In the area of professional development, Novitz wanted a thoughtful approach to programs in continuing education. Although he admitted one of the early programs he fostered – a cooperative effort with Westinghouse Corporation which, in effect, violated the letter of the Society's Code of Ethics – was "an unfortunate misstep," it didn't deter him from pursuing the basic goal. "I was extremely conscious that despite the agreed value of this type of program, I had seen such programs done by other organizations costing a great deal of money prove to be totally ineffective, leaving the sponsoring organization with nothing but a debt and failure," he said. "I didn't want a big splash type of treatment on this. My priority during that time was to use regional conferences and some of our outstanding chapters to sponsor professional development programs. I contacted a few publisher-types I knew, planting the idea of utilizing their staff members, inviting them in to talk about topical issues and making it a Sigma Delta Chi event."

The 1982 priority for freedom of information received its start at the Washington convention when the Society's First Amendment counsel, Bruce Sanford, led a lobbying effort on Capitol Hill, asking delegates to that convention to visit with their local representatives and senators about pending FOI legislation. Out of that came an expansion of the state FOI system to include efforts to establish a network of members and nonmembers who could lobby at grass roots levels on issues of national import. "We wanted to be able to ask a person with direct and personal contact with a congressman to pick up the phone and call, expressing support for or opposition to a particular bill or issue as soon as it surfaced," Sanford said. He and FOI committee chair Bob Lewis kept the network informed through "media alerts" and "FOI bulletins" and were able to mobilize the network quickly on any issue while it was still in the formulative stages.

Meanwhile, Record's planning committee established two new goals and priorities for the Society adopted by the board in Williamsburg, Virginia, in April 1982. Supporting Novitz's lead, the committee made development of sources of revenue for *The Quill* an "official" priority of the Society. In addition, it set improving the image and visibility of the Society as a goal to be reached in time for the 1984 convention, which would mark the seventy-fifth anniversary of the Society's founding. "We knew this would take several forms, but we saw our continuing work in freedom of information as the first step in the process," Record said.

Relating to the diamond jubilee celebration, Record, who would be national president in 1984, was named chairman of that event by Graves. One of the earliest steps taken was approval by the officers and the board in 1981 for the writing of the official history of the Society from 1959 through 1984. Clayton's book had covered the history of Sigma Delta Chi from its founding through the fiftieth anniversary. Bostrom completed his term on the board in 1981 and arranged for a sabbatical leave from his teaching duties at Northern Arizona University during the spring of 1982 to do the research and begin the writing. Expenses for the project would be covered by the Society, but his services were donated as a contribution to the seventy-fifth anniversary celebration.

The matter of a dues increase for professional members surfaced again in 1982 and was carried all the way to the November convention in Milwaukee. The $10 increase for professionals approved in New York in 1979 had carried the Society almost a year and one half further than Hurst's predictions had anticipated, but inflation had taken its toll. Moreover, dollars were needed to effect some of the new goals and priorities established. Thus, the board at its spring 1982 meeting in Williamsburg, Virginia voted to seek a two-year increase of $15. If adopted, the dues would have been raised from $30 to $37.50 for 1983 and from $37.50 to $45 for 1984.

Along with the proposed name change facing the Milwaukee delegates, the main topic of discussion there was the dues proposal. The delegates seemed to be divided into three camps – one for no dues increase, one for a dues increase of only $5 per year for the two years and one for the $7.50 increase proposed by the board. Delegates from a coalition of fourteen campus and professional chapters favoring the $5 increase met with representatives of the board and, after some stormy moments, it was decided the smaller increase would be offered as an amendment to the by-law change on the floor. Dornfeld opened the debate, calling attention to rising costs facing the Society and pointing out that other journalism organizations not only had higher dues than the Society of Professional Journalists, Sigma Delta Chi, but that those same organizations were considering raising dues further to meet inflationary pressures. He also pointed to the financial problems facing the younger professional members. "As the first reporter in line to become

president of this Society in more than forty years," Dornfeld told the delegates, "I am not here to do anything to price working journalists out of the market. They are the life blood of the Society. That is why we propose to phase the dues increase in over two years lest it be too much of a hardship on anyone at one time. I think this shows continued sensitivity on the part of our Society to the financial plight of our members. But of equal import is the question of just what we want this Society to be." Dornfeld said the Society would be able to get through the 1982-1983 fiscal year with a few cutbacks in program and services, but in shaping the following year's budget, he said, "We'll be faced with a much larger shortfall than we have been this year and the decisions will be much more painful. We'll have to be talking about such things as abandoning our efforts in Washington, severing our connection with our First Amendment attorney, and cutting back *The Quill* to six issues per year for lack of funds." Dornfeld applauded the compromise efforts by the delegates who offered the amendment as a method by which the needs of the Society could be met in the greater part along with those of a financial nature by young reporters, and he asked the delegates to support the compromise.

The debate continued for only fifteen minutes with the majority of speakers favoring the $5 increase for each of two years. When Novitz called for a decision, 179 votes were cast for the amendment, 114 against. On the amended main motion for a $5 increase in 1983 plus a $5 dues increase in 1984, Novitz ruled the "ayes" in a voice vote clearly carried the motion and the new dues structure was approved.

A MAJOR FUND DRIVE

As Novitz's term as president neared its end, incoming national president Dornfeld already had begun work on the most far-reaching goal set in 1981 – that of a major fund-raising drive. "We had been talking about fund-raising for a long time, but he [Novitz] had attempted to do it within the Society using past presidents, headquarters staff and the like. But we just didn't get anywhere," Dornfeld said. Tornabene agreed with earlier suggestions that there were two possible reasons for the minimum results. "First, newspeople are probably the worst possible group to try to raise money. They don't like to ask for money, they don't like to be in the role of salesman, and they don't want to appear to be beholden to anyone as journalists. Their whole psyche is totally opposite of those who must go out and ask for money," he said. "Second, members of the board over the years – all good people – had their own special projects. Some wanted to fund *The Quill*, some freedom of information instead of the magazine. Others preferred their own projects. So there were all kinds of fund-raising efforts with all kinds of quality of effort, none of which really paid off. This was the mentality which existed when I arrived, but the approach changed during Novitz's and Dornfeld's terms."

Boye, as part-time director of development, produced a report early in 1982 showing the most-promising possible foundations, and meetings were scheduled to approach those organizations with projects which it was hoped might be funded. But Dornfeld believed things were moving too slowly and had not waited for Boye's report. He had a feeling that perhaps another approach might be better. In late 1981, he had contacted Michael Washburn, a fund-raising consultant in New York City, to seek advice on the best approaches to a major fund drive. Washburn advised that persons inside the Society, although willing, probably did not have the expertise for such an effort. To have any real chance for success, the Society would be wise to hire a professional fund-raising organization, he told Dornfeld and Novitz.

Unable to convince the officers to move in this direction during the Novitz administration, Dornfeld waited until he became president in November 1982 to give it the high priority he believed it deserved. "It seemed to me that to be able raise the dollars we needed to fund our long-term projects in professional development and freedom of information and to provide the money needed to make *The Quill* what we wanted it to be, we needed to move beyond

depending on membership dues," Dornfeld said. "My fear was that we would venture into the fund-raising field in an unsophisticated and uncoordinated manner, and perhaps turn off or alienate media-related corporations and foundations that should be natural sources of funding." In mid-1982, Tornabene set up a meeting with the Ford Foundation in New York City to ask how the Society might go about receiving grants. "We found out fund-raising is a highly-sophisticated endeavor and that we didn't know how to go about doing it. But we became smarter," Tornabene said. Tornabene followed up by attending a full-day session on fund-raising in Chicago and learned there were opportunities to do it using experts and proper procedures.

Dornfeld and Tornabene received support from the officers in January 1983 to begin a full investigation of hiring a professional fund-raiser. Tornabene and Dornfeld contacted a Washington, DC consulting firm in February and were joined by Sutherland, Record and Dubin at a meeting March 10 in Chicago with two Chicago-based firms, seeking further input. On the basis of those sessions, Dornfeld knew it would take a strong financial commitment just to get started with a feasibility study. He wrote the members of the board March 15, 1983, stating, "When the board meets in Los Angeles, the officers hope to submit a proposal to hire a consultant who would help us develop plans for a major, three-to-five-year fund-raising campaign, test these plans among potential givers and begin implementing them....All of us are convinced that the Society never will succeed in tapping new sources of revenue – and financing the many important new programs on our wish list – without professional assistance."

At the May meeting in Los Angeles, Dornfeld provided more detail. "I told the board the cost would be $20,000 plus $5,000 in expenses for the first year just to do the study on what might be done. I said they should expect to spend as much as $100,000 per year for the next year and following years to raise the $3 to 5 million we hoped to bring in. The $100,000 per year would be for further work with consultants and potentially to hire a full-time director of development to work in our Chicago headquarters. And I told them if they didn't want to commit the $100,000 per year for as long as three years, don't even allocate the $25,000 to begin the study."

The board unanimously approved Dornfeld's plan and financial commitment. "I was absolutely stunned when we got the approval for the project," Dornfeld said. "It meant finally we were going to make the serious effort and back it up with the philosophy that you have to spend money to make money." Tornabene was delighted. The executive officer said the decision reached by the board was the perfect example of the "team" approach used by the officers since he had joined the headquarters staff. "The officers, in their way, have been humble, realizing that no one of them is the possessor of every good idea that is going to come out in their year as president," Tornabene said. "They may have come up with a good idea or have said something that led to a good idea, but they have used all of us as sounding boards to get something started. Once it starts, it takes off. The entire fund-raising program is an example of the right people nurturing an idea until the board unanimously approved the project."

Following the Los Angeles meeting, Dornfeld and his officers, along with Tornabene and Dubin, reviewed proposals and bids by several consulting firms, interviewed representatives of those firms and selected Charles Feldstein and Company, Inc. of Chicago as the fund-raising consultant to do the preliminary studies. In a June 8, 1983, letter to all of the Society's local and national leaders, Tornabene wrote, "The Society has embarked on an ambitious, vital project to help assure its future....The ability of the Society to continue its service in freedom of information, professional development, *The Quill*, and a score of other activities no longer is possible mainly through members' dues. While some members, foundations and media companies have directly supported the Society's goals with direct financial contributions, the economic well-being and future growth of the Society depend on developing alternate sources of

revenue." Meetings were scheduled with Feldstein and his associate, Charles Edwards, in June and July to get the project under way. Among the first topics discussed were efforts to raise the money from foundations and other sources for the feasibility study and perhaps additional dollars for a director of development so that Society program funds would not be jeopardized and services would not be cut back.

Dubin said those early meetings with the consultants changed the officers' attitudes about what kinds of money to seek. "For many years, the Society had been attempting to raise money to be placed in endowed accounts where the principal would remain intact and only the interest could be used for programs," he said. "We learned quickly that foundations and other grantors today don't want to place their capital funds in other organizations' endowed accounts. They would rather use the interest from their capital funds as grants and, at that, only for particular projects or programs which they are interested in supporting." A second lesson learned placed a temporary halt on the drive to build The Quill Endowment Fund. "We didn't want to go to a foundation and ask for money for *The Quill* today and six months later go back and ask for money for the larger fund-raising effort," Tornabene said. In addition, he said, a study was under way in 1983 to obtain a new Internal Revenue Service status for *The Quill* to make it tax exempt. This would allow tax-exempt foundations to make direct contributions to the magazine and individuals to be able to get a personal tax deduction for *Quill* contributions. "In effect," Tornabene said, "the Quill Endowment Fund drive was to be folded into the larger drive."

The project took shape further as the board, meeting in San Francisco in November 1983, approved a $2.4 million fund-raising drive to be completed in the next three years, including a $600,000 seventy-fifth anniversary special gifts campaign. That effort was aimed at soliciting gifts of from $1,000 to $3,000 from a limited group of Society members and smaller gifts from the total membership. In addition to the early $600,000 objective, the full campaign was aimed at raising as much as $800,000 in foundation grants, $750,000 from corporate and corporation foundations, and $250,000 in other gifts. The board and officers made it clear that all gifts would be solicited in line with the Society's Code of Ethics, meaning the funds would come from media-related sources. The board was encouraged by the fact that more than $50,000 in grants had been made to the Society and the Sigma Delta Chi Foundation in the 1982-1983 fiscal year, most of it going toward professional development and establishment of fellowships such as the Corrigan and Taishoff programs. In addition, the Robert R. McCormick Charitable Trust, affiliated with the Chicago *Tribune*, was approached to fund a new $100,000 visiting editor program. Under the proposed project, editors from strong daily newspapers would visit smaller newspapers as "editors in residence" to teach, critique, motivate and inspire local newspaper staff members and assist those newspapers to improve their products.

When Record became Society president in November 1983, he, along with Tornabene and the other officers, set about to organize a special national fund-raising committee. By mid-January 1984, fourteen media executives, ten of them past Society presidents, had agreed to work on the campaign. Robert U. Brown, president and editor of *Editor & Publisher*, agreed to serve as chairman and was joined by vice chairmen William J. Small, president of United Press International; Richard H. Leonard, editor, *The Milwaukee Journal*; Eugene S. Pulliam, publisher of the Indianapolis *Star* and *News*; Edward W. Scripps II, director, E.W. Scripps Co.; Morton Frank, chairman-emeritus, *Family Weekly*, and a cunsultant for CBS; John Chancellor, NBC News; Ralph Otwell, former editor, the Chicago *Sun-Times*; Lee Hills, editorial chairman-emeritus, Knight-Ridder Newspapers; George Watson, vice president, ABC News; John M. McClelland, Jr., chairman, Longview, Washington Publishing Co.; Staley McBrayer, News Citizen Newspapers; Robert M. White II, president and publisher, the Mexico,

Missouri *Ledger*; Frank Angelo, retired associate executive editor, the Detroit *Free Press*; John R. Finnegan, vice president and editor, St. Paul *Pioneer Press and Dispatch*, and Bill Kurtis, CBS News, New York.

While the designated use for the anticipated income from the three-year campaign were still being developed during 1984, it was clear that two priorities would be the hiring of a development director for the Society, and a director of continuing education.

With his primary 1983 long-range goal as president accomplished, Dornfeld turned to the year's program priorities, some of which he had already begun. In the area of professional development, the board approved a $5,000 appropriation to fund a pilot project whereby chapters would sponsor concentrated, educational workshops. Seven chapters received $700 grants during the spring of 1983 to produce those workshops and seminars. Dornfeld, the board and Legal Defense Fund chairman Mike Hammer campaigned for contributions to that fund from chapters and individual members, a project that raised more than $4,000 within weeks of its start.

Dornfeld also planted the seeds for a multi-year operation, "Project Watchdog," designed to get the Society involved more directly in promoting greater public awareness of the the watchdog role of the press and its importance in a free society. Slated to begin in 1984 and continue through 1987, the two hundredth anniversary of the United States Constitution, "Project Watchdog" would include an elaborate public relations campaign, headed by R.T. Kingman, public relations chief for General Motors, a longtime Society member, and involving prominent advertising and public relations executives across the nation. Using professionally-produced television, radio and print media spots, the campaign was to be aimed at the public to inform it that First Amendment rights are not the province of the press alone but were established for everyone and are worth protecting. Record said the project would be coordinated with the 1984 seventy-fifth anniversary celebration by the Society and would not only help in its freedom of information efforts, but would also help meet the goal of improving the image and visibility of the Society.

Dornfeld's final priority for the year was to seek to return women to membership on the national board of directors. He appointed Linda Kramer, a television assignment editor from Portland, Oregon, and Sutherland to a task force on women. Their work led to the election of two women – Rosanne Brooks and Georgiana Vines – to the board as directors of Region Two and Three in 1983, and laid the groundwork for expanding the role of women in leadership positions to an even greater extent.

In his report at the 1983 convention, Dornfeld noted that the Society still had image problems – internal and external – which remain to be solved. "SPJ,SDX is judged not on the basis of our national programs, but on what we are doing in Milwaukee or Muncie or Medford. Our image is only as good as that of our local chapters." He added that the Society must do a better job of communicating the changes made in the organization in recent years, especially the commitment of the Society to ethics in journalism and self-examination within the profession.

Membership, always a concern in terms of dollars and the representative nature of the Society, remained at a minimum-growth level. Had it not been for the work of the national membership committee, it would have declined in the first few years of the 1980's. The committee's direct-mail approach during 1982 and 1983 brought in more than 3,000 new members. Many of them continued to be news executives in both print and broadcast media, providing an additional benefit for the Society. With executives of more media as members, there was confidence that staff reporters and editors from those newspapers, radio and television stations would show an interest in the Society. The experiment of allowing the membership committee to use dollars generated from first-year dues of members it attracted to continue the national drive proved highly successful and was continued into 1984.

"THE YEAR OF CHALLENGE"

Phil Record had been laying the

groundwork for his presidential year since Graves named him chairman of the planning committee in 1980. Many of the goals he set for 1984 had already been determined long before he accepted the gavel from Dornfeld in San Francisco in November 1983. In fact, his administration's seven priorities – advancing higher ethical standards throughout the profession, seeking new sources of revenue, improving the image and visibility of the Society, continuing efforts to improve *The Quill*, increasing funding to continue the Society's leadership in freedom of information, expanding the Society's professional development programs, and expanding membership in the Society – were already underway as a continuation of programs Dornfeld had promoted. His selection of a theme for the year – "The Year of Challenge" – served to alert the membership that the goals set forth for the year would be achieved easily.

But Record was at work almost immediately on another important venture, one which had the potential of even greater long-range impact. In conversations with and letters to executives of other national media organization, including the American Newspaper Publishers Association, the American Society of Newspaper Editors, Radio Televison News Directors Association, Associated Press Managing Editors and the National Newspaper Association, he suggested a "mini-summit" might be appropriate to explore the organizations' current programs, priorities and plans to avoid duplication of effort. What Alf Goodykoontz, Phil Dessauer and Jean Otto had accomplished five years earlier which resulted in the First Amendment Congresses, might be useful again, Record thought. "I didn't know how the various organizations' executives and boards would react to such a session, but I was pleased when each responded favorably," he said.

Once again, SPJ,SDX was out front in linking the programs of each of the major national media organizations. Record, named to chair the session, called for a February 1, 1984, meeting in Washington, DC, to get the process of coordinating efforts underway. Although freedom of information was among the topics to be discussed, the

238

agenda was to be much broader. Record's January 17, 1984, letter to the participants called for exploration of programs aimed as improving higher professional standards; advancing continuing education; supporting journalism education, minority recruitment and education of minority students; raising funds; publishing various publications; and scheduling and planning conferences, conventions and meetings. "Obviously, such a coordinated effort had the potential of helping each organization in its planning," Record said. "We hoped the meeting would show when and where the groups can work together, can give each other a hand, rather than having each organization go off on its own in a similar task. And, of course, we knew it could have a major impact on the resources of each group."

The results, perhaps, were better than those for which even Record had hoped. The administrative officers of the groups found immediately that there were a substantial number of areas on which joint or cooperative efforts would benefit all involved. And they agreed February 1 that the meeting should be an annual event, sponsored by the Society. Among the specific decisions made was that SPJ,SDX would direct its efforts in minority recruitment and training toward assisting with the stronger minority programs sponsored by the American Society of Newspaper Editors. In another area, the Society agreed to assist the National Newspaper Association, and to work toward providing Society-sponsored professional development programs during the NNA national conventions. SPJ,SDX efforts in supplying continuing freedom of information alerts to members of the National Council of Editorial Writers was given a priority and the NNA agreed to disseminate those alerts to nearly 6,000 smaller newspapers affiliated with the NNA. With another mini-summit planned for January 1985, the heretofore independently operating national journalism organizations were on their way toward another new venture in cross-organization cooperation.

In October 1983, various representatives of American media had severely criticized the Reagan administration for its news blackout of the invasion of Grenada, an island under Marxist rule in the Caribbean Sea. Efforts to coordinate media challenges of what SPJ,SDX First Amendment Counsel Bruce Sanford called "a quantum leap in the Reagan administration's program of information control," seemed to have settled on a newspaper-oriented task force. When Record was asked to participate in the task force's work, he offered to do so, but only if the broadcast media were included. "I could not, in good conscience, have been a signatory to any document which left half of the media on the sidelines and forced those newsmen and women to come up with their own position paper," he said. "In addition, it could have been disastrous to media's need to be together in this fight, had the two groups taken different or opposing views on the significance of the news blackout in Grenada." Joined by several newsmen and the wire services, Record was able to convince the organizers of the task force to include representatives of all media in the final makeup of the group. The result was a strong report which carried the approval of all segments of the media in the United States. "It was a perfect example of how well we can work together if we simply remember we are all fighting for the same principles," Record said.

The Society, joined by the Radio-Television News Directors Association, the American Federation of Radio and Television Artists, and the Newspaper Guild, made another joint-media presentation on FOI matters February 2, 1984. On behalf of the four groups, Record presented Sen. Patrick Leahy, of Vermont, and Rep. Glenn English, of Oklahoma, with petitions bearing the signatures of 6,000 citizens, calling on Congress to keep the federal Freedom of Information Act strong and to resist attempts by the CIA, the FBI and other government and private interests to weaken the law. Upon receiving the petitions, Leahy praised the journalism organizations and encouraged them to continue their efforts on behalf of freedom of information. The process of maintaining the free flow of information is not a conservative or liberal issue, he said. It must be an issue addressed by those of all political persuasions.

239

Until Record became national president, he had remained chair of the planning committee which turned its attention in 1983 to the seventy-fifth anniversary celebration. The diamond jubilee's activities began early in 1984 and culminated in November when the convention delegates assembled in Indianapolis and returned to the Society's birthplace at DePauw University in Greencastle, Indiana. One of the earliest seventy-fifth anniversary projects was the distribution of a special postage meter stamp to media outlets across the nation. The stamp's impression, which was to be used on mail sent by newspapers, radio and television stations, carried the words, "SPJ,SDX: 75 Years of Service to the Profession." In addition, a resolution presented in San Francisco called for every chapter to cite an individual outside the Society for outstanding work in the freedom of information battle. The award, which, it was suggested, might be named in honor of James Madison, was presented on or near national Freedom of Information Day, March 16.

To attract national attention to the Society's anniversary, Record said application had been made to sponsor issuance of a postage stamp by the U.S. Postal Service. "We were encouraged by Postmaster General William Bolger that the Postal Service would be willing to unveil the design for a stamp honoring a free and independent press in America during planned convention ceremonies at Greencastle, November 16," Record said in February 1984.

Other major seventy-fifth anniversary projects included the April 1984 issue of *The Quill*, which carried an article marking the founding date of the Society – April 17, 1909. *The Quill's* November 1984 issue devoted itself in the main to the seventy-fifth anniversary celebration. Past president Otto coordinated an effort to have past presidents and Wells Memorial Key winners speak to a campus or professional chapter during 1984. In addition, those persons were honored at the 1984 convention in Indianapolis. Seizing on an idea by executive officer Tornabene, Record invited several hundred print and broadcast media executives and luminaries to write letters regarding "What a Free Press

Means to America." He negotiated a grant from Capital Cities Communications to print and distribute a special booklet containing the letters to schools and libraries across the nation during the year. The original letters were to have been bound and presented to DePauw University for its new Hall of Fame.

During the convention, delegates were transported to Greencastle for ceremonies at DePauw University's East College where the idea of the fraternity was conceived. On that day, a new "Hall of Fame" was unveiled with a plaque containing the names of 70 previous Wells Key winners plus five new ones. Members saw the founding site as described in Bostrom's book, which each had received as a part of the registration packet.

Sadness pervaded the Society's leadership when it was learned that Region Four director Michael Kelly died January 28, 1984, in Cleveland, Ohio. He was appointed to a one-year term to represent Michigan, Ohio, Western Pennsylvania, and West Virginia on the board in 1979 when David Lieberth resigned to devote full-time to his law practice. Kelly was elected to a three-year term in 1980. He was the first board member to die in office since national president Chester Wells died September 1, 1913. Only two other Sigma Delta Chi officials died while in office in the organization – part-time *Quill* editors Ralph Peters, August 30, 1944, and Carl Kesler, July 2, 1956. Kelly was a consciencious regional director, making himself available whenever he was needed to campus and professional chapters in his four-state area. He helped establish campus chapters at at least three universities and was constantly on the alert, providing needed inspiration to chapters which were on a down cycle. Society president Record said, "Mike was a friendly, thoughtful and helpful member of the national board. He was deliberate in his consideration of national issues and in key decisions, often challenged us, making us defend our positions, thereby helping us improve our service to the members. His death was a shock and we feel the loss deeply." A red-haired Irishman, a designation he relished, his most penetrating questions during board meetings focused on issues related to finance. He had been business editor of the Cleveland *Plain Dealer* and was its assistant city editor at the time of his death. The board had not yet appointed a successor for Kelly as Region Four director at the time this book went to press. He had just been re-elected to a second three-year term in November 1983.

As the seventy-fifth anniversary celebration approached, Tornabene reported that by early 1984, the Society had 142 professional chapters and 184 campus chapters. Efforts to clean up the membership roles and give "active membership" a more realistic meaning continued into 1984. Members were kept on the active roles for only one year after the year in which they last paid national dues. Tornabene told to board in a January 13 memo, "We are now using 24,000 to describe the number of members of the society." His figures included 18,451 professional members (of which 12,278 were men and 6,173 were women) and 3,576 student members (of which 1,149 were men and 2,427 were women).

Continuity: Past, Present, & Future

The first three units of this book have been devoted to major events in the Society's history. While *The Quill*, the professional and campus chapters, and the people who have served largely in non-official capacities for the Society have been discussed from time to time thus far, each of these topics must be treated as an entity in and of itself.

Certainly *The Quill* has been the strongest and most frequently used tool for communication within and without the Society. Each executive officer and most SPJ,SDX presidents have considered it the single, most important continuing project of the Society.

The campus chapters – from which the Society grew – and the professional chapters that were their offsprings have been and are the life blood of the Society. No other professional journalism organization in the world has such an extensive, grass-roots structure of local chapters. Their contributions to the national body and to the profession have had a major impact on the viability of American journalism today.

Finally, those persons who have served the Society without the spotlight of publicity, have earned a special place in its history and, thus, in this volume.

CHAPTER 13

███████████

The Evolution of *The Quill*

The birth of *The Quill* as a formal, fraternity publication in 1912 at Sigma Delta Chi's first convention was marked by optimism, first that the organization could produce a magazine and second, that the $1 per member assessment would pay the costs of an anticipated six issues per year. Although neither would prove to be true, *The Quill* was launched by its first editor Frank Pennell with an issue dated December 1912 but not circulated until February 1913. Among the series of editorials which appeared in that first twenty-page, six-by-nine inch magazine was one which stated, "It is to be expected that editors of the standard magazines and periodicals throughout this country will go green with jealousy at the appearance of a promising stranger in their field. Though we do not for a moment anticipate bouquets over this initial issue of the newcomer, *The Quill*, we are certain of its success in the future." Seventy-two volumes later, in 1984, *The Quill* had fulfilled that promise of success, although whether other magazines are "green with jealousy" certainly is questionable.

A reading of Clayton's *Fifty Years for Freedom*, covering the development of *The Quill* from 1912 through 1959, followed by a study of these pages, will demonstrate that the magazine has gone through thick and thin quite literally. Whether one talks about the magazine's financial stability, its number of pages, the quality and quantity of its editorial content or the volume of advertising carried, *The Quill's* prosperous and lean years are easily identified. The two constants have been the dedication of the leadership and members of the organization to continue its publication and the devotion of its fifteen editors toward producing the best possible product.

THE BEGINNING

Established on the philosophy that it would carry chapter news and ideas along with articles and opinion pieces, *The Quill* was published only three times during its first year on a budget of $20 per issue. Within three years, the magazine had had three editors – Pennell, Pike Johnson and Carl Getz – all of whom produced issues in their spare time and incurred a total debt of

Clarence O. Schlaver, executive editor of *The Quill* from 1961-1971, at his desk at national headquarters, 35 East Wacker Drive in Chicago. Known as "C.O.," Schlaver was the first full-time editor of the magazine and the first to manage *The Quill* from Society headquarters in Chicago. His first issue as editor was September 1961.

more than $200. Lee A White, editor from 1915 through 1920, began his tenure by borrowing $150 to keep the magazine going, but, by the time he turned the editorship over to professor Frank Martin at the University of Missouri in 1920, he had built a reserve of $825 despite the fact that publication costs had reached $200 per issue. Martin found raising funds and the time it took to produce *The Quill* more than he could handle. When Chester Cleveland became editor in 1922, the convention delegates decided to include a salary of $600 per year for the editor.

A year later, at the prodding of national president Ward Neff, *The Quill* was given some financial stability with the establishment of what would be called The Quill Endowment Fund. To do so, the initiation fee for membership was raised substantially with the greater part of those fees going toward the fund. The Quill Endowment Fund remained a permanent part of the fiscal support for the magazine and in 1984 had reached nearly $250,000. During all of that time, only the interest drawn on the fund was used to operate *The Quill*. Mark L. Haas became editor in 1925 and determined to make the magazine a professional publication rather than a fraternity organ comprised, as it had been, of clipped matter taken from other publications or from speeches. Although he was not able to pay fees to contributors and had little control on what might come in or when it would arrive, Haas was able to bring fresh editorial content to the magazine. Haas' tenure as editor lasted only one year, but at its close the magazine produced its largest issue to date – 70 pages – devoted entirely to Mitchell Charnley's "History of Sigma Delta Chi." Professor Lawrence Murphy of the University of Illinois took the editorial reins of the magazine from 1926-1928 and was followed by Franklin Reck, who remained as editor through 1930. Under Reck's leadership and that of his managing editor, Martin A. Klaver, the magazine made an important step forward in January 1930, becoming a monthly publication.

Ralph L. Peters, a rewrite man for the Detroit *News*, became interested in *The Quill* in 1930, took over as acting editor in the fall, and assumed the editorship in January 1931. Peters' fourteen years as editor were not only the longest served by any editor thus far in the history of the Society, but he took the magazine to new heights of acceptance and respect. Although he worked on the magazine only in his spare time, as each of the previous men, and received only $50 per issue in payment, Peters added to the dimension of the magazine in every respect. Clayton's history says it best: "It is not a reflection on any of his predecessors to say that under Ralph Peters *The Quill* became of age and attained the stature that won it recognition as one of the outstanding profesional publications in journalism. He set an example of editorial enterprise and judgment that has not been surpassed [through 1959]. Shortly after taking over, he added 'The Book Beat' and

Charles C. Clayton (center), editor of *The Quill* from 1956-1961, was honored at a testimonial dinner in Carbondale, Illinois, August 1, 1970. Clayton, the last part-time editor of the magazine, was photographed with (from left) Tom Phillips, president of the Southern Illinois professional chapter; Frank Angelo, 1969-1970 Society president; Bill Kong, Region Seven director; and Darrell Aherin, president of the Southern Illinois University campus chapter.

secured Charnley to conduct it. He added a column of his own entitled 'After Deadline' by Pete, in addition to his own editorials. He brightened up the format with larger heads and began to use magazine makeup techinques. In his first year, he widened the scope to include discussions of radio news writing, and with headquarters' approach to Meredith Publishing Company for free typographical design help, a new cover design and new type style were brought out. During the 1930's, many nationally-known bylines appeared in *The Quill.*" Revenue from advertising finally began to make a significant contribution to *The Quill* in the 1930's. Executive director James Kiper, in 1934, conducted a survey of *The Quill's* subscribers to tabulate occupations, buying habits and other information for advertisers. The depression discouraged immediate results, but, by 1942, advertising revenue began to come in again.

In 1943, Peters explained in his July-August issue that the picture was bleak.

Under wartime conditons, income from The Quill Endowment Fund dwindled and initiations of new members to the fraternity dropped to almost zero. Responding to the apparent crisis, the executive council agreed to cut back to a bi-monthly publication, drop color from the cover and reduce the size of the magazine to sixteen pages. In the 1930's and early 1940's, the average size of *The Quill* had been twenty pages. Peters died August 30, 1944, and *The Quill* was without a permanent editor until July 1945. Willard R. Smith, former executive director Albert Bates and Carl R. Kesler took over as interim editors until Kesler, a staff member on the Chicago *Daily News*, accepted the position. The 1946 national convention in Chicago, the first after the war, voted to resume monthly publication of *The Quill* and, in January 1947, it returned to that publication schedule, although financial restrictions kept down the number of pages in each issue for some time. Beginning in 1950, advertising revenue increased, and the

Charles F. Long, editor of *The Quill* from 1971-1980. Long joined the headquarters staff January 2, 1967, as an administrative/editorial assistant, spending only part time on the magazine. Named news editor of *The Quill* during 1969, he was appointed editor in September 1971.

convention issue that year contained sixty-four pages with substantial advertising. Kesler produced the magazine almost singlehandedly and had the double burden of serving both as editor of *The Quill* and as national president of the fraternity in 1949-1950. He turned to special issues to attract advertisers, producing one issue on radio and television news, another on industrial publications and another on the City of Chicago. He started an annual awards issue in June of each year, publicizing the winners of the Distinguished Service Awards, which attracted advertising from the media whose reporters and photographers received medallions. To offset criticism that *The Quill* was strictly a fraternity magazine, Kesler restricted Sigma Delta Chi "news" to the back of the magazine. And one of his outstanding contributions were his editorials, which Clayton called "some of the finest and most thoughtful writing in journalism." Kesler died at his desk at the *Daily News* July 2,

1956.

Clayton, who had been on the staff of the St. Louis *Globe-Democrat* for thirty years, had recently gone to Southern Illinois University as a visiting professor of journalism and completed the August 1956 issue for Kesler. Upon publication of that issue, Clayton was named editor of the magazine, returning the editorial offices of *The Quill* to the college campus for the first time since 1926. The business side remained in Chicago, where the executive director had been in charge of advertising sales since Bates had held that job. Circulation was also handled in Chicago by the executive director and the headquarters staff. Shortly after Clayton took over as editor, the executive council had determined the fraternity was on a "death trend" and Sigma Delta Chi had begun to agonize its way toward the McKinsey Report and total reorganization. Clayton continued Kesler's practice of writing one or more editorials per issue, but "I agreed that as long as I was editor of *The Quill*, I wouldn't take sides on those controversies," Clayton recalls. He believed the editorials were an important part of the magazine's content and said he regretted the practice was dropped in later years. "My editorials were generally accepted as the position of *The Quill* but not that of the Society, and I never became involved editorially in any internal matter," he said. He used editorial cartoons on freedom of the press and other journalistic issues done by some of the most prestigious cartoonists of the day. His philosophy for the magazine directed him to place an emphasis on news of executive council and chapter activities. He solicited articles on assigned topics from a variety of writers although able to pay them nothing. "We had an excellent group of writers and covered the issues of the day pretty well," he said. Although I didn't seek the recognition in any way, *The Quill* of those years was quoted more often in *The Congressional Record* than at any time before or since."

Clayton handled all the editorial duties from his home in Carbondale, Illinois. "Executive director Victor Bluedorn would send the advertising to be run down to me, and I would do the layout of the entire

Naomi Donson, the first woman named editor of *The Quill*, served in that capacity from September 1981 through August 1982. During her tenure, Donson helped to stabilize the magazine's fiscal condition, arranging, along with Hurst and *Quill* general manager, Roger Boye, for new typesetting and printing contracts.

magazine," he recalls. The copy was mailed to The Ovid Bell Press in Fulton, Missouri, and Clayton took pride in the fact that although the operation was run from three cities, he was able to get the magazine out on deadline nearly every month in his five years as editor. Among those issues, Clayton produced the largest single issue in the magazine's history to date – 132 pages – in November 1959 for the celebration of the fraternity's golden anniversary. "We had a great deal of advertising in that issue and I believe that Bluedorn got a little greedy," Clayton said. Bluedorn received a commission on all advertising sold for *The Quill*. "I tried to warn Vic about it, but he didn't listen and I think the advertising in that issue may have been more directly involved in his termination than anything

else." As part of the entire reorganizational effort, advertising commissions were removed as part of the salary benefits for the executive officer. Bluedorn was fired May 20, 1960. During the next few months, Arpan, Barnum and Pearl Luttrell handled the advertising and circulation for *The Quill* while Clayton continued to take care of the editorial content at a salary of $125 per issue. The magazine reached more than the 13,000 active members of the Society, and one could find an average of thirty-two pages in each issue with as many as forty-eight to fifty-six pages in the awards and convention issues.

SCHLAVER BECOMES EXECUTIVE EDITOR

The McKinsey Report, adopted by the 1960 national convention in New York City, had recommended that the editorship for *The Quill* be made a full-time, professional staff position housed at the national headquarters. As noted earlier, Clayton opposed the move vigorously and, when it was assured, he was committed to accept a Fulbright grant to lecture in journalism in Formosa. Thus, he did not apply for the position but said, "I had no interest in moving to Chicago nor in taking on the job full-time, something that I thought was unnecessary and too expensive." Clayton continued as editor through the August 1961 issue. *The Quill* reorganization committee, headed by Sidney R. Bernstein of *Advertising Age* in Chicago, selected Clarence O. Schlaver as the first executive editor for the magazine in June 1961. Schlaver, a veteran newspaper and magazine editor from Mount Prospect, Illinois, assumed his duties July 1 and was responsible for the September 1961 issue. For the first time in the organization's history, all aspects of *The Quill* were handled at the national headquarters in Chicago. With the McKinsey Report's program for *The Quill* in force, Schlaver was given responsibility for the editorial and advertising side of the magazine, both of which he enjoyed. Looking back to Schlaver's ten years as editor, Hurst characterized his colleague as one of the hardest-working and most totally-dedicated members he had known. Hurst said of Schlaver, "He was a man of great enterprise, an experienced newspaperman, and a capable editor. He had a legion of friends around the country, people he could call on as writers and for article ideas. He was a whirlwind worker. He had a cluttered desk and an ever-burning pipe of tobacco. He produced some of the largest issues of *The Quill* ever assembled – sixty, eighty, even 100 pages. He was an eminently fine individual and a professional journalist in every way. He did noble service for the Society during his years as editor."

Schlaver, known to his colleagues as "C.O.," produced those magazines from 1961 through 1966 primarily as a one-man operation. The magazine's masthead carried the names of Agee or Hurst as business manager through July 1962, with Clayton as advisory editor and Pearl Luttrell as circulation manager. With the June issue that year, Schlaver named professor Edmund Arnold of Syracuse University and Emmett Peter, Jr., editor of *The Daily Commercial* of Leesburg, Florida, as associate editors to provide counsel and critiques of the magazine. Hurst's title as executive officer replaced the business manager designation on the masthead in August 1962, a title which remained until Hurst was named publisher by the board, effective with the December 1978 issue.

Schlaver altered the "look" of the magazine, including a new cover design and interior section headings, upon taking charge. But, with the exception of his own "The Editor's Column Right" or "Column Write" as it became known in mid-1964, and the addition of some new monthly features, the content of the magazine followed generally the same pattern as it had under Clayton. The February 1962 cover article was a highly-popular Valentine Day essay by past-president Walter Humphrey. Titled, "A Newspaperman's Love Affair," the previous published *Quill* feature had been widely distributed by the Society in reprint form. Among Schlaver's early accomplishments was a 108-page issue of November 1962 marking the fiftieth anniversary of the first publication of *The Quill*. Through the early 1960's, growth in

Society membership and a steady stream of advertising dollars allowed Schlaver to keep the magazine at from thirty-two to forty pages or more, with the annual June awards issues and the semi-annual careers issues from seventy to ninety pages. Chapter news, still kept in the back of the book, occupied an important place with from six to ten pages per month devoted to national board meetings, along with stories and illustrations provided by chapers covering their meetings, initiations, charterings and special events. Capsule items about recent news events concerning journalism and the media, which became known as "For the Record," began to appear regularly as well. In September 1962, the printing contract was moved from Ovid Bell Press in Fulton, Missouri, to Wayside Press in Mendota, Illinois, close enough so that the headquarters-based staff could work directly with the printer on production. Schlaver made the trip each month to make final editorial changes.

The work load on *The Quill* and within the executive officer's area had grown to the extent that, early in 1966, the board agreed to expand the headquarters staff to allow for a person to spend half-time as an editorial assistant for the magazine and half-time as an administrative assistant to Hurst. Charles F. Long, a 28-year-old University of Oklahoma graduate with newspaper, broadcasting and magazine experience, had been a member of the Society since 1960 and had been an at-large member keeping up with Sigma Delta Chi activities through *The Quill*. He had been helping edit *Sooner* magazine and serving as an administrative assistant to the executive secretary of the University of Oklahoma Alumni Association when he was granted a nine-month leave to research and write a history of the University of Oklahoma. "I got so deeply involved in that," Long recalls, "that I began to lose interest in the former position and decided that, when I completed that project, I was going to look around to see what other career opportunities were available." Long was attracted by an advertisement in the July 1966 *Quill* inviting applications for the new position. The ad read, "Wanted: To join Sigma Delta Chi headquarters staff in Chicago this fall...Energetic young man with journalism degree and two-to-three-years' experience in news-editorial work plus administrative ability. To assist on *Quill* magazine editorial and production work, news releases, planning of regional and national meetings, correspondence and variety of other duties." Essentially, the job was parallel to the work Long had been doing at the University of Oklahoma. Although Long and his wife and two children had just moved into a new home in Norman, when the opportunity came to join the Sigma Delta Chi staff beginning on January 2, 1967, "I was eager to go. I looked forward to moving to the big city and expanding my horizons." The trip to Illinois was anything but pleasant as the family with one very ill child drove through blinding snowstorms in time for the biggest snowfall in the history of Chicago. "We lived out of a motel for a while and everything was shut down. I remember walking a mile to get powdered milk for the baby because even the milk trucks couldn't get through," Long remembers. "To counter all of that, the people in the headquarters office and Ralph Otwell at the *Sun-Times* were just tremendous. They all looked out for my welfare and that of my family."

Long's new duties on the job represented an experiment at headquarters. Hurst and Schlaver had not had help before and while they were eager to use their new assistant, they weren't sure in the beginning just what Long would do. "The nature of the job meant that it was picking up loose ends, writing letters and doing whatever Russ and C.O. needed to get done," Long said. "But it was an educational experience for me for it gave me the opportunity to learn what the Society was all about and meet a great many people by letter and phone much faster than I might have done otherwise. The dual job wasn't something I wanted to do for very long, for my interests were with the magazine. I was assigned half-time duties on each side, but I kept edging toward the editorial side of the magazine every time I could." The administrative assistant position, however, kept Long busy, especially prior to and during the twice-a-year national board meetings when he had the unenviable job of

Ron Dorfman became the fifteenth editor of *The Quill* in the magazine's seventy-year history, assuming the post November 1, 1982. A writer and editor with newspaper and magazine experience before joining the magazine, Dorfman was a 1963 political science graduate from the University of Chicago.

keeping the board minutes. During conventions, he covered proceedings and speakers for *The Quill*. "Those were tough duties because when the convention was over you had to return to Chicago and do both jobs at the same time," he said. "We had to get the post-convention work finished up and minutes sent out to the board. All the while we were on deadline for the next issue of *The Quill*."

Long was promoted to news editor of the magazine in June 1969, but he retained his split role as half-time administrative assistant to Hurst. Late that year, Hurst was hospitalized and placed in traction for a back problem and could not attend the 1969 national convention in San Diego. Long, who would be attending only his third national convention, was forced into the role of handling all the administrative duties at the officers' meeting and board meetings before the convention and tasks during the convention itself. "Pearl Luttrell was a great help at that convention. She was the only real continuity we had and was a major reason for the convention's success from a logistical standpoint." Long and president Arthur stayed in touch with Hurst by telephone at points during the convention. But Arthur pointed to Long's work in particular. "Long did a magnificent job for Hurst and for me there in San Diego. There were so many pressures, what with the votes on the admission of women and the name change. And with the Tom Forcade incident, the problems with the underground press, the Agnew speech in Des Moines and all, we were going in all directions at once."

Forcade was editor of the Underground Press Syndicate. Upon being invited to participate on a panel on the underground press, he showed up in San Diego and was arrested and jailed on charges of desecrating the American flag by wearing a part of it on his hat. Arthur, treasurer Guy Ryan and convention co-chairman Gene Gregston, managing editor of the San Diego *Evening Tribune*, along with Long, arranged to have Forcade released from custody on bail, but he was late in arriving for the panel. He went to the panel table, picked up a water glass and hurled it in the general direction of the press table, narrowly missing 81-year-old past SDX president Luther Huston, who was covering the convention for *Editor & Publisher*. Forcade accused Sigma Delta Chi of having had him arrested, for which he later apologized to Arthur. But Long and Forcade clashed the following spring at a regional conference in Chapel Hill, on the University of North Carolina campus, when Forcade again accused Sigma Delta Chi of having had him arrested in San Diego. Long challenged the statement from the floor, telling the delegates what had really happened, and demanding that Forcade provide documentation for his charges. Forcade refused to respond to Long except to say, "That's bull!," to which one of the conference delegates said, "There's your answer, Charlie."

On Wednesday of convention week, Vice President Spiro Agnew gave his famous anti-press speech in Des Moines, Iowa. Hurst remembers that from his hospital bed at about 10:30 pm he telephoned Arthur, calling him away from dinner that night to notify him by telephone of the Agnew speech and suggesting the Society probably ought to respond officially in some way. Long recalls the incident as one in which he, so early in his Sigma Delta Chi career, was called upon to be part of a major decision. "There I was in Bill Arthur's room at the El Cortez Hotel acting in this role representing Russ Hurst, along with several of the officers, trying to determine what the Society should say in response to Mr. Agnew. We did draft a statement, but that, along with everything else that happened in San Diego, was an experience I won't forget. I don't know how we pulled it off."

Long said he was fortunate to have been able to work with Schlaver. "He was a rolled-up-sleeves kind of man who had a marvelous personality and disposition, but his face would turn bright red when he was angry about something," he said. "C.O. was fascinated with the production side of the magazine, and I learned a great deal from him in that area. He was committed to his total role and loved the business and advertising sides as much or more, I think, as he enjoyed editing the magazine." Hurst was responsible for the fiscal integrity of the magazine but took an interest in the editorial side as well. He was a journalist at heart and, though he didn't interfere with Schlaver or Long on the editorial decisions, he offered his expertise and help. "Schlaver, Long and I had a very close working relationship. It was almost impossible for anyone to put out a magazine singlehanded for what was the most critical audience in the world, an audience of journalists," Hurst said. "It was a team effort." The three of them would discuss article ideas, and talk about potential authors, and all were scouting constantly for material for *The Quill*. However, a major portion of the manuscripts from 1967 through mid-1971 which were used in the magazine, Long said, were sent in on speculation from authors hoping to be published in *The Quill*. No fees were paid authors; the reward was in being published in such a prestigious magazine. Long recalls

Hurst was especially adept at reading proofs for that magazine, and that Hurst enjoyed it. "Russ was the only other person through the years [except Agee] who had come from a newspaper background, and I appreciated his willingness to give those galleys the extra reading they needed," he said.

Schlaver told the board he had decided to leave *The Quill* in June 1971 to become editor of the *American Press*, a magazine for newspaper management published in Wilmette, Illinois. The June issue of the magazine carried the announcement with president Chandler's accolade, "He has built *The Quill* into a truly excellent professional publication. The depth and bredth of the magazine's offerings over the past decade are a tribute to his skills and dedication." Schlaver died nine years later, February 12, 1980, at age 74.

LONG'S DECADE BEGINS

Long was named acting editor of the magazine and Otwell was selected to chair the search committee for a new, permanent editor. "I let Russ know immediately that I was interested in becoming editor of the magazine," Long remembers. "Russ told me he was pleased that I wanted to be considered, and he notified Ralph and Bob of my interest. I thought I had an inside track for the job because I had been with the magazine for more than four years and I would have the opportunity to show what I could do for the several issues I'd be producing as acting editor while the committee did its work." His own determination and the chance of history allowed him to demonstrate his writing skills and to put out a magazine on "the" hot journalism issues of the day under extreme deadline pressures. Long's first issue, July 1971, carried his byline on a story about editorial cartoonist Paul Conrad of the Los Angeles *Times*, who had just won his third Distinguished Service Award from the Society in May of that year. But it was the August issue that caught the eye of the search committee and brought Long and *The Quill* wide praise. CBS News had produced a documentary, "The Selling of the Pentagon," which, while it won nearly every journalistic prize in its field, brought with it

the wrath of the Nixon administration and a $12 million libel suit by May of 1971. While court and congressional battles over that documentary were in progress, *The New York Times* on June 13 published a summary of a top-secret government study, "A History of U.S. Decision Making Process on Vietnam Policy," to be known as "The Pentagon Papers." The decision of the U.S. Supreme Court in "The Pentagon Papers" case came June 30, while the congressional hearings on the CBS documentary continued into early July. "In addition to my piece on Paul Conrad, I had used up just about all of the other articles on hand for the July issue and I determined then and there that I was going to go out after writers to do articles for me rather than waiting for them to come in," Long said. "I saw those free press issues as perfect for us immediately, but I knew we'd have to get it out in a hurry." Hurst suggested that Jack Landau, an attorney and journalist who had won a Distinguished Service Award earlier, do the play-by-play and legal analysis article on "The Pentagon Papers," and recommended that J. Edward Gerald, a professor at the University of Minnesota, look at the case from a broader perspective. Long called each and was able to persuade them to contribute their services, and he took on the job of reviewing the controversy surrounding the CBS "Selling of the Pentagon" case in Congress. The August issue of *The Quill* carried each of the three articles and a theme cover prepared by Robert Tobaison with a blue pentagon surrounding the CBS "eye" and *The New York Times* logo outside each of the pentagon's five sides.

The September issue, Long's third as acting editor, concentrated on "The New Journalism," with articles by David McHam, then of Baylor University, and George Bailey of the University of Wisconsin at Milwaukee. McHam profiled journalists Tom Wolfe, Norman Mailer and Gay Talese as the "authentic" new journalists, while Bailey edited a debate between WBBM Radio commentator John Madigan and Northwestern University professor Curtis MacDougall over personal involvement in news by journalists.

Otwell and Chandler were impressed

with Long's work during the summer of 1971, and, when the search committee unanimously selected Long as its choice as permanent editor, Chandler announced the decision in the September issue of *The Quill*.

Hurst selected Roger C. Boye to take on Long's former role of administrative assistant to the executive officer and news editor of *The Quill*. Chandler said later, "Strange as it may seem, the editorship of *The Quill* was not that attractive as a job. The salary was low for what we demanded in ability from an editor in comparison to what a good newspaper reporter was getting. The magazine had to operate with almost no budget and with little prospect that any influx of money would be provided." But Long was optimistic. "If we were going to be a magazine for journalists, I wanted *The Quill* to be the best-written magazine it possibly could be," he said. "I wanted it to look graphically as good as it could be. If we were going to be talking about good writing, editing and layout, we had to be exemplary in the field. I realized we had only this modest budget, but I kept thinking, 'Wait until we get this thing rolling. We'll have so much advertising and budget that we'll have pages we won't know what to do with.'"

Long was an avid reader and his nearly five years with the national headquarters had provided opportunities to develop contacts with potential authors. Hurst believed that the contributed services of Sigma Delta Chi members as authors had been a successful way to do things, but Long went to the 1971 Washington, DC convention determined to ask the board for money for honoraria for his prospective writers. "I agreed with Russ to a point, but, at the same time, I thought no one would do it, and do the kind of job I wanted to see done, unless we could offer them something in the way of money," Long said. "Ralph [Otwell] and Bob [Chandler] beat me to the punch and told me and the board they had already agreed to add money for honoraria to *The Quill* budget for the first time."

Wearing two hats, directing both the editorial side and the advertising side of the magazine, was another matter for Long. "I told Russ, Bob and Ralph that I planned to be an editorial-type person and that I was not going to pursue advertising aggressively. As an editor, I did not think that was the proper thing to do. I told them I would not do it under any circumstances." The early 1970's were a prosperous time and advertising came in on a regular basis – not enough to expand the operation – but enough to stay alive. But when the beginning of the recession of the mid-1970's hit and advertising began to drop off dramatically, Long knew someone had to handle the advertising. Hurst and Long thought they had an answer in 1973 when they proposed that a part-time advertising representative be hired on a commission basis to solicit advertising for *The Quill*. Tom Cutler, an enthusiastic salesman whose offices were just a block from headquarters, was retained. "I felt great about that," Long said. "I thought it was a step in the right direction. We had nowhere to go but up and I was optimistic." *The Quill* never did see as much advertising income as had been hoped for during the seven years Cutler was on the job as advertising representative. In fact, Long said, "I had to interrupt my editorial work on many occasions to answer telephone calls inquiring about advertising and do what I thought Cutler should have been doing. I didn't go out and sell, but to a great extent, I ended up doing much of what I had said I did not want to do in handling advertising."

The Quill received a major face-lift in June 1973, with Long introducing a new cover design to make the magazine more distinctive and contemporary and he refined the photographic-oriented design with line illustrations by free-lance artist James Campbell, who also designed the new cover logo. Long and Campbell redesigned most of the sections of the magazine, from the table of contents to the book reviews, assigning some new titles and modifying others. In October of that year, Halina Czerniejewski replaced Boye as Hurst's administrative assistant and news editor for *The Quill*. Boye had joined the faculty of the Medill School of Journalism at Northwestern University. A twenty-three-year old honor graduate of Ohio University, Czerniejewski came to Sigma Delta Chi from a job as a staff writer for the Associated Press in Columbus, Ohio. The magazine from 1971 through 1974 usually contained as many as forty pages per issue, with a few at thirty-two pages and special issues still running to sixty and more.

FINANCIAL PROBLEMS FOR *THE QUILL*

Long's dream, however, for an expanded magazine with enough dollars to do the job he wanted to do received a double blow by 1974. A general recession had caused advertising linage to begin to drop, and inflation had begun to eat away at any working margin Long and Hurst had been able to maintain. The normal issue thereafter dropped more often to thirty-two pages, with only the awards and convention issues exceeding that in total pages. The Society's regular operating budget began to feel the effects of the same inflationary pressures, leaving no opportunity for part of its budget to be transferred to *The Quill*. This left Long with the dilemma of having to decide on quality in content versus quantity in pages or number of issues. Long opted quickly for what he hoped would be quality.

A first step to try to balance the fiscal problems was to produce eleven issues, combining the July-August 1975 issues into one magazine. That solved the problem only temporarily, because, in addition to the inflation factor, the Society (and primarily *The Quill*) was impacted by a slow-down in the rate of induction of new members. The surge of membership growth with the inclusion of women had peaked and the years of ten percent growth for the Society were over. Long wrestled continually with the problem of the section on news of the Society and its chapters. He wanted to address journalistic issues in the main and, while the chapter news was important, the space problems became evident more and more. "Russ did what he could to give me the pages I needed for as long as he could, but, eventually, we both knew we were stuck with thirty-two pages," Long said. Other cost-saving measures were instituted, including moving to a self-cover for the magazine – using the same paper stock for the cover as for the inside pages. Thus, the cover became part of the thirty-two pages.

To further diminish the "news hole" in the magazine, the advertisements, which did come in, quite naturally required space in the magazine. Long made his next move with the chapter news section. Going against a long-established tradition, he eliminated grip-and-grin photos of awards presentations. Some time earlier, he had eliminated photos of chapter initiates because, he said, "the information on what was happening in the chapters and at the national level was more important than those two-column photos which showed forty people in head sizes so small you couldn't recognize anyone anyway." Given space considerations as the size of the magazine diminished because of lack of finances – six of the eleven issues in 1976 had thirty-two pages and three had thirty-six pages – Long said he made a philosophical change to make chapter news better and more interesting to the full membership. He did away with "running a story and headline on the fact that a chapter had held a meeting with so-and-so as a speaker or that it had held its elections and that whoever had been chosen president," he said. While those items had been a part of the magazine for twenty years or more, in Long's estimation they had to go. "I was interested in the 'meat' of a speech to a chapter or the detail of a major project taken on by a chapter, but I seldom received that kind of story. More often than not, if we wanted the real news, Halina or I would have to get on the telephone and follow up on a story submitted with only the fact that an important news executive or a famous attorney had spoken to a chapter with nothing about what he had said." The stylized and philosophical changes in the Society news sections did not sit well with some members, but Long said he received almost no direct calls or letters of complaint – and, in fact, received compliments about the changes that had been made.

THE FIRST AMENDMENT ISSUE

Amid the frustrations of dealing with cut-backs, Long experienced one of the high points in his career as editor – The First Amendment issue. Hurst and Long talked about a U.S. bicentennial issue, but both wanted to avoid a trite repetition of what other magazines would be doing in 1976. They considered an issue which would look to the future but dismissed the idea. Early in the spring, it occurred to them that while the Bill of Rights had been made a part of the U.S. Constitution in 1791, it was still tied to the events surrounding the birth of the nation. Thus, it seemed to be natural to focus an issue on the First Amendment during the bicentennial year. The September issue was set aside for the special treatment. "I started with a determination to get Supreme Court Justice William O. Douglas to write for The First Amendment issue," Long recalls. Douglas had been very ill and had turned down every invitation to speak and write for many months. Long's "Editor's Notes" column in the February 1980 *Quill*, written on the occasion of Douglas's death, tells how the Justice came to write the introduction to the issue. "He had begged off at first. Persistently poor health prevented him from preparing the introduction we requested....We looked elsewhere. We studied a long list of authoritative figures. We kept returning to the fact that [the other man who could write such an introduction, Justice Hugo] Black was no longer alive. There was only Douglas. We asked again; again he said no. Two days passed by. From out of the blue, it arrived." "Submitted to *The Quill* Magazine, June 22, 1976," it said on the cover page. "The First Amendment: An Introduction by William O. Douglas, Associate Justice, Retired, Supreme Court of the United States." "The manuscript endures as a treasure, an ever-powerful beacon. It could have been written this morning," Long said. Douglas wrote, "The First Amendment is a weathervane and there are ominous signs everywhere that the values it embraces may be in for stormy weather. As a nation, our federalism cannot allow disparate treatment – for literature, movies, public debate, speech or press – dependent on the whims or prejudices of local groups. So far as basic freedoms are concerned, there must be national standards, lest the most illiterate and the least civilized factions lower us to their prejudices and condition the mass media and national publications to the lowest common denominator." Long said, "This

may well have been the last of Douglas' public writings. Unquestionably, it is one of the finest articles ever to appear in this magazine – and well worth repeating again and again."

With Douglas's introduction to the issue in hand, Long completed plans and assignments for the September 1976 issue. He arranged for the University of Minnesota's Gerald to submit two articles and for ASNE general counsel Richard Schmidt, Washington *Star* Supreme Court reporter Lyle Denniston, press critic Ben H. Bagdikian and immediate past president Bill Small to write articles. All illustrations for the issue, including a painting reproduced in full color as the cover, were done by Kenneth Stark. As his introduction to the issue, Long wrote of the apparent lack of knowledge by the American people of the Bill of Rights and their inability to recognize the forty-five words contained in the First Amendment. "Such evidence is no less alarming today," he wrote. "A monument may stand for a long time with the aid of a few caretakers; but that doesn't assure that passers-by will appreciate it – or even stop to look at it. Here, then, is an effort to stop the passers-by."

The special issue was advertised in advance and, by publication time, more than 2,500 extra copies had been ordered. Through the next six years, the First Amendment issue became the most widely-circulated single issue in the history of the magazine. With the financial help of Harte-Hanks Newspapers, Inc. of San Antonio, Texas, reprints of that issue were made available for sale. As the issue went into a third printing in 1979, it became a standard reference on the First Amendment through the early 1980's. All told, 22,500 copies of the First Amendment issue were reprinted and, by mid-1982, none was left to be sold.

Careers in journalism continued to have a place in issues of *The Quill*. Long produced a careers issue in 1972. Bostrom's article, "How to Apply for a Job in Media" in that issue, and an updated 1976 version, were reprinted. Thousands of copies of the articles were distributed until 1981 to newspapers, press associations, and college and university departments of journalism, making it one of the most popular reprints ever from *The Quill*. Long also kept the magazine in tune with collegiate journalism. His coverage of the state of journalism education through the years produced debates by educators and working newspersons.

From May 1977 to January 1982, former executive officer Agee wrote a monthly press review column for *The Quill*, reporting and commenting on approximately 200 articles about the news media that appeared in major newspapers and non-journalism magazines. In 1976, Czerniejewski was promoted to associate editor of *The Quill* and executive assistant to Hurst. She retained her split duties until May 1977, when Kathy Lieberman was hired as director of information and Czerniejewski moved all of her energies to *The Quill*. It was another landmark for the magazine – the first time *The Quill* had two full-time employees. Long and Czerniejewski introduced a new design to the interior of the magazine in September 1977. The primary change was the addition of a four-to-eight-page, tan-colored center section called "Report," which carried the news of the Society. "We believe this new format gives this department added strength and identity," Long wrote in his column that month.

Czerniejewski left the magazine in the summer of 1978 and was replaced by Helen Raece, who was given the title assistant editor. A graduate of the University of Illinois, Raece's name was listed in *The Quill* masthead beginning with the September issue, the same issue in which the magazine changed its type composition to cold type.

Inflation continued to plague the Society, as well as *The Quill*, and, beginning with the December 1978 issue, two of the next three issues were reduced to only twenty-four pages. The magazine began to be a topic of discussion at meetings of the officers and board of directors. They were concerned both about the diminished size of the magazine and its content. Although Hurst did not request it, the board formally named Hurst publisher of the magazine in December 1978, a role he had long before

played without the title. Because the size related directly to finances and the Society was facing what would be a $50,000 deficit for the year, the board hoped it could find ways to increase the size of the Quill Endowment Fund or gain new sources of revenue for the magazine. Advertising did not seem to be the answer, although Long hoped that Cutler might be replaced with a more aggressive advertising representative or a full-time ad salesman. During Cutler's tenure, advertising pages in *The Quill* surpassed, only once in the seven years he represented the magazine, the number in the year before he was contracted. The number of total pages, including advertising and editorial copy, hit a twenty-four-year low in 1979, while the number of pages of editorial matter was at a twenty-five-year low in 1980. In January 1980, the officers authorized Hurst to hire an in-house advertising sales person, and Hurst turned to Boye, who started February 1. Though not trained in sales work, Boye began to contact potential advertisers by phone and letter and by persistence alone increased the number of advertising pages by forty-eight percent by the end of 1980. Cutler's contract was terminated in May of 1980. The awards issue in June carried twenty-nine pages of advertising, second only in the Society's modern history in that category to the November 1959 issue which marked the fiftieth anniversary of the founding of Sigma Delta Chi. Boye's time available for advertising work was cut back when he was named to the dual role of general manager for *The Quill* and director of development for the Society in the fall of 1980. Yet another recession followed, and, while Boye was able to keep the volume of advertising pages well above that of each year in the 1970's, his efforts only effected a moratorium on deeper financial problems.

A DILEMMA FOR THE BOARD

The content of the magazine was a different matter. Unable to do anything significant about increasing the number of pages, the officers and board turned to discussing how the few pages available each month should be used. By personal feelings rather than in any formal way, the twenty-two board members aligned themselves into three camps: those who wanted the magazine to be a professional journal producing articles on the cutting edge of journalistic issues, those who wanted *The Quill* to be a membership magazine with its emphasis on the internal happenings in the Society, and those who wanted a combination of the two. The latter group was certainly in the majority but faced the near-impossible task of coming up with a way to get enough of both in any given issue to make the magazine what they wanted it to be, and they could not agree on what percentages ought to be given to each division of the magazine.

In retrospect, most of the officers who served from 1978 through mid-1980 agreed the board talked about *The Quill* at great lengths, but simply did not face up to the problem of deciding what it wanted the magazine to be. The divisions and the frustrations on the board led some to challenge Long's work on the magazine, but only in a general way. Long said he felt no pressure from the board in 1978 and 1979. "No one from the board talked to me directly about being unhappy with the job I was doing as editor," he said. "The occasional complaints I heard came through Russ, but I was also getting compliments from board members, so the signals were mixed at the least." In fact, Long said he thought that from the perspective of quality writing and editing and bringing the magazine to the highest point of his tenure as editor, he accomplished that during 1979 and early 1980. He pointed specifically to the issues which covered "The Press After Farber," "Fire Storm in Missoula," "That Story About the H-Bomb," and "Blowup at Baylor."

Long's role as editor of *The Quill* became entangled in the examination of the administrative and fiscal operation at national headquarters by the finance committee and the officers beginning in January 1980. They were intent on directing Hurst more toward the larger picture in the Society and away from the minutiae of the headquarters operation and from work with the magazine. Based on a preliminary report by the finance committee and

disussions with Hurst in Philadelphia, the officers accepted as fact their perception that Hurst was spending from as little as five to as much as twenty percent of his time on *The Quill*. Long was adamant in saying later that the actual figure was closer to five percent. "The magazine was my baby all the time that I was editor," Long said. "Russ read galleys, at my request, as an additional set of eyes looking for errors only, not for judgment in regard to content. He never ever read manuscripts for their final approval. That was my job."

Nonetheless, controversy continued to swirl among board members about Long's continued tenure as editor. A change of editors was inevitable. The situation was very much like that of a major league baseball manager who, after a championship season, was fired because, although the owner couldn't pinpoint a specific reason, the team wasn't doing as well as he wanted. The owner wasn't about to sell the club and couldn't fire the team, so the manager had to go. "The news of my dismissal came like a cold slap in the face." Long recalls. "I may have been naive, who knows? But, I was totally unprepared for it." Some weeks after a stormy session centered on *The Quill* during the Seattle board meeting May 8, 1980, Long submitted his letter of resignation as editor of *The Quill*, effective September 1.

Long's farewell statement said, "At the age of thirty-three to be given the opportunity to edit a national magazine, of course, was a great honor. To attempt to guide this particular magazine to a high quality expected by one of the most critical of audiences offered a significant challenge as well. I suppose I'll never know whether we could have reached the perfection I always thought was possible for us. But thanks to the good reporters and writers, artists and photographers around the country who worked for us, often out of love and loyalty, we did accomplish a few fine things. The Society's membership has more than doubled in the past ten years or so. I prefer to believe the constant attention given toward the growth and perfection of *The Quill* had something to do with that."

Hurst praised Long's total dedication to

The Quill and the highest standards of journalism. "He has upheld the magazine's traditions of quality and service to the profession, and he has contributed in innumerable ways to the development of a strong professional Society." President Otto added, "Mr. Long gave unstintingly of his time and energy both to the magazine and the Society. The magazine has improved markedly under his leadership. The Society is grateful for his services and wishes him success in the next phase of his journalistic career." After taking some time off, Long joined Cahners Publshing Co. in Chicago, where he became editor of a major business publication, directing his own staff of writers and editors. Helen Raece was named acting editor for the September issue of the magazine.

While a search committee led by past president Dessauer began to interview candidates for editor of *The Quill*, the officers met in Milwaukee and made decisions about the financial side of the magazine. *The Quill* had, of course, been operating with an annual deficit, receiving a $20,000 subsidy from SPJ,SDX operating funds each year. In looking over all of the Society's fiscal affairs, the officers determined that both the Society and *The Quill* would be required henceforth to operate in the black and mandated a three-year phase-out of the *Quill* subsidy. They also set a policy that the new editor of *The Quill* would be given total responsibility for the editorial content of the magazine – something Long maintained he had had all along, but which the officers wanted to clarify – and would be answerable to the officers and board for his or her performance. The executive officer would remain responsible for the fiscal integrity of the magazine.

Dessauer's search committee recommended Naomi Donson, a writer and editor with experience in the magazine, newspaper and book-publishing fields, to replace Long. Donson assumed her duties with the October 1980 issue with definite goals in mind. "I wanted to see *The Quill* deepen as well as broaden its coverage of the way various media handled vital stories. Within the space limitations, I hoped to raise the literary quality of the magazine." She found quickly that size and budgetary limitations made it difficult to move as quickly as she would have liked toward realization of her ambitions. "Also, there were overriding practical considerations, such as the outmoded publication process, a staff in flux and the move to new quarters." Raece had resigned as assistant editor after editing the September issue and was replaced for six issues by Anne Mason, a former junior editor for *McCall's* magazine in New York City. In June 1981, Laura McMurry, who had been hired as an editorial assistant shortly after Donson became editor, was named assistant editor.

The promised editorial autonomy for the editor was set in place officially, but the traditional convention and awards issues, and two other special issues requested by the officers and board during 1981, left only seven issues on which Donson could make all the decisions on editorial content. In addition, the tight financial limitations under which she had to work also controlled much of the decision-making process. "There was considerable input from all quarters, including the board, about everything to do with the magazine," she said. "Understandably, everyone was deeply interested in it. Big changes were under way."

Donson said she thought the magazine had begun to move in the right direction with the March 1981 issue, "Making It in the Washington Firmament," and she took pride in the July-August issue, which focused on "The Press." "The pieces added up to a well-rounded balance, running the gamut from in-city campus journalism to the international scene. Based on the many commendatory letters which came in, I thought of that issue as a teaching issue," she said. "I thought we made considerable headway in content and design during my time with the magazine. By prevailing on some illustrious journalists to contribute pieces for nothing or next to it, and getting academics who had considerable experience in the field but now had pressure to publish, fee or no fee, I managed to get some worthwhile articles for the magazine while operating on the proverbial shoestring. It was a challenge I grew to relish."

As editor, Donson was charged not only with improving the editorial content of the magazine and, of course, forced to live within the limited budget, but she and *Quill* general manager Boye were asked to come up with ways to improve the efficiency of the production process and save money on that side of the operation. "Having worked for publishers who had their own typesetting operation in-house, I knew that *The Quill* production system was inefficient and expensive," she said. "Aside from money, time was being lost. Turnaround on galleys was slow; two or more people had to go out-of-town to the supplier in order to turn out the magazine. I really pushed to assemble estimates and investigate bids. We were able to get a new typesetting and film-work deal with Central Photo Engraving Co. in Chicago accomplished before the heavy winter weather and the added chores of the move to the new headquarters on Lake Shore Drive. Certainly, the advantages of a possible twenty-four-hour turnaround on galleys saved wear and tear on personnel." Donson said she had hoped to help facilitate moving to in-house typesetting and had alerted Hurst and several officers of the advantages.

Meanwhile, Boye was moving toward obtaining better prices and service on the printing contract. Wayside Press in Mendota had been purchased by Progressive Graphics in Oregon, Illinois, and the new company made its Oregon plant the typesetting division and Mendota the printing division. Both were about eighty miles west of Chicago and about thirty miles apart. "We sent out information seeking bids for printing all over the country," Boye said. "We received many bids, the best coming from American Press in Gordonsville, Virginia. They had a business representative housed in Chicago, and they met our specifications perfectly. We wouldn't have had much flexibility with American, but as it turned out, their rather tight parameters fit us very well, and we were able to get the better price because of it." The contract with American Press began with the April 1981 issue. With the typesetting, pasteup and the making of page

negatives done in Chicago, and all Society staff production work done there for the first time since at least 1926, the negatives were shipped to Virginia by overnight delivery. Donson recalls, "I think we saved as much as $20,000 in the first year with the new typesetting and printing arrangements."

In order to solve the long-standing board of directors' problems of determining what the magazine should be, setting policy for *The Quill's* editor and assuring autonomy for that editor, Sutherland proposed establishment of a permanent publications committee of the board. The board agreed at its January 1981 meeting and president Graves appointed Sutherland chairman of the committee. "I sent out a questionnaire to every board member, every past president I could locate, and every national committee chairman in the organization asking a series of questions about what *The Quill* should be and what priorities should be given the magazine," Sutherland said. "The consensus was overwhelming that we had made a mistake in 1980 in cutting back on financial support for the magazine. *The Quill* was the Society's showpiece for all the members, and the needed improvements were so important that whatever needed to be done, including reinstituting the subsidy, should be done." In fairness to those who initiated that 1980 policy, it should be noted they remained convinced *The Quill* should be self-supporting. Sutherland and his committee were developing recommendations to the board when Donson resigned as editor, leaving the job in August 1981.

Donson's final project was the September 1981 issue, which served as a compass issue for the Society. The board and officers had asked to have *The Quill* for that month serve to inform the membership of the results of the myriad changes which had taken place during the previous two years and let them know how those changes were expected to mean positive growth for SPJ,SDX in the future. Titled "SPJ,SDX: The Journalism Society of the '80's: Visible, Vital, Visionary," the magazine included articles by Tornabene, who had become executive officer in June; several of the national officers; and chairs of the various national committees whose programs had become priorities for the Society. Bostrom acted as coordinator for the board, helping with the assignments, writing and editing of the magazine, which had an overrun of 7,500 copies to be used as a tool in recruiting new members.

RON DORFMAN TAKES THE HELM

Turning its attention to the search for a second new editor within a year, the publications committee made recommendations on what it believed the search committee should be looking for in an editor. Graves named Dornfeld to chair the search committee, which included Sutherland, past presidents Otwell and Otto, and University of Indiana journalism professor John Ahlhauser. Dornfeld and Sutherland came from the group on earlier boards which believed the magazine should be an issue-oriented publication dealing with provocative subjects. Each believed Long had edited a professionally-produced magazine but had not been on what they called, "the cutting edge of journalistic issues." They had not been satisfied with Donson's more recent product and were determined both to set a direction for the magazine which would bring *The Quill* to a much higher level of prominence in the journalism community and to select an editor who was an outstanding journalist and could fill their objectives. The search committee advertised widely and also made personal contacts in various cities inviting qualified candidates to apply. "We received 125 applications," Dornfeld said, "and because we did not want to make a mistake, after we narrowed the field to about a dozen, we asked each of the semifinalists to write a thorough critique of *The Quill* and propose changes to make the magazine better." The committee narrowed the field further to six finalists and interviewed each in Chicago. The final decision came down to two highly-qualified applicants, one strong in producing solid content and one with superior ability in packaging the magazine. Dornfeld said both were very strong candidates, but the committee came down on the side of content, selecting Ron Dorfman as the fifteenth editor of *The Quill*.

Dorfman, 41, was a 1963 graduate in political science from the University of Chicago who had newspaper experience with the City News Bureau of Chicago and *Chicago's American* before turning to the magazine industry in 1969. He had been editor of *Chicago Journalism Review*, a pioneer in the field of media criticism, been articles editor for *Chicago* magazine and had been a free-lance writer. In 1980 and 1981, he had been an editorial adviser to *China Reconstructs* in Peking, China, where his major task had been to improve the staff's English-language skills, teach the staff something about Western journalism and society and generally help to improve the quality of the publication.

If there was anything in Dorfman's background which caused any concern, it had been his work as editor of *Chicago Journalism Review*. The magazine had been organized in 1968 to do critical analysis of the news media in Chicago, and Dorfman had taken pot-shots at a number of the city's media executives and operations. Now he was applying for a position with what might be termed "an establishment publication," *The Quill*. "Dorfman's work at *Chicago Journalism Review* provoked concern for a moment, but here was Otwell on the Search Committee, and Otwell had been a target on occasion of some of Dorfman's barbs," Dornfeld said. "Otwell may have had some concerns along those lines, but when it came to voting, Otwell supported Dorfman and any fears I might have had dissolved at that point." As it had turned out, it was Otwell who had invited Dorfman to apply. "Shortly after I returned from China," Dorfman recalls, "I got a call from Otwell asking me if I would be interested in being editor of *The Quill*. The invitation certainly floored me, and I said I would be interested in talking about the position. After we talked, he said that if I were interested formally in the job, I should write to Dornfeld."

Tornabene had called on two Chicago-area journalists and SPJ,SDX members to serve as interim editor and associate editor while the search for a new permanent editor was conducted. He arranged for Oliver R. Witte, an award-winning magazine journalist, to be interim editor and Edmund

J. Rooney, assistant professor of journalism at Loyola University in Chicago, to be associate editor. The two men produced the magazine in October and November, and Boye took over as interim editor for the December 1981 issue.

Because the board would not meet until mid-November and the search committee was eager to allow Dorfman to begin work on his first issue for January 1982, Dornfeld notified the board of the search committee's recommendation by letter on October 20, asking for a response by telephone from each member. Dorfman was approved and began his work at SPJ,SDX headquarters November 2, 1981. Dorfman said he accepted the position, because, during the interviews and talks with Dornfeld, Sutherland and Otwell, he became convinced that they were serious about what they hoped to accomplish with the magazine and about autonomy for their new editor. "In my critique of past issues of *The Quill*, it was surprising how closely I had come to touching on the very issues Dornfeld had submitted in response to Sutherland's questionnaire," Dorfman said. "I said that the magazine had been too tame for my blood, that its contents were mundane and the magazine seemed to drift from issue to issue without any direction. It appeared that together we would have an opportunity to change all of that." In his statement as a part of his formal introduction as editor, Dorfman wrote, "I hope to turn the magazine into an important voice in the discussions and debates of the profession." To complete the editorial staff, Mark Rosner, a young free-lance writer with some public relations writing background, joined *The Quill* as assistant editor with the March 1982 issue. Rosner was graduated from Michigan State University with a degree in political science.

In August 1981, Tornabene sought board approval for the quarterly National News Council reports to be published in *The Quill*. The Council would pay for the publication, about $12,000 annually. The board approved, and on September 20, a joint announcement said the regular News Council report would begin in the December 1981 issue. The report, which recounted News Council decisions on press problems brought to it, had been printed in other publications, but it was thought *The Quill* audience would be an excellent outlet for the report. The National News Council, whose executive director was Bill Arthur, 1968-1969 Society president, agreed to have its staff write and edit the report.

With an editor hired and on the job, Sutherland's publications committee refocused its efforts on what its role would be. "We were very sensitive about wanting autonomy for the editor," he said. "The publications committee became an advisory board in the sense that we critiqued the magazine and served as a funnel for criticism, praise and anything else which came toward the magazine so that the editor could concentrate on the content and not have to deal constantly with board members and other outsiders." Dornfeld had supported that concept all along. "There's no editor who can take direction from twenty-two different people. Dorfman needed the publications committee as a sounding board and a buffer as well."

In his second issue, February 1982, Dorfman applied his philosophy of what the magazine should be. Further, he surprised his readers on two counts. First the non-Society content of the issue was devoted to a single article, "The Virtuous Journalist," by Michael J. Kirkhorn, an associate professor of journalism at the University of Kentucky. "I offered the 9,000-word essay in hopes that it would start an argument among the readers and draw an outpouring from the readers on Kirkhorn's views of how the media performs." Dorfman didn't get as much response as he had hoped on the article's content, but he did get response on the length of the article and his change to eight-point type with one point of leading to replace the nine-point type with two points leading of earlier issues. "The one-to-two-page article had been a 'religion' with earlier editors, and I would run another piece of that length if it were as well written," Dorfman said. But, he returned to nine-point type with the May issue.

Aside from his duties with the magazine, Dorfman joined regional directors Harry Fuller and Ron Lovell in a project to produce a book, *Reporting/Writing/Editing*, a collection of articles from *The Quill*. To be part of an expected series called "The *Quill* Guides to Journalism," the book was published by Kendall-Hunt and, offered to members, newspapers and journalism schools. Sales did not go as well as the board had hoped through the first two years, and prospects for continuing the series were up in the air in early 1984.

FINANCIAL HELP FOR THE FUTURE

Adequate finance for the magazine remained a problem. *The Quill's* budget carried only $6,000 per year for writers' fees. Dorfman was able to convince the board at its Washington, DC meeting to provide him with an additional $9,000 for the second half of the 1981-1982 fiscal year. His total honoraria budget for 1982-1983 was $24,000, and that was increased to $27,000 for 1983-1984, amounts that Long and Donson would have relished. While that seemed to some a great deal of money to pay authors in one year, Dorfman said, "It all depends on how you spread it around. I paid a $1,000 fee only once," he said in 1983. "Most of the time, I paid $750 or less and sometimes as little as $300 to get an article I wanted."

The publications committee had submitted a list of five priorities for *The Quill* resulting from the questionnaires, and the board adopted them as part of its 1982 goals and priorities. A major objective was to "fix" the 1980 decision to withdraw the subsidy from the magazine over a period of three years. With the 1982-1983 budget, the board altered the percentage of membership dues allocated to *The Quill*, giving the magazine thirty percent of the annual dues payment by each member. In late summer, the board approved the lease-purchase of a Mergenthaler CRTronic electronic phototypesetting machine, giving *The Quill* staff greater production control. Dubbed "Mergy" by the headquarters' staff, the desk-top, direct-entry digital system cost almost exactly the same as the contracted typesetting and would be owned by the Society in two and one-half years, promising substantial future production savings.

The long-discussed major fund drive for *The Quill* became a reality at the 1982 national convention in Milwaukee when formal preparation for a "70th Anniversary Capital Campaign" commenced. With the expertise of past presidents McCord and McBrayer, an attractive prospectus was prepared and luncheons were scheduled throughout 1983 to provide potential contributors an opportunity to make contributions to the $500,000 campaign. Among the specific projects the Society hoped to fund from the drive was fellowships, wherein a well-established reporter, editor or teacher would be offered money for a sabbatical leave each year during which he or she would probe some aspect of journalism, the results to be published in *The Quill*. Special projects and surveys, along with computerized research and data-checking, not affordable within the magazine's budget structure, were included, as was a request for funding additional pages for regular features in each issue of the magazine. No sooner was that project under way when the board, in May 1983, approved a Society-wide fund drive in an attempt to raise from $3 million to $5 million, and *The Quill's* solo effort was put on hold.

But, led by the publications committee, chaired by Region One director Jim Plante, the officers and board resolved one problem that had lingered since the late 1970's – the amount of Society and chapter news to be carried in the magazine. During their February 3, 1984 meeting in Washington, DC, the officers heartily endorsed the committee proposal to incorporate the chapter officers' newsletter, *News & Views*, into *The Quill*. Taking the funds used for production of the up-graded newsletter and applying them to the production costs of *The Quill*, the board approved adding four pages per issue for chapter and Society news in addition to the 15-20 percent of the magazine already given over to those topics. President Phil Record said, "The survey of delegates on how the magazine could be improved, taken during the 1982 Milwaukee convention, indicated a definite desire for more Society news in *The Quill*. The publications committee made its recommendation based on that information and input from others in the Society and the board simply endorsed the change."

Executive officer Tornabene added, *"News & Views* reached only about 1,500 members directly and, with the change, the board knew that through the modification, it could get important information on the Society's programs in the hands of the magazine's 25,000 readers every month." The first issue to include the expanded chapter and Society news section was scheduled to appear in late spring, 1984. Tornabene said national headquarters would publish one-page special bulletins to chapter officers on an "as-needed" basis to get vital information which could not wait for the next issue of *The Quill* to be published.

As the Society approached its seventy-fifth birthday, *The Quill* was still a much smaller magazine than the publications committee, the officers and the board wanted; but with the major fund drive in the offing, a drive which could impact the magazine in a positive way, things were looking brighter for the seventy-two-year-old magazine.

CHAPTER 14

■

The Chapters: Heart of the Society

Russell E. Hurst, executive officer for nineteen years, said in 1982, "The key to the future of the Society always has been in direct proportion to the amount of talent and energy each member and each chapter devotes to the Society's programs and activities." Those words could have been spoken by any of the nine executive officers who served the Society or by any of its first sixty-eight presidents. The life blood of SPJ,SDX has been its members, and the heart of the Society has been its chapters. Certainly the successes that the Society has enjoyed have been the result of the dedicated work of its members and chapters. There are those who believe the history of the Society could have been told better by focusing the major portion of this book on descriptions of the activities of each campus and professional chapter through the years.

Whether those efforts have been in fighting for freedom of information and First Amendment rights, promoting higher standards of journalistic performance, developing programs in journalism education, providing scholarships to encourage young men and women to enter journalism, communicating to the public to dispel the myths and misunderstandings about journalism or recognizing, stimulating and rewarding outstanding performance in journalistic work, the 326 chapters chartered since 1909 have been the central force that has kept the gears turning.

A LOOK AT THE NUMBERS

When Kenneth Whiting, an Associated Press copy editor, joined the fraternity through the Chicago Headline Club in June 1959, he became the 30,000th person to be inducted since the founding of Sigma Delta Chi and was among 12,000 active members. During that fiftieth anniversary year, the number of campus chapters reached seventy and the number of professional chapters fifty-three. Reorganization of the fraternity to a professional journalistic society in 1960 had a positive impact on growth, for by the time Hurst became executive officer in 1962 there were seventy-nine campus chapters and sixty-nine professional chapters. Four years later, Phil Flynn, assistant news director for WAGA-TV, Atlanta, Georgia, was assigned membership number 50,000. He was one of 21,000 considered active members at that time – 18,000 professionals and 3,000 students. In 1969, the number of chapters climbed past 200, with 101 campus and 101 professional chapters. Campus chapters were organized at a faster rate than professional chapters during the 1970's. In 1980, when the 300th chapter was chartered, there were 168 campus chapters and 132 professional chapters. Another landmark in membership came in 1982 when Brian K. Duncan, a city reporter for *The Columbia Record*, in Columbia, South Carolina, became the 100,000th member enrolled.

As the reader will have noted, the number of persons considered "active" members has fluctuated through the years as changes in policy have been made regarding what constitutes "active" membership. As noted above, that number was 12,000 in 1959 and 21,000 in 1966. By 1980, the Society's stationery listed the number at more than 35,000. However, the officers and board agreed in 1980 that it was time to "clean up" the membership roles, deleting those who had not paid national dues for more than one year and reducing the publicized number to about 28,000. Believing that even that number did not represent a true picture of the Society's "active" membership, executive officer Russell Tornabene announced in a January 13, 1984, memo that the phrase, "more than 24,000," would be used to describe the membership. Professional members made up 83 percent of that 1984 figure, with 17 percent identified as student members. Although the number of members listed as having "active" status had dropped by 11,000 in just four years because of the policy changes, it should be remembered that SPJ,SDX remained the largest journalism organization in the world and the only one with its national strength primarily at the local level – in 142 professional and 184 campus chapters.

THE PROFESSIONAL CHAPTERS

Professional chapters, as they are known today, began as alumni chapters soon after the first Sigma Delta Chi members had been graduated from college and gathered in numbers great enough in a given city to form a chapter. The first alumni chapter on record – made up of former members of area campus chapters – was established in Seattle, Washington, in 1915. Six years later, the first chapter that might be called a professional chapter by today's standards, was formed in Milwaukee, Wisconson – an outgrowth of interest in the fraternity aroused by the chartering of a campus chapter at Marquette University in 1920. The designation "professional chapters" would not come until 1937. From that time until November 1960, the care and development of professional chapters was in the hands of a national vice president for professional chapter affairs. Adoption of the McKinsey Report at the New York convention in 1960 eliminated that office and replaced it with eleven regional directors, giving the chapters – professional and campus – much closer contact with the national organization.

The door was opened for expansion to include international chapters when delegates to the 1960 convention changed the by-laws. The first attempt came when Thomas K. Curran, United Press International's vice president and general manager for Europe and the Middle East, interested fifteen American Sigma Delta Chi members working in London, England, to petition to organize an SDX professional chapter in that city. The British Isles professional chapter – the first of its kind – was chartered March 10, 1962, with Society president Buren McCormack presiding, and international expansion committee chairman James W. Irwin, Chicago, as chartering officer. In 1963, a second international chapter was chartered – the Peninsular Headline Club in Seoul, Korea. A Canadian professional chapter was chartered in Toronto in 1966. No other international chapters have been chartered since that time and instructions on how to do so disappeared from the Society's *Directory* after 1976. The names of the three organized international chapters also disappeared from the list beginning with the 1978 *Directory*. Some interest developed in reinstating the British Isles chapter in 1981, but, by 1984, the idea of international expansion of the Society again seemed to be dormant at best.

Professional chapters have always had the responsibility, under their charters, to send an offical delegate to each national convention at chapter expense. In fact, petitions to gain a charter for a professional chapter have had to include demonstration of enough financial stability to assure delegates would be present for the annual meeting. When the Washington, DC convention committee found itself with an unexpected $3,000 surplus in funds following the 1981 convention, it proposed that a subsidy be established to assist with travel costs for delegates from needy and deserving professional chapters. The national board agreed, matching the Washington DC committee's contribution and establishing a $6,000 pool for professional delegate travel. The first such allocations were made to nine professional chapters in time to assist with travel costs for the 1982 convention in Milwaukee. The Milwaukee convention committee, in turn, provided the Society with funds to underwrite travel subsidies for professional delegates to the 1983 convention in San Francisco and the practice was continued with another nine chapters receiving funds.

Almost incalculable is the Work by local professional chapters leading toward strengthening state FOI laws, raising scholarship money for high school and college journalists, increasing public awareness of First Amendment issues and raising the standards for journalistic performance. For instance, current open meetings and open records acts were passed in every state, in most cases, only after the persistent and dedicated efforts of chapter members. Furthermore, although there is no documented evidence of the total dollar volume of scholarship aid provided by local chapters, *The Quill*, in its July 1968 issue, reported that forty professional chapters annually gave almost $36,000 in scholarships. It is known that several chapters' scholarship programs have raised and awarded more than $100,000 through the years and that many professional chapters had scholarship program established for twenty or thirty years before 1968, Considering only a simple extrapolation of

that $36,000 from forty chapters through the sixteen years since 1968, and that many scholarship programs among the present 141 professional chapters have never been reported to national headquarters, it is probably conservative to estimate the value of SPJ,SDX-sponsored scholarships at more than $1 million, and perhaps approaching $2 million.

The First Amendment Congresses in 1980 helped to raise public awareness of First Amendment issues, as has national Freedom of Information Day. But, activities toward such an end, along with thousands of others, have been organized and carried out by professional chapters from coast to coast before and since 1980. And, on the matter of ethical standards for journalists, a national Code of Ethics is only a piece of paper unless local chapter members take it to heart, applying it to their own performance and working toward making the Code important to journalists who are not members of the Society. In all those cases, the Society's professional chapters have done exemplary work. To say that the work of the professional chapters is incalculable is not an exaggeration.

There is no doubt that nearly every professional chapter – large and small – has made contributions to the Society and to American journalism worthy of mention in this book. That, however, would expand the book to twice its size and would take years to document. Thus, given space and time limitations, only a few representative professional chapters can be included – those designated as the Society's top chapters through the years or those which have made significant singular contributions. And at that, it should be evident that the programs and activities mentioned for each chapter represent only a few of its accomplishments. Recognition of outstanding chapters began in 1948 with the Fort Worth professional chapter winning the prize in each of the first two years. A complete list of the winning chapters may be found in the Appendix.

•The **Fort Worth professional chapter**, always one of the Society's small chapters with seventy-five or fewer members, has been the "home" chapter for three national presidents – James A. Byron

(1958-1959), Staley McBrayer (1967-1968) and Phil Record (1983-1984) – and one executive officer – Warren K. Agee (1960-1962) – since its chartering in 1946. Walter R. Humphrey, national president in 1933-1934, was its initiation "editor" and guiding light for many years. The chapter, which often served as host to national SPJ,SDX presidents for their first speeches as president, won the outstanding chapter award nine times (1948, 1949, 1960, 1961, 1966, 1970, 1972, 1973, 1974) – more than any other chapter. Through the years, the chapter has raised more than $150,000 in scholarships for journalism students, primarily from proceeds earned through production of its "Texas Gridiron Show," which celebrated its thirty-eighth year in 1984. A regular major contributor to the Society's Legal Defense Fund, it has been a leader in battles with the Texas Legislature to effect stronger open meeting and open record statutes. Journalism education programs at Texas Christian University, North Texas State University, Baylor University, and the University of Texas at Arlington have been enhanced by speakers from the chapter, which has also provided financial and organizational assistance to nearby campus chapters and helped establish other professional chapters. Furthermore, if it was not host chapter for the annual Region Eight conferences each spring, it was co-sponsoring the event with another area chapter or, again, lending a hand with a financial contribution.

•Winner of the award as top professional chapter seven times (1953, 1954, 1957, 1959, 1971, 1978, 1982), the **Chicago Headline Club**, chartered in 1921, has seen five men become national president of the Society while members of that chapter – Ward Neff (1922-1923), Charles E. Snyder (1931-1933), George A. Brandenburg (1938-1939), Carl R. Kesler (1949-1950) and Ralph Otwell (1973-1974). In addition, the chapter was the host for four national conventions, most recently in 1970. Freedom of information, professional ethics, and work with high school and college journalism students have been the center of the chapter's programs. Among its activities, the chapter set up a committee in

1967, one of the first to do so, to establish lines of communication between the news media and the judiciary regarding the people's right to know; formed a committee to mediate disputes between the people and the media to evaluate professional standards and investigate journalistic performance; worked with other chapters and the media in seeking adoption of legislation to strengthen the state's open meeting laws; established liaison with other Illinois press groups to monitor proposed amendments to the state Open Meetings Act, Shield Law, and other legislation pertaining to First Amendment issues; monitored Chicago-area government agencies for violation of freedom of information statutes; and contributed several thousands of dollars to the Legal Defense Fund, including proceeds from a film festival and a film premiere. In the field of journalism education, the Headline Club has presented scores of scholarships to Chicago-area high school and college journalism students; set up a free consulting service in Cook County to help students working on high school newspapers; sponsored workshops for dozens of high school and college publications advisers; and invited college journalism students to tour Chicago newspapers, radio, television and magazine operations of their choice. In promoting journalism as a career, the chapter produced and distributed the booklet, "The Big Story," later adopted by the Society nationally as its primary national recruiting tool, and sponsored career seminars for area high school students and counselors.

•Frequently mentioned throughout this book for its work in freedom of information, ethical standards and training for minority journalists, the **Milwaukee professional chapter** is a seven-time winner of the national achievement award (1951, 1955, 1975, 1976, 1977, 1979, 1983). Two of its chapter presidents became SPJ,SDX national presidents – Richard Leonard (1976-1977) and Jean Otto (1979-1980). Probably no other chapter has had a greater impact on freedom of information and First Amendment legislation in its own state. Among a myriad of FOI efforts by the chapter, it was the driving force behind the organization of the

Wisconsin Freedom of Information Council, which has become, along with the chapter, the strongest voice for FOI in the state; played a major role in convincing the Wisconsin Supreme Court to allow cameras and recorders in all courtrooms in the state; successfully blocked adoption of an unacceptable open records bill in the state legislature and testified for a more acceptable bill, which became law; and was actively involved in drafting Wisconsin's first right to privacy bill, successfully persuading legislators to remove a proposed section that would have made journalists subject to damages if their stories caused someone to be viewed in a false light. In one of its most ambitious projects, the chapter produced a series of weekly television hour-long programs, "Milwaukee – Behind the Headlines," broadcast during prime time on the local public TV channel, opening a dialogue among local journalists and with the public on press problems. Its scholarships, Legal Defense Fund donations, and contributions to journalism education and the recruitment and training of minority journalists amount to tens of thousands of dollars. Its pilot program in recruiting minority journalists is detailed elsewhere in this book.

•At the mention of the admission of women to the Society, work toward freedom of information legislation and fighting First Amendment battles in California, and the awarding of thousands of dollars annually in scholarships, the **San Diego professional chapter** comes to mind immediately. Winner of the outstanding chapter award six times (1963, 1965, 1967, 1969, 1972, 1973), it is the most-recently organized professional chapter (1951) to be so honored so many times. The San Diego chapter served as host for national conventions in 1959 and 1969 and organized three regional conferences. And when it was not in charge of the conference, it sent $300 to host chapters for thirteen years when that amount went a long way toward meeting the expense budget. As might be expected, the chapter's years of leadership, including that of Ken Reiley, toward admitting women to the Society is fully documented in this book. But the chapter may be known best for its

work with high school and college journalism departments and students, inviting the latter to regular professional meetings, working on campuses during press days and workshops and granting hundreds of scholarship to deserving students. In 1970, the chapter organized its own Sigma Delta Chi Foundation, investing a substantial amount of money, with the interest going toward scholarships. In total, the chapter's contributions toward scholarships have surpassed $20,000. With larger interest amounts available from the endowment in the last three years, nearly $15,000 of that amount has been granted from 1981 through 1983. Mini-scholarships to help journalism students attend national conventions and regional conferences and a continuing education program which has brought nationally-prominent speakers to San Diego for professional seminars added another $3,000 to $5,000 to that amount.

•The **Washington, DC chapter**, a three-time winner as the nation's outstanding chapter (1950, 1952, 1956) was chartered nearly fifty years ago, in 1936. Because of its location, it has been the nerve center of the Society's freedom of information battles throughout the past twenty-five years. Several of its members have served as national FOI committee chairman, most recently Bob Lewis and Tony Mauro. The host chapter for national conventions in 1971 and 1981, it has been, along with the Richmond professional chapter, the hub of activities and programs for Region Two and supplied five of that region's eight directors since 1961.

•**Atlanta's professional chapter**, also a double winner as top chapter (1958, 1981), has centered its programs around a new, but well-endowed scholarship program with annual grants of $1,000, and its famous "Green Eyeshade Awards," in its thirty-fifth year in 1984, which recognizes outstanding journalistic performance throughout the Southeast. Working with minority journalists in the area, the organization helped charter a chapter on the Clark College campus. Its journalism education programs at both the high school and collegiate levels have had a strong influence in recruitment and training of journalists.

The chapter served as host for a national convention in 1968 as well as three Region Three conferences.

•Each of two other chapters – the Buckeye and the East Tennessee professional chapters – has twice been named outstanding chapter. Founded in 1954 in Akron, Ohio, the **Buckeye professional chapter**, winner in 1954 and 1977, has presented $18,000 in scholarships to high school and college students since 1956. In the FOI area, it worked to keep the public informed about investigations surrounding the May 1970 shooting of Kent State University students my members of the National Guard when local courts shut down the flow of information.

The **East Tennessee professional chapter**, named top chapter in 1981 and 1982, has been one of the most supportive of the Legal Defense Fund, donating more than $1,500 since 1981. With fewer than sixty members, it earned most of the money from its annual gridiron show, "The Front Page Follies." Proceeds from that show, which raised as much as $3,500 each year in its first six years through 1984, provided nearly $15,000 in new and continuing scholarships in addition to the Legal Defense Fund contributions. In 1983, it arranged for a debate between the gubernatorial candidates that was telecast statewide.

•Another small chapter with a strong record of service in FOI is the **Austin professional chapter**. Its "Pocket Guide to Texas Open Meetings Law and Open Records Law," which also contained developments in libel law and use of the Code of Ethics, was produced in 1978 and circulated to working press in the state and to journalism students, part of the reason it was named outstanding chapter in 1979. In 1981, it sponsored a seminar on legislative coverage for newcomers to the legislative reporting scene in Austin. The chapter's scholarship fund and the Legal Defense Fund have been benefactors of its annual gridiron show.

•At the height of the national press-court battles regarding the issuance of gag orders and the restriction of public records relating to trials, the **Des Moines, Iowa, professional chapter** provided instruction for reporters and editors on how to cope with the courts' orders. That project, along with its continuing work dealing with closures of public meetings, won it the award as top small professional chapter in 1976.

•With fewer than fifty members on its roles, the **Inland Empire professional chapter**, serving the Spokane, Washington, area, was the 1983 winner for small chapters. While it has built strong relationships with journalism programs in local high schools and with Washington State University in Pullman, providing scholarships and travel funds for campus chapter members to attend national and regional SPJ,SDX meetings, the chapter has focused primarily on the freedom of information area. It led the drive to introduce shield law protection for newspeople in Washington in 1983. While the effort did not pay off in a law being passed, the chapter believed it had gained a foothold and was ready to spend as long as necessary to accomplish its goal. Local police-press relations have been improved because of the chapter's continuing effort at providing a forum during which problems can be worked out between police and press. Much as the Atlanta chapter's "Green Eyeshade Awards" serve a several-state area, the Inland Empire chapter's five-state awards competition for journalists recognizes outstanding achievement by writers and editors.

•While it has won only one national award as the Society's outstanding professional chapter (1968), few if any chapters have compiled a record of total service equal to that of the **Los Angeles professional chapter**. On the cutting edge of every freedom of information problem that developed in California from the mid-1960's through the Bill Farr case in the mid-1970's (see the chapter on shield legislation) to battles over court closures in the 1980's, the Los Angeles chapter provided both manpower and dollars in substantial amounts. It helped to organize the California Freedom of Information Committee, one of the nation's most influential such groups, on which several of its members have served as chairmen. One of the nation's largest chapters since its founding in 1934, it initiated a program whereby representatives from each campus chapters in the Los Angeles metropolitan area became members of its board of directors.

•In contrast, another active group of journalists, just forty miles away, had formed a chapter in 1961. Although there was little money in the treasury and a great deal of work to do, the **Orange County professional chapter**, serving Santa Ana, Anaheim, Fullerton and other communities southeast of Los Angeles, used its thirty to forty active members effectively to win the national award in 1978. For a number of years, the chapter concentrated on working with journalism students at California State University at Fullerton and with local high schools, sponsoring workshops, providing "A Day on the Job" opportunities for prospective journalism students, and making members available as speakers for journalism classes. Taking on the role of host for a Region Eleven conference in 1978 seemed to spark the chapter toward greater goals and achievements, for it became a leader in innovative methods of raising money for the Legal Defense Fund. It sponsored one of the first "Celebrity Memorabilia Auctions," raising nearly $1,000 during two such events.

•Responsible for fostering interest in and establishing several campus and professional chapters in the New York City and Long Island areas, the **New York Deadline Club** has built an enviable record of service to the Society. It has concentrated a substantial portion of its energies on encouraging young people to enter journalism, and sponsoring workshops and seminars on writing and editing for students and faculty advisers in the many city high schools and colleges. Chartered in 1925, the Deadline Club's scholarship award program has provided more than $70,000 in aid to deserving students. Its 600 members were recognized as the Society's best professional chapter in 1980 after organizing the 1979 national convention, one of the most successful in SPJ,SDX history. The chapter has been involved in FOI issues with both

state and national implications, including problems in treatment of news reporters covering college campus and ghetto disturbances in 1967 and 1968; free press-fair trial conferences in 1975; the Myron Farber shield law case in 1978; and closure of pre-trial hearings in the early 1980's. the chapter. In 1984, the chapter filed an amicus brief in the case of newspaper columnist William Frye, a self-syndicated newspaper columnist for 150 newspapers from 1962-1970. Frye had been assessed nearly $8,000 for Unincorporated Business Tax – a tax from which professionals, including doctors, dentists, attorneys, and architects, were exempted. The Deadline Club, arguing that such self-employed newspaper columnists should be considered "professionals," along with doctors and dentists, etc., said, "Were there to be a 'disciplinary body which has the power to supervise' the free press – in the words of the (appellate) court – that body would have power to influence or control the flow of information to a free society. Surely this is constitutionally intolerable and violates the First Amendment."

•Efforts to organize a freedom of information council to serve the state of New Mexico and El Paso, Texas, along with acting as the watchdog on press issues for that area, earned the **New Mexico professional chapter** the 1975 outstanding small chapter award. The council, established one year later, named a member of the New Mexico chapter as its first president. In addition, the chapter worked closely with the University of New Mexico journalism department and Albuquerque high schools, providing scholarships, classroom speakers, and promoting career opportunities in journalism.

•As with other chapters from metropolitan areas with resources in dollars and membership, the **Greater Philadelphia professional chapter** found journalism education and the students enrolled in its area colleges an immediate place where help was needed. Within a couple of years after the chapter's founding in 1960, it was already involved in organizing a career night and a scholarship program at Temple University. Its annual gridiron show, begun in 1967, provided the funds and, within three years, the chapter was awarding six $500 scholarships each year. Named the top chapter in the nation in 1974, the Greater Philadelphia chapter had been involved in defending First Amendment rights of college journalists and has taken on city officials on several occasions on freedom of information issues.

•The **Utah professional chapter**, centered in Salt Lake City, earned its 1980 award as top small chapter by refusing to give up on several 1979 press freedom cases. The chapter had started its own legal defense fund in 1977 to be able to retain an attorney as needed. After filing suit to gain admittance for the press to the 1979 Gary Gilmore execution, a petition denied by the courts, the chapter went to the state legislature and was successful in lobbying for legislation that allows nine press representatives to be present for executions. Believing that the city of South Ogden was violating state open meetings laws, the chapter filed a suit to have the meetings open, only to hit another stumbling block when the city proved its municipal code exempted it from the law. It was back to the legislature, where the chapter again lobbied successfully, this time, for a state law that required cities to adhere to the state open meetings law. In yet another action, the chapter pressed the state's Supreme Court to initiate a one-year experiment in allowing cameras and recording devices in Utah's courtrooms. While that effort was not successful during 1979, it opened the door for continuing efforts that were successful in the early 1980's. In 1983, the chapter joined other state press organizations underwriting a "Media and the Law" handbook for reporters and editors.

It has been not only the award-winning chapters which have compiled records of achievement at the national and local levels: other chapters have noteworthy accomplishments including the following;

•The **Grand Canyon professional chapter**, with only $20 in its treasury and fewer than thirty members, decided it was time Arizona reporters and editors had a comprehensive, step-by-step guide on what to do if faced with failure to gain access to meetings, courtrooms or public records or if served with a subpoena. Replicating the Pennsylvania First Amendment Coalition's "Media Survival Kit," the chapter, located in Flagstaff, Arizona, obligated itself to raise $3,000 to publish and distribute an Arizona "Media Survival Kit" covering both state and federal laws. The kit, made available in 1978, received nationwide attention, has been the model for similar publications in other states, and was published on a continuing basis in 1981 in conjunction with the Arizona Newspapers Association and the law firm, Brown & Bain, under the title, "Arizona Reporter's Handbook on Media Law."

•Five years before the 1981 United States Supreme Court decision in *Chandler v. Florida* opening state courts to cameras, the **Central Florida professional chapter** in Orlando was at work doing the spade work that made that decision possible. Unable to mediate a stalemate among the media, the bar association, and the courts, the chapter's FOI committee challenged the Orange County Circuit court to permit media coverage of a "mock trial" under strict courtroom procedures. The demonstration made such a favorable impression on the bar and the courts that the entire argument was moved off dead center and contributed greatly to the Florida Supreme Court's allowing Florida to become one of the first states to experiment with cameras in the courtroom.

•Having to start in a small way in establishing a scholarship fund did not discourage the **Central Ohio professional chapter** in Columbus. In 1971 it began providing annual $100 scholarships to two journalism students. By 1973, the amounts had increased to $150 each. The chapter increased the amounts to $300 in 1974, to $400 in 1978 and to $500 in 1981. The awards presented in 1982 were for $1,000 each, bringing the total amount provided twenty-seven students by 1984 to more than $10,000.

•The **Northeast Georgia professional chapter** also started small in 1977, providing scholarships – two awards of $250 each to beginning journalism students at the University of Georgia –

proceeds from its annual Great Athenian Grill (GAG) dinner. By 1984, the twenty-five member chapter in Athens had contributed $4,000 in scholarships during the first seven years of the program.

•On a larger scale, the **Greater Miami professional chapter's** efforts to assist students with money for college, funded in the main by the chapter's "Ribs 'n Roast" political satire show, raised more than $100,000 for scholarships during the twenty-year history of the program.

•The **Greater Buffalo International chapter**, going beyond what might be considered normal activities in the area of journalism education – providing speakers, sponsoring seminars, etc. – established a committee to evaluate the journalism, broadcasting and speech department at Buffalo State College in 1980. The year-long comprehensive study of the department's curriculum, presented to the school's administration, was the first step in bringing journalism education at Buffalo State up to par with other state-funded departments.

•The **Minnesota professional chapter**, with its membership primarily from the Minneapolis and St. Paul area, was a prime mover in getting needed freedom of information legislation passed in that state. It played a role in the adoption of the state's first open meetings law in 1957; the 1974 amendments,providing civil penalties for those who violate the law; and the 1973 state shield law; and worked to block privacy legislation that would have effectively repealed the state's open records law. According to its members, it was among the first chapters to print and distribute wallet-size cards containing excerpts of the open meetings, open records and shield laws.

Local professional chapters' regular programs have played an important part in the Society's drive toward professional development, in addressing local media issues, educating the public to its First Amendment rights and to the how's and why's of media operation, and in providing a taste of the working journalists' world for members of nearby campus chapters. Among the professional chapters that have reported such activities:

•The **Central Ohio professional chapter**, in Columbus, began offering professional workshops in the mid-1970's, attracting as many as 100 print and broadcast journalists from throughout the state.

•The **Richmond, Virginia, professional chapter** – joined by the **Virginia Commonwealth University campus chapter** – sponsored two seminars for working journalists. Conducted on the VCU campus, one seminar addressed matters concerning the national economy and inflation in layman's terms while the other provided instruction on how to interpret simple, but accurate, public opinion polls.

•The **Willamette Valley professional chapter** in Portland, Oregon, sponsored an all-day workshop with four panels centering on different uses of public records, and published a twenty-page booklet listing all the sources for public records, indexing by topic and and by agency state and federal records available in Oregon.

•The **Montana professional chapter** in Helena and the **Empire State professional chapter**, Albany, New York, conducted adult education classes for academic credit on college campuses to explain newspaper, radio and television news operations to the public.

Throughout the nation, the formation of media-law enforcement and media-bar association mediation committees has developed because of chapter programs. A professional chapter simply invited a local police chief, sheriff, judge, or attorney to speak to the chapter and respond to questions on dissemination of information, only to find that more common ground existed than might have been thought. And coordinating those programs, among others, with those of nearby campus chapters has been a common project for scores of professional chapters. Standing invitations have been issued to student journalists across the nation to attend professional chapter meetings. In a growing number of cases, the professional chapter has even underwritten part or all of the cost of meals for students at luncheon or dinner meetings.

THE CAMPUS CHAPTERS

When the Alpha chapter at DePauw University was formed, April 17, 1909, those first ten members may have dreamed of spreading their ideals to other college campuses, but it is doubtful that they thought the organization would attract so much attention so soon. As we have documented in this book, the University of Kansas was granted the Beta charter in 1910, followed closely by the University of Michigan the same year. By 1911, five more chapters had been organized, extending from Ohio west to Washington. Before the fraternity was ten years old, twenty-three schools had chapters and an alumni chapter had been founded. It is not surprising that during the fraternity's fiftieth year, in 1959, seventy campus chapters, along with fifty-three professional chapters, could be found in nearly every state. Nor is it surprising that, in the most recent twenty-five years, another 115 schools have chosen to adopt the ideals, philosophies, and objectives of the founders at DePauw, bringing the total of campus chapters to 184.

In the early years, the campus chapters – known until 1937 as "active" chapters, and, from that date until 1962, as "undergraduate" chapters – had been operated with no special officer in charge of their welfare. But, in 1938, Willard R. Smith, Wisconsin manager for United Press, became the first national vice president for undergraduate chapter affairs. The first few vice presidents were working newsmen, but, in 1942, professor Frank Thayer, department of journalism, University of Wisconsin, became the first journalism educator to be elected to that position. Since 1957, all who have assumed that post have been journalism educators. The title was changed to vice president for campus chapter affairs in 1962. A complete list of the vice presidents may be found in the Appendix.

The national officers of the organization were, almost from the outset, alumni members of campus chapters – they were the only ones with time and resources to handle the duties – and thus the executive council and, later, the board of directors were in the hands of working professionals. For ten years after the reorganization of the

fraternity in 1960, students had little voice in matters of policy except as delegates at the national convention. They had no vote on the board of directors. Delegates to the 1970 convention in Chicago, however, voted to change the by-laws to elect four campus board representatives to the board and to give them full voting rights. The first four students were elected at large. They were Robert C. Kochersberger, St. Bonaventure University; Connie Larkin, University of Toledo; Gary Ruderman, Drake University; and Kirk Smith, California State University at Sacramento. One year later, the four campus board members were elected to represent districts – District A, including Regions One, Two and Four; District B, including Regions Three, and Eight; District C, including Regions Five, Six and Seven; and District D, including Regions Nine, Ten and Eleven. Among the campus board members elected in 1971 was Caroline Pokrzywinski, Iowa State University, the first woman to serve on the board of directors. When Region Twelve was organized in 1974, it became a part of District B.

Students, representing campus chapters as their official delegates to the national conventions, however, have always received favored treatment insofar as their travel to convention cities has been concerned. From the time alumni chapters were given voting rights at the national convention, each alumni – and later professional – chapter was assessed a pro-rata sum to help defray the travel expenses of official student delegates. This practice continued until the 1961 convention in Miami Beach, when the board of directors voted to set aside $10,000 from the Society's operating budget to pay for 100 percent of student delegate travel to the 1962 convention in Tulsa, Oklahoma, and eliminated the assessment against professional chapters. Since that time, the travel allotment has been a part of the Society's budget. The travel subsidy for students was cut in 1980 to fifty percent of the price of an air coach ticket, and students whose chapters were within a 400-mile radius of the convention city were provided no subsidy at all. The change, caused by the need to trim the national operating budget in view of inflationary pressures, especially increasing airline fares, remained in effect through 1984, although the percentage of an air coach ticket paid by the Society was reduced again in 1983.

Through the 1976 convention in Los Angeles, campus chapters did not have to qualify for the travel subsidies. Vice president for campus chapter affairs James Julian, of San Diego State University, had suggested in November 1975 that minimum program requirements, be tied to the awarding of travel funds. His successor, Ralph Izard, of Ohio University, followed up on Julian's idea and, at the April 23, 1976, board meeting in Rochester, New York, the board approved a one-year trial for the program, but, implementation was delayed for one year. First administered for the 1978 convention in Birmingham, Alabama, the board, at that convention, made the minimum program requirements permanent. Those requirements were: (1) file the chapter's annual report on time with national headquarters and the regional director; (2) have at least nine meetings each school year with five programs per year concentrating on professional issues, including one on freedom of information, and at least one to which the public is invited; (3) conduct an annual service project for some group other than the chapter; (4) increase the membership in the chapter or, at least, maintain the membership recorded in the previous year's report; and (5) maintain a chapter book to include the national by-laws, local by-laws, minutes of meetings, initiation data on new and continuing members, and copies of the annual reports. Through 1984, the vast majority of campus chapters met all conditions and were awarded the travel money.

Leadership roles in the campus chapters generally have been given to upperclassmen, primarily seniors, meaning that each year saw a near-total turnover among those who directed those chapters. Thus, advisers, more often than not, provided the continuity from year to year. While nearly everyone in the Society recognized that advisers were the key to the success of most campus chapters, they were given few perks. Until 1963, they paid their own travel expenses to national

conventions or requested college or university funds for that travel. The success of the travel subsidy for student delegates and the fact that there was money left over from the $10,000 set aside for the Tulsa convention in 1962, prompted the board, May 10, 1963, to add enough money to the budget to pay not only student delegate travel but also one-half of the advisers' travel costs to conventions, beginning with the 1963 Norfolk convention. That policy continued through 1974 when the advisers' subsidy was cut to one-fourth of air coach costs. With the 1979 cut in all student travel subsidies and the elimination of others, advisers whose chapters were within 400 miles of the convention cities, received no travel money from SPJ,SDX. When available travel money from their colleges and universities began to dwindle in the late 1970's and early 1980's, advisers were, again, personally paying most of the costs to attend the national meetings. Efforts to return the advisers' travel subsidy to a higher amount began with the 1983 San Francisco convention and the officers committed themselves in January 1984 to a continued effort to raise the subsidies even more.

Beginning in 1959, advisers had a voice in bringing about change in policies relating to campus chapters. When Maynard Hicks became vice president for undergraduate affairs, a campus chapter activities committee was established to assist the vice president in preparing recommendations to the board. As many as sixteen advisers served on that committee each year and, when students joined the board, they also became members. The committee, which operated continually through 1984 except for one year, 1982, initiated most of the changes affecting campus chapters and advisers, including the minimum program requirements, modifications in the Mark of Excellence competition, and the award for distinguished campus advisers (detailed in the chapter on the SDX Foundation and award programs).

Realizing that campus chapter advisers, on occasion, are the forgotten lot in the Society, James Julian, a professor of journalism at San Diego State University and vice president for campus chapter affairs from 1972 through 1975, contributed $2,300 in stocks in 1979, with instructions that a special endowment within the SDX Foundation be created with the interest to be used in assisting or rewarding campus chapter advisers. Although Julian did not establish any specific uses for the interest money, he asked that it be held until sufficient interest had accumulated to supplement travel funds or to honor outstanding advisers in some other way for their service. By 1984, the board had not begun any special programs using the interest accumulated – nearly $1,700 – in the Julian Fund.

Recognition for outstanding performance by campus chapters came early in the 1920's and has continued through 1960 with the annual awarding of the F.W. Beckman Chapter Efficiency Cup and the Kenneth C. Hogate Professional Achievement Award. It was mandatory for all chapters to enter the competition and the results of the judging, based on numerical calculations, often were published in *The Quill*. The Beckman Cup was presented to the chapter that compiled the best record based on programs, character of membership, national relationships and financial condition. The Hogate Award honored the chapter having the largest percentage of alumni engaged in journalism during the previous five years. From 1960 through 1972, no competition was conducted among campus chapters.

The board re-established a voluntary competition among campus chapters in 1973, providing a $100 cash prize for the outstanding campus chapter. Regional directors selected a winner from their regions, submitting those chapters as national finalists. Each chapter wishing to be considered was required to submit a scrapbook, showing its accomplishments in graphic form. Although the size, production techniques, and aesthetic value of the scrapbooks were not be be considered by the judges, the board, in 1979, believing that those with beautifully-produced entries had a decided edge over those that submitted simple scrapbooks, eliminated the scrapbooks. From that time, all chapters have been considered for the award automatically, based on the information in chapter annual reports, The University of Illinois was declared the outstanding campus chapter in 1973 and, since then, a total of seven chapters have earned the award, Iowa State University won three times (1981, 1982, 1983), and Marquette University and Ohio University have won twice each. A list of winning campus chapters may be found in the Appendix.

As is true for professional chapters, the great majority of campus chapters have had at least singular achievements worthy of mention here. But, again, the accomplishments of a group of representative chapters must suffice.

When it came to freedom of information battles, the campus chapters were not timid.

•The **Oklahoma State University chapter** joined in litigation to ensure that the Stillwater city council kept its meetings open and then helped to carry the fight for stronger open meetings laws all the way to the state legislature.

•At one of its meetings, the **Northern Arizona University chapter** learned from the evening's speaker that in just three days, the state legislature was likely to pass a bill that would severely restrict public and media access to law enforcement records. Chapter officers went to work the next morning, and, in a matter of hours, organized a lobbying effort, involving all six SPJ,SDX chapters in the state, Chapter members made telephone calls to legislative leaders and to members of the House and Senate from their own districts, urging them to vote against the restrictive measure. Before the bill was considered by the key committee in the Senate, several legislators, contacted by the Northern Arizona University students, had succeeded in pigeon-holing it permanently. Attorneys for the firm representing the Arizona Newspapers Association at the legislature wrote SPJ,SDX executive officer Russell Hurst reporting that, "...the NAU campus chapter was the significant force in getting the bill killed."

•**Ohio State University's campus chapter**, finding a void in intra-state communications on freedom of information issues, volunteered to research, write, edit and publish a statewide newsletter, distributing it to a wide range of journalists and media. The newsletter was still being published in the early 1980's.

•The **West Virginia University campus chapter** took on a similar task for two years, collecting information, and writing, editing and producing *The Mountain State FOI Report* for newspapers and broadcast stations.

•The **Virginia Commonwealth University campus chapter**, hoping to publicize nationally the Society's FOI Service Center in Washington, DC, produced and paid for thousands of bright orange, self-adhesive stickers containing the name and telephone number of the Service Center, to be placed on newsroom telephones. The stickers were mailed to every newspaper and broadcast station in Virginia and made available in large quantities to every chapter in the nation for distribution.

•**Ohio University's campus chapter** opposed the Athens, Ohio, police chief's policy of disseminating information through news conferences rather than allowing reporters free access to police records. The chapter, in 1978, also provided the impetus for the Legal Defense Fund drive at the Birmingham convention that raised more than $2,500 in just a few hours. When it was announced that the chapter had won the $100 prize as the nation's outstanding chapter, its president turned the check over to national president Alf Goodykoontz for the Legal Defense Fund, inspiring other chapters and individuals to make contributions at the covention.

•The **University of Wisconsin at Eau Claire chapter** launched a letter-writing campaign on behalf of a bill in the Wisconsin state legislature that would give full First Amendment rights to broadcasters in that state.

•The campus chapter at **California State University at Long Beach**, using a variety of fund-raising techniques, collected $200 in 1973, contributing it to the defense fund for William Farr in his shield law battle with the California courts.

•Relating to the same case, the **University of Illinois campus**

chapter members wrote the judge in the Farr case in support of Farr's refusal to testify as a First Amendment right.

•In Moorhead, Minnesota, the **Moorhead State University chapter** waged a successful campaign to force open meetings and records on that campus and joined with area media in fighting for open meetings of school baords and other public bodies in both Minnesota and North Dakota.

•At **Northeast Louisiana University**, the campus chapter scored a major victory in 1981 for open meetings on campus for all schools in the state. When the Student Government Association closed a meeting, calling it an executive session, the thirty-one SPJ,SDX chapter members left, but picketed during the thirteen hours the SGA met behind closed doors. They followed up by seeking the help of the Monroe, Louisiana, district attorney, who threatened to file suit against the Student Government Association if actions at the meeting were not declared null and void. The SGA gave in, and the case probably established a precedent under the Louisiana sunshine law: that school governing associations will be considered public bodies.

•**California State University at Fullerton's campus chapter** organized a continuing FOI Day on campus to bring to campus media and law experts to explore the problems of press restrictions. During one year, the program was aimed at providing information for high school students. In another year, the FOI Day activities were presented for community college journalists and teachers.

It has never been a secret that, given the cost of attending college, students have few dollars for discretionary purposes. But when the cause is right, they seem to come up with the money somehow. Scores of campus chapters have made continuing contributions of from $25 to $1,000 and more to the Legal Defense Fund since its renewal in 1978. Using fund-raising techniques from a campus follies, to long-distance runs, to rock-a-thons and bowl-a-thons, to the sale of "Warren Burgers," students had boosted the national defense fund by several tens of thousands of dollars by 1984.

But those Legal Defense Fund contributions were dollars which went outside the local university or college campus. While individual campus chapters have not been able to match the scholarship programs of the Fort Worth, New York and Miami International professional chapters, they have matched or exceeded the dollar amount provided in scholarships by many professional chapters. Scholarships of from $100 to $500, funded in money-raising projects by campus chapters, have been commonplace across the country for many years. While a number of the campus chapters mentioned as active in FOI matters also have substantial scholarship programs, two other schools, which reported their activities to the Society, are:

•**Drake University** in Des Moines, Iowa, which presented four $400 scholarships to journalism undergraduates in 1982, with money raised from three performances of a show, "Bulldog Tales."

•**California State University at Sacramento** which provided a $500 scholarship to an outstanding member each year.

Campus chapters programs have brought some of the nation's top journalists to campuses, not only providing members with opportunities to talk with the best in the field, but extending that opportunity to all students in their departments and schools of journalism. The SDX Foundation funds visits annually by three Fellows of the Society, elected each year by the national convention, to campus chapters selected in a national competition. Begun in 1948, that program has provided more than 100 speakers for nearly as many chapters. Students whose chapters are situated in metropolitan areas have been able to attract nationally-prominent speakers, often in conjunction with local professional chapters. Those in more isolated areas have taken advantage of the Editor-in-Residence program of The Newspaper Fund and American Society of Newspaper Editors to bring outstanding editors to campus with little or no cost involved. Still other chapters have relied on amplified telephone (Telelecture) programs, on which they have

been able to discuss contemporary issues in journalism by telephone with experts in the field, paying only the cost of a long-distance telephone call. In addition, the Society's national officers and regional directors have visited campus chapters regularly through the years maintaining the national Society's connection with those chapters.

Whether the topics have been professional ethics, how to get a job in media, the latest in new technology, learning how to lobby with state legislators or members of Congress on FOI matters, or getting an update on national SPJ,SDX goals and objectives, students in the Society's 184 campus chapters have become involved in every phase of journalism through hundreds of contacts with the profession each year. Certainly, these students have provided and will continue to provide the Society with a deep reservoir of regenerative power for years to come.

CONTINUING EDUCATION

Some call it professional development, others continuing education, but, whatever name may be attached to the effort, the Society's work in keeping its members current about the fast-changing world of journalism has become one of its most important challenges.

Providing opportunities for members to retool or add depth to their understanding of the field, had been a continuing program through chapter activities, national conventions and regional conferences for most of the Society's history and especially in the most recent twenty-five years. But in 1978, professional chapter activities committee chair, Lillian Lodge Kopenhaver, of the Department of Communication at Florida International University, Miami, was asked to direct her committee's attention to identifying professional development programs for the Society. The success of those efforts spurred national planning committee chair Phil Record and his committee to present continuing education/professional development as one of the Society's goals for the 1980's. The board made it a priority program in January 1981. Record's report stated, "To make SPJ,SDX a truly professional Society, one which will have real appeal to and provide genuine service for professional journalists, it will be necessary to: (1) Establish strong continuing education programs, working through universities and strong chapters. Long range, it may be desirable to hire an education specialist. (2) Possibly incorporate a strong education program on a key topic at the national convention which would help attract more professional delegates. (3) ...This effort must include strong encouragement and, perhaps more importantly, detailed information on process and resources."

Before she left office in November 1980, president Jean Otto asked former national vice president for campus chapter affairs, Ralph Izard, professor of journalism at Ohio University, to head a task force on continuing education and lay the groundwork for a drive, in concert with the Kopenhaver committee, toward a national program of workshops, seminars and training sessions. With the adoption of continuing education/professional development as a Society priority in January 1981, new president Howard Graves gave added impetus to the project, reappointing Izard to the leadership post with directions to move ahead quickly with formal proposals. Graves said, "In today's world of ethical problems and too-frequent examples of faulty journalism, this Society can be a leader in providing opportunities for all journalists to improve the execution of their craft. It's an effort in which we should step out, be bold and creative. It is a move that would be welcomed by graduating students, young reporters, seasoned veterans – those who belong to SPJ and those who do not. We serve all of America's journalists and what we do reflects on everyone."

Izard's committee presented a preliminary report on future plans at the board's spring 1981 meeting in Cincinnati and, by November, had proposed three main objectives: (1) to develop ideas about the proper role of SPJ,SDX in continuing education and to make recommendations designed to achieve that role; (2) to conduct a census of existing continuing education programs; and (3) to develop practical advice for local chapters on means of conducting such programs. In addition, the task force made eight recommendations for action including the following: that "the hiring of a full-time staff member at national headquarters to coordinate a major effort to provide continuing education opportunities," that, "the Society seek to channel its efforts by developing a nationally coordinated program," and that, "efforts be devoted to raising funds to support the total program." Among other recommendations, the taskforce also suggested that "how-to" guidelines be drawn up and distributed to local chapters, that funds be allocated and efforts be directed toward building a library of resources, and that the continuing education task force be made a permanent standing committee of the national Society.

In its report, the task force presented a census of existing programs upon which the Society might build, compiled by John DeMott, professor of journalism at Memphis State University. DeMott quoted the editors of a newsletter, produced by a Canadian newspaper organization. "A journalist's education never ends. Forget the adage, 'you can't teach an old dog new tricks.' With imagination and commitment, you *can* teach new tricks." And DeMott added a remark from London *Free Press* managing editor, Jack Briglia: "And not only can [teach new tricks]. You must. There is more to journalism education than journalism school. A journalism school is not a finishing school by any stretch of the imagination; it's preparation."

Task force members Charles and Kathy Fair, professors of journalism at Virginia Commonwealth University, in an article on how chapters can participate in continuing education they prepared for the report, noted that while a national program was being developed, local chapters could provide mid-career training and needed seminars on contemporary press problems at little or no cost – in fact, they could make money through sponsorship of such programs. The Fairs wrote, "Such programs have provided local professionals with opportunities to broaden or sharpen their skills. And, with enthusiasm and proper planning, they can be done on a minimum budget."

The Society's board, impressed and

pleased by the report of Izard's task force, made the body permanent, and incoming president Charles Novitz asked Izard to chair the new continuing education committee. Within a year, the committee had completed work on plans for two national programs, an economics conference for journalists in Philadelphia, December 4-5, 1982, and two energy seminar/workshops, co-sponsored by the Society under a grant from the Westinghouse Corporation. Interestingly, the energy conferences drew considerable opposition from some officers and members of the board because of possible violations of the Society's Code of Ethics, which prohibits funding for SPJ,SDX activities from non-media sources. Society co-sponsorship of the events was withdrawn on those grounds.

Realizing that the professional chapter activities committee, chaired by Kopenhaver, and the continuing education committee, chaired by Izard, were working with similar objectives, and that Kopenhaver had been a part of the original task force, 1982-1983 president Steve Dornfeld combined the two groups into a professional development committee with Izard and Kopenhaver as co-chairs. The two educators didn't waste time focusing their efforts on a program that would be the most important professional development through 1984. With the probability of the Society's hiring a director of continuing education not yet a reality, Izard and Kopenhaver moved toward involving local professional chapters to a greater extent in their programs. At the Saturday board meeting following the 1982 convention in Milwaukee, Izard and Kopenhaver suggested that the board fund a series of professional development grants. They asked for $5,000 to provide local chapters with dollars to sponsor specific professional development programs during 1983. The board agreed and information was distributed announcing the Society's new activity. The committee received thirteen proposals, selecting seven for funding at $700 each. Chapters receiving the money were: Montana professional chapter for a program, "Montana's Open Government Laws;" Greater Miami professional chapter for a seminar on "Business in the Sunshine;"

Grand Canyon professional chapter, "How to Cover the Courts;" Pittsburgh professional chapter, "High Tech Journalism;" Central Illinois professional chapter, "Newswriting for Professionals;" Willamette Valley professional chapter, "Media and the Law;" and the New England professional chapter, "Media in the Age of Change."

The connection between the committee and the chapters presenting the day-long seminars for working journalists and journalism students did not end with funding, however. Each chapter was asked to make a full report on the successes and failures in this pilot program, an outline of the program as presented, copies of materials used and a record of the costs involved. Izard and Kopenhaver, using the talents of committee members and students from Ohio University, produced their 1983 annual report, *OUTREACH*, focusing on those funded programs as prototypes for use by any chapter. The twenty-four-page booklet, made available to all chapters and all delegates to the 1983 national convention in San Francisco, also provided chapters with general advice on setting up professional development seminars on any topic. In June 1983, the Society's officers and board included another $5,000 in the SPJ,SDX budget to continue the grants through 1984.

But the committee wasn't satisfied only with the successes of its seven locally-oriented programs. Turning its attention to a second 1983 pilot program aimed at improving skills for working journalists, it conducted a set of five, three-hour professional development workshops for the opening day of the San Francisco convention. The committee brought nine experts to the convention to teach seminars on print design, writing for print, writing for television, investigative reporting, and how to use the Freedom of Information Act. Registered delegates were invited to enroll, at no extra cost, for the special short-courses with the number of participants limited to thirty-five in each workshop. All the sessions were filled by mid-October.

The Professional development committee planned, in 1984, to conduct two surveys – one of working journalists and

278

another of media management personnel – to further determine professional development needs. In addition, the committee hoped to sponsor at least one regional professional development program and to discuss jointly-sponsored workshops with other major national journalism organizations.

Looking back on the accomplishments of the various committees in little more than three years, Izard praised the national board for its support. "It was very generous in funding our proposals and in encouraging us to challenge it with the innovative programs we designed," Izard said in 1984. With continuing education/professional development near the top of its continuing priority list for the 1980's, it was not surprising that the hiring of a full-time, national director for the program – working from national headquarters – was among the primary projects established for money raised in the Society's 1984-1987, $2.4 million fund-raising campaign.

███████████

CHAPTER 15

Notes on Some Special People

The 1,500 or so persons whose names appear in this book have played a role – great or small – during the development of the Society in its seventy five years. Most of these involved in the history of the most recent twenty-five years were the Society's executive officers, *Quill* editors, national officers, regional directors and other board members, committee chairs, chapter presidents and advisers, award winners and delegates to national meetings.

If, however, this is to be as comprehensive a record as could be accomplished, a handful of others, mentioned only briefly or not at all, have earned a place of their own in this book. For, while they have been outside the bright light of the national spotlight, they have been an important part of the Society – some for as long as twenty-five or thirty years – and have made their special contributions, helping to make SPJ,SDX an organization of service and fellowship.

THE SOCIETY'S PEARL

Thousands of persons in the Society including officers, board members, chapter presidents and individual members knew executive director Victor Bluedorn and first executive officer Warren K. Agee. Thousands more have known Russell E. Hurst and Russell C. Tornabene. But all those who had reason to contact national headquarters, or attended a national convention since 1961 have known Pearl Luttrell. She worked with all of the men, mentioned above, in the twenty-seven years she has been on the job for the Society. It would take another volume to list the compliments this author had heard from the SPJ,SDX leaders with whom she has been associated. In many respects, the modern history of the Society is wrapped around this warm, affable and dedicated woman. There has never been anyone like her in the Society's first seventy-five years and, in all likelihood, there never will be again.

Pearl Luttrell came to Sigma Delta Chi in 1957 as a part-time staff assistant to Bluedorn and his secretary/bookkeeper Lorraine Swain. Luttrell joined the staff full-time as a clerical worker and Addressograph operator in 1959. Her

The computer had replaced the old equipment when this photo of Pearl Luttrell was taken at national headquarters in 1983. Probably the most knowledgeable person on the staff regarding Society operations, she celebrated her twenty-fifth anniversary with the Society in 1984.

responsibilities included handling the mail and, thus, almost from her first days on the job, she has had direct contact with individual members and chapters – something she has done every day since. When Bluedorn was fired in May 1960, and interim executive directors Floyd Arpan and Charles Barnum drove into Chicago almost daily from their Northwestern University teaching jobs in Evanston to help keep the fraternity afloat, Luttrell was a tower of strength to them. "Pearl was absolutely indispensable," Barnum recalls. "She occupied a relatively minor position but she was a major force in holding the organization together." Apran said that while Luttrell was in the middle of all the controversy going on in the office, "She was very non-political and didn't get involved in those problems. You could always rely on her to get you the information you needed and I depended on her a great deal." Although she did not have an official title related to *The Quill*, Clayton said it was Luttrell who handled much of the news releases, circulation and advertising work for the magazine while there was no executive director.

As Agee came on board as the new Society's first executive officer under the McKinsey reorganizational plan in 1960, Luttrell provided much of the continuity for him. "Pearl was a hidden gem," Agee said. "When I was able to change some of the office personnel who seemed fiercely loyal to Bluedorn, I replaced one with Pearl, assigning her as office manager – a most happy decision because she rapidly became the office mainstay. She was extremely competent in handling a large volume of work and her personality was perfect for the job of relating to hundreds of members and the public." Luttrell remembers, "The big changes in the Society headquarters operation with the McKinsey Report brought more work for the staff. For me, it was relatively easy. I was fairly new on the job and I saw the changes in a different light than those who had been there for a while and didn't like what had happened." Agee and Schlaver named Luttrell circulation manager for *The Quill* in September 1961, a job she has handled since that issue. "C.O. was a special kind of man," Luttrell said. "He taught us what deadlines were about and there was real communication between

Pearl Luttrell began her work for Sigma Delta Chi in 1959. In this early 1960's photo, staff is shown at Addressograph machines, preparing mailing plates and labels. Headquarters staff consisted only of the executive officer and two or three secretaries when she began her work at 35 East Wacker Drive.

the regular staff and *The Quill* once he was here and the magazine was produced at headquarters. I remember when his pipe accidentally got knocked off into a waste basket and set some papers on fire. Everyone thought it was going to be a repeat of the 1934 fire, but there was only minor damage and a lot of smoke."

Luttrell attended her first national convention in 1961 in Miami Beach. She did not miss a national convention between that time and 1984 although she did have to return to Chicago during the 1966 Pittsburgh convention because of the illness of her son. Agee decided to leave as executive officer in early 1962. "Warren loved teaching, I think, and he enjoyed working at headquarters, but he was a big stinker to leave," she said with a big smile. "I took the job as office manager only because I thought he was going to be around for a while." Hurst became executive officer in June 1962 and, once again, it was Luttrell who provided the thread which tied the non-*Quill* operations together. "We had to get

ready for the November convention in Tulsa where a great many important decisions were to be made." The headquarters staff in those years was very small and included only an enrollment clerk, an Addressograph operators, secretary and bookkeeper in addition to Hurst, Schlaver and Luttrell. "We did all of our own cutting of stencils, duplicating any materials that were sent out and we typed individual letters of congratulations and membership cards for new members," she said. Even as the membership grew and the volume of work increased in large measure, the size of staff remained the same. "We were able to get a machine so we could cut our own metal Addressograph plates and that helped in efficiency, but it also added to our work load."

At the end of August of each year, headquarters became the center of preparation for the annual national convention. "When I first worked on conventions, only Hurst, the secretary/bookkeeper and I did the basic

282

planning for the convention including contacts with the hotel. We handled registration and credentials for delegates, took care of the awards and head tables and all of the other hundreds of details that had to be done.'' The headquarters staff packed up dozens of boxes containing all of the materials and books that had to be taken to the host cities for the board meetings and the conventions themselves, saw to it that they were shipped to the host city and then unpacked and distributed them as they were needed. When the conventions ended, Luttrell and her staff repeated the same operation to take the remaining and new materials back to Chicago.

But it was at those conventions where members of the Society were able to meet and get to know the ''Pearl'' they had talked with on the telephone so often over the years. If delegates and members had problems when they arrived at the convention hotel, it was not Hurst for whom they looked most often. One could hear them say, ''Where can I find Pearl?'' The ever-present Pearl Luttrell always had the answer or knew where to find it. Despite the fact she might have been nearly exhausted after months of preparation, having worked many nights and weekends in Chicago, and was probably worn thin with all of the problems she faced in the convention city – ''We were numb when we got there,'' she said – the delegates were always first with her. She greeted and assisted them with a grace and cordiality belying her physical and mental condition. To the officers and board members, Hurst, and later, Tornabene, were the stabilizing factors to whom they turned. To the delegates and members at convention time, there was always Pearl. Delegates were constantly amazed at her ability to recognize their names and facts about them. However, she said it was a natural thing. ''During the long hours we worked with those names, it was like we got up in the morning and went to bed at night with all of those people. The wheels were going constantly. It was like a lot of things you remember about your job and when you get home, you can't remember where you put last month's bills.''

To those chapters which were host to

William C. (Bill) Burk, while never holding national office, became well known throughout the Society for years of dedicated work and service. For thirty years, Burk and his wife, Mary, were hosts for a popular and traditional hospitality suite at each national convention.

national conventions, the ultimate compliment on having organized the convention well was knowing that they had impressed Luttrell. She pointed to the conventions in Tulsa in 1962, Norfolk, Virginia, in 1963 and Los Angeles in 1965 as those she remembers with the greatest admiration. ''I suppose I looked at conventions in a way that no one else would look at them,'' she said. ''The Tidewater chapter hadn't even been recognized as an official chapter when they were given the opportunity to do the 1963 convention and they did an outstanding job. And with Hank Rieger of NBC and R.T. Kingman of General Motors running the 1965 convention in Los Angeles, it went like clockwork.'' While many delegates remember the 1974 convention in Phoenix with President Gerald Ford, Dan Rather of CBS and the unending hospitality of SDX founder Eugene C.

Pulliam as one of the best, Luttrell said, "That's one convention I'd like to forget. The advance team from President Ford's office and the Secret Service men turned our operation upside down." She doesn't remember much about the 1969 convention in San Diego despite its historic significance because "I didn't see a lot that went on there because Hurst wasn't there and Charles Long and I had to handle all of the detail by ourselves."

Among the people she grew to know through the years at convention, Luttrell was especially close to the campus chapter advisers with whom she worked so long and hard. And she worked alongside George Wolpert for the many years he handled credentials for delegates at the registration table. "While George and I did not always agree on many areas, he really believed in the things he worked on in the Society. We got into lots of hot discussions over the admission of women and other things with him behind the desk through the years." For her it was like old home week at the national conventions. "It was always great to see people like Bill Burk from Santa Fe, who had been at more conventions than I have. For once, out in San Francisco [in November 1983] someone was giving him a party instead of him giving the party." Through the years she kept up with members and even their families when sons and daughters were married. One of the most rewarding experiences for Luttrell was watching Dornfeld from the time he was a member of University of Minnesota campus chapter in 1967 until he became national president of the Society in 1982-1983. "It has been interesting to see the changes from what their opinions were as campus members to the time they become directly involved on a national level. It's like watching your own children grow up."

The headquarters staff grew in numbers very slowly and had reached only about a dozen full-time persons by the early 1980's. With the exception of occasional part-time help to aid with mailings for regional conferences and the various awards programs, the administrative/editorial assistant in 1967 was the only major addition to the staff until 1977, when Lieberman joined the staff and Luttrell became director of membership services. Since that time various other positions were established including a general manager, an assistant editor, and production and secretarial help for *The Quill*. Luttrell became director of chapter relations in 1982 when Jerry Eastman was added to the staff to handle membership services. What Luttrell did very much by herself or with a minimum of help for twenty years was spread among the new staff members during Hurst's last few years on the job and during Tornabene's tenure. But she was still answering as many as twenty to thirty telephone calls per day in addition to her other duties in 1984. "It's a good thing to talk to the chapter presidents and members to find out what the problems are. Often, now, I refer them to whoever is in charge of the area about which they want information." Even in recent years, however, when a problem arose in a local chapter, one officer would turn to another and say, "Call Pearl." Many of those officers didn't even know her last name. "I used to laugh," she recalled, "when one campus chapter adviser who couldn't remember my name would call in and say, 'I want to talk to that person who has the name of a jewel...is it Ruby or what?'"

No matter what her name, Pearl Luttrell has been the jewel in the Society's crown. Hurst who worked with her for nineteen years said of her, "She has been a person with an enormous capacity for work. She had a cheerful attitude, was willing to tackle anything we would hand her and almost never complained. She did a tremendous job of running our national conventions, handling membership matters, complaints and telephone inquiries. She had a tremendous memory and could not only find anything filed away in the office but she remembered almost everything that happened while she worked for the Society." Long said in 1982, "Pearl was and probably still is the glue that holds the Society together. We would all ask what would happen if Pearl ever left?" Tornabene recognized her value as he became executive officer. "Pearl was the history of the headquarters and much of the recent history of the Society wrapped up in one person," he said. "I drew on her memory and ability regularly as I learned about my job for many months. No executive officer could have been blessed with a more dedicated and willing person with whom to work." As Hurst said as he completed his thoughts about her, "She has become recognized universally as, pardon the pun, a genuine 'pearl.' "

THE BILL BURK STORY

It may seem incongruous to devote a portion of a book, primarily about news journalists and their achievements, to a public relations man. But, anyone who regularly attended national conventions from 1954 through 1983 or was active in Sigma Delta Chi in Kansas City or Chicago since the mid-1950's, knows a book about SPJ,SDX would not be complete without special attention to William C. and Mary Burk.

Bill Burk began his working life as a reporter and photographer for newspapers in Edmund, and Guthrie, Oklahoma, and as a stringer for the Oklahoma City *Daily Oklahoman* and *Times*, The Associated Press, United Press International and *The New York Times*. He covered everything from the oil fields to the criminal courts to sports. After serving with the United States Coast Guard in World War II, he went to work in 1946 for the Santa Fe Railway Co. in Los Angeles as a system photographer. He transferred to Chicago a year later and in 1953 he moved to Topeka, Kansas, where he was in charge of public relations in a six-state area. He was named Santa Fe's manager of public relations in Chicago in 1961 and became its vice president for public relations in 1973, a position he held until he completed a thirty-seven year career with Santa Fe Industries, January 7, 1984.

While working in Topeka in 1953, Burk attended Sigma Delta Chi's national convention at the Jefferson Hotel in St. Louis, Missouri as a guest. Public relations men were eligible for membership in the fraternity until 1959, and Burk joined the Kansas City professional chapter, March 16, 1954.

Until the Society adopted its Code of Ethics in 1973, it was common for non-media organizations to make contributions toward and sponsor events at Sigma Delta Chi conventions. Burk convinced Santa Fe to underwrite the cost of a hospitality suite in the hotel which served as headquarters for the 1954 national convention in Columbus, Ohio, beginning a thirty-year tradition at Society conventions. At each national convention from 1954 through 1983 – he missed only one convention (the 1961 Miami Beach meeting) – for many delegates, one of *the* places to go during convention was "The Santa Fe Suite." Bill and his wife, Mary, would greet their guests at the door and delegates would spend a leisurely hour or so talking with friends, enjoying a cocktail, and unwinding from the long day of meetings and speeches. Within a few years, evenings in the Santa Fe suite meant listening to Barney Kilgore or David Manning White play the piano – one was almost always available – singing, or listening to the quartet harmonies of a group of regulars, especially Bill Arthur; Ray Dyer; Ralph Sewell; Dorothy O'Brien, wife of Chicago Headline Club member Joe O'Brien; and, when he attended the convention, Texan and Chief Chili Head, George Haddaway, publisher of *Flight* magazine.

When the national convention was scheduled for a city somewhere along the Atchison, Topeka and Santa Fe line, Burk would arrange to have a special car or cars attached to a scheduled train, delegates would purchase a ticket for the special cars, and join their Sigma Delta Chi friends for a easy-going ride to the host city. Burk recalls he used only his business car for the trip from Kansas City to Tulsa for the 1962 convention. For the 1965 Los Angeles convention and the 1969 San Diego convention, he arranged for a lounge/dining car and a five-bedroom lounge car in addition to his business car. With the adoption of the Code of Ethics in 1973, all the non-media-sponsored events were dropped from the official convention program, and most were discontinued. But the Santa Fe Suite continued to have a place at national conventions as a private party, with informal invitations issued so as not to violate the spirit or letter of the Code.

Burk was known to his Society

colleagues not only for providing a special train or a hospitality suite, but he also was an active member of the Kansas City and Chicago professional chapters. He was the Kansas City professional chapter delegate until 1958, served as state chairman for the fraternity through 1960 and was a member of the national convention resolutions committee in 1969. To honor him upon his retirement from Santa Fe and for his thirty years of service to the Society, a testimonial dinner was planned by Dan and Shirley Friedlander and O'Brien of Chicago, Jim Plante of New York City, and Bill Kong of San Francisco for November 10, 1983, in San Francisco. More than fifty of Burk's friends, including eight past presidents, gathered at Sinbad's Restaurant for the surprise "roast." Master of ceremonies Howard Graves reported that when Mary Burk arrived and discovered what was happening, she said, "Oh my, who's going to open the suite tonight?" The festivities, which opened with group singing of "The Atchison, Topeka and the Santa Fe," were filled with laughs and tributes to Burk. Ralph Otwell, president in 1973-1974, said, "I have grown to respect him for his contributions to the Society – in many cases more than some of us have made in a more formal way. Bill Burk has always been at the perimeter of the Society; he has never held high office; but he has given a lot of himself to this organization." Phil Dessauer, president in 1978-1979, added with a smile, "It was appropriate that when the Code of Ethics was passed, it contained the 'silent Santa Fe clause,' which provided that journalists should accept nothing of value, except that the guidelines could not apply to the hospitality, the use of a piano, or the wonderful fellowship that was always available up at Bill and Mary's place. Those are the things of value that no one should be without." Two members of the quartet, Dyer and Sewell, that sang for years in the Santa Fe Suite, entertained the crowd with a few of the "old songs," while Arthur, who was unable to attend, sent a tape recorded message set to music. Executive officer Russell Tornabene presented Burk with a plaque inscribed, "For outstanding and faithful service to the

Society as a devoted supporter of professional journalism." Burk may be retired, living in Rogers, Arkansas, but the days of the Santa Fe Suite won't soon be forgotten.

THE HEADQUARTERS STAFF

During the Society's rapid growth period in membership and activities of the 1960's and early 1970's, the headquarters' staff in terms of number of personnel by no means kept up with the work load. Both Hurst and Luttrell knew that what dollars there were would be aimed at programs, although Hurst kept reminding the board that if it wanted the job done right, it would take additional staff. Both attributed the tremendous volume of work accomplished by so few persons to the dedication and teamwork by the office staff. Hurst, a member of an organization of association executives. noted that SPJ,SDX operated with far fewer staff members than most similar organizations with even fewer members. On one occasion he told the board the Society probably had only one-half the permanent, full-time staff employed by other such associations or societies.

It was impossible to account for all of the Chicago headquarters professional and clerical staff in preparing this volume, but to fail to include here the names of those whose names and positions were available and whose work contributed significantly to the Society would be inexcusable. Other than the executive officers and *Quill* staff members previously named, the professional staff included three other categories: director of information, manager for business affairs, and membership services.

Kathy Lieberman joined the staff as director of information in May 1977. A graduate of Ohio University, Lieberman was the first full-time assistant to the executive officer in the Society's history. Picking up on all of the tasks performed by her half-time predecessors Long, Boye and Czerniejewski, Lieberman handled the compilation and editing of "NEWSletter," assisted with the production of the Society's annual directory, took on a myriad of duties at the national conventions, and was responsible for the minutes at national board meetings. As part of the headquarters' "team" effort, she assisted with chapter and membership services, awards programs, regional conferences, and Society correspondence, among other duties. As she grew in her job through her four years on the staff, even persons who had been used to talking only to Hurst or Luttrell knew Lieberman could and would assist them courteously and quickly. She resigned in June 1981 to be married and moved with her husband to Philadelphia.

Tornabene selected as her replacement, a *cum laude* communications graduate of Elmira College in New York with a master's degree in journalism from Marquette University – Bette A.B. Mammone. She was given the title administrative assistant to the executive officer but performed basically the same duties as had Lieberman. Shortly before Mammone assumed her job, the officers and board had mandated that "NEWSletter" become a regular publication instead of being issued when there was enough information to fill it or enough time to do it. The publication, designed in its most-recent form to fill the gap left by the void of chapter news in *The Quill*, was distributed to chapter officers, campus chapter advisers, national committee chairs and board members as many as nine times each year during Mammone's eighteen months on the job. She left the Society to take a public relations position with the Public Broadcasting Service office in Chicago.

Virginia Holcomb, a 26-year-old Tennessee native with an undergraduate degree in English from Texas Christian University and a master's in journalism from Northwestern University, became the full-time administrative assistant as director of information in November 1982. In addition to performing her regular administrative responsibilities, Holcomb changed both the title and format for the monthly newsletter. Under her editorship, it became "News and Views" in February 1983 and took on a brighter look with large photographs and magazine-style layout.

With finances at the center of so much of the Society's work, the Society's bookkeeper and later its manager for business affairs, Grace Roberts, proved to be an effective and efficient staff member. After joining the headquarters staff in February 1980 as a bookkeeper, Roberts worked quietly and was all but unknown outside the office. When planning committee chairman Record recommended that she be given more responsibilities with the hiring of Tornabene as executive officer, she bloomed into one of the most knowledgeable and useful members of the staff. In mid-1981, she was given the title of manager for business affairs and attended all of the officers' and board meetings to assist in preparation of the annual budget, answering questions, explaining budgetary procedures and advising when requested on fiscal matters. "She made the immediate need for a business manager in 1981 unnecessary and, for all intents and purposes, has assumed that role for the Society and has done an outstanding job," Record said.

With the expansion of the headquarters operation to include computerization, Jerry Eastman was hired in June 1982. As assistant for membership services, Eastman coordinated the change from work with the service bureau to the use of in-house computer terminals. A 1973 Phi Beta Kappa graduate of the University of Michigan, Eastman quickly became the Society's fountain of knowledge on membership affairs, relieving Luttrell of those responsibilities. He was also responsible for working with Roberts on member dues mailings and collections and, as with all of the other staff members, became a "team" player, filling in during heavy work periods wherever tasks needed doing. In February 1984, Eastman was made manager of operations, with duties both at Society headquarters and during national conventions.

Among the secretarial and clerical help, two long-time employees are remembered well by their colleagues and anyone who visited the national headquarters or called in regularly. Lorraine Peters spent many years working as Hurst's secretary and along side Luttrell in both full-time and part-time capacities. Her wide variety of duties and her long tenure made her almost as knowledgable as Luttrell in many areas until her final "retirement" in 1981. The other was Lois Martin, who in 1984 was the Society's enrollment secretary. Martin became a part of the staff in January 1977 as the Addressograph operator. Through the years, her soft-spoken style and cautious smile made her a valuable member of that small and dedicated group of office personnel. Others who spent several years on the staff during the last three decades and who were valued employees included Janice Small, Virginia Bleeker, Nirmala Daiya, Marian Baesel, Marion Main, Diana Harding, Jarie Franczyk, Rhonda Perdue and Sandra Bell.

Tornabene hired Karen Kruty as his secretary shortly after he arrived in January 1982. Toni Henle took over that post late in 1982 until August 1983 when she left to study for a Master's degree and Deborah Ivan became Tornabene's secretary. Others on the headquarters staff in 1984 included Ruth Usheroff, receptionist and assistant in accounting, and Mike Tarpey, who was responsible for the Society's mailroom and folding and collating equipment.

Few members of the Society ever came to know those headquarters' staff members by name or title, but they provided a major plus through the years for The Society of Professional Journalists, Sigma Delta Chi.

APPENDIX

FOUNDERS OF SIGMA DELTA CHI

Gilbert G. Clippinger   Edward H. Lockwood
Charles A. Fisher   LeRoy H. Millikan
William M. Glenn   Eugene C. Pulliam
Marion H. Hedges   Paul M. Riddick
L. Aldis Hutchens   Laurence H. Sloan

EXECUTIVE OFFICERS

Name	Title	Years Service
George Courcier	Assistant Secretary	1928-1929
Theodore A. Berchtold	Assistant Secretary	July-Oct., 1929
Albert W. Bates	Executive Secretary	1929-1934
James C. Kiper	Executive Secretary	1934-1943
Albert W. Bates	Chairman, Headquarters Committee	1942-1946
Victor E. Bluedorn	Executive Director	1946-1960
Warren K. Agee	Executive Officer	1960-1962
Russell E. Hurst	Executive Officer	1962-1981
Russell C. Tornabene	Executive Officer	1981-

NATIONAL PRESIDENTS

1912-1913   Laurence H. Sloan, staff member, New York, N.Y. *American*; president, Standard and Poor, New York, N.Y.

1913   Chester Wells, instructor, Dept. of Journalism, University of Oklahoma, Norman.

1913-1914   Sol Lewis, journalism instructor, University of Kansas; publisher, Lynden, Washington *Tribune*.

1914-1916   Roger F. Steffan, editor, Durham, North Carolina *Sun*; Formosa economic adviser for President Dwight Eisenhower.

1916-1919   Robert C. Lowry, staff member, Austin, Texas *Statesman*; general traffic manager, Corporation Aeronautica de Transportes.

1919-1920   Felix M. Church, publisher, Cadillac, Michigan *Evening News*; state editor, Detroit *Free Press*.

1920-1921   Lee A. White, editorial staff, Detroit *News*; director, public relations, Cranbrook Institutions, Bloomfield Hills, Michigan.

1921-1922   Kenneth C. Hogate, Detroit correspondent, *The Wall Street Journal*; president, *The Wall Street Journal*, New York.

1922-1923   Ward A Neff, vice president Corn Belt Dailies, Chicago; president and publisher, Corn Belt Dailies, Chicago.

1923-1924   T. Hawley Tapping, staff correspondent, Booth Newspapers, Ann Arbor, Michigan; Silliman University, Dumaguete City, Philippines.

1924-1925   George F. Pierrot, editor, *American Boy*, Sprague Publications, Detroit; president and managing director, World Adventure Series, Detroit.

1925-1926   Donald H. Clark, editor, *Mid-Continent Banker*, St. Louis; president and publisher, Clark Publications, St. Louis.

1926-1927   Roy L. French, director, School of Journalism, University of Southern California; co-publisher and vice president, Chaifant Press, Bishop, California.

1927-1928   James A. Stuart, managing editor, Indianapolis *Star*; editor, Indianapolis *Star*.

1928-1929   Robert B. Tarr, reporter, Pontiac, Michigan *Press*; managing editor, Pontiac *Press*.

1929-1930   Edwin V. O'Neel, editorial department, Indianapolis *Times*; publisher, Hagerstown, Indiana *Exponent*.

1930-1931	Franklin M. Reck, assistant managing editor, *American Boy*, Detroit; author, Manchester, Michigan.
1931-1933	Charles E. Snyder, editor, Chicago *Daily Drovers Journal*.
1933-1934	Walter Humphrey, editor, Temple, Texas *Daily Telegram*, editor, Fort Worth, Texas *Press*.
1934-1935	John E. Stempel, copy editor, New York *Sun*; chairman, Department of Journalism, Indiana University, Bloomington.
1935-1936	Carl P. Miller, vice president and general manager, Pacific Coast edition, *The Wall Street Journal*; executive director, Pacific Coast edition, *The Wall Street Journal*.
1936-1937	Tully Nettleton, Washington, DC editorial writer, *Christian Science Monitor*; assistant chief editorial writer, *Christian Science Monitor*, Boston.
1937-1938	Ralph L. Peters, roto editor, Detroit *News*.
1938-1939	George A. Brandenburg, Chicago editor, *Editor and Publisher*; Midwest editor, *Editor and Publisher*.
1939-1940	Elmo Scott Watson, editor, *Publishers Auxiliary*, Chicago; chairman, Department of Journalism, Denver University.
1940-1941	Irving Dilliard, editorial writer, St. Louis *Post-Dispatch*; Ferris Professor of Journalism Emeritus, Princeton University.
1941-1943	Palmer Hoyt, publisher, Portland, Oregon *Oregonian*; editor and publisher, *The Denver Post*.
1943-1945	Willard R. Smith, associate editor, *Wisconsin State Journal*, Madison; manager, Madison News Bureau, *The Milwaukee Journal*.
1945-1946	Barry Faris, editor-in-chief, International News Service, New York; international editor, Hearst Metrotone News, New York.
1946-1947	George W. Healy, Jr., managing editor, New Orleans *Times-Picayune*; executive editor, New Orleans *Times-Picayune*.
1947-1948	Luther Huston, manager, Washington, DC Bureau, *The New York Times*.
1948-1949	Neal Van Sooy, editor and publisher, Santa Paula, California *Chronicle*.
1949-1950	Carl R. Kesler, state editor, Chicago *Daily News*; editorial writer, Chicago *Daily News*.
1950-1951	John M. McClelland, Jr., editor, Longview, Washington *Daily News*; editor and publisher, Longview *Daily News*.
1951-1952	Charles C. Clayton, editorial writer, St. Louis *Globe-Democrat*; professor, Department of Journalism, Southern Illinois University, Carbondale.
1952-1953	Lee Hills, executive editor, Detroit *Free Press* and Miami *Herald*; vice president, Knight Newspapers and Detroit *Free Press*.
1953-1954	Robert U. Brown, president and editor, *Editor and Publisher*, New York.
1954-1955	Alden C. Waite, president, Southern California Associated Newspapers, Glendale, California.
1955-1956	Mason Rossiter Smith, editor and publisher, *Tribune Press*, Gouverneur, New York.
1956-1957	Sol Taishoff, editor and publisher, *Broadcasting*, Washington, DC.
1957-1958	Robert J. Cavagnaro, general executive, The Associated Press, San Francisco; Associated Press general executive, New York.
1958-1959	James A. Byron, news director, WBAP AM-TV, Fort Worth, Texas; executive news director, WBAP AM-TV, Fort Worth.
1959-1960	V.M. Newton, Jr., managing editor, Tampa, Florida *Tribune*.
1960-1961	E. W. Scripps II, Washington, DC correspondent, United Press International; vice president, Scripps-Howard Newspapers.
1961-1962	Buren McCormack, vice president and editorial director, *The Wall Street Journal*; executive vice president, *The Wall Street Journal*.
1962-1963	Walter Burroughs, president and publisher, Orange Coast Publishing Company, Newport Beach, California.
1963-1964	Theodore F. Koop, vice president, Columbia Broadcasting Company, Washington, DC.
1964-1965	Ralph Sewell, assistant managing editor, *Daily Oklahoman*, Oklahoma City; professor, School of Journalism, University of Oklahoma, Norman.
1965-1966	Raymond L. Spangler, publisher, *The Tribune*, Redwood City, California.
1966-1967	Robert M. White II, editor and publisher, *The Ledger*, Mexico, Missouri.
1967-1968	Staley McBrayer, chairman of the board, News-Citizen Newspapers, Fort Worth, Texas.
1968-1969	William B. Arthur, editor, *Look* magazine, New York; executive director, National News Council, New York.
1969-1970	Frank Angelo, managing editor, Detroit *Free Press*; associate executive editor, Detroit *Free Press*.
1970-1971	Robert W. Chandler, editor, *The Bulletin*, Bend, Oregon.
1971-1972	Guy T. Ryan, special representative, Copley Newspapers, Inc., San Diego, California.
1972-1973	William C. Payette, president, United Feature Syndicate, New York.
1973-1974	Ralph Otwell, managing editor, Chicago *Sun-Times*; vice president and executive editor, Chicago *Sun-Times*.
1974-1975	William Small, senior vice president and director of news, CBS, New York City; president, NBC News, New York City; president, United Press International, New York City.

1975-1976	Robert McCord, executive editor, *Arkansas Democrat*, Little Rock; associate editor, *Arkansas Gazette*, Little Rock.
1976-1977	Richard Leonard, editor, *The Milwaukee Journal*
1977-1978	Alf Goodykoontz, executive editor, Richmond, Virginia *Times-Dispatch*.
1978-1979	Phil Dessauer, managing editor, Tulsa, Oklahoma *World*; professor, Department of Journalism, University of Tulsa.
1979-1980	Jean Otto, editor, Op-Ed Page, *The Milwaukee Journal*; editor, editorial page, *Rocky Mountain News*, Denver.
1980-1981	Howard Graves, chief of bureau, The Associated Press, Portland, Oregon
1981-1982	Charles R. Novitz, managing director, International Television News Agency; NBC News, New York.
1982-1983	Steven R. Dornfeld, Washington correspondent, Knight-Ridder Newspapers; deputy metro editor, St. Paul, Minnesota *Pioneer Press – Dispatch*.
1983-1984	Phil Record, associate executive editor, Fort Worth *Star-Telegram*.

NOTE: In addition to Record, members of the 1984 executive committee included Charles Fair, Virginia Commonwealth University, vice president for campus chapter affairs; Frank Sutherland, managing editor, Hattiesburg, Mississippi *American*, president-elect; Robert Lewis, Washington correspondent for Newhouse Newspapers, secretary; Robert Wills, editor, *The Milwaukee Sentinel*; and Steven Dornfeld, Washington correspondent, Knight-Ridder Newspapers, past president.

NOTE: Since 1960 when the "ladder system" was established under the McKinsey Report, all who served as Society president except for E. W. Scripps II (1960-1961), Buren McCormack (1961-1962) and Walter Burroughs (1962-1963) also served as treasurer, secretary and first vice president or president-elect. Burroughs started on the ladder as secretary and McCormack as first vice president while Scripps was the first president under the new system. In addition, through 1984, all who became national president except Jean Otto (1979-1980) served at least one year as a regional director before moving to the "ladder." Otto was elected treasurer after a second term as president of the Milwaukee professional chapter.

VICE PRESIDENTS FOR CAMPUS CHAPTER AFFAIRS
(Known from 1938 through 1962 as vice president for undergraduate chapter affairs)

1938-1939	Willard R. Smith, Wisconsin manager, United Press, Madison.
1939-1940	Irving Dilliard, editorial writer, St. Louis *Post-Dispatch*.
1940-1941	Palmer Hoyt, publisher, Portland, Oregon *Oregonian*.
1941-1942	Barry Faris, editor-in-chief, International News Service, New York.
1942-1947	Frank Thayer, School of Journalism, University of Wisconsin, Madison.
1947-1948	Kenneth Marvin, Department of Journalism, Iowa State College, Ames.
1948-1949	John M. McClelland, editor, Longview, Washington *Daily News*.
1949-1950	Floyd Arpan, Medill School of Journalism, Northwestern University, Evanston, Illinois.
1950-1951	Lee Hills, managing editor, Miami, Florida *Herald*.
1951-1952	Alden C. Waite, vice president and general manager, Southern California Associated Newspapers, Glendale.
1952-1954	Alvin E. Austin, Department of Journalism, University of North Dakota, Grand Forks.
1954-1956	Dale R. Spencer, School of Journalism, University of Missouri, Columbia.
1956-1957	Edward Lindsay, editor, Lindsay-Schaub Newspapers, Decatur, Illinois.
1957-1958	Burton Marvin, School of Journalism, University of Kansas, Lawrence.
1958-1959	Robert Root, School of Journalism, Syracuse University, New York.
1959-1960	Maynard Hicks, Department of Journalism, Washington State University, Pullman.
1960-1962	Floyd Arpan, School of Journalism, Indiana University, Bloomington.
1962-1964	A.L. Higginbotham, Department of Journalism, University of Nevada, Reno.
1964-1966	Charles Barnum, Medill School of Journalism, Northwestern University, Evanston, Illinois.
1966-1969	Warren K. Agee, William Allen White School of Journalism, University of Kansas, Lawrence.
1969-1972	H.G. (Buddy) Davis, Department of Journaism, University of Florida, Gainesville.
1972-1975	James L. Julian, Department of Journalism, San Diego State University.
1975-1978	Ralph Izard, School of Journalism, Ohio University, Athens.
1978-1981	Bert N. Bostrom, Department of Journalism, Northern Arizona University, Flagstaff.
1981-1982	Wallace B. Eberhard, Henry W. Grady School of Journalism, University of Georgia, Athens.
1982-1985	Charles Fair, School of Mass Communication, Virginia Commonwealth University, Richmond.

REGIONAL DIRECTORS

Region One
1960-1961   H. Eugene Goodwin, director, School of Journalism, Pennsylvania State University, State College.
1961-1962   James R. Doran, editor, *The Patriot* and *The News*, Harrisburg, Pennsylvania.
1962-1965   William B. Arthur, managing editor, *Look* magazine.
1965-1968   Al Neuharth, executive vice president, The Gannett Company.
1968-1969   William C. Payette, vice president, United Feature Syndicate, New York.
1969-1971   Don E. Carter, vice president and executive editor, the Bergen *Record*, Hackensack, New Jersey.
1971-1972   Robert McLean, editorial personnel training director, Boston *Globe*.
1972-1978   Charles R. Novitz, manager, news syndication, ABC Television, New York.
1978-1984   James Plante, editor/writer, ABC News, New York; director of domestic news, NBC News, New York; director, news services, NBC News, New York.

Region Two
1960-1966   R.K.T. Larson, associate editor, *The Virginian Pilot and Star-Ledger*, Norfolk, Virginia.

1966-1967   Don Carter, managing editor, *The National Observer*, Silver Spring. Maryland.
1967-1969   Eugene Methvin, associate editor, *The Reader's Digest*, Washington, DC.
1969-1971   William Small, director and bureau manager, CBS News, Washington, DC.
1971-1974   Alf Goodykoontz, managing editor, Richmond, Virginia *Times-Dispatch*.
1974-1980   Val Hymes, special Washington, DC correspondent, Group W Television.
1980-1983   Marvin Garrette, assistant managing editor, Richmond, Virginia *Times-Dispatch*; managing editor, *Times-Disptach*.
1983-1984   Rosanne Brooks, Fairchild Publications, Washington DC

Region Three
1960-1968   Edward G. Thomas, public information manager, Southern Bell, Atlanta.
1969-1970   G.W. Churchill, executive assistant to the publisher, Nashville *Tennessean*.
1970-1973   Rhea T. Eskew, southern division manager, United Press International, Atlanta.
1973-1977   Wallace B. Eberhard, School of Journalism, University of Georgia, Athens.
1978-1983   Pete Prince, managing editor, Morristown, Tennessee *Citizen-Tribune*; executive editor, *Citizen-Tribune*.
1983-1986   Georgiana Fry Vines, assistant metro editor, Knoxville, Tennessee *News-Sentinel*

Region Four
1960-1966   *Frank Angelo, managing editor, Detroit Free Press.*
1966-1974   William Day, assistant to the publisher, Toledo, Ohio *Blade*.
1974-1977   Scott Aiken, foreign news analyst and business writer, Cincinnati *Enquirer*.
1977-1979   David Lieberth, news director, WHLO Radio, Akron, Ohio; attorney at law, Akron, Ohio.
1979-1984   Michael Kelly, business editor, Cleveland *Plain Dealer*.
1984-   Nancy Clark, managing editor, Cincinnati *Suburban Press*.

Region Five
1960-1961   Edward Lindsay, editor, Lindsay-Schaub Newspapers, Decatur, Illinois.
1961-1963   Dennis Orphan, associate editor *Today's Health* magazine, Chicago.
1963-1966   Lawrence S. Fanning, executive editor, Chicago *Daily News*.
1966-1970   Ralph Otwell, assistant to the editor, Chicago *Sun-Times*; managing editor, *Sun-Times*.
1970-1973   Richard Leonard, editor, *The Milwaukee Journal*.
1973-1981   Casey Bukro, environment editor, Chicago *Tribune*.
1981-1984   Howard Dubin, president, Manufacturer's News, Chicago.

Region Six
1960-1963   James Bormann, news director, WCCO Radio, Minneapolis.
1963-1966   Richard P. Kleeman, education editor, Minneapolis *Tribune*.
1966-1970   Wallace Allen, assistant managing editor, Minneapolis *Tribune*; managing editor, Minneapolis *Tribune*.
1970-1973   Rev. James Whalen, chair, Department of Journalism, St. Thomas College, Minneapolis.
1973-1979   Steven R. Dornfeld, statehouse reporter, Minneapolis *Tribune*; political writer, Minneapolis *Tribune*.
1979-1985   David B. Offer, managing editor, LaCrosse, Wisconsin *Tribune*.

**Region
Seven**

1960-1963 Robert M. White II, co-editor and co-publisher, Mexico, Missouri *Ledger*.
1963-1967 Steve Fentress, news director, KMOX-TV, St. Louis.
1967-1974 William T. Kong, reporter, Des Moines, Iowa *Register and Tribune*; assistant city editor, *Register and Tribune*.
1974-1980 Ron Willnow, city editor, St. Louis *Post-Dispatch*; news editor, *Post-Dispatch*; assistant managing editor, *Post-Dispatch*.
1980-1986 G. Fred Wickman, reporter, Kansas City *Star*; editor, "At Your Service," Kansas City *Star*.

**Region
Eight**

1960-1961 Ralph Sewell, assistant managing editor, *The Daily Oklahoman*, Oklahoma City.
1961-1964 Staley McBrayer, publisher, *The Daily News-Texan*, Arlington, Texas.
1964-1968 William C. Payette, manager, southwestern division, United Press International, Dallas.
1968-1972 Robert McCord, associate editor, *Arkansas Democrat*, Little Rock.
1972-1975 Phil Dessauer, associate editor, Tulsa, Oklahoma *World*.
1976-1980 Phil Record, city editor, Fort Worth, Texas *Star-Telegram*; managing editor, *Star-Telegram*.
1980-1986 Mike Hammer, state capitol bureau chief, *The Daily Oklahoman*, Oklahoma City; editor, special assignments and investigations, *The Daily Oklahoman*.

Region Nine

11960-1963 William Kostka, president, publisher, *Colorado Transcript*, Golden, Colorado.
1963-1966 Arthur C. Deck, executive editor, Salt Lake City, Utah *Tribune*.
1966-1969 Zeke Scher, Denver *Post*.
1969-1972 Roy L. Gibson, news director, KCPX-TV, Salt Lake City.
1972-1977 Howard Graves, chief of bureau, The Associated Press, Albuquerque, New Mexico and Portland, Oregon.
1978-1984 Harry Fuller, Jr., editorial writer, Salt Lake City *Tribune*.

Region Ten

1960-1961 J. Ernest Knight, editor, Tacoma, Washington *News-Tribune*.
1961-1967 Robert W. Chandler, editor, Bend, Oregon *Bulletin*.
1967-1973 Frank Wetzel, chief of bureau, The Associated Press, Portland, Oregon.
1973-1976 Clifford G. Rowe, assistant city editor, Seattle *Times*.
1976-1979 Charles Rehberg, assistant city editor, Spokane, Washington *Daily Chronicle*.
1979-1982 Ronald P. Lovell, associate professor, Department of Journalism, Oregon State University, Corvallis.
1982-1985 Marlowe Churchill, military affairs writer, Tacoma, Washington *News-Tribune*.

**Region
Eleven**

1960-1962 Raymond L. Spangler, publisher, Redwood City, California *Tribune*.
1962-1968 Guy T. Ryan, assistant managing editor, San Diego, California *Evening Tribune*.
1968-1973 Henry Rieger, West Coast director, press and publicity, NBC; vice president, public information, West Coast, NBC.
1973-1976 Haig Keropian, associate editor, *Valley News*, Van Nuys, California.
1976-1979 Kenneth C. Reiley, western representative, King Features, Chula Vista, California; western states representative, United Features Syndicate, Chula Vista, California.
1979-1982 Bob Rawitch, reporter, Los Angeles*Times*; assistant metro editor, Los Angeles *Times*; editor, San Fernando Valley edition, Los Angeles *Times*.
1982-1985 Charles Roberts, state capitol correspondent, Santa Ana, California *Register*.

**Region
Twelve**

1974-1981 Frank Sutherland, reporter, Nashville *Tennessean*; city editor, *Tennessean*.
1981-1982 Henry A. Bailey, staff writer, Memphis, Tennessee *Press-Scimitar*.
1982-1985 Frank Gibson, reporter, Nashville *Tennessean*.

STUDENT MEMBERS OF THE BOARD

(The presidents of three outstanding campus chapters were appointed to serve as student advisers without vote to the board for many years. Delegates to the 1970 convention in Chicago voted to change the by-laws to elect four campus board representatives with voting privileges to the board of directors. For 1970-1971, the campus representatives were elected at large. Beginning in 1971-1972, the students were elected from four districts established by dividing up the regions in the Society.)

1970-1971 At-Large Representatives

Robert C. Kochersberger, St. Bonaventure, New York University.
Connie Larkin, University of Toledo, Ohio.
Gary Ruderman, Drake University, Des Moines, Iowa
Kirk Smith, Sacramento, California State College

District A
1971-1972	Marc Koslow, George Washington University, Washington, DC.
1972-1973	James H. Wigton, Ohio State University, Columbus, Ohio.
1973-1974	Lesley Ciarula, University of Bridgeport, Connecticut.
1974-1975	Marc Ferrara, Fordham University, Bronx, New York.
1975-1976	David Kirby, Virginia Commonwealth University, Richmond, Virginia.
1976-1977	Jerry Penacoli, University of Bridgeport, Connecticut.
1977-1978	Paul Neuwirth, University of Bridgeport, Connecticut.
1978-1979	Tim Smith, Ohio University, Athens, Ohio.
1979-1980	Teresa Squillace, Central Michigan University, Mt. Pleasant, Michigan.
1980-1981	Rich Zahradnik, George Washington University, Washington, DC.
1981-1982	Joann Noto, Central Michigan University, Mt. Pleasant, Michigan.
1982-1983	Phil Gutis, Pennsylvania State University, State College, Pennsylvania.
1983-1984	Gregory Gilligan, Ohio State University.

District B
1971-1972	John Head, Georgia State University.
1972-1973	Natalea Brown, Oklahoma State University, Stillwater, Oklahoma.
1973-1974	Jeff R. Boggess, Texas Christian University, Fort Worth, Texas.
1974-1975	Emily M. Phillips, Louisiana State University, Baton Rouge, Louisiana.
1975-1976	Kathy Ball, Memphis State University, Memphis, Tennessee.
1976-1977	Stephen Ward, Oklahoma State University, Stillwater, Oklahoma.
1977-1978	Rose Jackson, University of Mississippi, University, Mississippi.
1978-1979	Steve Anton, University of Texas, Austin, Texas.
1979-1980	Suzanne Monroe, University of Arkansas, Little Rock, Arkansas.
1980-1981	Andrew Lockett, University of Mississippi, University, Mississippi.
1981-1982	James Corbett, University of South Carolina, Columbia, South Carolina.
1982-1983	Viola G. Gienger, University of Tennessee, Knoxville, Tennessee.
1983-1984	Linda Knowles, Oklahoma State University.

District C
1971-1972	Caroline Pokrzywinski, Iowa State University, Ames, Iowa.
1972-1973	Craig Thomas, University of Missouri, Columbia, Missouri.
1973-1974	Jane Winebrenner, University of Illinois, Urbana, Illinois.
1974-1975	Jim Grinstead, Central Missouri State University, Warrensburg, Missouri.
1975-1976	Debbie Gump, University of Kansas, Lawrence, Kansas.
1976-1977	Anne Mason, University of Wisconsin, Madison, Wisconsin.
1977-1978	Julie Nicolay, University of Kansas, Lawrence, Kansas.
1978-1979	Roger Malone, Western Kentucky University, Bowling Green, Kentucky.
1980-1981	Margaret Shirley, Western Kentucky University, Bowling Green, Kentucky.
1981-1982	Sharon Applebaum, University of Kansas, Lawrence, Kansas.
1982-1983	Steve Scott, University of Wisconsin, Eau Claire.
1983-1984	Jeffrey Stein, University of Iowa.

District D
1971-1972	Richard Dore, California State College, Long Beach, California.
1972-1973	Gary L. Stewart, Oregon State University, Corvallis, Oregon.
1973-1974	Marti Weirich, Northern Arizona University, Flagstaff, Arizona.

1974-1975	Lynn Thompson, University of Washington, Seattle, Washington.
1975-1976	Jerry Large, New Mexico State University, Las Cruces, New Mexico.
1976-1977	Lynne Thomas, Washington State University, Pullman, Washington.
1977-1978	Vicki Schaffeld, Oregon State University, Corvallis, Oregon.
1978-1979	Keven Ann Willey, Northern Arizona University, Flagstaff, Arizona.
1979-1980	Tamara Chapman, University of Texas at El Paso.
1980-1981	Connie Compton, Western Washington University, Bellingham, Washington.
1981-1982	John Allison, California State University, Long Beach, California.
1982-1983	Eraldo "Dino" Chiecchi, University of Texas at El Paso.
1983-1984	Dave A. Dickstein, California State University, Long Beach.

EDITORS OF *THE QUILL*

1912-1913	Frank Pennell	1928-1930	Franklin Reck
1913-1914	Pike Johnson	1930-1944	Ralph L. Peters
1914-1915	Carl Getz	1944-1956	Carl R. Kesler
1915-1920	Lee A White	1956-1961	Charles C. Clayton
1920-1922	Frank Martin	1961-1971	Clarence O. Schlaver
1922-1925	Chester Cleveland	1971-1980	Charles F. Long
1925-1926	Mark Haas	1981-1982	Naomi Donson
1926-1928	Lawrence Murphy	1982-	Ron Dorfman

NATIONAL HONORARY PRESIDENTS

1912-1919	Chase S. Osborn, newspaper editor, publisher, author.
1919	H. F. Harrington, dean, Medill School of Journalism, Northwestern University, Evanston, Illinois.
1920	Willard C. Bleyer, chair, School of Journalism, University of Wisconsin, Madison.
1921	F.W. Beckman, Knoxville, Iowa *Journal*.
1922	Walter Williams, president, University of Missouri, Columbia.
1923	James W. Brown, president *Editor and Publisher*, New York.
1924	Eric W. Allen, dean, School of Journalism, University of Oregon, Eugene.
1925	William Allen White, publisher, Emporia, Kansas *Gazette*.
1926	Kent Cooper, executive director, The Associated Press, New York.
1927	Harvey Ingham, publisher, Des Moines, Iowa *Register and Tribune*.
1928	William P. Beazell, assistant to the chairman, New York State Saratoga Commission.
1929	Bristow Adams, chairman-emeritus, Department of Journalism, Cornell University, Ithica, New York.
1930	Frank E. Mason, New York City.
1931-1932	Marten Pew, *Editor and Publisher*, New York City.
1933	Frank Porter Stockbridge, editor, *The American Press*.
1934	Charles G. Ross, White House press secretary, Washington, DC.
1935	Walter M. Harrison, Oklahoma City, Oklahoma.
1936	Hugh Baille, president, United Press, New York City.
1937	W.W. Loomis, publisher, LaGrange, Illinois *Citizen*.
1938	Raymond Clapper, correspondent, Scripps-Howard Newspapers, Washington, DC.
1939	J. Roscoe Drummond, Washington, DC bureau, New York *Herald-Tribune*.
1940	George B. Dealey, president, Dallas *Morning News*.
1941-1946	Marco Morrow, president, Copper Publications, Topeka, Kansas.
1947	John S. Knight, president, Knight Newspapers, Akron, Ohio.
1948	Roy Allison Roberts, president and general manager, Kansas City, Missouri *Star*.
1949	Douglas Southall Freeman, editor, Richmond, Virginia *Times-Leader*.
1950-1951	Grove Patterson, editor-in-chief, Toledo, Ohio *Blade*.
1952	Arthur Hays Sulzberger, publisher, *The New York Times*.
1953	E. Lansing Ray, publisher and editor, St. Louis *Globe-Democrat*.
1954	John Cowles, publisher, Minneapolis *Star and Tribune*.
1955	Roy W. Howard, chairman, Executive Committee, Scripps-Howard Newspapers; editor, New York *World Telegram and Sun*.
1956	Alberto Gainza Paz, publisher, *La Prensa*, Buenos Aires, Argentina.
1957	Barry Bingham, editor-in-chief, Louisville, Kentucky *Courier-Journal and Times*.
1958	J. Donald Ferguson, president, *The Milwaukee Journal*.

1959	Eugene C. Pulliam, publisher, Indianapolis *Star and News* and the Phoenix, Arizona *Republic and Gazette*.
1960	Frank J. Starzel, general manager, The Associated Press, New York City.
1961	James S. Copley, chairman, The Copley Press, Inc. San Diego, California.
1962	Paul Miller, president, Gannett Newspapers, Rochester, New York.
1963	Gardner (Mike) Cowles, president and publisher, Des Moines, Iowa *Register and Tribune*.
1964	Benjamin M. McKelway, editor, Washington, DC *Star*.
1965	Bernard Kilgore, president *The Wall Street Journal*.
1966	Frank. H. Bartholonew, chairman of the board, United Press International, New York City.
1967	Thomas M. Storke, editor-emeritus, Santa Barbara, California *News-Press*.
1968	Dr. Frank Stanton, president, Columbia Broadcasting System, New York City.
1969	Mark Ethridge, lecturer, School of Journalism, University of North Carolina, Chapel Hill.
1970	Nelson Poynter, president, St. Petersburg, Florida *Times and Independent*.

WELLS MEMORIAL KEY

Year	Name	Year	Name
1913	Laurence H. Sloan	1949	Luther Huston
1914	Lee A White	1950	John T. Bills
1915	Roger Steffan	1951	Neal Van Sooy
1915	Carl Getz	1952	William Kostka
1919	Felix M. Church	1953	Floyd Arpan
1920	Kenneth C. Hogate	1954	John M. McClelland, Jr.
1921	Lee A White	1955	Alvin E. Austin
1922	T. Hawley Tapping	1956	Charles C. Clayton
1923	Ward A. Neff	1957	Virgil M. Newton, Jr.
1924	George F. Pierrot	1958	Mason Rossiter Smith
1925	Donald H. Clark	1959	Bernard Kilgore
1926	Roy L. French	1960	Sol Taishoff
1927	Lawrence W. Murphy	1961	Donald D. Hoover
1928	James A. Stuart	1962	George W. Wolpert
1929	Robert B. Tarr	1963	James A. Byron
1930	Edwin V. O'Neel	1964	Robert J. Cavagnaro
1931	John G. Earhart	1965	Walter Burroughs
1932	Franklin M. Reck	1966	Buren McCormack
1933	Charles E. Snyder	1967	Alfred W. Balk
1934	Walter Humphrey	1968	Theodore F. Koop
1935	John E. Stempel	1969	Eugene C. Pulliam
1936	Carl P. Miller	1970	Robert M. White II
1937	Tully Nettleton	1971	William B. Arthur
1938	Albert W. Bates	1972	Charles E. Barnum
1939	Ralph L. Peters	1973	James S. Copley
1940	John L. Meyer	1974	William T. Kong
1941	Floyd Shoemaker	1975	James L. Julian
1942	Willard R. Smith	1976	Henry Rieger
1943	Elmo Scott Watson	1977	H.G. (Buddy) Davis
1944	Palmer Hoyt	1978	Warren K. Agee
1945	Albert W. Bates	1979	William Small
1946	George A. Brandenburg	1980	Robert Lewis
1947	Carl B. Kesler	1981	Russell Hurst
1948	Kenneth R. Marvin	1981	Howard S. Dubin
		1982	Alf Goodykoontz
		1983	Casey Bukro

SIGMA DELTA CHI FELLOWS

1948	Erwin Canham, editor, *Christian Science Monitor*, Boston.
	Barry Faris, editor-in-chief, International News Service, New York City.
	Harry J. Grant, chairman of the board, *The Milwaukee Journal*.
1949	Palmer Hoyt, editor and publisher, the Denver *Post*.
	Frank Luther Mott, dean, School of Journalism, University of Missouri, Columbia.
	James G. Stahlman, publisher, Nashville, Tennessee *Banner*.

1950   Howard Blakeslee, science writer, The Associated Press, New York City.
Walter Lippmann, editorial columnist, New York *Herald-Tribune*.
Benjamin McKelway, editor, Washington, DC *Star*.
1951   Irving Dilliard, editorial page editor, St. Louis *Post-Dispatch*.
Edward R. Murrow, commentator, CBS, New York City.
Alberto Gainza Paz, publisher, *La Prensa*, Buenos Aires, Argentina.
1952   James S. Pope, executive editor, Louisville, Kentucky *Courier-Journal*.
James B. Reston, Washington, DC correspondent, *The New York Times*.
Louis B. Seltzer, editor, Cleveland *Press*.
1953   Hodding Carter, editor and publisher, Greenville, Mississippi *Delta Democrat-Times*.
William B. Henry, commentator, NBC, Washington, DC.
Basil L. Walters, executive editor, Knight Newspapers, Chicago.
1954   Kent Cooper, executive director, The Associated Press, New York City.
Virginius Dabney, editor, Richmond, Virginia *Times-Dispatch*.
DeWitt Wallace, founder and editor, Reader's Digest, Pleasantville, New York.
1955   Paul Bellamy, editor emeritus, Cleveland *Plain Dealer*.
Harold L. Cross, author and legal counsel, Skowhegan, Maine.
Walter Humphrey, editor, Fort Worth, Texas *Press*.
1956   Luther Huston, Washington, DC staff, *The New York Times*.
George Thelm, Springfield, Illinois correspondent, Chicago *Daily News*.
Ward A Neff, president, Corn Belt Dailies, Chicago.
1957   Frank Bartholomew, president, United Press Associations, New York City.
J. Montgomery Curtis, director, American Press Institute, Columbia University, New York City.
Tom Powell, Jr., editor and publisher, Anamosa, Iowa *Eureka and Journal*.
1958   J.N. Heiskell, president and editor, Little Rock, Arkansas *Gazette*.
Willard M. Kiplinger, editor, Washington, DC *Letters* and *Changing Times*.
Eric Sevareid, Washington, DC news staff chief, CBS.
1959   Houstoun Waring, editor, Littleton, Colorado *Independent* and *Arapahoe Herald*.
Byron Price, executive, The Associated Press, New York.
Hal O'Flaherty, foreign correspondent, Chicago *Daily News*.
1960   Isaac Gershman, managing editor, City News Bureau, Chicago.
Bernard Kilgore, president, *The Wall Street Journal*, New York.
Frank Stanton, president, CBS, New York.
1961   Lyle C. Wilson, vice president and Washington, DC general manager, United Press Internation.
James A. Stuart, editor, the Indianapolis *Star*.
William Theodore Evjue, editor and publisher, *The Capital Times*, Madison, Wisconsin.
1962   Alan J. Gould, executive editor, The Associated Press, New York.
Joseph C. John, editor, *Suffolk County News*, Sayville, Long Island, New York.
David Lawrence, editor, *U.S. News and World Report*, Washington, DC.
1963   James Strohn Copley, chairman, The Copley Press, San Diego, California.
Paul Miller, president, Gannett Newspapers, Rochester, New York; president The Associated Press.
Sol Taishoff, president, publisher and editor, Broadcasting Publications, Inc., Washington, DC.
1964   Robert U. Brown, publisher and editor, *Editor & Publisher*, New York.
Turner Catledge, executive editor, *The New York Times*.
Vermont Royster, editor, *The Wall Street Journal*, New York.
1965   David Dietz, Cleveland, Ohio *Press*.
Mark Foster Ethridge, lecturer, University of North Carolina, Chapel Hill.
Wes Gallagher, general manager, The Associated Press, New York.
1966   James L. Kilgallen, Hearst Newspapers, New York.
Ralph McGill, publisher, *Atlanta Constitution*.
Charles A. Sprague, editor and publisher, *The Oregon Statesman*, Salem, Oregon.
1967   Julian Goodman, president, NBC, New York.
Eugene C. Pulliam, president, Phoenix Newspapers, Inc. and Indianapolis Newspapers, Inc.
J.R. Wiggins, editor, the Washington, *Post*.
1968   Earl J. Johnson, editor and vice president, United Press International.
John S. Knight, editor chairman, Knight Newspapers, Miami, Florida.
Theodore H. White, reporter and author, New York.
1969   Herbert L. Block (Herblock), editorial cartoonist, the Washington *Post*.
Arthur Krock, retired Washington, DC correspondent, *The New York Times*.
Kenneth MacDonald, editor and publisher, Des Moines, Iowa *Register and Tribune*.

1970   Walter Cronkite, CBS News correspondent, New York.

John H. Johnson, president, Johnson Publishing Company, Chicago.

William H. (Bill) Mauldin, editorial cartoonist, Chicago *Sun-Times*.

1971   Katharine Graham, publisher, the Washington *Post*.

John M. McClelland, Jr., editor and publisher, Longview, Washington *News*.

Howard K. Smith, commentator, ABC News, New York.

1972   George Gallup, founder and chairman, American Institute of Public Opinion.

Mary McGrory, columnist and staff writer, Washington *Star-News*.

Roger Tatarian, former editor and vice president, United Press International.

1973   Benjamin C. Bradlee, executive editor, the Washington *Post*.

John Chancellor, NBC News, New York.

Harry Reasoner, ABC News, New York.

1974   Louis M. Lyons, reditred curator, Nieman Foundation for Journalism.

I.F. Stone, editor, *I.F. Stone's Weekly*.

Richard L. Stout, *Christian Science Monitor*.

1975   David S. Broder, correspondent, the Washington *Post*.

James Jackson Kilpatrick, columnist.

Mike Wallace, correspondent, CBS News.

1976   William F. Buckley, Jr., columnist.

Charlotte Curtis, associate editor, *The New York Times*.

Peter Lisagor, Washington, DC bureau chief, Chicago *Daily News*.

1977   Pauline Frederick, international affairs analyst, National Public Radio.

Lee Hills, chairman of the board, Knight-Ridder Newspapers, Inc.

Lowell Thomas, newscaster, commentator and author.

1978   Eugene Patterson, editor, president and chief executive officer, St. Petersburg, Florida *Times*; and president, Congressional Quarterly.

Jack Landau, law columnist, Newhouse Newspapers; director, Reporters Committee for Freedom of the Press

Richard Salant, president, CBS Nsws, New York

1979   Walter Mears, chief, The Associated Press, Washington, DC bureau.

Dan Rather, co-editor, CBS News "60 Minutes." New York.

Art Buchwald, syndicated columnist, Los Angeles *Times* Syndicate, Washington, DC.

1980   Clayton Kirkpatrick, president, Chicago *Tribune*.

Clark Mollenhoff, professor of journalism, Washington and Lee University, Lexington, Virginia.

Red Smith, sports writer, *The New York Times*.

1981   Charles Kuralt, CBS News, New York.

Allen H. Neuharth, chairman and president, The Gannett Company, Rochester, New York.

Richard M. Schmidt, Jr., general counsel, American Society of Newspaper Editors, Washington, DC.

1982   David Brinkley, analyst, ABC News, Washington, DC.

William Farr, reporter, the Los Angeles *Times*.

William Shawn, editor, *The New Yorker*.

1983   David Halberstam, journalist and author.

Elmer W. Lower, dean, University of Missouri School of Journalism and former president, ABC News.

Carl Rowan, syndicated columnist.

DISTINGUISHED TEACHING IN JOURNALISM

1966   A.L. Higginbotham, University of Nevada.

1967   Curtis D. MacDougall, Northwestern University.

1968   Mitchell V. Charnley, University of Minnesota.

1969   Chilton R. Bush, Stanford University.

1970   John L. Hulteng, University of Oregon.

1971   Ralph O. Nofziger, University of Wisconsin.

1972   Alvin E. Austin, University of North Dakota.

1973   DeWitt C. Reddick, University of Texas.

1974   John Hohenberg, Columbia University.

1975   J. Edward Gerald, University of Minnesota.

1976   R. Neale Copple, University of Nebraska.

1977	Edward Bliss, Jr., American University.
1978	Edmund C. Arnold, Virginia Commonwealth University.
1979	Floyd G. Arpan, Indiana University.
1980	Edwin Emery, University of Minnesota.
1981	Paul A. Atkins, West Virginia University.
1982	Russell N. Baird, Ohio University.
1983	George S. Hage, University of Minnesota.

FIRST AMENDMENT AWARD

1975	Reporters Committee for Freedom of the Press.
	Supreme Court Justice William O. Douglas.
1976	Medford, Oregon *Mail Tribune.*
	Media of Nebraska Committee.
	Daniel Schorr.
	The Fresno Four.
	Raymond Spangler.
	William Farr.
1977	Charleston, West Virginia *Gazette.*
	Great Falls, Montana *Tribune.*
1979	Scottsdale, Arizona *Daily Progress* and publisher Jonathan Marshall.
1980	Allen Neuharth.
	Retired U.S. Representative John E. Moss.
	Richard M. Schmidt, Jr., general counsel, American Society of Newspaper Editors.
	Freedom of Information Center and its director, Paul L. Fisher, University of Missouri.
	Milton B. Chilcott.
1981	WCBS-TV, New York City.
1982	*The Missoulian*, Missoula, Montana.
	Senator Patrick Leahy of Vermont.
	Jean Otto, chairperson, board of directors, First Amendment Congress, Inc.
	Richmond Newspapers, Inc., Richmond, Virginia.
	Bernie Wynn, Arizona First Amendment Coalition, Phoenix, Arizona.
1983	Brown and Bain, legal firm, Phoenix, Arizona.
	Frank Snepp, author.

DISTINGUISHED CAMPUS ADVISERS

1979	Paul Atkins, West Virginia University.
	Merrill Bankester, Memphis State University.
	James Highland, Western Kentucky University.
	Robert Warner, University of Wyoming.
1980	Charles Fair, Virginia Commonwealth University.
	King D. White, Oklahoma State University.
	Rob Daly, Kansas State University.
	Tom Heuterman, Washington State University.
1981	Ralph Izard, Ohio University.
	Brent Norlem, St. Cloud, Minnesota State University.
	David L. Bennett, Northern Arizona University.
	Roy G. Clark, Sam Houston State University.
1982	Lamar Bridges, Central Michigan University.
	Perry J. Ashley, University of South Carolina.
	Les Anderson, Wichita State University.
	Pete Wilson, California State University at Humboldt.
1983	William Fisher, Kent State University.
	Dick Lytle, Texas Tech University.
	Ted Stannard, Western Washington University.

BARNEY KILGORE MEMORIAL AWARD

1969 Douglas Stone, University of Minnesota
Finalists:
Michael V. Adams, Texas Christian University.
Roger C. Boye, University of Nebraska.
Albert C. Stepp, Jr., University of South Carolina.
Lawrence L. Thomas, San Diego State University.

1970 Howard J. Finberg, San Francisco State University.
Finalists:
Carl W. Schwartz, University of Illinois.
Steven E. Stewart, University of Georgia.
Roger W. Smith, University of Southern California.
June Ellen Tyhurst, Oklahoma State University

1971 James (Max) Woodfin, Southern Methodist University.
Finalists:
N. Christian Anderson, Oregon State University.
Louis M. Heldman, Ohio State University.
Allen Lipsett, Georgia State University.
Ronald Ragan, East Texas State University.

1972 Steven Wines, University of Kentucky.
Finalists:
John Balzar, California State University Northridge.
David G. Bartel, University of Kansas.
Michael Brock, San Francisco State University.
Linda Halsey, Ohio State University.

1973 Robert L. Simison, University of Kansas.
Finalists:
Rita Ciolli, Fordham University.
H.J. Cummins, University of Nebraska.
Randy Bellows, University of Florida.
Jane Weisman, San Diego State University.
Paul Parsons, University of Arkansas, Little Rock.

1974 Joseph R. Lapointe, Wayne State University.
Finalists:
James L. Adams, Indiana University.
Charles Durfey, Ohio State University.
Lesle Ciarula, University of Bridgeport.
Joyce Marie Murdoch, University of Georgia.

1975 Gregory Waskul, California State University Northridge.
Finalists:
Laura Allen, University of Texas at Arlington.
Diane Eng, Syracuse University.
Michael J. Mayham, University of Nebraska.
Jonnie Wilson, San Diego State University.

1976 C. Christine Morris, Indiana University.
Finalists:
Yael T. Abouhalkah, University of Kansas.
Matthew J. Bokor, University of South Florida.
Holly Kurtz, University of California at Los Angeles.
Karen Anne Welzel, Ohio State University.

1977 Cheryl Patterson, California State University Fullerton.
Finalists:
Bonita S. Brodt, University of Indiana.
Jacalyn V. Golston, California State University Fresno.
Leah Rozen, Pennsylvania State University.
Jerry Seib, University of Kansas.

1978 Linda Mari Taira, University of Hawaii.
Finalists:
Laura Hlavach, Indiana University.
Cynthia Kasabian, San Francisco State University.
Laurence W. Marscheck, Pepperdine University.
Thomas J. Petruno, Ohio State University.

1979	Robert E. Mackle, Oklahoma State University.

Finalists:
Scott Goldsmith, Indiana University.
Mark W. Harden, San Francisco State University.
John Hollar, Southern Methodist University.
Scott MacDougal, University of Wisconsin at Eau Claire.

1980	Carol A. Beier, University of Kansas.

Finalists:
Jeff Barton, Baylor University.
Thomas French, Indiana University.
Mary Jo Mosher, St. Cloud State University.
Carol Pitts, Drake University.

1981	Timothy J. Franklin, Indiana University.

Finalists:
Katherine Brussell, University of Kansas.
Paula Froke, Pennsylvania State University.
Ken Wysocky, University of Wisconsin at Oshkosh.
Mark Zoromski, University of Wisconsin at Eau Claire.

1982	Daniel M. Weintraub, San Diego State University.

Finalists:
Philip S. Gutis, Pennsylvania State University.
Karen Franklin, San Francisco State University.
Rebecca Chaney, University of Kansas.
Laurie A. Brink, University of Tennessee.

Barney Kilgore FOI Internships

1983
Sharon Appelbaum, University of Kansas
David Freedman, Columbia University

EUGENE C. PULLIAM FELLOWSHIP
FOR EDITORIAL WRITING

1978	Ross MacKenzie, Richmond, Virginia *News-Leader*.
1979	No Award Made
1980	Ralph B. Bennett, San Diego, California *Evening Tribune*.
1981	F.J. (Ted) Douglas, the Detroit *News*.
1982	No Award Made
1983	Ralph Johnson, Toledo, Ohio *Blade*.

OUTSTANDING PROFESSIONAL CHAPTER

NOTE: Only one outstanding professional chapter was chosen each year from 1948 until 1972 when two awards were presented – one for chapters with one hundred or more members and one for chapters with fewer than one hundred members. The dividing line between the large and small chapters was changed to seventy-five members in 1979.

1948	Fort Worth	1960	Fort Worth
1949	Fort Worth	1961	Fort Worth
1950	Washington, DC	1962	Atlanta
1951	Milwaukee	1963	San Diego
1952	Washington, DC	1964	Buckeye (Akron)
1953	Chicago	1965	San Diego
1954	Chicago	1966	Fort Worth
1955	Milwaukee	1967	San Diego
1956	Washington, DC	1968	Los Angeles
1957	Chicago	1969	San Diego
1958	Atlanta	1970	Fort Worth
1959	Chicago	1971	Chicago

Large Chapters		Small Chapters	
1972	San Diego	1972	Fort Worth
1973	San Diego	1973	Fort Worth
1974	Greater Philadelphia	1974	Fort Worth
1975	Milwaukee	1975	New Mexico
1976	Milwaukee	1976	Des Moines
1977	Milwaukee	1977	Buckeye
1978	Chicago	1978	Orange County
1979	Milwaukee	1979	Austin
1980	New York	1980	Utah
1981	Atlanta	1981	East Tennessee
1982	Chicago	1982	EastTennessee
1983	Milwaukee	1983	Inland Empire

OUTSTANDING CAMPUS CHAPTER
1973-1983

NOTE: From the early professional fraternity days, undergraduate chapters competed for the Beckman and Hogate awards given on the basis of points earned for chapter efficiency, activities and the number of student members who entered the profession. Those awards were not given after 1960 and no competition among campus chapters was begun again until 1973.

1973	University of Illinois	1979	St. Cloud State University
1974	Marquette University	1980	Virginia Commonwealth University
1975	Marquette University	1981	Iowa State University
1976	Ohio University	1982	Iowa State University
1977	University of Wisconsin-Eau Claire	1983	Iowa State University
1978	Ohio University		

DISTINGUISHED SERVICE AWARD WINNERS

Research About Journalism

1935	Oscar W. Riegel	1960	Leonard W. Levy
1936	Ralph O. Nafziger	1961	Burton Paulu
1937	Alfred McClung Lee	1962	Theodore E. Kruglak
1938	Frank Luther Mott	1963	David P. Forsyth
1939	Norval Neil Luxon	1964	John Hohenberg
1940	Paul F. Lazersfield	1965	William L. Rivers
1944	Earl English	1966	Kenneth E. Olson
1945	Frank Thayer	1967	John Hohenberg
1946	Ralph D. Casey, Bruce	1968	William A. Hachten
	Smith and H.D. Lasswell	1969	Ronald T. Farrar
1947	James E. Pollard	1970	William Small
1948	J. Edward Gerald	1971	John C. Merrill and
1949	Edwin Emery		Ralph L. Lowenstein
1959	Robert S. Harper	1972	William Small
1962	Curtis D. MacDougall	1973	Philip Meyer
1953	Harold L. Cross	1974	Loren Ghiglione
1954	Edwin Emery and	1975	Marvin Barrett
	Henry Ladd Smith	1977	Peter Braestrup
1956	Theodore B. Peterson	1978	John Hohenberg
1957	Frank Luther Mott	1979	Lloyd Wendt
1958	L. John Martin	1980	John Lofton
1959	Warren C. Price	1981	Robert W. Desmond
		1982	Robert W. Desmond

General Reporting

1939	Meigs O. Frost	1965	Alton Blakeslee
1940	Basil Brewer	1966	Stanley W. Penn and
1942	Jack Vincent		Monroe W. Karmin
1943	Julius M. Klein and	1967	Charles Nicodemus
	Ralph S. O'Leary	1968	Haynes Johnson
1943	Edward J. Doherty	1969	Seymour Hersh
1945	James P. McGuire and	1970	Washington Post staff writers
	John J. McPhaul	1971	James B. Steele and Donald L. Barlett
1946	John M. McCullough	1972	William Reed, Jr. & James Bolus
1947	George Goodwin	1973	James R. Polk
1948	Richard C. Looman	1974	Frank Sutherland
1949	Bob Considine	1975	William Mitchell, Billy Bowles
1950	Edward B. Simmons		Kirk Cheyfitz, Julie Morris, Tom
1951	Victor Cohn		Hennessey, James Harper
1952	Chalmers M. Roberts		and Jim Neubacher
1953	Carl T. Rowan	1976	George Reasons and Mike Goodman
1954	Richard Hyer and	1977	Fredric Tulsky and David Phelps
	William P. Walsh	1978	Pamela Zeckman, Zay Smith
1955	Victor Cohn		Eugene Pesek and James Frost
1956	Alfred Kuettner	1979	Gene Miller, Carl Hlaasen,
1957	Pierre J. Huss		Patrick Malone and William D.
1958	Victor Cohn		Montalbano
1959	Saul Pett	1980	Longview (Wash.) Daily News Staff
1960	Robert Colby Nelson	1981	Sydney Freedberg and
1961	Joseph Newman		David Ashenfelter
1962	Oscar Griffin	1982	Loretta Tofani
1963	Jimmy Breslin		
1964	J. Harold Brislin		

Editorial Writing

1939	W.W. Waymack	1962	Karl E. Meyer
1940	Allen Drury	1963	H.G. Davis, Jr.
1942	Alexander Kendrick	1964	J.O. Emmerich
1943	Milton Lehman	1965	Alfred G. Dickson
1944	Felix R. McKnight	1966	Duane Croft
1945	Francis P. Locke	1967	Robert E. Fisher
1946	John W. Hillman	1968	Robert M. White II
1947	Alan Barth	1969	Albert (Hap) Cawood
1948	Virginius Dabney	1970	John R. Harrison
1949	John Crider	1971	Joanna Wragg
1950	Bradley L. Morrison	1972	John R. Harrison
1951	Robert M. White II	1973	Frank Corrigan
1952	Virginius Dabney	1974	Michael Pakenham
1953	John N. Reddin	1975	William Duncliffe
1954	Robert Estabrook	1976	George W. Wilson
1955	James J. Kilpatrick	1977	Desmond Stone
1956	Sylvan Meyer	1978	Philip Goldsmith
1957	Vermont Royster	1979	Rick Sinding
1958	J.D. Maurice	1980	Louis J. Salome, William Hollstrom
1959	Cecil Prince		and Betsy Poller
1960	Hodding Carter III	1981	John T. Senderling
1961	James A. Clendinen	1982	David Rohn

Editorial Cartooning

1942	Jacob Burck	1962	Paul F. Conrad
1943	Charles Werner	1963	William H. (Bill) Mauldin
1944	Henry Barrow	1964	Charles O. Bissell
1945	Reuben L. Goldberg	1965	Roy Justus
1946	Dorman H. Smith	1966	Patrick B. Oliphant
1947	Bruce Russell	1967	Eugene C. Payne
1948	Herbert Block	1968	Paul F. Conrad
1949	Herbert Block	1969	William H. (Bill) Mauldin

1950	Bruce Russell	1970	Paul F. Conrad
1951	Herbert Block and Bruce Russell	1971	Hugh Haynie
		1972	William H. (Bill) Mauldin
1952	Cecil Jensen	1973	Paul Szep
1953	John Fischetti	1974	Mike Peters
1954	Calvin Alley	1975	Tony Auth
1955	John Fischetti	1976	Paul Szep
1956	Herbert Block	1977	Don Wright
1957	Scott Long	1978	James Mark Borgman
1958	Clifford Baldowski	1979	John P Trever
1959	Charles Gordon Brooks	1980	Paul F. Conrad
1960	Dan Dowling	1981	Paul F. Conrad
1961	Frank Interlandi	1982	Richard Locher

Foreign Correspondence

1939	Kenneth T. Downs	1962	William J. Woestendiek
1940	Leland Stowe	1963	Malcolm W. Browne
1942	Keith Wheeler	1964	Henry Shapiro
1943	Frederick Kuh	1965	James Nelson Goodsell
1944	Frederick Kuh	1966	Robert S. Elegant
1945	Arnaldo Cortesi	1967	Peter Arnett
1946	Charles Gratke	1968	Clyde H. Farnsworth, Henry Kamm
1947	Daniel DeLuce		and Tad Szulc
1948	Nat Barrows	1969	Anatole Shub
1949	Kingsbury Smith	1970	Hugh Mulligan
1952	Keyes Beech and	1971	Peter Arnett and Bernard Gavzer
	Don Whitehead	1972	Charlotte Salkowski
1951	Ferdinand Kuhn	1973	Jacques Leslie
1952	Ernest Pisko	1974	Donald L. Barlett and
1953	Alexander Campbell		James B. Steele
1954	Carl T. Rowan	1975	Sydney H. Schanberg
1955	Carl T. Rowan	1978	Joe Rigert
1956	Russell Jones	1977	Robert Toth
1957	Harrison E. Salisbury	1978	Charles Krause
1958	John Strohm	1979	Karen DeYoung
1959	William H. Stringer	1980	Edward Giradet
1960	Smith Hempstone, Jr.	1981	Richard Ben Cramer
1961	Gaston Coblentz	1982	Bob Rivard

Washington Correspondence

1942	Drew Pearson and Robert S. Allen	1964	Louis M. Kohlmeier
		1965	Nick Kotz
1943	Sam O'Neal	1966	Richard Harwood
1944	Marquis W. Childs	1967	Jack C. Landau
1945	Peter Edson	1968	Joe Western
1946	Wallace R. Deuel	1969	Robert J. Ostrow and
1947	Bert Andrews		Robert L. Jackson
1948	W. McNeil Lowry	1970	Jared D. Stout
1949	Jack Steele	1971	Neil Sheehan and the New York
1950	William K. Hutchinson		York Times
1951	John Hightower	1972	Carl Bernstein and
1952	Clark Mollenhoff		Robert Woodward
1953	Richard L. Wilson	1973	James M. Naughton, John M.
1954	Clark Mollenhoff		Crewdson, Ben A. Franklin, Chris-
1955	Joseph and		topher Lydon and Agis Salpukas
	Stewart Alsop	1974	Seth Kanton
1956	Bem Price	1975	James Risser
1957	Robert T. Hartmann	1976	Maxine Cheshire, Scott Armstrong
1958	James Reston	1977	Gaylord Shaw
1959	Vance Trimble	1978	Joseph Albright
1960	James Clayton, Julius	1979	Gordon Eliot White
	Duscha, Murrey Marder,	1980	Joseph Albright
	Bernard Nossiter	1981	Jerome Watson

1962	Jules Whitcover	1982	Judith Bender, James M.
1963	Jerry Landauer		Klurfeld, Earl B. Lane
			and Susan Page

Radio Reporting

1946	Allen Stout	1967	WJR News, Detroit
1947	James C. McNamara	1968	KFWB News Radio, Los Angeles
1948	Goerge J. O'Connor	1969	Ed Joyce, WCBS Radio, New York
1949	Sid Pietzsch	1970	Bob White, KRLD, Dallas, Texas
1950	Jack E. Krueger	1971	John Rich, NBC News
1951	Jim Monroe	1972	Val Hymes, WTOP Radio
1952	Charles and Eugene Jones		Washington, DC
1953	Gordon Gammack	1973	Eric Engberg, Group W
1954	Richard Chapman		Washington, DC
1955	John Chancellor	1974	Jim Mitchell, Gary Franklin
1956	Edward J Green		Hank Allison and Herb Humphries
1957	Dave Muhlstein		KFWB Radio, Los Angeles
1958	Winston Burdett	1975	WHBF AM-FM Radio News Team
1950	Donald H. Weston		Rock Island, IL.
1960	Frederick A. Goerner	1976	Mike Lee and Doug Tunnell
1961	KDKA Radio News Staff		CBS News
	Pittsburgh, Pa.; and	1977	Paul McGonigle, KOY Radio
	Wip Robinson and Frank		Phoenix, Arizona
	O'Roark, WSVA,		
	Harrisburg, Pa.	1978	WGST Newsradio 92, Atlanta
1962	WINS News Staff, New		
	York	1979	ABC Radio News
1963	WINS News Staff, New		
	York	1980	WHDH, Boston
1964	WNEW Radio, New York	1981	Jim McNabb, KVET-AM, Austin, TX
1965	WNEW Radio, New York	1982	WEEL, Boston
1966	KTBC Radio, Austin, TX.		

Editorializing on Radio

1963	WRTA, Altoona, Pa	1973	WGRG, Pittsfield, Mass.
1964	WXYZ, Detroit	1974	Jim Branch, WRFM, New York City
1965	KDKA, Pittsburgh	1975	Charles B. Cleveland
1966	WAIT, Chicago		WIND, Chicago
1967	WSBA Radio, York-	1976	Ed Hinshaw, WTMJ, Milwaukee
	Lancaster-Harrisburg, Pa.	1977	Jay Lewis, Alabama
1968	Theodore Jones, WCRB,		
	Waltham,		Information Network
	Mass.	1978	KYW Newsradio, Philadelphia
1969	WWDC, Washington, DC	1979	WTLC Radio, Indianapolis
1970	WLPR, Mobile, Ala.	1980	Lesley Crosson, WEEL, Boston
1971	WSOC-AM, Charlotte,		
	N.C.	1981	Michal Regunberg, WEEL, Boston
1972	Frank Reynolds, ABC		
	News	1982	Susan Nixon, WBBM-AM, Chicago

Television Reporting

1952	Charles and Eugene Jones	1968	KNXT, Los Angeles
1954	Spencer Allen	1969	WCCO, Minneapolis
1955	Paul Alexander and	1970	KBTV, Denver
	Gael Boden	1971	Robert Schakne, CBS News
1956	Ernest Lelser, Jerry	1972	Laurens Pierce
	Schwartzkopff, and Julian	1973	Steve Young and Roger Sims,
	Hoshal and Dick Hance		CBS News
1957	Jim Bennett	1974	Lee Louis, KGTV, San Diego
1958	WBBM-TV, Chicago	1975	WHAS, Louisville
1959	WGN-TV, Chicago	1976	KMJ-TV,,Fresno, California
1960	WTVJ, Miami, Fla.	1977	WPIX-TV, San Francisco

1961	WKY-TV, Oklahoma City	1978	Steve Howell and John Britton
1962	KWTV, Oklahoma City		KCST-TV, San Diego
1963	WBAP-TV, Fort Worth, TX	1979	ABC TV News and Bob Dyk
1964	WFGA-TV, Jacksonville, Fla.	1980	Bill Blakemore and Greg Dobbs
1965	Morley Safer, CBS News		ABC News
1966	WSB-TV, Atlanta	1981	WHAS-TV, Louisville
1967	John Laurence, CBS News	1982	KGTV, San Diego

Editorializing on Television

1963	Tom Martin, KFDA-TV Amarillo, TX	1974	Jay Lewis, WSFA-TV, Montgomery Alabama
1964	KDKA, Pittsburgh	1975	Don McGaffin and Charles Royer
1965	WTOP-TV, Washington, DCKING, Seattle		
1966	WFBM-TV, Indianapolis	1976	WCVB, Boston
1967	KWTV, Oklahoma City	1977	Rich Adams, WTOP-Tv
1968	WOOD-TV, Grand RapidsWashington, DC Michigan	1978	Peter Kohler, WCBS-TV New York
1969	KCPX, Salt Lake City		
1970	WCCO, Minneapolis	1979	KPIX-TV, San Francisco
1971	Robert Schulman, WHAS-TV Louisville	1980	Bill Moyers, WNET, New York
		1981	Jack Hurley, WHIO-TV, Dayton, OH
1972	WCKT-TV, Miami, Fla.	1982	Beth Konrad, WDIV-TV, Detroit
1973	KRON-TV, San Francisco		

News Photography

1946	Frank Q. Brown	1964	Dom Ligato
1947	Paul Calvert	1965	Henry Herr Gill
1948	Frank Jurkowski	1966	Ray Mews
1949	Chicago Daily News	1967	Catherine Leroy
1950	David Douglas Duncan	1968	Edward T. Adams
1951	Edward DeLuga and Roger Wrenn	1969	Horst Faas
		1970	John P. Filo
1952	Robert I. Wendlinger	1971	Dong Jun Kim
1953	Bill Wilson	1972	Huynh Cong (Nick) Ut
1954	Leslie Dodds	1973	Anthony K. Roberts
1955	Richard B. Yager	1974	Werner Baum
1956	Dan Tompkins	1975	Stanley J. Forman
1957	Eldred C. Reaney	1976	Bruce Fritz
1958	Andrew St. George	1977	Eddie Adams
1959	Andrew Lopez	1978	Norman Y. Lono
1960	J. Parke Randall	1979	Eddie Adams
1961	Peter Leibing	1980	Giovanni Foggia
1962	Cliff DeBear	1981	Ron Edmonds
1963	Bob Jackson	1982	Robert Fila

Magazine Reporting

1949	Lester Velie	1966	John G. Hubbell
1950	Gordon Schendel	1967	William Lambert
1951	Bill Davidson	1968	Kristin Hunter
1952	Bill Davidson	1969	William Lambert
1953	James P. O'Donnell	1970	David L. Chandler
1954	Marshall MacDuffie	1971	Arthur Hadley
1955	Fletcher Knebel	1972	Thomas Thompson
1956	John Bartlow Martin	1973	Floyd Miller
1957	Harold H. Martin	1974	John Guinther
1958	John L. Cobbs	1975	Mike Mallowe
2959	John Robert Coughlan	1976	Larry DuBois, Laurence Gonzales

1960	Hobart Rowen	1977	John Conroy
1961	Joseph Morschauser	1978	Tony Green
1962	Peter Goldman	1979	Michael W. Vargo
1963	Theodore H. White	1980	Penny Lernoux
1964	Sam Castan	1981	Seymour Hersh
1965	Ben H. Bagdikian	1982	Don Kowet, Sally Bedell

Public Service in Newspaper Journalism

(During years 1939-1948 this category was known as "Courage in Journalism.")

1939	New Orleans States	1959	Atlanta Constitution
1942	Guthrie County Vendette Panora, Iowa	1960	Leesburg (Fla) Daily Commercial
1943	Lowell (Mass) Sunday Telegram	1961	San Gabriel Valley Daily Tribune West Covina, California
1944	Milwaukee Journal	1962	Pascagoula Chronicle Pascagoula, Mississippi
1945	New Orleans States	1963	Chicago Daily News
1946	Kansas City (Mo.) Star	1964	McComb (Miss) Enterprise-Journal
1947	Memphis (Tenn.) Press-Scimitar	1965	Miami Herald
1948	Philadelphia Inquirer	1966	Los Angeles Times Long Island Press
1949	Moose Lake (Minn.) Star-Gazette	1967	Newsday, Garden City, New York
1950	Atlanta Journal	1968	St. Louis Globe Democrat
1951	Chicago Sun-Times	1969	Chicago Daily News
1952	The Wall Street Journal New York City	1970	Newsday, Garden City, New York
1953	Chicago Daily News and Houston Post	1971	Boston Globe
1954	Cleveland Plain Dealer	1972	Sun Newspapers, Omaha, Nebraska
1955	Watsonville (Calif.) Register-Pajaronian	1973	Newsday, Garden City, New York
1956	Portland Oregonian	1974	Indianapolis Star
1957	Des Moines Register and Tribune and the Minneapolis Star and Tribune	1975	Louisville Courier-Journal
		1976	The Wall Street Journal
		1977	Philadelphia Inquirer
		1978	Chicago Sun Times
		1979	Miami Herald
1958	Tampa (Fla.) Tribune	1980	Independent Press-Telegram Long Beach, California
		1981	Los Angeles Times
		1982	Gannett News Service

Public Service in Radio Journalism

1949	WTTS, Bloomington, Ind.	1966	WIBW, Topeka, Kansas
1950	WAVZ, New Haven, Conn.	1967	Westinghouse Broadcasting Co. Inc.
1951	WMAQ, Chicago	1968	WBZ Radio, Boston
1952	WMT, Cedar Rapids, Ia.	1969	WHN, New York
1953	CBS Radio Network	1970	WWDC, Washington, DC
1954	CBS Radio Network	1971	WBZ Radio, Boston
1955	WMAQ, Chicago	1972	WGAR, Cleveland
1956	CBS Radio Network	1973	WMAL, Washington, DC
1957	KNX Radio, Los Angeles	1974	WIND, Chicago
1958	CBS Radio Network	1975	WRVA Radio, Richmond, Va.
1959	WIP Radio, Philadelphia	1976	WCAU-AM, Philadelphia
1960	WBT, Charlotte, N.C.	1977	WSGN-AM Birmingham, Ala.
1961	KNUZ, Houston	1978	KXL, Portland, Ore.
1962	WBZ Radio, Boston	1979	WJR Radio, Detroit
1963	WSB, Atlanta	1980	WIND, Chicago
1964	KSEN, Shelby, Montana	1981	WJR Radio, Detroit
1965	WCCO, Minneapolis	1982	WRAL, Raleigh, N.C.

Public Service in Television Journalism

1952	WBNS-TV, Columbus, Ohio	1967	NBC
1953	WHAS-TV, Louisville	1968	WIBW-TV, Topeka, Kansas
1954	Dumont TV Network and ABC	1969	WDSU-TV, New Orleans
1955	KAKE-TV, Wichita, Kan.	1970	KING-TV, Seattle
1956	KPIX-TV, San Francisco	1971	CBS
1957	WBZ-TV, Boston	1972	WABC-TV, New York
1958	KNXT, Hollywood	1973	WSOC-TV, Charlotte, N.C.
1959	WBZ-TV, Boston	1974	ABC News, New York
1060	NBC Television, New York	1975	WCKT-TV, Miami, Fla.
1961	KHOU-TV, Houston	1976	KNXT, Los Angeles
1962	KGW-TV, Portland, Ore.	1977	KOOL-TV, Phoenix
1963	KDKA, Pittsburgh and NBC	1978	WCCO-TV, Minneapolis
		1979	KXAS-TV, Fort Worth
1964	CBS	1980	KSL, Salt Lake City
1965	WABC-TV, New York	1981	WNBC-TV, New York
1966	KLZ-TV, Denver	1982	WCCO-TV, Minneapolis

Public Service in Magazine Journalism

1949	Collier's	1966	LIFE
1950	Collier's	1967	Philadelphia Magazine
1951	McCall's	1968	LIFE
1952	LOOK	1969	Philadelphia Magazine
1953	LOOK	1970	Washingtonian Magazine
1954	Saturday Evening Post	1971	New Orleans Magazine
1955	LOOK	1972	Philadelphia Magazine
1956	LIFE	1973	Philadelphia Magazine
1957	The Reporter	1974	Philadelphia Magazine
1958	LIFE	1975	Philadelphia Magazine
1959	Saturday Evening Post	1976	Philadelphia Magazine
1960	The Saturday Review	1977	Mother Jones
1961	LOOK	1978	New West
1962	LOOK	1979	National Geographic
1963	LOOK	1980	Philadelphia Magazine
1964	LOOK	1981	National Geographic
1965	The Reader's Digest	1982	The New Yorker

Radio or Television Commentary
(Award Discontinued in 1960)

1939	Albert Warner	1952	Clifton Utley
1940	Cecil Brown	1953	Charles J. Chatfield
1942	Fulton Lewis, Jr.	1954	Reuven Frank
1946	Harry M. Cochran	1955	Charles Shaw
1947	Alex Dreier	1956	Howard K. Smith
1948	Merrill Mueller	1957	Jerry Rosholt
1949	Elmer Davis	1958	Harold R. Meier
1950	Leo O'Brien and Howard Maschmeier	1959	Gene Marine
1951	William E. Griffith, Jr.	1960	David Brinkley

Newspaper Cartooning
(Awarded only twice)

1948 Ed Dodd
1950 Milton Caniff

Radio or Television Newswriting
(Awarded only twice)
1961 KDKA, Pittsburgh
1962 Harold Keen, WFMB-TV, San Diego

War Correspondence
(Awarded only three times)
1943 Ernie Pyle – Raymond Clapper Memorial Award
1944 Ernie Pyle – Human interest and Henry T. Gorrell – Spot news
1945 John Graham Dowling

Special Awards
1943 Raymond Clapper (Posthumous) – William Allen White Memorial Award
1977 Investigative Reporters and Editors – Public Service

Gold Key Awards of 1932
Paul Scott Mowrer
Philip Hale
Franklin P. Adams
Alexander Dana Noyes
Jay N. (Ding) Darling
Casper S. Yost

MARK OF EXCELLENCE CONTEST WINNERS

1972
Newswriting . . . . William Choyke, Ohio University
Feature Writing . . . . Mary Huffman, University of Nebraska
Editorial Writing . . . . Steven B. Poulter, Iowa State University
Student Newspaper . . . . Miami *Hurricane*, University of Miama (Florida)
Magazine Nonfiction Article . . . . Barbara Ruth Woller, Syracuse University
Student Magazine . . . . *Orient*, Ball State University
Radio Reporting . . . . Stephen Paul Homan, Pennsylvania State University
Television Reporting . . . . C. Peter Deane, Jr., University of North Carolina
News Photography . . . . David Thurber, California State University, San Jose
Feature Photography . . . . Julie VanReyper, California State University, Fresno

1973
Newswriting Under Deadline . . . . Mark Wilson, University of Colorado
Newswriting Not Under Deadline . . . . Sara Fitzgerald, University of Michigan
Editorial Writing . . . . Otis R. Tims, University of Mississippi
Student Newspaper . . . . *Indiana Daily*, University of Indiana
Magazine Nonfiction Article . . . . Mary Ann F. Galante, University of Southern California
Student Magazine . . . . *MUSE*, Southern Illinois University, Edwardsville
Radio Reporting . . . . Gary L. Stewart, Oregon State University
Television Reporting . . . . Ed Fischhoff, Ohio University
News Photography . . . . John D. Copeland, University of Florida
Feature Photography . . . . Michael O'Brien, University of Tennessee

1974
Newswriting Under Deadline . . . . Chuck Gomez, University of Florida
Newswriting Not Under Deadline . . . . Robert Von Sternberg, Kent State University
Editorial Writing . . . . Andres Tevington, Oklahoma State University
Student Newspaper . . . . *Daily Illini*, University of Illinois
Magazine Nonfiction Article . . . . Christopher Wren, George Washington University
Student Magazine . . . . *IMAGE*, Texas Christian University
Radio Reporting . . . . Rich Finlinson, University of Utah
Television Reporting . . . . Steve Hess, Fullerton College
News Photography . . . . Albert Swainston, University of Kansas
Feature Photography . . . . Ray Wong, University of Missouri

1975

Newswriting Under Deadline	Steve Hess, University of Southern California
Newswriting Not Under Deadline	Sue Engstrom, University of Nevada
Editorial Writing	Danny Goodgame, University of Mississippe
Student Newspaper	*Diamondback*, University of Maryland
Magazine Nonfiction Article	Judith Murphy, University of Oklahoma
Student Magazine	*Athens*, Ohio University
Radio Reporting	Janet Fuhrman, Pennsylvania State University
Television Reporting	Radio-Television News Center, San Jose State University
News Photography	Mark Perlstein, University of Wisconsin, Madison
Feature Photography	David Varner, Indiana University

1976

Newswriting Under Deadline	Maria Lawlor, University of Iowa
Feature Writing	David Gregor, University of Washington
Editorial Writing	Barbara Huebner, University of Wisconsin, Eau Claire
Editorial Cartooning	Peter Wagner, University of Minnesota
Student Newspaper	*Diamondback*, University of Maryland
Magazine Nonfiction Article	Ricahrd A. Kelly and James E. Yavorcik, Ohio State University
Student Magazine	*By-Line*, Northwestern University
Radio Reporting	Michial L. Rausch, Ohio University
Television Reporting	Phillip Andres Benson, Drake University
News Photography	Gary Anbrose, California State University, Long Beach
Feature Photography	Joseph McNally, Syracuse University

1977

Editorial Writing	Rhonda Dickey, University of Iowa
Feature Writing	Robert M. Goldstein, Oregon State University
Editorial Cartoon	Brian Basset, Ohio State University
Student Newspaper	*Daily Illini*, University of Illinois
Magazine Nonfiction Article	Mark Sackett, Marquette University
Student Magazine	*Klipsun*, Western Washington State College
Radio Reporting	Laura Blookworth, Jackie Medley and Jerry Fannin, University of Georgia
Television Reporting	Phillip Benson, Drake University
News Photography	Craig Newman, Arizona State University
Feature Photography	David Griffin, Ohio University

1978

Newspaper Spot News	Dennis J. Sadowski, Bowling Green (Ohio) State University
Newspaper Depth Reporting	Cary Spivak, Northern Illinois University
Editorial Writing	Edward Lee Ranking III, University of North Carolina at Chapel Hill
Editorial Cartooning	Steve Sandstrom, University of Oregon
Student Newspaper	*Diamondback*, University of Maryland
Magazine Nonfiction Article	David T. Friendly, Northwestern University
Student Magazine	*Clifton*, University of Cincinnati
Radio Spot News	Stan Guy Jones, Southwest Texas State University
Radio In-Depth Reporting	Leah Keith, Roger Hunt, Jackie Medley and Laura Bloodworth, University of Georgia
Television Spot News	Bruce Kriegsies, University of Missouri
Television In-Depth Reporting	Leah Keith, University of Georgia
News Photography	Stewart Bowman, University of Kentucky
Feature Photography	Lewis Gardner, Western Kentucky University

1979

Newspaper Spot News	Donna Rouviere, Brigham Young University
Newspaper Depth Reporting	Jill M. Schultz, University of Wisconsin, Madison
Editorial Writing	Jay Rosen, State University of New York at Buffalo
Editorial Cartooning	Scott Willis, Ohio State University
Student Newspaper	*Daily Student*, Indiana University
Magazine Nonfiction Article	Diane Kiesel, June Nicholson, John Henkel and Geri Fuller-Col, American University

Student Magazine	*Clifton*, University of Cincinnati
Radio Spot News	WMUC, University of Maryland
Radio Depth Reporting	Robert J. Gilmartin, University of Missouri
Television Spot News	Al Tompkins, Western Kentucky University
Television Depth Reporting	Dan Hodgson, Brigham Young University
News Photography	Tom Powell, Ohio University
Feature Photography	Bill Wax, University of Florida

1980

Spot News Story	Mary Astadourian, Michael Mace, and Jay Alan Samit, UCLA
Depth Reporting	David L. Preston, University of Missouri
Editorial Writing	Larry Sandler, University of Illinois
Editorial Cartooning	Jack H. Ohman, University of Minnesota
Student Newspaper	*The Daily Texan*, University of Texas at Austin
Magazine Nonfiction Writing	Jeff Porteous, Western Washington University
Student Magazine	*The Memphis Statesman*, Memphis State University
Radio Spot News	Michael Williams, University of Florida
Radio Depth Reporting	Laurie Peterson, Northwest Missouri State University
Television Spot News	Dave Kelly, Drake University
Television Depth Reporting	Anthony Kalinowski, Margaret Herring, Cynthia Oldland, Mark Harmon, Peter Reinert and Warren Weidner, Pennsylvania State University
News Photography	Paul Gilbert, Southwest Texas State University
Feature Photography	Frank Breithaupt, Bowling Green (Ohio) State University

1981

Newswriting	Ralph Merkel, Northwestern University
Best Depth Reporting	Nunzio M. Lupo, Michigan State University
Editorial Writing	Jeff Barton, University of Texas, Austin
Editorial Cartooning	John R. Taylor, Brigham Young University
Feature Writing	Maria Riccardi, Syracuse University
Student Newspaper	*Minnesota Daily*, University of Minnesota
Magazine Nonfiction Article	William Booth, University of Texas at Austin
Student Magazine	*Marquette Journal*, Marquette University
Radio Spot News	Tom Trepiak, Humboldt State University
Radio Documentary	Mary Lou Clark, Duquesne University
Television Spot News	Mindy Mintz, Indiana University
Television Documentary	Ronald Fox, West Virginia University
Spot News Photography	Kirk D. McCoy, University of Maryland
Feature Photography	Betsy Brill, University of Houston

1982

Spot News Story	Henry Fuhrmann, Kendall In, Jeannie Wong, California State University at Los Angeles
Depth Reporting	Christopher Quinn, Temple University
Editorial Writing	Edward W. O'Donnell, Western Washington University
Editorial Cartooning	Mike Luckovich, University of Washington
Feature Article	D. Haynes Bayless, University of Minnesota
Student Newspaper	*The Daily Collegian*, Pennsylvania State University
Magazine Nonfiction Article	John Schwartz, University of Texas at Austin
Student Magazine	*UTmost*, University of Texas at Austin
Radio Spot News	Mark Hamrick, University of Kansas
Radio Documentary	Mark Hamrick, University of Kansas
Television Spot News	Mike McQuinn, Brigham Young University
Television Documentary	Dan Sanz, Oregon State University
News Photography	Michael Quan, Boston University
Feature Photography	Gary Harwood, Kent State University

1983

Spot New Story	David Simon, University of Maryland
Depth Reporting	Michele Andrus Dill, Brigham Young University
Editorial Writing	Joseph Perkins, Howard University
Editorial Cartooning	Jeff A. Koterba, University of Nebraska at Omaha
Feature Writing	Isabel Wilkerson, Howard University

Student Newspaper . . . .*Diamondback*, University of Maryland
Magazine Nonfiction Article . . . . David Simon, University of Maryland
Student Magazine . . . .*UTmost*, University of Texas at Austin
Radio Spot News Under Deadline . . . . Tara Sandler, Emerson College
Radio News Not Under Deadline . . . . Judy Jackus, Emerson College
Radio Documentary . . . . Joyce Wise, Xavier University
Television Spot News Under Deadline . . . . John Pertzborn, University of Wisconsin at Madison
Television News Not Under Deadline . . . . June Grasso, Columbia University
Television Documentary . . . . John Caplan, Jeff Rainford Schroeter and
Scott Miskimo, University of Missouri
News Photography . . . . Gary Harwood, Kent State University
Feature Photography . . . . C. Casey Madison, Western Washington University

NATIONAL CONVENTIONS: 1959-1984

(with site, city, dates, attendance, speakers, major events, and issues decided)

Nov. 11-14 1959: Claypool Hotel, Indianapolis, Indiana.
Attendance: 600.
Speakers: Vice President Richard Nixon; David Brinkley; Manchester, England *Guardian* Publisher Laurence P. Scott; SDX Founder Eugene C. Pulliam; Jules Dubois, Latin American Department, Chicago *Tribune*.
Major Events and Issues: (1) Celebrated Fiftieth Anniversary of the founding of Sigma Delta Chi. (2) Criticized Cuban Dictator Fidel Castro for repressive action against newspapers.

Nov. 30 - Dec. 3, 1960: Biltmore Hotel, New York City.
Attendance: 600.
Speakers: Gov. Nelson Rockefeller, New York; Gov. Michael DiSalle, Ohio; Rep. John Moss, California; Turner Catledge, managing editor *The New York Times*; Frank Stanton, president, Columbia Broadcasting System; Pierre Salinger, press secretary to President John F. Kennedy; Herb Klein, press secretary to Vice President Richard Nixon.
Major Events and Issues: (1) Warren Agee becomes executive officer. (2) Adopted the McKinsey Report reorganizing the fraternity to a professional society, establishing a board of directors and the office of first vice president, setting up regions and regional directors, increasing national dues from $5 to $10, calling for full-time professional editor of *The Quill*, and changing name of administrative head from executive director to executive officer. (3) Established two new "purposes" for the Society -- "To attract talented young people at the high school and college level to journalism," and "To raise the prestige of the journalist in the community."

Oct. 25-28, 1961: Hotel Fontainebleau, Miami Beach.
Attendance: 460.
Speakers: McGeorge Bundy, special assistant to President John F. Kennedy; Gov. Nelson Rockefeller, New York; Robert R. Gilruth, National Aeronautics and Space Administration; Gov. Ferris Bryant, Florida.
Major Events and Issues: (1) Appropriated $10,000 to underwrite travel expenses of official student delegates to and from the national convention in Tulsa, Oklahoma for 1962 eliminating the assessments of the Society's professional chapters which had provided pro-rata travel expenses for student delegates. (2) Established first international chapter -- British Isles professional chapter. (3) Changed by-laws so that students may join with pledge of their "intention" to pursue careers in journalism rather than the long-standing stipulation that they have "decided" to do so.

Nov. 14-17, 1962: Mayo Hotel, Tulsa, Oklahoma.
Attendance: 550.
Speakers: Merriman Smith, senior White House correspondent, United Press International; Elmer Lower, general news manager, National Broadcasting Company; Louis Harris, public opinion analyst; Sen. Robert Kerr, Oklahoma; Claude M. Blair, vice president, American Telephone and Telegraph Company; Jenkin Lloyd Jones, editor, Tulsa *Tribune*.
Major Events and Issues: (1) Established Sigma Delta Chi Foundation. (2) Defeated proposal for name change, retaining the wording, "Sigma Delta Chi, professional journalistic society." (3) First national convention for Russell Hurst as executive officer. (4) Voted to continue national convention travel subsidy for student delegates on a permanent basis and study a travel subsidy for campus chapter advisers. A subsidy of one half the travel cost for advisers was approved formally at the May 10, 1963 board meeting in Dallas, Texas. (5) Urged Congress to adopt a national Freedom of Information Act.

Nov. 6-9, 1963: Golden Triangle Motor Hotel, Norfolk, Virginia.
Attendance: 650.
Speakers: Walter Cronkite, CBS News; Gardner Cowles, president and publisher, *Look* Magazine; Fletcher

Knebel, Washington columnist and co-author, *Seven Days in May*; Dr. Glenn Seaborg, chairman Atomic Energy Commission; Barry Bingham, editor and publisher, Louisville *Courier-Journal*.
Major Events and Issues: (1) Held a luncheon meeting for all delegates aboard the aircraft carrier U.S.S. Enterprise. (2) Approved policy for expansion of effort to charter additional chapters outside the United States.

Dec. 2-5, 1964: Hotel Muehlebach, Kansas City, Missouri.
Attendance: 727.
Speakers: Benjamin M. McKelway, editorial chairman of the Washington, D.C. *Star*; Dan Rather, White House correspondent, CBS News; J.W. (Pat) Heffernan, Reuters news agency; Julian Goodman, vice president, National Broadcasting Company; Alfred Friendly, managing editor, the Washington *Post*; Eugene Patterson, editor, Atlanta *Constitution*; Harlan Cleveland, assistant secretary of state for international organization affairs.
Major Events and Issues: (1) Defeated attempt to change the name of the society to Sigma Delta Chi, The Society of Journalists. (2) Endorsed proposed legislation in Congress for absolute repeal of the equal-time provision of the Communications Act of 1934.

Nov. 10-13, 1965: Hotel Biltmore, Los Angeles.
Attendance: 893.
Speakers: Barney Kilgore, president, *The Wall Street Journal*; Rep. Gerald Ford, Michigan; Gov. Edmund G. (Pat) Brown, California; Julian Scheer, assistant administrator for public affairs, NASA; Malcomb W. Browne, former Associated Press Saigon correspondent in Viet Nam.
Major Events and Issues: (1) Voted to submit name change and admission of women questions to the 1966 national convention in Pittsburgh. (2) Changed the designation "undergraduate" chapters to "campus" chapters and the national office designation to vice president for campus chapter affairs. (3) Voted gift of $25,000 to the Sigma Delta Chi Foundation to provide it with operating capital.

Nov. 9-12, 1966: Gateway Center Hilton, Pittsburgh.
Attendance: 500.
Speakers: Julian Goodman, president, National Broadcasting Company; Bishop John J. Wright, head, Pittsburgh Catholic Diocese; William L. Ryan, Associated Press foreign news analyst; Clark Mollenhoff, Washington Bureau, Cowles Publications; Frank Bartholomew, board chairman, United Press International; George Gallup, director, American Institute of Public Opinion.
Major Events and Issues: (1) Defeated moves to admit women to membership and change the name of the Society. (2) Voted to restrict regional directors to two terms of three years each. (3) Previewed the SDX careers film, *That the People Shall Know*. (4) Awarded first Distinguished Teaching in Journalism prize to Professor A.L. Higginbotham of the University of Nevada.

Nov. 15-18, 1967: Hotel Radisson, Minneapolis.
Attendance: 600.
Speakers: Vice President Hubert H. Humphrey; Harrison Salisbury, assistant managing editor, *The New York Times*; Otis Chandler, publisher, The Los Angeles *Times*; Wes Gallagher, general manager, The Associated Press.
Major Events and Issues: (1) Voted to refer question of admission of women to membership to the 1968 convention in Atlanta and asked the UCLA campus chapter not to pursue plans for a mail referendum on the matter. (2) Noted the deaths of SDX founder William M. Glenn and of Barney Kilgore.

Nov. 20-23, 1968: Marriott Motor Hotel, Atlanta.
Attendance: 650.
Speakers: Dr. Frank Stanton, president, CBS; Edwin Newman, NBC News; Ralph McGill, editor, Atlanta *Constitution*; Roger Tatarian, editor, United Press International; Louis Harris, public opinion analyst.
Major Events and Issues: (1) Voted to submit admission of women question to the 1969 convention in San Diego. (2) Established the $2,500 Kilgore Memorial Award competition for college journalists. (3) Established permanent committee on recruitment of minority group members to journalism. (4) Increased national dues for professional members from $10 to $15. (5) Noted the Society had chartered its 100th professional chapter and its 101st campus chapter during 1968. (6) Approved a by-law change permitting initiation of first-semester sophomores to membership in campus chapters and eliminating the phrase "above-average scholastic standing" from requirements for campus members.

Nov. 12-15, 1969: El Cortez Hotel, San Diego.
Attendance: 750.
Speakers: Merriman Smith, White House correspondent, United Press International; Daniel Schorr, CBS News; Julian Bond, state legislator from Georgia; Mark Ethridge, former publisher, Louisville *Courier-Journal*; Fletcher Knebel, author and columnist.
Major Events and Issues: (1) Changed by-laws to admit women to membership in the Society. (2) Defeated effort to change name of the Society from Sigma Delta Chi to The Society of Journalists. (3) Eliminated the offices of national honorary president and national historian. (4) Presented first Kilgore Memorial Award to Douglas Stone, University of Minnesota. (5) Observed a stormy panel session on the underground press.

Nov. 11-14, 1970: Palmer House, Chicago.
Attendance: 815.
Speakers: Walter Cronkite, CBS News; Katharine Graham, president, Washington Post Company; Henry Ford II, chairman of the board, Ford Motor Company; Peter Arnett, Viet Nam war correspondent, The Associated Press; Ann Landers, syndicated columnist; Nelson Poynter, board chairman, St. Petersburg, Florida *Times and Independent*.
Major Events and Issues: (1) First national convention attended by women as members of the Society. (2) Elected first four students with full voting rights to the national board of directors. (3) Chartered the first campus chapter at a women's college.

Nov. 10-13, 1971: Statler Hilton Hotel, Washington, DC.
Attendance: 896.
Speakers: Secretary of State William P. Rogers; Rep. Morris Udall, Arizona; Reuven Frank, president, NBC News; Al Neuharth, president of The Gannett Company; Max Frankel, Washington bureau chief, *The New York Times*; Dick West, humor columnist, United Press International; Ron Ziegler, press secretary to President Richard Nixon; Dan Rather, White House correspondent, CBS News; Helen Thomas, White House correspondent, United Press International; Hugh Sidey, White House reporter, *Life* magazine; Peter Lisagor, Chicago *Daily News*; Sally Quinn, reporter, Washington *Post*; James J. Kilpatrick, syndicated columnist; Bill Lawrence, ABC News.
Major Events and Issues: (1) Rejected change in Society's name. (2) Elected first woman, a campus board representative, to national board of directors. (3) Established four campus board districts, each district to elect a representative to the national board.

Nov. 15-18, 1972: Statler Hilton Hotel, Dallas.
Attendance: 900.
Speakers: Jack Anderson, syndicated columnist; Hodding Carter III, editor, Greenville, Mississippi *Delta Democrat-Times*; Garrick Utley, correspondent, NBC News; Newbold Noyes, editor, Washington *Star-News*; Bill Farr, reporter, Los Angeles *Times*; Peter Bridge, reporter, Newark, New Jersey *News*; Peter Arnett, correspondent, The Associated Press; Erma Bombeck, syndicated humor columnist.
Major Events and Issues: (1) Approved a resolution directing national nominating committee to nominate more than one candidate for top national offices. (2) Rejected attempt to send name-change issue to the 1973 Buffalo convention.

Nov. 14-17, 1973: Statler Hilton Hotel, Buffalo, New York.
Attendance: 700.
Speakers: Charles Kuralt, CBS News; Marquis Childs, Washington correspondent, St. Louis *Post-Dispatch*; Wauhillau LaHay, writer, Scripps Howard; Judge David Brofman, American Bar Association; Marcel Cadieux, Canadian ambassador to the United States; John Chancellor, NBC News; Benjamin C. Bradlee, executive editor, the Washington *Post*; James Doyle, former reporter, the Washington *Evening Star*; William Small, vice president, CBS News.
Major Events and Issues: (1) Voted to change the name of the Society from Sigma Delta Chi, professional journalistic society to The Society of Professional Journalists, Sigma Delta Chi. (2) Adopted a Code of Ethics for the Society, to replace the American Society of Newspaper Editors Canons used by Sigma Delta Chi since 1926. (3) Approved a system of weighted voting for delegates at national conventions based on chapter membership. (4) Saw the first contested races for national officers in the modern history of the Society. (5) Adopted a by-laws change which provided that regional directors and campus board representatives be elected only by delegates from their own regions or districts. (6) Established a new region, Region Twelve, effective at the conclusion of the 1974 national convention to include western Tennessee, Arkansas, Mississippi and Louisiana.

Nov. 13-16, 1974: The Townehouse, Phoenix, Arizona.
Attendance: 950.
Speakers: President Gerald Ford; SDX founder, Eugune C. Pulliam; Dan Rather, CBS News; Reg Murphy, editor, Atlanta *Constitution*; Hugh Downs, television journalist; Gov. Dale Bumpers, Arkansas; Barbara Ward, international economist; Seymour Hersh, *The New York Times*; James Polk, Washington *Star-News*; Jules Whitcover, the Washington *Post*; Jack Nelson, the Los Angeles *Times*.
Major Events and Issues: (1) Elected Val Hymes from Region Two to the national board, the first woman to serve as a regional director. (2) President Ford became the first President of the United States to address a national SPJ,SDX convention. Ford held a nationally-televised press conference attended by all delegates. (3) Used the proportional voting system for the first time. (4) Last visit by one of the ten founders to a national convention. To open the convention, Pulliam entertained the delegates at his R & G Ranch with a barbecue. (5) Honored nineteen past presidents in a special ceremony. (6) Voted by-laws change to give the national board responsibility for maintaining fiscal integrity of the Society. (7) Changed by-laws to designate the first vice president of the Society as president-elect and allowing that officer to become national president without standing for election further. (8) Viewed a premier showing of the motion picture, *The Front Page*.

Nov. 12-15, 1975: Benjamin Franklin Hotel, Philadelphia.
Attendance: 1,100.

314

Speakers: Harry Reasoner, ABC News; Tom Wicker, *The New York Times*; Otis Chandler, the Los Angeles *Times*; Edwin Newman, NBC News; Rep. Barbara Jordan, Texas; William Rusher, publisher, *National Review*; J. R. Wiggins, former editor, the Washington *Post*, and publisher, Ellsworth, Maine *American*.

Major Events and Issues: (1) Eliminated reference to sex in the national by-laws. (2) Presentation of initial First Amendment Award by the Society to the Reporters Committee for Freedom of the Press. U.S. Supreme Court Justice William O. Douglas was announced as the second winner of the award. (3) Conducted a ceremony on Independence Mall marking the first-day issue of an eleven-cent stamp honoring freedom of the press. The stamp, co-sponsored by SPJ,SDX and the U.S. Postal Service, carried the words, "Liberty Depends on Freedom of the Press."

Nov. 10-13, 1976: Marriott Hotel, Los Angeles.
Attendance: 1,000.
Speakers: James J. Kilpatrick, syndicated columnist; Charles Seib, ombudsman, the Washington *Post*; Marlene Sanders, ABC News; David Shaw, press critic, the Los Angeles *Times*; Philip Kerby, editorial writer, the Los Angeles *Times*.
Major Events and Issues: (1) Elected Jean Otto as national treasurer, the first woman to become a national officer for the Society. (2) Raised national dues for professional members from $15 to $20 and initiation fee for campus chapter members from $17.50 to $22.50.

Nov. 16-19, 1977: Renaissance Center Plaza Hotel, Detroit.
Attendance: 950.
Speakers: Jane Pauley, NBC News; Ken Herman, Pulitzer prize-winning reporter, Lufkin, Texas *News*; Lewis Lapham, editor, *Harper's*; Eugene Patterson, editor, St. Petersburg, Florida *Times*, and president, American Society of Newspaper Editors; Maxine Cheshire, reporter, the Washington *Post*; Sam Donaldson, ABC News White House correspondent.
Major Events and Issues: (1) Established the Eugene C. Pulliam Fellowships for Editorial Writers. (2) Voted to support the Advisory Board of the Student Press Law Center.

Nov. 15-18, 1978; Hyatt House and The Civic Center, Birmingham, Alabama.
Attendance: 800.
Speakers: Keith Fuller, president and general manager, The Associated Press; Myron Farber, reporter, *The New York Times*; Jody Powell, press secretary to President Jimmy Carter; Bob Schieffer, CBS News; Peter Jacobi, professor of journalism, Northwestern University; Al Neuharth, president, The Gannett Company; Keith Jackson, ABC Sports; Paul (Bear) Bryant, head football coach, University of Alabama; Jack Landau, director, Reporters Committee for Freedom of the Press.
Major Events and Issues: (1) Raised $2,600 for the Legal Defense Fund through "Operation Breadbasket." (2) Established award for the Distinguished Campus Adviser in each district. (3) Established minimum professional program requirements for campus chapters. (4) Board and officers' actions on freedom of information and First Amendment rights led to formation of FOI Service Center and the First Amendment Congresses.

Nov. 14-17, 1979: Waldorf-Astoria, New York City.
Attendance: 1,050.
Speakers: Eugene Roberts, executive editor, Philadelphia *Inquirer*; Charles Osgood, CBS News; Don Ohlmeyer, executive producer, NBC Sports; Walter Cronkite, CBS News; Mary McGrory, syndicated columnist, Washington *Star*; William F. Buckley, Jr., syndicated columnist and moderator, *Firing Line*.
Major Events and Issues: (1) Installed Jean Otto as the first woman president of the Society. (2) Raised national dues for professional members from $20 to $30 and student initiation fees from $22.50 to $27.50. (3) Established a finance committee to study fiscal policies and procedures of the Society.

Nov. 19-22, 1980: Hyatt Regency and the Ohio Center, Columbus, Ohio.
Attendance: 850.
Speakers: John Henry Faulk, former CBS Radio humorist, Madisonville, Texas; Katharine Graham, chairman of the board, The Washington Post Company; David Brink, president-elect, American Bar Association; Reese Schonfeld, president, Cable News Network; Bill Small, president, CBS News.
Major Events and Issues: (1) Approved the hiring of Bruce Sanford as the Society's first legal counsel. (2) Raised nearly $1,000 for the Legal Defense Fund with a 5,000-meter "Run for the First Amendment" race through the streets of Columbus. (3) Established fellowships for journalism educators to Washington Journalism Center seminars.

Nov. 11-14, 1981: Hyatt Regency On Capitol Hill, Washington, DC.
Attendance: 1,240.
Speakers: Katharine Graham, chairman of the board, The Washington Post Company; Carl Rowan, syndicated columnist; Lesley Stahl, CBS News White House correspondent; John Naisbitt, author and economic forecaster; John Quinn, vice president, The Gannett Company; Sen. Alan Simpson, Wyoming; Rep. Millicent Fenwick, New Jersey; Phil Jones, CBS News, Rep. Barbara Mikulski, Maryland; Brit Hume, ABC News; Al Hunt, *The Wall Street Journal*; Carole Simpson, NBC News; Rep. Barney Frank, Massachusetts.

Major Events and Issues: (1) Approved a first-ever annual, national dues assessment of $10 per year for campus chapter members effective Jan. 1, 1984. (2) Returned office of vice president for campus chapter affairs to a three-year term for the first time since 1972. (3) Delegates went to Capitol Hill to testify on the Freedom of Information Act and met with congressmen regarding the Agents Identification Bill. (4) First national convention for Russell Tornabene as executive officer. (5) ABC News correspondent Sam Donaldson, president Howard Graves and secretary Phil Record served as auctioneers during an auction of celebrity memorabilia which raised $4,115 for the Legal Defense Fund. (6) Scheduled keynote speaker Dan Rather, CBS News, and Friday night banquet speaker Tom Brokaw, NBC News, were unable to attend the convention because of live network coverage in Florida and California of the Space Shuttle Columbia's delayed lift off and early return to earth. Stahl substituted for Rather and Quinn accepted a very last-minute invitation to fill in for Brokaw.

Nov. 10-13, 1982: Hyatt Regency, Mark Plaza and The MECCA, Milwaukee, Wisconsin.
Attendance: 800.
Speakers: Andy Rooney, CBS News humorist; Joel Garreau, reporter, the Washington *Post*m and author of *The Nine Nations of North America*; William P. Tavoulareas, president, Mobil Oil Corporation; Walter Williams, professor and political economist, George Mason University.
Major Events and Issues: (1) Voted to increase professional members' national dues from $30 to $35 in 1983 and to $40 in 1984. (2) Rejected an attempt to change the name of the Society to The Society of Professional Journalists deleting the words Sigma Delta Chi from the name of the Society. (3) Adopted a by-law allowing campus chapters to enroll members from nearby campuses where no chapter is chartered. (4) Established a $5,000 professional development program to fund continuing education seminars sponsored by local chapters. (5) Raised nearly $4,000 for the Legal Defense Fund through "The First Amendment Follies" planned and conducted by the campus board representatives. (6) Approved a 75th Anniversary Capital Campaign to raise $500,000 for *The Quill's* endowment fund.

Nov. 9-12, 1983: Fairmont Hotel and Golden Gateway Holiday Inn, San Francisco.
Attendance: 750
Major Speakers: Ben Bagdikian, professor of journalism, University of California at Berkeley; Dr. Michael Burgoon and Dr. Judee Burgoon, professors of communication, University of Arizona, Tucson; Van Gordon Sauter, president, CBS News; Jeff Greenfield, media critic, ABC News.
Major Events and Issues: (1) Board approved a three-year, $2.4 million fund-raising campaign to provide revenue for Society programs. (2) Convention adopted resolution condemning news blackout by the Reagan administration during the invasion of Grenada. (3) Board voted to phase out, in a three-year period, its joint sponsorship with the Reporters Committee for Freedom of the Press in the FOI Service Center. (4) Convention adopted a resolution providing for a by-laws change to be brought to the 1984 convention changing the terms of campus board representatives to two years. (5) Elected two women as regional directors, bringing women (other than campus board representatives) back to the board for the first time in three years. (6) Officers began a procedure wherein the president-elect of the Society would be responsible for the program and speakers at future national conventions, while the president would concentrate on conducting officers' and board meetings.

Nov. 14-17, 1984: Indianapolis and Greencastle, Indiana

NATIONAL HISTORIC SITES IN JOURNALISM
MARKED BY THE SOCIETY

1942	Bennington, Vermont. Anthony Haswell, editor and publisher, the Vermont *Gazette*. He was jailed for fighting the Sedition Act.
1946	San Francisco, California. James King of William, founder, editor and publisher, the San Francisco *Daily Evening Bulletin* He fought corruption in municipal government and was assassinated by a politician fater many threats on his life.
1947	St. Louis Missouri. Joseph Pulitzer, founder, the St. Louis *Post-Dispatch*.
1948	*Montgomery, Alabama. Grover Cleveland Hall, editor, the Montgomery Advertiser.* He fought the Ku Klux Klan.
1949	Emporia, Kansas. William Allen White, editor and publisher, the Emporia *Gazette*.
1950	Boston, Massachusetts. The Boston *Gazette*, second regularly-published paper in the nation.
1951	New Orleans, Louisiana. George Wilkins Kendall, co-founder of the New Orleans *Picayune*, first war correspondent to achieve fame as a regular reporter of military actions.
1952	Alton, Illinois. Elijah Parish Lovejoy, editor, *The Observer*, and a militant abolitionist assassinated by his enemies.
1953	Bloomington, Indiana. Ernie Pyle, editor, columnist, war correspondent for Scripps-Howard newspapers.
1954	New York City. Henry J. Raymond, co-founder and the first editor, *The New York Times*.
1955	Pittsburgh, Pennsylvania. Radio Station KDKA. Reported Harding's election in 1920. First radio coverage of a national event.

1956	Columbia, Missouri. Walter Williams and the University of Missouri School of Journalism. First school of journalism in the nation.
1957	Baltimore, Maryland. H.L. Mencken, author and newspaperman.
1958	New York City. The trial of John Peter Zenger.
1959	Cleveland, Ohio. Edward Wyllis Scripps and the Cleveland *Press*. Publisher, founder of the Cleveland *Press* and chain of newspapers, plus United Press and Newspaper Enterprise Association.
1960	Charlottesville, Virginia. Thomas Jefferson.
1961	Philadelphia, Pennsylvania. Banjamin Franklin, statesman and newspaperman.
1962	New York City. Horace Greeley, one of the most influential newspaper editors in American history.
1963	New York City. James Gordon Bennett.
1964	Hartford, Connecticut. the Hartford *Courant*, oldest newspaper of continuous publication in the United States.
1965	New York City. Adolph S. Ochs, largely responsible for the revival of *The New York Times*. Louisville, Kentucky. Henry Watterson, outstanding editorialist. Kansas City, Missouri. William Rockhill Nelson, founder, Kansas City *Star*.
1966	Little Rock, Arkansas. John N. Heiskell and the *Arkansas Gazette*, oldest newspaper west of the Mississippi. New York City. News department, Columbia Broadcasting System. Leadership in founding independent radio news system; distinguished reporting and interpretation exemplified by H.V. Kaltenborn and Edward R. Murrow. Washington, DC. *National Intelligencer* (1800-1865). Vital force in nation's political force and set high standards of journalistic responsibility.
1967	Philadelphia, Pennsylvania and Baltimore, Maryland. Richard Hoe and Ottmar Mergenthaler, for invention of the rotary press in 1847 and the "linotype" machine in 1886, respectively. New York City and Washington, DC. The Associated Press. Establishment of the world's first private, leased wire for news transmission (1875). Carmel, California. Lincoln Steffans (1866-1936), foremost exponent of journalistic crusaders known as "muckrakers," whose exposes of corruption and injustice aroused the public conscience. Greencastle, Indiana. DePauw University, where Sigma Delta Chi was founded, April 17, 1909.
1968	Gunston Hall, Virginia. Home of George Mason, author of Virginia Declaration of Rights (1776), which gave the first expression of a free press its binding, legal form. Boston, Massachussetts. James Franklin's *New England Courant*, first newspaper published in the United States without license or authority. Washington, DC. the Washington *Globe* (1831-1845), published by Francis Preston Blair and John C. Rives. Cincinnati, Ohio. *The Centinel of the North-Western Territory*, marking the 175th anniversary of the first newspaper in the Northwest Territory, published in 1793.
1969	Hannibal, Missouri. 206 Hill Street, boyhood home of Samuel Clemans (Mark Twain) and site of the Hannibal *Journal*, which started Twain on the way to fame as one of America's great writers. Lexington, Virginia. Reid Hall, the journalism building on the campus of Washington and Lee University. Here the first formal instruction in journalism in the history of education was initiated by General Robert E. Lee in 1869. Atlanta, Georgia. Henry Woodfin Grady (1850-1889), and the Atlanta *Constitution*, leaders in creating a more comprehensive, interpretative journalism in the South.
1970	Sacramento, California. The Sacramento *Union*, oldest daily in the West, founded in 1851. Madison, Wisconsin. The Wisconsin Press Association, oldest continuing state press association in the nation, existing since the 1830's. Des Moines, Iowa. J.N. (Ding) Darling and the Des Moines *Register and Tribune*. Darling's cartoons catapulted him into national prominence and were a factor in enhancing the great prestige of his newspaper in the first half of the 20th century.
1971	Chicago, Illinois. The Chicago *Daily News* and the nation's oldest foreign news service operated by a newspaper. San Francisco, California. William Randolph Hearst and the San Francisco *Examiner*. Calhoun, Georgia. The *Cherokee Phoenix*, the Indian-language newspaper of the Cherokee nation.
1972	Philadelphia, Pennsylvania. Sarah Josepha Hale and *Godey's Lady's Book*, first major woman's magazine of mass circulation published from 1830-1882. Baraboo, Wisconsin. Ansel N. Kellogg and the first newspaper syndicate developed in 1861. Chillicothe, Ohio. The Chillicothe *Gazette*, oldest newspaper in continuous publication west of the Allegheny Mountains, published since 1800.
1973	Augusta, Georgia. The Augusta *Chronicle*, the South's oldest newspaper presently publishing. Chicago, Illinois. The Chicago *Tribune*. Oologah, Oklahoma. The Will Rogers Home, birthplace of Will Rogers.
1974	University of Alabama. Supreme Court Justice Hugo L. Black, eloquent and effective for the principle of a free and untrammeled press.

Chicago, Illinois. The Chicago *Defender*, for pioneering and continuous leadership and strength in the Black press.

Gathland State Park, Maryland. Townsend's War Correspondents Arch, a memorial to Civil War correspondents of the North and the South.

1975   Worcester, Massachusetts. Isaiah Thomas, American revolutionary editor, printer, pioneer press historian and co-founder and first president of American Antiquarian Society.

New York City. *The Nation*, oldest opinion magazine in the United States.

Pittsburgh, Pennsylvania. John Scull, first editor to transport type and a press across the Alleghenies to establish journalism west of the peaks; founder of Pittsburgh *Gazette* in 1786.

1976   Philadelphia, Pennsylvania. *The Pennsylvania Packet or the General Advertiser*, the first successful daily newspaper in the United States and first to publish the Declaration of Independence and the U.S. Constitution.

Rochester, New York. Frederick Douglass, founder in 1847 of the *North Star*, which with its successor newspapers under Douglass's direction was the leading Black journal in the United States in the antebellum period.

Canton, Ohio. Donald Ring Mellett, publisher of the Candon *Daily News*, who was gunned down in front of his home after editorializing against Canton's lawless elements and city officials' ineptness.

1977   New York City. *The Wall Street Journal*.

Richmond, Virginia. John Mitchell, one of the South's leading Black reform journalists and editor of the Richmond *Planet*.

1978   Philadelphia, Pennsylvania. Cyrus H.K. Curtis, who played a major role in consolidating Philadelphia newspapers and founded the *Ladies' Home Journal*.

Toledo, Ohio. David Ross Locke (Petroleum Vesuvius Nasby), who created the Nasby Letters and was a forerunner of the muckrakers.

Milwaukee, Wisconsin. H.V. Kaltenborn, pioneer radio news analyst who was known for his analysis of World War II.

1979   Charleston, South Carolina. Elizabeth Timothy, first woman publisher of an American newspaper.

Milwaukee, Wisconsin. Christopher Latham Sholes, chief inventor of the first practical typewriter.

Memphis, Tennessee. The *Christian Index*, second oldest Black religious newspaper in the nation.

1980   Boston, Massachusetts. *The Christian Science Monitor*, founder Mary Baker Eddy and long-time editor Erwin D. Canham.

Newburyport, Massachusetts. William Lloyd Garrison, founder of the *Liberator*, anti-slavery journal.

Atlanta, Georgia. W.A. Scott II, founder of the Atlanta *Daily World*, oldest continuing Black owned and controlled daily newspaper in the United States.

1981   Philadelphia, Pennsylvania. Richard Harding Davis, one of the most adventurous war correspondents of his time who was known for his colorful reportage during six wars.

1982   Akron, Ohio. *Akron Beacon Journal*, in honor of John S. Knight, builder of the Knight-Ridder Newspapers Company.

1983   New York City. *Freedom's Journal*, the first Black newspaper published in America.

1984   New York City. Margaret Bourke-White (1904-1971), one of America's best-known photojournalists.

Washington, DC. United Press International.

FREEDOM OF INFORMATION COMMITTEE CHAIRMEN

1948	Charles Clayton	1970-1971	Dick Kleeman
1949	Richard Fitzpatrick	1972	Richard Fogel
1950	Lyle Wilson	1973	Courtney Sheldon
1951	Norman Isaacs	1974-1976	Grant Dillman
1952-1963	V.M. (Red) Newton	1977-1978	Scott Aiken
1964-1965	Julius Frandsen	1979-1983	Bob Lewis
1966-1969	Clark Mollenhoff	1984	Tony Mauro

ETHICS AND PROFESSIONAL DEVELOPMENT COMMITTEE CHAIRMEN

(NOTE: The committee was called the ethics committee from 1948 through 1963, the professional development committee from 1964 through 1979 and the ethics committee from 1979 through 1984.)

1948	Charles Clayton	1958-1961	Bill Small
1951-1955	None	1961-1963	None
1955-1956	Norman Isaacs	1964	Don Carter
1957	None	1965	James Hetherington

318

1966-1968	John DeMott	1972-1973	Casey Bukro
1969	Haig Keropian	1974-1979	David Offer
1970	None	1979-1980	Marvin Garrette
1971	Arthur Klein	1981-1984	Fred Behringer

MINORITY RECRUITMENT COMMITTEE
AND MINORITY TASK FORCE CHAIRMEN

1968	Paul Swensson (pre-committee coordinator)
1969	Ernest Dunbar
1970	DeWayne Johnson
1971-1982	Edward Trayes
1983-1984	Walter Morrison
	(Morrison also served as chair of the Minority Task Force in 1981 and 1982)

JOURNALISM CAREERS COMMITTEE

1964-1966	Al Balk	1970	DeWayne Johnson
1967-1969	Paul Swensson	1971-1972	Charles Novitz

HISTORIC SITES COMMITTEE

1959	Ed Emery	1968-1969	C. Richard King
1960	Richard Leonard	1970-1971	Calvin Manon
1961	A.L. Higginbotham	1972-1975	Richard Schwarzlose
1962	Ed Emery	1976-1979	Mary Ann Yodelis
1963	Edward Thompson	1980-1984	A.L. Lorenz
1964-1967	William T. Ames		

BY-LAWS COMMITTEE

1960	1961	1962-1983	1984
Robert J. Cavagnaro	Eugene Schroeder	Charles Barnum	David Offer

PROFESSIONAL CHAPTER ACTIVITIES
AND CONTINUING EDUCATION COMMITTEE

1978-1981
Lillian Lodge Kopenhaver
1981-1984
Ralph Izard
Lillian Lodge Kopenhaver

CAMPUS CHAPTER ACTIVITIES COMMITTEE

1959	Maynard Hicks	1970-1972	H.G. Davis
1960-1961	Eugene Goodwin	1973-1975	James Julian
1962-1964	A.L. Higginbotham	1976-1978	Ralph Izard
1965	Charles Barnum	1979-1981	Bert N. Bostrom
1966	DeWayne Johnson	1982	Wallace Eberhard
1967-1969	Warren K. Agee	1983-1985	Charles Fair

MEMBERSHIP COMMITTEE

1964-1965	Phil Dessauer	1977	Alf Goodykoontz
1966-1969	Ken Reiley	1978-1980	Howard Graves
1970-1976	No Committee	1981-1984	Bruce Itule

1956 MODEL OPEN RECORDS LAW

A Bill To Be Entitled
Public Records Open to Examination by Citizens

Section 1. All state, county and municipal records shall at all times be open for a personal inspection of any citizen of the state of _____, and those in charge of such records shall not refuse this privilege to any citizen.
Section 2. Penalty...Any official who shall violate the provisions of section 1 shall be subject to removal or impeachment and in addition shall be deemed guilty of a misdemeanor and upon conviction shall be punished by a fine not exceeding one hundred dollars, or imprisonment in the county jail not exceeding three months.
Section 3. Photographing public records...In all cases where the public or any person interested has a right to inspect or take extracts or make copies from any public records, instruments or documents, any such person shall hereafter have the right of access to said records, documents or instruments for the purpose of making photographs of the same while in the possession, custody and control of the lawful custodian thereof, or his authorized deputy. Such work shall be done under the supervision of the lawful custodian of the said records, who shall have the right to adopt and enforce reasonable rules governing the said work. Said work shall, where possible, be done in the room where the said records, documents or instruments are by law kept, but if the same in the judgment of the lawful custodian of the said records, documents or instruments, be impossible or impracticable, then the said work shall be done in such other room or place as nearly adjacent to the court house as may be, to be determined by the board of county commissioners of the said county. Where the providing of another room or place is necessary, the expense of the same shall be provided by the person desiring to photograph the said records, instruments or documents. While the said work hereinbefore mentioned is in progress, the lawful custodian of said records may charge the person desiring to make the said photographs for the services of a deputy of the lawful custodian of the same in so doing at a rate of compensation to be agreed upon by the person desiring to make the said photographs and the custodian of the said records, documents or instruments, or in case the same fail to agree as to the said charge, then the board of county commissioners of said county.

1956 MODEL OPEN MEETINGS LAW

A Bill To Be Entitled

An act requiring all meetings of the governing bodies of municipalities, counties, Boards of Public Instruction, Boards of County Commissioners and other bords, bureaus, commissions or organizations, except grand juries, support in whole or in part by public funds or expending public funds to be public meetings.

Be it enacted by the legislature of the state of _____:
Section 1. All meetings of the governing bodies of all municipalities, located within the state of _____, Boards of County Commissioners of the counties of the state of _____, Boards of Public Instruction of the counties in the state of _____, and all other boards, bureaus, commissions or organizations in the state of _____, excepting grand juries, supported in part by public funds or expending public funds shall be public meetings.
Section 2. Any person or persons violating any of the provisions of this act shall be guilty of a misdemeanor and upon conviction shall be punished by a fine not exceeding _____ dollars or by imprisonment in the county jail for a period not exceeding _____, or by both such fine and imprisonment.
Section 3. All laws, or parts of laws, in conflict herewith are hereby repealed.
Section 4. If any provisions of this act or its application to any person, board, bureau, commission or organization shall be held unconstitutional, such decision shall not affect the constitutionality of any other portion of the act or its application to any other municipality, board, bureau, commission or organization.
Section 5. This act shall become a law upon its passage and approval by the governor or become a law without such approval.

1971 MODEL SHIELD LAW

No person shall be required in any proceeding or hearing to disclose any information or the source of any information procured or obtained by him while he was (a) engaged in gathering, writing, photographing or editing news and (b) employed by or acting for any organization engaged in publishing or broadcasting news, unless the body proposing to require disclosure of such information or source shall have first obtained a final order of a court, made after a hearing, and expressly finding:
(1) The existence of probable cause to believe that the witness or his sources has evidence which is relevant and material to an issue properly pending before such body, and
(2) Disclosure by such person is the only method by which such evidence, or evidence of similar effect, can be obtained; and
(3) The failure of disclosure of such evidence will cause a miscarriage of justice.

THE TWENTY-FIVE YEAR GROWTH IN ENROLLMENT: 1959-1983

NOTE: By January 1, 1959, the fraternity had enrolled 29,207 members since its founding in 1909. The following numbers represent the students and professional members who have enrolled, year by year, since that time through December 31, 1983. It must be remembered that of the 55,489 students who have enrolled since January 1959, many of them remained as members only during their college years and they did not affiliate with the Society as professional members upon being graduated. Of course, attrition occurred among the 20,757 members who joined as professionals, but the rate was much smaller. Thus, the "active" membership roster of 24,000 plus, announced by executive officer Russell Tornabene early in 1984, reflects only a portion of the members enrolled in the past twenty-five years. The final membership number assigned during December 1983 – 105,519 – represents the number of members enrolled in the first seventy-four years of the organization.

YEAR	CAMPUS	PROFESSIONAL	TOTAL
1959	787	413	1,200
1960	885	359	1,244
1961	924	523	1,447
1962	846	530	1,376
1963	875	461	1,336
1964	1,048	720	1,768
1965	990	615	1,605
1966	1,253	659	1,912
1967	1,077	607	1,684
1868	1,151	650	1,801
1969	1,262	508	1,770
1970	2,308	1,007	3,315
1971	2,643	1,369	4,012
1972	3,133	747	3,880
1973	3,167	782	3,949
1974	3,297	894	4,191
1975	3,379	954	4,333
1976	4,224	865	5,089
1977	3,345	869	4,214
1978	3,171	1,014	4,185
1979	3,918	937	4,855
1980	3,189	745	3,934
1981	3,217	1,651	4,868
1982	2,611	1,576	4,187
1983	2,789	1,302	4,091
	55,489	20,757	76,246

Data provided by Society headquarters, February 1984.

BIBLIOGRAPHY

TAPE-RECORDED INTERVIEWS

Agee, Warren K. Telephone interview. 1 July 1982.
Angelo, Frank. Personal interview. 7 November 1982. Detroit, Michigan.
Arpan, Floyd. Telephone interview. 30 June 1982.
Arpan, Floyd. Telephone interview. 7 July 1983.
Arthur, William B. Personal interview. 10 March 1983. New York City.
Balk, Alfred. Telephone interview. 8 July 1983.
Barnum, Charles. Personal interview. 1 July 1982
Bohannon, James. Telephone interview. 16 June 1983.
Boye, Roger. Personal interview. 23 June 1983. Chicago.
Burroughs, Walter. Personal interview. 9 March 1982. Costa Mesa, California.
Chandler, Robert. Personal interview. 9 August 1982. Bend, Oregon.
Clayton, Charles. Telephone interview. 26 January 1982.
Clayton, Charles. Telephone interview. 9 July 1982.
Cope, Lew. Telephone interview. 29 June 1983.
Dessauer, Phil. Personal interview. 27 May 1982. Tulsa, Oklahoma.
Dorfman, Ron. Personal interview. 23 June 1983. Chicago.
Dornfeld, Steven. Personal interview. 26 June 1983. Chicago.
Dubin, Howard. Telephone interview. 27 July 1983.
Dunbar, Ernest. Telephone interview. 25 July 1983.
Goodykoontz, Alf. Personal interview. 23 March 1982. Flagstaff, Arizona.
Graves, Howard. Personal interview. 9 August 1982. Portland, Oregon.
Hurst, Russell. Personal interview. 3 June 1982.
Koop, Ted. Personal interview. 10 March 1983. Washington, DC.
Kramer, Linda. Telephone interview. 30 June 1983.
Leonard, Richard. Personal interview. 9 November 1982. Milwaukee, Wisconsin.
Lewis, Bob. Personal interview. 11 March 1983. Washington, DC.
Lockridge, Kay. Telephone interview. 7 July 1983.
Long, Charles. Personal interview. 4 June 1982. Chicago.
Luttrell, Pearl. Personal interview. 24 June 1983. Chicago.
McBrayer, Staley. Personal interview. 26 May 1982. Phoenix, Arizona.
McCord, Robert. Personal interview. 2 June 1982. Little Rock, Arkansas.
McCord, Robert, Telephone interview. 12 July 1983.
Mollenhoff, Clark. Personal interview. 11 July 1982. Flagstaff, Arizona.
Novitz, Charles. Personal interview. 25 June 1983. Evanston, Illinois.
Otto, Jean. Personal interview. 8 November 1982. Milwaukee, Wisconsin.
Otto, Jean. Telephone interview. 5 August 1983.
Payette, William. Personal interview. 26 May 1982. Dallas, Texas.
Record, Phil. Personal interview. 24 June 1983. Evanston, Illinois.
Rieger, Henry. Telephone interview. 31 December 1982.
Rush, Tonda. Telephone interview. 10 June 1983.
Ryan, Guy. Personal interview. 8 March 1982. Vista, California.
Sanford, Bruce. Personal interview. 11 March 1983. Washington, DC.
Scripps, E.W. (Ted). Personal interview. 10 August 1982. Reno, Nevada.
Sewell, Ralph. Personal interview. 26 May 1982. Norman, Oklahoma.
Shover, William. Telephone interview. 14 September 1982.
Small, William. Personal interview. 10 March 1983. New York City.
Spangler, Ray. Personal interview. 12 August 1982. Redwood City, California.
Sutherland, Frank. Personal interview. 24 June 1983. Evanston, Illinois.
Taishoff, Sol. Telephone interview. 8 July 1982.
Tornabene, Russell. Personal interview. 24 June 1983. Chicago.
White, Robert M. II. Telephone interview. 26 January 1982.
White, Robert M. II. Telephone interview. 29 June 1982.

322

LETTERS AND OTHER CORRESPONDENCE

Agee, Warren K. Letter to author. 1 August 1982.
Aiken, Scott. Letter to author. 21 September 1982.
Austin, Al. Letter to author. 11 August 1982.
Bates, Albert. Letter to author. 12 May 1982.
Bukro, Casey. Letter to author. 2 April 1982.
Bukro, Casey. Letters to members of professional development committee, national headquarters
    and national officers. September 1972 to November 1975.
Carter, Don. Letter to author. 30 September 1982.
Hicks, Maynard. Letters to author. 8 September to 1 November 1982.
Jandoli, Russell. Letter to Russell E. Hurst. 17 December 1969.
Kleeman, Richard. Letter to author. 1 March 1982.
Offer, David. Letter to author. 1 February 1982.
Offer, David. Letters to members of professional development and ethics committees,
    national headquarters and national officers. December 1972 through November 1978.
Reiley, Kenneth. Letter to author. 15 February 1983.
Reiley, Kenneth. Letters to members of membership committee, national headquarters,
    national officers, members of the Society, and members of Theta Sigma Phi.
    January 1962 through November 1969.
Swensson, Paul. Letter to author. 4 February 1983.
Sanford, Bruce. Letters to members of the freedom of information committeee, national board
    of directors and national headquarters. November 1980 to November 1983.
Savory, Gilbert. Letter to author. 11 June 1983.
Wolpert, George. Letter to author. 5 March 1983.
Wolpert, George. Letters to members of membership committee, national headquarters, national officers,
    members of Theta Sigma Phi, and members of the Society. January 1966 through November 1969.

BOOKS

Clayton, Charles C. *Fifty Years for Freedom: The Story of Sigma Delta Chi's Service to American Journalism*:
    1909-1959. Carbondale, Illinois: Southern Illinois University Press. 1959.
Francois, William E. *News Media Law and Regulations*, Third Edition.
    Columbus, Ohio: Grid Publishing Inc. 1982.
Glenn, William M. *The Sigma Delta Chi Story*. Coral Gables, Florida: Glade House. 1949.

PERIODICALS

The Quill. October 1926. Sigma Delta Chi. Chicago.
The Quill. Vols. 20 (1932) through 72 (1984). Society of Professional Journalists, Sigma Delta Chi. Chicago.
*Trading Post*1954-1960. Sigma Delta Chi. Chicago.
Here's How. 1958-1959. Sigma Delta Chi. Chicago.
Replate. 1963-1977. Society of Professional Journalists, Sigma Delta Chi. Chicago.
Newsletter. 1977-1982. Society of Professional Journalists, Sigma Delta Chi. Chicago.
News and Views. 1983-1984. Society of Professional Journalists, Sigma Delta Chi. Chicago.

MISCELLANEOUS MATERIALS

"A Plan of Action" (Author unknown). 1959. Sigma Delta Chi. Chicago.
Continuing Education Reports. 1981-1983. Society of Professional Journalists, Sigma Delta Chi. Chicago.
Directory. 1962-1984. Society of Professional Journalists, Sigma Delta Chi. Chicago.
Ethics Committee Reports. 1976-1983. Socity of Professional Journalists, Sigma Delta Chi. Chicago.
Freedom of Information Committee Reports. 1948-1983. Society of Professional Journalists,
    Sigma Delta Chi. Chicago.
McKinsey & Company. "Building an Organization to Meet Today's Objectives." 1960. Chicago.
Minutes: Executive Council and Board of Directors. 1957-1983. Society of Professional Journalists,
    Sigma Delta Chi. Chicago.
Minutes: Officers Meetings. 1957-1960 and 1981-1984. Society of Professional Journalists,
    Sigma Delta Chi. Chicago.
Transcripts: National Convention Business Sessions. 1958, 1960, 1969, 1973, and 1982. Society of Professional
    Journalists, Sigma Delta Chi. Chicago.
White, Robert M. II. "The White Report." April 14, 1959. Sigma Delta Chi. Chicago.

INDEX

About the author

DR. BERT N. BOSTROM is a professor of journalism at Northern Arizona University in Flagstaff, Arizona. With degrees in journalism and English, he was a reporter for *The Phoenix Gazette* and taught in the public schools for ten years before joining the Northern Arizona University journalism faculty in 1967. He earned his doctorate in education from Arizona State University in 1975. Bostrom was named the Outstanding Journalism Educator in Arizona by the Arizona Newspapers Association in 1981. He is the author of one other book on the history of a professional journalism association and numerous magazine articles including several for *The Quill*.

A member of The Society of Professional Journalists, Sigma Delta Chi, since 1968, he was the charter president of the Grand Canyon professional chapter, faculty adviser to the Northern Arizona University campus chapter, deputy director for Region Eleven, and a member of several SPJ,SDX national committees. He was elected national Vice President for Campus Chapter Affairs in 1978 and served on the Society's board of directors for three years through November 1981.

About the cover

Richard Locher is an editorial cartoonist for *The Chicago Tribune*. He served as an Air Force test pilot, then worked as an advertising illustrator before becoming the artist for the comic strip, Dick Tracy. Locher won the SPJ,SDX Distinguished Service Award in Editorial Cartooning for 1982.